Using *Texas Write Source*

Your **Texas Write Source** book is loaded with information to help you learn about writing. One section that will be especially helpful is the "Proofreader's Guide" at the back of the book. This section covers the rules for language and grammar.

The book also includes main units covering research writing as well as the types of writing that you may have to complete on district or state tests. In addition, a special section provides samples and tips for writing in science, social studies, math, the applied sciences, the arts, and the workplace.

Texas Write Source will help you with other learning skills, too—test taking, note taking, and making oral presentations. This makes *Texas Write Source* a valuable writing and learning guide in all of your classes. (The **Quick Tour** on pages iv–v highlights many of the key features in the book.)

Your *Texas Write Source* guide . . .

With practice, you will be able to find information in this book quickly using the guides explained below.

- The **Table of Contents** (starting on page **vi**) lists the five major sections in the book and the chapters found in each section.
- The **Index** (starting on page **795**) lists the topics covered in the book in alphabetical order. Use the index when you are interested in a specific topic.
- The **Color Coding** used for the "Proofreader's Guide" (yellow) makes this important section easy to find. Colorful side tabs also provide a handy reference.
- **Page References** in the book tell you where to turn for additional information about a specific topic. *Example:* (See page **350**.)

> If, at first, you're not sure how to find something in *Texas Write Source*, ask your teacher for help. With a little practice, you will find everything quickly and easily.

TEXAS WRITE SOURCE

Authors
Dave Kemper, Patrick Sebranek, and Verne Meyer

Consulting Author
Gretchen Bernabei

Illustrator
Chris Krenzke

HOUGHTON MIFFLIN HARCOURT

Trademarks and trade names are shown in this book strictly for illustrative purposes and are the property of their respective owners. The authors' references herein should not be regarded as affecting their validity.

Copyright © 2012 by Houghton Mifflin Harcourt Publishing Company

All rights reserved. No part of this work may be reproduced or transmitted in any form or by any means, electronic or mechanical, including photocopying or recording, or by any information storage and retrieval system, without the prior written permission of the copyright owner unless such copying is expressly permitted by federal copyright law. Requests for permission to make copies of any part of the work should be addressed to Houghton Mifflin Harcourt Publishing Company, Attn: Paralegal, 9400 South Park Center Loop, Orlando, Florida 32819.

Printed in the U.S.A.

ISBN-13 978-0-547-39504-3

2 3 4 5 6 7 8 9 10 0868 19 18 17 16 15 14 13 12 11   4500305870

BCDEFG

If you have received these materials as examination copies free of charge, Houghton Mifflin Harcourt Publishing Company retains title to the materials and they may not be resold. Resale of examination copies is strictly prohibited.

Possession of this publication in print format does not entitle users to convert this publication, or any portion of it, into electronic format.

Quick Guide

Why Write? — 1

The Writing Process

Using the Writing Process
- Understanding the Writing Process — 7
- One Writer's Process — 13
- Using the Holistic Scoring Guide — 33

Understanding the Traits
- Understanding the Traits of Writing — 47
- Focus and Coherence — 51
- Organization — 59
- Development of Ideas — 67
- Voice — 75
- Conventions — 83

Exploring the Writing Process
- Prewriting — 91
- Writing the First Draft — 99
- Revising — 107
- Peer Response — 115
- Editing — 121
- Publishing — 127

The Forms of Writing

Narrative Writing
- Writing a Personal Narrative — 135
- Writing the College Entrance Essay — 149

Expository Writing
- Writing an Analysis of Opposing Ideas — 157
- Writing a Problem Analysis — 199
- Responding to Expository Prompts — 209

Persuasive Writing
- Writing an Argumentative Essay — 217
- Writing an Editorial — 259
- Responding to Persuasive Prompts — 269

Interpretive Response
- Interpret the Theme of a Play — 277
- Interpret a Novel — 319
- Writing an Analysis of an Expository Text — 327
- Responding to Prompts About Literature — 333

Creative Writing
- Writing Stories — 343
- Writing Plays — 355
- Writing an Audio Play — 364
- Writing Poetry — 367

Research Writing
- Research Skills — 381
- MLA Research Paper — 391
- Writing Responsibly — 439
- Documenting Research — 447
- Making Oral Presentations — 461

Writing Across the Curriculum
- Recording Your Learning — 475
- Writing in Science — 481
- Writing in Social Studies — 493
- Writing in Math — 511
- Writing in the Applied Sciences — 521
- Writing in the Arts — 529
- Writing in the Workplace — 543

The Tools of Language
- Listening and Speaking — 557
- Using Reference Materials — 561
- Learning the Language of Writing — 565

Basic Elements of Writing
- Basic Paragraph Skills — 611
- Basic Essay Skills — 623
- Editing and Proofreading — 638

Proofreader's Guide
- Checking Mechanics — 641
- Understanding Idioms — 702
- Using the Right Word — 708
- Parts of Speech — 728
- Understanding Sentences — 762

TEKS and ELPS Appendix — 786

A Quick Tour of *Texas Write Source*

Texas Write Source contains many key features that will help you improve your writing and language skills. Once you become familiar with this book, you will begin to understand how helpful these features can be.

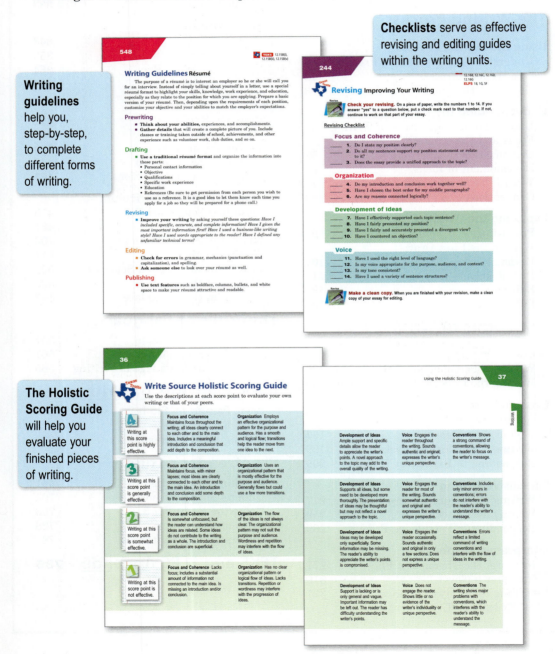

Writing guidelines help you, step-by-step, to complete different forms of writing.

Checklists serve as effective revising and editing guides within the writing units.

The Holistic Scoring Guide will help you evaluate your finished pieces of writing.

Texas Write Source

The **writing samples** will stimulate you to write your own effective essays.

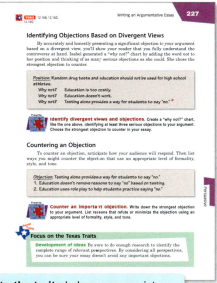

Links to the traits help you appreciate the importance of different traits at different points in the writing process.

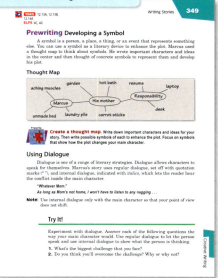

Graphic organizers show you how to organize your ideas for writing.

contents

The Writing Process

Why Write? **1**

USING THE WRITING PROCESS

Understanding the Writing Process **7**

One Writer's Process **13**
- **Prewriting:** Planning Your Writing — **15**
- **Drafting:** Developing Your Ideas — **18**
- **Revising:** Focus and Coherence, Organization, Development of Ideas, and Voice — **20**
- **Editing:** Conventions — **26**
- **Publishing:** Sharing Your Writing — **28**

Using the Holistic Scoring Guide **33**

UNDERSTANDING THE TRAITS

Understanding the Traits of Writing **47**
- Understanding and Using the Five Traits — **48**
- Checklist for Effective Writing — **50**

Focus and Coherence **51**
- Focusing — **52**
- Ensuring Completeness — **54**
- Writing a Focused Introduction — **55**
- Writing a Focused Conclusion — **56**
- Using Effective Support — **57**

Organization **59**
- Understanding the Big Picture — **60**
- Following the Thesis Statement's Lead — **61**
- Using a Logical Progression of Ideas — **62**
- Patterns of Organization — **63**
- Using Graphic Organizers — **64**
- Transitions — **66**

Development of Ideas **67**
- The Creative Mind in Action — **68**
- Reviewing Possible Starting Points — **69**
- Developing Your Ideas — **70**
- Presenting Your Ideas — **72**
- Avoiding Gaps — **74**

Voice **75**
- Developing and Adjusting Voice — **76**
- Using Dialogue — **78**
- Understanding Diction — **79**
- Working with Metaphors and Other Figures of Speech — **80**
- Using Adjectives Effectively — **82**

Conventions **83**
- Spelling and Punctuation — **84**
- Varying and Expanding Sentences — **86**
- Placing Modifiers — **88**
- Avoiding Awkward Sentences — **89**

EXPLORING THE WRITING PROCESS

Prewriting **91**
- Selecting a Genre and a Topic — **92**
- Gathering Details — **94**
- Forming Your Thesis Statement — **97**
- Organizing Your Details — **98**

Writing the First Draft **99**
- Writing the Beginning — **101**
- Developing the Middle — **102**
- Writing the Ending — **106**

Revising **107**
- Revising Checklist — **111**
- Revising in Action — **112**
- Checking for Depth — **114**

Peer Response **115**
- Peer-Response Guidelines — **116**
- Using the Traits to Respond — **118**

Editing **121**
- Checklist for Editing and Proofreading — **122**
- Errors to Watch For — **124**
- Special Editing Problems — **126**

Publishing **127**
- Preparing to Publish — **128**
- Places to Publish — **129**
- Preparing a Portfolio — **130**
- Creating Your Own Web Site — **133**

The Forms of Writing

NARRATIVE WRITING

Writing a Personal Narrative **135**
   STUDENT MODEL "A Greater Wealth" — 136
   Prewriting: Selecting a Topic, Gathering Details,
     and Considering the Story Line — 138
   Drafting: Creating a Beginning, a Middle,
     and an Ending — 140
   Revising: Including Background Information, Using
     Dialogue in a Narrative, Adjusting for Tone and Mood,
     Assessing Your Ending, and Improving Your Writing — 141
   Editing: Conventions, Checking Your Writing — 144
   Publishing: Sharing Your Writing — 145
   Evaluating a Personal Narrative — 146
   Reflecting on Your Writing — 148

Writing the College Entrance Essay **149**
   STUDENT MODEL "A New World of Cinema" — 150
   Prewriting: Focusing Your Efforts and
     Gathering Details — 152
   Drafting: Creating Your First Draft — 153
   Revising: Improving Your First Draft — 154
   Editing: Checking for Conventions — 154
   Example Prompts — 155

EXPOSITORY WRITING

Writing an Analysis of Opposing Ideas **157**
    Expository Writing Warm-Up and Paragraph   **158**
    Understanding Your Goal   **160**
    STUDENT MODEL "Are Third Parties Viable in
      U.S. Politics?"   **161**
    Prewriting   **163**
    Drafting   **169**
    Revising   **175**
      • **Focus and Coherence**   **176**
      • **Organization**   **178**
      • **Development of Ideas**   **180**
      • **Voice**   **182**
    Using a Checklist   **184**
    Editing   **185**
      • **Grammar**   **186**
      • **Sentence Structure**   **188**
      • **Mechanics:** Capitalization   **189**
    Using a Checklist   **190**
    Publishing   **191**
    Evaluating an Analysis of Opposing Ideas   **192**
    Evaluating and Reflecting on Your Writing   **198**

Writing Problem Analysis **199**
    STUDENT MODEL "Uncontrollable Invasion"   **200**
    Prewriting   **202**
    Drafting   **205**
    Revising   **207**
    Editing and **Publishing**   **208**

**Writing for Assessment: Responding to
Expository Prompts** **209**
    Prewriting   **210**
    Drafting   **212**
    STUDENT MODEL   **212**
    Revising and **Editing**   **214**
    Expository Writing on Tests   **215**

contents

PERSUASIVE WRITING

Writing an Argumentative Essay **217**
   Persuasive Writing Warm-Up and Paragraph   218
   Understanding Your Goal   220
   <u>STUDENT MODEL</u> "Ban Gifts and Fundraising by Lobbyists"   221
  Prewriting   223
  Drafting   229
  Revising   235
   • **Focus and Coherence**   236
   • **Organization**   238
   • **Development of Ideas**   240
   • **Voice**   242
   Improving Your Writing: Revising Checklist   244
  Editing   245
   • **Grammar**   246
   • **Sentence Structure**   248
   • **Mechanics:** Punctuation   249
   Checking for Conventions: Editing Checklist   250
  Publishing   251
   Evaluating an Argumentative Essay   252
   Reflecting on Your Writing   258

Writing an Editorial **259**
   <u>STUDENT MODEL</u> "Can Video Games Be Good for You?"   260
  Prewriting   262
  Drafting   265
  Revising   267
  Editing and **Publishing**   268

Writing for Assessment: Responding to Persuasive Prompts **269**
  Prewriting   270
  Drafting   272
   <u>STUDENT MODEL</u>   272
  Revising and **Editing**   274
   Persuasive Writing on Tests   275

INTERPRETIVE RESPONSE

Interpret the Theme of a Play **277**
    Writing Warm-Up and Paragraph   278
    Understanding Your Goal   280
    STUDENT MODEL "Stuck with Each Other"   281
    Prewriting   283
    Drafting   289
    Revising   295
      • Focus and Coherence   296
      • Organization   298
      • Development of Ideas   300
      • Voice   302
    Improving Your Writing: Revising Checklist   304
    Editing   305
      • Grammar   306
      • Sentence Structure   308
      • Mechanics: Punctuation   309
    Checking for Conventions: Editing Checklist   310
    Publishing   311
    Evaluating a Play Interpretation   312
    Reflecting on Your Writing   318

Interpret a Novel **319**
    STUDENT MODEL "The Limits of Being Normal"   320
    Prewriting   322
    Drafting   324
    Revising   325
    Editing and **Publishing**   326

Writing an Analysis of an Expository Text **327**
    Prewriting   330
    Drafting   331
    Revising, Editing, and **Publishing**   332

Writing for Assessment: Responding to Prompts About Literature **333**
    Prewriting   334
    Drafting   336
    STUDENT MODEL "Whose Reality?"   338
    Revising and **Editing**   340
    Responding to Literature on Tests   341

contents

CREATIVE WRITING

Writing Stories... **343**
    The Shape of Stories   344
    STUDENT MODEL "Soaking"   345
    Prewriting   348
    Drafting   351
    Revising and **Editing**   353
    Elements of Fiction   354

Writing Plays... **355**
    STUDENT MODEL "What's the Exchange Rate?"   356
    Prewriting   359
    Drafting   361
    Revising, Editing, and **Publishing**   363

Writing an Audio Play.. **364**
    STUDENT MODEL "Fireworks"   364
    Prewriting: An Audio Play Differs from a Stage Play   365
    Drafting, Revising, Editing, and **Publishing**   366

Writing Poetry... **367**
    Understanding Sonnets   368
    Prewriting   370
    Drafting   371
    Revising, Editing, and **Publishing**   373
    Using Poetry Conventions and Techniques   374
    Writing Free Verse   376
    Writing Cinquains   378

RESEARCH WRITING

Research Skills.. **381**
    Primary vs. Secondary Sources   382
    Evaluating Sources of Information   383
    Using the Internet   384
    Using the Library   385
    Using Reference Books   388

MLA Research Paper 391
Research Paper — 392
STUDENT MODEL "Roosevelt's New Deal: Success or Failure?" — 393
Prewriting — 401
Drafting — 414
Revising — 421
- Focus and Coherence — 422
- Organization — 424
- Development of Ideas — 426
- Voice — 428

Using a Checklist: Revising Checklist — 430
Editing — 431
- Grammar — 432
- Sentence Structure — 434
- Mechanics: Spelling — 435

Editing for Conventions: Using a Checklist — 436
Publishing — 437

Writing Responsibly 439
Using Sources — 440
Avoiding Plagiarism — 441
Writing Paraphrases — 444
Using Quoted Material — 446

Documenting Research 447
Guidelines for In-Text Citations — 448
MLA Works-Cited List — 451
APA Reference List — 459

Making Oral Presentations 461
Planning Your Presentation — 462
Creating Note Cards — 464
Considering Visual Aids — 466
Practicing Your Speech — 467
Delivering Your Presentation — 468
Evaluating a Presentation — 469
Preparing a Multimedia Report — 470
Multimedia Report Traits Checklist — 473

WRITING ACROSS THE CURRICULUM

Recording Your Learning **475**
    Taking Classroom Notes   476
    Taking Reading Notes   477
    Keeping a Learning Log   478

Writing in Science **481**
    Writing Guidelines: Cause-Effect Essay   482
    STUDENT MODEL "Avian Influenza (Bird Flu)"   483
    Writing Guidelines: Directions   487
    STUDENT MODEL "Building a Truss Bridge"   488
    Creating a Multimedia Presentation   490
    Writing Guidelines: Response to an Expository Prompt   491

Writing in Social Studies **493**
    Writing Guidelines: Historical Skit   494
    STUDENT MODEL "Decision at Ticonderoga"   496
    Planning a Multimedia Presentation   498
    Writing Guidelines: Report on Social Studies Research   500
    STUDENT MODEL "Fighting for the Right to Vote"   505

Writing in Math **511**
    Writing Guidelines: Article Summary   512
    Writing Guidelines: Statistical Argument   514
    STUDENT MODEL "Happily Ever After"   515
    Writing Guidelines: Response to a Math Prompt   518
    Other Forms of Writing in Math   520

Writing in the Applied Sciences **521**
    Writing Guidelines: Explanatory Essay   522
    STUDENT MODEL "More Than Weight Loss with High-Protein Diets"   523
    Writing Guidelines: Career Review   524
    STUDENT MODEL "Becoming a Radiology Technician"   525
    Writing Guidelines: Response to a Prompt   526
    STUDENT MODEL A Letter to Your Landlord   527
    Other Forms of Practical Writing   528

Writing in the Arts 529
Writing Guidelines: Research Report — 530
STUDENT MODEL "The Great Migration" — 531
Multimedia Presentation — 535
Writing Guidelines: Performance Review — 539
STUDENT MODEL "Feel the Rhythm" — 540
Writing Guidelines: Response to an Art Prompt — 541

Writing in the Workplace 543
Writing Guidelines: Business Letters — 544
Preparing a Letter for Mailing — 547
Writing Guidelines: Résumé — 548
Writing Guidelines: Memo — 550
Writing Guidelines: Job Application — 552
Writing Guidelines: Meeting Agenda — 554

contents

The Tools of Language

LISTENING AND SPEAKING

Listening and Speaking **557**
    Listening in Class   558
    Speaking in Class   559
    A Closer Look at Listening and Speaking   560

USING REFERENCE MATERIALS
    Using a Dictionary   562
    Using Other Reference Materials   564

LEARNING THE LANGUAGE OF WRITING

Learning the Language of Writing **565**
    Language Strategies   566
    Language of the Writing Process   568
    Language of the Writing Traits   572

Language of Narrative Writing **574**
    Reading the Narrative Model   576
    Oral Language: Narrative Writing   578

Language of Expository Writing **580**
    Reading the Expository Model   582
    Oral Language: Expository Writing   584

Language of Persuasive Essays **586**
    Reading the Persuasive Model   588
    Oral Language: Persuasive Writing   590

Language of Responding to Literature **592**
    Reading the Response to Literature Model   594
    Oral Language: Response to Literature   596

Language of Creative Writing **598**
    Reading the Creative Model   600
    Oral Language: Creative Writing   602

Language of Research Writing **604**
    Reading the Research Writing Model   606
    Oral Language: Research Writing   608

Basic Elements of Writing

Basic Paragraph Skills **611**

  The Parts of a Paragraph   612
  STUDENT MODEL "Hot-Air Ballooning"   612
  Types of Paragraphs   614
    • **Narrative Paragraph**
    STUDENT MODEL "A Good Start"   614
    • **Descriptive Paragraph**
    STUDENT MODEL "The Garden on the Balcony"   615
    • **Expository Paragraph**
    STUDENT MODEL "Hadrian's Wall"   616
    • **Persuasive Paragraph**
    STUDENT MODEL "Control the Pet Population"   617
  Patterns of Organization   618
    • **Classification Order**
    STUDENT MODEL "Types of Plastic"   618
    • **Comparison-Contrast Order**
    STUDENT MODEL "Marsupials and Monotremes"   619
    • **Cause-Effect Order**
    STUDENT MODEL "The Health Benefits of Laughter"   620
    • **Process Organization**
    STUDENT MODEL "Cheese Making"   621
    • **Climax Organization**
    STUDENT MODEL "Anxiously Waiting"   622

Basic Essay Skills **623**

  Understanding the Basic Parts   624
  Outlining Your Ideas   625
  Writing Thesis Statements   626
  Creating Great Beginnings   627
  Developing the Middle Part   628
  Using Transitions   629
  Shaping Great Endings   631
  Learning Key Writing Terms   632
  Using Writing Techniques   634
  Knowing the Different Forms   636

Editing and Proofreading **638**

contents

Proofreader's Guide

Checking Mechanics **641**
- Period, Exclamation Point 641
- Question Mark 642
- Comma 644
- Semicolon 654
- Colon 656
- Hyphen 658
- Apostrophe 662
- Quotation Marks 666
- Italics (Underlining) 670
- Parentheses and Diagonal 672
- Dash 674
- Ellipsis 676
- Brackets 678
- Capitalization 680
- Plurals 686
- Numbers 690
- Abbreviations 692
- Acronyms and Initialisms 694
- Spelling 696

Understanding Idioms **702**

Using the Right Word **708**

Parts of Speech **728**
- Noun 729
- Pronoun 732
- Verb and Verbal 740
- Adjective 754
- Adverb 756
- Preposition 758
- Conjunction and Interjection 760

Understanding Sentences **762**
- Constructing Sentences 762
- Using Sentence Variety 770
- Getting Sentence Parts to Agree ... 776
- Diagramming Sentences 782

TEKS and ELPS Appendix **786**

Why Write?

You write essays, develop research papers, and respond to writing prompts. These are important *practical* types of writing that you do in school. Be prepared. You'll continue to do a lot of practical writing when your schooling is completed. Whether you're applying for your dream job or writing a letter in support of something you believe in, your ability to express yourself and persuade others can make a difference in your future and the future of those around you. Regardless of the career you choose, your job might require writing reports, requests, or proposals, and emailing your managers, coworkers, or clients.

You may also keep a writer's notebook, write about your course work in a learning log, and share your ideas in online communities. These are important *personal* types of writing that help you figure things out and determine where you fit in. Writer Natalie Goldberg says that personal writing "allows you to penetrate your life and learn to trust your own mind." If you're not already doing personal writing, get started as soon as possible.

- **Using a Writer's Notebook**
- **Writing in Action**

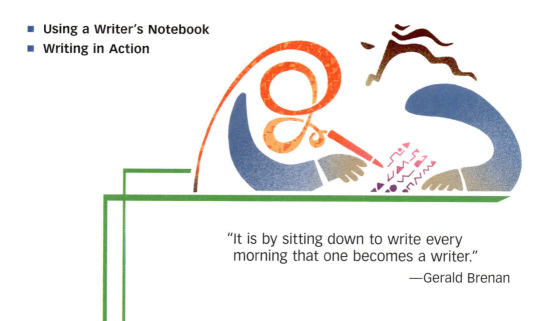

"It is by sitting down to write every morning that one becomes a writer."
—Gerald Brenan

Using a Writer's Notebook

A writer's notebook (also called a journal) is a place to record your thoughts on any topic. As you do so, you will make countless discoveries about your world. You may also find yourself inspired to create more polished forms of writing—stories, poems, and narratives.

Getting started may not be easy for you, but if you keep at it, you will find that writing in a notebook will become part of your regular routine. As writer Thomas Mallon states, "There comes a point when, like a marathon runner, you get through some sort of 'wall' and start running on automatic." To find out if this is true, write every day—no excuses!

Ensuring Success

To make sure that your writer's notebook is a success, consider the approach, quality, and variety of your entries.

- **Approach:** Begin each entry with a high level of enthusiasm. Write about things that matter to you and develop your ideas fully.
- **Quality:** Focus on exploring and developing your ideas, not on producing perfect copy. Your notebook is your place to experiment, take risks, and make mistakes.
- **Variety:** Write some of your entries from different points of view. For example, after a disagreement with a family member, write about the experience from the other person's point of view, or from the perspective of someone who overheard the discussion.

Rules for Notebook Writing

1. Date each entry. The date on an entry helps you find it later and places it in a context with other entries and experiences.
2. Write freely. Push to keep your pen moving or your fingers keyboarding. Continuous writing helps you make discoveries.
3. Write regularly. Develop the habit of writing daily. Then reread your entries to consider what you've discovered. Those ideas may prompt additional writing.

> "Have fun. Your sense of freedom and play will infuse your writing with energy, and that energy will make your words enjoyable to read."
> —Jack Heffron

Writing About Anything—and Everything

There are no limits to what you can write about—just as long as each of your entries connects with you personally. Write about people, places, and things; delve into your hopes, dreams, and memories; explore snippets of conversations that you overhear. Your notebook is the perfect place to explore these topics and form new understandings.

When you can't think of something to write about, refer to the following questions for ideas.

- **Observations:** What is happening around you right now? What are your thoughts and feelings about what's happening?
- **Memories:** What was the best moment of your day? The week? The year? What was the worst moment?
- **Hopes and dreams:** What do you want in life? What do you hope for in the future?
- **People:** What person means the most to you? What person do you most admire? What sort of person do you think you are or wish you were?
- **Places:** Where are you right now? Where do you wish you were? Where do you never want to be again?
- **Things:** What is your favorite possession? Your least favorite? What one thing most closely links you to your past?
- **Thoughts:** What is the most peculiar thing you've learned recently? What is the best piece of advice you've given or received?

Try It!

Find inspiration. Write freely for 8 to 10 minutes. The topic is you. Begin with *I wish I were* . . . and see where your writing takes you. Afterward, underline at least two discoveries that you made in this writing.

Taking It Personally

Here is a page from a student writer's notebook. This powerful entry focuses on the writer's future and does several important things. It . . .

- shows the depth of the writer's feelings,
- captures a time in her life,
- describes a place, and
- makes colorful comparisons.

Sample Notebook Entry

April 3, 2012

When I came home from school I headed right down to the lakefront. It had been a rough day, and it's always been easier to think when I'm looking at that big, blank expanse of water.

My guidance counselor was really upset with me when I told him I wasn't going to college next year. He kept going on about my good science grades, my potential, my future. That's just it. It's my future, but I just don't see college as part of it—at least not right now. My parents aren't thrilled about my decision, either, but it's too late to do anything about it now. I missed all the application deadlines.

Tomorrow I'm going down to enlist in the navy. I know it's kind of weird for a girl, but I want to experience those big ships, to spend time out on the ocean. I can study oceanography and meteorology in the navy better than at any school. There's always been something pulling me to the water. My biology teacher used to talk about how we all came from the sea, and I laughed and said I always thought I had seawater in my veins. I just know this is the right decision, and that I am finally steering the right course.

Note: Keeping a writer's notebook lets you look at ordinary things in new ways, describe your feelings, choose good descriptive words, and practice writing until you feel confident.

Try It!

Write freely for 5 to 10 minutes about an obstacle in your life. Use descriptive details to convey how you felt as you faced it.

Why Write

Writing in Action

A notebook can be a useful tool for sorting out your thoughts. Below are passages that show how three different students use their notebooks.

Examining Feelings

This student uses her notebook to sort out her feelings about her aunt.

> I still can't believe Aunt Tanya is gone, even though I was right there when she slipped away. It's not fair! She wasn't that old! That cancer worked so fast, and she was suffering so much, but at least she was fighting! She was so brave. Two weeks ago, she joked that she'd found a foolproof way to lose weight! Then the regression, and today she's gone. But she's out of pain now. Mom's a basket case, and I guess I can be strong for her. Strong like Aunt Tanya.

Reliving an Experience

Here a student reflects on a memorable time.

> Visiting New York with the choir was the best! I've never seen so many people or so much traffic! When Enrique and I asked directions from a pushcart owner, he gave us free hot dogs and said, "See, New Yorkers aren't so unfriendly!" We even got to sing on the steps of Lincoln Center. My favorite part was riding the ferry to see the Statue of Liberty. Suddenly someone started singing "America the Beautiful," and we all joined in. What an awesome moment! I'll always remember that feeling.

Questioning/Solidifying a Belief

This student explores her mistaken impression about a classmate.

> I don't know why I didn't like Luke. I guess I just figured he was this big popular jock. Then we got paired for this calculus lab. I thought I'd end up doing everything, but surprise! He really worked hard. He's actually had to help me with stuff I didn't understand, but he's been really nice about it. I liked working with him, and I think we can even be friends. I guess I shouldn't have judged him so quickly.

ELPS 2C, 3E, 3G, 4C

Using the Writing Process

Understanding the Writing Process	7
One Writer's Process	13
Using the Holistic Scoring Guide	33

Learning Language

Learning these words and expressions will help you understand this unit.

1. To **stumble upon** means "to discover."
   Discuss with a partner or in a small group something interesting you stumbled upon while doing research.

2. When something is **effective**, it has the intended result.
   What is the most effective way to budget time on a test?

3. If you **clarify** a point, you make it easier to understand.
   Describe a circumstance when someone clarified something for you and explain how your understanding of it changed.

4. To **analyze** is to examine thoroughly.
   How would you analyze the results of an experiment?

Understanding the Writing Process

Writing is mind traveling, destination unknown. Let this statement be a reminder that when you write, you may be engaged in uncharted thinking, mind traveling, so to speak. As you go along, you may stumble upon old memories, face realities of the present, and speculate on what might be. You won't necessarily know where your writing will take you. Your destination will only become clear as you travel further and further into your writing.

This is why writing may frustrate you. You feel you must know exactly where you are going before you start each journey. However, writing often works best when it is the product of an unexpected detour, a surprising thought burst, an ordinary idea gone haywire. That is why writing is thought of as a process; it can't be rushed, and it can't be fully scripted beforehand. In other words, it requires some mind traveling.

- **Becoming a Good Writer**
- **Understanding the Writing Process**
- **The Process in Action**
- **Learning from the Pros**

"There's a sureness to good writing . . . it comes only after writing every day, sometimes for years."

—Anne Bernays

ELPS 2D, 2I, 3E, 3G, 3H, 4G

> "The way around writer's block is to write every day and to give up judging. Just write the novel or story or essay or poem and keep writing."
>
> —Ron Koertge

Becoming a Good Writer

To become a good writer, you should act like one, which means that you should follow this advice:

- **Make reading an important part of your life.** Read anything and everything—books, magazines, and newspapers. Reading helps you internalize the traits of effective writing. Unless you become a regular reader, you can't expect to do your best as a writer.
- **Make writing an important part of your life.** Get into a regular writing routine, and stick to it! When writing becomes something that you want to do, rather than something that you have to do, you will begin to see improvement. (See pages **2–5** for more information.)
- **Explore meaningful topics.** In your personal writing, address your foremost thoughts, feelings, and experiences. In your assignments, write about topics that have special meaning to you. You will do your best work if you write about topics that truly interest you.
- **Set high standards.** If a first draft does not seem inviting, add more detail or voice to the writing. If the nouns and verbs in your writing are too general, replace them with more specific ones. Writer William Zinsser says, "Quality is its own reward." In other words, you will feel good about your writing if it is the result of a strong effort.
- **Try different genres.** Write essays, articles, stories, poems, and plays. Each genre can teach you something about writing.
- **Become a student of writing.** Learn about the traits of writing (see pages **47–50**) and build your writing vocabulary. For example, you should know what is meant by *focus, specific details,* and *transitions*. You should also know the difference between *narrative, descriptive, expository,* and *persuasive* writing.

FYI

Each writer's process is different. Some writers do a lot of planning in their heads, while others need to put everything on paper. In addition, some writers find it helpful to talk about their work throughout the process.

Try It!

Find one quotation that says something inspirational or insightful about writing. Discuss its meaning and significance with a partner.

Understanding the Writing Process

You should develop a piece of writing through a series of steps called the *writing process* before you share it. This page briefly describes these steps.

The Steps in the Writing Process

Prewriting

The first step in the writing process involves selecting a specific topic and genre for conveying the intended meaning to multiple audiences. Then the writer gathers details about the topic and organizes them into a writing plan centered on a thesis or controlling idea.

Drafting

During this step, the writer completes the first draft using the prewriting plan as a guide. This draft is a writer's *first* chance to get everything on paper.

Revising

During revising, the writer reviews the draft for five key traits: **focus and coherence, organization, development of ideas, voice,** and **conventions**. After deciding what changes to make, the writer deletes, moves, adds to, and rewrites parts of the text.

Editing

Then the writer edits the revised draft for grammar, mechanics, and spelling and proofreads the final copy before sharing it for review.

Publishing

Finally, the writer revises the final draft in response to teacher and peer feedback and publishes the work for appropriate audiences.

Analyze your own process. Are you a slow writer or a fast one? Do you do a lot of planning? Do you make many changes in a first draft? Explain.

The Process in Action

The next two pages give a detailed description of each step in the writing process. The graphic below reminds you that, at any time, you can move back and forth between the steps in the process. Also remember that carefully attending to the first steps in the writing process will make the final steps much easier.

Prewriting Planning Your Writing

- Select the correct genre for conveying your intended meaning to multiple audiences.
- Use strategies such as brainstorming, discussion, and background reading to decide on an appropriate topic.

Gathering and Organizing Details

- Gather as many ideas and details as you can about the topic.
- With the purpose of the assignment in mind, find one point to emphasize about the topic—either an interesting part or your personal feeling about it. This will be the thesis or controlling idea of your writing.
- Decide which details fit your topic.
- Organize your details into a writing plan using an outline, a chart, or some other method.

Drafting Developing Your Ideas

- When writing the first draft, concentrate on getting your ideas on paper. Don't try to produce a perfect piece of writing.
- Use your prewriting plan as a guide and include the details you collected, but feel free to add new ideas that occur to you as you go along.
- Be sure your writing has a beginning, a middle, and an ending.

Tip

Write on every other line and on only one side of the paper when using pen or pencil and paper. Double-space on a computer. This will give you room for revising, the next step in the process.

Revising Improving Your Writing

- Set aside your first draft for a while so you can return to it with a fresh perspective.
- Read your first draft slowly and critically.
- Use these questions as a revising guide:
  - Is my topic interesting for the reader?
  - Does the beginning catch the reader's attention?
  - Are the ideas in order and easy to understand?
  - Have I included enough details to clarify my meaning?
  - Does the ending leave the reader with something to think about?
  - Do I sound interested in and knowledgeable about the topic?
  - Does the whole piece have a consistent tone and logical organization?
- Ask at least one person to review your writing and offer suggestions.
- Make as many changes as necessary to improve your writing.

Editing Checking for Conventions

- Check for errors in grammar, mechanics, and spelling.
- Have another person check your writing for errors.
- Prepare a neat final copy.
- Proofread the final copy before publishing it.

Publishing Sharing Your Writing

- Share your final draft with your teacher and peers, and incorporate their feedback.
- Consider submitting your writing to a newspaper or other publication.
- Include the writing in your portfolio.

Tip

For assignments, save all your work. Refer to the earlier drafts and to the teacher's comments on the graded piece for ideas and inspiration for future writing projects.

Consider the process. Some experts say that revising is the most important step in the writing process. With a partner or in a small group, discuss why this may be true.

Learning from the Pros

Keep the following thoughts in mind as you develop your writing. They come from experienced authors who appreciate writing as a process of discovery.

"I don't pick subjects so much as they pick me."
—Andy Rooney

"When I speak to students about writing, I hold myself up as an example of that ancient axiom—write about what you know."
—Robert Cormier

"The inspiration comes while you write."
—Madeleine L'Engle

"Writing comes more easily if you have something to say."
—Sholem Asch

"I think one is constantly startled by the things that appear before you on the page while you write."
—Shirley Hazzard

"By the time I reach a fifth version, my writing begins to have its own voice."
—Ashley Bryan

"Half of my life is an act of revision."
—John Irving

"I am an obsessive rewriter, doing one draft and then another and another, usually five. In a way, I have nothing to say but a great deal to add."
—Gore Vidal

"I believe in impulse and naturalness, but followed by discipline in the cutting."
—Anaïs Nin

"Write visually, write clearly, and make every word count."
—Gloria D. Miklowitz

Try It!

Discuss your experience as a writer in a small group. Then create your own quotation that reflects this experience.

One Writer's Process

At your age, you probably know quite a lot about the steps in the writing process: prewriting, drafting, revising, editing, and publishing. You also probably know that using the process helps you to produce your best work, an effective, finished piece of writing. Since you already understand this, there's no real need to read further, is there?

Well, yes—in fact, reviewing the steps in the writing process is always a good idea. As you become a better writer, it may be tempting to slack off, take it easy, skip a step or two. However, *every* step in the process is essential to doing your best work. This chapter, which chronicles student writer Roberto Salazar's process for a persuasive essay, will serve as a simple reminder of that fact.

- **Previewing the Goals**
- **Prewriting**
- **Drafting**
- **Revising**
- **Editing**
- **Publishing**
- **Assessing the Final Copy**
- **Reflecting on Your Writing**

"If you want to write, or really to create anything, you have to risk falling on your face."

—Allegra Goodman

Previewing the Goals

Before Roberto Salazar began writing his essay, he previewed the goals for persuasive writing, which are shown below. He also looked over the Holistic Scoring Guide on pages 36–37. Both of these activities helped him get started.

Traits of Persuasive Writing

- **Focus and Coherence**
  Select a timely topic, a controversial issue that you care about. Form your opinion and clearly support it with logical reasons.

- **Organization**
  State your opinion in the beginning, defend your position with various forms of support in the middle, and end with a call for action. Use transitions throughout the piece to guide the reader from one idea to the next.

- **Development of Ideas**
  Support your ideas thoroughly with unique and thoughtful details. Include information on a range of relevant perspectives and craft your argument to move a disinterested or opposed audience.

- **Voice**
  Use a confident voice that engages the reader, balances facts and feelings, and sounds authentic and original.

- **Conventions**
  Follow rules of grammar, usage, mechanics (capitalization, punctuation), sentence structure, and spelling.

Try It!

List two or three topics that would be suitable for a persuasive essay. Considering voice, what tone would be appropriate for each topic? What important terms would you need to explain for each?

One Writer's Process

Prewriting Planning Your Writing

Roberto's economics teacher assigned the following topic. Roberto recognized that a persuasive essay is an appropriate genre for this prompt because it asks him to decide on a position and defend it.

> Recently we've discussed the government's obligations in a market economy—providing for national defense, overseeing health-care initiatives, addressing environmental concerns, among others. Based on what you've learned about the federal budget process, do you support greater reductions in military spending, or is the current spending level necessary? Support your thesis, or position, with valid reasons and evidence.

Reflecting on the Topic

Roberto made a list of pros and cons on the issue.

YES to reductions	NO to reductions
• The amount we spend on defense prevents us from effectively addressing other issues.	• Our military should be the best in the world.
• Spending a lot on defense encourages other countries to compete.	• We need to keep up with other countries.
• Having a strong military makes us vulnerable to involvement in conflicts.	• Defense industries have a big effect on the economy.
• We should focus on peaceful solutions.	• There will always be conflict in the world; we have to be ready.

Roberto found that he still had some questions. He wrote them down and researched them before forming his opinion.

> • How much does our military spend, especially in relation to other countries?
> • What do we spend on the nation's health and education?

Try It!

Which of Roberto's reasons is strongest? Weakest? Which of the opposing viewpoints would you address in a persuasive essay? Why?

Prewriting Gathering Details

Roberto gathered valid, reliable evidence about defense spending from primary and secondary sources. He recorded his source information on note cards, although he also could have used a computer document or application.

Sources of Information

Stockholm International Peace Research Institute. *SIPRI Yearbook 2009: Armaments, Disarmament and International Security.* Oxford: Oxford UP, 2009. Print.

Peña, Charles. "Record Defense Spending, Less Security." *Houston Chronicle* 13 Nov. 2008,

"Department of Defense." *Office of Management and Budget.* **The White House,** n.d. Web. 20 Feb. 2011 <http://www.whitehouse.gov/omb/>

Quotations and Paraphrases

Roberto used note cards to record quotations and paraphrases, too. He was sure to include the source for each.

Quotation

"The reality is: The United States would be just as secure if we reduced military spending, perhaps more so."

Source: Peña

Paraphrase

Worldwide military spending reached 1.4 trillion dollars in 2008, and the United States was responsible for a large portion of that amount.

Source: Stockholm

Try It!

Find some sources that would answer Roberto's questions from page 15.

Prewriting Forming a Thesis Statement

Once Roberto had formed his opinion and had enough information to support it, he was ready to write the *thesis, or position, statement* for his essay. An effective thesis statement consists of two parts: a specific topic plus a particular feeling or opinion about it. Roberto wrote this thesis statement:

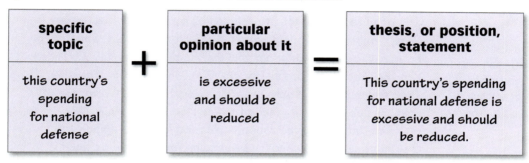

Organizing the Essay

Next, Roberto used an outline to plan an organizing structure appropriate to the purpose, audience, and context of his essay.

I. Introduction
II. Background
   A. Explanation of how federal budget is distributed
   B. National defense as nearly half of discretionary budget
   C. Comparison to budgets for education and health
III. Key Supporting Points
   A. Other countries' spending on defense far less than U.S.'s
   B. U.S. current level of preparedness
   C. Public support to reduce defense spending
IV. Concession
   A. Defense contractors benefiting from large budget
   B. Economic impact of losing some defense contracts not great
V. Conclusion

Try It!

Imagine that you had taken the opposite side of the issue. Write a thesis statement that reflects that opinion; then create an outline like the one above.

Drafting Developing Your Ideas

Roberto referred to his outline as he wrote his first draft. At this point, he wanted to get all his ideas down on paper without worrying about writing the perfect essay.

The first paragraph states the issue and ends with the thesis statement.

    It sure takes a lot of cash to make a country feel secure. China's military spending was $84.9 billion. Defense spending for France, the United Kingdom, and Germany totaled $177.8 billion. Yet the United States spent $607 billion ("Military Spending"). That amounts to 42 percent of the world's total. Worldwide military spending had reached 1.4 trillion dollars by 2008, with the United States responsible for a lopsided amount. It is obvious that this country's spending for national defense is excessive and should be reduced.

The second paragraph gives background information.

    In the United States, the federal budget is classified in two ways. National defense falls under a category of the federal budget called "discretionary" spending. Congress decides on the level of resources set aside for any specific area. Congress decides where to increase or decrease funds. Congress earmarks the other two-thirds of the budget for programs where the level of funding is decided by the number of people who is qualified for entitlements. Funding for the Department of Defense currently accounts for nearly half of the federal discretionary budget. The president's request for 2010 was $533.8 billion for the Department of Defense ("Dept. of Defense"). Besides this, the departments' budget does not include outlays for ongoing overseas military operations. In fact, when you include war spending and nuclear activities, an increase of nearly 80 percent is shown in defense spending from 2000 to 2009 ("Center for Arms Control"). The Department of Education merited a request of $46.7 billion—less than ten percent of the defense budget; and the amount budgeted for health was $80.5 billion ("FY '10"). Priorities seam a bit skewed here.

The next three paragraphs support the thesis.

    As the U.S. military gobbles up more and more of the world's military spending pie, here is a logicle thought: decreasing the amount spent on national defense would have little affect on U.S. military capability. Especially relative to other countries' military power. Even if the defense budget were cut in half, the next 2 big spenders combined wouldn't come near our level.

Further, the U.S. doesn't need the level of military preparedness it currently has. Another country is unlikely to wage a conventional war against us. Much of our defense preparedness is based on the premise of unrealistic scenarios. In the words of Charles Peña, "The real threat today is not the armies of other nations but the terrorist threat represented by al-Qaeda, which is relatively undeterred by massive U.S. military power" (Peña). In other words, continuously increasing military funding will do little to prevent terrorism. A change in terrorist thinking will come only with international cooperation to address poor conditions.

For another thing, there are lots of public support to reduce military spending. In a 2008 Gallup poll, 44 percent of the respondents thought the government spent too much on defense, 30 percent said it was about right, and only 22 percent thought spending was too little ("Gallup"). While more recent polls show an increase in the number of people who think defense spending is appropriate, a significant amount still believe we spend too much. In addition, there are dozens of organizations and Web sites that support decreased defense spending. Congress's leaders should take note.

While it is true that the current level of spending benefits many defense contractors and other businesses, their impact on the economy isn't important. If these businesses could no longer rely on government contracts, they could evolve to the market (convert their production to non-military use). This is exactly what many defense contractors did following WWII.

It is not crazy to believe that huge military budgets are outdated. Humanitarian efforts make a huge difference. Contrary to "hawkish" thinking, when conflict does arise, peaceful resolutions are possible. It is time to start taking apart the military machine and spend that money better.

Revising For Focus and Coherence and Organization

Roberto set his essay aside for a while before giving it a fresh look. When he did review it, he rechecked the goals on page 14. Then he wrote down some changes he planned to make in terms of focus and coherence and organization.

Focus and Coherence

"I could draw the reader's attention to my topic better in the opening. I need to clarify details in some places and delete one or two details that don't contribute to the reader's understanding of my topic."

Organization

"I should separate the second paragraph into two paragraphs to improve the organization. I need to be sure my ending is a strong finish for this essay."

Roberto's First Revision

Here are some of the revisions that Roberto made in his essay.

Using a rhetorical question in the opening immediately draws the reader's attention to the topic.

An explanation adds emphasis.

<del>It sure takes a lot of cash</del> **How much cash does it take** to make a country feel secure**?** China's military spending was $84.9 billion. Defense spending for France, the United Kingdom, and Germany totaled $177.8 billion. Yet the United States spent $607 billion ("Military Spending"). That amounts to 42 percent **—close to half—** of the world's total. Worldwide military spending had reached 1.4 trillion dollars by 2008, with the United States responsible for a lopsided

One Writer's Process

An unnecessary idea is deleted.	amount. It is obvious that this country's spending for national defense is excessive and should be reduced.
	In the United States, ~~the federal budget is classified in two ways.~~ National defense falls under a category of the federal budget called "discretionary" spending. Congress decides on the level of resources set aside for any specific area. Congress decides where to increase or decrease funds.
An added detail completes the explanation.	Congress earmarks the other two-thirds of the budget for "mandatory" spending: programs where the level of funding is decided by the number of people who is qualified for entitlements.
A new paragraph improves the organization.	¶ Funding for the Department of Defense currently accounts for nearly half of the federal discretionary budget. The president's request for 2010 was $533.8 billion for the Department of Defense ("Dept. of Defense"). Besides this, the departments' budget does not include ~~outlays~~ costs for ongoing overseas military
A few well-placed words clarify the statistics.	operations. In fact, when you include war spending ~~and nuclear~~ activities, an increase of nearly 80 percent is shown in defense spending from 2000 to 2009 ("Center for Arms Control"). The Department of Education meritted a request of just $46.7 billion—less than ten percent of the defense budget . . .

Try It!

Review the changes Roberto made to the beginning of his essay. Make similar revisions to the rest of the essay, suggesting at least one revision to improve focus and coherence and one to improve organization.

Revising Using a Peer Response Sheet

Kinsey evaluated Roberto's essay using a scoring guide like the one on pages 36–37. Her suggestions on the response sheet below showed Roberto where he could make additional improvements.

Peer Response Sheet

Writer: _Roberto_   Responder: _Kinsey_

Title: _Cut Defense Spending Now!_

What I liked about your writing:

I'm glad you included lots of facts and figures to support your thesis.

I can tell you really believe your opinion is right!

Changes I would suggest:

More details are needed in some areas (for instance, the year of the budgets you mention in the first paragraph). Also, it's hard to imagine how much $533 billion really is. Could you clarify that somehow?

Try It!

Review Kinsey's suggestions for improvement. Which suggestion seems to be the most important? What else would you suggest to improve the essay? (Look at the explanations of focus and coherence and organization on page 14 to refresh your memory.) Explain your ideas to a partner.

Roberto's Revision Using a Peer Response

Here are some revisions Roberto made, using Kinsey's comments.

> How much cash does it take to make a country feel secure? China's 2008 military spending was $84.9 billion. Defense spending for France, the United Kingdom, and Germany totaled $177.8 billion. Yet the United States spent $607 billion ("Military Spending"). That amounts to 42 percent—close to half—of the world's total. Worldwide military spending had reached 1.4 trillion dollars by 2008, with the United States responsible for a lopsided amount (Stockholm). It is obvious that this country's spending for national defense is excessive and should be reduced.
>
> In the United States, national defense falls under a category of the federal budget called "discretionary" spending. Congress decides on the level of resources set aside for any specific area. Congress decides where to increase or decrease funds. Congress earmarks the other two-thirds of the budget for "mandatory" spending: programs (such as social security) where the level of funding is decided by the number of people who is qualified for entitlements.
>
> Funding for the Department of Defense currently accounts for nearly half of the federal discretionary budget. The president's request for 2010 was $533.8 billion for the Department of Defense ("Dept. of Defense"). Besides this, To give some perspective on how much $533.8 billion is, a mere five percent of that budget, or $30 billion, is the estimated amount needed annually to end world hunger overseas military operations.... (Borgen 17).

- The year of the budget is added.
- A statistic is placed earlier in the paragraph for more impact, and the source of the figure is stated.
- An example that improves the definition of the term is added.
- A comparison helps the reader understand the enormity of a figure.

Revising For Development of Ideas and Voice

Roberto also reviewed his writing for its development of ideas and voice. His thoughts below tell you what changes he planned to make.

Development of Ideas

"I could combine related sentences to improve the flow. The reader will then be able to follow my argument from one point to the next. I could also expand a sentence here and there."

Voice

"I can use more formal language in some spots. I need to change some words to improve the style and tone. These changes will help me engage the reader."

Try It!

Review the second revision of Roberto's essay (page 23). Name two ways in which you would improve his development of ideas. What two or three changes would you make in his voice? Compare your ideas to Roberto's revisions on the next page.

"Learn to evaluate your own work with a dispassionate eye. . . . The lessons you acquire will be all the more valuable because you've mastered your craft from within."

—Sue Grafton

Roberto's Revisions for Development of Ideas and Voice

Here are the revisions Roberto made after reviewing the development of ideas and voice of his writing.

Sentences are combined and a statistic is revised to improve the development of ideas.

How much ~~cash~~ **money** does it take to make a country feel secure? Worldwide military spending had reached 1.4 trillion dollars by 2008, with the United States responsible for a ~~lopsided~~ **disproportionate** amount (Stockholm). **While** China's 2008 military spending was $84.9 billion, **and expenditures for Europe's top three spenders** ~~Defense spending for France, the United Kingdom, and Germany~~ totaled $177.8 billion, ~~Yet~~ the United States spent $607 billion ("Military Spending"). That amounts to 42 percent—close to half—of the world's total. **With the numbers telling the story,** ~~It~~ is obvious that this country's spending for national defense is excessive and should be reduced.

A phrase is added to further engage the reader.

In the United States, national defense falls under a category of the federal budget called "discretionary" spending. Congress decides on the level of resources ~~set aside for~~ **allocated to** any specific area. ~~Congress decides~~ **and** where to increase or decrease funds. ~~Congress earmarks~~ **is earmarked** the other two-thirds of the budget for "mandatory" spending: programs (such as social security) where the level of funding is ~~decided~~ **determined** by the number of people who is ~~qualified~~ **eligible** for ~~entitlements~~ **benefits.**

Sentence beginnings are varied.

The formality, style, and tone is addressed throughout.

Funding for the Department of Defense currently accounts for nearly half of the federal discretionary budget. The president's request for 2010 was $533.8 billion for the Department of Defense ("Dept. of Defense"). To give . . .

Editing For Conventions

Roberto's last step in the process was to check for grammar, mechanics, and spelling errors. He used the "Proofreader's Guide" in the back of his *Write Source* textbook and the checklist below.

Conventions

"I'll look carefully at my essay for errors in grammar, mechanics, and spelling."

GRAMMAR

_____ 1. Do I use the proper tense and voice for my verbs?

_____ 2. Do my subjects and verbs agree in number?

_____ 3. Do my pronouns clearly agree with their antecedents?

_____ 4. Do I use the right words (*there, their, they're*)?

SENTENCE STRUCTURE

_____ 5. Do I use a variety of correctly structured sentences that clearly communicate my ideas?

MECHANICS (CAPITALIZATION AND PUNCTUATION)

_____ 6. Do I use end punctuation correctly?

_____ 7. Do I use commas correctly?

_____ 8. Do I correctly italicize or use quotation marks for titles?

_____ 9. Do I use apostrophes correctly?

_____ 10. Have I capitalized all the proper nouns and adjectives?

SPELLING

_____ 11. Have I spelled words correctly?

_____ 12. Have I used the spell-checker on my computer?

_____ 13. Have I used abbreviations correctly?

Try It!

Find two errors in Roberto's revised draft on page **25**. Did you find the same errors as he found? (See page **27**.)

Roberto's Editing

Here is a sample of Roberto's editing. (See page **639** for common editing and proofreading marks.)

> ... Congress decides on the level of resources allocated to any specific area and where to increase or decrease funds. The other two-thirds of the budget is earmarked for "mandatory" spending: programs (such as social security) where the level of funding is determined by the number of people who ~~is~~ *are* eligible for benefits.
>
> Funding for the Department of Defense currently accounts for nearly half of the federal discretionary budget. The president's request for 2010 was $533.8 billion for the Department of Defense ("Dept. of Defense"). To give some perspective on how much $533.8 billion is, a mere ~~five~~ *5* percent of ~~t~~ that budget, or $30 billion, is the estimated amount needed annually to end world hunger (Borgen 17). Besides this, the department~~'~~s budget does not include costs for ongoing overseas military operations. In fact, when you include war spending activities, an increase of nearly 80 percent is seen from 2000 to 2009 ("Center for Arms Control"). The Department of Education ~~meritted~~ *merited* a request of just $46.7 billion—less than ~~ten~~ *10* percent of the defense budget; and the amount budgeted for health was $80.5 billion ("FY '10"). Priorities ~~seam~~ *seem* a bit skewed here.

A proper noun is capitalized, and subject-verb agreement is corrected.

Numeric expressions are corrected, and a misplaced apostrophe is fixed.

Misspelled and misused words are corrected.

Publishing Sharing Your Writing

Roberto met with his peer reviewer Kinsey again, who was impressed with the improvements Roberto had made. Then he used the information below to produce a clean and effective copy of his final essay.

Tips for Handwritten Copies

- Use blue or black ink and write clearly.
- Write your name according to your teacher's instructions.
- Skip a line and center your title on the first page; skip another line and begin your essay.
- Indent each paragraph and leave a one-inch margin on all four sides.

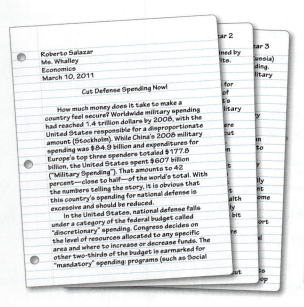

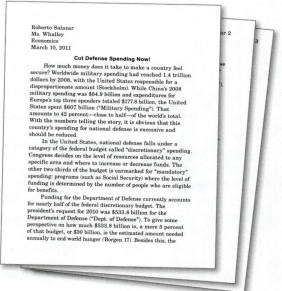

Tips for Computer Copies

- Use an easy-to-read font set at 12-point type size.
- Double-space the text and set your margins so that you have a one-inch space around the outside of each page.

Roberto's Final Copy

Roberto submitted his final essay with confidence. He felt that his writing met his goals and satisfied the terms of the assignment.

Roberto Salazar
Ms. Whalley
Economics
March 10, 2011

Cut Defense Spending Now!

How much money does it take to make a country feel secure? Worldwide military spending had reached 1.4 trillion dollars by 2008, with the United States responsible for a disproportionate amount (Stockholm). While China's 2008 military spending was $84.9 billion and expenditures for Europe's top three spenders totaled $177.8 billion, the United States spent $607 billion ("Military Spending"). That amounts to 42 percent—close to half—of the world's total. With the numbers telling the story, it is obvious that this country's spending for national defense is excessive and should be reduced.

In the United States, national defense falls under a category of the federal budget called "discretionary" spending. Congress decides on the level of resources allocated to any specific area and where to increase or decrease funds. The other two-thirds of the budget is earmarked for "mandatory" spending: programs (such as Social Security) where the level of funding is determined by the number of people who are eligible for benefits.

Funding for the Department of Defense currently accounts for nearly half of the federal discretionary budget. The president's request for 2010 was $533.8 billion for the Department of Defense ("Dept. of Defense"). To give some perspective on how much $533.8 billion is, a mere 5 percent of that budget, or $30 billion, is the estimated amount needed annually to end world hunger (Borgen 17). Besides this, the

Salazar 2

department's budget does not include costs for ongoing military operations. In fact, when you include war spending and activities, an increase of nearly 80 percent is shown between 2000 and 2009 ("Center for Arms Control"). The Department of Education merited a request of just $46.7 billion—less than 10 percent of the defense budget; and the amount budgeted for health was $80.5 billion ("FY '10"). Priorities seem a bit skewed here.

As the U.S. military devours more and more of the world's military spending pie, it is clear that decreasing our defense budget would have little effect on our military capability relative to that of other countries. Even if the defense budget were cut in half, the next two big spenders combined—China and France—wouldn't come near our level of spending. The U.S. would still have the richest military in the world.

Further, the need for our current level of military preparedness is questionable. Another country is unlikely to wage a conventional war against us. Charles Peña of the Coalition for a Realistic Foreign Policy and an analyst for MSNBC television says, "The real threat today is not the armies of other nations but the terrorist threat represented by al-Qaeda, which is relatively undeterred by massive U.S. military power" (Peña 17). In other words, increased military funding will not prevent terrorism. The terrorist legacy will change only as the world addresses conditions that generate unrest.

Additionally, a significant portion of the public supports reduced military spending. In a 2008 Gallup poll, 44 percent of the respondents thought the government spent too much on defense, 30 percent said it was about right, and only 22 percent thought spending was too little ("Gallup"). While more recent polls show an increase in the number of people who think defense spending is appropriate, a large constituency still believes we spend too much. There are also many organizations and Web sites that support decreased defense spending.

Congress should take note. Although defense spending benefits the defense contractors and other businesses, these businesses do not make or break the economy. If they lost some government contracts, they could adapt to the market (convert their production to nonmilitary use). Many defense contractors had to do this after WWII.

It is not idealistic to believe that huge military budgets are an antiquated way of dealing with potential conflict. Humanitarian efforts can make a huge difference in the very need for defense, and, contrary to "hawkish" thinking, when conflict does arise, peaceful resolutions are possible. It's time to dismantle the military behemoth and put those funds to better use.

Assessing the Final Copy

The teacher used a scoring guide like the one found on pages **36–37** to assess Roberto's final copy. (A **4** is the best score.) The teacher wrote comments under each trait.

Holistic Scoring Guide: Score Point 3

Focus and Coherence
Your reasoning is clear; all ideas connect to each other and your thesis.

Organization
You clearly state your thesis in the beginning, in each middle paragraph you offer background and support your opinion, and you make a call to action in the ending. You use transitions effectively, and your sentences read smoothly from one idea to the next.

Development of Ideas
Your choice of details makes your argument very convincing. However, opposing arguments could have been addressed in greater detail. This was the weakest aspect of your essay.

Voice
Your voice conveys a sense of urgency that engages the reader. Your formality, style, and tone is appropriate for the audience.

Conventions
Your writing follows conventions rules and is free of careless errors.

Reflecting on Your Writing

Roberto filled out a reflection sheet to help him think about how he would revise his final draft in response to his teacher's feedback.

Roberto Salazar
Ms. Whalley
Economics
March 13, 2011

Persuasive Essay: Cut Defense Spending Now!

1. The best part of my essay is . . .

    the ending. It expresses my feelings concisely and powerfully.

2. The part that still needs work is . . .

    the opposing argument. It's a little weak.

3. The most important part of my prewriting and planning was . . .

    my fact finding. I was alarmed at what I found, and I think this came through in my voice.

4. During revising, I spent a lot of time dealing with . . .

    adding details and refining word choice.

5. What I've learned about this type of essay is . . .

    that it's important to care about my topic. Without that, it would be difficult to convince others to support my position.

6. Here is one question I still have . . .

    If I derive a figure, fact, or detail from a source's statistics, do I cite that source?

Using the Holistic Scoring Guide

The scoring guides in this book include descriptions of accepted standards for the five traits of good writing (focus and coherence, organization, development of ideas, voice, and conventions). You can use these descriptions to evaluate your writing according to a given scale.

Using a scoring guide throughout the process of your formal writing will result in a better paragraph, essay, or report. During prewriting, review the scoring guide so you know what is expected. During drafting and revising, compare your writing to the ratings in the scoring guide. When you finish writing, check the scoring guide once more. Use a scoring guide throughout the process, and your writing will be the best it can be.

- **Understanding the Holistic Scoring Guide**
- **Reading the Holistic Scoring Guide**
- **Write Source Holistic Scoring Guide**
- **Evaluating an Essay**
- **Assessing an Essay**

"It is only through evaluation that value exists: and without evaluation the nut of existence would be hollow."

—Friedrich Nietzsche

Understanding the Holistic Scoring Guide

Have you ever rated something on a scale of 1 (terrible) to 10 (fantastic)? The Holistic Scoring Guide is a rating scale for evaluating an entire piece of writing. The scoring guide rates a piece of writing on a scale of 1 (not effective) to 4 (highly effective). It provides a description of writing traits that match each score point on the scale.

The Holistic Scoring Guide can help you to create a highly effective response to a writing assignment. Here's how it works.

Understanding an Assignment

Read through the assignment and the scoring guide. Familiarize yourself with the criteria for an effective piece of writing, such as "Maintains focus throughout the writing" and "All ideas clearly connect to each other and to the main idea." Ask questions if you are unsure about any part of the assignment.

Using the Writing Process

As you move through the different stages of the writing process, focus on the descriptions in the scoring guide.

Evaluation Guide

The holistic scoring guide uses a 4-point system to evaluate writing. Scores of 4 or 3 indicate strong levels of mastery in most aspects of writing. Scores of 2 or 1 show that the writer has not yet mastered many aspects of writing.

A **4** means that the writing is **highly effective.**
It shows an overall mastery of the five writing traits.

A **3** means that the writing is very **generally effective.**
It clearly shows some mastery of most of the five traits.

A **2** means that the writing is **somewhat effective.**
It shows that the writer has little mastery of most traits.

A **1** means that the writing is **not effective.**
It indicates that the writer needs to work to master most of the traits.

Using the Holistic Scoring Guide

Reading the Holistic Scoring Guide

The scoring guide in this book is color coded for the four score points. There is a description for each score point to help you assess your writing.

Score Points

Writing at this score point is highly effective.

Focus and Coherence Maintains focus throughout the writing; all ideas clearly connect to each other and to the main idea. Includes a meaningful introduction and conclusion that add depth to the composition.

Organization Employs an effective organizational pattern for the purpose and audience. Has a smooth and logical flow; transitions help the reader move from one idea to the next.

Writing at this score point is generally effective.

Focus and Coherence Maintains focus, with minor lapses; most ideas are clearly connected to each other and to the main idea. An introduction and conclusion add some depth to the composition.

Organization Uses an organizational pattern that is mostly effective for the purpose and audience. Generally flows but could use a few more transitions.

Guiding Your Writing

The holistic scoring guide helps you . . .

- **plan your work**—knowing what is expected;
- **create a strong first draft**—emphasizing *focus and coherence, organization,* and *voice;*
- **revise and edit your work**—considering each trait; and
- **assess your final draft**—evaluating the traits throughout your entire piece of writing.

Analyze the differences. Look at the descriptions of "Focus and Coherence" at a 4-point score and at a 3-point score. Write a few sentences explaining the differences between the two descriptions in your own words. Then do the same for one of the other traits.

Write Source Holistic Scoring Guide

Use the descriptions at each score point to evaluate your own writing or that of your peers.

Writing at this score point is highly effective.

Focus and Coherence Maintains focus throughout the writing; all ideas clearly connect to each other and to the main idea. Includes a meaningful introduction and conclusion that add depth to the composition.

Organization Employs an effective organizational pattern for the purpose and audience. Has a smooth and logical flow; transitions help the reader move from one idea to the next.

Writing at this score point is generally effective.

Focus and Coherence Maintains focus, with minor lapses; most ideas are clearly connected to each other and to the main idea. An introduction and conclusion add some depth to the composition.

Organization Uses an organizational pattern that is mostly effective for the purpose and audience. Generally flows but could use a few more transitions.

Writing at this score point is somewhat effective.

Focus and Coherence Is somewhat unfocused, but the reader can understand how ideas are related. Some ideas do not contribute to the writing as a whole. The introduction and conclusion are superficial.

Organization The flow of the ideas is not always clear. The organizational pattern may not suit the purpose and audience. Wordiness and repetition may interfere with the flow of ideas.

Writing at this score point is not effective.

Focus and Coherence Lacks focus; includes a substantial amount of information not connected to the main idea. Is missing an introduction and/or conclusion.

Organization Has no clear organizational pattern or logical flow of ideas. Lacks transitions. Repetition or wordiness may interfere with the progression of ideas.

Using the Holistic Scoring Guide

Development of Ideas Ample support and specific details allow the reader to appreciate the writer's points. A novel approach to the topic may add to the overall quality of the writing.

Voice Engages the reader throughout the writing. Sounds authentic and original; expresses the writer's unique perspective.

Conventions Shows a strong command of conventions, allowing the reader to focus on the writer's message.

Development of Ideas Supports all ideas, but some need to be developed more thoroughly. The presentation of ideas may be thoughtful but may not reflect a novel approach to the topic.

Voice Engages the reader for most of the writing. Sounds somewhat authentic and original and expresses the writer's unique perspective.

Conventions Includes only minor errors in conventions; errors do not interfere with the reader's ability to understand the writer's message.

Development of Ideas Ideas may be developed only superficially. Some information may be missing. The reader's ability to appreciate the writer's points is compromised.

Voice Engages the reader occasionally. Sounds authentic and original in only a few sections. Does not express a unique perspective.

Conventions Errors reflect a limited command of writing conventions and interfere with the flow of ideas in the writing.

Development of Ideas Support is lacking or is only general and vague. Important information may be left out. The reader has difficulty understanding the writer's points.

Voice Does not engage the reader. Shows little or no evidence of the writer's individuality or unique perspective.

Conventions The writing shows major problems with conventions, which interferes with the reader's ability to understand the message.

Evaluating an Essay

To learn how to evaluate a persuasive essay, you will use the holistic scoring guide on pages **36–37** and the essays that follow. These essays are examples of writing for each score on the scoring guide (1–4).

Notice that the first essay received a score of 4. Read the description for a score of 4 on pages **36–37**. Then read the persuasive essay. Use the same steps to study the other examples. As you read, concentrate on the overall quality of the writing in each example.

Writing that fits a score of 4 is very strong.

Support the Green River Trail

Can a relic from long ago be recycled for the benefit of our community? That's the question Carstensville residents explored at last week's city council meeting. The people were responding to a proposal to convert the old railroad line through the city to a multiple-use recreation trail. After experiencing such a trail firsthand and researching how rail trails can positively impact a community, I am ready to support the proposal. The Green River Rail Trail will provide health, safety, economic, and environmental benefits to Carstensville. That is why voters should agree to fund the trail.

During a recent vacation trip to Dallas, I had the pleasure of bicycling on the Katy Trail, a rail-to-trail conversion. All along the trail, I experienced a part of Dallas many people have never seen. Rolling along through a vivid green landscape, I saw flowers in bloom and heard birds sing. I watched hundreds of other people enjoying the trail and discovering its wonders on foot, by bicycle, and on in-line skates. It was one of the best experiences of my vacation.

Personal enjoyment is only one of the benefits offered by rail trails. Perhaps first among those additional benefits is the opportunity to improve public health. According to the US Centers for Disease Control (CDC), too many Americans are overweight. In 2008, every state except Colorado had a population in which more than 20% of the people were obese and at risk for diabetes, heart disease, and other chronic illnesses. According to the CDC, one remedy for this problem is more

Clearly states the main idea: voters should support the trail.

Personal anecdote helps create a strong voice.

exercise. Rail trails provide a way for people of all ages to get the exercise they need.

Many towns and cities lack safe places for outdoor recreation. In our town, many streets do not have sidewalks. People who wish to walk, ride, or skate are forced to put themselves at risk by traveling in the road. The proposed trail crosses only two roads, and those roads are seldom traveled by vehicles. By avoiding major roadways, the Green River Trail will create a safe recreation space for all.

This trail will improve our community's economic health as well. A 2004 study by the Institute for Transportation Research and Education at North Carolina State University showed that bicycle trails attract $60 million in tourist spending to the state's Outer Banks region every year. Carstensville already includes one tourist attraction—Green River Park. The proposed trail will link the park to downtown, bringing more people—and more money—to our town's businesses.

Finally, the position of the trail along commuter routes will encourage people to walk or cycle to work. Taking cars off the road will lessen the traffic burden that has created traffic jams downtown. It will also mean fewer cars sending pollutants into the air and a reduction in greenhouse gases, which contribute to global warming.

As you can see, the proposed Green River Trail would provide numerous benefits to the people of our community—and not only those who plan to use the trail. Improved health and safety, a healthy economy, less downtown car traffic, and a cleaner environment benefit us all. So please vote to support the Green River Trail. You'll find yourself enjoying its benefits soon!

Callouts:
- No errors in conventions.
- Ideas are supported by specific details.
- Conclusion supports main idea by connecting to the reader.

Writing that fits a score of 3 is strong in most ways.

Focuses on one main idea.

Farmers' Markets: A Bargain for Everyone

Saturday, my family and I went shopping for produce. My dad chose some ripe tomatoes. My mom picked out some green beans and eggplant. My brother Carlos and I went straight for the sweets—peaches so tasty we couldn't wait to eat them. If you think we were at the supermarket, think again. We shopped at the Austin Farmers' Market. It was the first time we did this, but it won't be the last. We discovered what many Americans are learning: farmers' markets are a bargain for everyone.

The idea behind farmers' markets is simple. People who grow fruits and vegetables can bring their products straight to the consumer. This simple formula can make a big difference in a farmer's ability to make a profit. Since farmers can make more money, they are happier. And happier farmers are more productive.

The economic benefit of farmers' markets extends beyond individual farm owners. Local farm businesses tend to spend their profits locally. And that means a boost for the local economy. In order to raise, process, and sell their crops, farmers need to buy seeds, grains, and equipment like tractors. Most often, they buy from local farm supply stores. Local farmers also hire people to work on their farms. That means more jobs for people who live here.

Another critical benefit for the consumer is freshness. Much of the produce in large supermarkets is brought in from, hundreds, or even thousands of miles away. Before they arrive in the store, strawberries and corn, beets and broccoli may have been sitting for weeks in a refrigerated warehouse. Carlos and I once got some blueberries at the supermarket that were not fresh. They tasted terrible, and I felt a little bit sick after eating them.

Buying locally grown products at a farmers market benefits

Progression of thought from sentence to sentence is generally smooth.

Using the Holistic Scoring Guide

Minor errors in conventions create few disruptions.

Ideas are developed and show some depth of thought.

Voice sustains connection to the reader.

Buying locally grown products at a farmers market benefits the envirnment as well. Bringing produce to supermarkets from thousands of miles away means feuling trucks, boats, and even planes for long journeys. Long distance transport pollutes the air. In addition, many local farmers grow their food organically. This means they don't use chemical fertilizers and pesticides that polluter our water supplies.

Food safety is another reason to give farmers' markets a try. In recent years, thousands of illnesses and even some deaths have been caused by contamination of food in huge warehouses and processing facilities. When so much food is being handled at one time, it can be hard to keep track of things like contamination. So contamination can happen. In contrast, local farmers handle much smaller amounts of food. They can easily tell when their is a problem.

Farmers' markets provide a chance for farmers to make a better profit. They boost the local economy, and help local businesses stay healthy and strong. They help you keep healthy, too, by providing nutritious food without danger of contamination. And they keep the environment healthy by cutting down on air pollution and dangerous chemicals. If you still aren't convinced that farmers' markets are a great place to shop, take this challenge. Visit a local farmers' market. Find your favorite fruits and vegetables. Then buy some from the farmer. I think you'll taste the difference.

Writing that fits a score of 2 is strong in some ways.

> The opening paragraph is somewhat focused.

> At points, the writer engages the reader.

> Development of ideas is superficial.

> Several errors in conventions.

Parents Should Limit Kids' Screen Time

Do you know any kids who spend all of their time on the computer or watching television. If you are like most people, you do. More and more kids are spending hours every day watching television and playing computer games. If you asked them, they would say they are enjoying themselves. I disagree. Too much "screen time" is making them miss out on a lot of other things they should be doing or would enjoy better. If there parents would limit kids' screen time, they could do these things.

Take my sister for examples. She lives for television! As soon as she gets home from school she eats a snack and then she feeds her Rabbit and then she starts to watch TV and she doesn't stop until my mom or dad tells her she has to. By this time, it is too late for her to get her homework done. So that's just one thing she is missing out on doing when she should be.

Kids who spend too much screen time don't have any time to enjoy sports either. Our gym teacher Mr. Simmons told us that many kids should be exercising more, not less. He also said that video games are not really exercise, even if you have to move around to play them. But I can tell you how much fun sports can be because I played soccer last year and the year before. I will probably play this yea, too.

Finally, think of what else kids could be doing instead of looking at a screen. They could be cooking, or reading, or leaning how to play the gatar. They could be talking with their friends or learning how to fix cars. If there parents would limit kids' screen time, they could do these things.

Using the Holistic Scoring Guide

Writing that fits a score of 1 is weak.

Focus is not clear.

Mainly a list with few specific details.

Many errors in conventions.

Ideas are repeated over and over.

More Money for Theter

The school says we need more money for theter. Some think so and some don't. Thiose who do not maybe don't like playes. But there are a lot of plays to like. Such as the spring play we had last year, which everybody loved. The fall play too it was great but even a little short. Even if some people do not like plays, others like them. So I think the should spend more money.

Plenty of stuedents take part in plays. Like Jenn, who played Mrs. Thompson. She did a great job. Or Luisa, who played a mean hair stilist. She is not even means! Roberto and Lynn were in the play last year, too. They aren't a brother or sister, but they portraide them.

What is there to do after school. Not a lot besides just sports and vieo games. So kids can't do those all the time. They can do theter instead. Sports teams get plenty of money every year. Like football, for example, and soccer gets money and so does even swimming. They all get money. Besides, theter is expensive. They need to buy props and costoms. Those cost lots of money.

Someday one kid from our school might be an actor and be rich. He could give money to the theter program. That would solv all of our problem. Maybe he give money to football, to. And that would make things easier for all of us. Wuldn't that make everyone feel better, since some people like plays. We could have money for theter too. So I think the school should spend the money.

Assessing an Essay

Read the essay below, focusing on its strengths and weaknesses. Then follow the directions at the bottom of the following page. **(The essay may contain errors.)**

Naomi Badalamenti
Ms. Sharp
English III
February 24, 2011

Make Financial Literacy Mandatory

A few months ago, an Arlington student named Damon started a job at a local grocery store. He gets paid by direct deposit. He opened a checking account and got a debit card. Within a month, Damon got a notice in the mail that he had overdrawn his account and the bank was charging him $29. Obviously, Damon mismanaged his money, but this really isn't a surprise since he was never taught how to plan a budget or use money from a bank account. His education, and that of all juniors and seniors at Arlington High, would be better if it included a mandatory course in money management.

Students should be taught how to plan their spending to help control expenses. They should develop 'practice' budgets that account for food, clothing, transportation, entertainment, computer, and communications expenses. This would help them understand that their income must cover their outlays (or cuts must be made!) They also need to know what will happen if they don't pay their bills on time.

Teachers could help students understand the maze of bank accounts. They could explain how to balance a checkbook and how to record every single transaction in order to do so. If someone doesn't tell students that an unpaid bounced check will result in their names being placed in a national database, preventing them from opening another checking account for five years ("Talking"), how will they know? They might think they're being smart and thrifty to hang on to a paycheck for months—but they'd certainly be disappointed to find that they couldn't cash it after only three or six months.

And what about those offers for credit cards that they're already getting? Young adults don't understand how interest compounds. They are falling deep into debt because of credit cards, according to figures such as the following from Nellie Mae. Of undergraduate college students in 2008, 76% had at least one card; nearly half of those carried balances more than $1,000; and only 21% paid their balances in full each month ("Undergraduate"). High school is a good time for students to learn that although good credit is important to many aspects of their later lives, they have to manage their first credit card accounts well. Otherwise, they risk damaged credit or even bankruptcy.

Is financial literacy something that students should learn from their parents? Perhaps, and many parents are able to provide that education. Some, however, don't know enough about it themselves. Some don't have time. Some think it's a school's responsibility. In any case, a teacher, it seems, could devote more time to these important issues than parents or other adults could. High school students also may be more inclined to listen to a teacher.

A good number of students will be leaving home after high school, and they don't want to be dependent on their parents. There are many reasons why young people get in financial trouble; it would be great for them to know something about budgets and credit before they're faced with it head-on. Arlington should develop such a course to help students better prepare for their real-world futures.

Exercise

Use the holistic scoring guide on pages 36–37 to assess the essay you have just read. Record your rating and comments on a separate piece of paper.

ELPS 2C, 4C, 4D, 5G

Understanding the Traits

Understanding the Traits of Writing	47
Focus and Coherence	51
Organization	59
Development of Ideas	67
Voice	75
Conventions	83

Learning Language

Learning these words and expressions will help you understand this unit. Answer these questions with a partner.

1. To **maintain** is to keep the same or continue.
   What does it mean to maintain a home?
2. **Focusing** involves narrowing and sharpening your view.
   Why does a photographer focus a camera?
3. To **link** is to connect two things.
   What kinds of things could you link together?
4. When you reach a **conclusion**, you come to an end.
   Think of the conclusion to a movie you have seen. Did it surprise you? Why or why not?

Understanding the Traits of Writing

When a doctor does a physical examination, he or she checks a patient's blood pressure, height, weight, posture, circulation, breathing, and so on. When someone is in good health, all of these elements are in good working order. If, on the other hand, any of the elements are "out of order," the patient's health will suffer.

Similarly, a piece of writing can be evaluated by reviewing five key traits: *focus and coherence, organization, development of ideas, voice,* and *conventions.* If all of these five traits are strong, then the piece of writing will be effective. However, if there are problems with any of these traits, then the essay or article will not be as effective as it could be.

In this chapter, you'll get a quick overview of the five traits of writing, and you'll see how these traits fit into the writing process.

- **Understanding the Five Traits**
- **Using the Traits**
- **Checklist for Effective Writing**

"What is written without effort is in general read without pleasure."

—Samuel Johnson

Understanding the Five Traits

Throughout this book, you'll use the five traits to make your writing the best it can be. Here is a brief description of each trait.

Focus and Coherence

Focus and Coherence refers to individual paragraphs and the composition as a whole. An effective composition maintains the focus on a topic or thesis and has a sense of completeness. A clear, sustained focus helps your reader understand how the ideas in the composition are related. A meaningful introduction and conclusion can also help you achieve this goal.

Organization

Organization refers to your movement from sentence to sentence and paragraph to paragraph. You may choose from a variety of strategies to organize your composition. By using logic and transitions, you can lead your reader step-by-step through your ideas.

Development of Ideas

The thorough and specific **development of ideas** helps your reader appreciate your unique or personal approach to a topic. Your approach may reflect your own view of the world, offer a unique perspective, or show new connections between ideas.

Voice

Your writing **voice** refers to the unique way you use language to share your ideas. Maintaining this voice throughout the composition will make your reader want to read every word.

Conventions

Conventions are the rules of grammar (usage and sentence structure), mechanics (capitalization, punctuation, using italics, number styling, etc.), and spelling. Paying attention to these rules is especially important near the end of the writing process, as you revise and proofread your work. Gaining a command over these conventions will help you be more effective in communicating your ideas.

Try It!

Reflect on the traits by discussing the following questions in a small group or with a partner:

1. Which trait challenges me the most? Explain.
2. Which trait is strongest in my writing? Explain.

Using the Traits

Since no one can focus on all five traits at once, different traits are important at different stages in the writing process.

Prewriting	
Focus and Coherence	Select a genre and topic, gather details, choose your focus (thesis or controlling idea), and decide on main points. Think about your likely audience.
Organization	Write your thesis statement and topic sentences, decide on a method of organization, and create a list, outline, or graphic organizer.

Drafting	
Development of Ideas	Thoroughly develop each idea.
Organization	Write a beginning, a middle, and an ending, using your plan. Use transitional words and phrases and make logical connections.
Voice	Use a voice appropriate to your personality, topic, purpose, and reader.

Revising	
Focus and Coherence	Revise your focus, main points, and details.
Organization	Check the order and unity of your paragraphs.
Voice	Adjust your voice as needed.

Editing, Proofreading, and Publishing	
Conventions	Edit your work for correct grammar, mechanics, and spelling.

Try It!

Write a notebook entry explaining which traits are most important early in the writing process and which are most important toward the end.

Checklist for Effective Writing

If a piece of writing meets the following standards, it exhibits the traits of effective writing. Check your work using these standards.

Traits Checklist

Focus and Coherence

_____ 1. Is the genre appropriate?
_____ 2. Is the topic interesting?
_____ 3. Is a specific focus maintained throughout the essay?
_____ 4. Do a variety of details support the focus?
_____ 5. Do the introduction and conclusion add depth to the composition?
_____ 6. Are the ideas in the composition clearly related?

Organization

_____ 7. Is there a clear thesis statement?
_____ 8. Is there a clear beginning, middle, and ending?
_____ 9. Is the writing logically organized, with meaningful transitions?

Development of Ideas

_____ 10. Are the ideas thoroughly developed?
_____ 11. Are the ideas presented with specific and thoughtful details?

Voice

_____ 12. Does the voice fit the topic and the purpose?
_____ 13. Does the voice sound authentic and original?
_____ 14. Does the voice express individuality?

Conventions

_____ 15. Does the work follow the rules of grammar, mechanics and spelling?
_____ 16. Is the work presented in a clear, correct format?

Focus and Coherence

Have you ever started reading something that quickly grabbed your attention but you soon lost interest in it? Perhaps the focus shifted from one idea to another or it lacked coherence, making you feel like something important had been left out.

You want readers to be engaged in your writing from start to finish, pulling them in with the first paragraph and sustaining their interest until the very last word. You want to give readers relevant information, and you don't want unnecessary information or details to get in the way of your main point.

- **Focusing**
- **Ensuring Completeness**
- **Writing a Focused Introduction**
- **Writing a Focused Conclusion**
- **Using Effective Support**

"Writing became such a process of discovery that I couldn't wait to get to work in the morning: I wanted to know what I was going to say."

—Sharon O'Brien

"Always make room for the unexpected in yourself."
—Steve Martin

Focusing

Read the following writing assignment:

- Write an essay about two things you would like to see changed in your school.

To begin, make a list of your ideas and then choose the two that you think are most important. Then, ask yourself how you will present your ideas in the essay. What supporting details will you provide? What is the best way to present these details in your argument?

Finally, before you begin writing, think of what you must do to clearly communicate your ideas in the essay.

- You want to write a strong thesis. What do you think about the topic?
- You want to be persuasive. Who is your audience, and what is your purpose? Are you trying to convince the school administration to implement your ideas, or do you want to persuade your fellow students to support your plan?
- You want to describe clearly the two things you think should change. Do you have specific suggestions for how these changes could happen?
- You want to present strong supporting details to support your argument throughout the essay. What are they?
- You want to keep your focus on your thesis. As you write, you may think of other changes you would like to see, in your school and elsewhere, but you don't want to lose track of your thesis. How can you remember to stay focused?

As you compose your essay, make sure that each paragraph has a clear topic sentence. This will help you maintain the focus as you incorporate supporting details. Review each paragraph to make sure that you are maintaining the focus of your thesis in the introductory paragraph. For example, if you had decided that you were going to appeal to the school administration to make the changes you recommend, make sure that you are not getting off track and shifting your focus to trying to convince your fellow students to support your ideas.

Focus and Coherence

One student decided to respond to the writing assignment by addressing her essay to the principal of her school. She settled on two changes that she most wanted to see: less overcrowding in classrooms, and more classes in the arts.

Here is an example of a response that strays from the topic:

> Although there are many good things about Hartnett High, I would like to see a few changes. For the most part, the teachers are very good, and a wide variety of electives is offered. However, the classes are overcrowded. In English we've been reading Russian novels, which is great, but it's difficult to concentrate. Also, I believe there should be more classes in the arts. Last weekend I went to an exhibit of Russian paintings at the museum. I would like to be able to study them and learn to paint myself. I also think that seniors should be allowed to go off campus without a pass when they don't have classes.

Here is an example of a student's response that maintains a better focus on the topic:

> Although there are many good things about Hartnett High, I would like to see two important changes. My first recommendation is to find a way to reduce class size. Too many classes are overcrowded, and it is difficult to concentrate in such an uncomfortable situation. Another important change I would like to see is for the school to offer more classes in the arts. I will offer some proposals for the school administration to consider.

Try It!

Reread the writing assignment at the top of the previous page. Then in a small group, discuss some of the things you would like to see changed in your school. Try to come up with a list of three topics. Choose one topic to discuss. Then let each person take a turn arguing in favor of that change. Take notes as you listen to each speaker and give each other feedback on how each speaker might improve the focus of his or her argument.

Ensuring Completeness

Your introductory paragraph should lay out the scope of your essay. In just a few words, you should give your readers a picture of where you are going and how you plan to go there. First of all, you need to be clear about how you are going to communicate your ideas. Then, decide on a strategy and narrow or expand your focus, depending on the topic. Your introductory paragraph does not have to be long. However, it does need to be complete.

As you write the body of your essay, you should deliver on the promise of your introduction. You have unrolled the red carpet. Now invite your readers to walk forward as you present your ideas and support the ideas with facts, details, and input from other sources.

At the end of the essay, when you have presented all your ideas, it is important to write a strong conclusion tying it all together. How would you feel if you loved a book and just couldn't put it down, but when you got to the end, the last words were "and they lived happily ever after"? You would not feel satisfied.

The principles of writing a good essay also apply to writing good paragraphs. Each paragraph in the body of your essay should begin with a strong topic sentence that tells readers what they are going to learn. The supporting sentences in the paragraph give them that information. Then the conclusion wraps it up.

As a writer, you want to do more than just follow a formula. Your overall intention should be to dig deep, to explore your topic in such a way that both you and your reader will have new, surprising insights.

Tips for Ensuring Completeness

- Sleep on it. One of the best ways to review your writing is to leave it alone—but just overnight. When you reread your writing after you have been away from it for a day you are more likely to notice key pieces of information that are missing, or unclear connections.
- Check with peers. Your favorite books and stories didn't go directly from the author's desk to your library shelf. Authors almost always get comments on their writing from friends, family members, or editors. Having others read your work will help you figure out if you have been successful in linking ideas in a clear, coherent way.
- Read it out loud. Become an audience of one as you read your piece of writing aloud. Listen for gaps, or bits of information that you thought you had included but didn't. Try to imagine the questions you would ask, or what you would want to know more about.

Try It!

Working with a partner, think of a process and in five minutes describe it as completely as you can. Then discuss with your partner what you may have left out. How might you improve your description?

Focus and Coherence

Writing a Focused Introduction

As you know, a good composition begins with a strong introduction. This is your chance to grab the reader's attention, to invite him or her to explore the topic with you. Your introduction should be meaningful and add depth to the composition. A superficial opening may lead to a superficial essay. A strong introductory paragraph should include the following elements:

- a clear statement of your thesis
- an attention-grabbing detail or idea
- a preview of the essay's contents
- a suggestion about what new insights the reader might gain

Read the following introductory paragraph in a student essay about the advantages and disadvantages of living in a big city.

> **The opening is not very interesting.**
>
> **Unclear statement of thesis**
>
> **Lacks preview**
>
> Twice a week, the garbage pickup wakes me up really early. Sometimes I think it might be better to live in a small town. Living in a city has its drawbacks. For example, nearly every day the school bus gets stuck in traffic. It's really annoying, but I guess I like living in the city pretty well. I would probably get bored living in a small town.

Now read this revision of the paragraph. Notice how the writer pulls the reader into the essay and how the thesis statement and preview give the essay its focus.

> **Attention grabber**
>
> **Thesis statement**
>
> **Preview**
>
> Twice a week, at 5:30 a.m., I am torn out of my dreams by the clanging of garbage cans and the screeching brakes of the garbage truck as it lumbers down our street. Even before I get out of bed, I have a splitting headache and am very grouchy. Nearly every day, on my way to school, I get impatient when our bus gets stuck in commuter traffic. Well, this is big city living. In spite of these and other annoyances, I still think living in a big city is better than living in a small town. The advantages of big city living outweigh the disadvantages. There are several reasons why this is so, which I will discuss in this essay.

Try It!

Read the above paragraphs aloud with a partner. Compare the openings and discuss why the second paragraph's opening is more interesting. Be specific.

Writing a Focused Conclusion

By the time a reader comes to the end of the composition, he or she has learned a lot about your ideas and is interested in your final word on the subject. How will you tie it all together? Will your reader have a sense of completeness about what he or she has read? Your concluding paragraph should summarize or elaborate on the body paragraphs.

Read the following conclusion to the essay begun on the previous page. The body of the essay discussed the advantages and disadvantages of living in a big city, comparing these factors and offering supporting details to prove the writer's point. The writer wants to deliver the final one-two punch.

Summary is too general.
Incomplete restatement of thesis
Does not offer new perspective on the subject

> I have convinced myself to accept the annoyances of living in the big city. There are many reasons to support my point of view. Living in a small town would be boring, and there wouldn't be as many things to do. It's better to live in the city, I think.

Now read this revision of the paragraph. Notice how the writer clearly restates the thesis, summarizes the main points, and adds new perspective.

Summary or elaboration of main points
Restatement of thesis
New perspective on the subject

> In the end, I have convinced myself to accept the annoyances of living in the big city as part of the package. There are many reasons to support my point of view. I would be bored to tears in a small town. There are fewer activities for teens, and I wouldn't get to meet the variety of people who live in the big city. The advantages of the big city definitely outweigh its disadvantages. Besides, there are worse things than being awakened early or being stuck in traffic. That gives me plenty of opportunities to study!

Try It!

Reread the introductory paragraphs on page 55 and the concluding paragraphs on this page. Discuss with your classmates why it is important to write a focused conclusion.

Using Effective Support

There are many types of details you can use when writing about your topic. Your main idea, along with the purpose of your writing, determines which details are most effective. The key types of details are explained on these pages.

Facts are details that can be *proven*.

> In 2009, for the first time ever, an Asian-born player won the PGA golf tournament. Y.E. Yang, from South Korea, beat the famous player Tiger Woods, who had won 14 major championships and seemed unbeatable.

> When Senator Arlen Specter of Pennsylvania faced losing the primary for reelection in 2010, he switched from the Republican Party to the Democratic Party.

Statistics present *numerical information* about a specific topic.

> Making the *Lord of the Rings* films included shooting more than 600 million feet of film, using 2,700 special-effects shots, and creating 1,600 pairs of Hobbit feet.

> With more than 1,000 wins and a winning percentage of .844, Tennessee coach Pat Summitt is the most successful coach in college basketball history.

Examples are statements that *illustrate a main point*.

> During the Victorian period of architecture, the Stick style was often overshadowed by other styles, but it had its own unique characteristics. The Stick style is known for its stickwork, the decorative patterns of boards on a house's exterior. The stickwork created horizontal, vertical, or diagonal patterns on the siding, which imitated architecture from medieval Europe.

Anecdotes are *brief stories* that help to make a point about an idea. They are usually interesting and entertaining and can be more effective than a static list of details.

> Sometimes people need to take the time to look up information. Explaining his embarrassing "potatoe" spelling incident, former vice president Dan Quayle admitted, "I should have caught the mistake on that spelling bee card, but as Mark Twain once said, 'You should never trust a man who has only one way to spell a word.' " When told that it was President Andrew Jackson and not Mark Twain he quoted, Quayle said, "I should have remembered that was Andrew Jackson who said that since he got his nickname 'Stonewall' by vetoing bills passed by Congress." Quayle was wrong again. He had confused Andrew Jackson with the Confederate general Thomas Jackson, who received the nickname "Stonewall" during the Civil War.

Quotations are *people's statements* repeated word for word. They usually offer powerful supporting evidence.

> Sometimes a comic observation can make a person think about an important topic. For example, comedian Jay London observed, "I told my therapist I was having nightmares about nuclear explosions. He said, 'Don't worry, it's not the end of the world.' " People may laugh at the idea, but when they actually think about it, the statement does remind them that they live in the nuclear age.

Definitions present the *meaning* of unfamiliar terms. Defining technical terms can be beneficial for the reader and clarify your writing.

> Greener vehicles may run on biodiesel, a renewable fuel derived from vegetable oil or animal fat.

Reasons answer *why* and can explain or justify ideas.

> Filmmakers should not be allowed to make sequels, especially ones with successive numbers in the titles. Producers should know that sequels lose money. Although these movies are made to capitalize on the success of the first film, no sequel has topped an original at the box office. With few exceptions, such as *Spiderman II* and *Spiderman III*, sequels almost never approach the quality of the original film. With each increasing title number, the film's originality decreases. Did moviegoers really need *Jason X* after eight sequels to *Friday the 13th*? Most importantly, each sequel loses one or more "A" stars from the one before it. This clearly makes each movie less watchable.

Comparisons address the *similarities or differences* between two ideas or things. It is especially helpful to compare something new or unknown to something your reader understands.

> Although they were fought about 40 years apart, the war in Iraq is still similar to the Vietnam War. The U.S. entered both wars because of a perceived threat: Vietnam because of Communism and Iraq because of terrorism. Both wars were fought against a stubborn enemy that used guerrilla tactics. Early in each war, both Lyndon Johnson and George W. Bush declared that the mission was accomplished. They then saw their approval ratings plummet as the wars continued.

Try It!

Find an article that shows four of the detail types explained on this page and the previous one. On your own paper, write the examples that you find.

Organization

Once you have discovered an interesting writing idea and gathered supporting details, you must decide on an organizational pattern. Without clear organization, great ideas just get lost.

Often a topic fits easily into a particular pattern. For example, writing about the first time you met a friend would naturally fall into a narrative or storytelling pattern with a chronological order. Describing how to make the perfect pizza would fit the process pattern. A topic may fit more than one pattern, and it is up to you to determine the best method for presenting your ideas.

At times, an idea deserves a more creative approach. Writing that breaks out of an organizational pattern and takes its own path is often more exciting and dynamic. Do not be afraid to experiment.

This chapter provides background information about organizing ideas effectively. It will help you learn different ways to structure your writing.

- **Understanding the Big Picture**
- **Following the Thesis Statement's Lead**
- **Using a Logical Progression of Ideas**
- **Patterns of Organization**
- **Using Graphic Organizers**
- **Transitions**

"Complicated outlines tempt you to think too much about the fine points of organization, at a time when you should be blocking out the overall structure."

—Donald Hall

Understanding the Big Picture

The basic structure of informational writing is simple. Essays, articles, and reports contain three main parts: the beginning, the middle, and the ending. Each part plays an equally important role in an effective piece of writing.

Beginning The opening paragraph should capture the reader's attention and state your thesis. Here are some ways to capture your reader's attention:

- Tell a dramatic or exciting story (anecdote) about the topic.
- Ask an intriguing question or two.
- Provide a few surprising facts or statistics.
- Provide an interesting quotation.
- Explain your personal experiences or involvement with the topic.

Middle The middle paragraphs should support your thesis statement. For example, in an essay about improved safety in NASCAR racing, each middle paragraph would focus on one main aspect of improved safety. (An outline can help you write this section.)

Ending The closing paragraph should summarize your thesis and leave the reader with a final thought. Here are some strategies for creating a strong closing:

- Review your main points.
- Emphasize the special importance of one main point.
- Answer any questions the reader may still have.
- Draw a conclusion and put the information in perspective.
- Provide a final significant thought for the reader.

Try It!

Select an essay from this book or an article from a magazine. Outline the three parts of the essay or article to show how it is organized.

Following the Thesis Statement's Lead

An organizing pattern may be built into your essay assignment. For example, you may be asked specifically to develop an argument or to write a process paper. When a pattern is not assigned, one may still evolve quite naturally during your initial thinking and planning. If this doesn't happen, take a careful look at your thesis statement (and supporting information). An effective thesis will almost always suggest an organizing pattern; if it doesn't provide this "controlling vision," consider rewriting it.

Review the following thesis statements and notice how they present the writer's focus and tell how the topic will be developed.

Sample Thesis

> Miners looking for gold during the 1849 Gold Rush had a much different experience of life in the West than pioneers who came to the West as farmers.

Discussion: This thesis shows how the writer will compare the experiences of two groups of people in the West. Alternate paragraphs will discuss each group, or each paragraph may compare and contrast these two groups.

Sample Thesis

> Applying for college has become a complicated, stressful process.

Discussion: This thesis indicates that the writer will explain a process. Information must be presented in a logical order, describing each step from beginning to end. The statement also suggests that besides describing each step in this complicated process, the writer will discuss the stress involved.

Sample Thesis

> The National Parks Service can reduce damage to Yellowstone National Park by limiting automobile traffic, increasing fees, and hiring additional staff.

Discussion: The writer of this thesis presents a problem and suggests ways to solve it. The statement suggests that after describing the problem the writer will explain each solution.

Try It!

List the thesis statements for two different essays in this book. Explain how each thesis suggests an organizing pattern for the essay. Discuss your findings with your classmates.

"It is a capital mistake to theorize before one has data."

—Sherlock Holmes

Using a Logical Progression of Ideas

Most people are familiar with Sherlock Holmes and his extraordinary powers of deduction. Holmes would make a surprising statement, back it up with many supporting details, and leave Dr. Watson in awe of his conclusion. For example, here is how Holmes deduced Watson had returned from Afghanistan at their first meeting in *A Study in Scarlet*:

"I *knew* you came from Afghanistan. . . . The train of reasoning ran, 'Here is a gentleman of a medical type, but with the air of a military man. Clearly an army doctor, then. He has just come from the tropics, for his face is dark, and that is not the natural tint of his skin, for his wrists are fair. He has undergone hardship and sickness, as his haggard face says clearly. His left arm has been injured. He holds it in a stiff and unnatural manner. Where in the tropics could an English army doctor have seen much hardship and got his arm wounded? Clearly in Afghanistan.'"

Confronted with all that evidence, Watson can only say, "It is simple enough as you explain it." That is the same reaction you want from your readers, especially when you are trying to persuade them with your ideas.

Most of your academic writing should be organized deductively. *Deduction* comes from a Latin word meaning "to lead." When writing deductively, you lead the reader to your conclusion by presenting a main idea, or thesis, and then supporting it with specific details. The organizational pattern looks like this:

Deductive Arrangement
- Start with the main idea or thesis.
- Present supporting details and examples.
- Conclude by restating the thesis and/or summarizing the key support.

Deductive writing presents an idea and leads the reader smoothly through the evidence. Supporting details either define the idea, expand it, or illustrate it.

Try It!

Study a building, house, or vehicle. Write down your observations and see what you can deduce from them. *When was it built? What was it used for previously? What condition is it in?* Then write a deductive paragraph about your findings.

Patterns of Organization

As a writer, you know that the main idea or topic sentence in a paragraph is developed and explained by supporting details. This process can be organized in different ways, depending on the focus and purpose of your composition. To show the relationships or connections among ideas, you can use different patterns of organization, including *chronological order, problem/solution, order of importance, comparison/contrast,* and *cause and effect.*

Chronological order arranges events in the time order in which they happened. This method of organization is used to tell a story, to present a series of events, or to describe the steps in a process. You might use chronological order in an essay about historical events, a famous person's life, or a scientific discovery.

Problem/solution order states a problem followed by a solution. Problem/solution order is often used in a piece of writing that promotes change or calls for specific action. An example might be an argument about motorcycle helmet laws.

Order of importance arranges details from least to most important, or the reverse. This might be used in discussing the things to look for when buying a new car.

Comparison/contrast order shows the similarities and differences between two subjects. For example, you might explore the similarities and differences between dress codes at different schools.

Cause-and-effect order shows the relationships between events and their results. You might use this strategy in an essay about the events leading up to an election.

Try It!

With a partner, look for examples of each kind of organization in your textbook. Then brainstorm the kinds of topics that would be most effectively described by each kind of organizational strategy.

Using Graphic Organizers

Graphic organizers can help you gather and organize details for your writing. The next two pages list and model several useful organizers. (Re-create the organizer on your own paper to gather details for an essay.)

Cause-Effect Organizer

Use to collect and organize details for cause-effect essays.

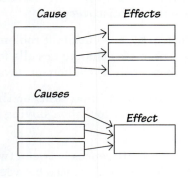

Problem-Solution Web

Use to map out problem-solution essays.

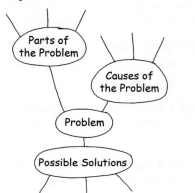

Time Line

Use for personal narratives to list actions or events in the order they occurred.

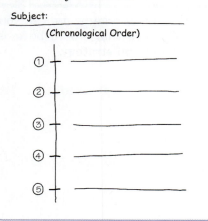

Evaluation Collection Grid

Use to collect supporting details for essays of evaluation.

Subject: _____

Points to Evaluate	Supporting Details
1.	
2.	
3.	
4.	

Organization **65**

Venn Diagram

Use to collect details to compare and contrast two topics.

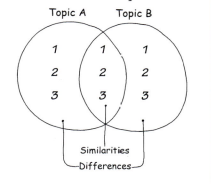

Line Diagram

Use to collect and organize details for academic essays.

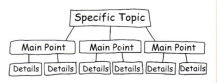

Process (Cycle) Diagrams

Use to collect details for science-related writing, such as how a process or cycle works.

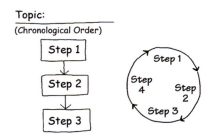

5 W's Chart

Use to collect the *who? what? when? where?* and *why?* details for personal narratives and news stories.

Subject: _____

Who?	What?	When?	Where?	Why?

Definition Diagram

Use to gather information for extended-definition essays.

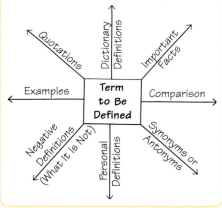

Sensory Chart

Use to collect details for descriptive essays and observation reports.

Subject: _____

Sights	Sounds	Smells	Tastes	Textures

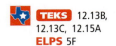

> "Start with something interesting and promising; wind up with something the reader will remember."
>
> —Rudolf Flesch

Transitions

Imagine this: You have an appointment for a job interview in a nearby town. You have to drive a short distance on the freeway between your town and the town where your interview is taking place. You know how to get to the freeway entrance, and you have a map of your destination. Once you are on the freeway, however, which exit should you take? Should you turn to the right or the left after you take the exit? Your prospective employer has not given you that information. She has not given you the signals that you need to complete your journey.

Writing a composition is like taking a reader on a journey through new territory. Your composition is more than several sentences or paragraphs lined up next to each other. If your sentences and paragraphs are not linked in a way that makes sense, your reader will get lost or be confused. In the same way that a freeway connects two towns, transitional words and phrases help to show how ideas are related.

Here are some of the transitional words and phrases you can use in your compositions or in timed-writing activities. Notice that the kinds of transitions you use depend on the organizational structure you have chosen.

Type of Organization	Transitional Words and Phrases
Chronological Order	in the beginning, after, next, before, finally, then, first, later
Problem/Solution	because, in spite of, therefore
Cause-and-Effect	as a result, because, since, so, therefore, consequently
Comparison/Contrast	comparison: also, like, and, too, another, in addition contrast: on the other hand, although, but, however, instead
Order of Importance	first, last, mainly, most important

Try It!

Choose one of the organizational strategies above and write a paragraph about a topic that fits the strategy. Challenge yourself to use as many transitional words and phrases within the paragraph as you can.

Development of Ideas

Writing effectively means more than just summarizing the plot of a book you have read or making a list of facts you have uncovered by doing research. To be a highly effective writer, you need to develop ideas and present them thoughtfully so that readers will understand and appreciate them.

Coming up with original ideas can be a challenge. One way to make this task easier is to focus on the part of an assignment that is most interesting to you. What facts that you uncovered were most surprising or compelling? Why? How did your research change your thinking about the topic? Chances are that if you found certain aspects of an assignment interesting, many of your readers will, too.

This is only one strategy for developing original ideas. This section will help you learn other strategies for developing ideas that will make your writing powerful, engaging, and effective.

- **The Creative Mind in Action**
- **Reviewing Possible Starting Points**
- **Developing Your Ideas**
- **Presenting Your Ideas**
- **Avoiding Gaps**

"Words—so innocent and powerless as they are, as standing in a dictionary, how potent for good and evil they become in the hands of one who knows how to combine them."

—Nathaniel Hawthorne

The Creative Mind in Action

Making a sculpture, composing a song, cooking a new dish, and writing a persuasive essay are all creative acts. You have probably done at least one of those things, but you still might not think of yourself as a creative person. Don't worry; creativity is not as hard as you might think. In writing, being creative means taking materials that you have on hand and using them to express ideas. Anyone can do it!

The materials that you have on hand as a writer can vary. Those materials can include information you already know, information you have uncovered during research, observations you make about the world around you, or experiences you have. In order to express original ideas, you need to think creatively about your materials.

Thinking Creatively

One way to start thinking creatively is to make some careful observations. Here, your senses play a critical role. Touch, taste, hearing, smell, and sight all contribute to the complete picture.

The Story of a Cap

What if your teacher gave you a baseball cap and asked you to write about it? You could start by making some careful observations and taking some notes:

- What color is the cap? Are its bill and crown the same color?
- What is the logo? Is it recognizable as a sports team from a city like Dallas or is it the symbol of a Texas college or university? Does it contain a written message or symbol you have never seen before?
- Is the bill short or long? Is it relatively flat—or bent into a curve?
- Is the cap clean or dirty? Is it stained with sweat?
- Feel the fabric. Is it smooth or scratchy? Cotton or polyester?

Now do some creative thinking. Try asking some questions about the cap. This will put your creative mind in action and help you to generate the original ideas you need.

- Where did the cap come from?
- Who made it in the factory? What might that person's life be like?
- How might the cap have gotten to your town? What might have happened to it along the way?
- Who was the original owner of the cap?
- If the cap could tell you its story, what would it be?

Try It!

Put your creative mind to work. Focus on another common object. Make some observations while a classmate takes notes. Then discuss and record the questions that come to mind.

Reviewing Possible Starting Points

How do writers identify writing topics? Many start with the world around them. Every day, you encounter people, places, experiences, activities, trends, and ideas that could become a writing topic. All you need to do is apply a little creative thinking. Listed below are a number of topics inspired by a person's everyday experiences. Reviewing these ideas should prompt you to uncover interesting starting points for your own writing.

Expository

- Discuss the impact of a natural disaster.
- Explain how to make mouth-watering barbeque.
- Explore how social media have changed communications.
- Explain how a particular movie or novel affected you emotionally.
- Discuss the effects of global climate change.

Persuasive

- Persuade a doubter of the reasons your favorite sports team will win.
- Identify the country's biggest problem and convince Congress to solve it using your recommendations.
- Explain how expanding public transportation will improve life in Houston.
- Encourage Texas lawmakers to ban cell phone use for all drivers.

Narrative

- Write about a day in which almost everything went wrong.
- Tell how a friend has changed your life for the better.
- Recall a memorable family gathering.
- Write about a vacation experience that you will never forget.
- Tell about the greatest game you ever played—on a sports field, a game board, or a computer.

Descriptive

- Describe an interesting place you recently visited.
- Describe a work of art that dazzled you with its beauty.
- Describe an influential teacher and how he or she changed your life.
- Describe the music of your favorite performer or group.

Try It!

Create four topic ideas that interest you by examining the people, places, experiences, and activities of your everyday life. Try to find one topic for each writing mode listed above.

Developing Your Ideas

Presenting well-developed ideas means more than just stating facts or summarizing the plot of a story.

To understand the difference between undeveloped and developed ideas, it's helpful to look at a few examples. The following paragraphs show the differences between undeveloped and well-developed ideas.

Reviewing a Book

Undeveloped: The writer merely summarizes.

In the novel, *Thompson's Grocery*, Joanna Thompson opens a small grocery store. Right away she has trouble. The store burns down. She almost decides to quit, but then becomes a success.

Developed: The writer expresses her opinions and supports them with details.

The novel *Thompson's Grocery* shows that with work, people can overcome incredible odds. Joanna Thompson struggles to succeed in business, facing adversity and overcoming community indifference, a fire, and tough competition. Her struggles are dramatic, but her hard work is an inspiration. Her life contains an important message: giving up is the worst mistake you can make.

Describing a Memorable Meal

Undeveloped: The writer lists the dishes served.

Last Friday, I ate at La Taquita. The meal started with an appetizer of black bean soup with shredded pork. My main dish was chiles rellenos. When it was time for dessert, I ordered flan.

Developed: The writer explains what made the meal memorable.

The meal I had at La Taquita was like nothing I had ever experienced in a restaurant. When I arrived, the delicious smells wafting from the kitchen made my taste buds tingle. The appetizer, a thick, hearty black bean and shredded pork soup, was cooked to perfection with just the right amount of chile pepper to satisfy my need for heat. My chiles rellenos were loaded with melted cheese and perfectly tender. It was like eating my Aunt Elena's home cooking all over again—until dessert. The flan they served me was even better than Aunt Elena's. It was a truly memorable dining experience.

Asking Some Questions

How can you turn a boring list or a bland plot summary into writing full of well-developed ideas? Start by asking some questions about the facts you've uncovered. This will help you to develop your own unique perspective about the topic and create writing with depth and insight.

Depending upon the form of writing you choose, you may want to ask different questions. Here are some sample questions to help you get started.

Expository
- How will the facts I uncovered impact people's lives?
- What parts of the process will I have to explain?
- What makes the book, story, or poem worth reading?
- How does the film comment on our lives today?
- How are two things alike? How are they different?

Persuasive
- What is the problem that I am focusing on?
- Why is the problem important?
- What action do I think will solve the problem?
- What aspects of the situation are most interesting to me?
- What arguments would persuade people to take my side?

Narrative
- What parts of the story are most important?
- What is the "message" of the story?
- What made the events that happened memorable to me?
- How might other people relate to the events?

Descriptive
- What makes the thing I am describing unique?
- Why is it worth my readers' attention?
- How will my description affect readers?
- What sensory details can enhance readers' experiences?

Presenting Your Ideas

Presenting your ideas means more than stating them. In order to present your ideas effectively, you need to provide effective support for them. You can do this by using a number of tools. You can use the tools across all forms of writing, from persuasive and expository to narrative and descriptive. Just choose the tools that best support your ideas.

The Writer's Toolkit

Here are some of the tools you can use to develop and support your ideas.

Dialogue or Quotations

In this excerpt from a movie review, quoting a respected authority helps add weight to an argument.

"There is little doubt," critic Edward Rodriguez declared, "that the use of special effects in the film has set a new standard for Hollywood."

Description

In this excerpt from a persuasive essay, effective description creates a powerful emotional response.

A heavy black oil slick floated on the surface of the water. Dead seabirds coated with tar bobbed in the waves. The stench of petroleum and rotting flesh filled the air. Scenes like this don't have to happen, and if you support the new oil shipping regulations, they will not.

Comparison and Contrast

In this excerpt from the description of an art show, the writer provides insight by showing how two things are alike and different.

Most of the watercolor paintings depict realistic scenes of everyday life in Dawson County. James Halloran uses watercolors to a dramatically different effect. His colorful abstract paintings of livestock, ranch buildings, and farm equipment provide a fresh, exciting new perspective on life in our area.

Development of Ideas

Facts and Examples

In this excerpt from an expository essay about fire departments, a fact that can be proven and a real-life example support a main idea.

Not all fire departments have the money they need for equipment. According to a recent survey, 26% of volunteer fire departments are short on protective gear. Of those fire departments, 85% cite a lack of funds to buy the gear as the reason they don't have it yet. Last year, 35 firefighters in the city were injured while fighting fires. More than half those injuries could have been prevented with proper protective gear. Sergeant James LaRue was among those who were hurt. Last January, he fought a fire without necessary protective gear and was burned badly as a result.

Point and Counterpoint

In this excerpt from a narrative essay about the writer's vacation, she presents another side of the argument, and then she refutes it. This makes her point stronger.

Some people say that the best way to experience the ocean is to spend a day lounging on the beach. I think that the people who say that have probably never gone scuba diving. I did recently, and it was one of the most incredible experiences of my life. Swimming around with barracudas, moray eels, and thousands of other undersea animals is more rewarding than sitting around working on a tan any day.

Reasons

In this excerpt from an expository essay, the writer gives reasons to support the idea that social media have changed the way people communicate.

Social media have transformed the way in which news travels from one person to the other. Traditionally, individuals did not have the power to broadcast information. They could gather information and pass it on in person, by letter, or by phone, usually to only a few people at a time. Now one person can post to a social media site and inform hundreds of friends at once who won the football game or what the weather is like in his location. Turning people into broadcasters has changed communication forever.

Try It!

What if your teacher asked you to write an expository essay explaining the role of country music in attracting tourists to Austin? Make a list of the writing tools you might use to support your ideas. With a partner, discuss which writing tools would work best.

Avoiding Gaps

Sometimes a writer can come up with great ideas, but readers can still miss the point. When this happens, it's often because the writer leaves gaps that prevent his or her ideas from being explained clearly. The result is that the ideas are not developed fully, and the argument, description, or explanation is weak and incomplete.

To provide the necessary depth, you need to paint a complete picture so that your reader can understand the situation as clearly as you do. Remember, you won't get credit for what you leave out!

Filling in Weak Spots

To see how leaving gaps can weaken a piece of writing, consider this example. The writer's main idea is that a lack of transportation services for students is decreasing participation in the arts.

Without transportation, fewer students can attend our concerts, plays, and other arts events. Last week, two tenth graders, Aaron Johnston and Emilio Santos, told me that they wouldn't be performing in this fall's school play because their parents were unable to drive them to rehearsal.

The writer names two students affected by the transportation problem. Do two students out of a large school represent a large problem? It doesn't seem so, but look at how the perspective changes when the writer closes the "information gap."

Without transportation, fewer students can attend our concerts, plays, and other arts events. Last week, two tenth graders, Aaron Johnston and Emilio Santos, told me that they wouldn't be performing in this fall's school play because their parents were unable to drive them to rehearsal. They are just two of more than 50 students who wrote letters to the school board asking for a better transportation solution for play rehearsal. It's little wonder that play participation has dropped 20 percent since the school stopped running shuttles to the auditorium on rehearsal nights.

Voice

Voice is what distinguishes one writer from another. It is how your writing expresses your individuality; it is who the reader hears. Everyone's speaking voice is unique and almost instantly recognizable. Writers try to make their writing voice distinct as well.

A reader only has a writer's words to react to, which is why a writer's voice is so important. The reader senses when you use your own natural voice because your words feel authentic. Your words connect with the reader. Developing a writing voice takes time, but it will make your writing more engaging. This chapter suggests ways to develop and adjust your voice. It also explains how to use dialogue, understand diction, work with metaphors and other figures of speech, and use adjectives effectively.

- **Developing Voice**
- **Adjusting Voice**
- **Using Dialogue**
- **Understanding Diction**
- **Working with Metaphors**
- **Using Other Figures of Speech**
- **Using Adjectives Effectively**

"Writers should use their own voices as much as possible, for their own voices have power, control, and courage."

—Peter Elbow

Developing Voice

Your speaking voice is filled with your personality, and your writing voice should reflect your individuality as well. Writing often, whether in a notebook or in class assignments, will help you develop an authentic voice. Here are some other tips for developing your voice:

- **Write about a topic that interests you.** Your interests help make you who you are. Let readers know you are interested in your topic.
- **Be passionate.** If you feel strongly about your writing, these feelings will permeate your voice.
- **Be honest and genuine.** Don't try to be someone else to impress readers.
- **Write freely.** Don't edit your voice out of your writing.
- **Read your writing out loud.** Does it sound like you?

Read the following notebook entry. The thoughts and feelings reflect the writer's unique perspective and individuality.

Sample Notebook Entry

> I don't know why cops get such a bad rap around here. Jaci and I were walking home yesterday, and a cop car zipped by, flashers and siren and all, and Jaci said, "Yeah, they must need donuts pretty bad." She laughed, but I didn't think it was funny. I mean, they were probably going to help someone. I didn't tell Jaci, but I think I want to be a cop. When my little brother Luis wandered away from Mom, a cop helped find him, and he was really nice. When Tia Bonita got hit by the cab and broke her leg, a cop got to her in a couple of minutes, and he sat and talked to her until the paramedics got there. And I've seen cops working at fires and accidents. I mean, they don't just hand out tickets and arrest people. They help people, and I think that must feel pretty good.

Try It!

Becoming familiar with other writers' voices may help you discover your own voice. Read the following quotation and then rewrite it in your voice, trying to express a comparable thought.

> "The sun escaping from the breaking clouds, as it sank toward the hills they had left, was now shining brightly again. Their fear left them, though they still felt uneasy."
> —J. R. R. Tolkien, *The Fellowship of the Ring*

Adjusting Voice

You adjust your speaking voice to the audience you are addressing and to your purpose. The same is true of your writing voice.

Adjusting for Audience

A personal, informal writing voice is closest to your usual way of talking. You should use it for writing narratives, sending e-mail to friends, or writing personal letters. It is often colorful and visual. To the reader, it is friendly and familiar.

On the other hand, you wouldn't use this voice when you are applying for a job, writing a research paper, or petitioning your senator. For those readers, you would adopt a more formal voice, but without losing your unique perspective.

Adjusting for Purpose

You can adjust your writing voice to match your purpose—to relate an experience, to share information, or to persuade a reader.

- **Relating an experience:** When you describe an experience, your writing voice should be authentic, engaging, animated, and personal, similar to the way you sound when talking to a group of friends.

    Jack Smith gave a speech at our school yesterday that really got us pumped up. I would like to see him elected, but he's a third-party candidate with about as much chance of winning as I have of being named captain of the football team.

- **Sharing information:** Writing to inform demands an interested, knowledgeable voice that tells the reader you know your topic well.

    The electoral college favors a two-party system, as shown by Ross Perot's receiving 18 percent of the popular vote, but not a single electoral vote, in the 1992 presidential election.

- **Persuading a reader:** Think of how you tried to persuade your parents to let you use the family car, or a teacher to extend an assignment deadline. To persuade the reader, your writing voice must be convincing and informed.

    With the death-hold grip the electoral college has on elections, third-parties should not throw their candidates into the ring with the two main parties.

Try It!

Select a topic, choose one of the purposes above, and write a sentence or two that fits this purpose. Then adjust your voice and rewrite the passage to fit each of the other two purposes.

Using Dialogue

In creative writing, dialogue is used to give the reader information and to advance the story. Dialogue also breaks up the wall of text, making a story easier to read.

Writing realistic dialogue requires more than just copying what people say. Real speech is not planned or precise. People repeat phrases, add unnecessary words, contract words, and leave out words. They talk at the same time and interrupt each other. As a writer, you need to make use of these characteristics while keeping dialogue engaging and to the point.

When writing dialogue . . .

- mix in some narrative description to help describe a speaker's tone,
- be sure every line has a purpose, and
- read it out loud to be sure it sounds realistic and authentic.

Read the following sample. See how the dialogue adds information and develops the unique perspectives of the speakers. It sounds authentic and original.

Sample Dialogue

> While waiting in line to audition for <u>The Last Great Average American Survival Race</u>, Jack handed Dana the application. "Here. We have to pretend to be a couple for a few minutes. All you have to do is memorize these answers. I made a few changes to fit your . . ."
>
> "Favorite food, spaghetti?" Shaking her head, Dana scowled. "No way, I hate spaghetti. It's a disgusting mess of slimy . . ."
>
> "You don't have to eat any. You just have to say you like it. We need to show them that we're a happy, average, compatible couple."
>
> "Why?"
>
> "Why? Because that's what they're looking for," Jack replied, jabbing the clipboard with his finger. "It's in the name of the show. It's in the contest guidelines."
>
> "Well, if the producers followed my guidelines, I'd be the next great pop diva," Dana said hotly.

Try It!

Ask a classmate about what he or she did last weekend. Record your classmate's response. Write it down as accurately as you can. Then rewrite your conversation as if it were dialogue for a story. Add descriptive phrases, keep it authentic, and give every line a purpose.

Understanding Diction

Diction is the level of language you use based on your purpose and intended audience. Knowing about levels of diction will help you better understand your options for voice. You will use two basic levels of diction for most of your writing.

Formal English

Your essays, research papers, and business letters should meet the standards of formal English. This level of language pays careful attention to word choice, follows the conventions for grammar and usage, and maintains a serious, objective (factual) tone throughout. Formal English does not sound personal or conversational.

> **Researchers are developing alternative fuels to decrease the world's dependency on fossil fuels. Automakers believe that re-forming ethanol into hydrogen will create the fuel of the future for flexible-fuel vehicles. Currently, one experimental ethanol re-former is able to produce 110 pounds of hydrogen per day, with its only by-product being one ounce of carbon dioxide per every four ounces of hydrogen.**

Tip

Generally, avoid using *I, we,* and *you* in academic writing. Instead, focus on the topic itself and let your personal viewpoint be revealed indirectly.

Informal English

You may write many other pieces, such as personal narratives and feature articles, using a more informal level of language. Informal English usually includes some personal references, a few popular expressions, and shorter sentences.

> **Almost two years ago, I passed my driver's test. I was so excited that day. Now, looking ahead, I wonder how much driving I will do. Gas prices are skyrocketing, and each trip I take pollutes the world a little more. Our government must help scientists find new sources of fuel that are less harmful.**

Other Forms of Diction

- **Colloquial language** refers to the expressions that are accepted in informal situations and certain locations: **You wanna shoot hoops later or just hang out?**
- **Slang** is language used by a particular group of people among themselves: **During rehearsal, I really got ticked off.**
- **Jargon** (technical diction) is the specialized language used by a specific group, such as those who use computers: **The operating system notifies the user if an application installer requires administrator privileges.**

Working with Metaphors

A metaphor is a figure of speech comparing two things without using the words *like* or *as*. Metaphors invite new ways of thinking about key ideas, and they do so in a very stylized way. Well-written metaphors enliven ordinary language and help engage the reader. There are many ways to develop metaphors, including the three explained below.

Creating Metaphors with Nouns

The usual way to develop a metaphor is to compare two nouns: **A conversation with Barry is a meaty stew of politics, philosophy, and history.** In this example, the reader understands that a conversation with Barry is stimulating and challenging.

Creating Metaphors with Verbs

Another way to develop a metaphor is to use a verb: **My brain boiled over with competing ideas.** In this example, the verb *boiled over* metaphorically compares an agitated mind (brain) to a boiling pot of liquid.

It is also possible to enhance a comparison of two nouns with a participial phrase. A participial phrase begins with a participle, a verb form ending in *-ing* or *-ed*. (See page 752). Note the following example: **My brain was a boiling teakettle, shrieking with competing ideas.**

Using Extended Metaphors

A metaphor doesn't have to be expressed in a single sentence. Sometimes it can serve as a unifying element throughout a series of sentences. Extending a metaphor in this way helps you expand or clarify an idea in your writing.

> The whole of human understanding is an intricate spider's web of thought. Each filament of insight connects discrete bits of knowledge. Where much knowledge has been accumulated, the dense netting snags increasingly finer details and adds to the richness of our understanding. But oh, the gaps remaining in that web!

Note: Be careful with extended metaphors. Your writing may sound forced or inauthentic if you extend a metaphor through too many sentences.

Try It!

Pair up with a partner to find two effective metaphors in an article or a story. Then write your own metaphors modeled after the examples that you have found. Be original! After reading each other's metaphors, share your work with the entire class.

Using Other Figures of Speech

Fiction and personal essays often include *figures of speech,* which are used to communicate ideas in indirect or symbolic ways. Figures of speech go beyond the words' literal meanings. Using original figures of speech is a way to present ordinary things or situations in unusual and unexpected ways. They can help readers stay engaged in your writing. The information below covers three common figures of speech.

Personification

Personification is a figure of speech in which an animal, object, or idea is given human characteristics. (This makes personification a form of metaphor.) When used effectively, personification can create a powerful image and help establish the voice in a piece of writing.

Example: That car had it in for her. It always waited to break down until she absolutely had to be somewhere important, and whenever she worked on it, it always managed to draw blood. Even when she filled the gas tank, it would be sure to spit some back on her shoes.

Hyperbole

Hyperbole is an extreme form of exaggeration used to make a point by drawing special attention to the subject. Often, the result is humorous.

Example: You think you have a lot of brothers and sisters? I have so many siblings that when we were growing up, the U.S. government gave our house its own ZIP code.

Understatement

Like hyperbole, understatement draws special attention to a subject in order to make a point. Whereas hyperbole exaggerates, understatement does the opposite, using overly restrained language. Its effect is typically ironic or sarcastic.

Example: He [our new dog] turned out to be a good traveler, and except for an interruption caused by my wife's falling out of the car, the journey went very well.
—E. B. White, "A Report in Spring"

Try It!

Write one brief passage about a topic of interest using personification, another passage about the topic using hyperbole, and a last passage about the topic using understatement.

Using Adjectives Effectively

Mark Twain wrote, "When you catch an adjective, kill it. No, I don't mean utterly, but kill most of them—then the rest will be valuable." Obviously, adjectives have their purpose. When used properly, they can clarify the nouns that they modify. When used carelessly, adjectives can bloat a text, muddying its meaning. Writing that uses adjectives ineffectively fails to establish a connection with the reader.

Knowing What to Look For

Watch for the following types of problems in your writing.

- **Unnecessary adjectives:** Don't add an adjective to modify a noun when a more specific noun would serve.
  Original: An awful smell rose from the pit.
  Improved: A stench rose from the pit.

- **Empty adjectives:** Remove adjectives that add no real meaning to your sentence.
  Original: The slow turtle crept across the sidewalk.
  Improved: The turtle crept across the sidewalk.

- **Overused adjectives:** At times, the first adjective that comes to mind will be overused. Replace worn-out adjectives with original ones.
  Original: We strained to see in the pitch-black darkness.
  Improved: We strained to see in the relentless darkness.

Note: These overused adjectives contain little meaning: *neat, big, pretty, small, cute, fun, bad, nice, good, funny,* and so on.

- **Multiple adjectives:** Avoid stringing together multiple adjectives before a noun; very often a single adjective can effectively express the meaning that you are looking for.
  Original: Angelita bit into a juicy, runny, soggy barbecue sandwich.
  Improved: Angelita bit into a sloppy barbecue sandwich.

Try It!

Read the following passage. Work in a small group to rewrite it, addressing problems with the use of unnecessary, empty, overused, and multiple adjectives. Then take turns reading each other's passages aloud.

Our adorable, cute, cuddly kitten rubbed its downy fur against my cheek. Its little cries reminded me it was hungry. I poured some creamy milk into a bowl and watched as the tiny feline happily lapped it up. I marveled at the beauty of its brown, tortoiseshell coat.

Conventions

Errors in grammar, mechanics, spelling, or sentence structure can make a piece of writing unclear or difficult to read. No matter how interesting the subject, these types of errors detract from the overall fluency of the writing. Careless errors, in particular, can rob your message of its impact, suggesting to the reader that the quality of ideas may be less than trustworthy. Before you present your work, it is important, then, for you and a trusted classmate to check for conventions. Professional writers rely on editors and proofreaders for just these reasons.

There are many ways to improve your mastery of the conventions. One way is to review the rules from time to time. For example, you can browse the "Proofreader's Guide" in the back of this book to remind yourself of the rules. It also helps to keep a list of errors that you commonly make. Then you can refer to this list whenever you are editing a piece of writing.

- **Spelling**
- **Punctuation**
- **Varying Sentences**
- **Expanding Sentences**
- **Placing Modifiers**
- **Avoiding Awkward Sentences**

"Ignorant people think it is the noise which fighting cats make that is so aggravating, but it ain't so; it is the sickening grammar that they use."

—Mark Twain

Spelling

Few errors detract more from a piece of writing than misspelled words. The idea that the English language is too unpredictable and confusing to make sense of is a myth. Knowing how to spell words correctly is an important skill. Like any other skill, basic spelling rules can be learned. Two spelling rules are listed here. Browse the Spelling section in the back of this book to remind yourself of other basic spelling rules.

Regular Plurals

Most nouns in the English language change from the single form to the plural form by adding *-s*. For most nouns ending in *-s*, *-x*, *-ch*, or *-sh*, add *-es*. For example, *waltz* becomes *waltzes*. These nouns form regular plurals.

Irregular Plurals

Some nouns are irregular and do not follow the same rule. Use a dictionary to look up the correct spelling of words that have irregular plurals.

If a noun ends with -fe, change -f to -v, then add -s	knife, knives
If a noun ends with -f, change -f to -v, then add -es	half, halves
If a noun ending with -o is preceded by a vowel, add -s	igloo, igloos
If a noun ending with -o is preceded by a consonant, add -es	potato, potatoes

Using Spell-Checking Software

Some people might argue that learning to spell is unnecessary because of spell-checking software. Spell checkers *are* good tools for catching minor mistakes that even good spellers make, such as typing *teh* instead of *the*. However, spell-checking software does not work properly when the misspelled word creates another legitimate word. For example, if you have typed *your* for *you're*, *reins* for *reigns*, or *to* instead of *too*, spell-checking will not recognize the mistake because the word you typed is, in fact, spelled correctly. Therefore, do not rely too heavily on spell-checking software. It should never be used as your only means of proofreading, nor should it take the place of using a dictionary.

Punctuation

Accurate punctuation is an important component of good writing. Proper punctuation is essential for the effective written communication of ideas. It helps readers to know when to pause or where to stop. Punctuation can connect certain ideas or set one idea apart from another idea.

Punctuation mistakes lead to ambiguity and interfere with the reader's comprehension. In order to be clearly understood, your punctuation must be correct. The chart below shows some of the most commonly used punctuation marks. These and other punctuation marks will be covered in-depth later in this book.

Common Punctuation Marks

apostrophe '	parentheses ( )
colon :	period .
comma ,	question mark ?
exclamation mark !	quotation marks " "
hyphen -	semicolon ;

The Big Picture: Checking to be sure that your work is free of errors becomes especially important near the end of a writing project. When you check for conventions, try to focus on one type of error at a time.

- **Punctuation:** Review your work for all forms of punctuation; however, the most common errors involve commas and apostrophes. (See pages **124–126**, **644–653**, and **662–665**.)
- **Spelling:** Check your writing for capitalization and spelling. (See pages **680–685** and **696–700**.)

Punctuation Checklist

Use this checklist as a guide when you edit and proofread your writing.

_____ Does every sentence end with the proper punctuation?
_____ Are all commas used correctly?
_____ Are all apostrophes used correctly?

Varying Sentences

If all of your sentences follow the same basic pattern, your writing will be lifeless. By varying your sentences in different ways, you can spice up your writing and increase your reader's enjoyment. Varying sentences also enhances the effectiveness of the ideas you are communicating.

Varying Sentence Beginnings

Sentences that begin the same way start to plod along. To avoid this problem, vary the way you start them.

Starting with the Main Subject

Original version: Many European countries have megalithic stone monuments. England has the famous Stonehenge circle. France has the Cordon des Druides. Italy has the site near Fossa in Abruzzo. Europe also has many more examples.

Varied Beginnings

Revised version: Megalithic stone monuments can be found in many places in Europe. The famous Stonehenge circle stands in England. In France, there is the Cordon des Druides. Italy has the site near Fossa in Abruzzo. These are only three examples of Europe's many ancient stone structures.

Varying Sentence Lengths

To avoid plodding sentences, combine some of them to vary their lengths.

Similar Length

Original version: Today, students take the electronic calculator for granted. Until about 50 years ago, there was no such thing. Before then, people used pencil and paper or a slide rule. A slide rule helps a person multiply and divide large numbers. It adds or subtracts logarithmic distances to do this.

Varied Lengths

Revised version: Today, students take the electronic calculator for granted, but it was not invented until about 50 years ago. Before then, people used pencil and paper or a slide rule. A slide rule helps people to multiply and divide large numbers by adding or subtracting logarithmic distances.

Try It!

Find a passage in one of your essays in which sentences begin in the same way or are close in length. Rewrite the passage, varying the sentences.

Expanding Sentences

Details seem to spill out of accomplished writers' minds naturally. Readers marvel at how effectively these authors can expand a basic idea with engaging details. Maybe you envy good writers because of this special ability and wish you could write in the same way. The truth is you can by writing *cumulative sentences*, or sentences with modifying clauses and phrases coming before and after the main clause. (See page 774.) You can communicate complex ideas with this sophisticated sentence structure. In the following cumulative sentence, the main clause (in blue) precedes the modifying phrases.

Tony is laughing, halfheartedly, with his hands on his face, looking puzzled.

In the cumulative sentence below, modifiers are placed both before and after the main clause (in blue).

As the storm continued, the river rose, **rapidly overflowing its banks and sending waves of dirty water over the field.**

FYI

Below are six ways to expand your sentences.

1. With **individual words**: *halfheartedly*
2. With **prepositional phrases**: *with his hands on his face*
3. With **participial (-ing or -ed) phrases**: *looking puzzled*
4. With **infinitive phrases**: *to hide his embarrassment*
5. With **subordinate clauses**: *while his friend talks*
6. With **relative clauses**: *who isn't laughing at all*

Try It!

Expand each of these main clauses by adding at least two modifying words, phrases, or clauses. Then trade papers with a classmate and read aloud the sentences that he or she wrote.

1. A dog howled.
2. Mary started the car.
3. The moon cast an eerie glow.
4. My father tried to fix the bike.
5. The leaves blew.

Placing Modifiers

Sentence modifiers add information to the sentence. One way to vary the rhythm of your writing and make your composition more effective is to vary the placement of sentence modifiers.

Using Trailing Modifiers

The most common placement for a sentence modifier is after the main clause. In this pattern, the main clause provides basic information, and the sentence modifiers add detail. In the following sentence, the main clause (in blue) is followed by a long modifying phrase.

> Some people take high doses of vitamin E, hoping to combat free radicals (molecules) that have been blamed for damaging cells and promoting illnesses.

Note: The main clause in the sentence above serves as a foundation for the information that follows it.

Trying Sentence Anticipators

It is also possible to place sentence modifiers before the main clause, in which case the modifiers lead up to the main point of the sentence. In the following sentence, the modifying phrases are in black.

> Having reexamined studies of 136,000 people and finding no evidence of beneficial effects, scientists now warn against taking large doses of any vitamin.

Note: The introductory modifiers in the sentence above build support for the concluding thought in the main clause.

Including Sentence Interrupters

Finally, sentence modifiers can interrupt the main clause, giving additional information and adding emphasis or drama to the second part of the clause. Consider the phrases in black in the following example.

> Vitamin C, vitamin E, selenium, and beta carotene, the four most popular antioxidants that many people have assumed to be life extenders, can cause severe illness in large doses.

Try It!

Review one of your textbooks for examples of sentences with trailing modifiers, sentence anticipators, and sentence interrupters. (Find at least one of each.) Then rewrite each sentence by placing the modifier or modifiers in a different position. Notice the effect this has on the meaning.

Avoiding Awkward Sentences

Complete, correct sentences may be made up of several ideas. The trick is getting those ideas to work together. Incorrect sentence structure disrupts the flow of ideas in your writing. The most common errors are explained below.

Watching for Fragments

A sentence fragment lacks a subject, a verb, or some other essential part. Because of the missing part, the thought is incomplete.

> **Fragment:** Business transactions in colonial America. (This fragment lacks a verb.)
>
> **Sentence:** Business transactions in colonial America often did not involve money.

Checking for Comma Splices

A comma splice results when two independent clauses are connected with only a comma. A period, semicolon, or conjunction is needed to correct this error.

> **Comma splice:** Countless writers and artists since Aristotle's time have believed that creativity and madness are linked, experts today say that isn't true.
>
> **Corrected:** Countless writers and artists since Aristotle's time have believed that creativity and madness are linked, but experts today say that isn't true.

Watching for Run-On Sentences

A run-on is two (or more) sentences joined without adequate punctuation or a connecting word. Turn them into two sentences or into a compound sentence.

> **Run-on:** Some people prefer to watch sports others like to participate in them.
>
> **Corrected:** Some people prefer to watch sports. Others like to participate in them.
>
> **Corrected:** Some people prefer to watch sports, but others like to participate in them.

Try It!

Rewrite the following sentences, correcting any errors that you find.

1. The closet in our living room. Under our attic stairs.
2. Commuters had been stuck on the freeway for hours, some of them had a crazed look in their eyes, the others were napping.
3. I thought the test would never end I had a classic case of finger cramps. In addition, I had severe brain-drain complications only a long nap would restore me.

Exploring the Writing Process

Prewriting	91
Writing the First Draft	99
Revising	107
Peer Response	115
Editing	121
Publishing	127

Learning Language

Learning these words and expressions will help you understand this unit.

1. A **genre** is a particular style of art or writing.
   What genre do you enjoy reading the most?
2. **Redundant** means repetitive.
   Why would redundant ideas weaken an essay?
3. When people look at the **big picture**, they consider all the parts of something as a whole.
   Describe how your class fits in the big picture at school.

Prewriting

Author Barry Lane says writers "continually move back and forth between the sea and the mountain" during a writing project. As Lane explains it, writing begins in the "sea of experience," which contains the memories, experiences, and information that writers work with. When they actually write, writers begin to climb the "mountain of perception," forming new understandings, linking ideas, and drawing conclusions. If they need more details, they head back to the sea.

Prewriting refers to the beginning of a writing project—when you're still at sea—selecting a genre and topic, gathering information about the topic, structuring your ideas, formulating a research question, and so on. Prewriting also refers to trips back to the sea—when you need to carry out additional research and planning in the middle of a writing project to be sure your ideas are sustained and persuasive. If you give prewriting the proper attention, you've laid a solid foundation for all of the other steps in the writing process.

- **Selecting a Genre**
- **Selecting a Topic**
- **Gathering Details**
- **Finding Additional Information**
- **A Closer Look at Prewriting**
- **Forming Your Thesis Statement**
- **Organizing Your Details**

"Writing is an exploration. You start from nothing and learn as you go."

—E. L. Doctorow

Selecting a Genre

A genre will be selected for you in many assignments. For broader assignments, you may need to determine your audience and select the genre that will convey your meaning most effectively. For example, you might choose *biography* to tell the story of a favorite person and choose *personal narrative* to describe your own experiences.

Selecting a Topic

Your teacher may provide you with a general subject and ask that you narrow it to a specific topic.

General Subject: The Endocrine System

Specific Topic: Glands and Hormones of the Endocrine System

Depending on the assignment, you might discuss the topic with others, do some background reading, consider your personal interests, or even do preliminary interviews. You can use one of the following strategies to select an effective, specific writing topic.

Keeping a Writer's Notebook

Write on a regular basis in a personal notebook (journal), exploring your experiences and thoughts. Review your entries on occasion and underline ideas that you could explore in writing assignments. (See pages **1–5** for more information.)

Developing a Cluster

Begin a cluster with a nucleus word, usually a general term or idea related to your writing assignment. Then cluster related words around it. After 3 or 4 minutes, scan your cluster for a word or an idea that interests you. Write nonstop about that idea for 5 to 8 minutes. A few writing topics should begin to occur to you.

Making a List

Begin with a thought or a key word related to your assignment and simply start listing words and ideas. Listing ideas with a group of classmates (brainstorming) is also an effective way to search for writing topics.

Trying Freewriting

Begin writing with a particular focus in mind—one that is related to your assignment. Write nonstop for 5 to 10 minutes to discover possible writing topics.

- Don't stop to judge, edit, or correct your writing.
- Keep writing even when you seem to be drawing a blank. If necessary, write "I'm drawing a blank" until a new idea comes to mind.
- Review your writing and underline ideas you like.
- Continue freewriting about ideas you want to explore further.

Sample Freewriting

> Most people think of doctors and nurses when they hear you're interested in a medical career. It's really amazing, the kinds of jobs there are in health care. With some medical careers, people don't even have to see or touch another human being. In others, that's what they do all day. Also, think about how important computers are to health care now!...

Considering the "Basics of Life" List

Below you will find a list of the essential elements in our lives. The list provides an endless variety of topic possibilities. For example, the category *education* led to the following writing ideas:

- internships for high school students
- community service requirements
- open campus vs. closed campus

Basics of Life

clothing	education	love	entertainment
communication	machines	rules/laws	health/medicine
exercise/training	faith/religion	science/technology	recreation
housing	family	energy	literature/books
community	trade/money	land/property	tools/utensils
food	agriculture	work/occupation	freedom/rights
arts/music	heat/fuel		

Try It!

List four or five possible writing ideas for any two categories in the "Basics of Life" list. (For your next writing assignment, use one of the strategies above to identify possible topics.)

Gathering Details

In most cases, it's a good idea to first collect your initial thoughts about the topic you've selected, including personal experiences and interests and past knowledge. Then, if necessary, do research to find more information.

Gathering Your Thoughts

These strategies will help you to recall what you already know and establish your personal feelings about the topic.

- **Freewriting:** Approach freewriting in one of two ways. (1) Do a focused freewriting, exploring your topic from a number of different angles. (2) Approach freewriting as if it were a quick version of the actual paper.
- **Audience appeal:** Address a specific audience as you write. Consider a group of parents, a television audience, or the readers of a popular teen magazine.
- **Questioning:** Ask yourself or others questions to gather information about your topic. If your topic falls into the categories of *problems*, *policies*, or *concepts*, you can use the questions in this chart.

	Description	Function	History	Value
Problems	What is the problem?	Who or what is affected by it?	What is the current status of the problem?	Why is it important?
Policies	What type of policy is it? What are its features?	What is the policy designed to do?	What brought this policy about?	Is the policy working? Why or why not?
Concepts	What type of concept is it? Who or what is related to it?	Who has been influenced by this concept?	When did it originate? How has it changed?	What value does it hold? What is its social worth?

Try It!

Gather your thoughts. Use one of these strategies to collect your own thoughts about a writing topic.

Finding Additional Information

For most writing assignments, it won't suffice to simply gather your own thoughts about a topic. Expository and persuasive essays, for example, will almost always require a research plan that includes other sources of information. These sources can be divided into two categories—*primary* and *secondary*.

Exploring a Variety of Sources

- **Primary sources** include interviews, personal observations, firsthand experiences, surveys, experiments, and so on. A primary source informs you directly, not through another person's explanation or interpretation. Some of the best primary sources are from experts on the topic.
- **Secondary sources** include periodicals, books, references, Web sites, and so on. A secondary source is one that contains information other people have gathered and interpreted. It is at least once removed from the original. Many reliable secondary sources are written for informed audiences in the field.

Tips for Gathering Information

- Whenever possible, use both primary and secondary sources to get a thorough understanding of your topic.
- Read secondary sources with a critical eye, always evaluating the quality and the purpose of the information.
- Take careful notes, writing down important facts, opinions, and quotations. Record any source information you will need to cite.
- Consider using a graphic organizer such as a gathering grid to keep track of the facts and details your research uncovers.
- Consult librarians and teachers if you have trouble finding information.

Try It!

Imagine that you've been assigned to write an essay about immigration in the United States. Examine each of the following sources of information, differentiating between primary or secondary. Label each with a "P" or an "S."

1. An e-mail message from a member of the National Immigration Forum, responding to your questions from a previous e-mail
2. An interview concerning immigration in *In Motion*, an online magazine
3. Your participation in an immigration-rights rally
4. A newspaper report, reviewing new immigration legislation

> "As soon as you connect with your true subject, you will write."
> —Rachel Carson

A Closer Look at Prewriting

After you've selected a genre and topic and gathered details about it, you can plan and write your first draft, or you can consider how well you match up with your topic before you go any further.

Taking Inventory of Your Thoughts

After carefully considering the questions that follow, you will be ready to (1) move ahead with your writing or (2) change your genre or topic.

Audience and Genre

- Who are my readers?
- How much do they already know about my topic?
- How can I keep them interested in my ideas?
- How should I present my ideas—in a story, an essay, a report, a multimedia presentation?
- What form of writing should I use—narrative, descriptive, persuasive, expository?

Focus and Purpose

- Does my topic meet the requirements of the assignment?
- Am I writing to explain, persuade, describe, entertain, or retell?

Self

- How do I feel about the topic? Have I made a personal connection with it?
- Do I have enough time to develop it?

Topic

- How much more do I need to know about this topic?
- Has my research changed my thinking about the topic?
- What part of the topic will I focus on?

Forming Your Thesis Statement

After you have explored the topic and collected information, you should begin to develop a more focused interest in your topic. If all goes well, this interest will become the thesis of your writing. **A thesis statement identifies the focus of an academic essay.** It is sometimes called a controlling idea and usually highlights a particular condition, feature, or feeling about the topic or takes a stand.

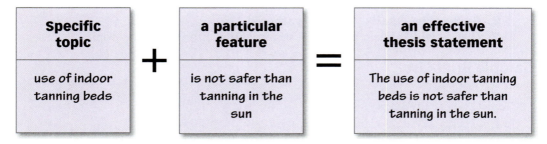

Sample Thesis Statements

Writing Assignment: Essay on some aspect of the '60s generation
Specific Topic: Social issues of the decade
Thesis Statement: The social issues of the 1960s (**specific topic**) continue to play a role in our current culture (**particular feature**).

Writing Assignment: Essay about the introduction of new species into the ecosystem
Specific Topic: The Asian carp in the Great Lakes
Thesis Statement: The introduction of the Asian carp into the Great Lakes (**specific topic**) could lead to a radical change in the lakes' ecosystem (**particular feature**).

Try It!

Write thesis statements. Listed below are specific topics students have used for essays. For two of them, write a thesis statement that focuses on a particular feature of the topic.

General Subject:	Specific Topic:
the Internet	peer-to-peer sharing programs
a nineteenth-century author	Edgar Allan Poe
"helpful" insects	butterflies and dragonflies
a natural disaster	the 2005 earthquake in northern Pakistan

Organizing Your Details

After forming a thesis statement, you may need to design a writing plan before you start your first draft. Your plan can be anything from a brief list of ideas to a detailed sentence outline. Your goal is to structure your ideas in a sustained and persuasive way. Use the guidelines that follow to help organize your details for writing.

1. Study your thesis statement. It may suggest a logical method of organization for your essay.
2. Review the details you have gathered.
3. Decide which basic pattern of organization fits your essay topic.

Sample Brief List

Topic: Hunger in Africa
- Natural resources
- India as an example
- The "Harare Declaration"

Sample Sentence Outline

Topic: Hunger in Africa

I. Africa is a land of many valuable resources.
   A. It contains great areas of unused land, water, and minerals.
   B. There are enough resources to feed all of Africa.
   C. Developing these resources will take time and cooperation.
II. India should give African countries hope.
   A. It experienced a similar hunger problem.
   B. The government began producing enough food for its people.
   C. Today, India is in much better shape than it was 25 years ago.

Writing the First Draft

Once you have chosen your topic, gathered details, and organized your details, you're ready to write your first draft. This is your first attempt at developing your prewriting into a complete, structured unit of writing that supports central ideas, concepts, and themes.

Writing a first draft can be exciting and satisfying as you see your initial thinking about a topic take shape. Try to write your first draft freely without being overly concerned about correctness. Your goal is to get all your ideas on paper in a form that is easy to follow. Use the planning you've done (outline) as a basic guide, but be open to new ideas that come to mind as you write.

If you are writing an essay or a research paper, systematically develop each of your main points in a separate paragraph. Also connect the paragraphs with linking words or transitions. The information in this chapter provides additional tips and strategies for writing your first draft.

- **Considering the Big Picture**
- **Writing the Beginning**
- **Developing the Middle**
- **Writing the Ending**

"The first draft is the down draft—you just get it down. The second draft is the up draft—you fix it up."

—Anne Lamott

Considering the Big Picture

As you prepare to write a first draft, keep in mind these three traits of good writing: *organization, development of ideas,* and *voice.*

Organization Use your planning as a guide and try to get all of your thoughts on paper. Be sure to include a beginning, a middle, and an ending. (See below.)

Development of Ideas Start with a specific focus. Develop your main supporting points and add new ideas, concepts, and themes as they come to you.

Voice Let your words flow naturally and freely, as if you were in a conversation with the reader.

Drafting Hints

- Review your prewriting materials before you begin. This will help you get started.
- If you are drafting by hand, write on every other line; if you are using a computer, double-space your work so you will have room to revise.
- Focus on the writing and don't be overly concerned about being neat and avoiding errors. You can make corrections later on.

Organizing Your Writing

As you write, keep in mind the three parts of any piece of writing: the beginning, the middle, and the ending.

The Beginning

- Gets the reader's attention.
- Identifies the thesis or purpose of your writing.

The Middle

- Systematically presents the main points that support the thesis.
- Includes details that develop the main points.

The Ending

- Restates the thesis.
- Presents a final insight about the topic.

Try It!

Be sure to review this page before you write your next first draft. Afterward, assess your results. *Did you get all of your ideas on paper? Did you include all three parts—beginning, middle, and ending?*

Writing the Beginning

Informative and interesting opening paragraphs hook the reader.

Grabbing Your Reader's Attention

Develop an opening statement that reflects the focus and tone of your writing. Here are some ways to attract the reader's interest.

- Give a surprising fact or statement.
  Although the wild dogs called dingoes are generally considered Australian natives, they originated in and still roam Southeast Asia.
- Ask a question.
  When is a dog not a dog? When it is a dingo: part wolf, part dog, and all danger.
- Use a relevant quotation.
  "They're the devil in fur, that's what they are!" This is how an angry sheep rancher refers to dingoes, the wild dogs of the Australian outback.
- Present an interesting detail about the topic.
  Dingoes, often considered pests, play an important role in Australia's ecosystem.

Shaping Your Beginning Paragraph

The first part of your opening paragraph should identify your topic and hook the reader. Follow with any necessary background information. End with your thesis statement, identifying the specific part of the topic you plan to emphasize.

Attention-getting opening	"They're the devil in fur, that's what they are!" This is how an angry sheep rancher refers to dingoes, the wild dogs of the Australian outback. Descended from wolves, these lean, shrewd creatures roam northern Australia, living off their wits and whatever small animals they can find. Farmers who suffer the loss of chickens or sheep to these predators consider dingoes little more than a headache. Yet these long-legged interlopers are actually an important part of the Australian ecosystem.
Background information	
Thesis statement	

Try It!

Share the beginning paragraph of a current assignment in a small group. Discuss how strongly the opening grabs the reader's attention, and identify possible improvements using the strategies above.

Developing the Middle

Your middle paragraphs should provide the persuasive details that support your thesis. Use your planning materials to systematically organize your support in a logical order. Here are some ways to support your thesis.

Explain: Provide facts, details, and examples to illustrate a concept.
Narrate: Share a brief story (anecdote) to illustrate or clarify an idea.
Describe: Tell how someone appears or how something works.
Summarize: Present only the most important ideas.
Define: Identify or clarify the meaning of a specific term or idea.
Argue: Use logic and evidence to prove something is true.
Compare: Show how two things are alike or different.
Analyze: Examine the parts of something to better understand the whole.
Reflect: Express your thoughts or feelings about something.

FYI

Most essays, articles, and research papers require a number of these methods to thoroughly develop their theses. For example, an essay of definition may contain two or more definitions, a comparison, a brief story, and so on.

Using Various Types of Support

Below and on the next page are some examples of how one student used various types of support in his paper about dingoes, wild dogs of Australia.

Explain: Provide important facts, details, and examples.

> Dingoes have proven a real menace to Australian sheep and cattle farmers, who have gone to great lengths to protect their animals by building the Dingo Fence. Built in the 1880s, the fence stretches across New South Wales and southern Queensland, the country's major farming area. It effectively separates the cattle and sheep areas from dingoes. At six feet high, it is also sunk nearly a foot below ground to prevent the predators from digging underneath. At the time this 3,000-mile-long fence was built, it was the longest man-made structure in the world, showing just how far some people will go to protect their investments.

Describe: Create a mental picture of your subject.

> Although dingoes look somewhat like dogs, they have physical characteristics that link them to wolves. Their coats are generally ginger colored but may vary in color from sandy to dark red to black, with white markings on their feet, throats, and bushy tails. There

are even white dingoes found in the Australian Alps. Dingoes stand about one and a half to two feet high at the shoulder, and are about five feet long. They are long legged and lean with long, pointed muzzles and pointed ears that stick straight up at the tops of their heads. Although related to dogs, dingoes have larger teeth and do not bark but howl instead, much like wolves and coyotes. Once considered close relatives to domestic dogs *(Canus familiaris)*, dingoes have been given feral status and their own scientific name, *Canus dingo.*

Argue: Present a case for or against a topic.

Ironically, the Dingo Fence has shown that although dingoes may seem like pests, they are an important part of the Australian ecosystem. As predators, dingoes help control the rabbit population. An unchecked rabbit population decimates grazing lands, negatively affecting sheep and cattle ranching. In fact, on the protected side of the Dingo Fence, rabbit and kangaroo populations have depleted grass and water. On the dingo side of the fence, these populations have been effectively reduced, allowing for more luxuriant grasslands. This indicates that dingoes help maintain an ecological balance.

Reflect: Consider the impact of your topic.

Dingoes have been considered pests—ostracized by special fences and overcome by poison, traps, and shooting. Scientists worry about the possible extinction of these animals, so they have set up conservation areas. However, a threat that is less easily controlled is that of dingoes interbreeding with domestic dogs. Scientists fear that in the not-too-distant future, the pure dingo strain may disappear forever.

Analyze: Examine the parts of something to better understand the whole.

Ever since the cry "Dingoes ate my baby!" appeared in a sensationalist tabloid newspaper, people have been concerned about dingo attacks. Scientists exploring the phenomena suggest that attacks on humans are not characteristic of purebred dingoes. The problem comes from offspring of dingoes and domestic dogs. The resulting hybrid pups are larger and more aggressive with characteristics of a dog and a dingo. Whereas a pure dingo might eat whatever bugs or lizards it finds, a hybrid craves meat, leading to more and more attacks on sheep, cattle, and even humans.

Try It!

Select one of the techniques on pages **102–103** to illustrate a topic of your choice in a brief paragraph. Then read aloud your paragraph to a partner and ask your partner to identify the technique you used.

Developing the Middle

Using Different Levels of Detail

In most cases each main point is developed in a separate paragraph. Remember that specific details add meaning to your writing and make it worth reading, while writing that lacks effective detail leaves the reader with an incomplete picture and is not persuasive. A well-written paragraph often contains three levels of detail.

Level 1: A controlling sentence names the topic.

> Ironically, the Dingo Fence has shown that although dingoes may seem like pests, they are an important part of the Australian ecosystem.

Level 2: Clarifying sentences provide supporting points for the idea or concept.

> As predators, dingoes help control the rabbit population. An unchecked rabbit population decimates grazing lands, negatively affecting sheep and cattle ranching. In fact, on the protected side of the Dingo Fence, rabbit and kangaroo populations have depleted grass and water. On the dingo side of the fence, these populations have been effectively reduced, allowing for more luxuriant grasslands.

Level 3: A completing sentence adds details to make the paragraph persuasive.

> This indicates that dingoes help maintain an ecological balance.

Try It!

Identify one set of sentences that show the three levels of detail in the paragraph below. Label each sentence after writing it down. (The topic sentence is the one controlling sentence in the paragraph.)

1. Until a few years ago, dingo watching was a popular tourist attraction
2. on Fraser Island, Australia's top vacation spot. Dingoes have traditionally
3. displayed a mild temperament around humans, but
4. aggressive behaviors began appearing in 2001, with
5. a fatal attack on a child. Since that time, another
6. 20 attacks have been documented. It appears that
7. through continued contact with tourists, the dingoes
8. have lost their innate fear of humans. Because the
9. animals are by nature carnivores, this newfound
10. aggression poses obvious dangers. While dingo
11. watching is not discouraged, it now comes with
12. governmental warnings and regulations.

Integrating Quotations

Always choose quotations that are appropriate for your writing. Quotations should support your ideas, not replace them.

Strategies for Using Quotations

Use the strategies below to make the most effective use of quoted material in your writing.

- **Use quotations to support your own thoughts and ideas.**
  Effective quotations can back up your main points or support your arguments.

  Even in the early twentieth century, pollution was a growing concern, as shown in this comment by Franklin D. Roosevelt: "Government cannot close its eyes to the pollution of waters, to the erosion of soil, to the slashing of forests any more than it can close its eyes to the need for slum clearance and schools."

- **Use quotations to lend authority to your writing.**
  Quoting an expert shows that you have researched your topic and understand its significance.

  Despite vociferous opposition to the arms race, the development of the bomb was an important part of world peace. As nuclear physicist Edward Teller explained, "We had a wonderful record on the hydrogen bomb. We tested it, perfected it, and never used it—and that served to win the Cold War."

- **Use quotations that are succinct and powerful.**
  Distinctive quotations add value to your writing.

  Country music's power doesn't come from complicated structures or deep political undertones; it is popular simply because it touches people's lives. As legendary songwriter Harlan Howard once put it, "Country music is three chords and the truth."

Common Quotation Problems to Avoid

Avoid these problems as you choose quotations.

- **Plagiarism**
  Cite sources for all quotations (and paraphrases).
- **Long quotations**
  Keep quotations brief and to the point.
- **Overused quotations**
  Use a quotation only when you cannot share its message as powerfully or effectively in another way.

Writing the Ending

Your ending paragraph allows you to tie together the important ideas and concepts in your essay. Your ending should do at least two of the following things:

- Restate or revisit the thesis of your paper.
- Review the main points.
- Leave the reader with something to think about.

Connecting with the thesis

Reviewing the main points

A final thought

The dingoes of Australia provide an interesting quandary for the government. The animals have been important to maintaining an ecological balance, even though they pose an increasing threat to domestic animals, and, more recently, to humans. Tourists still love watching dingoes, and scientists still worry about the pure dingo strain dying out due to mixed breeding. The dilemma remains: Will preserving the species be worth the growing danger?

Forming a Final Thought

Here are three different ways to structure a persuasive final thought.

A call to action directs the reader to do something.

> Only the city council can save Heathrow Park from the bulldozers. Call, e-mail, or write your representative to ask that our beautiful city park be preserved.

A lingering question encourages the reader to further examine the subject.

> Help save unwanted dogs and cats by having your pet spayed or neutered. Thousands of animals are put to death each year because people didn't take action. Don't you want to do your part to avoid these unnecessary deaths?

A good-or-bad conclusion suggests that your topic poses a possible benefit or threat the reader should be aware of.

> The Starlight Players is the only community theater group in the area. If people don't support it, the company could disband. That would give people another reason to find entertainment elsewhere, and a valuable family activity would be lost. It's your choice.

Try It!

Write an ending for a current writing assignment. Try reworking it using the suggestions above. Select the one you like best.

Revising

In a first draft, you communicate your initial sense of a topic. You do your best to connect all of your ideas. When you revisit a first draft, after setting it aside for a day or two, you will see different parts that you would like to change.

You may spot redundant information, which needs to be cut. You may note places that would benefit from adding details to clarify your meaning. You may want to strengthen weak arguments or rearrange ideas to improve the logical organization and flow. These are all the basic revising moves.

Revising may be the most important step in the writing process. It helps you improve the thoughts and details that carry your message. This chapter will give you a better understanding of this step, covering everything from a review of basic revising guidelines to an explanation of a valuable revising strategy.

- **Basic Revising Guidelines**
- **A Revising Strategy That Works**
- **A Closer Look at Revising**
- **Revising Checklist**
- **Revising in Action**
- **Checking for Depth**

"To the confident [change] is inspiring because the challenge exists to make things better."

—King Whitney, Jr.

Basic Revising Guidelines

No writer gets it right the first time. Few writers even get it right the second time. In fact, professional writers almost always carry out many revisions before they are satisfied with their work. As writer Virginia Hamilton says, "The real work comes in the rewriting stage." The following guidelines will help you make the best revising moves.

- **Set your writing aside.** Get away from it for a day or two. This will help you see your first draft more clearly when you are ready to revise.
- **Carefully review your draft.** Read it at least two times: once silently and once aloud. Also ask another person to react to your writing—someone whose opinion you trust.
- **Consider the big picture.** Decide if your organization is logical and if you've effectively developed your thesis.
- **Look at the specific parts.** Rewrite any parts that aren't clear or effective. Cut information that doesn't support your thesis and add ideas that clarify your meaning.
- **Assess your opening and closing paragraphs.** Be sure that they effectively introduce and wrap up your writing.

Revising a Timed Writing

When you have little time to make changes, writer Peter Elbow recommends "cut and paste revising." For example, if you are responding to a writing prompt on a test or for an in-class assignment, you may have just 10 to 15 minutes to revise your writing. The steps that follow describe this quick revising strategy.

1. Don't add any new information.
2. Cut unnecessary details.
3. Check for basic organization.
4. Do whatever rewriting is necessary.

Try It!

Find an essay you wrote but haven't read in a while. Read it aloud, either alone or to someone else, paying careful attention to every word and every punctuation mark. *What trouble spots do you notice? Why do you notice them more when reading your work aloud? How would you fix these parts?*

A Revising Strategy That Works

The strategy below covers everything from reading the first draft to improving specific ideas. Use this strategy when you have time for in-depth revising.

Read: Sometimes it's hard to keep an open mind when you read your first draft. It's good to put some distance between yourself and your writing.

- Whenever possible, put your writing aside for a day or two.
- When you return to it, read your first draft aloud.
- Ask others (peers, family members) to read it aloud to you.
- Listen to your writing: What does it say? How does it sound?

React: Use these questions to help you react to your writing:

- What parts of my writing work for me?
- Is there a consistent tone?
- Have I arranged the parts in the best possible order?
- What other revising should I do?

Rework: Make changes until all parts of your writing work equally well. There is usually plenty of reworking to do in the early stages of revising, when you are still trying to bring a clear focus to a topic and share it effectively.

Reflect: Write comments in the margins of your paper (or in a notebook) as you revise. Here are some guidelines for reflecting:

- Explore your reactions freely. Be honest about your writing.
- Note what you plan to cut, rearrange, clarify, and so on.
- Reflect on the changes you make. (How do they work?)
- If you are unsure of what to do, write down a question to answer later.

Refine: Refining is checking specific ideas for clarity, logic, readability, and consistency. Use these questions to help you refine your ideas:

- Will the reader be able to follow my train of thought from idea to idea?
- Do I use transitional words or phrases to link ideas?
- Have I overdeveloped or underdeveloped certain points?

Tip

Remember that revising is the process of improving the ideas and the details that carry the message in your writing. Don't pay undue attention to conventions too early in the process; just concentrate on improving your message.

A Closer Look at Revising

The later stage of revising allows you to deal with those aspects of your writing that may make it seem boring. Use the questions that follow to check for any uninspired "badlands" in your writing.

- **Is your topic worn out?** An essay entitled "Lead Poisoning" sounds uninteresting. With a new twist, you can enliven it: "Get the Lead Out!"
- **Is your approach stale?** If you are writing primarily to please your teacher, start again. Try writing to learn something or to trigger a particular emotion within the reader.
- **Do you sound uninterested or unnatural?** If you do ("A good time was had by all"), try another approach. This time, be honest. Be real.
- **Do parts of your writing seem boring?** Maybe those parts are boring because they don't say enough, or they say too much. To rework these parts, think of them as a series of snapshots. Each picture needs to be clear and balanced between its main idea and the supporting details.
- **Is your writing constrained by overly tight organization?** The structure of an essay provides you with a frame to build on. However, if the frame is followed too closely, your writing may become predictable. If the "formula" is obvious when you read your draft, change the structure in order to more freely present your ideas.

Try It!

In a small group, discuss these two paragraphs using the questions above as a guide. Then report your opinions to the class.

Adventures in Cairo

Cairo is a sprawling city of 15.2 million people. Bazaars, small stalls or storefronts selling various goods, cater mostly to tourists. The prices are quite reasonable, but the vendors are pushy to the point of actually grabbing some people and pulling them into their shops. Adding to the commotion, many poor people beg for "bakshish" or tips (essentially for doing an unrequested "favor").

Traffic is just incredible—but it moves! Drivers are absolutely obsessed about getting where they want to go. There are no lanes; drivers just squeeze in and out of traffic however they can. The few traffic lights seem not to work. If there is too much traffic on one side of a divided highway, well, drivers go the wrong way on the other side. They make left turns from the middle lanes. There is a LOT of honking going on at all times. Also sharing the road are donkey-drawn carts. It's crazy! And although there are police everywhere, they do not seem very concerned about any of this.

Revising

> "Any activity becomes creative when the doer cares about doing it right or doing it better."
> —John Updike

Texas Traits Revising Checklist

Use this checklist as a guide when you revise your writing. *Remember:* When you revise, you improve the thoughts and details that carry your message.

Focus and Coherence

_____ 1. Is my topic important and relevant?
_____ 2. Have I developed a specific focus or thesis statement?
_____ 3. Does each paragraph support my thesis?
_____ 4. Do I avoid repetition and redundancy?

Organization

_____ 5. Does my writing follow a clear pattern of organization?
_____ 6. Have I developed effective beginning, middle, and ending parts?
_____ 7. Do I need to reorder any parts?

Development of Ideas

_____ 8. Have I included enough details to make my ideas clear?
_____ 9. Do my sentences flow smoothly?

Voice

_____ 10. Does my voice fit the purpose of my writing?
_____ 11. Do I sound interested in and knowledgeable about my topic?
_____ 12. Do I use specific nouns and vivid verbs to engage the reader?
_____ 13. Have I used an appropriate level of formality?

Conventions

_____ 14. Are my sentences complete and clearly written?
_____ 15. Is my essay free of errors in mechanics and spelling?

Revising in Action

When you revise a first draft, focus on improving the writing overall. You can improve a piece by adding, deleting, rearranging, or reworking information. (See the next page for examples.)

Adding Information

Add information to your writing if you need to . . .

- share more details to make a point,
- clarify or complete an interesting idea, or
- link sentences or paragraphs with transitional words or phrases to improve clarity and flow.

Deleting Information

Delete material from your draft when the ideas . . .

- do not support your focus or
- are redundant or repetitious.

Rearranging Material

Rearrange material in your writing in order to . . .

- create a clear flow of ideas,
- present points in order, or
- make a dramatic impact.

Reworking Material

Rework material in your writing if it . . .

- is confusing or unclear,
- does not maintain a consistent tone or the proper voice, or
- needs to be simplified.

Being Your Own Critic

When revising, try to anticipate your reader's concerns. Doing so will help you determine what changes to make. Here are some questions and concerns a reader may have:

- What is the main point of this essay?
- Is the writer's voice consistent, interested, and authoritative?
- Can I follow the writer's ideas smoothly?
- Does the ending wrap up the essay in a clear way?

Sample Revision

The writer revised this essay by rearranging, adding, deleting, and reworking. (See the inside back cover of this text for editing and proofreading marks.)

> ### The Sky's Not the Limit
>
> Ever since movies began, filmmakers have tried to put imaginary things on film. *Still, the effects never seemed real enough.* People used model building, hand-drawn cartoons, or stop-motion animation. In the last 20 years, however, computer-generated imagery (CGI) has made it possible to create believable special effects in movies. *Anything that can be imagined can be put on-screen and look real.* CGI allows filmmakers to show things realistically on-screen that people could only imagine before.
>
> CGI can create totally imaginary characters that look real. An early example is a knight leaping out of a stained-glass window in *Young Sherlock Holmes* (1985). ~~Dinosaurs are the most popular creatures for special effects over the years, starting with the stop-motion puppets of *The Lost World* (1925).~~ Later on, CGI showed us believable dinosaurs in *Jurassic Park* (1993). More recently, CGI and the voice and acting of Andy Serkis created the incredible character of Gollum (*Lord of the Rings: The Two Towers*, 2002). ~~Even though I loved and believed in Yoda as a puppet in *The Empire Strikes Back* (1980), the technology is outmoded and too limited.~~ *Today, CGI even replaces older special effects technologies like the Yoda puppet from The Empire Strikes Back (1980).* Many of the aliens in the newer *Star Wars* films are all CGI creations (*Revenge of the Sith*, 2005). Now, even the most fantastic creatures from folklore to science fiction can seem real on-screen.

Sentences are rearranged for better organization.

An interesting detail is added to develop an idea.

An unnecessary detail is deleted.

An important idea is reworded for appropriate voice.

Checking for Depth

One important consideration when revising an essay is to determine whether or not the level of detail is appropriate. Some ideas can be expressed perfectly well without a lot of specifics (and, in fact, may suffer from too many details). If, however, you realize during revision that a particular passage needs more support, the addition of specific details will help the reader better understand your writing.

Different types of writing require different types of details. For instance, facts, statistics, and examples support expository and persuasive writing, while narrative and creative writing benefit from sensory and memory details.

Adding Depth

As Alahandra was reviewing her essay about the process of digestion, she came upon these two sentences:

> In the mouth, saliva helps break down food. When someone swallows, a movement called peristalsis pushes the food down into the stomach.

Alahandra then added details to better explain the process.

> In the mouth, the chewing of food causes the exocrine glands to release saliva. Enzymes in saliva help break down food. Saliva also helps condense the chewed-up food into small balls that can pass into the esophagus when swallowed. In the esophagus, peristalsis, or contraction of the smooth muscle tissues, pushes the food down toward the stomach, where it enters through a one-way "gate" called the cardiac sphincter.

Try It!

This passage is from an essay about the body's healing process. In a small group, discuss why the writer should or should not add details.

> As soon as you receive a minor cut, your body's healing process begins. Blood from tiny blood vessels fills the wound and begins to clot. Then a scab forms.

Peer Response

If you had some poppy seeds stuck between your teeth, surely you'd want someone to politely and discreetly point out your little *faux pas*. Similarly, if there is a problem in your writing, you would appreciate a friend or classmate directing your attention to it. That's what peer responding is all about. When you ask your peers for their honest opinions about your writing, they can show you things you don't see yourself—good and bad. Once you have this feedback, you can decide on the best way to address any problem areas.

Feedback from your fellow writers is valuable throughout the writing process, but it is especially helpful during the early stages of revising when you are evaluating your first draft. Some experts go so far as to say that talking about your work will help you more than anything else you do during the writing process.

- **Peer-Response Guidelines**
- **Using the Traits to Respond**
- **Trying a New Strategy**

"Criticism, like rain, should be gentle enough to nourish a man's growth without destroying his roots."

—Frank A. Clark

> "The first rule in listening to comments about your work is 'Never defend yourself' unless you can tell that your critic has misunderstood something."
>
> —Ken Macrorie

Peer-Response Guidelines

The guidelines below will help you participate in peer-response sessions. (If you're just starting out, work in small groups of two or three classmates.)

Considering the Writer's Role

Come to the session with a meaningful piece of your writing—perhaps a recently completed first draft. Make a copy for each member of the group (if this is what the group usually does).

- **Introduce your writing.** Give a brief explanation of what your piece is about without going into too much detail.
- **Read your writing aloud.** If you don't feel comfortable reading aloud, ask group members to read your piece silently.
- **Ask for feedback.** Listen carefully and consider all suggestions. Don't be defensive, because this may stop some members from commenting honestly.
- **Take notes.** Record your classmates' comments on your copy so you can decide later what to change.
- **Answer questions.** If you're unsure of an answer, it's okay to say, "I don't know" or "I'll look into that."
- **Seek assistance.** If you have trouble with a specific part of your writing, ask for help.

Seeking Constructive Criticism

To get constructive criticism, you may need to ask the responders some direct questions. Consider your purpose, your intended audience, and the focus of your writing. Knowing these three things will help you form your questions.

Try It!

Practice your role as the writer in a peer-response session with a classmate, friend, or family member. First, share the information on the next page about the responder's role. Then follow the guidelines for the writer listed above. Afterward, assess the effectiveness of the session: *Did the session help you see parts of your writing that could be improved? Did the responder answer any questions that you had? Did he or she make any other helpful suggestions?*

Peer Response

Considering the Responder's Role

You need to be honest in your feedback without hurting the writer's feelings. Your comments should always be polite and constructive.

Giving Constructive Criticism

Don't make demands . . . "Change the ending so the reader has something to think about."	**Do** make suggestions . . . "The ending could be stronger if you leave the reader with a question to think about."
Don't focus on the writer . . . "Nobody understands what you're trying to say in the middle part."	**Do** focus on the writing . . . "Don't you think your ideas would be easier to follow if you switched paragraphs two and three?"
Don't focus on the problem . . . "The beginning paragraph is boring."	**Do** focus on the solution . . . "Descriptive details might make the beginning more interesting."
Don't give general comments . . . "Your sentences aren't very interesting."	**Do** give specific advice . . . "Changing from passive to active voice in a few places could liven things up."

Response Tips

- Listen carefully to the writer's reading and questions.
- Take notes in the margins of your copy.
- Ask questions. If you are not sure of something, ask for clarification.

Try It!

Using the tips above, write three strong criticisms about this paragraph.

> In the northwest part of Utah lie the remnants of a sizable lake from the Ice Age. All that remains of the ancient Lake Bonneville is salt—up to six feet deep in some areas. The Bonneville Salt Flats, which occupy approximately 160 square miles, are extremely flat and devoid of plant life. As such, the area is well suited for motor sports, and the state's highway department now maintains a part of the Flats known as the Bonneville Speedway. It was here that numerous land speed records were set, beginning in 1935 when Malcolm Campbell, driving a specially designed Rolls-Royce, passed the 300-mph mark for the first time. For the next 62 years, each of the world's land speed records was broken at the Bonneville Speedway, until Andy Green's rocket-powered record of 763 mph in October 1997 at Black Rock Desert in Nevada.

Using the Traits to Respond

Responders help writers rethink, refocus, and revise their writing. As a responder, you may find it helpful to base your responses on the traits of writing.

Addressing Focus and Coherence, Organization, and Development of Ideas Early in the Process

Focus and Coherence: Helping the Author with Focus and Coherence
- Can you tell us the main idea of your writing?
- It seems like you're trying to say . . . . Is that right?
- Are these points the main ideas in your writing?
- Your writing left me thinking . . . . Is that what you intended?
- This sentence seems to state your focus. Is that correct?

Organization: Helping the Author Focus on Organization
- You got my attention in the beginning by . . .
- Are the middle paragraphs organized according to . . . ?
- Why did you place the information about . . . in the fourth paragraph?
- A transition might help between the . . . paragraphs.

Development of Ideas: Helping the Author Focus on Development of Ideas
- The most convincing details are . . .
- A few details like . . . may make this part more interesting.
- In my opinion, details like . . . may distract from your main idea.

Try It!

Find and read any student writer's paragraph in this book. Afterward, write two constructive criticisms based on the *focus and coherence, organization,* and *development of ideas* in the writing.

Addressing Voice and Conventions Later in the Process

Voice: Helping the Author Focus on Voice
- The sentences that most clearly show your personality are . . .
- How would you describe your attitude about this topic?
- What audience did you have in mind when you wrote this?
- The third paragraph sounds too formal to me. Do you think it fits in with the rest of your writing?
- The overall feeling I get from your writing is . . .
- The middle part of your essay might be too subjective.

Conventions: Helping the Author Focus on Conventions
- I'm confused by the meaning of . . . . Can you define it, please?
- The words . . . feel wrong to me. You could use . . . instead.
- Have you used . . . too often in the first part of your writing?
- A few misplaced commas in the first paragraph make your message a little confusing.
- Could some of the sentences in the second paragraph be combined?

Try It!

Read the following paragraph. Then write a few constructive criticisms about the *voice* and *conventions* in the writing.

> When I was about six years old, my friend Luisa and I happily spent our summer afternoons exploring the world of our neighborhood. Venturing a block or two away, we'd find an orchard in someone's backyard and help ourselves to a fresh pear. Or we'd hunt for fossils in the stone landscaping near the church parking lot down the street. One afternoon Luisa and I found a caterpillar, and brought it home to put in a jar with a branch. We let the caterpillar crawl up and down our little arms. Gradually I became aware that I wasn't feeling well, so I went home. When I reported to my mom, she lifted my shirt and looked at my back, proclaiming that I had chicken pox. For years after that, I believed there was a link between handling a caterpillar and feeling sick.

Reacting to Criticism

You don't have to incorporate all of your classmates' suggestions. The following tips will help you get the most out of response sessions.

- Trust your own judgment about your writing.
- Determine which issues are most important.
- Pay attention to comments made by more than one responder.
- Get another opinion if you are not sure about something.

Trying a New Strategy

Two strategies are provided on this page for evaluating a piece of writing.

Reacting to Writing

Peter Elbow, in *Writing Without Teachers,* offers four types of reactions peer responders might have to a piece of writing:

- **Pointing** refers to a reaction in which a group member "points out" words, phrases, or ideas that impress him or her.
- **Summarizing** is a list of main ideas or a single sentence that sums up the work. It's a reader's general reaction to the writing.
- **Telling** involves the reader describing what happens in a piece of writing: first this happens, then that happens, and so on.
- **Showing** refers to speaking metaphorically about the piece. A reader might speak of a quality as if it were a voice, color, shape, or piece of clothing ("Your writing has a neat, tailored quality").

Critiquing a Paper

Use this checklist as a guide when you assess a piece of writing-in-progress.

_____ **Purpose:** Is it clear what the writer is trying to do—entertain, inform, persuade, describe? Explain.

_____ **Audience:** Does the writing address a specific audience? Will the reader understand and appreciate the subject? Why?

_____ **Development of Ideas:** Does the writer develop the topic with enough information?

_____ **Organization:** Are the ideas arranged in the best way?

_____ **Voice:** Does the writer sound sincere and honest? Does the writer speak to his or her audience? Does the level of language fit the audience?

_____ **Conventions:** Has the writer ensured that no errors in conventions interfere with the flow of ideas?

_____ **Purpose Again:** Does the writing succeed in making the reader smile, nod, or react in some other way?

Try It!

Try one of these strategies the next time you respond to one of your peers' essays or papers. Afterward, assess the effectiveness of the strategy.

Editing

Editing is the final step before publishing anything you've written. When you edit, you check your revised writing for errors in grammar, mechanics such as punctuation and capitalization, and spelling. Your goal is to produce a clean, correct final draft—a necessity if you want the reader to take you seriously as a writer. Errors not only interrupt the reading; they also reduce the reader's confidence in your message.

Editing is most easily accomplished with the appropriate tools: a dictionary, a thesaurus, spell- and grammar-checkers, and the "Proofreader's Guide" in this book (pages **640–785**). These resources will help as you prepare your writing for publication. The information in this chapter will help you improve your editing and proofreading skills.

- **Checklist for Editing and Proofreading**
- **Editing in Action**
- **Errors to Watch For**
- **Special Editing Problems**

"When something can be read without effort, great effort has gone into its writing."

—Enrique Jardiel Poncela

"Grammar is a tricky, inconsistent thing. Being the backbone of speech and writing, it should, we think, be eminently logical, make perfect sense, like the human skeleton. But, of course, the skeleton is arbitrary, too."

—John Simon

Checklist for Editing and Proofreading

Use this checklist as a guide when you edit and proofread your revised writing. Also refer to "Errors to Watch For" on pages 124–125.

Tip
Always have a trusted friend or peer serve as a second editor. You're too close to your work to catch every error.

Conventions

MECHANICS (PUNCTUATION) (See pages 641–679.)
- _____ Do my sentences end with the proper punctuation?
- _____ Do I use commas correctly in compound sentences?
- _____ Do I use commas correctly in a series and after long introductory phrases or clauses?
- _____ Do I use apostrophes correctly?

MECHANICS (CAPITALIZATION) AND SPELLING (See pages 680–700.)
- _____ Do I start my sentences with capital letters?
- _____ Do I capitalize proper nouns?
- _____ Have I checked for spelling errors (including those the spell-checker may have missed)?

GRAMMAR (See pages 728–785.)
- _____ Do the subjects and verbs agree in my sentences?
- _____ Do my sentences use correct and consistent verb tenses?
- _____ Do my pronouns agree with their antecedents?
- _____ Have I avoided any other usage errors?

PRESENTATION
- _____ Does the title effectively lead into the writing?
- _____ Are sources of information properly presented and documented?
- _____ Does my writing meet the requirements for final presentation?

Editing in Action

Note the grammar, mechanics, and spelling corrections made in these paragraphs from a student essay. See the inside back cover of this book for an explanation of the editing symbols.

> A comma is inserted after a long introductory phrase.
>
> Apostrophe and spelling mistakes are corrected.
>
> Abbreviations are spelled out.
>
> Placement of punctuation with quotation marks is corrected.
>
> The name of the ship is marked for italics.
>
> Usage errors are corrected.

About 450 miles off the coast of Newfoundland in 12,000 feet of water, scientists discovered the remains of the great ocean liner, the R.M.S. *Titanic*. The 73-year search for the *Titanic*, which went down in what is considered the world's greatest sea disaster, was a challenging one. It concluded finally in September 1985.

When it was first launched in 1912, the British steamer was the largest ship in the world. An incredible 882 feet long and 175 feet high, the *Titanic* was proclaimed the most expensive and luxurious ship ever built. It was said to be "unsinkable." It was equipped with a double bottom, and the hull was divided into 16 separate watertight compartments.

Despite its reputation, the mighty *Titanic* did sink—on its maiden voyage. Carrying approximately 2,200 passengers and over $420,000 worth of cargo, the *Titanic* set sail from England in April 1912, bound for New York. Just a few days out of port, however, on the night of April 14, the *Titanic* collided with an iceberg in the north Atlantic Ocean, damaging steel plates along its starboard side. The great "floating palace" sank in a matter of 2 1/2 hours, taking with it all of its cargo and 1,522 of its passengers and crew.

Errors to Watch For

These two pages show 10 common errors to check for in your writing.

1. **Problem:** Missing Comma After Long Introductory Phrase
   Solution: Place a comma after a long introductory phrase.

   > Growing up in suburban Chicago**,** I longed for a dog of my own.

2. **Problem:** Confusing Pronoun Reference
   Solution: Be sure the reader knows whom or what your pronoun refers to.

   > Although Ty pointed out the error to Diego, ~~he~~ **Ty** didn't fix it.

3. **Problem:** Missing Comma in Compound Sentence
   Solution: Use a comma between two independent clauses joined by a coordinating conjunction—*and, but, or, nor, so, for,* or *yet.*

   > Maria just turned 16 years old**,** yet she is starting her senior year.

4. **Problem:** Missing Comma(s) with Nonrestrictive Phrases or Clauses
   Solution: Use commas to set off a phrase or clause that is not needed to understand the sentence. (See page **648**.)

   > I ordered a tostada**,** which is my favorite Mexican food.

5. **Problem:** Comma Splice
   Solution: When only a comma separates two independent clauses, add a conjunction, replace the comma with a semicolon, or create two sentences.

   > First water the vegetable garden**;** then cut the front lawn.

6. **Problem:** Subject-Verb Agreement Error
   Solution: Verbs must agree in number with their subjects.

   > Tomatoes from the farmers' market ~~tastes~~ **taste** the best.

Editing

7. **Problem:** Missing Comma in a Series
   Solution: Use commas to separate individual words, phrases, or clauses in a series.

   > Mr. Taneka was loaded down with balloonsˏ giftsˏ and games.

8. **Problem:** Pronoun-Antecedent Agreement Error
   Solution: A pronoun must agree in number with the word that the pronoun refers to. (See page **780**.)

   > Either Carmen or her girlfriends left ~~her~~ *their* books on the bus.

9. **Problem:** Missing Apostrophe to Show Ownership
   Solution: Use an apostrophe after a noun to show possession.

   > Our school'ˇs mascot is a bulldog.

10. **Problem:** Misusing *Its* and *It's*
    Solution: *Its* is a possessive pronoun meaning "belonging to it." *It's* is a contraction of "it is" or "it has."

    > The cute little sports car was missing one of ~~it's~~ *its* taillights.

Try It!

Find the errors in the passage below. Write the paragraph correctly on your paper.

   Felipe wants to attend a four-year college but his family can't afford it. His parents who both work for the telephone company haven't been able to maintain a college savings fund. None of Felipes cousins have attended college, either. Maybe Felipe will get one or more of the scholarships he applied for, he deserves a chance to continue his education. Its not an easy time of life for him.

Process

Special Editing Problems

The spell-checker and grammar-checker on your computer are great—but they're not foolproof. You still have to look for errors that they may not recognize. For example, a grammar-checker is not likely to catch the following kinds of errors.

Use of a Comma with "Who" Clauses

A dependent clause that begins with the relative pronoun *who* can be a nonrestrictive clause, which requires one or more commas to set it off, or it can be restrictive, requiring no commas. (See page **648**.)

My neighbor,**who retired from the workforce several years ago**,**volunteers at the local senior day-care center.** (This "who" clause is not needed to understand the point of the sentence. Commas should set off the clause.)

Joel and Marcus are juniors,**who often practice their guitars together**. (This "who" clause is needed to understand the point of the sentence. Commas should not set off the clause.)

Apostrophes to Show Possession

When two people individually own things, an apostrophe is needed with both names. For joint ownership, however, the apostrophe belongs only with the last owner listed.

Freddy suspiciously eyed ~~Pete~~ Pete's **and Jorge's snowboards**. (Since Pete and Jorge each own a snowboard, both names need apostrophes.)

We can ride in Carlo's and Carol's car. (Carlo and Carol own the car together, so only one apostrophe and *s* is needed.)

Object Pronouns

Trouble sometimes arises when a prepositional phrase contains a pronoun as part of the compound object.

Natalia wants to go to the beach with Mom and ~~I~~ me. ("I" is a subject pronoun and shouldn't be used in a prepositional phrase. The correct pronoun to use is "me," an object pronoun.)

Try It!

Write your own sample sentences that illustrate the rules explained above. Afterward, discuss your sentences with a partner and help each other correct your samples.

Publishing

According to *The American Heritage Dictionary*, the word *publish* means "to prepare and issue (printed material) for public distribution." What better destiny for your writing? This chapter offers guidelines for preparing to publish as well as suggestions on where you might submit your work.

This chapter also explains how to prepare a writing portfolio. A writing portfolio shows your teacher (and other readers of your work) your progress as a writer. It gives you yet another reason to put forth your best effort on writing assignments.

- **Preparing to Publish**
- **Places to Publish**
- **Preparing a Portfolio**
- **Parts of a Portfolio**
- **Creating Your Own Web Site**

"To write well, express yourself like the common people, but think like a wise man."

—Aristotle

> "An essential element for good writing is a good ear. One must listen to the sound of one's prose."
> —Barbara Tuchman

Preparing to Publish

Publishing is the final step in the writing process, offering your readers a chance to enjoy your writing. The following guidelines will help you prepare your writing for publishing.

Tasks to Complete

- **Work with your writing** until you feel good about it from start to finish. If any parts still need work, then it isn't ready to publish.
- **Ask for input and advice** during the writing process. Your writing should answer any questions the reader may have about your topic. Confusing parts must be made clear.
- **Save all drafts for each writing project** so you can keep track of the changes you have made and monitor the development of your ideas. If you are preparing a portfolio, you may be required to include early drafts as well as finished pieces.
- **Check for the traits of writing** to be sure that you have effectively addressed *focus and coherence, organization, development of ideas, voice,* and *conventions* in your work. (See pages 51–89.)
- **Carefully edit and proofread your work** after you have completed all of your revisions.
- **Prepare a neat final copy** to share with the reader. Use pen (blue or black ink) and one side of the paper if you are writing by hand. If you are using a computer, avoid fancy, hard-to-read fonts and odd margins.
- **Know your publishing options** since there are many ways to publish. (See page 129.)
- **Follow the requirements** indicated by the publisher. Each publisher has its own set of requirements, which must be followed exactly.

Try It!

Use these guidelines once you decide to publish a piece of writing. Be sure to ask your teacher for help if you have any questions about the publishing process.

Places to Publish

Think back to the day you started writing a particular piece. You decided what you would write about with two fundamental ideas in mind: a topic that interested you and a thesis or controlling idea about that topic. At this point, you've done a lot of work to perfect your writing. Peers and teachers probably reviewed it as you went along. Now it's time to share the finished product.

School Days

If you have written about a topic that interests or affects others in your age group, school publications provide some good publishing options.

- Your school's newspaper is a good choice for expository or persuasive writing about school-related topics.
- A student literary magazine offers publishing opportunities for a variety of writing forms, but especially for narrative writing, literary criticism, and poetry.

Your Own Backyard

The people in a community generally share some interests or background—that's what brought them together as a community in the first place. As a result, ideas that draw your attention may also appeal to your community as a whole. You may find that local publications are interested in publishing your writing.

- A local newspaper or newsletter may be interested in an insider's view of school events, or a young person's opinions on current issues.
- Depending on what you have written about, special-interest Web sites may provide a publishing opportunity. Look for clubs and organizations that have a connection to your writing topic.

Explore the Possibilities

Traditional publishers of magazines and books may also be an option to investigate. If you have a favorite national magazine, it may accept writing from outside writers on certain topics. A librarian can help you to research the possibilities. You can also look in the *Writer's Market* for more places to publish.

> **Tip**
>
> Before submitting your work to a publication, check the submission guidelines to be sure your writing is in an acceptable form and style. Include a self-addressed stamped envelope (SASE) when submitting your work to help ensure that you receive a response and that your work will be returned if that's what you want.

Preparing a Portfolio

A writing portfolio is a collection of your work that shows your skill as a writer. Your teacher will probably ask you to compile a *showcase portfolio*—a collection of your best writing for a quarter or a semester. Compiling a showcase portfolio allows you to participate in the assessment process. You decide which writing samples to include, and you reflect upon your writing progress.

Working Smart

Use the following information as a guide when you compile a showcase portfolio. There are no shortcuts when it comes to putting together an effective portfolio, so don't skip any of these suggestions.

1. Organize and keep track of your writing (including planning notes and drafts).
2. Be sure that you understand all of the requirements for your portfolio. If you have any questions, ask your teacher for help.
3. Keep your work in a safe place. Use a good-quality expandable folder for your portfolio to avoid dog-eared or ripped pages.
4. Maintain a regular writing/compiling schedule. It will be impossible to create an effective portfolio if you approach it as a last-minute project.
5. Develop a feeling of pride in your portfolio. Make sure that it reflects a positive image of yourself. Look your best! (Remember that your teacher will be reviewing your portfolio for assessment.)

Try It!

Create a chart—similar to the one below—to help you keep track of writing you may want to include in a portfolio. For each piece, put a check next to each step you complete.

	Social Studies: "Urban Sprawl"	Literature: Great Gatsby
Prewriting Notes	✓	✓
First Draft	✓	✓
Revision	✓	
Edited Copy		
Final Draft	✓	
Cover Sheet		

Parts of a Portfolio

Check with your teacher about specific requirements for your portfolio. Most showcase portfolios contain the following parts:

- **A table of contents** listing the pieces included in the portfolio
- **An opening essay or letter** detailing the story behind your portfolio (how you organized it, what it represents to you, and so on)
- **Specific finished pieces** representing your best writing (Your teacher may ask you to include all of the planning, drafting, and revising for one or more of your writing samples.)
- **A best "other" piece** related to your work in another content area
- **A cover sheet** attached to each piece of writing, discussing the reason for its selection, the work that went into it, and so on
- **Evaluation sheets or checklists** charting the basic skills you have mastered as well as the skills you still need to work on. (Your teacher will supply these sheets.)

Writing Your Opening Pages

The first two pages of a showcase portfolio are shown here.

Table of Contents

Showcase Portfolio
Jenna Bosworth

Table of Contents

Letter from Jenna Bosworth 1

Persuasive Essay:
"The U.S. Department of Peace: Why Not?"
    Cover Sheet 2
    Planning Notes 3
    Graphic Organizer 4
    First Draft 5
    First Revision 7
    Second Revision/Edit 9
    Final Draft 11

Feature Article:
"Misery in Missouri"
    Cover Sheet 13
    Peer Reviews 14
    Revision 16
    Final Draft 18

Letter to the Editor 20

Opening Letter

Dear Ms. _____,

    I first thought compiling a portfolio was just another assignment. However, as the semester progressed, I realized that I wanted to "show off" my writing. As a result, I put a lot of effort into the enclosed pieces of writing. You will be able to see that by looking at the different steps I took in writing them.

    The first piece—"The U.S. Department of Peace: Why Not?"—is a persuasive essay that I wrote for my current-events class. The essay stems from a resolution by Senator Mark Dayton, who proposed that the United States have a Department of Peace. Writing about this resolution helped me feel more connected to the affairs of government. I paid careful attention to both sides of the argument as I crafted this essay. I am pleased to include it in my portfolio.

    The second selection—"Misery in Missouri"—is a feature article I wrote in Honors Composition. It depicts a few summer days in hot, humid St. Louis and how various people cope with the heat. I enjoyed profiling the different personalities. Developing this piece certainly improved my interviewing skills.

    My third piece is a letter to the editor that I submitted to the *Bugle-Call*. I was both surprised and happy when it was published. The letter expresses my displeasure with the new rules regarding Senior Prom. I discovered my civil-but-angry voice while writing this letter. This experience gave me new confidence in my writing ability.

Sincerely,
Jenna Bosworth

Creating a Cover Sheet

When you create your showcase portfolio, you should attach a cover sheet to each writing project you include. (See the sample below written for a student's persuasive essay.) Your cover sheet should do one or more of the following things:

- Explain why you chose the piece for your portfolio.
- Tell about the process of writing you used, including problems you encountered.
- Describe the strong points and the weak points in the writing.
- Reflect on the writing's importance to you.

Sample Cover Sheet

I chose this essay because I am proud of how I expressed myself about an important issue. Our assignment was to write a persuasive essay based on any of the issues we'd been discussing in Current Events. One issue, a resolution by Senator Mark Dayton to create a federal Department of Peace and Nonviolence, really struck me as a commonsense approach to preventing conflict. The resolution, unfortunately, never went anywhere in Congress, but I decided I would write an essay in support of it.

An article from *Time* magazine provided some background information. I researched the issue further using congressional sites on the Internet and the senator's own Web site. I did some personal research, as well, getting the opinions of friends and family members. Then I organized my information using a line diagram before writing my first draft.

The strongest point in this paper is my confident voice. I'm sure it's because I felt so strongly about the topic. The weakest point is probably the flow of my ideas. I was more concerned with presenting my thoughts than with sentence fluency.

Writing this essay helped me see that persuading someone to accept my viewpoint is more than being passionate about a particular issue. Being persuasive requires a logical presentation of an argument and paying careful attention to opposing points of view.

Try It!

Write a cover sheet for a piece of writing that you would like to include in your portfolio.

Creating Your Own Web Site

Creating a Web site is one way to showcase your work. Check with your Internet service provider to find out how to get started. If you are designing your page at school, ask your teacher for help. The questions and answers below will help you get started.

Q. How do I begin planning my site?

A. Think about the number of pages you want on your site. Do you want just one page to showcase a piece of your work, or do you want multiple pages (a home page, a page of poetry, a short-story page, a page of favorite links, and so on)? Check out other students' Web pages for ideas. Then sketch out your pages. Note how the pages will be linked by marking the "hot spots" on your sketches.

Q. How do I make the pages?

A. Each page is created as a separate file. Many word-processing programs let you save a file as a Web page. Otherwise, you may have to learn HTML (hypertext markup language). This is a code that allows you to add text and graphics to a page. Your teacher may be able to help you with it. If not, you can find instructions on the Internet.

Q. How do I know if my pages work?

A. You should always test your pages. Using your browser, open your first page. Then follow the links to make sure they work correctly.

Q. How do I get my pages on the Web?

A. You must upload your finished pages to your Internet provider's computer. Ask your provider how to do this. (If you're working on your home computer, get a parent's approval. If you're using a school computer, work with your teacher.) Your provider will tell you how to access the pages later, in case you want to make changes. After you upload a page, visit your site and make sure it still works.

Try It!

Get the word out about your site. E-mail your friends and ask them to visit your site. Your service provider can offer tips on how to get your site listed on various Web search engines.

Narrative Writing

Writing Focus
Writing a Personal Narrative   **135**
Writing the College Entrance Essay   **149**

Grammar Focus
Adjective Phrases   **144**

Learning Language
Learning these words and expressions will help you understand this unit.

1. An **audience** is a group of people seeing, listening, or reading something.
   Describe a time when you have been in the audience.
2. An **experience** is something that you live through, or something that happens to you.
   Explain your experience of your first day of school.
3. A person who is uncertain and anxious is in **suspense**.
   Why do you think people like suspense in books?
4. People who **weave tales** are telling a story with characters.
   Weave a tale about your family or friends.

Narrative Writing
Writing a Personal Narrative

In his book *Writing About Your Life*, William Zinsser says, "Be surprised by the crazy wonderful events that will come dancing out of your past when you stir the pot of memory." Writing personal narratives provides an opportunity to write literary texts to express your ideas and feelings about real or imagined people, events, and ideas. This form of writing allows you to write engaging stories that have complex and non-stereotypical characters that connect you with your life in meaningful ways.

In this chapter, you will read a personal narrative in which the writer uses sensory details to describe charming his grandmother for selfish reasons. Despite his less than honorable intentions, he ends up making the right decision. Then you will learn how to write your own narrative about a time you acted appropriately, but for the wrong reason. Special attention is given to creating an engaging story and to including a range of literary devices to enhance the plot.

Writing Guidelines

Subject: Making the right decision for the wrong reason
Purpose: To share a meaningful experience
Genre/Form: Personal narrative
Audience: Classmates

"Wrong reasoning sometimes lands poor mortals in right conclusions."
—George Eliot

Personal Narrative

In the following personal narrative, Kenny writes about a time he did the right thing for the wrong reason.

Beginning
The writer describes a conflict.

Middle
Background information adds details to enhance the plot and theme.

The writer's "wrongful" reason is revealed.

A Greater Wealth

Most young kids are very self-centered most of the time. It's like their brain meters are stuck on "Selfish." In just about any situation in which they have a choice, first they wonder what's in it for them. This certainly described me, until I met my dear grandmother.

My father had been born in Japan, and he had many old, old photographs of the palatial estate that had belonged to his family through many generations. He told me stories of gorgeous homes full of lacquered furniture, silk wall panels, and polished cedar platforms. He also described magnificent gardens, full of the sweet scents of exotic flowers and the gentle trickle of graceful fountains.

From all this, I figured my grandmother must be rich. I had never met her before she came from Japan, but at eight, I reasoned that if I were nice to her, she would take me back to Japan to live in luxury. It was a good plan, I thought, and I vowed to spend time with my grandmother so she would grow to love me and want me to accompany her upon her return.

"There she is!" my father called. I expected to see some regal kimono-clad creature riding in a satin litter like I'd seen in pictures. Instead, I saw a tiny woman with silver hair, wearing a modern blue suit. She did not look wealthy to me. Still, I vowed to be attentive, to make myself indispensable to her during her stay.

To get closer to her, I flattered her into telling me stories about old Japan. She enjoyed making temari, fabric balls wound tightly with delicate designs, and as she worked, she wove tales of Japanese legends and history as intricate and beautiful as the designs she created. I listened, fascinated. Her words were a mix of the two languages, so I didn't completely understand everything at first. Interestingly, as her English improved, so did my understanding of Japanese.

Dialogue builds suspense.

No one spoke of her going back, and I was anxious to commence my life of Japanese luxury, so one evening I worked up my courage to ask.

"Obaasan?" I began timidly. She looked up from her embroidery, her amber eyes peeking lovingly over her half-glasses.

"Yes, Kenny-chan?" She always added the traditional endearment to my name.

"When you go back to Japan, will you take me?"

She seemed surprised by the question, and she stopped her winding and rested her hands on her lap.

The narrative builds to a moment of discovery.

"Kenny-Chan, I am no going back. I live here now. But why you want to leave? Here is so wonderful."

"But aren't you rich in Japan? Don't you have beautiful things there?"

"Why you think that?" she asked, surprised.

I told her about my father's stories.

"Yes," she smiled. "I told those stories to your father when he little. My father told them me. Once they all true, and my family had great wealth. But then war came, and it all disappeared. Your sohu—your grandfather—and I worked very hard make good life. Not rich life, but good life. Now he gone, and I wish to remain here with family."

Resolution
The writer reveals his new understanding.

My dreams of a luxurious life had been dashed. At first I was disappointed. Then I remembered that she was staying with us, and my sadness disappeared. I had tried to make her love me so that I could join her in Japan. I quickly understood that I didn't need the wealth of Japan. My grandmother had given me great riches right here at home.

 Respond to the reading. Answer the following questions about the sample narrative.

Focus and Coherence (1) How does the introduction help to focus the narrative? (2) Does the conclusion reinforce the main idea? How?

Organization (3) Where is time order used in the narrative?

Voice (4) What does the dialogue reveal about the writer's unique perspective?

Prewriting Selecting a Topic

To get started, Kenny listed a few times when he did the right thing, but not for the right reason. He then put an asterisk next to the one time he would write about.

Topics List

- gaining my grandmother's attention so she would take me to Japan*
- mowing Mrs. Havel's lawn so I could use her swimming pool
- practicing the guitar to become famous
- befriending a certain classmate to help me in calculus

Select a topic. List at least three personal experiences in which you did the right thing, but not for the right reason. Put an asterisk next to the one experience that you would like to write about.

Gathering Details

Kenny then completed a Q-and-A chart to gather his initial thoughts.

Q-and-A Chart

Questions	Answers
What did I want?	I wanted to have my grandmother take me to Japan.
Why did I want this?	I wanted to live in luxury.
What did I do?	I was especially nice to her.
What was the result?	I really grew to love her.
What did I learn?	I learned that real wealth comes from love.

Learn about your experience. Complete a Q-and-A chart about your experience.

Focus on the Texas Traits

Focus and Coherence The narrative genre is appropriate when you want to express your ideas about real or imagined people, events, and ideas. Try to work in sensory details that build suspense and lead up to a turning point—a moment of realization.

Considering the Story Line

Since a personal narrative is essentially a true story, it should contain the basic elements that create an engaging story or plot line, including a conflict to get things started, complications, a moment of truth, and so on. Here's how Kenny's narrative develops according to the base elements of a story or plot. (Also see page **344**.)

Determining the Conflict

Kenny believes he would live a life of luxury in Japan, so he needs to convince his grandmother to take him back with her.

Working in Complications

Kenny learns a great deal about life in Japan from his father and his grandmother. No one talks about the grandmother going back, yet Kenny is anxious to start his new life. A conversation between Kenny and his grandmother builds to the moment of truth.

Identifying the Climax or Moment of Truth

Kenny discovers that his grandmother isn't rich and that she isn't returning to Japan.

Bringing the Story to a Close

In the resolution, Kenny discovers that living without luxury will be okay, and interacting with his grandmother is its own reward—one that is much more valuable than material wealth.

Develop your story line. Identify the main parts for your narrative: conflict, complications, climax, and resolution. (During the actual writing, change or add to any part as needed.)

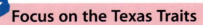

Focus on the Texas Traits

Organization It is important to organize your narrative so that it makes sense to your audience. One way to organize information is in chronological order. This means writing events in the sequence in which they occurred and using words such as *before, at first, now,* and *once* to help the reader understand the sequence of events. See if you can find at least one example of chronological order in the sample narrative.

"Your opening has to be good—or the rest of the story won't have a chance because nobody'll stick around to read it."
—Lawrence Block

Drafting Creating a Beginning, a Middle, and an Ending

A personal narrative expresses and reflects upon a pivotal moment in the writer's life. All narratives have a beginning, a middle, and an ending.

The Beginning **Draw the reader in.** The beginning must hook the reader and introduce the situation. You can engage the reader in several ways:

- Start with an interesting statement about a conflict.
- Begin with dialogue to pull the reader into the action.
- Make a statement that piques the reader's curiosity.
- Share information that sets the scene.

Kenny selected the fourth technique. In his introduction, he discusses a common childhood condition—self-centeredness—that every reader can identify with.

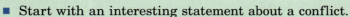

The Middle **Build suspense through action, dialogue, and sensory details.** The middle uses literary devices to enhance the plot and support the main idea of your narrative. In the sample narrative, Kenny works to make his grandmother love him; and at the moment of truth, he discovers that his grandmother is not returning to Japan.

The Ending **Explain what you learned from the situation.** Wrap up your story in a resolution and explain what you have learned. Remember that the purpose of your narrative is to explore a time when you made the right decision for the wrong reason. In his resolution, Kenny explains that great wealth is not limited to money and luxury.

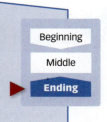

Develop your first draft. Catch your reader's interest, build suspense through actions and sensory details, and reveal the lesson you learned.

Revising Including Background Information

In a personal narrative, be sure that your audience has enough background information to understand the history of complex characters and the significance of your experiences. This is sometimes called the *backstory,* events that occurred before the experience begins.

Kenny's second paragraph helps the reader appreciate how Kenny developed expectations about his grandmother. We understand why he gets the wrong ideas about his grandmother—why he is surprised when he meets her that she wears a "modern blue suit" and not an elegant kimono.

Sample "Backstory"

> My father had been born in Japan, and he had many old, old photographs of the palatial estate that had belonged to his family through many generations. He told me stories of gorgeous homes full of lacquered furniture, silk wall panels, and polished cedar platforms. He also described magnificent gardens, full of the sweet scents of exotic flowers and the gentle trickle of graceful fountains.

Check for background information. As you review your first draft, determine if you have included, or need, background information. Remember that specific details can bring complex characters to life.

Using Dialogue in a Narrative

Including dialogue is a literary strategy that can do several things to bring your narrative alive. It helps develop the personalities of the characters. It also can further the action and build suspense. Finally, it can serve as a transitional device to move from one part of the experience to the next.

Sample Dialogue

> "When you go back to Japan, will you take me?"
> She seemed surprised by the question, and she stopped her winding and rested her hands on her lap.
> "Kenny-Chan, I am no going back. I live here now. But why you want to leave? Here is so wonderful."
> "But aren't you rich in Japan? Don't you have beautiful things there?"
> "Why you think that?" she asked, surprised.

Revising Adjusting for Tone and Mood

Your narrative might include the basic "facts" of your experience, but tone and mood can make your reader share your feelings about the events.

Tone

Tone, a writer's attitude toward a subject and an audience, is shaped through word choice and sensory details. Notice how the words *regal kimono-clad creature, vowed, attentive,* and *indispensable* create a humorous tone.

> I expected to see some regal kimono-clad creature riding in a satin litter like I'd seen in pictures. Instead, I saw a tiny woman with silver hair, wearing a modern blue suit. She did not look wealthy to me. Still, I vowed to be attentive, to make myself indispensable to her during her stay.

Mood

Mood is the atmosphere a writer creates. Notice how the details in the following passage create a warm atmosphere:

> To get closer to her, I flattered her into telling me stories about old Japan. She enjoyed making temari, fabric balls wound tightly with delicate designs, and as she worked, she wove tales of Japanese legends and history as intricate and beautiful as the designs she created. I listened, fascinated. Her words were a mix of the two languages, so I didn't completely understand everything at first. Interestingly, as her English improved, so did my understanding of Japanese.

Check for Mood and Tone To achieve consistency of tone, try rearranging words, sentences, and paragraphs and use transitions. To enhance the mood, consider adding more sensory details.

Assessing Your Ending

Your closing paragraph should reflect on the experience or discovery.

Sample Reflective Closing

> My dreams of a luxurious life had been dashed. At first I was disappointed. Then I remembered that she was staying with us, and my sadness disappeared. I had tried to make her love me so that I could join her in Japan. I quickly understood that I didn't need the wealth of Japan. My grandmother had given me great riches right here at home.

Check your ending. Be sure that you have reflected on your experience in the closing paragraph.

Revising Improving Your Writing

Use a checklist. On your own paper, write the numbers 1 to 16. Put a check next to the number if you can answer "yes" to that question. If not, go back and revise that part of your personal narrative.

<u>Revising Checklist</u>

Focus and Coherence

_____ 1. Is the narrative focused on one main experience?
_____ 2. Do I include details that support the focus?
_____ 3. Do I include sensory details that define tone and mood?
_____ 4. Is the tone consistent throughout the narrative?
_____ 5. Do I include a meaningful introduction and conclusion?
_____ 6. Are the ideas clearly related to each other?

Organization

_____ 7. Do I include an interesting opening that draws in the reader?
_____ 8. Does the narrative build to a climax?
_____ 9. Does my ending reflect on the experience?
_____ 10. Do I include meaningful transitions?

Development of Ideas

_____ 11. Do I identify the reasons for my actions?
_____ 12. Do I include essential background information?
_____ 13. Do I include specific details and dialogue?
_____ 14. Are the ideas thoroughly developed?

Voice

_____ 15. Does my dialogue sound realistic?
_____ 16. Do the tone and mood help readers share my experiences?

Make a clean copy. After you've finished your revisions, make a fresh copy of your writing to edit.

Editing for Conventions

When you edit for conventions, you check grammar, mechanics (punctuation, capitalization), spelling, and sentence structure. Use the following activity to improve your use of adjective phrases.

Adjective phrases

An adjective modifies a noun or pronoun. An adjective phrase does the same thing.

The history *of Europe* **can be fascinating.** [adjective phrase *of Europe* modifies *history*]

The students *with preparation* **did well on the exam.** [adjective phrase *with preparation* modifies *students*]

An adjective phrase usually follows the noun or pronoun it modifies. It tells *"what kind," "which one," "how much,"* and *"how many."*

My sister locked her keys in the trunk *of her car.* [modifies the noun *trunk*, tells "which one."]

He is *extremely generous.* [modifies the pronoun *He*; tells "how much."]

One kind of adjective phrase is a prepositional phrase. Prepositional phrases show relationships and begin with prepositions such as *on, in, with, from, of, under, above, before,* and so on.

The cat *on my lap* **got tired and jumped down.**

Not all adjective phrases are prepositional phrases.

The *very loud* **clock kept me awake all night.**

Exercise

Identify the adjectives and adjective phrases in the following sentences. Some sentences have more than one adjective phrase.
1. He told me stories of gorgeous homes full of lacquered furniture.
2. He also described large gardens, full of the sweet scents of exotic flowers.
3. I expected to see some regal kimono-clad creature riding in a satin litter like I'd seen in pictures.

Edit for adjective phrases. As you revise your narrative, ask yourself if you have used adjective phrases effectively. Add adjective phrases to add more variety to your writing.

Writing a Personal Narrative

Editing Checking Your Writing

Use a checklist. On your own paper, write the numbers 1 to 13. For each of the questions below, put a check by the number if you can answer "yes" to that question. If not, go back and edit your narrative for that convention.

Editing Checklist

Conventions

GRAMMAR
_____ 1. Do I use correct forms of verbs?
_____ 2. Do my pronouns agree with their antecedents?
_____ 3. Do my verbs agree with their subjects?

SENTENCE STRUCTURE
_____ 4. Do I use a variety of correctly structured sentences that clearly communicate my ideas?

MECHANICS (CAPITALIZATION AND PUNCTUATION)
_____ 5. Do I begin all my sentences with capital letters?
_____ 6. Do I capitalize all proper nouns?
_____ 7. Do I use punctuation after all my sentences?
_____ 8. Do I use commas after long introductory word groups?
_____ 9. Do I use commas correctly in compound and complex sentences?
_____ 10. Do I punctuate dialogue correctly?
_____ 11. Do I use apostrophes correctly?

SPELLING
_____ 12. Have I spelled all my words correctly?
_____ 13. Have I double-checked the words my spell-checker may have missed?

Publishing Sharing Your Writing

There are several ways to publish your personal narrative.

- Read your story out loud to the class.
- Submit the story to your school's creative writing magazine.
- Send your story to a student-writing magazine.

Evaluating a Personal Narrative

To learn how to evaluate a narrative essay, you will use the holistic scoring guide on pages 36–37 and the essay that follows. This highly effective essay fits a score of 4.

Writing that fits a score of 4 is highly effective.

Girls' Night Out

"I'll pick you up at 6:30!" Roberto's voice on the phone was excited.

"Great! I can't wait!" I said and hung up.

I lied. It wasn't great at all. I wanted to go to a new chick flick with the girls, not sit alone in uncomfortable bleachers watching bulky guys getting their faces smashed into a wrestling mat. Even so, Roberto had sounded pleased when I impulsively offered to go to the match. I sighed and called my friend Carly.

"What do you mean, you can't go?" Carly nearly shrieked, and I held the phone away from my ear. "What about me and Isabel and Kate? Friday night is always Girls' Night Out!" I explained that I felt I had to support Roberto during his tournament.

"Well, that's noble of you," she said, somewhat sarcastically. "But really, Jan, you must become your own person. We're going to miss you tonight."

"I'm sorry. I promise that I'll make it next week," I said.

"Yeah, unless Mr. Wonderful wants to drag you to a fly-fishing festival or something!"

I hung up, mentally kicking myself. Carly was right. I was putting my boyfriend before my friends. It had been a rough week, and I had really been looking forward to our weekly evening of girly giggles. There was nothing appealing about spending the evening in a gym that reeked of sweat! But there was no way I could cancel my date with Roberto—not this late in the game.

At the gym, Roberto disappeared into the locker room, and I picked my way up through the crowded bleachers to get a good spot. I settled onto a hard wooden seat. I was glad I had brought

The writer uses realistic dialogue to set the scene.

Sensory details help define the tone.

The writer's "wrongful" reason is revealed.

The writer's ambivalence is developed more thoroughly.

Details support the focus and define the mood.

along a novel to read between matches, because I didn't know any of my neighbors and I knew it was going to be a long night.

I cheered when Roberto won his match with a late takedown, even though I winced at the painful-looking contortions he had to go through to do it. All of his teammates had their turn. After what seemed like forever, the match ended. I sighed with relief as I stood up from the hard bleachers and stretched.

> A meaningful transition here could help build suspense.

The team had done pretty well, coming in second, and the coach announced a pizza party at his house. Spending the rest of the evening with Roberto's teammates was not what I had in mind when I canceled the date with my friends. I must have looked pretty unhappy, and Roberto pulled me aside.

"You don't have to go, Jan," he said. "It's just the guys, and I know it won't be much fun for you."

"You mean you'd go without me? Roberto, I gave up Girls' Night Out for you!" He seemed genuinely surprised.

"Jan, you didn't have to do that!"

"I wanted to show you how much I support you, how much I care about what you do." I blinked hard to stop the stinging in my eyes.

> Realistic dialogue supports the focus.

"Look, I know that sometimes my 'stuff' is boring for you, and that's okay. We don't have to do everything together. Imagine me tagging along on your Girls' Night Out! Sometimes you need your friends, just like I need mine."

He was right. We like each other for who we are, not for who we might try to be. I felt even closer to Roberto after what he said. I realized that he had a very mature attitude about our relationship, and I decided then and there to follow his example.

> The writer reveals her new understanding.

After Roberto dropped me off, I called and left a message for Carly on her cell phone.

"I hope you guys had a great time tonight," I said. "I don't think wrestling is for me. I can't wait to see you next week!"

Reflecting on Your Writing

You've worked hard to write a personal narrative that your classmates will enjoy. Now take some time to think about your writing. Finish each of the sentence starters below on your own paper. Thinking about your writing will help you see how you are growing as a writer.

My Narrative

1. The strongest part of my personal narrative is . . .

2. The part that still needs work is . . .

3. The main thing I learned about writing a personal narrative is . . .

4. In my next personal narrative, I would like to . . .

5. One question I still have about writing personal narratives is . . .

Writing the College Entrance Essay

For some college applications, you will be asked to write a personal essay in response to a given prompt. Your goal in this essay is to address the prompt specifically, while at the same time telling something about yourself—how you think and why you are drawn to the particular school or program. One option is to tell a story that includes a clear theme and uses a tone that illustrates your thoughts and experiences.

Before you begin your essay, be sure that you understand what you are being asked to write about and why. Remember that the reader is trying to gain a better understanding of you, the student and the person, so be sure to present your ideas honestly and sincerely.

This chapter includes a sample entrance essay, writing guidelines, and a list of typical writing prompts you might see on applications. Also refer to online sources that provide additional tips for writing entrance essays.

Writing Guidelines

Subject: **Application prompt**
Purpose: **To reveal something about you as a student and as a person**
Form: **Personal essay**
Audience: **School admissions officer**

"Be honest with yourself and your readers. Don't try to write only what you think readers want to hear."

—Verne Meyer

College Entrance Essay

As part of his college application, David Lopez was asked to write a personal essay in response to this prompt: "In 500 words or fewer, explain something about yourself and what you would contribute to this college."

In his response, David uses an anecdote from his own experience to introduce his goal. He then provides details on how his goal might be fulfilled in a particular program at the college. Margin notes point out important features in his essay.

Beginning The writer uses a personal experience with dialogue to get the reader's attention.

Middle The writer explores the point of the experience and establishes a theme.

Introductory phrases link the paragraphs.

A New World of Cinema

As one of my duties as a student council member, I helped new students learn about our school. Earlier this year, I was doing this by introducing Anastasia Korkoff (a foreign-exchange student from Moscow) to other students. As we talked, a picture of a woman taped on the inside of a locker door caught Anastasia's eye. "Rachel McAdams!" she said. "I loved *The Notebook!*"

"You saw that?" I replied. I was shocked. "Where?" I asked.

"In a theater in Moscow," she replied, "but I could have seen it on my computer. I watch all kinds of movies, not just American, but French, Indian, German, and Russian, too."

That conversation stuck in my mind for days. This girl from Russia had been affected by an American movie that was not a blockbuster, and knew the name of the actress—not even a major celebrity.

I've come to realize that film can be a major source of shared experience—not just with my friends or with others in this country, but also with people throughout the world. While I had always enjoyed movies as a form of entertainment, I had never realized before how broadly they shape culture—from Miami to Moscow.

A few weeks later, I explained these ideas to Ms. Crane, my English teacher. She listened, smiled, and suggested that I read the essay "Cinema Is the New Cathedral." As I read the piece, suddenly everything clicked. The writer argued that movies have replaced many other forms of communal experience, and even serve a religious-like function. At that point, I knew that

Writing the College Entrance Essay   151

Personal observations establish an inquisitive, motivated tone.	understanding film was critical to understanding culture—both culture in this country and in others. Since then, understanding film and filmmaking has been my goal. From that point, I realized that my future would be in filmmaking. I began to dream of studying international film and the relationship between a film and its national culture. Also, because films have such a broad international audience, I began making plans to study how Hollywood movies affect cultures outside the United States.
The writer offers details that explain his educational goal.	
Personal details reinforce motivated tone.	While I'm not sure yet exactly where my passion for film might lead, I am sure that the trip will be interesting and worth the effort. For example, my mom suggests that I combine film study with communication and think about a career in journalism. My counselor says that the film-study program could be a springboard into the filmmaking industry. But Ms. Crane suggests that I study film and culture—and then teach the subject either in high school or in college. Wherever the film-study path leads, I'd like to start the journey at Burnley College.
Ending In closing, the writer links the college with the career path he has chosen.	

 Respond to the reading. Answer the following questions about the sample college entrance essay.

Organization (1) In which paragraph does the author explain his goal? (2) What purpose is served by the paragraphs before that?

Development of Ideas (3) What field of study does the writer want to pursue? (4) Why does he find this field of study appealing?

Voice (5) How would you describe the author's voice in this essay—enthusiastic, sincere, negative, confident? Explain. (6) What words or phrases in the essay help develop the desired tone? Name two or three.

# TEKS 12.13A, 12.14A

Prewriting Focusing Your Efforts

The first step in writing your college application essay is to establish a clear focus for your work. To begin, consider the following questions:

- **What is the genre?** How can you use it to convey your ideas?
- **What does the prompt ask for?** Try restating it in your own words.
- **Who is your audience?** In most cases, the goal of a college application essay is to help admissions officials get to know you.
- **How does the prompt relate to the college or program?** Admission decisions are partly based upon how well an applicant's abilities and interests match those of the institution.
- **What specific instructions are given in the prompt?** Note specifically what the prompt asks you to do (*analyze*, *explain*, *describe*, *evaluate*, and so on) and how long your response should be.

Sample Controlling Ideas

- After studying computer graphics at Norrid College (the program), I hope to expand what can be achieved in Internet films (personal goal).

- I believe that Waterworth University (the college) can help me to become the sort of leader who inspires others to greatness (personal goal).

Gathering Details

Experts agree that these strategies will help you prepare a strong essay.

1. **List your strengths and weaknesses with the prompt clearly in mind.** Be honest with yourself in this evaluation.
2. **Select a positive quality related to your goal.** An upbeat essay that focuses on hopeful results has the best chance of catching the attention of admissions officers.
3. **Choose a personal story to illustrate that quality and goal.** Think of experiences that describe you as a person and a student. Then choose one (or more) experiences to include. Use dialogue or develop characters or conflict to help your essay come alive.

Prewrite

Develop a controlling idea and gather details. Choose a prompt from page 155 or use an actual prompt from a college. Analyze the prompt, develop a controlling idea, and gather details to support your focus.

Writing the College Entrance Essay

Drafting Creating Your First Draft

Admissions personnel face a staggering number of application essays each year. For yours to get the attention it deserves, it must be compelling, honest, and personal. As you write your first draft, be sure each section does its job well.

Beginning Paragraph

The beginning paragraph should catch the reader's interest and smoothly lead up to your controlling idea. Here are different ways to begin your essay.

- **Open with a personal anecdote.** This is the approach that we recommend. Be sure that the anecdote reveals something positive about you and relates to the prompt. You can use dialogue or describe a compelling character or conflict to bring the anecdote to life.
- **Start with a revealing quotation.** Select a quotation that truly reflects your thoughts and feelings about your goal and the school in question. It can help establish your theme.
- **Begin with an eye-catching fact or statistic.** Of course, this statement should effectively introduce the rest of your essay.

Middle Paragraphs

As you develop the main part of your essay, use an honest, sincere voice with a consistent tone. Also keep these tips in mind.

- **Develop your controlling idea.** Each paragraph in your essay should advance or develop the main point of your response.
- **Include specific details.** Instead of stating *I grew up in the country near a medium-sized city,* write *I grew up on a huge dairy farm near Muncie, Indiana, a medium-sized city northeast of Indianapolis.*
- **Use transitional words and phrases.** To ensure that your essay flows smoothly, link paragraphs with connecting words or phrases such as "From events like this" and "A few weeks later."

Ending Paragraph

The ending part should bring the reader to a satisfying sense of resolution and leave him or her with a favorable impression of you. Here are two ways to conclude your essay.

- **Revisit your controlling idea.** Bring your reader back to the main point of your essay.
- **End positively.** State politely but confidently that you look forward to attending the college in question.

Draft your college entrance essay. Write freely without worrying about length just yet. Get your ideas on paper. You will have time to revise later.

Revising Improving Your First Draft

Once the first draft of your application essay is complete, review and revise it to achieve specific rhetorical purposes using the following questions as a guide:

- **Organization** Does your essay grab the reader's attention from the beginning? Does the middle of your essay develop your controlling idea? Does the ending revisit the controlling idea and end on a positive note? Do you use transitions to lead the reader from paragraph to paragraph? Do your sentences flow and have a consistent tone?
- **Development of Ideas** Is your controlling idea clear, logically developed, and well supported? Are your sentences and paragraphs arranged to use tropes, such as metaphors or analogies, to advance your controlling idea? Is the connection clear between your goal and the school or program? Is your theme clear?
- **Voice** Does your essay sound personal, sincere, and positive? Does it give the reader a sense of your personality? Does the dialogue, if you've used it, sound realistic? Have you added details which establish your intended mood or tone?

FYI

The Most Important Rule

The most important rule for a college application essay is this: **Be yourself.** Admissions readers must judge whether your goals, experiences, and abilities match well with their school. So don't try to impress them with words borrowed from a thesaurus. Instead, **focus on yourself and your goals.**

Revise your essay. Use the questions above to guide your revision. Also ask a trusted classmate to read your essay and give feedback to help you revise.

Editing Checking for Conventions

With an application essay, first impressions are critical. As a result, careful attention to grammar, mechanics, and spelling is also critical. Take time to check your essay for errors and ask a trusted friend, teacher, or parent to check it as well. Then prepare a clean final copy to submit with your application.

Edit your work. Carefully check your grammar, mechanics, and spelling.

Example Prompts

The following types of writing prompts are typically found on college applications. Most college application prompts also include the words "in one page or less" or a similar instruction about the length of your response.

Open-Ended Prompts

Prompts such as these leave a lot of leeway for possible answers. This means you will have to work extra hard to shape a focused response.

- Please include a personal statement with your application.
- Why is our college a good choice for you?
- Tell us your goals after college. How might our program contribute to those goals?

Influences in Your Life

Prompts like these ask you to write about people, places, and things that are important to you. Remember to relate their influence to your goals and to how the school can help you meet those goals.

- Describe a creative work in literature, art, music, or science that has affected you, and explain the effect.
- Identify a person who has had a significant influence on your life, and describe that influence.

General Subject Prompts

These types of general subject prompts ask you to reflect on your thoughts, feelings, and beliefs.

- What is the value of community service in our society? Tell us how it relates to your life and plans.
- Do you believe there is a "generation gap"? Describe the differences between your generation and others.
- Think of a time when you have taken a risk: What was the effect (whether positive or negative) on your life?

Try It!

Choose one of the prompts above and write a one-page application essay in response. Carefully follow the steps outlined in this chapter. When you are finished, ask a friend, teacher, or parent for feedback. Then try again, using a different prompt.

ELPS 2C, 4C, 5B

Expository Writing

Writing Focus
Writing an Analysis of Opposing Ideas   **157**
Writing a Problem Analysis   **199**
Responding to Expository Prompts   **209**

Grammar Focus
Pronoun Case   **186**
Parallel Series   **187**

Learning Language
Work with a partner to learn the following words and expressions from this unit.

1. A **controversy** involves differing opinions on an issue.
   Tell about a controversy in your school or community.
2. When something is **relevant** to a topic, it clearly connects.
   What details would be relevant to a discussion about your homework?
3. **Logic** is a system of reasoning.
   Describe your logic in making an important decision.
4. To **grab people's attention** means to capture their interest.
   How would you grab the attention of a large audience?

Expository Writing
Writing an Analysis of Opposing Ideas

The world of politics is filled with strong opinions and vigorous debates. Much writing about politics presents ideas persuasively: The writer chooses one side of a political argument and uses facts and ideas to defend it. But in a world full of strong opinions and opposing ideas, it's often helpful to know both sides of an argument.

An analysis of opposing ideas thoroughly examines a controversial situation by presenting both sides of an argument without favoring either. To present both sides fairly, you'll need to research valid, reliable, and relevant primary and secondary sources and provide information on the strengths and weaknesses of each position.

In this chapter, you'll learn the steps necessary to write a thoroughly researched, well-organized, and objective analysis of opposing ideas. Your analysis should be suitable for publication in a local or school newspaper.

Writing Guidelines

- **Subject:** A controversy with two sides
- **Purpose:** To examine both positions fairly
- **Form:** Analysis of opposing ideas
- **Audience:** Readers of local or school newspapers

"A lot of good arguments are spoiled by some fool who knows what he is talking about."
—Miguel de Unamuno

 TEKS 12.13A, 12.15A(vii)

Expository Writing Warm-Up Mapping a Controversy

Your analytical essay should include an analysis of views and information that contradict the opposing ideas presented in the thesis statement. A controversy map can help you select an appropriate controversy for a topic and identify both sides of the issue. Kyreesha created the following map to understand a book-banning controversy at her high school.

Controversy Map

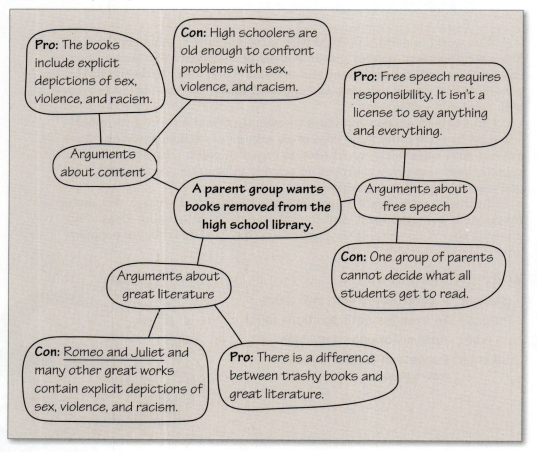

Try It!

Think of a controversy that you can be objective about. Create a map or cluster, writing the controversy in the center and creating branches for different arguments. Write down both sides of the argument and try to be fair to each position.

TEKS 12.13A, 12.15A(i), 12.15A(iii–vi)

Writing an Analysis of Opposing Ideas

Writing an Expository Paragraph

Kyreesha used her controversy map (page 158) to write the following introductory paragraph for an analytical essay. Her paragraph has three parts.

- The **topic sentence** introduces the controversy and grabs the reader's attention.
- The **body sentences** use a variety of well-chosen details to present information on relevant perspectives.
- The **closing sentence** states the thesis, or controlling idea.

A Battle over Books

Topic Sentence: Do parents have the right to call for book banning at a public high school?

Body Sentences: Examples of books that parents at Wilson High want banned include Kurt Vonnegut's *Slaughterhouse Five* and Toni Morrison's *Beloved,* deemed to have explicit depictions of sex, violence, and racism. Other parents disagree, citing explicit material in more than 100 classics—including *Romeo and Juliet* and *The Scarlet Letter.* These opponents of the ban argue that high schoolers are old enough to wrestle with such issues, and that their rights to free speech cannot be denied by one group of parents. The parents for the ban draw a distinction, however, between great literature and books they consider "trash." They also indicate that free speech requires responsibility.

Closing Sentence: In a battle over books with the Wilson High School Board, parents voiced their arguments about why they believed certain books were either offensive or essential.

Write your own introductory paragraph. Write about the controversy you chose. Create a topic sentence that grabs the reader's attention, include information on relevant perspectives in the body, and write a closing sentence that clearly states the thesis.

"You don't notice the referee during the game unless he makes a bad call."
—Drew Curtis

TEKS 12.13A, 12.15A(i), 12.15A(iii–vi)
ELPS 4K, 5D, 5E, 5F

Understanding Your Goal

Your goal in this chapter is to write a well-organized analysis of opposing ideas that fairly examines both sides of an argument. The traits listed in the chart below will help you plan and write your analysis of opposing ideas.

Traits of an Analysis of Opposing Ideas

- **Focus and Coherence**
  Choose an appropriate topic that will fit the genre and interest the audience. Write a clear thesis statement, and make sure all details relate clearly to your thesis or controlling idea.

- **Organization**
  Start with an introduction that captures your reader's attention and states your thesis. Use middle paragraphs to fairly present both sides of the argument. End with a conclusion that puts the debate in perspective.

- **Development of Ideas**
  Develop your analysis with well-chosen details that support your ideas. Include information on all relevant perspectives.

- **Voice**
  Use an informative, engaging voice that shows respect for both sides of the argument. Choose words that have the right denotation (meaning) and appropriate connotation (feeling).

- **Conventions**
  Avoid errors in grammar, mechanics, and spelling. Include a variety of sentence structures to help readers focus on your message.

Get the big picture. Look at the scoring guide on pages 36–37. You can use this guide to assess your progress as you write. Your goal is to write an analysis of opposing ideas that fairly explains both sides of a controversy.

Literature Connection You can find an expository analysis in daily newspapers or general news interest magazines such as *Time* and *Newsweek*. Read critically to determine if the author represents both sides objectively.

Analysis of Opposing Ideas

An analysis of opposing ideas fairly presents both sides of an argument. It uses facts, statistics, examples, and quotations to support each side. In this article, a student writer presents both sides of the argument about "third parties."

Introduction
An effective introductory paragraph identifies the topic and presents the thesis statement (underlined).

Middle
The relevant perspectives of proponents are presented first. Citations demonstrate consideration of primary and secondary sources.

Middle
Rhetorical devices, such as the simile comparing politicians to puppets, help convey meaning.

Are Third Parties Viable in U.S. Politics?

Since the Republican Party gained major party status in the 1850s, candidates from the Democratic or Republican parties have won the vast majority of United States elections ("Political"). Yet candidates from much smaller "third parties" have participated in many elections, and have even won local and state contests. Often, third-party platforms differ widely from the platforms of the two major parties. Perhaps for this reason, third parties have played a controversial role in U.S. politics. While proponents of third parties laud them for the new ideas they bring to the political arena, critics consider third parties an insignificant or damaging influence on U.S. politics.

Those who support third parties insist that the two-party system is one of the main reasons that new ideas are never tried. In an effort to win a majority vote, proponents say, the Democratic and Republican parties have often adopted watered-down platforms that attract the necessary number of voters but fail to solve society's problems. As long as Democrats and Republicans enjoy an unshakable hold on power, this situation will continue. The official homepages of third parties such as the Green Party, however, reveal bold solutions to society's problems (Green Party). According to political analyst Raul Lopez, their participation in the electoral system is invaluable ("Fresh Look").

Proponents also argue that the two major parties have created a system of money politics in which politicians are like puppets carrying out the will of their masters—big corporations and other wealthy donors. Since third parties are generally more dependent on grassroots support, they are more likely to be responsive to the concerns of the voters. Third-party supporters also cite the success of third-party candidates in state, local, and even national elections as evidence that a significant number of U.S. voters want fresh ideas and grassroots activism.

Middle
Relevant opposing perspectives are presented next.

A transition between paragraphs indicates an additional opposing view.

Conclusion
Effective concluding paragraphs identify points of agreement between the two sides and raise questions about the future of the debate.

    Those who oppose third parties insist that the participation of such parties more often results in skewed election results than in any kind of meaningful reform. Often, they cite the "spoiler" role of third-party candidates ("Spoiler"). For example, if a third-party candidate mainly draws votes from one of the major-party candidates, the election might sway in favor of the other. This is a particular concern in close elections when people ask, "Who would win if the third-party candidates did not appear on the ballot?"

    In addition to the "spoiler" argument, those who oppose third-party candidacies insist that when people abandon major parties for third parties, they only reinforce the major parties' fear of new ideas. Without new ideas, these partisans argue, the major parties will remain stagnant, and the problem of an unresponsive, money-driven political system will remain (Greenbald 84).

    Although both sides disagree on the effectiveness of third parties, they tend to agree that the U.S. political system needs an influx of new ideas. Chronic problems such as health care, the national debt, poverty, and homelessness have resisted solution, despite a range of attempts by the major parties. People on both sides of the third-party debate hope that new ideas capable of solving these problems will be brought to the forefront of our political process.

    As major-party politics and pressing social problems remain a focus in U.S. politics, it's likely that third parties will also remain a part of the political system. Whether they will be able to effect meaningful change remains to be seen. Much of their effectiveness—or lack of effectiveness—results from the ability of those on either side of the debate to convince voters to either support or abandon third parties.

Respond to the reading. Answer the following questions.

Organization (1) What is the writer's organizational structure or schema?

Development of Ideas (2) What are the different perspectives of the debate? (3) How does the writer demonstrate consideration of primary and secondary sources to support the analysis?

Voice (4) How does the writer use rhetorical devices and other techniques to engage the reader and express an original voice?

 12.13A, 12.13B, 12.15A(iii), 12.15A(iv), 12.15A(vi), 12.15A(vii)

Writing an Analysis of Opposing Ideas

Prewriting

In the prewriting stage, you'll identify a controversial issue, explore both sides of the argument, and create a clear organizational scheme for your essay.

Keys to Effective Prewriting

1. Choose a political controversy in which two major positions are in opposition.

2. Gather relevant, valid, and reliable evidence from primary and secondary sources that clearly presents and supports both sides of the argument.

3. Identify areas of agreement between the two positions.

4. Write a thesis statement that summarizes the controversy.

5. Plan your essay using a clear organizational schema, or structure, such as an outline.

Prewriting Planning Your Writing

An analysis of opposing ideas is an appropriate genre for exploring two sides of a controversy objectively. To create an effective analysis, you need to find a current controversial issue that will interest you and your classmates. Think of controversies at your school, in your community, in the nation, and in the world.

A student named Paulo gathered topics by reading local and national newspapers and watching news shows. He made a controversies chart and put an asterisk next to the topic he wanted to write about.

Controversies Chart

School	Community	Nation	World
– funding for new gymnasium	– city council resignations	– congressional redistricting	– genocides in Africa
– MySpace.com limits	– community service requirement	– electronic voting *	– globalization and free trade
– special education overhaul	– subsidy for construction	– congressional ethics reform	– third-world debt relief
			– global warming

Create a controversies chart. Create a chart like the one above with the headings "School," "Community," "Nation," and "World." List topics that interest you from local and national news articles. Place an asterisk (*) next to the controversy you choose to write about.

Focus on the Texas Traits

Development of Ideas Select a controversy that (1) has strong support from both sides and (2) you can be objective about. Keep an open mind as you research all relevant perspectives. Gather relevant, substantial evidence and well chosen details that support the strengths and weaknesses of both sides.

Writing an Analysis of Opposing Ideas

Using Sources Effectively

Once you have selected a controversy to write about, you need to research the issue to fully understand it. Solid research requires a variety of valid, reliable, and relevant primary and secondary sources.

Choosing Valid, Reliable, and Relevant Sources

A **primary source** will provide you with first-hand information or descriptions of an event or issue. A **secondary source,** however, presents information that has been published elsewhere.

Not all sources are appropriate for a given topic. A **valid** source will provide you (and your readers) with information that actually addresses your topic. For example, a memoir (primary source) or scholarly article (secondary source) about why people do or do not like politicians might not be a valid source for an analysis of the electronic voting issue.

A **reliable** primary or secondary source provides information that is trustworthy. If reviews of a documentary (primary source) or nonfiction book (secondary source) suggest that a filmmaker or author may have included clearly false information, you should look for a different source. Your sources should be accurate and honest.

Relevant sources are closely connected to the events or issues of your topic. For example, an eyewitness account (primary source) or TV special (secondary source) about a contested election in Victorian England might not be relevant to a discussion of electronic voting in modern times. Those sources may provide historical perspective, but you could not cite them as evidence for what is happening today.

Paulo created the following list to be sure that he had gathered primary and secondary sources that were valid, reliable, and relevant.

Sources List

Print Media:
  "How To Trust Electronic Voting." The New York Times 21 June 2009: A20. Print.
  Morozov, Evgeny. "We Do Not Trust Machines." Newsweek 1 June 2009: 33. Print.

Online Media:
  "H.R. 2894 Voter Confidence and Increased Accessibility Act of 2009 (Introduced in House)." The Library of Congress THOMAS. Library of Congress, 16 June 2009. Web. 27 Sept. 2010.

Primary Sources:
  Parks, Betty. Personal Interview. 15 Oct. 2010.

Prewrite

Create a sources list. Look for a variety of sources and closely consider the validity, reliability, and relevance of each.

TEKS 12.15A(v), 12.15A(vi)
ELPS 2E, 3G, 4G

Prewriting Gathering Details

As you conduct research, you need to consider the validity, reliability, and relevance of your primary and secondary sources. Note cards are a convenient way to keep track of your research to help ensure that you have substantial evidence to support all relevant perspectives on your issue. Here are sample note cards that Paulo prepared during his research.

Note Cards

Why are people thinking about electronic voting?
"Public confidence in the electoral system is critical for our nation's democracy."

Source: "Building Confidence in U.S. Elections"

What problems happened in the past?
In the 2000 presidential election, voting problems led to a disputed result.

Voting Machines created problems in the 2004 and 2008 elections.

Sources: "Election 2000"; Weiss

What are the benefits of electronic voting?
- Quicker and easier
- Can check results before submitting
- Totaled faster
- Counted more accurately

Source: "Electronic Voting"

What are the problems with electronic voting?
- Errors occur
- Unreliable software
- No paper trail
- Hacking

Source: Morozov

Prewrite

Research your topic and take notes. What kinds of primary and secondary sources did you use? To help assess the validity, reliability, and relevance of your evidence, discuss your research results with a teacher or peer.

Writing an Analysis of Opposing Ideas

Organizing Your Essay

Once you have completed your research, it is time to write a thesis statement.

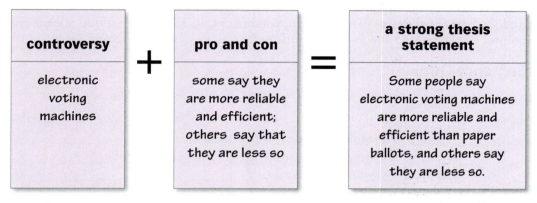

controversy		pro and con		a strong thesis statement
electronic voting machines	**+**	some say they are more reliable and efficient; others say that they are less so	**=**	Some people say electronic voting machines are more reliable and efficient than paper ballots, and others say they are less so.

Write your thesis statement. Use the model above to create a thesis statement for your essay. Try different versions until you are satisfied.

Writing Topic Sentences

Write topic sentences first for the "pro" side, then for the "con" side, and last for the common ground. Here are Paulo's topic sentences.

Topic Sentences

Pro (convenience):	Proponents of electronic voting systems say they allow people to vote quickly and easily.
Pro (accuracy):	Proponents also point out that electronic voting makes vote counting faster and easier.
Con (unreliability):	Opponents of electronic voting insist that such systems are unreliable.
Con (tampering):	Opponents of electronic voting also fear that computer hackers could tamper with election results.
Common ground:	While people disagree about the effectiveness of electronic voting, many agree that election systems should be standardized to improve voter confidence.

Write topic sentences. Focus first on the "pro" argument, then on the "con" argument, and finally on the common ground.

Prewriting Outlining Your Analysis

Before writing your analysis, develop a clear organizational schema, or structure, for conveying your ideas. To create an outline, write your thesis statement and your topic sentences. Then add supporting details that help explain your main points. Paulo created the following outline for his analysis of opposing ideas.

Sentence Outline

Thesis Statement: Some people say electronic voting machines are more reliable and efficient than paper ballots, and others say they are less so.
  I. Proponents of electronic voting systems say they allow people to vote quickly and easily.
     A. Voters simply touch a certain candidate's name.
     B. Voters can review choices before submitting the ballot.
 II. Proponents also point out that electronic voting makes vote counting faster and easier.
     A. The computer keeps a running tally.
     B. Election results are available sooner.
III. Opponents of electronic voting insist that such systems are unreliable.
     A. Software glitches can cause errors.
     B. Some machines fail completely, losing votes forever.
 IV. Opponents of electronic voting also fear that computer hackers could tamper with election results.
     A. Users can fool the machines to allow multiple votes.
     B. Hackers could cause skewed results.
  V. While people disagree about the effectiveness of electronic voting, many agree that election systems should be standardized to improve voter confidence.
     A. Voting machines created problems in past elections.
     B. Election practices vary greatly from state to state.

Organize your ideas. Create an outline like the one above to help you plan an organizational schema for your analysis.

Writing an Analysis of Opposing Ideas

Drafting

Now that you have gathered and organized your ideas and details, you can begin drafting your essay.

Keys to Effective Drafting

1. Use your outline or list as a writing guide. Be sure to include information on all relevant perspectives.

2. Write on every other line or double-space if you are using a computer. This will allow room for changes.

3. Identify the topic and clearly state your thesis in the introductory paragraph.

4. Include your topic sentences in the middle paragraphs. Use a variety of details and sentence structures to support each idea. Draw on valid, reliable, and relevant primary and secondary sources.

5. Put the opposing arguments in perspective in your concluding paragraph.

Drafting Getting the Big Picture

The graphic below shows how the genre elements of an analysis of opposing ideas work together to present a clear picture of an appropriate topic. Use this graphic as a guide when preparing to write your first draft. (The examples are from the student essay on pages **171–174**.)

Beginning
The **introduction** identifies the controversy and states the writer's thesis.

Thesis Statement
Some people argue that electronic voting machines are more reliable and efficient than paper ballots, and others say they are less so.

Middle
The **middle** paragraphs clearly explain both sides of the controversy. Rhetorical devices such as parallelism are used to convey meaning.

Topic Sentences
Proponents of electronic voting systems say they allow people to vote quickly and easily.

Proponents also point out that electronic voting makes vote counting faster and easier.

Opponents of electronic voting insist that such systems are unreliable.

Opponents of electronic voting also fear that computer hackers could tamper with election results.

While people disagree about the effectiveness of electronic voting, many agree that election systems should be standardized to improve voter confidence.

Ending
The **ending** includes a conclusion that puts the controversy in perspective.

Closing Sentences
If Congress followed the recommendations of the Commission on Federal Election Reform and passed a bill to implement an electronic counting system with the accountability of a paper trail, citizens could be more confident that their votes count. . .

TEKS 12.15A(i), 12.15A(ii)
ELPS 5G

Writing an Analysis of Opposing Ideas   171

Introducing Your Analysis

The introductory paragraph of your analysis of opposing ideas should engage your reader, identify your topic, and provide your thesis statement.

- **Engage your reader.** Consider using a rhetorical device, such as a provocative question, to capture your reader's attention and to introduce the controversy.
  How can citizens be sure that their votes count?

- **Identify your topic.** Be sure to include details that expand on your opening sentence and provide necessary background information.
  Since the Supreme Court decided the closest presidential election in U.S. history in 2000, various solutions have been suggested to protect voters' rights and promote voter confidence.

- **End with a thesis statement.** Summarize the controversy in a sentence that broadly states both sides of the argument.
  <u>Some people argue that electronic voting machines are more reliable and efficient than paper ballots, and others say they are less so.</u>

Introductory Paragraph

Paulo drafted the following introductory paragraph.

The writer engages the reader, introduces the topic, and states his thesis (underlined).

> How can citizens be sure their votes count? Since the Supreme Court decided the closest presidential election in U.S. history in 2000, various solutions have been suggested to protect voters' rights and promote voter confidence. Because the 2000 election results were muddled by unclear markings on traditional paper ballots, technology companies and government agencies have since proposed using direct recording electronic (DRE) voting machines. However, DREs caused problems in the 2004 and 2008 elections. A political battle has ensued. <u>Some people argue that electronic voting machines are more reliable and efficient than paper ballots, and others say they are less so.</u>

Expository

Write an introductory paragraph. Use the guidelines above as you begin your analysis of opposing ideas. (Also refer to the beginning of the analysis on page 161.)

Drafting Developing the Middle

The middle part of your essay should include an analysis of views and information that support and contradict both sides of the controversy as they are presented in the thesis statement. The middle paragraphs analyze the "pro" position, the "con" position, and the common ground. As you write, use **transitions** to connect your ideas. Paulo made the following chart to consider how he could use transitions to show different relationships.

Time	Extra Information	Compare/Contrast	Cause and Effect
after	in fact	both	thus
sometimes	also	even	as a result
during	in addition	while	consequently

Middle Paragraphs

Notice how Paulo uses topic sentences, facts, statistics, examples, quotations, and transitions to build his middle paragraphs.

> The first middle paragraphs present the "pro" side of the argument.

Proponents of electronic voting systems say they allow people to vote quickly and easily. Most DRE systems use touch-screen computer monitors, which are now common across the United States. In fact, millions of people use touch screen technology regularly to bank at automated teller machines (ATMs) or purchase items at self-service checkouts in stores. After choosing a slate of candidates, the user of a DRE machine can review and even change choices before submitting a final ballot—something that is possible but sometimes difficult with paper ballots. As poll worker Betty Parks notes, "There's been a lot less confusion in my district since we started using DREs."

> Each paragraph begins with a topic sentence. Supporting sentences have a variety of structures.

Proponents also point out that electronic voting makes vote counting faster and easier. Most DRE machines are capable of compiling both ongoing and final vote counts immediately. This eliminates human error from the vote count and allows faster reporting of election results ("Electronic Voting").

> Next, the writer explains the "con" side of the argument, which contradicts the "pro" side.

Opponents of electronic voting insist that such systems are unreliable. Studies have shown that in a number of elections, DRE machines produced errors in vote counts ("Accessibility"). In the presidential elections of 2004 and 2008, DRE machines gave some candidates extra votes, while other machines failed completely (Weiss). In addition, detractors point to another major factor in muddled elections—human error. Many of the people confused by paper ballots would be even less comfortable poking a screen to indicate their choice. Consequently, voters would make errors in their selections, though this time there would be no paper trail for a recount.

Opponents of electronic voting also fear that computer hackers could tamper with election results. A skilled computer programmer could rewrite the code that controls electronic voting machines to skew the results toward a particular candidate. Since DRE machines do not always offer a paper record of a voter's choices, there is no way to prove the validity of vote counts (Morozov).

> The last middle paragraph addresses areas of agreement and recent developments.

While people disagree about the effectiveness of electronic voting, many agree that election systems should be standardized to improve voter confidence. Both sides also believe that voting and vote counting should be easy and efficient. The nonpartisan Commission on Election Reform issued a statement saying that "public confidence in the electoral system is critical for our nation's democracy" ("Building Confidence"). The Commission recommended a combination of electronic voting with the accountability of a permanent record, and recent bills before Congress have attempted to carry out this recommendation ("H.R. 2894"; "S. 1431").

Write your middle paragraphs. Use your outline (page 168) to create paragraphs that present both sides of the controversy and explain the common ground. Include facts, statistics, examples, quotations, and transitions.

Drafting Concluding Your Essay

You have presented both sides of the political controversy, as well as outlined points on which both sides agree. Now that you have explained the controversy in detail, you are ready to write your concluding paragraph. Follow these guidelines:

- Put the controversy in perspective.
- Summarize the current situation.
- Include an insight that makes the reader think.

Concluding Paragraph

In his concluding paragraph, Paulo connects the ideas in his essay with his ideas about the future of the controversy.

The writer creates a thoughtful ending for his essay.

> The United States has not yet adopted a uniform voting process for federal elections. If Congress followed the recommendations of the Commission on Federal Election Reform and passed a bill to implement an electronic counting system with the accountability of a paper trail, citizens could be more confident that their votes count. The debate over electronic voting might be finally put to rest. However, a candidate's best defense against voting irregularities will probably always be to win not by a few percentage points, but by a landslide. In a hotly contested election, people on either side of the aisle will always look for a reason to call foul.

Write your concluding paragraph. Put the controversy in perspective, summarize current ideas about the controversy, and leave your reader with something to think about.

Prepare a complete first draft. Double-space if you use a computer, or write on every other line if you write by hand. This makes the draft easier to review and gives you room to make revisions.

Writing an Analysis of Opposing Ideas

Revising

Thorough revision helps ensure that the controversy you chose has been clearly explained. When you revise, you check your logic, rearrange parts of your writing to clarify meaning, and create a more engaging, informative voice. You also check your word choice and improve sentence structure and variety.

Keys to Effective Revising

1. Read your essay aloud to yourself or to a friend.

2. Be sure you have thoroughly analyzed the controversy. Consider how well your analysis reflects the genre and addresses your audience and purpose.

3. Check your topic sentences and details to confirm that you have followed your outline. If necessary, rearrange words, sentences, and paragraphs to clarify your meaning.

4. Locate and eliminate any errors in logic.

5. Check your draft for an engaging voice and variety in sentence length and structure.

6. To mark revisions on your draft copy, use the editing and proofreading marks found on pages 638–639.

TEKS 12.13C, 12.15A(i)
ELPS 1B, 2D, 2E, 2G, 2I, 3G, 3H, 4C, 4G

Revising for Focus and Coherence

When you revise for *focus and coherence,* you make sure all parts of your writing are related and support your thesis. Your sustained focus enables the reader to understand and appreciate how the ideas included in your writing are related. A meaningful introduction should add depth to your essay.

Does my first paragraph effectively introduce my analysis?

Your introduction is effective if it captures the reader's attention, clearly identifies the topic, provides necessary background information, and logically leads to the thesis statement.

Exercise

Read the following introductory paragraph and identify the topic and the thesis. Suggest an opening statement that might better capture the reader's attention and engage the reader in the topic. Then tell which background information seems to be missing and how you might rearrange words and sentences to logically lead to the thesis.

> The Bill of Rights is the foundation of freedom and liberty in the United States. Americans on both sides of the "right to bear arms" debate are hoping the Supreme Court will rule in their favor. Gun owners are challenging a local ban on handguns on the basis that it violates the Constitution. Similar cases have been brought before the high court in the past, but rulings involved the application of federal law and the regulation of militias. Although a local ban on handguns was struck down in 2008, the ruling applied to the federal jurisdiction of Washington, D.C. Supporters of the Second Amendment believe that it should apply to state and local laws, while others say it should only apply to federal laws.

Check your introduction. Read aloud your introductory paragraph while a partner takes notes on your topic, background information, and thesis. Discuss any ideas that were unclear to your partner and revise your introduction as needed. Then switch roles.

Do unnecessary or unconnected details interfere with my analysis?

Your details support your analysis if you can answer "yes" to this question about each one: *Does this detail relate clearly to my thesis?*

Exercise

Read the following topic sentence and check each detail by answering the question *Does this detail support the topic sentence (main idea)?* Identify which details are not needed.

Topic sentence: Gun-rights advocates argue that the right to bear arms is a basic freedom protected by the U.S. Constitution.

Detail: Firearms regulation is a right of the states, and recent court rulings support states' rights.

Detail: Groups such as the National Rifle Association have challenged numerous gun regulations in court.

Detail: These gun-rights advocates point out that people have the right to challenge state and local laws under the Fourteenth Amendment.

Detail: The First Amendment guarantees freedom of speech.

Check your focus. Be sure all parts of the writing support or relate to the thesis. If a detail seems unnecessary or unconnected, consider cutting it.

Focus and Coherence
Unnecessary details are cut.

> Because the 2000 election results were muddled by unclear markings on traditional paper ballots, technology companies and government agencies have since proposed using direct recording electronic (DRE) voting machines ("Election 2000"). However, DREs caused problems in the 2004 and 2008 elections (Weiss). ~~The popular vote was within 3 percentage points in 2004. In 2008, Barack Obama received nearly 10 million more votes than John McCain.~~ A political battle has ensued. Some people argue that electronic voting machines are more reliable and efficient than paper ballots, and others say they are less so.

Revising for Organization

When you revise for *organization*, you check the overall structure or schema of your essay to be sure that you have effectively arranged and clearly conveyed your ideas.

How can I check the overall structure of my essay?

You can check the overall structure of your essay by using the essay structure checklist below.

Essay Structure Checklist

BEGINNING PARAGRAPH

_____ 1. Does my first sentence capture the reader's interest?

_____ 2. Do I provide background information that leads to my thesis statement?

MIDDLE PARAGRAPHS

_____ 3. Do my first middle paragraphs explain the "pro" position?

_____ 4. Do my next middle paragraphs explain the "con" position?

_____ 5. Does my last middle paragraph address the common ground?

_____ 6. Does each middle paragraph include a topic sentence with supporting details?

_____ 7. Do transitions between paragraphs help achieve a logical organization?

ENDING PARAGRAPH

_____ 8. Does my conclusion sum up my analysis?

_____ 9. Do I leave the reader with a final thought?

Revise

Check your overall structure. Write numbers 1 to 9 on a piece of paper. Then ask yourself the questions above. If you can answer "yes" to a question, check off the number. If not, revise until you can answer the question with a "yes."

Writing an Analysis of Opposing Ideas

How can signal words make my structure clear?

Signal words help convey your ideas by making your organizational structure clear. They remind the reader where he or she is in your argument. Here are some sample signal words:

Proponents say . . .	Many people argue . . .	Those who favor . . .
Opponents contend . . .	Both sides agree . . .	Those who oppose . . .

Exercise

Read the following thesis statement and main points for an analysis of opposing ideas. Add signal words to make the structure of the analysis clear.

Thesis Statement: The proposal to drill for oil in the Arctic National Wildlife Refuge has inspired heated debate.

1. Drilling for oil would help alleviate U.S. dependence on foreign oil.
2. Drilling would create new jobs in Alaska and new revenue for the country.
3. The Arctic National Wildlife Refuge is meant for wildlife, not big oil companies.
4. The United States should search for alternative energies to decrease its oil dependence.
5. The question is "What is right for Alaska and for the nation?"

Check your topic sentences. Use signal words to help the reader know where she or he is in your argument.

Organization
Signal words help the reader keep track of the argument.

<u>Proponents of</u> Electronic voting systems <u>say they</u> allow people to vote quickly and easily. Most DRE systems use touch-screen computer monitors, which are now common across the United States. . . .

Revising for Development of Ideas

When you revise for *development of ideas,* you check for substantial, relevant evidence and well-chosen details that help the reader understand and appreciate your message.

Do I provide substantial evidence to explain my analysis?

Different types of evidence can help you achieve specific purposes in explaining your analysis:

- **Facts** are details that can be proven. Use facts to clearly explain your topic and create a knowledgeable voice.

- **Statistics** are facts that include a numerical amount. Use statistics to make your information precise.

- **Examples** are specific events or situations that illustrate a general idea. Use examples to make your writing concrete.

- **Quotations** are the exact words of a speaker. Use quotations to share an expert's knowledge.

Exercise

Find different types of evidence in this paragraph and tell what effect each type has.

> Opponents of Austin's new water treatment facility argue that the city does not need it and cannot afford it. According to the Austin Water Utility, the new plant will cost nearly $1 billion. Environmentalists argue that Austin is in the midst of a drought and a recession, and all efforts should be focused on conservation. As Bill Bunch of Save Our Springs describes the proposal, "It's a boondoggle. A potential fiasco. Conserving water is our cheapest supply source. It's our only path to water security." As a recent report by a water conservation task force concluded, conserving water is the best means to extend resources and save money.

Check your evidence. Read your analysis to review how you have used facts, statistics, examples, and quotations to develop your ideas. Provide more substantial evidence where needed.

Writing an Analysis of Opposing Ideas

Do my details help the reader appreciate my ideas?

An effective analysis uses well-chosen details to thoroughly develop ideas.

Exercise

Read the following thesis statement. Then decide which details would help support the thesis.

Thesis Statement: City leaders argue that another water treatment facility must be built, while environmentalists think the focus must be placed on conservation.

Details

information about why environmentalists think conservation is important

statistics on how much water the city uses

the city's projected population growth

city leaders' arguments about the need for another facility

the name of the company that built the existing facilities

the age and condition of the existing facilities

biographical information about the candidates for mayor

Check your support. Read your analysis to consider whether adding details might help develop your ideas more thoroughly.

Development of Ideas
A quotation, paraphrase, and fact help the reader appreciate areas of agreement and recent developments.

Both sides also believe that voting and vote counting should be easy and efficient. ~~Civil rights groups and election officials agree that voting irregularities endanger the fundamentals of our democracy.~~ The nonpartisan Commission on Election Reform issued a statement saying that "public confidence in the electoral system is critical for our nation's democracy" ("Building Confidence"). The ~~Many believe that the best means of success would be to combine~~ commision recommended a combination of electronic voting with the accountability of a permanent record. and recent bills before Congress have attempted to carry out this recommendation ("H.R. 2894"; "S.1431").

Revising for Voice

When you revise for *voice,* you try to make your essay more informative, engaging, and enjoyable to read. You check that the words you have chosen have the appropriate connotation and correct denotation.

How can I check the connotation of my words?

You can check the connotation of your words by making sure each word helps engage the reader and creates the feeling you intend. Not all synonyms are created equal. Note how the feeling of the following sentence changes as different synonyms are inserted:

Congress passed the immigration reform bill.

approved	rubber-stamped	pushed through	mandated
(friendly)	*(jaded)*	*(aggressive)*	*(dictatorial)*

Exercise

In the following sentences, choose a synonym for the italicized words, noting each synonym's connotation or feeling. Write down an adjective that describes the feeling of each word.

1. Protesters *gathered* outside the Capitol building.
2. Police *monitored* the *crowd*.
3. Many people thought the turnout was *weak*.
4. The new legislation faces an *uncertain* future.
5. Security forces *detained* any unruly *protestors*.
6. Inside the Capitol, legislators *discussed* amendments to the bill.
7. The president welcomes the *reform*.
8. Some critics say the bill is *costly* without yielding many *results*.
9. Others feel the bill is *unfair* to those who have already immigrated.
10. The politicians who voted against the legislation face a *terrible* reelection campaign.

Revise

Check your connotation. Read your essay and weigh the feeling created by each word. If you find a word that doesn't engage the reader or creates the wrong feeling, search for a synonym that has a more appropriate connotation.

TEKS 12.13C
ELPS 1B, 1E, 4C, 5B

Writing an Analysis of Opposing Ideas

How can I check the denotation of my words?

You can check your denotation by making sure that you understand the precise dictionary definition for each technical term you use. Note the incorrect denotation of the words in blue:

> National Guard troops enforce the immigration **bill.**
> (Troops enforce *laws,* not *bills.*)
> They **ticket** illegal immigrants crossing the border.
> (Troops *arrest* or *detain* illegal immigrants, they don't *ticket* them.)

Exercise

Replace each word in italics with a word that has the correct denotation. Use a dictionary if you need it.

1. Despite patrols, hundreds of immigrants cross the *state line* every day.
2. Many of them find work, though they don't have a *license.*
3. The law allows some resident aliens to apply for *membership.*
4. Critics say the law lets illegal aliens remain, providing them *sanctuary.*

Revise

Check your denotation. Read your essay and look up each technical term in a dictionary, making sure it has the right denotation. If you find words that have the wrong denotation, replace them with correct terms.

Voice
Changes improve connotation and correct denotation.

Opponents of electronic voting also fear that computer ~~technicians~~ hackers could ~~change~~ tamper with election results. A skilled computer ~~designer~~ programmer could rewrite the ~~language~~ code that controls electronic voting machines to skew the results toward a particular . . .

Expository

Revising Using a Checklist

Check your revising. On a piece of paper, write the numbers 1 to 10. If you answer "yes" to a question, put a check mark next to that number. If not, continue to work on that part of your essay.

Revising Checklist

Focus and Coherence

_____ 1. Do I introduce my topic effectively and state my thesis clearly?
_____ 2. Do my details clearly relate to my thesis?

Organization

_____ 3. Does the overall structure of my essay work well?
_____ 4. Have I used transitions to connect my ideas?
_____ 5. Have I also used signal words to help my reader understand the argument?

Development of Ideas

_____ 6. Have I included substantial and relevant evidence and well-chosen details to explain my analysis?
_____ 7. Have I thoroughly explored each idea, so that the reader can truly appreciate the argument?

Voice

_____ 8. Have I used an active, engaging voice?
_____ 9. Do my words have the appropriate connotation?
_____ 10. Have I used words with the correct denotation?

Make a clean copy. When you are finished with your revision, make a clean copy of your analysis for editing.

Writing an Analysis of Opposing Ideas

Editing

Now that you have finished revising your essay of opposing ideas, you are ready to edit for conventions: grammar, sentence structure, capitalization, punctuation, and spelling.

Keys to Effective Editing

1. Use a dictionary, a thesaurus, and the "Proofreader's Guide" on pages 640–785 as editing resources.

2. Check your writing for correctness of grammar, sentence structure, capitalization, punctuation, and spelling.

3. Edit on a clean revised copy of your essay. Then either enter the corrections on your computer file or write a new handwritten copy that includes the corrections.

4. Use the editing and proofreading marks on pages 638–639.

Grammar

When you edit for *conventions,* you correct errors in pronoun case, subject-verb agreement, and usage.

How can I check the case of my pronouns?

You can check the case of your pronouns by paying attention to how each pronoun is used in the sentence. (See **738.1**.)

- Use **nominative case** for subjects and predicate nouns.
  he   she   it   they

  He applied for a permit with the city clerk, but **she** informed him that there was a violation.

- Use **possessive case** to show ownership.
  Before the noun: his   her   their   its
  After the noun: his   hers   theirs   its

  He asked for **his** waiver, but the decision to grant it was not **hers**.

- Use **objective case** for any objects (direct or indirect objects; objects of prepositions or infinitives).
  him   her   it   them

  The city clerk told **him** that a waiver seemed reasonable to **her**, but **it** would need public approval and a committee vote.

Grammar Exercise

Replace each underlined pronoun with a pronoun of the correct case.

1. The contractor promised <u>she</u> that <u>him</u> would remedy the code violation.
2. The purpose of <u>her</u> meeting was to discuss conditions of the waiver and address any difficulties he might have with <u>its</u>.
3. The public was allowed to address <u>them</u> concerns, and the committee made <u>it</u> vote.

Check the case of your pronouns. Follow the rules above to check pronoun use in your analysis.

Writing an Analysis of Opposing Ideas

How can I create parallel series?

To correctly structure sentences, you can create parallel series by making sure that each item in a group of three or more is the same kind of grammatical element: three present-tense verbs or three past-tense verbs or three participles, and so on.

Not parallel: Residents complained that the project was violating city code, created a safety hazard, and made too much noise.

Parallel: Residents complained that the project violated city code, created a safety hazard, and made too much noise.

Grammar Exercise

Rewrite each series below to make it parallel.

1. The contractor introduced himself, was outlining the project, and presented his case for a waiver.
2. Opponents of the project argued that it was hurting businesses, disturbing residents, and created conflict in the community.
3. The committee is listening to the arguments, discussed the proposal, and postponed ruling on the matter until more evidence could be presented.

Check for parallel series. Read your analysis to make sure that each item in a series of three or more has the same grammatical structure.

Learning Language

To check for parallel series, be aware of irregular verbs, or verbs that do not form the past tense by adding the usual –ed, –d, or –t ending. The following is a list of common irregular verbs. Write a sentence using one of the present-tense verb forms from the list in a parallel series and read it aloud to a partner. Then have your partner restate the sentence using the past-tense verb form for the series. Switch roles and repeat using other words from the list.

Present	Past
know	knew
understand	understood
teach	taught
think	thought
speak	spoke
go	went

Sentence Structure

How can I make passive sentences active?

You can make a passive sentence active by rewriting it so that the subject of the sentence is doing the action of the verb. Active sentences are clearer, shorter, and more energetic than passive sentences. (See **748.2**)

Passive
All public schools have been affected by No Child Left Behind.
The subject, *schools,* is not doing the action.

Active
No Child Left Behind has affected all public schools.
The subject, *No Child Left Behind,* is doing the action.

Exercise

Rewrite the passive sentences below to make them active.

1. The system for federal funding of schools was reformed by the No Child Left Behind law.
2. Schools are required by the law to meet certain standards and show improvement.
3. The legislation has been praised by conservatives.
4. The law has been criticized by liberals.
5. Since its creation, public education has been reformed almost continuously by the government.
6. The public school system was created by the government to educate students and prepare them to be citizens.

Check for active sentences. Read your analysis and watch for sentences in which the subject does not do the action of the verb. Rewrite these passive sentences to make them active.

Mechanics: Capitalization

What words should I capitalize?

Capitalize proper nouns and proper adjectives:

Britain ⟶ British   Arthur ⟶ Arthurian
Islam ⟶ Islamic   Newton ⟶ Newtonian

Capitalize geographic directions if they are part of a proper name, unit, or regional term:

South Carolina   South Pole   the East Coast (but the eastern U.S.)
North Dakota   Western Hemisphere   the Northwest Passage (but northwestern states)

Capitalize titles preceding names:
President Obama   **Aunt Rosa**   **Professor Juarez**

Capitalize historical periods and events:
Jazz Age   **Renaissance**   **Civil War**

Exercise

In the following paragraph, correct any errors in capitalizing adjectives.

   The people of north Korea live under totalitarian rule, while the people of south Korea live in a democracy. The korean War was fought because the Northern part of the country had fallen under a stalinist model of government, while the southern part aspired to a jeffersonian democracy.

Check your capitalization. Be sure your writing follows the capitalization rules above. Make any changes necessary to correct your work.

Editing Using a Checklist

Check your editing. On a piece of paper, write the numbers 1 to 12. If you can answer "yes," put a check mark after that number. If you can't, continue to edit for that convention.

Editing Checklist

Conventions

GRAMMAR
_____ 1. Have I checked the case of my pronouns?
_____ 2. Do my pronouns agree with their antecedents?
_____ 3. Do my subjects and verbs agree?

SENTENCE STRUCTURE
_____ 4. Do I use a variety of correctly structured sentences that clearly communicate my ideas?
_____ 5. Do the subjects of my sentences do the action of the verbs?

MECHANICS (CAPITALIZATION AND PUNCTUATION)
_____ 6. Do I use end punctuation after all my sentences?
_____ 7. Do I use commas after long introductory phrases and clauses?
_____ 8. Have I used quotation marks correctly for quotations?
_____ 9. Do I start all of my sentences with capital letters?
_____ 10. Do I capitalize all proper adjectives and nouns?

SPELLING
_____ 11. Have I spelled all words correctly?
_____ 12. Have I double-checked for errors my spell-checker may have missed?

Creating a Title

After your editing is complete, add a title that engages your reader and sums up your content. Here are a few ways to create an effective title:

- Use a hook: **A Closer Look at Electronic Voting**
- Ask a question: **Does Electronic Voting Get the Job Done?**
- Identify the controversy: **The Battle over Electronic Voting**

Publishing

The purpose of your analysis of opposing ideas is to present a clear, evenhanded examination of a political controversy. After you've incorporated feedback from your teacher and peers, share your ideas with appropriate audiences. The following guidelines will help you publish your work.

Focusing on Presentation

- Write neatly using blue or black ink.
- Place your name in the upper left corner of page 1.
- Skip a line and center your title; skip another line and start your essay.
- Indent every paragraph and leave a one-inch margin on all four sides.
- Write your last name and the page number in the upper right corner of every page after page 1.

Publish Your Essay
School and local newspapers often welcome writing that clearly examines political controversies. Send your article to a local or school-based newspaper using e-mail or postal mail. Before sending your article, make sure it conforms to the publication's submission guidelines and would interest the publication's audience.

Go Online!
Upload your analysis of opposing ideas for others to read.

Add It to a Blog
Many students create Web logs, or blogs, to share their ideas online. If you have a blog, consider publishing your article on it. Add photographs, charts, and other visual elements to support your ideas. You may also invite comments from your readers.

Format your final copy. To format a handwritten essay, use the guidelines above or follow your teacher's instructions. Make a clean copy and carefully proofread it.

Evaluating an Analysis of Opposing Ideas

To learn how to evaluate an analysis of opposing ideas, you will use the holistic scoring guide on pages 36–37 and the essays that follow. These essays are examples of writing for each score on the scoring guide (1–4).

Notice that the first essay received a score of 4. Read the description for a score of 4 on pages 36–37. Then read the analysis of opposing ideas. Use the same steps to study the other examples. As you read, concentrate on the overall quality of the writing in each example.

Writing that fits a score of 4 is very strong.

4

Is It Right to Limit Campaign Contributions?

If you are like most people, you understand that money influences federal elections. Many people believe that money is turning politics into a contest in which elections and political influence can be bought. These people believe that the way to solve the problem is through campaign finance reform—limiting campaign contributions or funding campaigns through tax dollars. Others think that while the current system is not perfect, campaign finance reform could only make matters worse. A look at both sides of the argument reveals that both have valid points.

Those who favor campaign finance reform insist that under the current system, many potential candidates are shut out. Candidates must be wealthy or collect large amounts of money from donors in order to buy the advertising they need to get elected. Candidates with access to large amounts of money can use it to overwhelm candidates with less money by using dishonest "attack ads" spread across the media.

In addition, those who favor campaign finance reform point out that problems continue after an election is over. Senators, Congresspeople, and other elected officials must immediately begin raising money for their next campaign. This opens a pathway for those willing to donate money in return for influence. Donating money to a congressperson's campaign fund, for example, could persuade the congressperson to vote in a certain way.

Finally, supporters of campaign finance reform point out that unlimited donations help keep politicians in office even if they

The introductory paragraph is meaningful and outlines the purpose of the analysis.

Transitions help readers move from one idea to the next.

do not act in the best interests of the people who elected them. Constant campaign donations allow elected officials to build campaign funds that make them almost impossible to defeat. Less turnover in the government limits the number of new ideas, yet the best way for a government to work is for the government to explore as many ideas for solving problems as possible.

Those who oppose campaign finance reform point out that while candidates spend huge amounts of money, many of the donations given to them are small amounts. According to the Center for Responsive Politics, most individuals donate less that $200 per election cycle. They insist that it would harm the political system to limit the ability of individuals to support a candidate with a good idea. It is reasonable to assume, they say, that the best ideas and the best candidates will attract the greatest amount of financial support.

In addition, those who oppose campaign finance reform cite legal concerns. If elections were funded through taxes, that would mean that voters' tax dollars could be used to support candidates whose ideas they oppose. Forcing a person to provide money for a candidate he or she did not support would be a violation of election laws.

Reform opponents also say that donating money to a candidate is a way of expressing a donor's ideas about how the government should be run. If you believe that sentences for certain crimes should be longer, for example, you can donate money to a candidate who supports your position. Limiting your ability to donate money to that candidate would be the same as limiting your right to free speech.

According to the Center for Responsive Politics, candidates, political parties, and interest groups spent $5.3 billion on the 2008 presidential and congressional elections. That's a huge amount of money, and the money spent on future campaigns will probably be greater. That ensures that no matter which side is correct, the debate over campaign finance reform is likely to continue.

Writing that fits a score of 3 is strong in most ways.

3

Should Minor Party Candidates Be in Presidential Debates?

In recent years, nationally televised debates have played a critical role in presidential elections. Debates among major candidates have allowed people across the nation to understand candidates' ideas, see how they react under pressure, and get a feel for how they might do the job if elected. Yet the number of candidates who have been allowed to participate in these debates has been limited. Television networks and organizations that sponsor the debates often set these limits based on the level of support for a party by the voting public. Under these formulas, candidates from so-called "minor" parties are often shut out. Is this the best way to run a debate.

Those who support limits on debate participation often point out that the number of candidates plays a role. In any given presidential election, there are dozens of candidates who have qualified to be placed on the ballot. Since major debates take place on television, they are very expensive to produce and the time for each debate must be limited.

It is overwhelmingly likely that a major party candidate will win most elections. Indeed, in the entire history of the United States, no minor party candidate has been elected to the presidency. The closest a minor party candidate came to winning the presidency was in 1912. Theodore Roosevelt, running as the Progressive Party candidate, won 88 electoral votes. The winner, Woodrow wilson, received 435. Given this evidence, those who favor limited debates say, including minor-party candidates is a waste of time. It's better to give voters a chance to listen to the ideas of candidates who have a chance.

Those who support the inclusion of minor party candidates insist that ideas are key to a healthy democracy. My uncle, for example, has many ideas about politics. Every day, our nation faces new challenges, and we need new ideas for solving problems. Elections should be about offering a broad variety of viewpoints, but if only major parties are heard from, the number of good ideas will be limited. Given the opportunity, a third party candidate's

> Minor errors in conventions don't interfere with effectiveness of analysis.

> Idea could be developed more thoroughly with additional details.

> Paragraph shows a minor lapse in focus and fails to support the controlling idea.

ideas could attract the support necessary to win an election. But if minor party candidate's aren't allowed in a debate, this can never happen.

In addition, supporters of increased access point out that even if they don't win, minor party candidates can bring about change. Two examples, they say are presidential candidates Ross Perot and Ron Paul. Even though both candidates came from minor parties, they were allowed to participate in presidential debates. Their ideas about government accountability, economics, and political corruption found support among many citizens. Because of this, candidates from the Demeocratic and Republican parties were forced to respond to these concerns. Although they were not elected, minor party candidates influenced the election.

In a democracy all citizens should be able to have their views represented. During their campaigns, minor party candidates represent the voters who support them. Only if these candidates can participate in debates will their supporters' viewpoints be presented in a large public forum. If these candidates are shut out, so are the people who support them.

While it is likely that the battle over who gets included in presidential debates will continue, new technologies may make the argument less important. The Internet gives even minor candidates the chance to express their views to millions. And social networking tools enable these views to spread quickly. In fact, in years to come, televised presidential debates may even become a thing of the past.

> The text could use a transition here to help the reader connect ideas.

Writing that fits a score of 2 is strong in some ways.

The introductory paragraph is superficial and not fully developed. Repetition interferes with flow of ideas.

Errors in conventions interfere with the flow of writing.

Ideas are not fully developed and lack substantial evidence.

Concluding paragraph is weak and does not support the thesis.

Should Judges Be Appointed or Elected?

Being a judge is a serious job. Every day, you have to make dcesions that affect people's lives. How do you get to be a judge? That depends on where you live. In some places, voters elect the judges by voting in the voting booth. Those votes by the voters make the decision. In other places, the judges get appointed by a governor or other official. There is no voting involved..

Some people think voting is the best way to pick a judge. People have the right to vote when they are 18 years of age an somme think this is too young, but most agrre that it is the right age when voters choose a judge, the judge will reflect their values. If they don't like the judge, they can vot the judge. But the judge can make plenty of bad decision before that. Some people think an appointed judge will do just what the person in charge of the appointments wants. This would be bad.

Other people think a judge should be appointed. That's because judges have to make some decisions that are unpopular but fair. What if a judge can be voted out, how fair is that. Like if the judge sent a burglar to jail, but the burglar had lots of friends who could vote against the judge. The judge might vote a lighter sennence.

Considering both sides of the argument, I think both have their points. Judges are always under pressure one way or the other. They must try to do their jobs no matter what. Whether they are voted in or appointed, they are judged by the public. Most of them probably do a pretty good job, and I think you'll agree.

Writing an Analysis of Opposing Ideas

Writing that fits a score of 1 is weak.

The introductory paragraph includes a substantial amount of information not related to the thesis.

Does not show a clear organizational schema for conveying ideas.

Problems with conventions make the message hard to understand.

Missing a meaningful concluding paragraph.

Should Politicians Be Allowed to Take Gifts.

Ab big argument is happening right now. About gfts for politicns. Like people given them to htem. One biog item is football tickets. M uncld egot some, but he isn't a politician. But if he was, he would probably like them just as much. To him football is an important part of life. And gifts are something he is always wanting to get.

Some people think why shouldn't you be able to give a gift if you want to? A politician is a person, and could even be you friend. My friends give me gifts sometimes. Last year Carla gave me a new CD, and I even worte her a thank you leter for it in return. What is wrong with that? I don't think anything, and that is the main pint. I think lots of people agrey.

Other peple thing gifts are bad I mean for politicians if you gave a new tennis rackett to a politician, he might vote the way you ask him to. But he might not. Maybe if yu gave him a car, would be worse there should be laws against this, they say. Plus if another politician does not get a gift, it woud not be fair?

Politicians could get gifts sometimes, but not all the time. And the gifts couldn't be as big as a car. Maybe something smaller like a caerma or a wach wuld be OK. That way fewer people would care about what they got. And they would probably just do the same thing anyway. That is the way it has always been and you can't stop it so what's the use?

Expository

Evaluating and Reflecting on Your Writing

Now that you have completed your analysis of opposing ideas, take some time to reflect on the process of writing it. On a separate sheet of paper, complete each sentence below. This personal reflection will help reinforce what you've learned about writing an analysis of opposing ideas.

My Analysis of Opposing Ideas

1. The strongest part of my analysis is . . .

2. The part that still needs work is . . .

3. The prewriting activity that worked best for me was . . .

4. The main thing I learned about writing an analysis of opposing ideas is . . .

5. In my next analysis of opposing ideas, I would like to . . .

6. One question I still have about writing an analysis of opposing ideas is . . .

Expository Writing
Writing a Problem Analysis

You analyze issues and situations every day. Perhaps you help resolve a disagreement between friends or family members. You might have to figure out how to juggle work and school responsibilities. You might try to assemble something complicated, or even think about how you are going to afford something you really want to buy. Analysis involves careful research and logical thinking—looking at every aspect of a problem. It is important to include an analysis of views that contradict your thesis and evidence in order to make your writing balanced and effective.

In this chapter, you will read a problem analysis about an invasive ground cover—crown vetch—that is causing serious problems in the United States. Then you will be guided through the process of developing your own problem analysis. Remember: For this type of essay, you should examine all aspects of the problem to provide a balanced analysis.

Writing Guidelines

Subject: A timely topic
Purpose: To analyze a problem and its consequences
Form: Problem analysis
Audience: Classmates

"Common sense in an uncommon degree is what the world calls wisdom."
—Samuel Taylor Coleridge

Problem Analysis

In the following essay, Carla analyzes the problem of crown vetch, an invasive plant often planted along highways.

Introductory Paragraph
The writer introduces the topic and clearly states her thesis (underlined).

Middle
The middle paragraphs include evidence and details that support and contradict the thesis.

The writer cites valid, relevant, and reliable sources.

Uncontrollable Invasion

Fifty years ago, road crews began planting crown vetch along newly constructed highways to prevent soil erosion. Crown vetch is a ground-cover plant with appealing foliage and flowers. Road improvement scars were quickly covered, and erosion was no longer a concern. Then planners discovered a problem. Crown vetch didn't like staying in one place. Instead, it started taking root in land adjacent to the roadsides. As a result, it became clear that crown vetch could not be planted carelessly or left unchecked. <u>Crown vetch is a dangerous, invasive plant that, if left unchecked, could change the nation's landscape as we know it.</u>

Most people pay little attention to this plant along the nation's highways and freeways. Crown vetch matures into an 18-inch-high creeping plant that grows in all climates—wet or dry, hot or cold. As the road crews discovered, it is an effective ground cover that serves an important purpose. However, if not controlled, it can take over a roadside and nearby land, overwhelming any vegetation in its path, including small trees (Fernald). When this happens, even the most unobservant driver begins to notice a sameness in the vegetation mile after mile.

In areas where crown vetch really takes hold, local crops and gardens are put at risk. According to Art Gover of Pennsylvania State University, crown vetch sprouts from rhizomes (underground root runners) and seeds, which makes it fast growing and difficult to eradicate. The rhizomes can be up to ten feet in length. As a result, crown vetch can easily overwhelm backyard gardens or crops near roadsides. To control the plant, strong chemicals can be applied to the area. Unfortunately, chemicals may also kill any nearby desirable plants or contaminate the soil. Another way to control the plant is to set fires in these areas year after year.

Each middle paragraph begins with a topic sentence, followed by supporting details.

A variety of sentence structures helps to communicate ideas.

Conclusion The concluding paragraph summarizes the writer's thesis.

The greatest danger posed by crown vetch is its potential to invade and destroy native prairie habitats. Native prairie land is unique to interior parts of the United States, primarily in the Great Plains. Most of the original prairie is gone, and crown vetch could threaten what remains (Heim). A prairie needs to maintain a special balance of native plants and animals to thrive, and the introduction of crown vetch into the area could certainly destroy that balance. Fires, historically caused by lightning storms, help maintain the health and vitality of the prairies. However, if crown vetch were in the area, the plant would burn too quickly and without the necessary heat to aid in prairie regeneration. If chemicals were used to control the crown vetch, it would be important not to affect the prairie plants. Workers could be trained to use the chemicals properly. However, it would be a tragedy to lose what remains of the nation's prairie lands because of an invasive plant such as crown vetch.

Crown vetch has helped control erosion along U.S. roadways, but it has the potential to do as much harm as good. Crops, gardens, and prairies are the areas where an infestation of crown vetch could be harmful. Most plants in their rightful place benefit the landscape or ecosystem, but in the wrong place, without the proper restraint, they may cause serious, long-term problems.

Respond to the reading. Answer the following questions about the sample problem analysis.

Focus and Coherence (1) What is the thesis of this essay? (2) Do the paragraphs reinforce the thesis?

Organization (3) Is the essay logically organized? (4) Does it have smooth transitions? Give examples.

Voice (5) Does the writer sound interested in and knowledgeable about the topic? (6) Does the writer convey a unique perspective? Explain.

Prewriting Considering Current Issues

The purpose of a problem analysis is to identify a problem and then examine its various aspects. To get started, Carla made a list of current issues. She thought about whether she would like to write a personal narrative about how an issue affected her or if it would be better to write a more objective essay. She decided that an objective analysis would more effectively achieve her purpose.

Current-Issues List

terrorism	diminishing oil resources
urban sprawl	invasive plant species *
fresh water	global warming

Think of current issues. Make a list of current issues. Then choose one to explore further. Place an asterisk (*) next to the issue you choose.

Selecting a Specific Topic

Carla had discussed issues about invasive plant species in her botany class. She decided it would be interesting to investigate one of these species and explore the specific kinds of problems that it causes. After reviewing her class notes and researching on the Internet, she came up with this list. Then she put an asterisk next to the species of plant she wanted to write about.

Topics List

Invasive Plants		
pepper trees	hydrilla	kudzu
crown vetch *	leafy spurge	garlic mustard

Choose a topic. List topics related to the current issue that you chose. Put an asterisk (*) next to the topic you would like to write about.

Focus on the Texas Traits

Development of Ideas The goal of a problem analysis is to identify a problem and then examine its aspects, including ideas that contradict the thesis. You will need to develop ideas with specific details. If you can't find enough information about your topic, consider another topic.

Consideration of Sources

You will find a variety of sources as you research your topic. These can be classified into two categories:

A **primary source** is original material that has not been interpreted by other writers. Examples of primary sources include eyewitness accounts, interviews, letters, and photographs.	A **secondary source** is based on other sources. Information from these sources is interpreted, summarized, or retold by another writer. Examples of secondary sources are encyclopedias, many newspaper and magazine articles, and textbooks.

It is critical that you consider and evaluate potential primary and secondary sources for validity, reliability, and relevance. Dependable sources add value and merit to your analysis. Unreliable or irrelevant sources will weaken your essay.

Considering Validity

A **valid** source explicitly addresses your topic. When you consider a source's validity, ask yourself the following questions:

- Does the information directly relate to my topic?
- Can I find sources that better relate to my topic?

Evaluating Reliability

A **reliable** source is fair and accurate. Primary sources, such as eyewitness accounts and interviews, can be reliable sources for firsthand statements of information. However, remember that primary sources may include only one person's perspective and may be subjective, based on opinion or emotion. A secondary source often covers a topic more broadly and is generally more objective, or factual. When you consider a source's reliability, ask yourself the following questions:

- Is the information sound and accurate, well-supported by facts?
- Does the source provide unbiased facts on my topic?

Determining Relevance

When you are writing about a current issue, a **relevant** source is up to date and closely connected to your issue. When you consider a source's relevance, ask yourself the following questions:

- Is the source appropriate for my topic?
- Is the information in the source still meaningful and current?

Analyze your sources. As you research your primary and secondary sources, consider and analyze their validity, reliability, and relevance. Remember to cite the proper references (see page 440).

Writing a Thesis Statement

Once you have gained a thorough understanding of your topic, write a clear thesis statement expressing why your topic is a problem. You will remain focused on this thesis throughout your essay. Here is Carla's thesis statement.

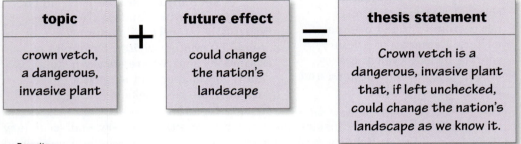

Learn about your topic. Research your topic to learn as much as you can about it. Then write a thesis statement that expresses why it is a problem. (Use the example above as a guide.)

Organizing Your Information

Organizing the facts and details that support and contradict your thesis statement is the next step in the drafting process. Different graphic organizers can help writers compare and contrast information, classify information, or list main points and details. Carla chose to use a **two-column chart** to organize her main points and related details.

Main Points	Related Details
grows on roadsides	• forms dense cover, controls erosion • creates an unnatural sameness • overwhelms other vegetation
puts local crops and gardens at risk	• grows fast and works well as ground cover • needs strong chemicals or annual fires to control
could destroy native prairie habitats	• threatens prairie lands unique to U.S. • upsets balance of native plants and animals • hinders prairie regeneration

Organize your support. Complete a two-column chart like the one above in which you list the main points and related details that support and contradict your thesis. List main points in the order you will write about them.

Drafting Creating Your First Draft

The following tips will help you develop your first draft.

Introductory Paragraph

First, introduce your topic and clearly state your thesis.

- Open with interesting information that introduces your topic.
  Fifty years ago, road crews began planting crown vetch along newly constructed highways to prevent soil erosion. Crown vetch is a ground-cover plant with appealing foliage and flowers.

- End with your thesis statement.
  Crown vetch is a dangerous, invasive plant that, if left unchecked, could change the nation's landscape as we know it.

Middle Paragraphs

The middle paragraphs explain the main points that support the thesis.

- Start with an effective topic sentence to state the main idea.
  Most people pay little attention to this plant along the nation's highways and freeways.

- Support your thesis with relevant and substantial details.
  Crown vetch matures into an 18-inch-high creeping plant that grows in all climates . . .

- Include valid, reliable, and relevant sources.
  According to Art Gover of Pennsylvania State University . . .

- Use transitions and rhetorical devices to connect your ideas.
  However, if not controlled, it can take over . . .

- Use a variety of sentence structures.
  The rhizomes can be up to ten feet in length. As a result, crown vetch can easily overwhelm . . .

Concluding Paragraph

Finally, restate the thesis and summarize the main supporting points.

- Restate your thesis.
  Crown vetch has helped control erosion along the U.S. roadways, but it has the potential to do as much harm as good.

Write your first draft. Write an initial draft of your essay, using the sample essay, your prewriting work, and the information above as a guide.

Choosing the Best Details and Evidence

As you research your topic, you will find more information than you can use in your problem analysis. The details may be interesting, but they will not all be relevant to your topic. How can you decide which details to include in your essay and which details to leave out?

Choosing the Best Details and Evidence

After you have gathered information, ask yourself the following questions:

- **Which details relate specifically to my thesis statement?** Carla found interesting details about additional efforts to prevent erosion along highways. Because her intent was to focus on crown vetch, however, she set that information aside and included only the information about her topic.

- **Are there enough details and enough evidence to support the main idea of each middle paragraph?** Details and evidence in the middle paragraphs should all support the main point.

- **Have I included the most interesting and relevant details?** You may have found a source that expresses an idea in a more interesting way than other sources, or that makes the analysis more substantial. For example, a professor at Pennsylvania State University gave Carla some specific details that explained why crown vetch is particularly invasive. She decided to include these details in her analysis.

Considering Evidence that Contradicts the Thesis

In her research, Carla came across an article claiming that the spread of crown vetch is not as serious a problem as is widely believed. The article's author, a scientist, had done studies that she believed were authoritative. Although the other evidence Carla had found overwhelmingly supported her thesis, she included some contradictory evidence in her problem analysis. This made it possible for her to make an even stronger case for her position.

As you research, you may find evidence and details that contradict your thesis. Consider including some of this information, and then use more valid and reliable evidence to prove why it is not accurate. This can make your essay stronger.

Focus on the Texas Traits

Focus and Coherence It is important to maintain your focus throughout the analysis. Make sure that all the details are relevant to the topic. Be careful not to shift abruptly from one idea to the next. Instead, show how all ideas connect to each other and to the main idea.

TEKS 12.13C, 12.15A(ii)
ELPS 1B, 5G

Revising Improving Your First Draft

As you revise, use the checklist below as a guide.

Revising Checklist

Focus and Coherence

_____ 1. Do I maintain a specific focus throughout the analysis?
_____ 2. Do a variety of details support and contradict the focus?
_____ 3. Do the introduction and conclusion add depth to the analysis?
_____ 4. Are the ideas in the analysis clearly related?

Organization

_____ 5. Is there a clear thesis statement?
_____ 6. Does my analysis have a strong introduction, middle, and conclusion?
_____ 7. Have I presented my points in a logical order?
_____ 8. Have I used rhetorical devices to evoke a specific response from the reader?
_____ 9. Are there meaningful transitions between paragraphs?

Development of Ideas

_____ 10. Are the ideas thoroughly developed with well-chosen details?
_____ 11. Do I effectively develop each middle paragraph?

Voice

_____ 12. Does my voice sound confident and knowledgeable?

Revise your first draft. Read your analysis carefully. Then use the checklist above to improve your first draft.

Creating a Title

- Draw on your thesis: **Uncontrollable Invasion**
- Ask a question: **Is Crown Vetch Ruining America's Landscape?**
- Use your imagination: **A "Vetching" Problem**

Editing Checking for Conventions

After revising your analysis, use the following checklist to edit your writing for grammar, mechanics (punctuation and capitalization), and spelling errors.

Editing Checklist

Conventions

GRAMMAR

_____ 1. Have I used the correct forms of verbs?

_____ 2. Do my subjects and verbs agree in number?

_____ 3. Do my pronouns agree with their antecedents?

SENTENCE STRUCTURE

_____ 4. Do I use a variety of correctly structured sentences that clearly communicate my ideas?

MECHANICS (CAPITALIZATION AND PUNCTUATION)

_____ 5. Do I capitalize the first word in every sentence?

_____ 6. Do I capitalize all proper nouns and adjectives?

_____ 7. Have I ended my sentences with the correct punctuation?

_____ 8. Have I used commas, semicolons, and colons correctly?

_____ 9. Have I punctuated quotations correctly?

SPELLING

_____ 10. Have I spelled all my words correctly?

_____ 11. Have I double-checked for easily confused words that my spell-checker would miss?

Edit your analysis. Use the checklist above to edit for grammar, mechanics, and spelling. Also, ask a partner to check your work for errors. Then prepare a final copy and proofread it.

Publishing Sharing Your Work

The purpose of this step is to share information with your audience.

Publish your analysis. Share your writing by reading it aloud in class, followed by a question-and-answer session, or by posting it on a bulletin board. Also, consider presenting it as a speech or submitting it to a Web site.

Writing for Assessment
Responding to Expository Prompts

Expository writing is basically informational writing. Depending on the topic, you might summarize, illustrate, analyze, explain, classify, or compare. For most expository assignments, you will be given plenty of time to complete your work. However, when you are asked to respond to an expository prompt on an assessment test, you will have to complete your work within a set period of time.

When responding to an expository prompt, you will need to plan, write, and revise your writing quickly. In this chapter, you will learn how to analyze an expository prompt and create an effective, well-organized response—all within specific time constraints. Having the ability to write on demand is a valuable skill that you will use now and later—when you go on to college or enter the workplace.

Writing Guidelines

    Subject: An expository prompt
       Form: Response essay
  Purpose: To demonstrate competence
 Audience: Instructor or test evaluator

"I see only one rule: to be clear. If I am not clear, then my entire world crumbles into nothing."

—Stendhal

Prewriting Analyzing an Expository Prompt

To respond effectively to an expository prompt, you will first need to analyze it. If you do a thorough job of analyzing the prompt, you'll have a much better chance of producing a successful essay. To analyze a prompt, use the STRAP questions:

> **Subject:** What topic should I write about?
>
> **Type:** What form of writing should I create (essay, letter, editorial, article, report)?
>
> **Role:** What role should I assume as the writer (student, son or daughter, friend, employee, citizen)?
>
> **Audience:** Who (teacher, parents, classmates, employer, official) is the intended audience?
>
> **Purpose:** What is the goal of my writing (inform, summarize, illustrate, analyze, classify, compare)?

Subject
Type
Role
Audience
Purpose

Some people always stand out as individuals. These people don't follow trends; they set them. **Assuming the role of a historian,** write a brief essay for your classmates about someone you admire for individuality. Explain what makes the person stand out in the crowd and how the person's unique traits make you admire him or her.

Note: One of the following key words or phrases is often found in an expository prompt: *outline, analyze, inform, compare and contrast, explain,* or *define.*

Try It!

Analyze this prompt by answering the STRAP questions. (Some answers may be implied or left open. Use your best judgment.)

People under the age of 20 have grown up with computers and are well-versed in the language of computers. Write an essay that explains to the older generation the role of computers in the lives of today's teens. Consider the positive and negative effects of computer use.

Planning Your Response

After you have analyzed the prompt using the STRAP questions, it's time to start planning and organizing your response. One good way to do this is to use a graphic organizer. The organizers below all provide ways to organize an effective response to an expository prompt.

Quick List (Any Essay)
1. First Point
   —Detail 1
   —Detail 2
2. Second Point
   —Detail 1
   —Detail 2
3. Third Point
   —Detail 1
   —Detail 2

Time Line (How-To/Process)
First
Next
Then
After
Last

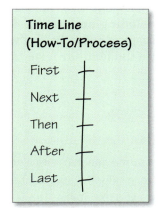

T-Chart (Two-Part Essay)

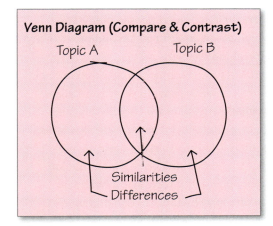

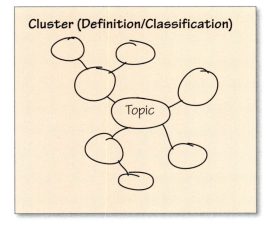

Use a graphic organizer. Reread the expository prompts on page 210. Choose one and use a graphic organizer to plan and organize your response to the prompt. Keep the STRAP questions in mind as you work.

Tip

When it comes to responding to a prompt, good time management is critical. If you have 45 minutes to respond to a prompt, use the first 5 to 10 minutes to analyze the prompt and plan your response, the last 5 to 10 minutes to revise and edit your response, and the time in between for the actual writing.

Drafting Responding to a Prompt

Once you have answered the STRAP questions and planned your response using a graphic organizer, you can begin writing. Before you begin, take a look at the following student essay for an example of an effective response.

Student writer Marta Rodriguez wrote the following expository essay in response to the second prompt on page 210. Marta chose to organize her essay by stating main points and including supporting details to support her thesis. Picking up on the prompt's concept of teens being "well-versed in the language of computers," Marta decided to use the familiar term "digital natives" to describe her generation.

Sample Response

Introduction
The introductory paragraph clearly states the thesis (underlined).

Just as some generations were raised listening to radio and others were raised watching television, my generation was raised using computers. These young people are "digital natives" who speak the language of computers and use them throughout life. <u>Computers provide young people many tools for schoolwork, for communication, and for entertainment; they also present a few dangers along the way.</u>

To begin with, computers have become indispensable tools for processing information. Word-processing programs allow students to write more quickly, revise more thoroughly, and edit more accurately than ever before. Internet search engines allow students to find exactly the information they need with only a few mouse clicks. As the old saying goes, "information is power." However, not every piece of information from the Internet is reliable, and an unwary researcher can end up with material that is biased or downright wrong. Also, computers make it more tempting to plagiarize. Teens have to be savvy and conscientious to avoid bad information and plagiarism. The "power" gained by access to an endless supply of information is offset by responsibility and risk.

The writer uses a familiar saying to communicate the opposite meaning.

> **Transitions** connect the middle paragraphs.

In addition to processing information, modern teens use computers for communication. Through instant messaging, online games, chat rooms, and group sites, teens connect with old friends and meet new ones. Many young people also write their own blogs or create their own videos and podcasts, sharing their ideas with the world. But while communicating online, teens must beware of "stranger danger." Spammers clog up e-mail boxes, hackers develop viruses, and predators lurk on group sites. Even if a computer user can avoid these dangers, having a friend online is no substitute for having one in person. Teens must learn to use computers to enhance friendships, not replace them.

Today's teens also use computers as a source of entertainment. Instead of going to a store, most teens buy music and movies online, either to be delivered or downloaded. They also prefer to buy one or two songs at a time rather than a whole album. Some sites even allow teens to share their files. This can cause problems. Illegal file sharing and downloads might seem a cheap way to get entertainment—until the person is caught and fined, or even sent to prison. An illegal download also cheats the person's favorite artist out of the chance to make a living. If teens can steer clear of illegal music and movies, though, there is still plenty of listening and watching to do.

> **Conclusion** A meaningful conclusion adds depth to the composition.

For teens today, computers shape everyday life. The question is whether teens can manage the power of these great tools. When handled well, a computer provides homework help, connects people to friends, and even sets the world to music. On the other hand, unwise computer use can result in plagiarized documents, dangerous predators, and even fines and jail time. Most teens avoid these pitfalls almost instinctively. After all, these "digital natives" grew up understanding computers and speaking their language.

Now write your own response. Look over the planning you did for the prompt on page 210.

Revising Improving Your Response

Most writing tests allow you to make corrections to improve your work, though you should find out ahead of time how many changes are allowed. If changes are allowed, make them as neatly as possible. Use the STRAP questions as a guide.

Subject: Does my response focus on the prompt topic?
Do my main points support my thesis statement?

Type: Have I followed the correct form (essay, letter, article)?

Role: Have I assumed the role called for in the prompt?

Audience: Have I effectively addressed my audience?

Purpose: Does my response accomplish the goal of the prompt?

Improve your work. Using the STRAP questions above as your guide, revise your response within the allowed time period.

Editing Checking Your Response

Check your expository response for punctuation, capitalization, spelling, and grammar. You don't want any careless errors that confuse the reader.

Editing Checklist

Conventions

_____ 1. Have I used end punctuation for every sentence?
_____ 2. Have I capitalized all proper nouns and first words of sentences?
_____ 3. Have I checked my spelling?
_____ 4. Have I made sure my subjects and verbs agree?
_____ 5. Have I used the right words (*their, they're, there*)?

Check for conventions. Review your response for any errors in punctuation, capitalization, spelling, and grammar. Make neat corrections.

Expository Writing on Tests

Before you write . . .

- **Study the prompt.**
  Use the STRAP questions listed on page 210. Remember that an expository prompt asks you to explain or inform.
- **Budget your time carefully.**
  Spend several minutes planning and organizing your response. Use the last few minutes to read over what you have written.

As you write . . .

- **Choose a clear focus or thesis for your response.**
  Keep your main idea or purpose in mind as you write.
- **Be selective.**
  Use examples that support your focus.
- **End in a meaningful way.**
  Remind the reader about the importance of the topic.

After you've written a first draft . . .

- **Check for completeness.**
  Use the STRAP questions on page 214 to revise your work.
- **Check for correctness.**
  Check your punctuation, capitalization, spelling, and grammar.

Learning Language

Analyze one of the prompts below using the STRAP questions. Then plan and write a response. Complete your work within the time your teacher gives you.

- In recent years, political debate has often taken a negative, even angry tone. As someone concerned with the tone of political debate, write a set of guidelines to keep debates civil and focused on solving problems at hand.

- People spend their leisure time in a variety of ways. Some play team sports while others pursue pastimes such as cooking and playing music. Write a brief essay explaining one leisure-time activity that you find rewarding. Include details that provide a clear explanation for your classmates.

Persuasive Writing

Writing Focus

Writing an Argumentative Essay	217
Writing an Editorial	259
Responding to Persuasive Prompts	269

Grammar Focus

Subject-Verb Agreement	246
Adjective Clauses	247

Learning Language

Learning these words will help you understand this unit.

1. A **debate** involves presenting opposing ideas on a subject.
   What subjects are debated at your school?

2. To **counter** an argument, explain why it isn't the best idea.
   How might you counter an argument for raising the voting age?

3. Something chosen at **random** is chosen without a reason.
   If you and a friend chose numbers at random, do you think they would be the same?

4. **Leveling the playing field** means making a situation fair.
   In what situation would you level the playing field?

Persuasive Writing
Writing an Argumentative Essay

Perhaps more than any other leader in American history, Abraham Lincoln understood the value of a logical argument. As president, he led the nation during many fierce debates over the ethics of slavery. Lincoln observed, "I am a firm believer in the people. If given the truth, they can be depended upon to meet any national crises. The great point is to bring them the real facts." He believed that people would make the right choice if they understood divergent views and relevant perspectives.

Today, the people of our country are engaging in debate and making decisions about many issues. Some of these issues involve ethics, or moral controversies.

One way to participate in these ethical debates is to write an argumentative essay. An argumentative essay takes a position on one side of a controversy and supports the position with logical, well-organized reasons and details. In this chapter, you'll learn the steps necessary to create an effective argumentative essay that is crafted to move a disinterested or opposed audience.

Writing Guidelines

Subject: **An ethical issue**
Purpose: **To argue for a position**
Form: **Argumentative essay**
Audience: **Classmates, readers of a local newspaper**

"Let me give you a definition of ethics: It is good to maintain and further life; it is bad to damage and destroy life."

—Albert Schweitzer

Persuasive Writing Warm-Up Taking a Stand

When you take a stand, you give your position (opinion) on a controversial issue and support it with logical support. Most current newspapers and magazines will present several issues to choose from. Once you have found a controversy, filling in a pro-con chart is a way to record facts that support each side.

Pro-Con Chart

Issue: Drug companies spend billions of dollars each year advertising prescription drugs directly to people in hopes that they will request the drug from their doctor.

Pro	Con
–Ads help inform people about certain conditions and make them more likely to contact a doctor.	–Ads use marketing techniques that may mislead patients or cause false impressions.
–It is necessary for medical professionals to discuss a prescription drug with a patient before it is prescribed and used.	–Ads may encourage patients to request drugs that are unnecessary and may be harmful.
–Ads increase profits for drug companies, which is their right; they may invest more money in research.	–The money spent on advertising is passed on to patients by raising the prices of the drugs.
–Research and development costs make it necessary for drug companies to make large profits.	–Ads may encourage patients to take drugs when a condition might be treated through diet or exercise without drugs.
–Other medical providers such as doctors, hospitals, and insurance companies can advertise; it's only fair that drug companies can, too.	–Doctors may feel pressured to prescribe a requested drug even if it isn't the best because they fear losing patients.

My Position: Drug companies should be prevented from advertising directly to patients.

Try It!

Look for controversial issues in newspapers and magazines. Select an issue, write it down, and create a pro-con chart to list arguments for each side. Then write your position.

Writing a Persuasive Paragraph

A persuasive paragraph states a position about a controversial topic and uses logical support to defend it. A persuasive paragraph has three main parts:

- The **topic sentence** states the position.
- The **body sentences** support the position and respond to an objection.
- The **closing sentence** restates the position.

Sample Persuasive Paragraph

In the following persuasive paragraph, a writer expresses her position about prescription drug advertising. She uses facts, statistics, and examples she has gathered in her pro-con chart.

Drug Advertising Helps Drug Companies, Not Patients

Topic Sentence: Drug companies should be prevented from advertising their prescription products directly to patients. In 1999, Congress passed more lenient guidelines for drug companies advertising on TV ("The Impact of Direct-to-Consumer Advertising" 1). By 2007, advertising expenses for broadcast media increased to nearly $5 billion. Supporters suggest that advertising helps educate the public about some health conditions and makes it more likely that a patient will discuss a sensitive condition with a doctor. They also believe that drug companies should be able to earn back their large expenditures on research and development using the same advertising options as doctors and other health care providers. However, ads use aggressive marketing techniques that may mislead patients and create false impressions to increase profits. Patients may demand advertised drugs without understanding the side effects or other treatment options. Doctors may be hesitant to refuse a patient's demand because they fear losing patients. *Closing Sentence:* The government should prohibit consumer marketing of prescription drugs like all the other countries in the world (except New Zealand) (ProCon.org).

Write a persuasive paragraph. State your position about the controversy you chose (page **218**), provide reasons from your pro-con chart, respond to an objection, and end by restating or reinforcing your position.

Understanding Your Goal

Your goal in this chapter is to write an argumentative essay that states a thesis about an ethical issue and uses logical reasons to support the position. The traits listed below will help you plan and write your argumentative essay.

Traits of an Argumentative Essay

- **Focus and Coherence**
  Select a topic that involves an ethical controversy, write a position statement, and include logical reasons that support the position.

- **Organization**
  Create a beginning that states your position, a middle that provides support and answers an objection, and an ending that restates your position. Use transition words and phrases to connect your ideas.

- **Development of Ideas**
  Be sure that your position statement is based on logical reasons. Include a range of relevant perspectives and various forms of support.

- **Voice**
  Use a voice that shows understanding of the controversy and commitment to a specific position. Choose fair and precise words to state and defend your position. Write clear, complete sentences with varied beginnings and lengths.

- **Conventions**
  Eliminate errors in grammar, sentence structure, capitalization, punctuation, and spelling.

Literature Connection. Op-ed articles in newspapers give people a chance to present a persuasive argument for a position which may be opposite ("op") from other editorials ("ed"). They feature argumentative essays on current controversies. As you read an op-ed article, it's your job to evaluate the reasons given in support of the writer's position. You can find many op-ed articles in your local daily newspaper.

Writing an Argumentative Essay

Argumentative Essay

An argumentative essay states a position on a controversy and defends it with logically organized reasons and details. In this sample essay, a student writer takes a position on lobbyists giving gifts and raising funds for members of Congress.

Beginning
The introductory paragraph introduces the controversy and states the writer's position (underlined).

Middle
The first middle paragraph presents the first logical reason to support the writer's argument.

The middle paragraphs include facts and examples from reliable, valid sources.

Ban Gifts and Fundraising by Lobbyists

Since the invention of political systems, people have tried to use money and other gifts to influence the actions of politicians. In New York City in the 1800s, William "Boss" Tweed used bribery to corrupt city agencies and rob the city of millions (Martin 434). More recently, in 2006, a scandal involving millions of dollars of payments by lobbyist Jack Abramoff in exchange for preferential treatment for his clients' interests in Congress resulted in the convictions of Abramoff, a member of the House of Representatives, and several other government officials including two White House aides (Abramoff Scandal 1). The current system allows lobbyists to give gifts, provide favors, and raise election funds for members of Congress, a practice that creates a conflict of interest. <u>The best way to remove this conflict from the political system is to ban lobbyists from giving gifts or raising funds for politicians.</u>

First of all, banning all gifts and fundraising by lobbyists will eliminate long-standing relationships in which they purchase political access and influence. Although Congress has tried to tighten restrictions on lobbying activities, there has been little change in the influence of lobbyists or their actions (Spulak 1). Direct gifts to members of Congress and their staff are limited to small amounts, but lobbyists are not prevented from helping raise funds for reelection. In one poll, 65% of Americans said that most elected officials make policy decisions or take actions as a direct result of campaign contributions (*FOXNews.com*). Sometimes, lobbyists even assist directly in writing legislation, adding passages favorable to their corporate clients (LobbyWatch 2).

Banning gifts and fundraising by lobbyists will restore Americans' trust in Congress. Again and again, members of Congress must defend their actions after taking positions favorable to lobbyists who gave them gifts. In another poll, 38% of people indicated that they believed most members of Congress were corrupt (*USAToday.com*). Distrust in public

Persuasive

> **The third middle paragraph presents the writer's most important reason.**

> **The final middle paragraph accurately and honestly represents a divergent view and responds to that objection.**

> **Ending** The concluding paragraph restates the writer's position and adds perspective.

officials has become an epidemic; gifts and fundraising by lobbyists for Congress contribute greatly to that distrust. A ban would create an honest, open environment in which respect for our leaders can grow.

Perhaps most importantly, banning gifts will give typical citizens more opportunity to be heard in Washington. In the same poll, 58% of people believed most members of Congress were more focused on meeting the needs of special interests than on the needs of their constituents. Because many lobbyists are former politicians, they already have more access to members of Congress than common people. Forbidding gifts and fundraising by lobbyists can help level the playing field in Washington so that regular voters can be heard.

Some people might argue that a ban will do little to reduce the buying of influence since such gifts and actions can easily be hidden. However, the same could be said for any number of illegal activities. A ban forces those who wish to buy influence to break the law, and sets up a system of punishment for those who do. An outright ban would be a deterrent and help to prevent corruption.

When many voters look at Congress, they see an institution in which lobbyists are able to buy power and favorable treatment. Sometimes this is true, and sometimes it isn't. In either case, the ability of lobbyists to give gifts and raise funds for politicians stirs controversy and contributes to an environment of mistrust that makes it easy for citizens to turn their backs on the political process. Banning these gifts will not only reduce the undue influence of lobbyists, but it will also bring ordinary citizens back into the political process—and that might improve life for everyone.

Respond to the reading. Answer the following questions.

Organization (1) What is the purpose of the first three middle paragraphs? (2) What is the purpose of the final middle paragraph?

Development of Ideas (3) What is the writer's position on gifts and fundraising by lobbyists? (4) What are the three main reasons that support the writer's position?

Voice (5) Find two or three examples of sentences that illustrate the author's unfavorable view on gifts and fundraising by lobbyists.

Writing an Argumentative Essay

Prewriting

Prewriting begins when you are still deciding on the appropriate genre and topic and ends when you are ready to write your first draft. By breaking an essay into small steps, you'll be well prepared to begin writing.

Keys to Effective Prewriting

1. Choose an ethical controversy of interest to your audience and select a suitable genre.

2. Gather logical reasons and details to help form and support your position. Think about which valid, reliable sources you can include.

3. Write a position statement that focuses your thoughts.

4. Choose a divergent view to address in the middle part of your essay.

5. Create an outline or list to plan your essay.

Prewriting Planning Your Writing

To write in the genre of an argumentative essay, Isabel needed to find an ethical controversy. She searched newspapers, magazines, and news shows and listed controversies. Finally, she put an asterisk beside her choice.

Newspapers and Magazines	News Shows
drug testing for student athletes*	free speech for student newspapers
universal Internet access	mandatory sentencing laws
animal testing for cosmetics	high cost of prescription drugs
federal budget cuts for housing	carbon emissions laws

Select a controversy. Read national newspapers and magazines and watch news broadcasts, making a list of ethical controversies. Put an asterisk (*) next to the controversy you'd like to write about.

Finding Sources

Once you have selected a controversy, you need to use valid, reliable sources for research. Isabel listed primary (firsthand) and secondary (secondhand) sources.

Primary Sources	Secondary Sources
Interviews with: • Coach Colton • school nurse • suspended student • student athletes	Pesca, Mike. "Do Random Tests Keep Teen Athletes Off Steroids?" National Public Radio, 4 Sept. 2009. Web. 25 Sept. 2010. Peterson, Matt. "A Year Later: The Effectiveness of Mandatory High-School Athlete Steroid Testing Under Microscope." Dallas Morning News, 8 Aug. 2009. Web. 25 Sept. 2010. Woolf, Jules. 2009 North American Society for Sports Management Conference. Columbia, South Carolina. 29 May 2010. Speech.

List research sources. Make a source list like the one above. List a variety of sources that may be valid and reliable before checking them more closely.

Identifying and Selecting Support

A well-written argumentative essay uses a variety of details.

- **Facts** are bits of information that can be proven to be true. Use facts from valid and reliable sources to lay the foundation of the controversy.
  Texas began randomly testing high school athletes in 2007, . . . (Peterson)

- **Statistics** are facts that include a numerical value. Use statistics to provide examples that help to illustrate the controversy.
  After spending about $6 million, the testing only returned 19 positive results, 1/20th of 1% of all athletes, . . . (Peterson)

- **Quotations** are the exact words of people involved in the topic. Use quotations to let experts and authorities speak for themselves.
  "Pro sports have, for a long while, forgotten the reason for competition—the love of the game, the pursuit of excellence. Instead of our high school athletes learning from drug-using pros, the pros ought to learn from our kids." (Coach Colton)

- **Anecdotes** are brief stories that make a point. Use anecdotes to demonstrate an abstract idea in a concrete way.
  None of the athletes at Millard Fillmore were tested because the school wasn't selected for testing, and the athletes knew that before the school year began.

Selecting Sources

Consider the validity and reliability of sources before choosing them to use in your research. In general, valid and reliable sources may take a stand on a controversial issue, but they do so on the basis of factual evidence and logical reasoning. Sources may differ on their positions, but they back up their positions with facts and logic. Ask these questions when considering both primary and secondary sources.

- Are your sources objective or do the authors have a biased view they want to promote?
- Are the statistics current?
- Are the quotes from a recognized authority or someone with extensive experience in the area?

Evaluate and select resources. Review your source list using the questions above. Then choose three or four sources to use for your research.

Prewriting Stating Your Position

The next step is writing a preliminary position statement. An effective position statement names the controversy and gives a specific stand or opinion about it.

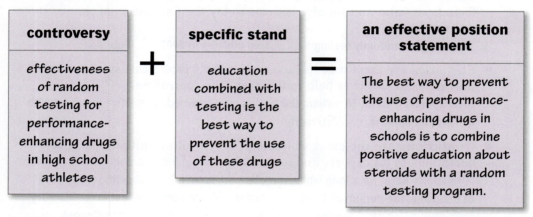

Write a position statement. Use the formula above to create a position statement for your essay. Try two or three versions until you are satisfied.

Supporting Your Position

After taking a position, you need to offer logical reasons and supporting details from your research. Isabel created the chart below to list her support.

Position: Education and random drug tests should be used for high school athletes.

	Reasons	Details
Why?	Education has proven effective.	Costs about 1/10th of testing Tough economy makes education a bargain
Why?	Current fear factor is not effective.	Not enough athletes are tested Creating fear would require too many tests
Why?	Positive education has proven effective.	Relies on students to make good decisions Coaches and parents participate More effective than negative education

Organize support for your position. Create a chart of your own. Write your position. Then add reasons and details that support each reason.

 **TEKS** 12.16B, 12.16D, 12.16G

Writing an Argumentative Essay

Identifying Objections Based on Divergent Views

By accurately and honestly presenting a significant objection to your argument based on a divergent view, you'll show your reader that you fully understand the controversy at hand. Isabel generated a "why not?" chart by adding the word *not* to her position and thinking of as many serious objections as she could. She chose the strongest objection to counter.

Position: Random drug tests and education should *not* be used for high school athletes.
- Why not?   Education is too costly.
- Why not?   Education doesn't work.
- Why not?   Testing alone provides a way for students to say "no." *

 Identify divergent views and objections. Create a "why not?" chart, like the one above, identifying at least three serious objections to your argument. Choose the strongest objection to counter in your essay.

Countering an Objection

To counter an objection, anticipate how your audience will respond. Then list ways you might counter the objection that use an appropriate level of formality, style, and tone.

Objection: Testing alone provides a way for students to say "no."
1. Education doesn't remove reasons to say "no" based on testing.
2. Education uses role play to help students practice saying "no."

 Counter an important objection. Write down the strongest objection to your argument. List reasons that refute or minimize the objection using an appropriate level of formality, style, and tone.

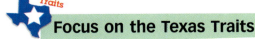

Focus on the Texas Traits

Development of Ideas Be sure to do enough research to identify the complete range of relevant perspectives. By considering all perspectives, you can be sure your essay doesn't avoid any important objections.

Prewriting Outlining Your Essay

Before actually writing your essay, it is a good idea to organize your reasons and supporting details in an outline or a list. Isabel created a sentence outline. Always consider the purpose of your essay, your audience, and the context as you plan.

Sentence Outline

Position Statement: The best way to prevent the use of performance-enhancing drugs in our schools is to combine positive education with a random testing program.

I. The cost of education compared to testing is minimal.
   A. Dr. Elliott said some programs cost 1/10 of testing.
   B. Education seems to be a bargain when budgets are small.

II. The "fear factor" of getting caught using steroids in random tests isn't strong enough to make a big difference.
   A. 97% of athletes weren't tested in Texas in 2007–2008.
   B. None of the athletes at Millard Fillmore were tested.
   C. Athletes knew they wouldn't be tested during the summer.
   D. An Oregon study showed that nearly 50% needed to be tested for the fear factor to be powerful.

III. Positive education about steroid use has been shown to work.
   A. Students can make good decisions with accurate information.
   B. It supplies information on improving performance in healthy ways.
   C. Coaches and parents often participate in the programs.
   D. These programs are more effective than ones focusing on only negative effects.

IV. Supporters of testing point to the need to give students a way to resist peer pressure or pressure from adults.
   A. Education programs add to students' skills at saying "no" by using role play and simulations to practice.
   B. Adding education to random testing gives students a reason to say "no" and experience at doing it.

Create an outline. Organize your reasons and supporting details in an outline or a list. Consider the purpose, audience, and context for your essay.

Writing an Argumentative Essay

Drafting

After selecting a topic, researching it, writing a position statement, and organizing your essay, you are ready to write your first draft.

Keys to Effective Drafting

1. Use your outline or list as a writing guide, closely following it as you work.

2. Write on every other line or double-space if you are using a computer. This will allow room for changes.

3. In the first paragraph, introduce the controversy and provide your thesis statement.

4. Include a topic sentence in each middle paragraph. These paragraphs provide support for your thesis.

5. In the last middle paragraph, answer a significant objection from a range of relevant perspectives.

6. End by restating your position and sharing an insight with your audience.

Drafting Getting the Big Picture

The graphic below shows how the elements of an argumentative essay work together. Use this graphic as a guide to help you write your first draft. (The examples are from the student essay on pages 231–234.)

Beginning

The **introductory** paragraph introduces the controversy and states the writer's position.

Position Statement
The best way to prevent the use of performance-enhancing drugs in schools is to combine positive education about steroids with a random testing program.

Middle

Each **middle** paragraph supports the writer's position statement in a way that is appropriate for the purpose, audience, and context.

The last middle paragraph accurately and honestly responds to an objection with logical reasons.

Topic Sentences
First, the cost of education compared to testing is minimal.

Second, the "fear factor" associated with getting caught using steroids through random testing isn't strong enough to make a great difference.

Most importantly, positive education about steroid use has been shown to work in several studies.

Of, course, supporters of random drug testing alone point to the need to give students a way to resist peer pressure or pressure from adults.

Ending

The **concluding** paragraph puts the controversy in perspective.

Closing Sentence
It's time to level the playing field again, *without* steroids in the balance.

Writing an Argumentative Essay

Beginning Your Essay

The introductory paragraph of your essay should engage your reader, introduce your topic, and provide your position statement.

- **Engage your reader.** Begin with a sentence that will capture your reader's interest and attention.

  In 2005, scandal rocked the world of professional baseball as allegations of the use of steroids and other performance-enhancing drugs hit the headlines.

- **Introduce your topic.** Include details that expand on your opening.

  Since then, leagues, Congress, state legislatures, and health officials have all weighed in on ways to prevent adults and teenagers from using these potentially deadly drugs.

- **Provide your position statement.** The thesis statement clearly and concisely states your position on the controversy.

  The best way to prevent the use of performance-enhancing drugs in schools is to combine positive education about steroids with a random testing program.

> Beginning
> Middle
> Ending

Introductory Paragraph

The controversy is introduced.

In 2005, scandal rocked the world of professional baseball as allegations of the use of steroids and other performance-enhancing drugs hit the headlines. Since then, leagues, Congress, state legislatures, and health officials have all weighed in on ways to prevent adults and teenagers from using these potentially deadly drugs. Texas began randomly testing high school athletes in 2007, testing about 3% of athletes—about 45,000—over a two-year period. It was the largest and most expensive testing program in history. After spending about $6 million, the testing only returned 19 positive results, 1/20th of 1% of all athletes, and funding was greatly reduced for the next year (Peterson). But efforts to prevent steroid use shouldn't be abandoned or continued without change. <u>The best way to prevent the use of performance-enhancing drugs in schools is to combine positive education about steroids with a random testing program.</u>

The position statement is given (underlined).

Write an introductory paragraph. Be sure to engage your reader, introduce your topic, and provide a clear thesis statement.

Drafting Developing the Middle Part

The middle part of your essay supports your position with reasons and details appropriate to your purpose, audience and context. It also answers a significant objection to your position. Remember to refer to your outline or list (page 228) as you write.

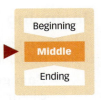

Linking Your Ideas

Transition words and phrases help you connect your ideas. You can use transitions to connect your paragraphs, showing the order of importance of your reasons and signaling your answer to an objection.

Reason 1	Reason 2	Reason 3	Answer to Objection
First of all	Secondly	Most importantly	Even so, some people . . .
To begin	In addition	The biggest reason	Granted, opponents say . . .
For starters	Also	The main issue	Of course, critics allege . . .

You can also use transitions to show other relationships between ideas, such as time, cause and effect, comparison and contrast, and added information.

Time	Cause	Contrast	More Information
When	Consequently	Although	For example
After	As a result	However	Besides
At first	Because	Nevertheless	In addition

Middle Paragraphs

A topic sentence (underlined) introduces the main idea of each middle paragraph.

<u>First, the cost of education compared to testing is minimal.</u> Dr. Diane Elliott, professor of medicine and a researcher on random drug testing at Oregon Health and Science University, said there are programs that are proven to work that cost the same as three sports drinks per student. "It's one tenth of what one drug test costs," she said (Peterson). At a time when school districts are struggling to pay for even basic programs because of the slow economy, effective education on steroids seems to be a bargain.

<u>Second, the "fear factor" associated with getting caught using steroids through random testing isn't strong enough to make a great difference.</u> Even with the extensive and costly

Writing an Argumentative Essay

The body of each paragraph supports the paragraph's topic sentence.

testing program used in Texas in 2007–2008, 97% of athletes knew they weren't going to be tested. None of the athletes at Millard Fillmore were tested because the school wasn't selected for testing and the athletes knew that before the school year began. Athletes also knew that no tests would be administered during the summer, giving them a window for steroid use without fear. An Oregon study showed that for the fear of getting caught to become significant in students' minds, the number tested needed to be nearly 50%, which would involve more than 350,000 tests each year in Texas—more than ten times the number administered in 2007 and 2008 (Pesca).

The middle paragraphs build to the most important reason.

Most importantly, positive education about steroid use has been shown to work in several studies. This type of education provides the facts about steroids, both positive and negative, relying on high school students to make good decisions when given accurate information. It also supplies information on ways to improve athletic performance in healthy ways, such as improved nutrition and weight training. Coaches and parents, who have a strong effect on players' attitudes and actions, often participate in the educational programs and discussions. These types of programs have been shown to be more effective in changing attitudes about steroids than ones that only focus on the negative effects of steroids (Woolf).

The last middle paragraph responds to a significant objection.

Of course, supporters of random drug testing alone point to the need to give students a way to resist peer pressure or pressure from adults. They say that the possibility of drug testing provides them with an easy answer for turning down steroids. While this is true, educational programs add to students' skills at saying "no" by using role plays and simulations to practice those skills. Adding education to random testing gives students both a reason to say "no" and some experience at doing it (Woolf).

Write the middle. Using your outline (page 228), write middle paragraphs that are appropriate for your purpose, audience, and context. These paragraphs should effectively support your position and counter an objection.

Drafting Ending Your Essay

You have stated your position, supported it with reasons and details, and responded to an objection. Now you are ready to write your concluding paragraph. To do the job effectively, consider your purpose, audience, and context and use the following guidelines:

- Restate your position clearly and concisely.
- Sum up the main reasons for supporting your position.
- Summarize your response to the significant objection.
- Include an insight for your reader.

Concluding Paragraph

The position is restated.

The paragraph sums up the support and ends with a final thought.

Combining positive education with random testing for high school athletes is the best way to prevent kids from using steroids. Right now, all across the United States, thousands of kids are risking their lives for the sake of bigger muscles. Carl Colton, coach of the Fillmore High School wrestling team, said, "Pro sports have, for a long while, forgotten the reason for competition—the love of the game, the pursuit of excellence. Instead of our high school athletes learning from drug-using pros, the pros ought to learn from our kids." The best way to stop this trend is to make education and random drug testing of high school athletes mandatory and give them the knowledge, reasons, and experience to say "no." It's time to level the playing field again, without steroids in the balance.

Write your conclusion. Write a concluding paragraph to summarize your position and your answer to an objection. Include a final thought or an insight for the reader.

Prepare a complete first draft. Write a clean copy of your entire essay. Double-space if you use a computer, or write on every other line if you write by hand, so that you have room to make revision notes.

Revising

The revision process makes your initial draft better. When you revise, you add or delete details, reorganize parts of your writing, and improve your writing voice. You also check word choice and sentence style.

Keys to Effective Revising

1. Read your essay aloud and note parts where you need to clarify your meaning or that sound unconvincing.

2. Make sure you have clearly stated your position.

3. Check the order and unity of your middle paragraphs. Rearrange them as necessary.

4. Be sure you use an informed, confident, and persuasive voice. Add transitional words or phrases to help the flow.

5. Check your essay for strong word choice, a variety of sentence structures, and a consistent tone.

6. Use the editing and proofreading marks on pages 638–639.

Revising for Focus and Coherence

When you revise for *focus and coherence,* you make sure that your position statement is focused and clear. All parts of your essay should support your position or relate to it.

Is my position statement focused and clear?

Your position statement is focused and clear if it presents an issue that can be addressed in an essay and if there is no doubt about your position. Here are three problems to avoid.

- **Position statements that are too general** prevent you from arguing a specific point.

  Seniors should have a lot more freedom at school.
  (A better position statement would be "Seniors should have an open campus if they meet certain guidelines.")

- **Position statements that are uncertain** leave readers with doubt about your position.

  A universal health care plan might work in the United States.
  (A better position statement would be "A universal health care plan would cut costs and improve medical care in the United States.")

- **Position statements that don't rely on facts** prevent you from arguing for a position using valid sources.

  Movies today are more exciting than they were 50 years ago.
  (A better position statement would be "Advanced technology has made modern movies more reliant on special effects and less attentive to character development.")

Exercise

Read the following position statements and write an improved statement for each one.

1. Michael Jordan was a great basketball player.
2. Spending on schools doesn't seem high enough.
3. Parents shouldn't have too much say in school decisions.
4. People convicted of crimes shouldn't have the same rights as others.
5. Nuclear power costs a lot, but it doesn't pollute the air.

Review your position statement. Does it present an issue that can be addressed in an essay? Is there any doubt about your position? If necessary, revise your position statement so it is more focused.

Writing an Argumentative Essay

Is my essay coherent?

Every paragraph and sentence in a coherent argumentative essay supports or relates to your position statement. A coherent essay also presents a complete, unified approach to the topic. Remove or change sentences such as those that follow:

- Interesting facts or anecdotes don't always relate to your position.

    Position: Our town needs to invest more in our schools.
    Sentence: The first school in our town was built in 1827.
    (The sentence doesn't relate to the current school situation.)

- Some facts don't provide support for your position.

    Position: Downloading music from the Internet should be free.
    Sentence: Most Web sites provide information at no cost.
    (The sentence doesn't address the issue of music copyrights.)

- Introducing other topics may weaken the coherence.

    Position: Health insurance companies should not be allowed to decide what medical treatments are needed.
    Sentence: Doctors get paid too much money to perform routine tests.
    (The issue of doctors' payments is a separate issue from insurance company power.)

Exercise

Read the following position statement and indicate whether you would use, eliminate, or change each sentence to increase focus and coherence.

Position: The federal government should not bail out large banks or corporations with taxpayers' money.

1. Smaller companies are forced to succeed or fail on their own.
2. Our family has bought cars made in America for nearly one hundred years.
3. Small businesses need to get more tax breaks so they can compete.
4. Our taxes should not go to help private companies or individuals make profits.
5. One way to support new business ideas and investments is to let older companies fail.
6. If the government wants to help the economy, it should lower taxes.

Review your essay. Do all of your sentences support your position or relate to it? Does your essay present a complete, unified approach to the subject? If necessary, eliminate or change sentences that detract from the focus and coherence.

 Revising for Organization

When you revise for *organization,* you make sure your introduction and conclusion work together and your middle paragraphs are in the best order. The order of your reasons should be clear, and the ideas in your sentences should be connected.

Do my introduction and conclusion work together?

Your introduction and conclusion work together if they use the same persuasive strategy to convince the reader. Consider the purpose of your essay, your audience, and the context. Here are three strategies to make your introduction and conclusion work together as a team:

1. Begin with a **problem** and end with your **solution**.
2. Begin with a **question** and end with your **answer**.
3. Begin with a **common belief** and end with your **specific position**.

Exercise

For each introduction and conclusion listed below, indicate which strategy (1, 2, or 3) is used.

1. **Introduction:** Aside from diet, exercise, and lifestyle, what other factor most affects longevity?
   Conclusion: The other factor that affects longevity is money—and the access it provides to health care. This situation is unfair, and it needs to change.
2. **Introduction:** Every person in the United States has a heart, a stomach, and a brain, but over 45 million of those people do not have health care coverage.
   Conclusion: Government of the people, by the people, and for the people must make sure that all the people receive adequate health care coverage.
3. **Introduction:** Health insurance companies, in order to protect their profitability, are free to deny coverage to those who most need it.
   Conclusion: A government-sponsored health care program is a more equitable way to ensure adequate health care for everyone.

Revise

Check your introduction and conclusion. Make sure your introduction and conclusion work together for your argumentative essay's purpose, audience, and context. If they do not, revise them using one of the strategies above.

Writing an Argumentative Essay

Are my middle paragraphs in the best order?

In an ideal argumentative essay, all of your arguments and support would be equally strong. In reality, that is not always the case. It is important to remember that your middle paragraphs should not be arranged randomly. When middle paragraphs are arranged in the best order for your purpose, audience, and context, they are organized by importance. Here are three strategies for organizing your middle paragraphs:

1. **Start strong.** You may want to place your most important reason first, give other reasons next, and end your argumentative essay with your answer to an objection.
2. **End strong.** You may want to begin with your least important reason and build to the most important reason. Then answer an objection in your last middle paragraph.
3. **Try 2-3-1.** You may want to begin with your second most important reason, provide your least important reason, and finish with your strongest reason. Then answer an objection in the last middle paragraph of your argumentative essay.

Exercise

Read the following reasons for universal health care and decide on an order for them. Indicate which strategy you chose and why.

1. Lack of universal health care harms children most.
2. Though some people point to higher taxes for socialized medicine, U.S. citizens already pay exorbitant amounts for medical insurance.
3. Citizens of Western nations with socialized medicine live an average of five years longer than citizens of the United States.
4. Universal health care would reduce infant mortality rates.
5. The United States is the only industrialized nation without universal health care coverage.
6. Tens of millions of Americans go uninsured each day.

Check the order of your reasons. If your reasons do not have a clear order, use one of the strategies above to reorganize them. Remember your purpose, audience, and context.

Organization
Changes ensure that the introduction and conclusion work together.

Combining positive
∧ ~~Education and~~ random testing for high school athletes is the
　　　　　∧ with
best way to prevent kids from using steroids.

When you revise for the *development of ideas,* you make sure you have dealt fairly with your own position as well as with opposing views. Your goal is to move a disinterested or opposed audience, but you must do so by backing up your assertions and treating divergent views fairly.

Have I presented my ideas fairly?

When you revise your work, you will want to be sure that you have presented your ideas fairly and avoided using logical fallacies. Consider these examples:

- **Fair:** Most Europeans oppose testing cosmetics on animals for ethical reasons.
  Unfair: Most Europeans oppose testing cosmetics on animals, so we should, too.
  (Avoid bandwagoning, which implies that the reader should agree because most other people do. The better argument states why we should oppose it.)

- **Fair:** About 10 percent of the animals used for scientific research are involved in product testing, amounting to millions of animals each year.
  Unfair: Who knows how many animals die in product testing each year?
  (Avoid appeals to ignorance, which use a lack of evidence to try to prove something. A little research would tell how many animals are involved.)

- **Fair:** Scientists could be researching alternative product-testing methods.
  Unfair: Scientists should be curing cancer, not putting lipstick on rats.
  (Scientists who specialize in cosmetics probably are not experts on cancer. Avoid oversimplification, which reduces complex situations to overly simple ones.)

Exercise

Read the sentences below and identify the logical fallacy in each one.

1. If the government banned animal testing of cosmetics and drugs, all that would happen is that people wouldn't have such nice mascara.
2. Whenever you buy blush, imagine how many animals were tortured for it.
3. Millions of caring people reject cosmetic testing on animals, and you should, too!
4. You don't put eyeliner on your cat, and neither should scientists.

Present your position fairly. As you present your views, avoid bandwagoning, appeals to ignorance or strong emotions, and oversimplification. If necessary, rewrite statements to eliminate errors in logic.

Writing an Argumentative Essay

Have I presented divergent views fairly?

In trying to move a disinterested or opposed audience, you need to have presented divergent views accurately and honestly. You will also need to anticipate reasonable objections to your argument and describe them fairly. Then you will need to address the divergent views decisively, demonstrating that your argument is the stronger one.

- **Fair:** Proponents of animal testing believe it is important for scientific advancement as well as for the benefit of human health.
  Unfair: Either we end all testing of cosmetics on animals, or we have no compassion at all.
  (It's unfair to assume opponents have no compassion. Avoid either-or thinking, which allows for no other viewpoints.)

- **Fair:** Many people think that animal testing is an important part of determining a product's safety.
  Unfair: Of course, the animal haters see no problem with cosmetics testing.
  (It's unfair to call opponents "animal haters." Avoid slanted language that insults the person or position instead of arguing against it.)

Exercise

Read the sentences below and identify the logical fallacy in each one.

1. People who support animal testing must love seeing chimps with rouge.
2. Either we ban cosmetics testing, or every animal in the world will be in danger.
3. If we don't stop animal testing right now, we'll face a "gorilla" war.
4. Heartless scientists should try to remember their childhoods—if they ever were children.

Development of Ideas
Slanted language is removed.

> Some ~~people just~~ [civil rights activists] want to ~~cover up the problem and get rid of~~ [end] testing completely. But efforts to prevent steroid use [believing that it violates student privacy rights] shouldn't be abandoned or continued without change.

Revise

Be fair to divergent views. Read your essay and watch for either-or thinking and slanted language. Remove any you find.

Revising for Voice

When you revise for *voice,* you make sure you have used the correct level of language to move a disinterested or opposed audience. Different levels of language also help you adjust your style and tone appropriately.

Have I used the correct level of language?

You have used the correct level of language if you use a semiformal voice. Here are three levels of voice:

- **Formal voice** avoids contractions, humor, colloquial expressions, slang, and personal references to the writer. A formal voice often has complex sentence structures and uses a wide vocabulary.
- **Semiformal voice** occasionally uses contractions and appropriate humor, colloquial expressions, and personal references to the writer. A semiformal voice avoids slang.
- **Informal voice** is full of contractions, humor, colloquial expressions, slang, and many personal references to the writer. An informal voice resembles an everyday conversation and is used in casual writing, such as friendly notes and letters.

Exercise

Read each sentence below and decide whether the level of language is formal, semiformal, or informal. Rewrite formal or informal sentences to create an appropriate level of language.

1. Governmental interventions into the privacy of citizens through such means as non-court-ordered wiretaps should be eliminated.
2. Those Washington bigwigs maybe got it in their brains they can do whatever they want, but they got a big-time wake-up call coming.
3. Private phone lines are called private for a reason, and the government doesn't have the right to listen in on every call I make to Aunt Millie.
4. I say it's time to toss the fat cats from Capitol Hill.
5. Well, Washington's politicians have done it again, butting their noses where they don't belong.

Check your level of language. Read your draft, making sure that you have used a semiformal level of language to create an appropriate style and tone. Revise parts that sound too formal or informal.

How can I move a disinterested or opposed audience?

One way to sway a disinterested or opposed audience is through the use of a rhetorical device such as an anecdote, a brief story that touches on a person's sense of logic, emotions, or ethical beliefs. Attentively crafted anecdotes used to back up assertions are more engaging than simple lists of details. The following example of an anecdote appeals to both the reader's sense of humor and to feelings of respect.

> *Thomas Jefferson was America's ambassador to France in the 1780s. Soon after taking the position, Jefferson was visited by a French minister for foreign affairs. The French foreign minister remarked, "You replace Monsieur [Benjamin] Franklin," to which Jefferson replied, "I* succeed *him. No one could replace him."*

Anecdotes in argumentative essays convey a semiformal tone. They may have the effect of making the style of the essay more personal by relating specific examples for the reader.

To identify an appropriate anecdote to include in your argumentative essay, ask yourself the following questions:

1. What experiences have I had that demonstrate the problem?
2. What experiences have people in my school had that show the effects of the controversy?
3. What experiences have people in my community had that show the effects of the controversy?
4. What stories in the news media provide examples that support my position?
5. Are there any historical anecdotes that are relevant to my position?

In addition to anecdotes, other examples of rhetorical devices that can move disinterested or opposed readers include simile, metaphor, allusion, analogy, irony, paradox, and understatement. See pages **634–635** for definitions and examples.

Revise

Use an anecdote. Consider adding an anecdote or other rhetorical device to back up your assertions and move a disinterested or opposing audience by appealing to the audience's logic, emotions, or ethical beliefs.

Revising Improving Your Writing

Check your revising. On a piece of paper, write the numbers 1 to 14. If you answer "yes" to a question below, put a check mark next to that number. If not, continue to work on that part of your essay.

Revising Checklist

Focus and Coherence

_____ 1. Do I state my position clearly?
_____ 2. Do all my sentences support my position statement or relate to it?
_____ 3. Does the essay provide a unified approach to the topic?

Organization

_____ 4. Do my introduction and conclusion work together well?
_____ 5. Have I chosen the best order for my middle paragraphs?
_____ 6. Are my reasons connected logically?

Development of Ideas

_____ 7. Have I effectively supported each topic sentence?
_____ 8. Have I fairly presented my position?
_____ 9. Have I fairly and accurately presented a divergent view?
_____ 10. Have I countered an objection?

Voice

_____ 11. Have I used the right level of language?
_____ 12. Is my voice appropriate for the purpose, audience, and context?
_____ 13. Is my tone consistent?
_____ 14. Have I used a variety of sentence structures?

Make a clean copy. When you are finished with your revision, make a clean copy of your essay for editing.

Writing an Argumentative Essay

Editing

Now that you have finished revising your argumentative essay, you are ready to edit for grammar, sentence structure, capitalization, punctuation, and spelling.

Keys to Effective Editing

1. Use a dictionary, a thesaurus, and the "Proofreader's Guide" in the back of this book to check your writing.

2. Check your writing for errors in grammar, sentence structure, capitalization, punctuation, and spelling.

3. Edit on a clean, revised copy of your essay. Then either enter the changes on your computer file or write a new handwritten copy that includes the changes.

4. Use the editing and proofreading marks on pages 638–639.

Grammar

When you edit for *conventions,* you correct errors in grammar, sentence structure, capitalization, punctuation, and spelling.

How can I check subject-verb agreement?

Check subject-verb agreement by making sure subjects and verbs have the same number. If the subject is singular, the verb must be singular. If the subject is plural, the verb must be plural.

> The **doctrine** of preemptive war **has** many detractors.
> **Critics argue** that preemptive war is like punishing a person before any crime has been committed.

Note: In the first example, a prepositional phrase comes between the subject and verb. It does not affect subject-verb agreement.

Compound Subjects

If the compound subjects are joined by *and,* use a plural verb.

> The **president** and **the secretary of defense contend** that it is better to preempt an attack than retaliate after one has taken place.

If the subjects are joined by *or* or *nor,* match the verb to the nearest subject.

> Even so, neither **diplomacy** *nor* **war has eliminated** terrorism.

Indefinite Pronouns

Some indefinite pronouns are singular: *each, either, neither, one, everybody, another, anybody, everyone, nobody, everything, somebody,* and *someone.*

> **Nobody wants** war.

Some indefinite pronouns are plural: *both, few, many,* and *several.*

> **Many believe** that war is necessary to stop tyranny.

Some indefinite pronouns are singular or plural, depending on the object in the prepositional phrase that follows the pronoun: *all, any, most, none,* and *some.*

> **Most** of the **world participates** in the war on terrorism.
> **Most** of the **nations,** however, **oppose** the doctrine of preemptive war.

Check agreement. Read your argumentative essay and check for the agreement of your subjects and verbs. Make any necessary corrections.

Have I used adjective clauses effectively?

An adjective clause is a subordinate clause that, like an adjective, modifies a noun or pronoun. A subordinate clause, which cannot stand alone as a sentence, is a group of words containing a subject and predicate.

Examples The house where he was born has been made into a museum.
(The clause *where he was born* modifies the word *house*.)

She is the one who earned her awards.
(The clause *who earned her awards* modifies the noun *one*.)

This poem, which I wrote last year, is about the first home I lived in.
(The clause *which I wrote last year* modifies the noun *poem*.)

He is an author whose works have influenced generations of readers.
(The clause *whose works have influenced generations of readers* modifies the noun *author*.)

Exercise

Rewrite each item below to form one sentence that contains an adjective clause.

1. Every member of Congress must vote his conscience. Each member represents a different district.
2. Each voter must cherish their right to vote. Our ancestors fought for that right.
3. The politician should take his or her responsibilities seriously. The politician wants to be reelected.
4. Both senators and representatives should work together on the bills. The bills deal with climate change.

Edit

Check your use of adjective clauses. Read your essay carefully, checking to make sure that you are using adjective clauses to improve your writing. Make any necessary corrections.

Try It!

Form pairs to write down four sentences that contain adjective clauses. You might want to use the examples above as models. Then, check to make sure the subject-verb agreement in each sentence is correct. Pairs should then alternate reading the sentences aloud with the listener identifying the antecedent, or modified noun or pronoun, in each sentence.

Sentence Structure

When you revise for *sentence structure,* you check to see whether you have used long and short sentences effectively.

What are the best ways to use long and short sentences?

Writers often use short, simple sentences to make an important point. When constructed carefully, short sentences pack a powerful punch—and improve sentence rhythm.

Longer sentences may be used to provide detailed information about a complicated issue. These longer sentences answer questions about *who, what, when, where, how,* and *why* an action takes place. Consider this sentence:

Stem-cell researchers conduct experiments.

This short sentence answers *who* (stem-cell researchers) and *what* (conduct experiments), but it does not provide other details the reader needs, such as *where, why,* and *how*. By adding these answers to the original short sentence, you can create a long sentence that is full of detail. Review the following paragraph:

Both sides of the stem-cell research controversy believe they hold the moral high ground. Those who oppose stem-cell research feel they are advocating for the tens of thousands of frozen embryos that scientists may use in their research. Those who favor stem-cell research feel they are advocating for the millions of people living with neuromuscular diseases. Both sides are correct. Albert Schweitzer once said, "It is good to maintain and further life; it is bad to damage and destroy life." These are wise words. The best use of stem-cell research maintains and furthers life on both ends of the scale—using adult instead of embryonic stem cells. In states where it is allowed, stem-cell researchers conduct experiments by injecting undifferentiated cells into damaged areas to reconstruct tissues.

Exercise

Using the paragraph above, answer the following questions.

1. Find the two short, simple sentences. Why are they so powerful?
2. Select two other longer sentences. Identify which of the following questions they answer: Who? What? When? Where? How? Why?

Revise

Review your sentences. Read your writing and identify short and long sentences. Is there enough variety to keep the reader interested? Do you use short sentences to make important points? Do the longer sentences provide needed details? If not, vary your sentence structure to meet the needs of your purpose, audience, and context.

Mechanics: Punctuation

Commas after introductory words, phrases, and clauses

Introductory words, phrases, and clauses should be separated from the main, independent clause by a comma to make reading easier and to prevent misreading. Look at the samples below, which indicate correct usage, to see how the sentence might be misread without the comma.

> **Underneath, the ground was dry.**
>
> Misread without the comma: **Underneath the ground . . . .**
>
> **In all, the class created fifteen stories.**
>
> Misread without the comma: **In all the class . . . .**
>
> **Although she angrily fought, the group was eventually convinced.**
>
> Misread without the comma: **Although she angrily fought the group. . . .**

Exercise

Each of the sentences below was taken from the sample argumentative essay. Select the right place to insert a comma to separate an introductory word, phrase, or clause from the main, independent clause.

1. First the cost of education compared to testing is minimal.
2. At a time when school districts are struggling to pay for even basic programs because of the slow economy effective education on steroids seems to be a bargain.
3. Most importantly positive education about steroid use has been shown to work in several studies.
4. While this is true educational programs add to students' skills at saying "no" by using role plays and simulations to practice those skills.
5. Right now all across the United States, thousands of kids are risking their lives for the sake of bigger muscles.

Revise

Review your use of commas. Read your writing. Identify sentences with introductory words, phrases or clauses. Have you separated them from the main, independent clause with a comma? If not, add commas to make reading easier.

Editing Checking for Conventions

Check your editing. On a piece of paper, write the numbers 1 to 12. If you can answer "yes" to a question below, put a check mark beside that number. If you can't, continue to edit for that convention.

Editing Checklist

Conventions

GRAMMAR

_____ 1. Do my subjects and verbs agree in number?
_____ 2. Have I effectively used adjective clauses?
_____ 3. Do the subjects of my clauses agree with their antecedents, or the words they modify?

SENTENCE STRUCTURE

_____ 4. Do I use and form complex sentences correctly?
_____ 5. Do I use a variety of long and short sentences?

MECHANICS (CAPITALIZATION AND PUNCTUATION)

_____ 6. Do I start all my sentences with capital letters?
_____ 7. Do I capitalize all proper nouns and adjectives?
_____ 8. Do I use end punctuation after all my sentences?
_____ 9. Do I use commas after long introductory phrases and clauses?
_____ 10. Have I correctly punctuated quotations?

SPELLING

_____ 11. Have I checked for commonly misused pairs?
_____ 12. Have I consulted a dictionary to determine or check spellings of words my spell-checker may have missed?

Creating a Title

After your editing is complete, add a title that engages your reader and sums up the content of your essay. Here are a few ways to create an effective essay title.

- Call the reader to action: **Test for Performance Drugs Now**
- Take a position: **Performance Drug Testing Just Makes Sense**
- Be creative: **Stop Steroids Cold**

Publishing

Feedback, Revising and Publishing

The purpose of an argumentative essay is to take a position on a controversial issue and defend that position with various forms of support. The final steps in the process involve gaining feedback from peers and teachers, revising in accordance with the feedback, selecting an appropriate audience for publishing, and creating a final copy for publishing.

Gaining Feedback

After you have revised and edited your essay, it's always best to have at least one person read and comment on your work. This might involve peers or teachers. Follow these guidelines in selecting your reviewers.

- Ask peers and teachers if they would be willing to review your work.
- Ask them to be honest in their appraisal without criticizing you personally.
- Determine if they are more comfortable providing written or verbal feedback. If they choose verbal feedback, be prepared to take notes on their views.

Revising in Accordance with Feedback

Consider the comments by peers and teachers seriously. Also remember that your own thoughts and voice are what make your writing unique and powerful. Try revisions that your reviewers suggest and then decide whether they have improved your essay. Revise your essay accordingly.

Selecting an Appropriate Audience

- Review the topic of your essay to help select an appropriate audience for publishing it.
- If your topic relates only to your school or local community, consider publishing to your class or school, relatives and friends, or local Web sites or newspapers.
- If your topic relates to state, national, or international issues, consider publishing to Web sites and newspapers that serve a larger audience.

Creating a Final Copy

Review the guidelines for submission to your chosen publishing site and prepare your essay to meet the requirements.

Evaluating an Argumentative Essay

To learn how to evaluate an argumentative essay, you will use the holistic scoring guide on pages **36–37** and the essays below. These essays are examples of writing for each score on the scoring guide (1–4).

Notice that the first essay received a score of 4. Read the description for a score of 4 on pages **36–37**. Then read the persuasive essay. Use the same steps to study the other examples. As you read, concentrate on the overall quality of the writing in each example.

Writing that fits a score of 4 is very strong.

4

Stop Testing Cosmetics on Animals

> The essay has a meaningful, focused introduction.

What is your definition of a bad day? Imagine this one. You are strapped down to a table so you cannot move. One of your eyelids is permanently pried open. A cosmetic product such as shampoo, mascara, or hair spray is dripped into your eye. That's what life is like for rabbits subjected to the Draize test, which is just one of the cruel ways in which animals are used to test cosmetics products. The Draize test helps determine how human eyes might respond to the product being tested. However, there are other ways to test cosmetics that don't involve cruelty to animals. That's why animal testing of cosmetics should stop immediately.

> Specific details illustrate the writer's main points.

There is little doubt that cosmetics products need to be tested for safety before people can use them. Unsafe or poorly tested cosmetics products have the potential to severely injure or even kill the their users. But the problem is that animals are dying every day to ensure this safety. Each year, hundreds of thousands of rabbits, mice, and other small mammals die painful, prolonged, and unnecessary deaths. Is it really necessary to kill this many animals in order to ensure that products are safe? And more important, is it fair?

Further, testing cosmetic products on laboratory animals does not always predict how the products may affect people. Each year, for example, thousands of laboratory animals are force-fed cosmetics and cosmetics ingredients to see if they will die. But not all things that are poisonous to animals are poisonous to humans. Laboratory animals may be experiencing pain and even death for no reason.

Perhaps the most important reason for eliminating animal-based cosmetics testing is that cost-effective and accurate alternatives exist. Long ago when the Draize test was invented, there was no alternative to using live animals for testing. Now, laboratories can use human tissue grown in a laboratory culture to test products. Computer and mathematical models can also be used. This combination of alternatives can produce safe cosmetics without cruelty.

In addition, many cosmetics makers have discovered that using ingredients from nature is a great way to avoid the need for animal testing and to sell more products. People have known the effect of herbs, vegetable oils, and other natural ingredients for years. Today's health-conscious consumers are asking for products that use these natural ingredients instead of chemicals. The companies who use them in their products are getting more attention than ever.

The companies that still use animal testing for their cosmetics products might argue that animal testing is necessary, and that without such tests, they would need to go out of business. The success of hundreds of cosmetics companies that do not use animal testing proves that this argument is false. By using a combination of all-natural ingredients and cruelty-free testing, these companies are creating high-quality products that attract loyal customers and produce profits.

In the end, those who continue to use cruel animal testing will probably be forced to change their methods anyway. Starting in 2009, the nations of the European Union (EU) banned animal testing for most ingredients; a complete ban will take effect in 2013. Those companies that do the right thing now by eliminating animal testing will be sparing the lives of innocent animals and improving their chances to sell their products. That combination is a win for animals and for humans.

Smooth transitions help the reader move from one idea to the next.

The author addresses and responds to an objection.

The unique voice of the writer is apparent.

Writing that fits a score of 3 is effective in most ways.

Americans Need Relief From High Prescription Costs

A key focus of the debate over healthcare reform is how we can make prescription drugs more affordable for the people who need them. American consumers have faced this problem for more than a decade, and members of Congress have debated possible solutions. As the debate has raged on, prescription drug prices have continued to rise, and many people who need medication have paid the price. It is time for the debate to end, and for Congress to pass a bill limiting drug price increases. Such limits would benefit us all.

In recent years, the price of prescription drugs has skyrocketed, making them unaffordable for many Americans. The cost of a month's supply for medication for many common conditions can run into hundreds or even, thousands of dollars. All evidence shows that these prices will continue to rise at rates that are astronomical. At the same time, worker salaries are staying the same or even dropping. This means that the affordability gap for prescription drugs will continue to grow unless reform occurs.

Insurance coverage for prescription drugs is falling short. During the past decade, the cost of employer-supported health insurance premiums has increased by more than 100%. Much of this increase is due to the rise in cost of prescription drugs. Rather than cover the increase themselves, employers are asking their workers to pay for a greater portion of their insurance costs. This means even people with insurance are struggling to pay. Limits on price increases will slow the rise of premium costs.

Senior citizens face the one-two punch of an increasing needs for prescriptions and lower incomes. Because of their age, more seniors are more likely to face chronic conditions such as diabetes and heart disease. At the same time, many seniors are retired and living on lower incomes. A limit on drug price increases will bnefit seniors, too.

> Errors in conventions are few and do not interfere with the writer's message.

> The essay could use more transitions to improve flow.

> This paragraph loses focus and does not fully support the argument.

One way to lower costs of drugs is to negotiate lower prices with drug companies. Everyone knows that the best way to get a low price is to buy a product in large amounts. To get lower prices, the government can simply notify pharmaceutical companies that purchases of drugs will be made to the companies that offer the lowest prices, and that other companies will be shut out. Other countries negotiate drugs purchases. So do insurance companies. The government can, too.

> The writer identifies and responds to an opposing argument.

Some might argue that drug companies cannot lower their prices. They need to charge a lot for prescription drugs because the cost of producing such drugs is so high. There's little doubt that the research needed to produce prescription drugs costs a great deal of money. But a huge amount of the money spent each year by pharmaceutical companies goes toward advertising their drugs and influencing consumers to buy them and doctors to prescribe them. In addition, many drug companies are enjoying record profits.

> The conclusion could be more completely developed.

While it is necessary for drug companies to make a profit, they should not do so at the expense of consumer's physical and financial fitness. People everywhere are suffering because the cost of prescription drugs is too high and growing too fast.

Writing that fits a score of 2 is effective in some ways.

- The introduction is not fully developed, and the writer's position is unclear.

- Errors in conventions interfere with the flow of the writing.

- Ideas are not fully developed and focus wanders.

Eliminate Mandatory Prison Sentences

Crime is a problem for communities everywhere. Robberies and burglaire shappen every day. Even murder. Drugs ar ea huge problem, and they cost communities millions every year. Mandatory sentences only make these problems worse by locking people up who do not need to be prisoned for so long. The reponbility for fighting crime is shared by all.

Locking people in prison for years is not always the best solution, for example jail is a place where people with problems do not get a chance to slove them only mk wrose? What happens is someone is jail? They might not get counel or even the mental health atentun, and alsow met people who are other criminals. What is wrong with this. They are likely bad ifuences on on them. Outside of jail, the nonviolent criminals have a chance. to change there ways.

The cost of keeping people in jail is a big strain. Think about feeidng and housing a person for 20 years. Now think about if that person was not even in jail. How can a person find a job to support himself if he is in jail? And the cost of rent or even buying a house is high. Not to mention the cost of food and clothing.

Mandatory sentences will only make problems worse. The cost of prison time makes things harder for communities. Jail makes it harder for a person to learn good choices. It's better to let our judges decides. who should go to jail for a long time and who should not.

Writing that fits a score of 1 is weak.

- Includes a substantial amount of information not related to the topic.

- The essay lacks a logical flow of ideas.

- Problems with conventions make the message hard to understand.

- The conclusion is missing.

Don't Share Music Downloads

When the last time you pyaid for music off the Internet? My favorite badn ofres songs for free, so I can get thos and why not. But not all music is free. Some of it costs money. Money is soming you urn for youself. I make about $60 a week at the maull, and I doant want to spned it all of mucis even if I can but what is the best way to do this!

Some people share music downloads, which is ilehalk unless you payed for them. the peple working in law inforsemint would like to know if you are doing this, because it is there job to arest peple who brake law. SO would rekkered companies and shold not do this or else you will be in trueble the sam as anyone else. Even with your prent.s and at school.

Downloads mak sharing exsy/ pop in a disck and thgere you go. Yu can put hunnerds of songs even on your little emp3 plyer, and lissen to them any tim yo want. my player has shuffle so you cn micks them up or lissen one at a time. it's yore chose. I like to use sufle sometime but not all the time. But it is still wrong.

Think if you was a musishion. You made a livving off you're songs and records. That is how you paye you're bills and feed youself. That is what many many musicians do today, and it is hard work.

Reflecting on Your Writing

Now that you have completed your argumentative essay, take some time to reflect on your writing experience. On a separate sheet of paper, complete each sentence below.

My Argumentative Essay

1. The strongest part of my essay is . . .

2. The part that still needs work is . . .

3. The prewriting activity that worked best for me was . . .

4. The main thing I learned about writing an argumentative essay is . . .

5. In my next argumentative essay, I would like to . . .

6. One question I still have about writing an argumentative essay is . . .

Persuasive Writing
Writing an Editorial

What do you do when you feel strongly about a topic? Do you try to convince your friends and family members to share your point of view? Do you post your opinion on a blog? Do you ask your neighbors to take action by signing a petition?

A good way to persuade other people to adopt your point of view or to take action on a particular issue is to write an editorial. An editorial is a type of argumentative essay that presents a strong position and backs it up with logical reasons and other forms of support.

In this chapter, you will read a sample editorial in which a student argues that playing video games can have positive effects. Then you will write your own editorial. Choose a clear position that you can defend with solid reasoning and facts. Consider the reliability of the primary and secondary sources that you use. Remember to represent the views of those who disagree with you accurately and honestly—doing so is not only fair, but it will also help make your argument more convincing.

Writing Guidelines

   Subject: A timely topic that is important to you
      Form: Editorial
  Purpose: To present a convincing persuasive argument
 Audience: Classmates

"Whatever is popular deserves attention."
—James Mackintosh

Editorial

An editorial is an essay or an article that gives an opinion about a current topic or issue. It clearly states a position then supports it with reliable facts and details. The following editorial focuses on the positive effects of video games.

Beginning
The beginning introduces the topic and provides a clear position (underlined).

Middle
The writer supports his or her position with logical reasoning and reliable sources.

Can Video Games Be Good for You?

Let's face it, we have all heard the warnings of the negative effects of video and computer games from our parents and from the media. Video games encourage violence; they destroy our brain cells; they turn us into couch potatoes. In short, the message has been that nothing positive comes from playing video games. Apparently, our town librarians have taken these ideas to heart. Our town library has decided against offering video game rentals. As a gamer, I strongly feel that this decision should be reversed. <u>The library should offer video game rentals because, according to the latest research, playing them has hidden benefits and may even be good for you.</u>

The first study I read was published in a popular parenting magazine. In it, parents saw improvements in their children's hand/eye coordination and problem-solving skills from playing video games. Their children were able to follow directions and make quick decisions in order to advance to the next level or to win a game. Eighty-four percent of parents surveyed reported that their children's typing skills improved because they played online or computer games (Franklin). To be fair, a major video game manufacturer funded this study. While I would not consider it the best or only source, when combined with other valid, reliable sources, it does help to make the case that video games can be beneficial educational tools.

Recent research commissioned by the U.S. National Institute of Health suggests that people who regularly play video games have better visual skills than people who do not play. Gamers are really good at picking out details in the midst of chaotic scenes. Scientists found that gamers are far better at coping with a variety of visual distractions than non-gamers. In the study, scientists also found that, "Although video game playing may seem to be rather mindless, it is capable of radically altering visual attention processing" (BBC News).

TEKS 12.16B, 12.16E, 12.16F, 12.16G
ELPS 1G, 4G, 4I, 4K

Writing an Editorial

The writer uses rhetorical devices to appeal to logic and emotions.

My interview with my friend Ben—a serious gamer—backed up that research. Ben thinks playing video games helped to make him a better driver. He said, "Driving on busy streets, when cars slam on their brakes and pedestrians dart out into traffic, requires drivers to make fast decisions. That's what video games are all about."

I think that video games are a great tool to help teenagers with their driving skills. Quick reaction times are key to avoiding accidents. The library has driver's education books, so why not offer video games that could help people with their driving skills as well?

Teenagers and children are not the only people who benefit from playing video games. Elderly video game players become better and faster at switching tasks than those who do not play. In addition, their memory and their ability to reason both improved (Alleyne). So, video games are a way for everyone to stay mentally fit.

The writer includes an accurate, honest representation of divergent views.

Still, critics may say that video games are violent and an excuse to sit, staring at a screen. While some games are violent, not all of them are. Many are brain teasers that require logical thinking skills, such as finding your way out of a maze. A lot of video games are also interactive. The entire family can get active, whether they are singing along to their favorite band, learning the latest dance craze, or fine-tuning their athletic skills.

Ending
The author's semiformal voice creates an appropriate style.

Our town library could avoid games that are too violent, but they should not lump all video games together. Video games can help bring friends and family members together. Reliable research suggests that video games provide exercise for both the mind and the body. I think *that* is something our town library should be supporting and encouraging, don't you?

Texas Traits

★ **Respond to the reading.** Answer the following questions.

Focus and Coherence (1) What position does the writer of the editorial take? (2) Does all of the information relate to that idea?

Development of Ideas (3) Are the writer's ideas developed thoroughly enough for the reader to understand?

Voice (4) How does the writer try to engage the reader? (5) How does the writer make the editorial sound authentic and original?

Prewriting Planning Your Writing

The purpose of an editorial is to persuade others to adopt your point of view on a timely topic. Enzo began by listing potential topics that interested him.

Topics List

School
- student council elections
- community service requirements
- drama skills class

Community
- video game rentals at library *
- crime watch program
- new supercenter

Popular Trends
- latest MP3 player
- blogging
- energy drinks

At first Enzo thought he would write about the impact of the new supercenter in his community, but he wasn't sure that his classmates would be interested in this topic. So, he talked with his friends and classmates about which topic most interested them. Based on his and their personal interests, he decided to write about video game rentals at the town library. Then he decided that an editorial would be the best way to approach this topic.

Prewrite

Choose your topic. List possible topics related to school, community, and popular trends. (Try to list at least three topics under each category.) Then put an asterisk next to the topic that you want to write about.

Focus on the Texas Traits

Development of Ideas The goal of an editorial is to present a well developed opinion about a timely topic, supported by facts. You will need to consider all aspects of your topic (significance, strengths, weaknesses, and so on).

Including Relevant Perspectives

Once you have chosen the topic that you will address, you need to consider all of the perspectives relative to the argument. To plan his essay, Enzo used an argument/counter-argument chart, listing the various perspectives of the educational value of video games.

Argument/Counter-Argument Chart

Argument	Counter-Argument
Increase visual skills	Encourage violence
Encourage mental and physical exercise	Promote sedentary lifestyle
Improve hand/eye coordination	

Include different perspectives. Use an argument/counter-argument chart to list information for your editorial. Try to include at least two or three points under each label.

Evaluating Primary and Secondary Sources

To write a well-informed editorial, you need accurate facts to support and defend your argument. To ensure that the facts you cite are accurate, carefully evaluate the validity of the research and the reliability of your sources.

To determine the reliability of your primary sources, ask these questions:

- Is my interview subject an authority on the topic?
- Is my interview subject biased in any way?
- Does the primary source material seem credible and reliable?

To determine the validity of your secondary sources, ask these questions:

- Is the source from an educational or government publication?
- Is the source biased or trying to sell something?
- Does the source have accurate and up-to-date information?
- Does the source contain grammatical errors and spelling mistakes?

Evaluate your sources. Use the information above as a guide to evaluate the validity and reliability of your primary and secondary sources.

Representing Opposing Viewpoints

While it is often easy to defend and support your own viewpoint, it can be difficult to respond to other viewpoints without distorting them. To avoid having the audience dismiss your viewpoint by misrepresenting other valid viewpoints, you should anticipate objections and make some concessions to other viewpoints.

Opposing Viewpoint-Concession Chart

Opposing Viewpoint	Concession
Critics charge that video games contain content that is violent.	While it is true that some video games are violent, not all video games contain violent content. The library could stock only non-violent video games.

Represent opposing viewpoints. Use an opposing viewpoint/concession chart to list information for your editorial.

Writing a Thesis Statement

A thesis or position states the focus of your editorial and guides your writing. An effective thesis statement takes a stand or expresses a specific feeling about your topic. Use the following formula to form your thesis or position.

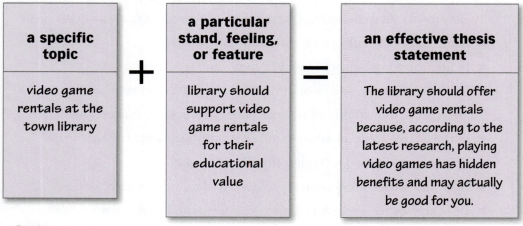

Write your thesis statement. Use the information above as a guide to create your thesis. Remember that your thesis or position statement needs to be based on logical reasons with various forms of support.

Writing an Editorial

Drafting Creating Your First Draft

As you write your editorial, use your planning from the previous page and refer to the following guidelines.

Introductory Paragraph

Your introductory paragraph should introduce your topic in an interesting way and state your position. Let the audience know the purpose of your editorial.

- Capture your audience's attention in the first sentence.
  Let's face it, we have all heard the warnings of the negative effects of video and computer games from our parents and from the media.

- Provide background information and end with your position.
  The library should offer video game rentals because, according to the latest research, playing video games has hidden benefits and may even be good for you.

Middle Paragraphs

The middle paragraphs should develop the main points in your editorial. Organize these paragraphs in a logical way that is appropriate to the audience and to the context of your editorial.

- Provide a topic sentence for each paragraph.
  Teenagers and children are not the only people who benefit from playing video games.

- Develop each paragraph with supporting details, facts, and examples.
  Elderly video game players become better and faster at switching tasks than those who do not play.

Concluding Paragraph

Your concluding paragraph should restate your position, summarize your main points, and leave the audience with a final important thought.

- Summarize your evaluation.
  Reliable research suggests that video games provide exercise for both the mind and the body.

- Provide a closing thought that will remain with the reader.
  I think that is something our town library should be supporting and encouraging, don't you?

Write your first draft. Use the guidelines above and your prewriting work to help you complete your first draft.

Using Persuasive Strategies

Rhetorical devices can help you persuade an audience. An effective editorial can appeal to logic, emotions, and ethical beliefs, depending on the topic and the audience. Statistics, projections, or personal stories can illustrate the topic. To determine which persuasive strategies should you use, ask yourself the following questions:

- Which strategy is most likely to persuade readers?
- What objections are readers most likely to have? What persuasive strategies will work best for my counter-argument?
- How strong is my argument? How can examples, facts, and statistics help to persuade readers?

Use persuasive strategies. Make a list of the logical, emotional, and ethical information that you can use in your persuasive argument.

Anticipating Audience Responses

Understanding your audience is an important part of developing and organizing your argument. There are three important elements that you need to consider when writing your editorial: the level of formality, the style, and the tone. Select words that create a tone and style that match the purpose of the argument.

Formality	Tone	Style
The level of formality that writers use is determined by their audience and their purpose. Formal English is used to discuss an important subject in a serious way; informal English is used to convey a more conversational tone.	Tone refers to a writer's attitude toward his or her subject: admiring, hopeful, critical, humorous, angry, and so on. It indicates how the writer feels about the topic.	Style is the way that a writer uses words, phrases, and sentences to express ideas. It involves unique word choice, sentence structure and variety, and literary devices.

Use the correct formality, tone, and style. Does your editorial sound too formal, too informal, or just right? Write down some of the words and phrases that convey a specific tone. Does your style get your point across?

Focus on the Texas Traits

Voice Remember to use language that shows that you care about your position. Your tone should be respectful of opposing viewpoints. Your editorial should sound engaging, original, and authentic.

Revising Improving Your First Draft

When you revise your first draft, you clarify your ideas, check your organization, and improve your voice. The guidelines below can help you revise.

Revising Checklist

Focus and Coherence

_____ 1. Do I use transitional words and phrases?
_____ 2. Do I achieve a consistency of tone and style?
_____ 3. Is my editorial coherent throughout?

Organization

_____ 4. Does my essay have a strong introductory paragraph, middle, and concluding paragraph?
_____ 5. Have I presented my points in a logical manner?

Development of Ideas

_____ 6. Do I clearly introduce my topic?
_____ 7. Have I stated my position on the topic clearly?
_____ 8. Have I developed my ideas thoroughly and consistently?

Voice

_____ 9. Is my voice engaging, confident, and convincing?
_____ 10. Do I use appeals to logic, emotion, or ethical beliefs?

Revise your first draft. Carefully review your editorial using the checklist above. Make the necessary improvements.

Creating a Title

A good title introduces your topic and catches the reader's interest. Here are some different ways to approach writing a title.

- Use a line from the evaluation: **Hidden Benefits of Video Games**
- Be clever: **Can Video Games be Good for You?**
- Create an interesting rhythm: **Video Games and More**

Editing Checking for Conventions

After revising your editorial, you'll need to edit it for conventions: punctuation, capitalization, spelling, and grammar. If your conventions are correct, the reader will be more likely to respect your editorial.

Editing Checklist

Conventions

GRAMMAR
_____ **1.** Did I use the correct forms of verbs?
_____ **2.** Do my subjects and verbs agree in number?

SENTENCE STRUCTURE
_____ **3.** Do I use a variety of correctly structured sentences that clearly communicate my ideas?
_____ **4.** Do I use a variety of sentence lengths and beginnings?

MECHANICS (CAPITALIZATION AND PUNCTUATION)
_____ **5.** Did I capitalize the first word in every sentence?
_____ **6.** Did I capitalize all proper nouns and adjectives?

SPELLING
_____ **7.** Did I spell all my words correctly?
_____ **8.** Did I double-check for words that my spell-checker might miss?

Edit your editorial. Use the checklist above to edit for conventions. Then prepare a final copy of your editorial and proofread it.

Publishing Sharing Your Work

Share your editorial with students and your teacher. (See pages 115–120). Encourage readers to respond to your ideas.

Publish your editorial. Revise your editorial one final time in response to your peer review and your teacher's feedback. Then publish your editorial. Choose one of these methods.

- Submit your editorial to your school or local newspaper.
- Post your editorial on a Web site.

Writing for Assessment
Responding to Persuasive Prompts

Sometimes it's necessary to create and present a persuasive argument quickly. For example, imagine that you're trying to convince your parents to let you borrow their car to drive to the home of a friend in another town. Your parents are reluctant, but you feel you have good reasons to support your argument. Creating an organized argument quickly may mean the difference between visiting your friend and staying home for the evening.

Writing tests also require you to organize and present an argument in a relatively short period of time. After reading a prompt, you'll need to choose a position; structure your argument; and write, revise, and edit your response—all within a predetermined time limit. This chapter will show you how to respond to a persuasive writing prompt quickly and effectively.

Writing Guidelines

  Subject: **A persuasive prompt**
     Form: **Response essay**
  Purpose: **To demonstrate competence**
 Audience: **Instructor or test evaluator**

"Opinions cannot survive if one has no chance to fight for them."

—Thomas Mann

Prewriting Analyzing a Persuasive Prompt

To respond to a persuasive prompt, begin by analyzing the prompt. A thorough analysis of the prompt will give you your topic, the form of your response, your role in writing, your expected audience, and your purpose for writing. To analyze a prompt quickly and effectively, use the STRAP questions:

Subject: What topic should I write about (policy, proposal, decision)?
Type: What form of writing should I create (essay, letter, editorial, article, report)?
Role: What role should I assume as the writer (student, son or daughter, friend, employee, citizen)?
Audience: To whom am I writing (teacher, parents, classmates, employer, official)?
Purpose: What is the goal of my writing (persuade, respond, evaluate, tell, describe)?

Subject
Type
Role
Audience
Purpose

In response to problems with traffic on the roads in your community, a council member has proposed assessing a $50 fee on each car. The money collected will be used to reduce the cost of local bus service. As an *automobile owner who commutes to work by bus,* write a letter to the city council to persuade them to vote for or against this new fee.

Note: The following key words are often found in persuasive prompts: *convince, argue, defend, persuade.*

Try It!

Analyze this prompt by answering the STRAP questions.

A recent documentary about young people highlighted ways in which high school students are making a difference in their communities. As a high school student, write a letter to your school newspaper that invites students to get involved in a positive way in your community.

Responding to Persuasive Prompts

Planning Your Response

After answering the STRAP questions, you need to begin planning your persuasive response. One of the following graphic organizers can help you to plan your response quickly.

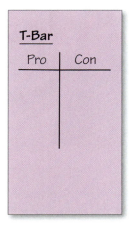
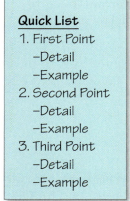
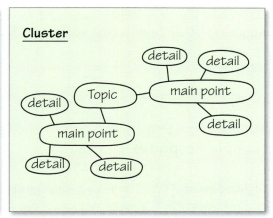

Choosing a Side

Persuasive prompts often ask you to choose one side or the other of an argument. In order to do this, you'll need to consider the ideas on both sides first, and then choose the side with the strongest reasons behind it.

One way to thoroughly examine both sides of an argument is to use a graphic organizer. Placing the "pros" and "cons" side by side will make it easier for you to determine the stronger side.

Considering both sides of an argument will also help you to find an important objection to respond to. By explaining how the objection is wrong or weak, you will demonstrate that you have considered both sides of the issue; this can strengthen your argument.

Prewrite

Use a graphic organizer. Reread the persuasive prompts on page 270. Choose one and use a graphic organizer to plan your response to the prompt.

Tip

One secret to success with writing prompts is careful time management. For example, if you have 45 minutes to respond, use the first 5 minutes to analyze the prompt and plan your response, the last 5 minutes to revise and edit your response, and the 35 minutes in between for drafting your response.

Drafting Responding to a Prompt

Once you have answered the STRAP questions and planned your response using a graphic organizer, you can begin writing.

In response to the second prompt on page 270, student writer Zabel Aroyan chose to write about donating blood. She used her own experience and an informal voice to appeal to other high school students. The following is her response.

Sample Response

Introduction
The introductory paragraph hooks the reader with an interesting question and introduces the subject.

> How would you like to help save lives without spending years training to be a doctor, a nurse, or a firefighter? You can make a life-changing difference, and it won't take much of your time. I'm talking about giving blood.
>
> Last July I volunteered to help out at a Red Cross blood drive at the Solano Mall. I learned a lot about the many ways that donated blood can help save lives. For example, transfusions help people who are in a crisis as a result of surgery, accidents, and illness. Patients undergoing heart surgery, treatment for cancer, and recovery from accidents can all be helped. Each donation of blood is like a life raft that can bring many people on board.

A simile underscores the writer's point.

> It's easy to find a local blood drive if you go to www.givelife.org. You can also find out about one through public service announcements on the radio or TV—even billboards and ads on buses. Keep your eyes peeled!

Middle
The middle paragraphs express reasons for supporting the position.

> After you find out where to donate blood, the rest is even easier. The process only takes about 20 minutes, and snacks and juice are provided. You need a valid ID and a parental permission slip if you are under 18. Students must be at least 17 years old, weigh at least 110 pounds, and be in good health.
>
> There are some reasons that you might not be allowed to give blood. Tests and restrictions are in place to keep the nation's blood supply safe. Those who have had a tattoo or a body

Responding to Persuasive Prompts

piercing (not including ears) are not allowed to give blood for one year. Those on medication or those who have traveled to another country should talk to the technicians to find out if they can safely donate blood.

The final middle paragraphs cite objections and respond to them.

You may want to give blood, but you fear the process. You may worry about getting AIDS or just hate needles. You may think you'll feel faint or be at risk until your blood supply is back to normal. The donor program has anticipated all these concerns. The needles used are new and sterile, so you won't contract AIDS or any other blood-borne disease. The needles are also extremely sharp and generally cause little discomfort. Finally, only about one pint of blood is taken, so your blood supply is not drastically reduced. Just remember, your discomfort will be outweighed by a lifesaving gift.

What if you can't donate blood? There are still plenty of ways you can participate. One way to help is to organize a blood drive at your school or another location. During the drive, you can help with registration and refreshments and in general help donors feel comfortable when they are giving blood. You can also recruit donors—family members, friends, classmates, teachers, and neighbors.

Conclusion
The concluding paragraphs strengthen the essay's focus by restating the writer's position and making a call to action.

When I volunteered for the blood drive at the mall, I learned that somebody in the United States needs blood approximately every two seconds. This means that every day, an average of over 43,000 Americans may need blood. Yet only five percent of eligible donors actually give blood each year.

The writer's voice sounds authentic and original.

We can do better than five percent! I give blood each year. It feels great to help someone I don't even know, and I'm sure you'll get the same feeling of satisfaction. Find a blood drive near you, and give the gift of life.

Draft

Now write your own response. Look over the planning you did for the prompt on page 271 to write a response. Finish your response in the time allotted by your teacher.

Revising Improving Your Response

Before you begin a writing test, find out if you are allowed to make changes to your draft copy. If changes are allowed, make them as clear and neat as possible. Use the STRAP questions to guide your revisions.

Subject: Have I responded to the topic of the prompt? Do all my main points support my position?

Type: Have I responded in the form requested (essay, letter, editorial, article, report)?

Role: Have I assumed the role called for in the prompt?

Audience: Have I addressed the audience identified in the prompt?

Purpose: Does my response accomplish the goal indicated in the prompt?

Improve your work. Carefully review your response, using the STRAP questions above as your guide. Within the time allowed, make changes to revise your response.

Editing Checking Your Response

After revising, be sure to read through your response one final time. Correct any errors in conventions: punctuation, capitalization, spelling, and grammar.

Editing Checklist

Conventions

_____ 1. Have I used end punctuation for every sentence?

_____ 2. Have I capitalized all proper nouns and the first word of every sentence?

_____ 3. Have I spelled all words correctly?

_____ 4. Have I made sure my subjects and verbs agree?

_____ 5. Have I used the right words (*to, too, two; there, their, they're*)?

Check your conventions. Read through your response one final time. In the time allowed, neatly correct any errors in punctuation, capitalization, spelling, and grammar.

Persuasive Writing on Tests

Before you write . . .

- **Analyze the prompt.**
  Use the STRAP questions. Remember that a persuasive prompt asks you to use facts and logical reasons to persuade or convince.
- **Plan your response.**
  Carefully allot the time you will spend on planning, writing, revising, and checking conventions. Use a graphic organizer to gather your details and organize your response.

As you write . . .

- **Stay focused.**
  Keep your main idea or argument in mind as you write. All your reasons should clearly support your argument.
- **Answer a significant objection.**
  Make your argument stronger by responding to a likely objection.
- **Summarize your argument.**
  In the final paragraph, summarize your opinion and supporting reasons to make a final plea to the reader.

After you've written a first draft . . .

- **Revise and edit.**
  Use the STRAP questions to revise your response. Correct any errors in punctuation, capitalization, spelling, and grammar.

Try It!

Choose one of the prompts below. First, analyze it using the STRAP questions. Then use a graphic organizer to gather details and plan. Finally, write, revise, and edit your response.

- Swordfish populations are declining due to overfishing. Local restaurants are campaigning for people to give swordfish a break by choosing other fish on the menu. Write a letter to the local newspaper editor asking people to support or oppose this campaign.

- Many people in this country do not get enough exercise. Yet exercise is known to help maintain an appropriate weight, reduce the risk of heart disease, and improve general health. As a health-care professional, write an essay for a fitness Web site that seeks to convince people to exercise more.

ELPS 2C, 4C, 5B

www.hmheducation.com/tx/writesource

Interpretive Response

Writing Focus
Interpret the Theme of a Play	**277**
Interpret a Novel	**319**
Writing an Analysis of an Expository Text	**327**
Responding to Prompts About Literature	**333**

Grammar Focus
Adverb Clauses	**306**
Adverb Phrases	**307**

Learning Language

With a partner, discuss the following words and expressions from this unit.

1. An **element** is one part of something, such as a play.
   Which element of books do you find most interesting?
2. A **formula** is a statement that describes a relationship.
   Describe a formula for success in school.
3. Speaking **at the top of your lungs** means to speak very loudly.
   When is it rude to speak at the top of your lungs?

Interpretive Response
Interpret the Theme of a Play

In this chapter, you will learn how to interpret a literary text, beginning with the characters, setting, and plot. Through these basic elements, you will gain a deeper understanding of how theme is developed in a text. Then you will apply what you have learned by writing your own interpretation of a text.

The example of a literary text in this chapter is a play. Before television and film, before theaters and amphitheaters, before writing itself, plays fired the imagination of ancient people. Some plays entertained. Others enlightened. As people viewed these plays, they interpreted the meaning of what they were seeing and hearing. Almost all plays helped people explain the meaning of life and how their world worked.

Plays have always had an effect on viewers. The ancient Greeks said that plays create *catharsis*—literally washing the soul. Today, interpreting literary texts such as tragedies and comedies allows people to experience events without being hurt, or to laugh and forget their troubles. Interpreting literary texts helps people understand ideas and themes in their own lives.

Writing Guidelines
- **Subject:** A play
- **Purpose:** To interpret a main theme
- **Form:** Literary analysis
- **Audience:** Classmates

"A good drama critic is one who perceives what is happening in the theater of his time. A great drama critic also perceives what is not happening."

—Kenneth Tynan

Writing Warm-Up **Thinking About Drama**

Almost all plays contain the same elements: characters, conflict, action, dialogue, plot, and theme. Even TV dramas have these elements. To better understand the basic elements of one particular play, a student named Leon filled out a play map.

Play Map

- **Title:** Party at the End of the World
- **Playwright:** Dedra Runningcloud
- **Characters:** Jonas Jenkins (a drifter prophet), Sheriff Smith, Lyndsey Peck (owner of the Eel Creek General Store)
- **Setting:** Eel Creek, Alaska, a remote village above the Arctic Circle
- **Conflict:** Jonas Jenkins says the world will end, but most people won't believe him.
- **Plot:**
  - **Event 1:** Sheriff Smith tries but fails to run Jonas off.
  - **Event 2:** Jonas meets Lindsey in the general store.
  - **Event 3:** Jonas's dire predictions start to come true.
- **Climax:** Lyndsey holds an "End of the World Party" on the rooftop of the general store, and Jonas and the others who attend see a spectacular meteor shower. It seems the world is really coming to an end.
- **Resolution:** The sun rises on a new day, proving Jonas wrong, except that he had passed away during the party. He had predicted the end of the world for himself.
- **Theme:** Look at life through a wide-angle lens.

Prewrite

Create a play map. Think of a play or TV drama you have recently seen or read. Discuss each element with a partner. Then both partners complete a play map. Make sure to listen to each other and help each other express ideas clearly.

Interpret the Theme of a Play

Writing an Analysis Paragraph

Using his play map, Leon wrote a one-paragraph interpretation of the play. Note that his interpretation has the following parts:

- The **thesis statement** names the play and playwright and summarizes the interpretation.
- The **body sentences** describe the characters, setting, and plot and indicate the theme using quotations and stylistic and rhetorical devices.
- The **closing sentence** provides a thoughtful conclusion.

Look Out for Jonas

Thesis Statement

<u>In *Party at the End of the World*, playwright Dedra Runningcloud explores how different points of view bring people together—and drive them apart.</u> The play centers on Jonas Jenkins, a "drifter prophet" who arrives in the small town of Eel Creek, Alaska, and proclaims that the world will end that night. Jenkins's predictions startle the people of the town. "Look out for Jonas!" a child cries. Sheriff Smith arrives to run Jonas out of town but can't find the prophet, who has wandered into the Eel Creek General Store.

Body Sentences

There, Jonas meets the storekeeper, Lyndsey Peck, and tells her the world will end that night. Instead of fearing him, Lyndsey joins in the fantasy and declares an "End of the World Party" on the store roof. Lyndsey hosts the celebration, and Jonas and an eclectic group of townsfolk lie in lawn chairs and watch a spectacular meteor shower. When the sun rises the next day, those who were partying discover that the world didn't end, but Jonas has had a heart attack. From his point of view, it really was the end of the world. Runningcloud contrasts the close-minded suspicion of Sheriff Smith with the open-minded acceptance of Lyndsey Peck. Both agree with the child—"Look out for Jonas!"—but in opposite ways.

Closing Sentence

By accepting and even celebrating Jonas's point of view, Lyndsey brings the community together.

Write a thesis statement. Use the play map you created on page 278 to write a thesis statement you could use in an interpretation of the play and its main theme. Think about what you want to say about the play before you write.

TEKS 12.13B, 12.13D, 12.15C(i-ii)
ELPS 5C, 5E, 5G

> "You need three things in the theater—the play, the actors, and the audience—and each must give something."
> —Kenneth Haigh

Understanding Your Goal

Your goal in this chapter is to write an essay that interprets a theme of a play. The key traits for this assignment follow. Read these independently or with a partner.

Traits of a Play Interpretation

■ Focus and Coherence
Focus your interpretation so that the reader can understand and appreciate how the ideas are related. Correctly use play terminology in your interpretation and choose words that capture a precise meaning.

■ Organization
Create an introduction that identifies the play and the thesis, a middle that logically interprets the theme with meaningful transitions to move from idea to idea, and a conclusion that puts the play in perspective.

■ Development of Ideas
Write a thesis statement that names the play and focuses on a main theme. Then interpret that theme by connecting it to the characters, setting, and plot. Include textual evidence from the play.

■ Voice
Show your knowledge and understanding of the play while also creating a narrative flow, allowing the reader to experience the play's action through your unique perspective.

■ Conventions
Check your writing for grammar, mechanics (punctuation, capitalization), and spelling errors.

Literature Connection: Your interpretation can focus on a short play, such as J. M. Synge's *Riders to the Sea*, or a full-length play, such as Shakespeare's *Macbeth*. Both plays contain strong thematic elements. You can find a review of a film version of *Macbeth* in Robert Hatch's essay "Bloody, Bold, & Resolute."

Play Interpretation

In the following essay, Arella analyzes *Sisters,* a play by Marsha A. Jackson.

Beginning
The introductory paragraph catches the reader's interest, introduces the play, and advances a clear thesis statement (underlined).

Middle
The first middle paragraph sets the scene and includes commentary on a quotation from the author's notes before the play.

Another middle paragraph summarizes the action and supports the thesis while using stylistic devices to advance the theme.

Stuck with Each Other

In the dark theater, children sing a haunting tune: "Don't Play with the Alley Children." It's a singsong chant that young Olivia Williams and her friends would sing in their upper-middle-class apartments while young Cassie Charles and her friends played among the garbage cans below. Though both girls are African Americans, they are divided by their social class, their experience, and their strategies for living in a white world. Then, one New Year's Eve, the grown-up Olivia is stranded in her ad-agency office along with the grown-up Cassie, a cleaning woman. <u>In her play *Sisters,* Marsha A. Jackson contrasts the two women's lives, showing how color and gender make two very different women into true sisters.</u>

The action of the play begins on New Year's Eve in Olivia's office at Peat, Montgriff, and Simon, an ad agency in Atlanta, Georgia. Olivia kneels on the floor among boxes and is packing up her office when Cassie arrives singing "I'm Every Woman" at the top of her lungs. The two women could not be more different. Olivia is 30, single, stiff, proper, and sad, listening to MUZAK as she packs up her life. Cassie is 40, a mom, loose and happy, listening to Whitney Houston. As Jackson points out in her notes before the play, "Both characters are intentionally broadly drawn in Act I, such that the laughter is the medium of entry into the complexity of each character and situation" (104). These two women begin as stereotypes, but when they get stuck together, both characters start to unfold.

A storm begins outside, lightning strikes, and the power in the building goes out. Olivia and Cassie, alone in the building, must rely on each other. They walk down twenty flights of stairs so that Olivia can drive Cassie home, but Olivia has forgotten her car keys, and the storm has turned to a blizzard. All traffic is stopped, and the trains that Cassie would ride aren't running because of the blackout.

The women climb back up the stairs, and Cassie reluctantly helps Olivia pack up her office while the two women unpack their lives. Olivia reveals that she is leaving because she has hit the "glass ceiling" and, despite her hard

The interpretation continues with quotations from the play that support the thesis statement.

work, is getting passed over for promotions. Cassie says that Olivia's ambition is a curse: "Being ungrateful for what you got, and wishing for things you can't have. If that ain't a curse, I ain't seen one" (134). Cassie has her own hang-ups. She has taken care of others her whole life: first her grandmother and now her son. Olivia points out, "Who's taking care of you, Cassie? You've been so busy working, trying to convince yourself you don't deserve a life, you didn't even feel it when you gave up" (144). As they talk, Olivia and Cassie grow to understand each other.

In this paragraph, nuances and ambiguities within the play are identified and analyzed.

Jackson seems to be showing that the things that keep people apart—walls and alleys, work and money—aren't as powerful as the forces that draw them together. Simply by setting these two women in the same space, Jackson undoes the years and dollars that had kept them apart. Stuck with each other on New Year's Eve, Olivia and Cassie create their own celebration. They trade stories, listen to music, dance, and even make resolutions. Olivia resolves to find her way in a "white man's world" and have fun doing it. Cassie resolves to start her own cleaning business and move up in the world.

Ending
The concluding paragraph reflects on the main theme of the play.

By the end of their time together, Olivia and Cassie are more than friends: They are sisters. Their theme song no longer is "Don't Play with the Alley Children" but "Blest Be the Tie That Binds." Marsha Jackson has brought two very different women together—two different aspects of the playwright herself. Jackson not only wrote the play but starred as Olivia during its run. As a classically trained playwright and a leading light in the theater scenes of Atlanta and Houston, Jackson is very much like Olivia. But the loving way in which she writes Cassie's part—and her own experience of being an "alley child" in a white world—show that part of Jackson is and always will be Cassie.

Respond to the reading. Answer the following questions about the essay.

Organization (1) How are the middle paragraphs organized?

Development of Ideas (2) What theme does Arella focus on in her interpretation? (3) How do the characters, the setting, and the plot demonstrate the theme?

Voice (4) Where does the writer's voice sound most analytical? Explain. (5) Where does the writer's voice sound most narrative? Explain.

Interpret the Theme of a Play 283

Prewriting

To get started on your interpretation, you need to unlock the secrets of a play. The keys to prewriting can help you. Once you finish the activities on the next pages, you'll be ready to write.

Keys to Effective Prewriting

1. Write a clear thesis statement that identifies the theme you will interpret. Research the background of the play and identify quotations that help support your thesis and topic ideas.

2. Plan your essay using an outline or an organized list.

3. Gather information about the stylistic and rhetorical devices the author uses and their aesthetic effects. Take notes on how details in the play affect the reader and support the theme.

4. Identify ambiguities and nuances within the text and analyze their meanings for your readers.

5. Anticipate and answer questions that readers might have. Make sure to address information that is contradictory to your thesis.

Prewriting Planning Your Writing

You may already know what play you would like to interpret. If not, follow the instructions on this page.

Think about plays you have read and plays that you have seen performed—in or out of school. Also consider famous plays that have been made into movies. To select a play, Julius created a topics list.

Topics List

Plays I've Read	Plays I've Seen	Plays Made into Movies
Romeo and Juliet	The Fantasticks	The Night of the Iguana
Julius Caesar	Godspell	Death of a Salesman
Inherit the Wind	The Lion King	Chicago
The Glass Menagerie *		

Brainstorm a topics list. Work with a partner and write "Plays I've Read," "Plays I've Seen," and "Plays Made into Movies" on a piece of paper. Underneath, list topic ideas. Place an asterisk (*) next to the play you'd like to write about.

Focus on the Texas Traits

Development of Ideas To create a thorough interpretation for your readers, try to select a play that you can both read and see onstage. If you've read but haven't seen a certain play, find the video of a performance. Then explain or describe your ideas with unique and thoughtful details.

Interpret the Theme of a Play

Writing Down Main Events

After you have selected a play to write about, you need to read (or reread) it and, if possible, view it. Then consider the play's basic elements. Julius created the following play map for *The Glass Menagerie*.

Play Map

Title:	The Glass Menagerie
Playwright:	Tennessee Williams
Characters:	Amanda Wingfield (the mother), Laura Wingfield (the shy daughter), Tom Wingfield (the son), and Jim O'Connor (the gentleman caller)
Setting:	The Wingfield apartment in an overcrowded city tenement
Conflict:	Laura has withdrawn from life, and her mother and brother want to bring her out.
Plot:	
Event 1:	Amanda reminisces about her gentleman callers.
Event 2:	Amanda learns Laura has quit business school.
Event 3:	Tom arranges for a friend to come to dinner.
Climax:	The gentleman caller, Jim O'Connor, kisses Laura, but then reveals that he is already "going steady" with someone else.
Resolution:	Laura is left desolate, and Tom, tired of working to support his mother and sister, runs away, chasing his military dreams.
Theme:	Life may be fragile, but it can't be lived in a glass case, without risk.

Prewrite

Create a play map. Using the same format as shown above, write out the main elements of the play you have chosen.

Prewriting Writing a Thesis Statement

Your interpretation of the play should advance a clear thesis statement on the theme you plan to explore. The following formula can help you.

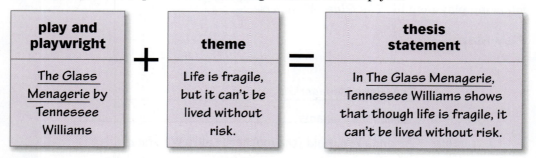

Write your thesis statement. Use the formula above as you develop a clear thesis statement for your essay. Try two or three versions until you are satisfied.

Organizing the Middle of Your Essay

The middle of your essay should set the scene, highlight key actions in the plot, give insights into the characters' actions, and discuss the theme. In interpreting the play, it is important to try to anticipate and answer questions that readers might have. In addition, you need to respond to ideas that might be contradictory to your thesis statement. Here are some possible reader questions and a contradictory idea that Julius wants to address in his essay.

Why is Amanda shocked to learn what Tom and Laura are doing?
Amanda is frustrated to learn about the secret lives her two children are leading because she thought they were satisfied with their plans.

Why is Jim O'Connor important to the play and to the other characters?
Jim O'Connor supports the theme that life can't be lived without risk. He seems to be everything the Wingfields need—romance, adventure, confidence, and risk.

People shouldn't take risks because they and others might get hurt.
Even though there is a risk of getting hurt, the Wingfields need to change their lives because they are all very unhappy and dissatisfied.

Explore questions and contradictory ideas. Follow the pattern that Julius used above, or create your own pattern. Write questions that your readers might ask and make notes for answers. Explore at least one idea that is contradictory to your thesis statement.

Supporting Your Interpretation

To fully interpret a play, you need to think about the details of the play, the playwright, and the background of the play. This kind of information can be found in primary and secondary sources. Some information will help you interpret the play, while other information will provide details that you want to include in your essay. For example, you can include quotations from the introduction, preface, or appendix of the published play. You can also include quotations directly from the play in your essay. Commenting on information from primary and secondary sources will help support your thesis statement. Julius formed a set of questions to help interpret the play and choose quotations to include in his essay.

Background Information to Help Me Interpret:

Who is the playwright, and when and where did the playwright live?
Tennessee Williams was born on March 26, 1914, in Columbus, Ohio. His real name was Thomas Lanier Williams.

What did the audiences and critics think of the play?
Audiences and critics loved The Glass Menagerie, and its success made Tennessee Williams an overnight star. He talked about the success being a "catastrophe" for him because it was so sudden.

Quotations to Help Strengthen My Interpretation:

What did the playwright think of this play?
Tennessee Williams called The Glass Menagerie a "memory play," one that portrays life not with stark realism, but with "a closer approach, a more penetrating and vivid expression of things as they are."

What quotations from the play support the thesis that life can't be lived without risk?
When talking to his mother, Tom says "Man is by instinct a lover, a hunter, a fighter, and none of those instincts are given much play at the warehouse." Laura shows that she wants to understand risk too, when she says, "I'll just imagine he had an operation. The horn was removed to make him feel less freakish! . . . Now he will feel more at home with the other horses, the ones that don't have horns."

Prewrite

Gather background and quotations. Read the material printed with the play and do your own research. Write down background information and quotations from or about the play to support your interpretation.

 12.13A, 12.13B

Prewriting Planning Your Essay

Julius planned his essay with a sentence outline, but if your teacher prefers, you can create a topic outline, or even a simple list.

Sentence Outline

Thesis Statement: In The Glass Menagerie, Tennessee Williams shows that though life is fragile, it can't be lived without risk.

I. Each of the Wingfields—mother Amanda, son Tom, and daughter Laura—lives physically in the apartment but psychologically very far from it.
  A. Amanda grew up with Southern gentility.
  B. Tom works at a factory to support the family but wants to be a poet.
  C. Laura collects glass animals and "attends" a business college.

II. Soon after the characters are introduced, Amanda is shocked to learn about the secret lives her two children are leading.
  A. Laura has dropped out of business college.
  B. Tom goes to movies, dreaming of adventure.
  C. Amanda gets Tom to invite a "gentleman caller" to meet Laura.

III. When the "gentleman caller," Jim O'Connor, arrives at the Wingfield apartment, he brings life to the whole place.
  A. He believes in adventure, just as Tom does.
  B. Jim represents the genteel past to Amanda.
  C. He is the boy Laura had a crush on in high school.

IV. Jim O'Connor seems to be everything the Wingfields need—romance, adventure, confidence, and risk.
  A. Jim remembers Laura as "Blue Roses."
  B. Jim accidentally breaks her glass unicorn.
  C. He kisses her, but then tells her he is "going steady" with another girl.

Plan your essay. Work with a partner or independently to plan your essay. Use your thesis statement, background information, questions, and ideas to create an outline or list to plan your essay. Add details to support each topic or idea.

Drafting

After thinking carefully about the elements of the play and planning your interpretation, you are ready to start writing. By following your plan, you can get all of your ideas on paper.

Keys to Effective Writing

1. Use your outline or list to guide your writing.

2. Write on every other line or double-space if you are using a computer. This will allow room for changes.

3. Create an introduction that discusses the play and playwright and states your thesis.

4. In the middle paragraphs, support your topic sentences with commentary on quotations and paraphrases from the play.

5. Analyze the theme, focusing on characters, setting, and plot. Interpret ambiguities and nuances in the text for your readers.

6. Anticipate and respond to readers' questions and to contradictory information.

7. Write a conclusion that expands on the theme.

Drafting Getting the Big Picture

Your interpretation should be structured to include three parts: an introduction, a middle, and a conclusion. The chart below shows how the three parts of a play interpretation fit together. The examples are from the essay on pages 291–294.

Beginning

The **introductory paragraph** captures the reader's interest, names the play and playwright, and states the thesis.

Thesis Statement
In The Glass Menagerie, Tennessee Williams shows that though life is fragile, it can't be lived without risk.

Middle

The **middle** paragraphs analyze the theme by focusing on character, setting, and plot.

Topic Sentences
Each of the Wingfields—mother Amanda, son Tom, and daughter Laura—lives physically in the apartment but psychologically very far from it.

Soon after the characters are introduced, Amanda is shocked to learn about the secret lives her two children are leading.

Jim O'Connor seems to be everything the Wingfields need—romance, adventure, confidence, and risk.

Ending

The **concluding paragraph** expands on the main theme.

Closing Sentences
When Jim O'Connor leaves the apartment, he takes the newfound hope away with him. That's because he can't live life for the Wingfields. Everyone must take his or her own fragile soul out into the world and risk it—as Jim does.

Starting Your Essay

The opening of your interpretation should capture the reader's interest, introduce the play and playwright, and state your thesis. Here are some strategies for capturing your reader's interest:

- **Start with a strong image.**
  Aside from her mother and brother, Laura Wingfield's only companions in life are tiny, fragile glass creatures—her "glass menagerie."

- **Use and comment on a quotation from the play.**
  "The Wingfield apartment is in the rear of the building, one of those vast hive-like conglomerations of cellular living-units that flower as warty growths in overcrowded urban centers of lower middle-class population" (27). It's a location most people can imagine, a location many people can simply look around and see. . . .

- **Begin with an intriguing idea.**
  From the moment the curtain opens, the audience wonders about the smiling portrait of the sailor—the one Wingfield who no longer remains . . .

Introductory Paragraph

Julius chooses to begin his essay with an intriguing idea and then provides background information before stating his thesis.

> From the moment the curtain opens, the audience wonders about the smiling portrait of the sailor—the one Wingfield who no longer remains in the cramped apartment. The father has escaped the claustrophobic world where the mother and her two grown children still live. The whole play takes place in this small space, with an occasional breath of fresh air out on the fire escape in the alley. The family has withdrawn to this apartment as if it is a safe haven from the world, but their unhappiness demonstrates that the apartment is anything but safe. The Wingfields aren't really living. <u>In The Glass Menagerie, Tennessee Williams shows that though life is fragile, it can't be lived without risk.</u>

The introductory paragraph catches the reader's interest and states a clear thesis (underlined).

Write your introduction. Use one of the strategies above to capture the reader's interest. Consider commenting on a quotation from the play to intrigue your readers. Then provide background information and present your thesis.

Drafting Developing the Middle Part

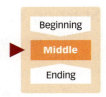

In the middle part of your essay, you systematically interpret the theme. First, focus on characters, setting, and plot. Next, analyze the aesthetic effects, or artistic impact, of the author's use of stylistic and rhetorical devices (see pages 634–635 for a list of devices). Then, interpret the theme itself.

> The first middle paragraph uses characters and setting to analyze the theme.

Each of the Wingfields—mother Amanda, son Tom, and daughter Laura—lives physically in the apartment but psychologically very far from it. Amanda is an older woman brought up in the traditions of the Old South, with lemonade on verandas and gentlemen callers. She lives in this bygone age and discusses her days of dating, even though they resulted in a broken marriage. The playwrite includes numerous references to the "gentleman caller" in the play. The man symbolizes the characters' hopes for change, and the references also help the reader understand the futility the characters feel.

> Julius discusses how the author uses the stylistic device of allusion to help readers understand the characters and the theme.

To begin with, Tom also feels trapped like a bug, working in a shoe factory, though he wishes to be a poet. Coworkers call him "Shakespeare" (92). Tom works simply to make money to support his mother and sister, though he spends nights at the movies, wishing for grand adventures. Laura is the most lost and fragile of them all. She had been shy in high school, with a crippled leg and lungs weakened by "pleurosis." Laura has withdrawn from the world, spending her time with a collection of animal statues, her "glass menagerie." Her favorite is a unicorn that tries to fit in with a shelf full of horses. This unicorn symbolizes Laura, who doesn't fit in and is so very fragile.

> The next middle paragraphs use plot to analyze the theme.

Soon after the characters are introduced, Amanda is shocked to learn about the secret lives her two children are leading. When Amanda stops at Rubicam's Business College, where her daughter is supposed to be taking classes, she learns that Laura became so nervous in the first week of class that she dropped out. She has been going to the library and walking instead of going to class. Shortly afterward, Amanda learns of Tom's dreams of adventure and his plans to join the military. "Man is by instinct a lover, a hunter, a fighter, and none of those

> Analyzing how Tennessee Williams uses rhetorical devices reveals the effect of the author's style on the theme of the play.

instincts are given much play at the warehouse," Tom tells his mother (64). To help express Tom's frustration, Tennessee Williams has Tom's character use rhetorical questions when he speaks to his mother. This shows that Tom is struggling with difficult questions about life that he is trying to answer.

Frustrated with her children, Amanda asks Tom to help Laura find a man. Tom at first says no, but then arranges for a gentleman caller. When the "gentleman caller," Jim O'Connor, arrives at the Wingfield apartment, he brings life to the whole place. Jim is Tom's only friend and confidant at the factory, and he understands Tom's desire for adventure. Jim also enlivens Amanda, who redecorates the apartment to make ready for him. To Amanda, Jim represents the return of the gracious past. But Jim's strongest effect is on Laura, who has secretly loved him since high school. Back then, she had been absent for a while, and Jim asked why. When Laura said "pleurosis," Jim heard "blue roses," and called her that name (112). The name is another symbol of Laura's odd and fragile beauty.

Jim O'Connor seems to be everything the Wingfields need—romance, adventure, confidence, and risk. Perhaps Amanda has found a way back to bygone days; perhaps Tom has found a coconspirator to help him escape the factory; perhaps Laura has found a gentleman who would lift her out of her fragile glass world and into life. Laura trusts Jim with the unicorn, and he gently sets it on a table. Later, as he tries to teach Laura to dance, they knock the unicorn off the table, and its horn is broken away. Laura says, "I'll just imagine he had an operation. The horn was removed to make him feel less—freakish! . . . Now he will feel more at home with the other horses, the ones that don't have horns" (125). Jim steals a kiss from Laura, but calls himself "stumblejohn" for doing it, given that he has a steady girlfriend. This is just what Laura needs—to take risks, even possibly to get broken, if only to fit in better. The problem is that she isn't like her unicorn—she doesn't lose her horn or learn to fit in with the other horses.

> The last middle paragraph focuses directly on the theme.

Write your middle paragraphs. Use your outline (page 288) as a guide. Analyze the aesthetic effects, or artistic impact, of the author's use of stylistic and rhetorical devices to support your interpretation of the theme.

Drafting Concluding Your Essay

The conclusion of your interpretation should expand on the main theme of the play. Here are strategies you can try:

- **Connect the theme to life in general.**
  When Jim O'Connor leaves the apartment, he takes the newfound hope away with him. That's because he can't live life for the Wingfields. Everyone must take his or her own fragile soul out into the world and risk it—as Jim does.

- **Relate the theme of the play to the playwright's life.**
  When Tom Wingfield leaves home, abandoning his job at the shoe warehouse, Tennessee Williams is reliving his own escape from the shoe warehouse where he worked before becoming a successful playwright.

- **Provide a powerful quotation from the play.**
  After leaving home, Tom is haunted by thoughts of his sister and her glass menagerie: "The window is filled with pieces of colored glass . . . like bits of a shattered rainbow. . . . Oh, Laura, Laura, I tried to leave you behind me, but I am more faithful than I intended to be!" (137).

Concluding Paragraph

In his concluding paragraph, Julius connects the play to life in general.

> The concluding paragraph expands on the theme and responds to the idea that people should not takes risks because they will get hurt.

> When Jim O'Connor leaves the apartment, he takes the newfound hope away with him. That's because he can't live life for the Wingfields. Everyone must take his or her own fragile soul out into the world and risk it—as Jim does. Amanda's hope that a gentleman caller would make her life perfect was dashed when her husband left, and now Laura's hope for a similar knight in shining armor is also dashed. Such rescuers don't exist. Only Tom escapes the apartment, but he can't be free either, because he knows his mother and sister are still there, waiting for their lives to begin.

Draft

Write your ending and complete a first draft. Work with a partner or independently to develop the last paragraph of your essay, using one or more of the suggestions listed above. Make a complete copy of your essay, double-spacing or writing on every other line to leave room for revising.

Revising

When you write, you allow your thoughts to pour out onto the page. When you revise, you reexamine those thoughts to improve your paper, deciding what to add, delete, move, or rework. The points below give you an overview of the revision process.

Keys to Effective Revising

1. Read your essay aloud to see whether the individual paragraphs and composition as a whole are focused on the thesis statement.

2. Review your introduction and conclusion. These paragraphs should be meaningful and add depth to the essay.

3. Make sure you have used stylistic and rhetorical devices to write an engaging essay.

4. Consider how clearly you analyzed ambiguities, nuances, and complexities in your writing. Make references to the text and use quotations from it to support your interpretation.

5. Check that you have anticipated and responded to readers' questions and contradictory information.

6. Use the editing and proofreading marks on pages 638–639.

Revising for Focus and Coherence

When you revise for *focus and coherence,* check that all of your ideas are related to your thesis statement. This enables the reader to explore various aspects of the text without losing focus on the central theme of your interpretation.

Are my analyses of ambiguities and nuances in the text related to my thesis?

An ambiguity is a question or uncertainty that arises in the text. A nuance is a small difference in meaning that is seen in a text. For example, in a play a character might say something that has more than one meaning or a deeper meaning. A strong interpretation helps the reader understand confusing ideas or hidden meanings within a text. When identifying and analyzing these ambiguities and nuances, make sure you maintain the focus of the essay. Ask yourself the following questions:

1. What is my thesis statement?
2. Does my analysis relate directly to my thesis?

Exercise

Read the examples below and decide which analysis best maintains its focus on the thesis statement.

Thesis Statement: The passage of time is a recurring theme in *Romeo and Juliet,* playing a key role in the destruction of the title characters.

Analysis #1: Juliet declares that her love for Romeo is "too rash, too unadvis'd, too sudden/Too like the lightning" (Act II, Scene II). Her words emphasize how quickly her relationship with Romeo is moving. Yet, in a subtle nuance, her comparison to lightning also describes their love as a bright light amidst the darkness that surrounds them.

Analysis #2: The play's multiple references to time may seem ambiguous to some readers. Romeo's lament toward the beginning of the play that "sad hours seem long" (Act I, Scene I) shows time passing slowly. However, the passage of time is hastened when Juliet must marry Paris a day early. This development forces Juliet to take action—action that ultimately proves fatal.

Review your analyses. Read aloud the sentences in which you identify and analyze ambiguities and nuances of the play. Make any changes necessary to maintain focus on your thesis statement.

Interpret the Theme of a Play

Have I maintained focus on my thesis while analyzing complexities in the text?

When you identify and analyze complexities in a text, you are helping your readers understand your interpretation of the play. In order for your essay to remain focused and coherent you need to choose carefully what you analyze. There may be many interesting ambiguities and nuances that you could bring to the readers' attention. However, you need to make sure that you present analyses that maintain the focus of your essay.

Exercise

Read the example below and think about how it relates to the thesis statement on the previous page. Make revisions to the paragraph so that the analysis focuses directly on the thesis.

A complexity within the text becomes evident with Romeo's exclamation, "Look, love, what envious streaks/Do lace the severing clouds in yonder east./Night's candles are burnt out, and jocund day/Stands tiptoe on the misty mountaintops" (Act III, Scene V). Until now, light has been a positive symbol for the couple. At dawn, however, Romeo and Juliet must part ways, and light has now become their enemy.

Revise your ideas. Find places in your essay where you identify and analyze complexities of the play for the reader. If necessary, make revisions so that the ambiguities and nuances that you examine maintain a clear focus on your thesis statement.

Focus and Coherence
Revise ideas to fit your thesis.

The playwrite includes ~~a few~~ numerous allusions to the "~~glass menagerie~~ gentleman caller" in the play. This allusion refers to the characters' ~~desire to~~ hopes for change ~~stay protected~~, but also helps the reader understand the ~~hope~~ futility the characters feel.

Revising for Organization

When you revise for organization, you check the overall structure of your essay and the unity of each paragraph. One aspect involves determining if you have clearly answered readers' possible questions and have responded to ideas that contradict your thesis.

Have I anticipated readers' questions and responded to contradictory information?

- **Readers' Questions**—As you wrote the essay, you tried to anticipate readers' questions. Now, as you revise your work, try to read the essay as your readers might. Are there questions that you haven't answered? Have you left out details that might help your readers understand?
- **Contradictory Ideas**—Contradictory ideas are another aspect of the kinds of questions readers might ask. For example, a reader might want to contradict the thesis of Julius's essay and say that the play shows that people shouldn't take risks because of the consequences. In his essay, Julius addressed this anticipated contradictory idea by examining the dialogue and the characters' actions and showing that risk is a necessary part of living.

Exercise

Think about questions readers' might have. Read the following thesis statement and sentences. For each sentence, identify a possible readers' question being answered or the contradictory information that is being discussed.

Thesis Statement: In *The Final Adventure,* playwright Stephen Dietz explores the uses of deception.

1. By focusing on two great deceivers—Sherlock Holmes and Professor Moriarty—Dietz differentiates between "good" and "bad" deception.
2. At the climax, Dietz pits his two deceivers in a battle to the death atop Reichenbach Falls in Switzerland.
3. Looking at the theme in a larger context, Dietz himself is a "good deceiver," using actors, costumes, and sets to fool the audience.
4. The theme of deception expands, taking in the whole play and its many costumes, sets, and sound effects.

Review your paragraphs. Read through your essay and make sure you have considered and responded to questions that your readers might have and/or ideas that are in contradiction to your thesis.

Have I used transitions and rhetorical devices to help readers understand my ideas?

One way to make your essay organization stronger is to make use of your outlines, notes, lists, and other planning work to structure your ideas in a sustained and persuasive way. Another way is to include transitions and rhetorical devices to help your readers understand your ideas.

Some Rhetorical Devices You Can Use to Strengthen Your Organization	Transitional Words and Phrases for Different Types of Organization
• Metaphor • Simile • Analogy • Hyperbole • Irony	• **Time Order:** first, soon, in the end • **Point by Point:** considering the characters, as to the plot, in the climactic scene • **Logical Order:** to begin with, furthermore, as a result

Exercise

Identify the transitional words and rhetorical devices in the sentences below.

To begin with, Holmes and Moriarty each weave webs of deception in *The Final Adventure.* Holmes's web is, in fact, the larger of the two, constructed to slowly contract around his prey. The prey, Moriarty, escapes the outer strands of the web only to be caught in the center. In the end, he cannot escape the central strand because it is not a deception but the truth—evidence to convict the crime boss and destroy his syndicate.

Revise

Check your sentences. Have you connected your sentences with transitional words and phrases? Have you used rhetorical devices to strengthen your ideas? If not, add some to clarify and improve the flow of your ideas.

Organization
Transitions and rhetorical devices help connect the ideas in sentences.

> To begin with, Tom also feels trapped, like a bug working in a shoe factory, and though he wishes to be a poet. Coworkers Friends call him "Shakespeare" (92). Tom makes works simply to make money to support his mother and sister, though he spends nights at the movies, wishing for grand adventure. . . .

Revising for Development of Ideas

When you revise for the *development of ideas*, you check your thesis statement, topic sentences, and details. These two pages will also help you balance your ideas with ideas from primary and secondary sources. As you revise, also look for places to include effective quotations.

Have I balanced my views with those from other sources?

Your personal interpretation of a play is the basis for your work and should not be overshadowed by other sources. Still, reviewing primary and secondary sources can help you support your thesis in a powerful way. Primary sources include the work itself and, possibly, any direct interviews with the author, actors, or director of the play. Secondary sources include other reviewers who can help you support your thesis with pertinent thoughts or quotations.

Exercise

Read the paragraph that follows. Identify each sentence as a personal view or observation or one from a primary or secondary source. Describe how the other sources reinforce the personal views.

In *Dear World,* the main character, Countess Aurelia, is initially hard to understand. In a dark and dreary Paris just after World War II, she refuses to accept what has happened in the war and often what is happening before her eyes. In the play she believes that "the sun is always shining, just behind the clouds" (13). As one reviewer observed, "She takes Pollyanna's optimism and advances it to the next level: full blown insanity." But gradually, the dedication to her own vision and resistance to the pessimism voiced by others is infectious, not just to other characters in the play, but to the audience as well.

Check your sources. Be sure you have balanced your own views with those from other sources. Ask yourself the following questions:

1. Have I clearly represented my own views?
2. Have I used primary and secondary sources to support my thesis?
3. Are my sources valid, reliable, and relevant to the topic and thesis?

Interpret the Theme of a Play

Have I used effective quotations?

You have used effective quotations in your interpretive essay if you have quoted only those passages that make a strong, clear point. Quotations from the primary source of the text illustrate a general opinion with a specific example. An interpretation with too many quotations becomes cumbersome, while one with too few quotations gives the reader little insight into the play.

Exercise

In the following paragraph, decide which quotation should remain and which should be deleted. Give reasons for your decision.

1   The madwomen enlist the aid of the Sewerman who poles around the sewers
2   of Paris on a gondola. The Sewerman seems to have the same madness as the
3   ladies, reveling in garbage: "It used to be if garbage smelled a little strange, it was
4   only because it was a little confused. Everything was there: sardines, cologne,
5   iodine, roses. Ah! The feast you found floating by" (43). The Sewerman's madness
6   allows him to see beauty in everything, even garbage. A stark contrast is drawn
7   between the Sewerman's madness and the madness of rampant capitalism, which
8   sees beauty in nothing. As the politician sings: "There will be a sweet taste in the
9   air, of industrial waste in the air" (32).

Revise

Check your quotations. Be sure that each one strongly supports your point and that you have not used too many or too few quotations.

Development of Ideas
An ineffective quotation is deleted.

When Laura said "pleurosis," Jim heard "blue roses," and called her that name (112). The name is another symbol of Laura's odd and fragile beauty. ~~Jim apologizes about the nickname, saying, "I hope you didn't mind" (113).~~

Revising for Voice

When you revise your play interpretation for voice, make sure you effectively narrate the plot and analyze the theme.

Have I used a compelling narrative voice?

You have used a compelling narrative voice if your summary of the plot is vivid and inviting and your character descriptions are revealing. A compelling narrative voice achieves consistency of tone by doing the following things:

1. **Describes** people, places, and things using tropes, such as metaphors, similes, analogies, hyperbole, or rhetorical questions.
2. **Shows** important action with vivid words and by employing schemes such as parallelism, antithesis, inverted word order, repetition, and reversed structures.
3. **Provides** dialogue that reveals personalities and uses transitional words and phrases to improve tone.

Exercise

For each pair of sentences, indicate which sentence has a better consistency of tone and why.

1. **a.** The game show host, Brad Bowers, doesn't seem very genuine.
   b. The game show host, Brad Bowers, wears a perpetual plastic smile and an obvious toupee.
2. **a.** Brad Bowers bursts through the curtain opening, leaps down from the stage like a kangaroo, and grabs audience members to join in the game show, *King of the Mountain*.
   b. Brad Bowers comes out on stage and then goes down in the audience and asks questions to see who knows the answers.
3. **a.** Bowers is so vain that he refuses to wear glasses, though he needs them.
   b. Bowers declares, "There's nothing wrong with my eyes," just before he runs into a couch and tumbles headlong.

Refine your narrative voice. Review the part of your essay that focuses on the plot and characters. Make sure you achieve a consistency of tone with clear descriptions, vivid verbs, and dialogue that reveals personality. Review your use of tropes, schemes, and transitional words and phrases.

Interpret the Theme of a Play

Have I used an effective analytical voice?

You have used an effective analytical voice if your writing consistantly does the following things:

1. **Divides** a topic into parts.
2. **Defines** each part.
3. **Shows** how the parts relate to each other and to the whole.
4. **Includes** references and commentary on quotations from the text.

Exercise

Read the paragraph below and identify how the writer divides the theme into parts, defines each part, shows the relationship between the parts, and comments on quotations.

> All of the contestants in *Game Show* hope for a shot at the American Dream. Ethel Tinsley wants to win enough money to publish her book. She stated with great conviction that, "I am sure that with my background, I have a shot at winning," when interviewed by a reporter backstage. Dolly Perkins hopes to be able to move out of the "retirement villa" where she lives. Kathy Burns and Steve Nystrom both want to advance their film careers—and perhaps rekindle their romance. Most of the contestants are destined not for the American Dream but for the American Reality: that competition results in one winner and many losers.

Review your analytical voice. Read the part of your essay that analyzes the theme. Be sure you have divided the theme into parts and shown how the parts relate to each other. Consider including a quote from the play to strengthen your interpretation.

Voice
The writer includes a quotation from the play to strengthen the interpretation of the theme.

Shortly afterward, Amanda learns of Tom's dreams of adventure and his plans to join the military. "Man is by instinct a lover, a hunter, a fighter, and none of those instincts are given much play at the warehouse," Tom tells his mother (64).

Revising Improving Your Writing

Check your revising. On a piece of paper, write the numbers 1 to 11. If you can answer "yes" to a question, put a check mark after that number. If not, continue to revise that part of your essay.

Revising Checklist

Focus and Coherence

_____ 1. Does my thesis statement focus on a major theme of the play?
_____ 2. Have I analyzed the theme using details that are focused on the theme and topics?
_____ 3. Have I created an effective introduction and conclusion and used appropriate quotations?

Organization

_____ 4. Is my writing logically organized and easy to follow?
_____ 5. Have I used transitional words and phrases and rhetorical devices to connect ideas?
_____ 6. Does the conclusion expand upon the theme?

Development of Ideas

_____ 7. Are my ideas explained or described with unique and thoughtful details?
_____ 8. Have I included enough specific details to help the reader understand and appreciate my ideas?
_____ 9. Do the ideas flow from paragraph to paragraph without significant gaps?

Voice

_____ 10. Have I used an engaging narrative voice to summarize the play?
_____ 11. Have I used a strong analytical voice to explain the theme?

Make a clean copy. When you finish revising your essay, make a clean copy for editing.

Interpret the Theme of a Play

305

Editing

Once you have finished revising your work for its content, you need to edit it for punctuation, capitalization, spelling, and grammar.

Keys to Effective Editing

1. Use a dictionary, a thesaurus, and the "Proofreader's Guide" in the back of this book to check your writing.

2. Check your use of semicolons as well as other punctuation, capitalization, spelling, and grammar.

3. Edit on a clean revised copy of your essay. Then either enter your changes on the computer file or create a new handwritten copy that includes the corrections.

4. Use the editing and proofreading marks on pages 638–639.

Grammar

When you edit for *conventions,* you check punctuation, capitalization, spelling, and grammar.

Have I used adverb clauses correctly?

There are two types of clauses—independent and dependent. An independent clause is a complete thought that can stand alone as a sentence. A dependent clause, sometimes called a subordinate clause, is not a complete thought, so it cannot stand alone as a sentence. An **adverb clause** is one type of dependent clause.

- An adverb clause is a dependent clause that is used like an adverb. An adverb clause can modify a verb, an adjective, or an adverb.
- Adverb clauses can answer any of the following questions about the words they modify: *When? Where? Why? To what extent? For what purpose? Under what condition?*
- Adverb clauses always begin with a subordinating conjunction. Some of the most common subordinating conjunctions appear in the list below.

Subordinating Conjunctions List

after	in order that	before	even though
as long as	because	since	so that
if	until	when	whenever
unless	wherever	whether	while
where	as	as if	

Grammar Exercise

Combine each pair of sentences into one sentence by making one of them an adverb clause. Use a different subordinating conjunction in each sentence.

1. Marisol's day got off to a bad start. She did not hear her alarm go off.
2. Marisol's tire was nearly flat. She was able to pull safely off the road and call for assistance.
3. The bridge construction was finished. She could not take her usual route to work.
4. She did not make it to work on time. The meeting would have to be rescheduled for next week.

Check your adverb clauses. Make sure you have followed the rules shown above for correctly using adverb clauses.

Interpret the Theme of a Play

Have I used adverb phrases correctly?

You already know that an adverb is a word that gives an additional detail about the meaning of a verb, an adjective, or another adverb. **Adverb phrases** modify the same parts of speech. A prepositional phrase that does the work of an adverb is called an adverb phrase. Adverb phrases answer the following questions: *Where? When? How? How long? To what degree? Why?*

Adverb: Paulita is travelling abroad.
Adverb phrase: Paulita is travelling to Greece.

- An adverb phrase can modify a verb:
  Teodor walks in a swift manner to get to his locker between classes.
- An adverb phrase can modify an adjective:
  Teodor's sister was tall for her age.
- An adverb phrase can modify an adverb:
  Teodor likes to practice his swimming strokes early in the morning.

Note: Adverb phrases are not always located near the words that they modify. They can appear anywhere in a sentence. Two or more adverb phrases can also be located in one sentence, modifying the same word.

Grammar Exercise

Read the ten prepositional phrases below. Then write ten sentences, using them as adverb phrases.

1. in a hurry
2. for my sake
3. before the party
4. at the train station
5. at the corner
6. in her last message
7. by the bay
8. to the airplane pilot
9. by chance
10. about our victory

Edit for grammar. Read your essay, underlining the adverb clauses and phrases that you find. If there are none, look for places to add some. Check to see if there are two sentences that you can combine into one sentence with an adverb clause, using a subordinating conjunction.

Sentence Structure

When you edit for *sentence structure,* you check to see whether you have used a variety of sentence structures.

Have I used compound and complex sentences correctly?

Sentences can be classified according to the number and kinds of clauses that they contain. Three types of sentence structure are *compound, complex,* and *compound-complex.* They are formed by using the following rules:

- A **compound sentence** has two or more independent clauses. They are joined together either by a comma and a coordinating conjunction or by a semicolon.
  Felix started a band, so his sister bought a new guitar.
  Felix started a band; his sister bought a new guitar.

- A **complex sentence** has at least one independent clause (called the *main clause)* and at least one subordinate clause. The main clause and the subordinate clause each has its own subject and verb.
  As soon as Felix started a band, his sister bought a new guitar.

- A **compound-complex sentence** has at least two main clauses and at least one subordinate clause.
  As soon as Felix started a band, his sister bought a new guitar; the next day, they practiced for three hours.

Grammar Exercise

Identify the structure of each of the following sentences as *compound, complex,* or *compound-complex.*

1. The road was washed away after the storm struck last Wednesday, and it hasn't been repaired yet.
2. The sky was blue, but the forecast called for rain.
3. The minute it started to hail, everyone dashed indoors.

Check your sentence structure. Make sure that your essay contains a variety of compound, complex, and compound-complex sentence structures.

Mechanics: Punctuation

Have I used semicolons correctly?

The semicolon can be used to mark the connection of sentences that are closely related. It is a stronger mark of punctuation than a comma, but it is weaker than a period. Semicolons join complete ideas within sentences and are also used to avoid confusion in sentences that already contain commas.

- Use a semicolon between independent clauses that are not connected by the conjunctions *and, or, nor, for, but, so,* or *yet.*
  The antique vase had been stored in the attic for 15 years; the owner had forgotten all about it.

- Use a semicolon before a conjunctive adverb (*however, therefore, hence,* and so on) or a transitional phrase (*in fact, on the other hand,* and so on) that introduces an independent clause.
  The antique vase had been stored in the attic for 15 years; however, the owner had forgotten all about it.

- Use a semicolon to separate a series of items that already contain commas. This use of the semicolon is for clarity.
  The owner of the house kept a treasure-trove of items up in the attic: the antique vase, a gift from her father; a set of bone china, for very special meals; and a painting of the French countryside, a souvenir from her time spent abroad.

Exercise

Indicate where a semicolon is needed in the following sentences.

1. Luz received tips for taking care of her pets from friends in San Antonio, Texas, Riverside, California, and Tulsa, Oklahoma.
2. She placed six Japanese koi fish in the pond. Their orange scales shimmered in the sun.
3. Luz's household was expanding by the minute. She was taking care of six koi fish, who were growing rapidly, a Great Dane with an enormous appetite, and a stray cat who was desperate for attention.
4. Luz's household was expanding all the time. In fact, it had doubled in less than a year.

Check your punctuation. Review your essay for punctuation usage. Look for places that semicolons can be used. Remember that semicolons are only used between two independent clauses or between two or more items in a series.

Editing Checking for Conventions

Check your editing. On a piece of paper, write the numbers 1 to 10. Put a check by the number if you can answer "yes" to that question. If not, continue to edit your essay for that convention.

Editing Checklist

Conventions

GRAMMAR

_____ 1. Have I used correct verb tenses throughout?
_____ 2. Do all of my adverb clauses begin with a subordinating conjunction?
_____ 3. Have I correctly combined sentences with adverb phrases?
_____ 4. Have I avoided comma errors?

SENTENCE STRUCTURE

_____ 5. Do I use a variety of correctly structured sentences that clearly communicate my ideas?
_____ 6. Have I included a variety of compound, complex, and compound-complex sentences?

MECHANICS (CAPITALIZATION AND PUNCTUATION)

_____ 7. Do I start all of my sentences with capital letters?
_____ 8. Have I used semicolons and other punctuation marks correctly and consistently?

SPELLING

_____ 9. Have I spelled all of my words correctly?
_____ 10. Have I used a dictionary to identify spellings of unfamiliar words or words my spell-checker may have missed?

Creating a Title

Be sure to give your interpretation a title that attracts the reader's attention and represents your essay well. Try one of these strategies:

- Create a play on words: **Glass People**
- Use a common expression: **Those Who Live in Glass Apartments**
- Take a line from the essay: **Broken to Fit In**

Interpret the Theme of a Play

Publishing

Sharing Your Essay

You're nearly done! You've selected a topic, gathered and organized details, written a first draft, revised it, and edited it. Now it's time to share your interpretation of a play with others.

 Make a final copy. Follow your teacher's instructions on how to format your paper. Prepare a final copy of your essay and proofread it for errors.

Getting Feedback

- Ask your peers and your teacher to review your work.
- Ask them to give you honest feedback about what works and what does not work in your essay.
- Ask your peer and teacher reviewers how they would like to give you their feedback. Would they rather provide verbal feedback in a discussion or give you written feedback? If they choose to give you verbal feedback, remember to take notes.

Using Feedback to Revise

Review the feedback that your peers and teacher have given you. Which comments are the most helpful? Which suggestions will make your essay stronger? Revise your essay by working these comments into it.

Selecting an Audience

Search online for the play that you wrote about. Find Web sites that have bulletin boards. Post your essay where others interested in the play can read it.

Creating a Final Copy

Carefully review the guidelines for any submission requirements to the Web site that you have chosen. Be sure to prepare your essay to meet those requirements before you publish it online.

Evaluating a Play Interpretation

To evaluate your essay, use the holistic scoring guide on pages 36–37 and the essays below. These essays are examples of writing for each score on the scoring guide (1–4). Notice that the first essay received a score of 4. Read the description for a score of 4 on pages 36–37. Then read the essay. Use the same steps to study the other examples.

Writing that fits a score of 4 is very strong.

Pygmalion

You have probably heard the expression "you can't tell a book by its cover." The expression makes the statement that appearance does not always reflect reality. Of course, this idea is often applied to people. As we all know, a person's outward appearance, including the person's way of dressing, speaking, and acting, is not always an accurate reflection of that person's true character. The idea that people's appearances differ from their inner selves is the main theme of George Bernard Shaw's play <u>Pygmalion</u>.

Shaw set <u>Pygmalion</u> during England's Victorian era of the late nineteenth and early twentieth centuries. During this period, social roles in that country were largely static, and the rules of conduct were strict. It would be almost impossible, for example, for a working class person to achieve a high social status. In contrast, a person born into the upper class would stay there, no matter what. The classes did not mix among each other. Everyone was treated according to his or her social status. Appearance meant everything.

<u>Pygmalion</u> begins with an encounter between a poverty-stricken girl named Eliza and Freddy Eynsford-Hills, a young man from a genteel family. Eliza is selling flowers on the street corner to survive. Freddy bumps into her, knocks her flowers to the ground. Because she is of a lower class, Freddy scarcely notices her. However, two gentlemen, Professor Henry Higgins and Colonel Pickering, do notice Eliza. Higgins, a linguistics teacher, bets Pickering that by correcting Eliza's low-class Cockney accent, he can convince anyone she is from the upper class.

The introduction is meaningful and clearly states the essay's main idea.

The organization of the essay puts this necessary background information in the correct order.

Main characters and plot are effectively outlined.

As the play progresses, so does Eliza's outward transformation. Professor Higgins helps Eliza to eliminate her accent, and he and Pickering provide her with the clothes and jewelry she needs to look the part of an upper-class woman. The first real test for Liza is when she meets the Eynsford-Hills and their son Freddy, the very young man who failed to notice her at all as a flower girl. Seeing the "new" Liza, Freddy falls deeply in love. Later, Liza attends an upper-class ball where she successfully masquerades as a member of that class. Higgins wins his bet.

What might seem like a simple story—the rise of a poor girl into high society—is actually a complex look at social attitudes. Though Eliza looks and sounds like a member of the upper class, she does not have the education, the money, and most important, the family connections to become one. She is too graceful and well-behaved to fit in as a lower-class woman either. "What am I fit for? What have you left me fit for? Where am I to go? What am I to do? What's to become of me?" Liza asks. The experiment has caused her great harm.

However, the story ends with a twist. Liza has grown on the inside by learning manners and human decency, and she knows it. She can keep what she has learned no matter what her outside appearance. If society judges her differently because of how she looks, it is society's loss. If any of these ideas stir a response in you, it may be because you can relate to them in your own life. While Pygmalion was first performed in 1913, its theme—that you can't judge a book by its cover—is a timeless one, and is completely relevant today.

> The author explores nuances and complexities in the text.

> The conclusion reinforces the main idea and makes a personal connection to the reader.

Writing that fits a score of 3 is strong in most ways.

3

Macbeth, or Why It's Bad to Be Too Ambitious

People often dream of having wealth and power. What would you do to be the all-powerful ruler of a medieval kingdom? If you are the character Macbeth in William Shakespeare's tragedy Macbeth, the answer is just about anything, including commit murder. Written in the early 1600s, the play addresses a theme that is timeless: human ambition. And its commentary on the theme is that ambition—or at least too much of it, anyway—is a very, very bad thing.

As the play opens, Macbeth, who is a general in King Duncan's army, is returning home to Scotland after a great military victory. Along with his friend Banquo, Macbeth has defeated the combined armies of Norway and Ireland. In the battle, Macbeth has shown bravery, heroism, and loyalty. But these traits will soon be lost.

Macbeth and Banquo meet three witches, who greet them with prophecies. Macbeth, they say, will be named "Thane of Cawdor," and will "be king hereafter." Neither Macbeth nor Banquo believe the prophecies, but one soon comes true. For his heroism, Macbeth is named Thane of Cawdor by King Duncan.

Initially, Macbeth is a good man, but his scheming wife Lady Macbeth helps increase his ambition. She convinces Macbeth to murder King Duncan so Macbeth can claim the thrown. Macbeth does so, then blames the killing on two servants and kills them before they can testify. Fearing for their lives, Dunca's airs flee, and Macbeth takes the throne.

As a rich and powerful king, Macbeth might be happy, but Shakespeare has a lot to say about using murder to gain power. In a dark relentless style, he lets the man once honored as a hero sink deeper into depravity. Driven insane with ambition, Macbeth arranges the death of anyone who could threaten his power. He hires two assassings to kill his friend Banquo. even the bonds of friendship are broken by ambition.

Macbeth visits the witches again. They speak some more prophecies, which lead Macbeth to believe that no man can kill

Side notes:
- The main idea is clearly explained. The writer's unique voice is evident.
- A transition sentence would make the start of this paragraph smoother.
- Minor errors in conventions do not interfere with the reader's understanding.

> A quotation from the play could better explain the witches' prophecies.

him. But Macbeth, has misinterpreted the prophecies, and a man that is able to kill him will soon return to the scene. His name is MacDuff, the Thane of Fife, and he is loyal to King Duncan. If Macbeth is a model of blind ambition, MacDuff is a model of honorable behavior.

> This paragraph could make a better connection to the play's theme.

From the moment of Duncan's murder, MacDuff suspects Macbeth is responsible. While MacDuff is in England, Macbeth has his entire family murdered. As discontent over Macbeth's bloody rule grows, MacDuff returns with an army to attack Macbeth. Lady Macbeth's death, possibley by suicide, makes things even bleaker. Macbeth's world is completely unraveling, and soon, he is killed by MacDuff.

> The conclusion is weakened by redundancy.

Macbeth is a ruinous tragedy, and one of Shakespeare's darkest works. Still, it uses its power to explore an important human theme—that of unlimited ambition. In trying to gain power at any cost, Macbeth loses his humanity. And by doing this, he becomes less human than he was before.

Writing that fits a score of 2 is strong in some ways.

The Impoertance of Being Earnest

<u>The Importance of Being Earnest</u> is by Oscar Wilde. It was first performed in 1895, and is one of his most famous plays. The play is about two freinds. Who both pretend to be someone who they are not. Being who they are not causes problems for both of them. That is what almost everyone is.

One of the main characters claimes to be someone named Ernest Worthing. But that is not his real name. His real name is Jack. At least that's his name in the countrey because he has a double identity. He is honest and good and claims to have a brother named Ernest in the city. In the city, he goes by the name Earnest and is a fun-loving bachelor. So both places he goes he is someone he is not.

Jack wanst to date his friend Algernon's cousin Gwendolen. Algernon is leading a double life as well, he go off to an inamginary sick friend named "Bunbury." Algernon is also someone he is not.

To be earnest means to be honest or sincere. At the time people acted like they was, but they was not. They just acted that way, honest or reponib;e, but they're image was all that counted. Lady Bracknell, Algernon's cousin and Gwendolin's aunt, tries to act like she is better than everyone else. She interviews Ernest about his past before he can date Gwendolin for example. But she is just a bad person.

So I am sure Ocar Wilde would like to say that we should be earnest. And not many of his characters are. But there is a happy ending anyway. Jack turns out to be an abandoned baby who was named Earnest afer all. He and Gwendolyn fall in love. So do Algernon and Cecily. So everything ends happily.

- The introduction is superficial.
- Wordiness and repetition interfere with the flow of ideas.
- Errors in conventions interfere with meaning.
- Ideas are poorly organized and somewhat unclear.
- The conclusion is superficial.

Interpret the Theme of a Play   317

Writing that fits a score of 1 is weak.

1

Statement of main idea about theme is missing.

There are major problems with conventions. It also lacks a logical flow of ideas.

Problems with conventions make the message hard to understand.

Organization is poor and the conclusion is missing.

Riders to the Sea

Some playes are happy and some are sad. This one I think the saddest playe ever. It is called Riders to the Sea it was writen by John Millington Singe, and every body dies and when they doe it is very trajic and sad. It is sad that they die, which makes Maurya fel terrible. She is the mother, but she do not die.

The playe abut Maurya he life is sad because five of her sone plus her husbind was drowened in the oceana nd they are all died except Michael who will soon die but they need to know if his clothes. Shwab, Shamuss, Patch, And Stepehen plus her husbind have died at sea. Now Bartley go to sea which is dangeuis work as a salor on a boat she worie he drown, too witch wuld be very sad and trajic too.

So Maurya is very upset. Ansd sh is angry at Bartley, and they have an argumint. The Brtley rides off his horse and he dorwns. But Maurya doesn't noe yet hat he have ben killed. But if she did noe it, how would you feel the same as her? The women kene which is lik cryieng. They crye and Maurya does too because of Bartley. It is a sadplaye as I have said befour.

Now Maurya finds out and that is the saddest part. She has lost everthing to the sea and she is a widoe and she says that no one can live for ever. It is the saddest play I have ever red.

Reflecting on Your Writing

Take a few moments to think back on your experience of interpreting a play. Reflection helps you to retain what you have learned and prepare for future writing assignments.

My Play Interpretation

1. The strongest part of my interpretation is . . .

2. The part that most needs to be changed is . . .

3. The main thing I learned about interpreting a play is . . .

4. Next time I interpret a play or another work of literature, I would like to . . .

5. One question I still have about analyzing ambiguities, nuances, and complexities in a play is . . .

6. Right now, I would describe my writing ability as (excellent, good, fair, poor) because . . .

Interpretive Response
Interpret a Novel

An interpretation of a literary text requires a different focus than a personal response or a review of a work's merits. When interpreting a novel, you will present your understanding, or interpretation, of the work. One way to do this is by using quotations effectively; analyzing the author's use of rhetorical and stylistic devices; and identifying ambiguities, nuances, and complexities within the text. Anticipating and responding to readers' questions will make your interpretation even stronger.

In this section, you will read a sample interpretation of the novel *The Curious Incident of the Dog in the Night-Time* by Mark Haddon, tracing the theme of mystery that runs through the novel. Then you will write your own interpretation of a literary text, developing the theme by addressing the elements you have identified in the sample essay and connecting all of your main points with specific references to the text.

Writing Guidelines

Subject: A novel
Purpose: To analyze a main theme
Form: Literary interpretation
Audience: Classmates

"A good novel tells us the truth about its hero; but a bad novel tells us the truth about its author."

—G. K. Chesterton

Novel Interpretation

In the following interpretation, Andrew examines a main theme in the novel *The Curious Incident of the Dog in the Night-Time*. The side notes highlight important features in the interpretation.

The Limits of Being Normal

Introduction
The interpretation opens with an intriguing quotation and ends with the thesis statement (underlined).

Sherlock Holmes once asked Dr. Watson about "the curious incident of the dog in the night-time." When Watson pointed out that the dog did nothing in the night-time, Holmes responded, "That was the curious incident." In *The Curious Incident of the Dog in the Night-Time*, Mark Haddon introduces another detective obsessed with discovering the truth. Christopher John Francis Boone is a 15-year-old autistic savant who has trouble understanding other people but knows every prime number up to 7,057. <u>As Christopher investigates the mysterious death of a neighborhood dog, Haddon uses the theme of mystery to explore the complexities of human interaction.</u>

Middle
Use of the word *cradle* suggests Christopher's close connection with animals.

The story begins when Christopher discovers a crime scene across the street. A large black poodle named Wellington lies dead, and Christopher kneels to cradle the dog. When the dog's owner discovers him there, Christopher says he did not kill the dog, but he gets in a scuffle with the police and lands in jail. After his father comes to get him out, Christopher pledges to solve the mystery of Wellington's death.

Christopher's inability to read facial expressions adds complexity to the novel.

The reader is given more information about people with autism.

As Christopher investigates the killing, Haddon brings him into direct confrontation with a deeper mystery: other human beings. Like most people with autism, Christopher has trouble reading even simple facial expressions. At one point, he says that people look at him when they speak, trying to see what he is thinking, but he can't see what they are thinking. People are confusing to Christopher. By contrast, he likes dogs because he can always tell what they are thinking; they have only four moods — "happy, sad, cross and concentrating" — and they don't lie since they can't talk (4). All these facts make Christopher alone in his social world and demonstrate the very meaning of the word *autism*. In fact, Christopher has a recurrent, favorite dream: "And in the dream nearly everyone on the earth is dead . . . and eventually there is no one left in the world" except people with autism (198).

A rhetorical device—an idiom—illustrates another aspect of Christopher's uniqueness.

Haddon deepens the theme of mystery by exploring the complexities of human language. For example, Christopher never lies. A lie means saying something happened that didn't happen, and Christopher cannot see the point of it. For him, the only things worth speaking about are facts and mathematics. Christopher also doesn't understand jokes and metaphors, such as "apple of my eye." He writes, "When I try and make a picture of the phrase in my head, it just confuses me because imagining an apple in someone's eye doesn't have anything to do with liking someone a lot . . . " (15).

The writer identifies a key ambiguity in the novel.

Christopher's quest for truth leads him inevitably to discover even deeper mysteries. Two years before the beginning of the story, Christopher's mother died of a sudden heart attack. At that time, Mrs. Shears, the neighbor woman who owned Wellington, became a family friend who helped them deal with their grief. Her friendship with the Boones ended on the night that Wellington was killed—but the question is whether the friendship ended because of the dog's death, or the dog died because the friendship ended. As Christopher investigates, he strips away years' worth of lies and discovers the truth.

Conclusion Quoting the main character in the conclusion adds depth to the interpretation and reinforces the theme.

At the beginning of the book, Christopher writes, "This is a murder mystery novel" (4), but it is much more than that. Haddon uses the theme of mystery to show how deeply mysterious human expressions, language, and relationships are to a person with autism. At first, the book seems to show the limits of being autistic, but in the end, it shows the limits of being normal. Christopher himself describes it best in the final sentence of the book: "And I know I can do this because I went to London on my own, and because I solved the mystery of Who Killed Wellington? . . . and I was brave and I wrote a book and that means I can do anything" (221).

Respond to the reading. Answer the following questions.

Focus and Coherence (1) What is the focus, or main idea, of the interpretation? (2) Are the ideas clearly connected?

Organization (3) Is there a logical progression of ideas that makes the interpretation easy for the reader to follow?

Development of Ideas (4) How does the writer's analysis of stylistic and rhetorical devices help develop the theme?

Prewriting Considering the Elements of a Novel

Using Quotations

When you write a literary interpretation, quoting dialogue and other passages from the work helps develop your ideas and gives your reader a real feel for the characters. Keep in mind, however, that it is possible to include too many quotations—or too few. Not using enough quotations may mean that you are not adequately supporting your main points; on the other hand, relying too much on quotations can limit your interpretation.

Look at the following quotations from the novel.

> "And in the dream nearly everyone on the earth is dead . . . and eventually there is no one left in the world . . ."
>
> "When I try and make a picture of the phrase in my head, it just confuses me because imagining an apple in someone's eye doesn't have anything to do with liking someone a lot . . ."

By weaving these quotations into the analysis, Andrew not only helps a reader understand the subject of autism but also fleshes out the main character's personality.

Novel Quotations

As you are planning your interpretation, look for key quotations in the novel that will support your thesis statement and help you develop your theme. You will probably find more quotations than you will end up using, but it is good to have several to choose from.

Anticipating Your Readers' Response

When interpreting a novel, put yourself in your readers' shoes. How much background information will they need? What questions will they have? Think about these questions as you are planning your interpretation. Be sure to give your readers enough information about the subject so that they will be able to understand your main points.

Andrew wanted to make sure that his readers learned some important facts about autism in his novel interpretation. He has included enough detail to support his view of the subject. When writing your interpretation, be sure to back up your statements with support so that your analysis will hold water.

Writing the Thesis Statement

Once you have analyzed the elements of your novel, write a thesis statement about the theme you will focus on. Andrew used the following formula to focus on one theme of *The Curious Incident of the Dog in the Night-Time*.

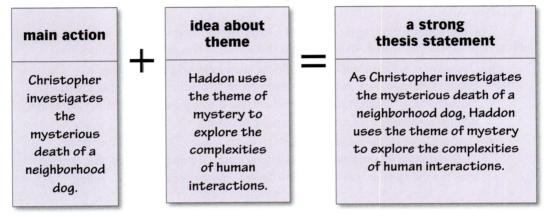

Write your thesis statement. Use the model above to meld the story and theme of your novel into a strong thesis statement. Try two or three versions if necessary.

Analyzing Stylistic or Rhetorical Devices

As you read the novel, pay special attention to the author's use of stylistic or rhetorical devices. Your interpretation should analyze the aesthetic effects, or artistic impact, of these devices. There are many types of stylistic or rhetorical devices (see pages **634–635**), including the following:

	**sentence structure**: long or short, complex or simple **imagery**: language that appeals to the senses **word choice**: informal or formal, descriptive or plain
	**repetition**: repeated words and phrases to make a point **parallelism**: parallel sentence structure emphasizes ideas **figures of speech**: comparisons between unlike things

Develop the theme. Look up additional examples of these devices. Then create a chart like the one above and identify some rhetorical and stylistic devices in your novel. Decide which details you would like to include in your interpretation to support your thesis.

Drafting Creating Your First Draft

As you write your interpretation, use your previous planning and the following guidelines.

Introduction

The introductory paragraph should introduce the theme of your analysis and end with your thesis statement. (Also include the name of the novel and its author.)

- Open with an interesting insight or background information.
  Sherlock Holmes once asked Dr. Watson about "the curious incident of the dog in the night-time." When Watson pointed out that the dog did nothing in the night-time, Holmes responded, "That was the curious incident."
- End with your thesis statement.
  As Christopher investigates the mysterious death of a neighborhood dog, Haddon uses the theme of mystery to explore the complexities of human interaction.

Middle Paragraphs

The middle paragraphs identify and analyze ambiguities, nuances, and complexities within the text. (Note: Cite text evidence to support your ideas.)

- Identify and analyze complexities and ambiguity—multiple interpretations of the text.
  The question is whether the friendship ended because of the dog's death, or the dog died because the friendship ended.
- Identify and analyze nuances—subtle or slight differences in meaning.
  Christopher's quest for truth leads him inevitably to discover even deeper mysteries.

Conclusion

Your concluding paragraph provides a final interpretation of the theme.

- Restate your thesis.
  . . . Haddon uses the theme of mystery to show how deeply mysterious human . . . relationships are to a person with autism.
- Give the reader something new to think about.
  At first, the book seems to show the limits of being autistic, but in the end, it shows the limits of being normal.

Write your first draft. Use the guidelines above and your prewriting work to help you complete the first draft of your interpretation.

Interpret a Novel 325

Revising Improving Your First Draft

After you have written a first draft, put it aside for a while to get a fresh perspective. Then revise your work.

Revise your analysis. Carefully review your writing using the checklist below. Make the necessary improvements.

Revising Checklist

Focus and Coherence

_____ 1. Do I maintain a specific focus throughout the interpretation?
_____ 2. Do I include a meaningful introduction and conclusion?
_____ 3. Are the ideas clearly connected to each other and to my thesis statement?

Organization

_____ 4. Have I clearly stated the thesis in the introduction?
_____ 5. Does my interpretation have a strong beginning, middle, and ending?
_____ 6. Are my ideas presented logically?

Development of Ideas

_____ 7. Do I include quotations from the text?
_____ 8. Do I analyze rhetorical and stylistic devices to help develop my ideas?
_____ 9. Do I anticipate readers' questions and contradictory information?
_____ 10. Have I analyzed ambiguities, nuances, and complexities?

Voice

_____ 11. Does my voice sound authentic and original?

Editing Checking for Conventions

After you have made the necessary improvements in your interpretation, edit your work for errors in grammar, sentence structure, mechanics (punctuation and capitalization), and spelling.

Editing Checklist

Conventions

_____ 1. Have I used correct end punctuation after each sentence?
_____ 2. Have I used commas correctly?
_____ 3. Have I spelled all words correctly?
_____ 4. Do my subjects and verbs agree in number?
_____ 5. Do my pronouns refer to clear antecedents and agree with them in number and gender?
_____ 6. Have I placed quotation marks around exact words quoted from the novel?
_____ 7. Have I included page numbers in parentheses after quoted material?

Edit your interpretation. Use the checklist above to edit for conventions. Then, exchange papers with a classmate. Give each other feedback and suggestions for revision. Finally, prepare a final copy of your essay and proofread it.

Publishing Sharing Your Interpretation

When you complete your interpretation, it's time to share your ideas. Here are a number of options:

- **Read your interpretation aloud.** Read aloud portions of your interpretation that you think are especially good.
- **Send your interpretation to a newspaper or magazine.** Check the submission guidelines and format the work as a review of a book.
- **Post your interpretation at a library.** Ask your school or local librarian for permission.
- **E-mail your interpretation to the publisher or author.** Search a Web site for a "contact us" link. Publishers and authors appreciate hearing from readers—especially those who like their books!

Publish your interpretation. Choose one of the methods above, format your interpretation accordingly, and share your work with others.

Interpretive Response
Writing an Analysis of an Expository Text

A novel analysis explores elements of plot, character, and structure. An analysis of an expository text, on the other hand, examines a writer's presentation of facts, details, opinions, and examples to achieve a specific purpose, such as summarizing, explaining, or comparing various subjects. When writing an analysis of an expository text, you will examine the ways the author has incorporated various elements. There are several ways to do this, including using quotations; analyzing the author's use of rhetorical and stylistic devices; and identifying ambiguities, nuances, and complexities within the text. Anticipating and responding to readers' questions will make your analysis even stronger.

In this section, you will read a sample analysis of the essay *Of Studies* by Francis Bacon. Then you will plan, develop, and present an analysis of an expository text, using the strategies you identify in the sample analysis.

Writing Guidelines

Subject: An expository text
Form: Expository analysis
Purpose: To analyze an expository essay
Audience: Classmates

"Either we write something worth reading or do something worth writing."
—Benjamin Franklin

Analysis of an Expository Text

In the following sample, the writer analyzes an essay extolling the value of reading and study, which was written about 400 years ago by the British author Sir Francis Bacon. The side notes highlight important features in the analysis.

Beginning
The writer introduces the subject and ends the first paragraph with the thesis statement (underlined).

Middle
The writer points out a complexity in Bacon's argument.

A transition connects ideas.

A strong metaphor compares reading to eating.

The Benefits of Studying

Perhaps every student has asked at one time or another: What is the point of studying history or literature? Why learn physics or foreign languages? Well, a 400-year-old essay just might have the answer. Sir Francis Bacon's essay "Of Studies" argues that reading and studying in a disciplined way help us develop the capacity to think and thus to be "full" and "ready" and "exact"—all useful qualities in the world. <u>Bacon's argument about the benefits of studying is as fresh and relevant today as it was when he wrote this famous essay centuries ago.</u>

Bacon begins with the claim that "[s]tudies serve for delight, for ornament, and for ability." That is, we can study for our own enjoyment, for the pleasure of conversing with others, and for success in various professions. Bacon warns, however, that studying in and of itself is not necessarily productive. Excessive studying can be a form of "sloth," and some people can use their learning as a kind of "affectation" to impress others. According to Bacon, studies "perfect nature and are perfected by experience." They improve our minds by reining in our lazy and shallow tendencies.

Bacon next explains what kind of study he thinks is most beneficial and how to make the most of the material that we read. More than anything, he says, read in order to "weigh and consider," not to argue or to accept superficial beliefs. Bacon explains how some books have less value than others: a book might be tasted, swallowed, or "chewed and digested." Because "[r]eading makes a full man," we must eat good "food." This is also applicable to students today, who have the opportunity to learn deeply or to gain only superficial learning.

Study, according to Bacon, is good for you. It can help to alleviate intellectual and moral difficulties in the same way that some physical activities can improve various physical problems. "Histories make men wise; poets, witty; the mathematics, subtle; natural philosophy, deep . . ."

Writing an Analysis of an Expository Text   329

> Bacon concludes this argument by stating that "every defect of the mind may have a special receipt [remedy; prescription]."
>
> Bacon's "prescription" for studying is as relevant today as it was 400 years ago. Some might doubt this statement, noting that in Bacon's time only a few people could read and write. His audience was a small, privileged group of people like Bacon himself, who had studied law and become part of the inner circle of the royal court. Today there are more remedies for "defects of the mind" than there were in Bacon's time. While these historical details are interesting, the fact that Bacon's "prescription" is now available to more people does not make it less potent. Indeed, the opposite is true. Literacy is widespread, and the word *education* has a much broader meaning. Books (and the Internet) are available to all who desire knowledge or who wish to improve their skills. People still read "for delight, for ornament, and for ability."
>
> Sir Francis Bacon's argument that studies must be "perfected by experience" is still valid today. Studying a foreign language without applying it in conversation is not very productive. Studying history is of no use to a citizen unless he or she applies its lessons to current events. Ultimately, the relevance or irrelevance of study depends on the degree of effort a student is willing to apply.

Here as elsewhere, quoting Bacon's precise language helps the reader appreciate its nuances.

The writer mentions information that might contradict his or her thesis.

Ending The writer restates the thesis and provides a contemporary example to underscore the main point.

Respond to the reading. Answer the following questions.

Focus and Coherence (1) What is the writer's focus in the analysis? (2) Is the focus sustained throughout the analysis? (3) Are the writer's ideas clearly connected?

Organization (4) How is the analysis organized? (5) Does a logical progression of ideas make it easy for the reader to follow?

Development of Ideas (6) How does the writer use quotations and an analysis of stylistic and rhetorical devices to help develop his or her ideas?

Voice (7) Where in the analysis is the writer's voice most engaging?

Prewriting Considering the Elements of an Expository Text

There are many factors to consider when you are planning your analysis. Each of the following elements can contribute to an effective piece of writing.

Write the Thesis Statement

Once you have analyzed the essay and decided how to focus on the topic, write a thesis statement. The writer of this analysis thought about the main arguments of "Of Studies," and came up with a thesis statement about its relevance today.

Organize Your Analysis and Gather Support

Next, decide how you want to organize your analysis. Consider using a graphic organizer, such as a two-column chart or a cluster diagram, to gather your details and to help you structure your ideas.

Find Quotations

Look for key quotations in the expository text that will support your thesis statement and help you develop your ideas.

Identify Stylistic or Rhetorical Devices

As you read the expository text, be on the lookout for the author's use of stylistic or rhetorical devices. These might include:
- allusions,
- repetition,
- parallelism,
- or one of the other devices defined on pages 634–635.

When you do identify a stylistic or rhetorical device, consider the aesthetic effect on the text. Does it change your perception of the author's tone? Does the use of a particular stylistic or rhetorical device cause you to reconsider the author's goals or main idea?

Plan your analysis. Use the guidelines above to help organize your ideas and plan your analysis.

 TEKS 12.15C(i), 12.15C(iv)
ELPS 5G

Writing an Analysis of an Expository Text

Drafting Creating Your First Draft

As you write your analysis, use your planning from the previous page and refer to the following guidelines.

Introductory Paragraph

The introductory paragraph should introduce the topic of your analysis and end with your thesis statement.

- Open with an interesting insight or background information.
  Perhaps every student has asked at one time or another: What is the point of studying history or literature? . . . Well, a 400-year-old essay might have the answer.
- End with your thesis statement.
  Bacon's argument about the benefits of studying remains as fresh and relevant today as when he wrote this famous essay centuries ago.

Middle Paragraphs

The middle paragraphs identify and analyze ambiguities, nuances, and complexities within the text.

- Identify and analyze ambiguity—the interpretations of the text.
  [T]he fact that Bacon's "prescription" is now available to more people does not make it less potent.
- Identify and analyze nuances—subtle or slight differences in meaning.
  Bacon [states] that "every defect of the mind may have a special receipt [prescription]."
- Identify and analyze complexity.
  According to Bacon, studies "perfect nature and are perfected by experience."

Concluding Paragraph

Your ending paragraph wraps up your analysis.

- Restate your thesis.
  Bacon's argument that studies must be "perfected by experience" is still valid today.
- Give the reader something new to think about.
  Studying history is of no use to a citizen unless he or she applies its lessons to current events.

 Draft

Write your first draft. Use the guidelines above and your prewriting work to help you complete the first draft of your analysis.

Editing Checking for Conventions

After you have written a first draft, put it aside for a while to get a fresh perspective. Then carefully review your writing using the checklists below.

Revising Checklist

_____ 1. Do I keep focused on my thesis throughout the analysis?
_____ 2. Does my analysis have a strong introduction, middle, and conclusion?
_____ 3. Have I presented my ideas logically?
_____ 4. Do I include quotations from the text?
_____ 5. Do I analyze rhetorical and stylistic devices to develop my ideas?
_____ 6. Do I anticipate readers' questions and contradictory information?
_____ 7. Have I analyzed ambiguities, nuances, and complexities?
_____ 8. Does my voice sound authentic and original?

Editing Checklist

Conventions

_____ 1. Have I used end punctuation for every sentence?
_____ 2. Have I capitalized all proper nouns and first words of sentences?
_____ 3. Have I checked my spelling?
_____ 4. Have I made sure my subjects and verbs agree?
_____ 5. Have I used a variety of correctly structured sentences?

Improve your work. Review your analysis and make all necessary revisions. Correct any errors in grammar, sentence structure, mechanics (capitalization and punctuation), and spelling.

Publishing Sharing Your Analysis

When you complete your analysis, it's time to share your ideas. Read your analysis aloud and invite classmates to ask questions. You might also consider sending your work to a newspaper, magazine, or Web site for possible publication.

Publish your analysis. Choose one of the formats above to publish your analysis of an expository text.

Writing for Assessment
Responding to Prompts About Literature

Many assessment tests now include writing about literature. The test will typically include a prompt asking you to respond to one or two specific aspects of a given literary selection. For instance, you may be asked to focus on the plot of a novel, the theme of a poem, or a character in a story. Your writing will show how well you understand these elements of literature.

In this chapter, you are reminded of the value of using the writing process—even in a timed test situation. You'll read an example of an effective fiction response, and you'll get a chance to respond to some prompts on your own.

Writing Guidelines

- **Subject:** Literature prompt
- **Form:** Response to a prompt
- **Purpose:** To demonstrate competence
- **Audience:** Instructor or test evaluator

"To understand a literary style, consider what it omits."

—Mason Cooley

"Surely that's the whole point about literature—that for a body of fiction to constitute literature, it must rise above its origins, its setting, even its language, to render accessible to a reader anywhere some insight into the human condition."

—Shashi Tharoor

Prewriting Analyzing a Literature Prompt

A prompt about literature asks you to respond to specific characteristics of a story, a poem, a novel, or a nonfiction selection. As you read a prompt, look for key words that tell you exactly what the prompt requires (such as *explain, describe,* or *compare*). In the sample prompt below, key words and phrases are underlined. The word *discuss* gives the main direction or focus for the response.

Sample Prompt

> *John Milton's* Paradise Lost *follows Adam and Eve's defiance and fall from grace.* In an essay, discuss how Milton uses images of light and darkness to express other opposites appearing throughout the poem. How does this pattern lead to your understanding of the epic poem's major theme? Support your thesis with examples from the text.

Try It!

Copy the following sample prompts on a sheet of paper. Underline key words and phrases for each prompt and make notes about the kinds of supporting information that you would need for a response.

1. *Go Tell It on the Mountain* is James Baldwin's account of a Southern family's move to Harlem and young John's struggle with his identity. Write an essay that compares John's feelings about white people to those of Gabriel (his stepfather) and to those of Richard (his natural father). Quote the characters in your response.

2. F. Scott Fitzgerald's short story "The Diamond as Big as the Ritz" tells about the Washingtons, a ridiculously wealthy family, who think they are entirely above the law and general social customs. In a brief essay, discuss how Fitzgerald portrays the family and their vision of reality.

Prewriting Planning Your Response

Once you analyze and understand a prompt, you are ready to plan your response. If a reading selection is provided, read it with the prompt in mind, picking out the information you need for your response. Then form your topic sentence and organize the details.

Sample Prompt and Selection

> *This excerpt from Thoreau's Walden focuses on the author's surroundings. In a paragraph, describe the feeling or mood created in this passage.*
>
> My nearest neighbor is a mile distant, and no house is visible from any place but the hill-tops within half a mile of my own. I have my horizon bounded by woods all to myself; a distant view of the railroad where it touches the pond on the one hand, and of the fence which skirts the woodland road on the other. But for the most part it is as solitary where I live as on the prairies. . . . I have, as it were, my own sun and moon and stars, and a little world all to myself.

The underlined words connote solitude.

Writing a Topic Sentence

After reading the prompt and selection, one student wrote this topic sentence.

> **Thoreau's description of** his **surroundings** (specific topic) **creates a feeling of pleasing solitude** (focus related to the prompt).

Creating a Graphic Organizer

The student also used a graphic organizer to gather details.

Author's terms	Feeling created
nearest neighbor is . . . distant	privacy
horizon bounded by woods	security
solitary . . . as on the prairies	isolation
little world all to myself	satisfaction

Drafting Responding to a Literature Prompt

Note below how student writer Adrian Hernandez underlined key phrases and added side notes on a copy of the selection from "The Diamond as Big as the Ritz." He used these notes to address the focus of the last prompt on page 334. These notes helped Adrian begin planning his response.

Sample Selection

The awestruck young visitor learns that the owner had workers kidnapped for his personal use and yet was disappointed by their conventionalism.

John was enchanted by the wonders of the château and the valley. Braddock Washington, so Percy told him, had caused to be kidnapped a landscape gardener, an architect, a designer of state settings, and a French decadent poet left over from the last century. He . . . left them to work out some ideas of their own. But one by one they had shown their uselessness. . . . And as for the architect and the landscape gardener, they thought only in terms of convention. They must make this like this and that like that.

But . . . they all went mad early one morning . . . and were now confined comfortably in an insane asylum at Westport, Connecticut.

"But," inquired John curiously, "who did plan all your wonderful reception rooms and halls, and approaches and bathrooms—?"

"Well," answered Percy, "I blush to tell you, but it was a moving-picture fella. He was the only man we found who was used to playing with an unlimited amount of money, though he did tuck his napkin in his collar and couldn't read or write."

Even someone who met their standards in terms of being able to spend enough money comes up short in other ways.

As August drew to a close, John began to regret that he must soon go back to school. He and Kismine had decided to elope the following June.

"It would be nicer to be married here," Kismine confessed, "but of course I could never get father's permission to marry you at all. Next to that I'd rather elope. It's terrible for wealthy people to be married in America at present—they always have to send out bulletins to the press saying that they're going to be married in remnants, when what they mean is just a peck of old second-hand pearls and some used lace worn once by the Empress Eugenie."

Responding to Prompts About Literature

> The dialogue reveals how the speakers feel about what they see as the "struggle" of wealthy people.
>
> "I know," agreed John fervently. ". . . Gwendolyn married a man whose father owns half of West Virginia. She wrote home saying what a tough struggle she was carrying on on his salary as a bank clerk—and then she ended up by saying that 'Thank God, I have four good maids anyhow, and that helps a little.' "
>
> "It's absurd," commented Kismine. "Think of the millions and millions of people in the world, labourers and all, who get along with only two maids."

Writing a Thesis Statement

After reading the excerpt and making notes, Adrian wrote the following thesis statement for his response essay.

> The Washingtons' perception of life (specific topic) shows that they are, in fact, out of touch with reality (particular focus related to the prompt).

Creating a Graphic Organizer

Adrian used a line diagram to organize the main points and supporting details for an essay response.

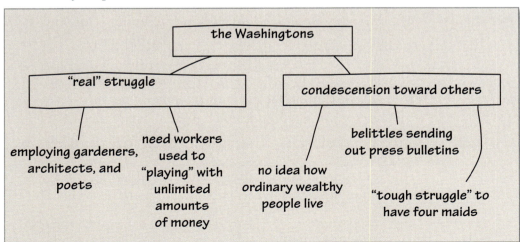

Student Response

In his response to the excerpt from "The Diamond as Big as the Ritz," note how Adrian used details from the story to support the thesis statement.

Introduction
The introductory paragraph contains the thesis statement (underlined).

Middle
This paragraph supports the claim that these people are out of touch with reality.

Whose Reality?

This excerpt from F. Scott Fitzgerald's story "The Diamond as Big as the Ritz" is an ironic look at "poor rich people." Most individuals strive to improve their lives, but they can only wish for what the Washingtons perceive as a burden or strain. <u>The Washingtons' perception of life shows that they are, in fact, out of touch with reality.</u>

The characters in this story seem somewhat pathetic as they describe what they perceive as real struggles in their lives. In the realm of extreme wealth portrayed here, chateaus and villas require gardeners and architects—and poets! After going through all the trouble to kidnap these workers, however, Braddock Washington is disappointed to find that they think "only in terms of convention." Their uselessness evident, he finds someone "used to playing with an unlimited amount of money"—obviously an important attribute. Braddock seems unaware that inhabitants of the average household, by contrast, maintain a comfortable home all by themselves. In doing so, they deal with more immediate and pressing struggles, both financial and physical.

Fitzgerald reveals how condescending the Washingtons are toward those who aren't like them.

TEKS 12.13A
ELPS 3E, 4G, 4H, 4K

Responding to Prompts About Literature   **339**

> **A transition points to a specific detail that supports the main idea.**
>
> The Washingtons don't have any idea how most wealthy people live. Toward the end of the excerpt, Kismine relates how wealthy people feel obligated to "send out bulletins to the press" about their valuable wedding clothes, but then she goes on to belittle this practice: "what they mean is just a peck of old second-hand pearls and some used lace." John agrees with her, scoffing at the "tough struggle" of a wealthy family with four maids. Again, Kismine demeans such suffering as "absurd"; but then she betrays her ignorance by commenting on how well most people, "labourers and all," do with only two!
>
> Fitzgerald acknowledges that wealthy people suffer, too, but he implies that their perception of life and its struggles is so far from the reality of most people as to make them almost laughable. This excerpt adds just one more aspect to a phrase famously attributed to Fitzgerald: "The very rich are different from you and me."
>
> **Conclusion** The conclusion restates the thesis and provides a final thought.

Respond to the reading. Answer the following questions about the student response. Explain your answers.

Focus and Coherence (1) What is the focus of the student writer's thesis statement? (2) Does each paragraph sustain that focus?

Organization (3) How is the response organized? (4) Is there a logical progression of ideas that makes it easy for the reader to follow?

Voice (5) Does the writer's voice seem original and authentic?

Respond to the Prompt Choose a prompt from page 334 and develop a thesis statement. Describe to a partner how you would organize your ideas. Then respond to the prompt.

Revising Improving Your Response

Always review your response at the end of a writing test. Make any changes and corrections as neatly as possible. Use the following questions to help you revise your response.

- **Focus and Coherence** Does my thesis statement directly address the prompt? Have I maintained my focus? Are the ideas clearly connected to each other and to the main idea?
- **Organization** Does my response have a strong beginning, middle, and ending? Are my ideas presented logically?
- **Development of Ideas** Are the ideas thoroughly developed with well-chosen details? Do I effectively develop each middle paragraph?
- **Voice** Does my voice sound authentic and original? Do I sound knowledgeable and confident?

Improve your work. Reread your practice response, asking yourself the questions above. Make any necessary changes neatly.

Editing Checking Your Response

In your final read-through, check your punctuation, capitalization, spelling, and grammar.

Editing Checklist

Conventions

_____ 1. Have I used end punctuation for every sentence?
_____ 2. Have I capitalized all proper nouns and first words of sentences?
_____ 3. Have I checked the spelling in my work?
_____ 4. Have I made sure my subjects and verbs agree?
_____ 5. Have I put quotation marks around the exact words that I quoted from the selection?

Check your response. Read over your work, looking for errors in punctuation, capitalization, spelling, and grammar. Make corrections neatly.

TEKS 12.13B, 12.13C, 12.13D
ELPS 4F, 4G, 5D, 5G

Responding to Prompts About Literature

Responding to Literature on Tests

Use the following tips as a guide whenever you respond to a prompt about literature. These tips will help you respond to both fiction and nonfiction selections.

Before you write . . .

- **Be clear about the time limit.**
  Plan enough time for prewriting, writing, and revising.
- **Understand the prompt.**
  Be sure that you know what the prompt requires. Pay special attention to the key words that tell you what you need to do.
- **Read the selection with the focus of the prompt in mind.**
  Take notes that will help you form your thesis. If you're working on a copy of the selection, underline important details.
- **Form your thesis statement.**
  Your thesis statement should identify the specific topic plus the focus of the prompt.
- **Fill in a graphic organizer.**
  Jot down main points and possible quotations for your essay.

As you write . . .

- **Maintain the focus of your essay.**
  Keep your thesis in mind as you write.
- **Be selective.**
  Use examples from your graphic organizer and the selection to support your thesis.
- **End in a meaningful way.**
  Start by revisiting the thesis. Then try to share a final insight about the topic with the reader.

After you've written a first draft . . .

- **Check for completeness and correctness.**
  Use the questions on page 340 to revise your essay. Then check for errors in punctuation, capitalization, spelling, and grammar.

Try It!

Read and analyze a prompt and literary selection your teacher supplies. Form a thesis statement that reflects the focus of the prompt, list supporting ideas in a graphic organizer, and write your essay. Then revise and edit your response.

Creative Writing

Writing Focus
Writing Stories   **343**
Writing Plays   **355**
Writing Poetry   **367**

Learning Language
Work with a partner to learn the following words and expressions from this unit.

1. A **stereotype** is an oversimplified generalization.
   How might a member of a group defy a stereotype?
2. A **strategy** is a plan to achieve a goal.
   What strategy would you use to improve your grades?
3. To **indicate** is to show or express.
   How would you indicate worry or surprise?
4. When you **pick up where you left off**, you resume doing something at the same point where you previously stopped.
   Describe a time when you took a break from something and later picked up where you left off.

 12.14A

Writing Stories

Stories can do many things. They can take us to faraway places and let us experience cultures other than our own. They can make us laugh or cry through exciting plots that keep us reading. But stories can offer more than just excitement or inventiveness. They also explore a character's inner feelings, sharing with us moments that can be very familiar, very similar to our own experiences. They allow us to examine those feelings and maybe understand ourselves a little better.

In this chapter, you will be writing an engaging story with a complex and non-stereotypical main character. A well-developed conflict will test the character's beliefs, and the resolution will reveal how the character has changed. As you write, you will explore how to use literary strategies and devices to enhance plot and define the mood and tone.

Writing Guidelines

- **Subject:** A character's inner feelings
- **Purpose:** To engage and entertain
- **Form:** Short story
- **Audience:** Classmates

"The American imagination releases itself very easily in the short story—and has done so since the beginning of our national history."

—Henry Seidel Canby

The Shape of Stories

A well-developed conflict and resolution help make a story engaging. The exposition introduces characters and complications, dramatic tension builds in the climax, and the falling action leads to a resolution that leaves the reader with something to think about. The graphic shows the basic structure of most stories.

Plot Line

The **exposition** introduces the main character(s), the settings, and the conflict. It gives background information the reader needs to understand the story.

The **rising action** is a series of events, called *complications,* that build suspense. Each event develops the conflict. During the rising action, the drama builds as the character faces complications that block his or her way.

The **crisis** is a moment of realization for the main character, when he or she comes to some decision or does something that will determine the outcome of the story. The crisis is not the climax but will lead to it.

The **climax** is the moment of truth, or the emotional high point of the story, when the main character either triumphs or fails. The climax should also somehow cause a change, either obvious or subtle, in the main character.

The **falling action** shows how the main character adjusts to the change.

The **resolution,** also called the *denouement,* is the ending. The resolution should be well-developed but short, bringing the story to a satisfying close.

Try It!

Think about a story you read recently and answer these questions.

1. Who was the main character, and what was the setting? (exposition)
2. What challenges did the main character face? (rising action)
3. When did the main character make a difficult decision? (crisis)
4. What was the high point of the story? (climax)
5. What happened afterward? (falling action and resolution)

Short Story

Every story has conflict, but sometimes that conflict is subtle. Some stories revolve around characters and the forces that motivate and change them. Marcus's theme focused on how a single moment can change someone's life.

Soaking

"Whatever Mom," Alejandro recalled the last words he had spoken to his mother as he neared the front steps. She had been nagging at him as he walked out the door that morning, and he expected her to pick up where they had left off as soon as he walked in. He was not in the mood. All three job interviews had gone horribly. Working out afterward failed to lift his spirits, and now his muscles ached too. Seeing his mother would only make him feel like more of a failure. Every fiber of his being was calling out for a hot, soaking bath. He decided to go straight to the tub and avoid her until she left for her book club.

He dragged himself up the stairs and was surprised to find the door locked. Odd. His mother usually left the door open. Digging around in the garden, he found the "secret" rock that hid the spare key and let himself in. The house was unusually quiet.

"Mom?" he called out, but got no answer. He shrugged. Strange. She always made it a point of being there when his sister Sonia got home. Otherwise, she would have called to make sure Alejandro would be home in time.

This is my golden opportunity. As long as Mom's not home, I won't have to listen to any nagging about what I should be doing to cheer up and get my life in order.

Alejandro went to the kitchen, opened the fridge, and crouched down, staring in. On the bottom shelf sat a plastic container with baby carrots in water, what Mom called the perfect healthy snack. She had a strange idea of perfection. If she were here, Alejandro would probably be crunching carrots and listening to another one of her lectures. Since she wasn't, he helped himself to a piece of cake. *My sugar intake will be the least of her worries when she finds out I blew my interviews.* Finishing his snack, Alejandro hauled himself upstairs for a long, hot soak.

He stepped into the bathroom, leaned down to the tub, and grasped the porcelain handle. Twisting it brought

---

A flashback from earlier in the morning is used as a literary strategy to introduce Alejandro's conflict with his mother. The following sentences reveal his inner conflict.

*The **rising action** adds complications.*

out a gurgling column of water. Once it was hot, Alejandro plugged the tub, pulled Mom's bath salts from the closet, and poured some in. *This is just what I need right now,* he thought, anticipating the comfort of the warm water enveloping his body.

As the tub filled, Alejandro went to his room to get some clean clothes. A pile of clean laundry waited on the bed. *I probably should have folded these.* Alejandro scooped up the clothes, carried them to the big chair by the window, and dumped them atop last week's pile. Then he plucked a wrinkled T-shirt, sweats, underwear, and mismatched socks from the mess and carried them with him toward the bathroom.

Halfway there, his eye snagged on the resumes and transcripts on his desk. He could almost hear his mother suggesting that he widen his job search. He ought to network better, too, she would say. . . .

The telephone rang. Alejandro startled. "It's probably her, making sure I'm home for Sonia." He went out into the hallway, grabbed the cordless, and went in to check on the bathwater.

"Alejandro?" It was his father's voice.

"Hey, Dad! You still at work?"

"Alejandro, listen!" His father's sharp voice cut him off.

"Dad? What's wrong?" Alejandro asked, quickly turning off the water.

"I'm at the hospital, son. Your mother's been in an accident." Alejandro sat on the side of the tub, suddenly unable to breathe, as though he'd been dunked in a tank of ice water.

"Is she—okay?" he heard himself say.

"The doctors said she'll pull through, but she's pretty well banged up. Her leg's broken, she's got some cracked ribs, and her shoulder was crushed. She'll be in the hospital for a while, and then she'll have a long recovery period."

"I'll be right there," Alejandro said.

"No, don't. She'll be asleep for a while. Besides, I need you to wait for Sonia. When she gets home from her Scout meeting, you'll have to tell her. You can bring her here with you then."

> **Transitions** guide the reader through the time order of events.

> **New complications** are presented through dialogue, leading up to a **crisis** for the main character.

Alejandro couldn't speak, but finally managed to squeak out a sound. "Okay. Tell her I love her, will you?"

"I will," his father said, and then he started to cry. Alejandro had never heard his father cry before.

He hung up, and Alejandro sat numbly, phone in hand, for a long time. When he finally looked at his bath, the water had cooled. He opened the drain and went back into his room to change into clean clothes. Afterward, he sat down, feeling out of breath.

> The sensory detail of cooling bathwater reflects the change in mood.

Sitting on his unmade bed, Alejandro gazed around the room, so familiar and suddenly so strange. Clothes and books were everywhere—he had barely unpacked since he moved home after college. His mother was always after him to pick up, and she usually just got disgusted and cleaned it for him. He'd never even thought about it, or the million other little things she was always doing to try to help him out. Now it would be his turn to take care of her as she recovered. He would finally get his act together—not just for his sake, but for hers.

Alejandro sat down on the floor by the big chair and slowly began folding his laundry. *After I finish this, I'll clean the rest of this dump. I'll bring the laptop with me to the hospital so I can write follow-up thank you letters for the interviews I had today and search for more options. I'll make sure Sonia has a healthy snack before we head to the hospital, too. . . .* Alejandro continued folding clothes, letting the eerie quiet of the empty house rise up around him. The only sound was the gentle gurgle of bathwater spiraling down the drain.

> A metaphor in the resolution is used as a literary device to represent the change in the character's life.

Respond to the reading. Answer the following questions.

Organization (1) How does the story build in suspense?

Development of Ideas (2) What is the conflict? (3) How does the writer develop the conflict in the story? (4) What is the theme of the story?

Voice (5) How do sensory details help convey the tone?
(6) How does the dialogue help create a feeling?

TEKS 12.13A, 12.13B, 12.14A
ELPS 3G, 4G

Prewriting Finding Your Focus

Before you get started, decide on a theme for your story: What central idea or message about life, human nature, or society do you want to share with the audience? Marcus made a list of possible themes for his story. He starred the one he decided to focus on.

> Possible Themes
> – good intentions don't always lead to the expected results
> – people can be blind to problems in their society
> – a person's life can change in an instant*
> – grieving is a slow, gradual process

Marcus thought about how he would convey his theme.

> How to Convey My Theme
> a car accident will change my character's outlook on life

Explore possible themes. List possible themes for your story. Once you select a theme, think about how you will structure your plot to convey it.

Building a Complex Character

Your main character should be complex and non-stereotypical. He or she should experience a range of emotions, and the results of the story's conflict should change your character in some way. To make your character more believable, try including traits that might surprise your readers. This will also help readers identify with your character. For example, at the start of Marcus's story, Alejandro sounds like just an average teenager arguing with his mother. Readers learn, however, that he has recently moved home, and his fear of failure seems to be hampering his will to succeed.

Create your main character. Share your idea for a main character with a partner. Then answer questions your partner has about your character. Incorporate these answers into your story.

Prewriting Developing a Symbol

A symbol is a person, a place, a thing, or an event that represents something else. You can use a symbol as a literary device to enhance the plot. Marcus used a thought map to think about symbols. He wrote important characters and ideas in the center and then thought of concrete symbols to represent them and develop his plot.

Thought Map

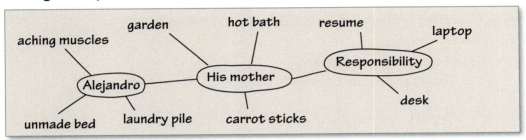

 Create a thought map. Write down important characters and ideas for your story. Then write possible symbols of each to enhance the plot. Focus on symbols that show how the plot changes your main character.

Using Dialogue

Dialogue is one of a range of literary strategies. Dialogue allows characters to speak for themselves. Marcus's story uses regular dialogue, set off with quotation marks (" "), and internal dialogue, indicated with *italics*, which lets the reader hear the conflict inside the main character.

"Whatever Mom."
As long as Mom's not home, I won't have to listen to any nagging . . .

Note: Use internal dialogue only with the main character so that your point of view does not shift.

Try It!

Experiment with dialogue. Answer each of the following questions the way your main character would. Use regular dialogue to let the person speak and use internal dialogue to show what the person is thinking.

1. What's the biggest challenge that you face?
2. Do you think you'll overcome the challenge? Why or why not?

Prewriting Finding Your Voice

Sensory details appeal to the reader's sense of sight, sound, smell, touch, or taste. They help engage the reader and can be used to define the mood and tone of a story.

Defining Mood

As you write, think about the feeling you want the story to create for the reader. Sensory details can help define the mood. Marcus appealed to the reader's sense of hearing to create an eerie feeling for his audience:

Sensory details:

> **The house was unusually quiet.**
>
> **His father's sharp voice cut him off.**

Try It!

Use sensory details to create mood. Make a list of the following:

1. sounds and sights that would convey excitement
2. tastes and smells to suggest relaxation
3. feelings and images that would show anger

Conveying Tone

Tone is the writer's attitude toward the subject. Tone can be conveyed in the following ways:

- Sensory details
  Details that appeal to the sense of touch convey a sympathetic tone.
  comfort of the warm water enveloping his body

- Sentence length and structure
  Brief sentences help create an informal tone.
  He shrugged. Strange.

- Word choice
  Marcus's choice of words shows his empathy for his character.
  Working out afterward failed to lift his spirits . . . Every fiber of his being was calling out for a hot, soaking bath.

Consider your tone. Decide what feelings you want your voice to convey in your writing. Think of sensory details, sentence structures, and words that would convey these feelings.

Drafting Developing the First Draft

Your story should include a beginning, a middle, and an ending that work together to show how the main character changes.

Starting Strong

Introduce the main character, setting, and conflict in your introduction. Here are some rhetorical devices you can use to engage the reader and convey your meaning.

- **Start with a flashback.**
  "Whatever Mom," Alejandro recalled the last words he had spoken to his mother as neared the front steps.

- **Begin with repetition.**
  He dragged himself up the street, up the sidewalk, and up the stairs, and then found the door locked.

- **Begin with dialogue.**
  "Hey, Mom," Alejandro said, walking through the front door. "You home?"

- **Use figurative language, such as a simile.**
  Alejandro pulled into his driveway, turned off the engine, and collapsed like a house of cards.

Introducing the Characters, Setting, and Conflict

Remember, provide complications that develop the conflict. Follow these tips:
- Use **action** that shows what the main character is experiencing.
- Use **dialogue** to let characters speak, and use **internal dialogue** to show the thoughts of your main character.
- Use **symbols** and **rhetorical devices** to convey meaning.
- Introduce complications to develop the conflict.
    First: Alejandro is going to try to avoid his mother.
    Next: Alejandro's mom isn't home.
    Then: He's glad she's not there.

Try It!

Experiment with different types of openings for your story. Choose the one that you think is most engaging.

Drafting Building Your Story

Developing the Conflict

Suspense is a literary strategy used to engage the reader. It is what keeps people glued to their seats in movies and turning pages when reading. The events in your rising action should build up to a crisis and the climax. This should be the moment of greatest suspension in your story.

Notice how Marcus builds tension in his crisis:

- **Crisis**

    Alejandro learns that his mother has been in an accident.

- **Climax**

    Alejandro realizes he shouldn't take his mother for granted, and he needs to accept more responsibility.

Try It!

Create a plot line for your story. Use the diagram on page **344** as a guide to be sure that your story has dramatic tension, is suspenseful, and builds to a climax.

Bringing the Story to a Close

Your falling action and resolution should bring the story to a satisfying ending. Indicate how life will be different for your character, and finish with a thoughtful ending tied to your theme.

In Marcus's falling action and resolution, Alejandro sits down and begins folding his laundry and thinking about his immediate plans. The reader is satisfied that the conflict has been resolved but is left wondering if Alejandro will be able to follow through.

Draft

Write your first draft. Use your planning from pages **348–352** to guide your writing. Develop your theme using an engaging conflict. Remember to use sensory details and natural language to make your story come to life for your readers. Finally, close the story with a satisfying ending.

Writing Stories

Revising Improving Your Writing

Use the following checklists as you revise and edit your story.

Revising Checklist

Focus and Coherence

_____ 1. Have I described the setting (place and time) clearly?
_____ 2. Do I focus on the conflict?
_____ 3. Is the theme clear?

Organization

_____ 4. Does my beginning capture the reader's interest and introduce the main character, setting, and conflict?
_____ 5. Does my middle provide complications that lead to the climax?
_____ 6. Does my resolution identify the outcome of the conflict and show how the character changed?

Development of Ideas

_____ 7. Is my main character complex and non-stereotypical?
_____ 8. Do my literary strategies and devices enhance the plot?

Voice

_____ 9. Does my dialogue (regular and internal) sound natural?
_____ 10. Do I use sensory details to clearly define the mood and tone?

Editing Checking for Conventions

When you edit, check your *grammar, mechanics,* and *spelling.*

Editing Checklist

Conventions

_____ 1. Do I use a variety of correctly structured sentences that clearly communicate my ideas?
_____ 2. Have I correctly punctuated dialogue (regular and internal)?

Creative Writing

Elements of Fiction

The following terms will help you write about and discuss literature.

Antagonist	The person or force that works against the hero of the story (See *protagonist*.)
Character	A person or an animal in a story
Climax	The moment of change when the protagonist either succeeds or fails and is somehow changed by the action
Conflict	A problem or clash between two forces in a story ■ **Person vs. person** A problem between characters ■ **Person vs. self** A problem within a character's own mind ■ **Person vs. society** A problem between a character and society, the law, or some tradition ■ **Person vs. nature** A problem with an element of nature, such as a blizzard or a hurricane ■ **Person vs. destiny** A problem or struggle that appears to be beyond a character's control
Mood	The feeling the story creates for the reader
Narrator	The person or character who tells the story, gives background information, and fills in details between dialogue
Plot, Plot Line	See page 344.
Point of View	The angle from which a story is told ■ In **first-person point of view,** one character is telling the story. ■ In **third-person point of view,** someone outside the story, a narrator, is telling it. ■ In **omniscient point of view,** the narrator tells the thoughts and feelings of all the characters. ■ In **limited omniscient point of view,** the narrator tells the thoughts of only one character.
Protagonist	The main character or hero in a story (See *antagonist*.)
Resolution	The story's ending, in which the author reveals the outcome of the conflict, ties up loose ends, and leaves the reader with something to think about
Setting	The place and time period in which a story takes place
Theme	The author's message about life or human nature
Tone	The writer's attitude toward her or his subject (*angry, humorous,* and so on)

Writing Plays

A play is an exciting writing challenge. Because a play is intended to be watched rather than read, its story is told with action and speech rather than with long sections of description. Even so, the script must be clearly written, allowing the reader to understand the characters, their motivations, and what happens to them.

In terms of plot, writing a play is like writing any other narrative. The main character desires something and faces conflict before finally succeeding or failing. At the climax, the character changes in some way, realizing a universal truth about the world or about himself or herself. This theme may be explicit or implicit.

In this chapter you will read a short play about a character who faces a personal dilemma and must make a decision. Then, you will write a short play and use stage directions to explain your characters' actions on stage. You will also read a short audio play and write one of your own, using dialogue and sound effects to suggest the character's actions.

Writing Guidelines

Subject: Facing a personal dilemma
Purpose: To entertain and enlighten
Form: Brief play
Audience: Classmates

"The structure of a play is always the story of how the birds came home to roost."

—Arthur Miller

Brief Play

Dolores wrote the following play in which a character must make an important personal decision.

What's the Exchange Rate?

Characters: **Eva,** who wants to be an exchange student
Tess, her friend
Miguel, Eva's boyfriend

(*The stage is bare. The lights come up on Eva, Center, as Tess rushes in to her.*)

- The theme is introduced and made explicit.

TESS: Eva, I can't believe you're going to France as an exchange student for a year! What a change!
EVA: Isn't it awesome! A whole year of traveling, learning the customs, meeting new people . . .
TESS: Especially those French boys! Ooooo . . . !
EVA: I don't care about that! I've got Miguel.

- Background is given and the conflict is suggested.

TESS: Um, yeah, but you won't have him for a whole year! Aren't you worried about that?
EVA: We'll be okay. We can write and e-mail.
TESS: He can't take an e-mail to homecoming or out to a party on Saturday night. Come on, Eva. Miguel, all alone, for a year? I don't think so!

- A rhetorical question highlights the conflict.

EVA: I never thought of that. I mean, Miguel and I—we've talked about it, we're together forever!!
TESS: Eva, senior year might be longer than forever.
EVA: Maybe I shouldn't go. (*Frowning*) This is hard.
TESS: (*Gently*) I know.

- Hyperbole emphasizes the conflict.

(*The lights go down. Eva moves Down Right, where the lights come up on Miguel, who is sitting, working on a computer. He stops and Eva stands next to him.*)

- A third character is introduced.

MIGUEL: Wow. What a great opportunity for you.
EVA: Yeah, but I'm wondering if I should pass it up.
MIGUEL: Are you crazy? Why?
EVA: Miguel, it's a year. I'll miss you too much!
MIGUEL: And I'll miss you, too, but we can write and e-mail. It's a change, but we can do it, Eva. (*Pause*) We can handle anything.

- The explicit theme is reinforced.

(*The lights go down and Eva moves Stage Left, where the lights come up on Tess.*)

A complication is added.	EVA: See? He's fine with it. TESS: Sure. He loves you and wants you to be happy. But do you really think it will be that easy? EVA: Why not? TESS: So, he'll put his life on hold here, and you'll be in France telling people "No," you can't go out?
A metaphor makes the options vivid.	EVA: I don't know, Tess. I love what we have now, but I don't want to put Miguel in a box and I don't want to live in one either. I really want to go, but . . . I don't know what to do. TESS: *(Gently)* I know. *(She moves to hug Eva.)*

(Their light goes down and Eva moves Center, where the lights come up on Miguel, who is examining a fishing reel.)

	EVA: It's not so bad, I'll be back in June. *(Casually)* And you'll be going out with other girls . . . MIGUEL: *(Shocked)* Why would I do that? EVA: It's your senior year. You should have fun. MIGUEL: But you're wearing my ring. We're exclusive.
Figurative language enhances the dialogue.	EVA: Miguel, it's going to be a whole year. I don't want you to freeze-dry yourself until I get back. MIGUEL: Eva, I don't want to date anyone else.
Stage directions indicate Eva's struggles.	EVA: Oh. *(Hesitantly she walks away, then speaks as if she is thinking out loud.)* Well . . . maybe I do. MIGUEL: What? EVA: I mean, I'll be in Paris, Miguel. Think of it! I'll be going to museums and plays and parties . . . MIGUEL: Eva, are you breaking up with me?
Stage directions reveal Eva's feelings.	EVA: *(It's painful for her to say this.)* I just thought, maybe we should take a little time off. See what's what. MIGUEL: You ARE breaking up with me! Eva, I thought you loved me! We talked, we planned . . .
The theme is reinforced.	EVA: *(Weakly)* People change. MIGUEL: Yeah, so I see.
Eva's forced attitude is ironic.	EVA: I mean, *(forcing a casual attitude)* I'm going to be traveling, changing, seeing the world. MIGUEL: So, I can just stagnate in the home pond, huh? EVA: Oh, I'm sure you'll be moving right along, too.

> MIGUEL: You bet I will! Listen, why don't you just give me back my ring right now, before you take off for your new, exciting life.
>
> EVA: Oh! Oh. Sure. *(Turns away and slips off the ring. Stares at it a minute before plastering a smile on her face.)* Here! I feel lighter already.
>
> MIGUEL: I'll bet. Sorry it was weighing you down for so long. *(Softly)* I thought you'd wear it forever. *(Eva makes a move toward him, then checks herself.)*
>
> EVA: Well! I guess that's that.
>
> MIGUEL: Yeah. Have fun in France, and don't waste any time worrying about me. I'll be having a great life!
>
> EVA: *(Softly)* That's all I ever wanted for you. *(Pause)* And for me. I just don't know if it's together.
>
> MIGUEL: *(Softly)* You really are amazing, you know.
>
> EVA: I don't have to go, Miguel.
>
> MIGUEL: Yes, you do.
>
> EVA: I can say no and stay here. We'd have the best senior year . . .
>
> MIGUEL: You can't do that, Eva. You've always wanted this. Maybe this will be a good test for us. If we can stand this, we're meant to be together.
>
> EVA: If we do, we'll be sure of it.
>
> MIGUEL: What about my ring? *(Holds it out to her.)*
>
> EVA: Maybe you'll want to give it to someone else.
>
> MIGUEL: Maybe I'll hold on to it until June.
>
> EVA: Maybe you will. *(Looks at him.)* Maybe you won't. Miguel, I'm going to go to France. I have to go. *(She looks back.)* But I really do love you.
>
> MIGUEL: *(Softly)* I know.
>
> *(She runs to him, and they hug.)*

- Miguel's use of sarcasm sharpens the dialogue.
- The conflict is revisited.
- The theme of the need for change is reinforced.
- The decision is made, the conflict resolved, and the play ends.

Texas Traits

Respond to the reading. Answer the following questions about the play.

Focus and Coherence (1) What is the explicit theme of the play?

Organization (2) How does the author build the suspense?

Development of Ideas (3) What does Eva want? (4) What is her conflict?

Voice (5) Find three stage directions that help you understand how the actor should say the line.

Prewriting Inventing a Main Character

One way to start planning a play is to select a main character who wants something. That something is called the character's **objective**, and the reason the character wants it is called the **motivation**. Dolores wanted to write about a teenage girl, so she made a list of things her character might want.

- To have a car
- To host a surprise party for a friend
- To be an exchange student
- To be admitted to a prestigious college

Dolores decided to explore the idea of becoming an exchange student.

Invent your main character. Think about a possible character. Then explore potential objectives before deciding on your character's objective.

Choosing a Conflict

Conflict is the heart of drama. To write a good play, you must include an **obstacle** that prevents your character from achieving his or her goal. This conflict is usually central to the implicit or explicit theme. There are two types of conflict.

- **Internal conflict**: The main character struggles to make a decision.
- **External conflict**: The main character struggles against an outside force, such as another person, society, an idea, or nature.

Dolores made the following chart to look at the possible conflicts her character could face. She starred the one she decided to use.

External Conflicts	Internal Conflicts
– Her boyfriend/parents/gymnastics coach/friends ask her not to go.	– She doesn't want to leave her friends.
– She has to come up with money to pay for the trip.	* – She doesn't want to lose her boyfriend, but she doesn't want either of them to be unhappy.
– Her host family sounds unfriendly.	– She knows she will be homesick.
– She will probably have to repeat her senior year when she returns.	– She is afraid of flying.

Choose your character's conflict. Make a list of possible obstacles to your character's objective and select the one you would like to write about.

Prewriting Planning Your Resolution

In the sample play, Eva's obstacle to becoming an exchange student is her desire both to keep her boyfriend and for both of them to be happy. The explicit theme becomes the need for change. To overcome her internal conflict, Eva tries several strategies.

Character	Options
Eva	– do not go to avoid separation – stay "together" but see other people – break up – wait and see what the future brings

Developing Secondary Characters

Secondary characters should be used selectively—especially in a short play. Each should have a specific role. Secondary characters can play the following roles:

- Give background information.
- Provide a sounding board for the main character.
- Introduce complications that block the main character's goal.

Create your secondary characters. Invent a few secondary characters and determine the purpose for each.

Considering Irony

Irony is the use of words to express something other than what is really meant. There are three kinds of dramatic irony:

- **Verbal:** A character says one thing but means another.
  "Oh, sure, I just love making a fool of myself in front of others!"

- **Dramatic:** The audience knows something the character does not.
  In *Romeo and Juliet,* Romeo thinks Juliet is dead so he kills himself, but we know Juliet is alive.

- **Situational:** What is expected to happen and what does happen are very different things.
  Willy Loman thinks his life insurance money will make his family happy, but his death just brings them sorrow.

Dolores uses dramatic irony when she has Eva speak casually to Miguel about breaking up. The reader knows she doesn't feel casual, but Miguel does not.

 12.14C

Drafting Writing Your First Draft

Remember to let your characters tell the story and reveal their personalities. Their words and actions may state an explicit theme or suggest an implicit theme. Keep in mind the interplay of action and dialogue.

Beginning

1. **Give the opening stage directions.** Include any information that will help the reader visualize the scene.
2. **Introduce your characters and conflict.** Include enough background information to explain to the audience how the characters arrived at this opening situation.

Middle

3. **Use dialogue and action to move the play along.** Include complications to add suspense and keep the audience interested. Write stage directions that convey the subtext.
4. **Divide into scenes if necessary.** Use separate scenes to condense time or to present a new development.
5. **Present the climax.** Bring the main character to a point where the conflict is resolved.

Ending

6. **Bring your play to a close.** Show how the character has changed and wrap up the action with a definite ending.

Building Scenes

A scene is like a mini-play with its own beginning, middle, and ending. Each scene should advance the action, build upon the character's objective, create complications, and move toward the resolution. In the sample play, each of the scenes has a specific purpose:

- **Scene 1:** To present the theme, background information, and the conflict
- **Scene 2:** To introduce Miguel and provide one solution: That he and Eva "stay together" while she is gone
- **Scene 3:** To build suspense as Tess suggests to Eva that it might not be realistic for Miguel and Eva to restrict their social activities
- **Scene 4:** To present the final confrontation, the climax, and the end of the play

Write your play. Write your play, using your prewriting as a guide. Use at least two scenes and include new ideas that occur to you as you write.

Drafting Creating Subtext

Subtext is the unspoken emotions of your characters—what they really think and feel, even while their actions suggest something else. The subtext may help establish an implicit theme. The playwright may include stage directions to help actors understand their character's motivation.

In the sample play, the subtext of the action is suggested through the stage directions. For example, when Eva removes Miguel's ring, the dialogue suggests she is happy to break up. However, the stage directions present the subtext.

> EVA: Oh! Oh. Sure. *(Turns away and slips off the ring. Stares at it a minute before plastering a smile on her face.)* Here! I feel lighter already.

These stage directions help the reader see that Eva isn't sure about giving Miguel his ring. We know that she is trying to make a good decision for both of them. That she still cares is further emphasized by the later stage directions.

> *(Eva makes a move toward him, then checks herself.)*

Thinking About Stage Directions

As you write stage directions, consider using stage shorthand to indicate the acting areas. The diagram below identifies the shorthand.

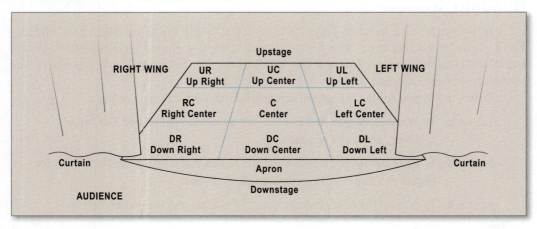

Writing Plays

Revising Improving Your Writing

Read your play out loud or have someone else read it to you. Change any lines that sound forced or unnatural. Use these questions to guide your revisions.

Revising Checklist

Focus and Coherence

_____ 1. Is there an explicit or implicit theme?
_____ 2. Do the stage directions make sense?

Organization

_____ 3. Does my play move logically from one scene to the next?
_____ 4. Does my play build to a logical conclusion?

Development of Ideas

_____ 5. Are the characters and conflict believable?
_____ 6. Have I included complications?

Voice

_____ 7. Does the dialogue sound natural and move smoothly?
_____ 8. Does the tone convey the intended meaning and purpose of the play?

Editing Checking for Conventions

Editing Checklist

_____ 1. Does the play follow correct script form?
_____ 2. Have I used parentheses for directions?
_____ 3. Have I checked my punctuation?
_____ 4. Have I consulted a dictionary to determine or check the spelling of words my spell-checker may have missed?

Publishing Presenting Your Play

Share your play with an audience. Have some students act it out in class, or post it on your (or your school's) Web site.

Audio Play

One of the best things about audio plays is that both the writer and the audience can really use their imaginations. The stories come to life entirely through the voices of the actors and the sound effects. With this in mind, Stephon developed a script. Note how the setting and sound effects are symbolic of the actions and feelings of the characters.

Fireworks

(SCENE: A PARK, FOURTH OF JULY. WE HEAR FIREWORKS IN THE DISTANCE PUNCTUATED BY THE CROWD'S "OOOHS" AND "AAAHS.")

    LUC: Wow, Cher! These are the best Fourth of July fireworks.
    CHER: They're nice, Luc.

(SOUND: A LOUD BOOM AND THE CROWD'S OOOOH!)

    LUC: Nice? They're spectacular!
    CHER: Yes. Listen, Luc, we have to talk.

(SOUND: A CRACKLING NOISE AND THE CROWD'S AAAAH!)

    LUC: That one was really cool! Talk about what?
    CHER: About us, Luc. I mean, I think we should see other people.

(SOUND: A POP FOLLOWED BY SMALLER POPS, AND THE SOUND OF LAUGHTER AND APPLAUSE.)

    LUC: Wow, that was—What?
    CHER: I think we should break up.
    LUC: But, Cher, we had the whole summer planned! We were going to go on nature hikes, go bird-watching, . . .
    CHER: YOU had the whole summer planned!
    LUC: I thought you'd like doing those things, too.
    CHER: Listen, Luc, it's more than just the things we like to do.

(SOUND: BOOM AND AUDIENCE REACTION.)

    LUC: What else is it, then?
    CHER: It's us, Luc. We don't click. There's just no magic between us, no—fireworks. I'm really sorry, Luc.
    LUC: But—
    CHER: Goodbye, Luc.

(SOUND: A WHISTLING BUILDUP AND THEN A FIZZLE. AUDIENCE GROANS IN DISAPPOINTMENT.)

Prewriting An Audio Play Differs from a Stage Play

Audio plays differ from stage plays in several ways.

- **No stage directions.** The actors will never be seen, so their movements must be implied through sound effects and the actors' dialogue.

  > John: Will you come in for a moment?
  > (SOUND OF DOOR OPENING AND CLOSING)
  > Marilyn: What a beautiful house you have.

  The writer has effectively shown that both John and Marilyn have entered John's home.

- **No physical actions by actors.** In a stage play, actors can convey actions, moods and thoughts by movements which cannot be seen in an audio play. The dialogue must be explicit, or one character must describe the actions of another.

  > Tony: What are you doing, Alberto? Put down the phone! I would never . . .

  The writer has made Alberto's actions apparent through Tony's dialogue.

- **Sound effects can set the scene.** Sound effects and background noise can help a listener visualize the action. For example, two people might speak to each other over background noise from a crowded restaurant, a football game, or a walk in the woods.

An Audio Play Is Similar to a Stage Play

- **A main character experiences conflict that is resolved during the play.** The conflict is central to the explicit or implicit theme of the play.
- **The play moves through a beginning, middle, and ending.**
- **The author builds interest and suspense using a variety of literary techniques,** such as irony, hyperbole, figurative language, and so on.
- **Dialogue presents characters' thoughts, feelings, and conflicts.**
- **The setting may be symbolic of the conflict** and should provide a natural opportunity for the dialogue.

Select a character and a conflict. Use the same process you did for your longer play, but remember the limitations of an audio play. The conflict, setting, dialogue, literary techniques, and theme must be presented in a single scene.

Drafting Writing Dialogue

An audio play relies on dialogue. Try closing your eyes and listening to your characters' dialogue, and write it down.

Introduction
1. Give the setting and background noises in just one sentence.
2. Establish characters and relationships in the first few lines.

Middle
3. Use the characters' dialogue to establish the conflict.
4. Use sound effects or background noise to indicate changes.

Conclusion
5. Close your play indicating how your characters have changed.

Draft your play. Write a first draft, using your prewriting as a guide.

Revising

Read your play aloud and revise it using this checklist.

Revising Checklist

Focus and Coherence
_____ 1. Is the relationship between the characters clear and believable?

Development of Ideas
_____ 2. Is the conflict resolved by the end?
_____ 3. Is there an explicit or implicit theme?

Voice
_____ 4. Does the dialogue sound natural?

Editing Checking for Conventions
_____ Does the play use the correct script form?

Publishing Presenting Your Play

Share your play with an audience. Have some students read it in class.

Writing Poetry

Some people think poetry is just for literature books. Others think it's mainly for greeting cards. But the earliest poetry was used for public performance, and much of the best modern poetry is written by everyday people for other everyday people.

In essence, a poem is "heightened" language—carefully chosen words with sounds and rhythms that are fun to hear, and with imagery and ideas that surprise or delight. In this chapter, you will find various examples of poetic traditions within particular forms, as well as definitions and demonstrations of common poetic conventions. As the examples show, poetry is for everybody!

By following the instructions in this chapter, you will learn to write your own sonnets, free-verse poems, and cinquains. We hope that you will return to this chapter often, whenever you have an idea that deserves to be expressed in a poem.

Writing Guidelines

    Subject: Man and machine
    Purpose: To entertain
       Form: Sonnet
  Audience: Friends, family, and classmates

> "The future masters of technology will have to be lighthearted and intelligent. The machine easily masters the grim and the dumb."
>
> —Marshall McLuhan

Understanding Sonnets

The sonnet originated in Italy during the Middle Ages. The form migrated to England around the time of William Shakespeare. The English made some changes to the Italian tradition, but kept the main characteristics. All sonnets are 14 lines long, with a logical structure, a regular rhythm, and—usually—a rhyme scheme.

English Sonnets

The English sonnet is sometimes called the Shakespearean sonnet. It consists of three *quatrains* (four lines each) that present a theme, followed by a *couplet* (two lines) that responds to the theme. The rhythm is generally iambic pentameter (see pages 371 and 375), and the rhyme scheme is usually *abab cdcd efef gg*. Shakespeare's Sonnet 18 is a classic example.

> This sonnet follows the English form of three quatrains and a couplet.

> The rhyme scheme is very tight *(abab cdcd efef gg)*.

> All lines are iambic pentameter.

Sonnet 18

Shall I compare thee to a summer's day?
Thou art more lovely and more temperate:
Rough winds do shake the darling buds of May,
And summer's lease hath too short a date:

Sometime too hot the eye of heaven shines,
And often is his gold complexion dimmed,
And every fair from fair sometimes declines,
By chance or nature's changing course untrimmed:

But thy eternal summer shall not fade,
Nor lose possession of that fair thou ow'st,
Nor shall Death brag thou wander'st in his shade,
When in eternal lines to time thou grow'st,

So long as men can breathe or eyes can see,
So long lives this and this gives life to thee.

Respond to the reading. On your own paper, reflect on the organization, development of ideas, and voice of the sonnet above.

Organization (1) What theme do the first two lines present? (2) How does the couplet sum up the writer's thoughts?

Development of Ideas (3) Summarize the main idea of the poem in your own words.

Voice (4) What is the writer's attitude or tone in the poem?

Writing Poetry 369

Italian Sonnets

Italian sonnets are sometimes called Petrarchan sonnets after Francesco Petrarch, a scholar and poet of the 1300s, who wrote 366 sonnets and other poems to a woman he loved. His sonnets helped establish the tradition of sonnets as love poems, and his adherence to the strict sonnet form showed the possibilities for brilliance while working within rigidly defined boundaries.

The Italian sonnet offers a unified theme in an *octave* (eight lines—often as two quatrains), followed by a *sestet* (six lines) which serves as a response to that theme. Italian sonnets usually present an *abababab* or *abbaabba* scheme in the octave and a *cdecde* or *cdccdc* scheme in the sestet. The rhythm of Italian sonnets is also generally iambic pentameter (see pages 371 and 375). The ninth line is called *the turn* because it indicates a change in the rhyme scheme and a turn in subject to a reflection on the theme.

Although Shakespeare and Petrarch wrote sonnets that explored love, a sonnet may be written about any topic. Boyce Pappan wrote about his car:

This sonnet follows the Italian form of octave and sestet.

The rhyme scheme is very loose **(abcbdefe ghihjh)**.

Most lines are iambic pentameter. Exceptions add emphasis to individual words and phrases.

Old Junker

My car is old as me—in car years, that's
middle-aged—an unappreciated
stretch of time between "brand new" and "classic"
when one's value is depreciated.
In other words, it's simply out of style,
so it doesn't get as much attention
as it once did. No one admires it. (I
never wash or wax it, I should mention.)

Still, I love this car and it's comfortable
as only an old car can be. No fear
of spilling something—the upholstery's
already stained. And you will never hear
me complain about gas mileage. Now if
I could only get the thing in gear!

Respond to the reading. On your own paper, reflect on the organization, development of ideas, and voice of the sonnet above.

Organization (1) What theme does the octave present?
(2) What response does the sestet provide?

Development of Ideas (3) Summarize the main idea of the poem in your own words.

Voice (4) What is the writer's attitude or tone in the poem?

Prewriting Choosing a Topic and a Focus

To decide on a topic, Boyce used freewriting. Here's part of what he wrote:

> What does "man and machine" mean to me? Machines are tools we use to enhance our abilities. Maybe I could write about a screwdriver or a hammer. Not a lot to say about something that simple. How about something more complex, like a car? Yeah! I could come up with lots of ideas about my car! I couldn't get by without my old . . .

Select a focus. Use freewriting to brainstorm for a topic related to "man and machine." Keep writing whatever comes to mind until you discover something exciting.

Gathering Details

Make a list of thoughts about your topic. List descriptive details, feelings, or ideas you have. Your list may also include poetic techniques, such as possible figures of speech, to use in your poem. (See page **374**.) Here's part of Boyce's list:

> It's as old as I am.
> Ugly and rusty outside, but comfortable inside
> I never wash it!
> Not very powerful, but great gas mileage
> At that awkward age between new and classic
> Tricky to start on cold days
> It's my one private spot on the planet.
> Like my locker, it's full of books, old papers, clothes, and junk!
> In its day, it was "stylish"; what happened?
> Don't have to worry about scratching it (like I would a new car)

Organizing Details

Next, arrange your ideas, placing similar ideas together. Think about what each section of your sonnet might cover. (*Remember:* The conventions and traditions for sonnets are generally three quatrains and an answering couplet or an octave and an answering sestet.) Review Boyce's sonnet on page **369** to see how he used his details.

Gather details. Make a list of descriptive details, feelings, and ideas about your topic. Include poetic techniques, such as figures of speech.

Drafting Writing Your First Draft

Write a first draft of your poem. Watch for opportunities to use the various poetic techniques described below and on pages **374–375**. Remember the traditional conventions for sonnets: 14 lines long, a logical structure, a regular rhythm, usually a rhyme scheme. However, don't get so bogged down with the conventions that you forget your goal: to create a poem with sounds and rhythms that are fun and images and ideas that surprise and delight.

Using Rhythm

The standard rhythm for a sonnet is iambic pentameter. (See page **375**.) As you write, let this rhythm guide your phrases. But remember, it's okay to vary the rhythm, especially for emphasis.

> ⏑ / ⏑ / ⏑ / ⏑ / ⏑ /
> My car is old as me. In car years, that's

Using Rhyme

While you are drafting your poem, a rhyme scheme may begin to suggest itself. If so, allow it to guide your word choice. However, don't work too hard at rhyming yet. Just focus on completing your first draft.

> In other words, it's simply out of style,
> so it doesn't get as much **attention**
> as it once did. No one admires it. (I
> never wash or wax it, I should **mention**.)

Using Enjambment

Poems with lines that always end on a rhyme can sometimes sound singsongy, like a nursery rhyme. When you use enjambment—carrying sentences from line to line and ending them inside a line—your poems will flow more naturally. Enjambment also makes rhyming simpler. (It's easier to fit a rhyme inside a sentence than at the end.)

> as only an old car can be. **No fear**
> of spilling something—the upholstery's
> already **stained**. And you will never hear

Using Personification

Personification gives human traits to something that is not human. (See page **374**.) This use of figurative language can help readers form striking images they have never imagined. It can also help establish a mood and tone for a poem, depending on the human traits you describe.

> My car is old as me—in car years, that's
> middle-aged—an unappreciated

Using Alliteration

Alliteration is the repetition of consonant sounds at the beginning of words. (See page **374**.) Alliteration can make a poem fun to read aloud and can make connections between words that begin with the same consonant sound. Some poets will use a long list of alliterative adjectives to highlight an object or action.

> of spilling something—the upholstery's
> already stained. And you will never hear

Using Assonance

Assonance is the repetition of vowel sounds anywhere in words. (See page **374**.) It can serve some of the same purposes as alliteration by enhancing the spoken and heard sounds of the words. However, to be effective in your poem, both alliteration and assonance must come naturally and serve a purpose in the poem's content.

> as only an old car can be. No fear

Draft

Write your first draft. Use your plan as a guide. Pay attention to the conventions of writing a sonnet, and watch for opportunities to use poetic techniques such as rhythm, rhyme, enjambment, personification, alliteration, and assonance to make your sonnet read effectively.

Revising Improving Your Poem

After drafting a sonnet, let it sit for a while. Later, when you return to it with fresh eyes, you will notice which parts work and which parts could be improved. Also have a trusted friend respond to the poem. Then make any needed changes, based on the traits of good writing.

- **Focus and Coherence** Does my poem have a well-developed theme?
- **Organization** Does my poem follow a sonnet structure in the English or Italian tradition? Does it introduce an idea in the quatrains or octave and a response in the couplet or sestet?
- **Development of Ideas** Do I use effective details? Does my poem show my feelings without telling the reader what to think?
- **Voice** Do my rhymes work well? Do I use poetic conventions to enhance the imagery of my poem? Are my ideas set—at least loosely—in iambic pentameter? (See pages **374–375**.) Does my poem show inventiveness and personality? Are my words precise and interesting? Do my phrases and ideas flow smoothly?

Revise your poem. Using the questions above as a guide, keep revising until your poem is the best that it can be.

Editing Checking for Errors

Because poetry is a concise form, every word, every punctuation mark, is important. Careful editing is essential.

Edit your poem. Be sure that every element of your poem accomplishes the purpose you intend.

Publishing Sharing Your Poem

There are many ways in which you can share a sonnet. Here are a few ideas:

- **Post it.** Put it on a bulletin board or a Web site.
- **Submit it.** Send your poem to a contest or a magazine.
- **Perform it**. Have an "open-mike" poetry reading in your class.
- **Send it** to friends and family members in a card or by e-mail.

Publish your poem. Share your poem with others and discuss the ideas and feelings it presents. Ask your teacher for other publishing ideas.

Using Poetry Conventions and Techniques

Poets use a variety of special techniques in their work. This page and the next define some of the most important ones.

Figures of Speech

- A **simile** (sĭm´ə-lē) compares two unlike things with the word *like* or *as*.

    The washing machine coughed
    like a dying stegosaurus.

- A **metaphor** (mĕt´ə-fôr) compares two unlike things without using *like* or *as*.

    That radio was more
    than tubes and speakers;
    it was the wide world come to visit
    in her parlor.

- **Personification** (pər-sŏn´ə-fĭ-kā´shən) is a technique that gives human traits to something that is nonhuman.

    The mailbox gaped
    with open mouth,
    speechless.

- **Hyperbole** (hī-pûr´bə-lē) is an exaggerated statement, often humorous.

    A bicycle sped past
    with a sonic boom!

Sounds of Poetry

- **Alliteration** (ə-lĭt´ə-rā´shən) is the repetition of consonant sounds at the beginning of words.

    I never wash or wax it, I should mention.

- **Assonance** (ăs´ə-nəns) is the repetition of vowel sounds anywhere in words.

    just catching dust in the sun

- **Consonance** (kŏn´sə-nəns) is the repetition of consonant sounds anywhere in words.

    No fear of spilling something—the upholstery's already stained.

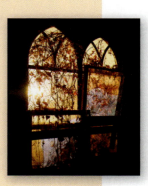

- **Enjambment** *(ĕn-jăm´mənt)* is running a sentence across more than one line of verse or from one stanza to another.

  a clunky machine
  with which she wrote letters
  starting, "Dear Niece"

- **Line breaks** help control the rhythm of a poem. The reader naturally pauses at the end of a line, the last word of which receives added emphasis.

  Branches reaching out,
  stretching,
  as though fingers yearning
  to strum the wind.

- **Onomatopoeia** *(ŏn´ə-măt´ə-pē´ə)* is the use of words that sound like what they name.

  that clackety old thing?

- **Repetition** *(rĕp´ĭ-tĭsh´ən)* uses the same word, phrase, or pattern of words more than once, for emphasis or for rhythm.

  What flames shot from the tailpipes!
  What smoke rolled from the spinning tires!
  What gasps rose from the crowd!

- **Rhyme** *(rīm)* means using words whose endings sound alike. *End rhyme* happens at the end of lines.

  so it doesn't get as much attention
  as it once did. No one admires it. (I
  never wash or wax it, I should mention.)

  Internal rhyme happens within lines.

  Finding her way in blinding snow.

- **Rhythm** *(rĭth´əm)* is the pattern of accented and unaccented syllables in a poem.
    - **Iambic:** an unstressed followed by a stressed syllable *(Ĭ ám´)*
    - **Trochaic:** a stressed followed by an unstressed syllable *(lá´-tĕr)*
    - **Anapestic:** two unstressed followed by a stressed syllable *(tŏ thĕ moón´)*
    - **Dactylic:** a stressed followed by two unstressed syllables *(stealth´-ĭ-lў)*

The rhythm of free-verse poetry tends to flow naturally, like speaking. Traditional poetry follows a more regular pattern, as in the following example.

  Moon´ on snow´
  Evening glow´

Writing Free Verse

At first glance, free verse may seem to follow no rules at all. Actually, each free-verse poem creates its own form—using traditional poetic techniques such as consonance, assonance, repetition, and rhythm. (See pages 374–375.) One tradition in free verse is that it almost never uses end rhymes.

Free verse does not use the strict rules of some other poetic forms, but it is easy to distinguish from prose because the words and rhythms are carefully chosen. They present surprising imagery and ideas in words that are fun to hear. Justine Fredrickson wrote the following free-verse poem about an old-fashioned typewriter. Notice the poetic techniques she used.

Consonance is used in the repeated "t" of line 2.

The words "Dear Niece" echo the poem's title. Assonance is used with the words "just," "dust," and "sun" in line 9.

Periods are left out to avoid abrupt pauses at the ends of sentences.

The ending recalls an earlier thought in the poem.

"Dear Aunt Janie"

My Aunt Janie
left me a typewriter—
a clunky machine

with which she wrote letters
starting, "Dear Niece"
and spilling her thoughts

It sat on my dresser for weeks
near the window,
just catching dust in the sun

When friends asked,
"Where'd you get
that clackety old thing?"

I'd shrug
and change the subject

This afternoon I came home
to find a white sheet of paper
waiting in the roller

As I touched the keys,
this poem spilled out

Tip

Notice how the sparseness of language in this poem invites you to fill in the meaning for yourself. In creative writing, it's best not to tell the reader how to think.

Writing Poetry 377

12.14B

Writing Guidelines Free Verse Poem

Prewriting

- **Choose a topic and focus.** Concentrate on vivid personal images, especially events that have changed your life or attitudes. Identify a scene and your emotions in connection to it.
- **Gather details.** Make a list of thoughts and feelings associated with the scene you have chosen, as well as descriptive details that help it come alive.
- **Organize details.** Arrange the ideas in your list by grouping related details together. This may suggest an organization for your poem.

Drafting

- **Consider poetic techniques.** Look for ways to make your poem vivid and your feelings clear by using conventions such as rhythm, similes and metaphors, repetition, alliteration, and so on.
- **Write a draft.** Try to tell the story or describe the scene as naturally as possible without worrying too much about things like line breaks or punctuation.

Revising

- **Work with a partner.** Read the poem aloud to a trusted partner and ask for an honest response.
- **Fine tune your language.** Review each line and word to be sure they work exactly as you would like. Avoid general statements and vague words in favor of specific ones.

Editing

- **Decide how you will use poetic conventions.** Free verse may avoid punctuation and use line breaks to allow easy reading and a natural flow.
- **Make a neat final copy.**

Write a free-verse poem. Follow the writing process to write a free-verse poem of your own. Use techniques such as consonance, assonance, repetition, and rhythm (see pages 374–375) to make your poem a work of art.

Creative Writing

Writing Cinquains

A cinquain (sometimes called a quintet) is a carefully structured poem of five lines. The first line has two syllables, the second has four, the third six, the fourth eight, and the final line just two again. One tradition in cinquains is for the rhythm to be iambic, although this is not a strict rule. Generally, both syllables in the first and last lines are strongly accented. Most cinquains are unrhymed, although rhyme is sometimes used for humorous effect.

Some cinquains follow a slightly different pattern although the number of syllables per line is the same. The first line is one word that gives the poem a title and subject, followed by two descriptive adjectives, three action verbs describing what the subject does, a phrase indicating feelings about the subject, and one word that essentially renames the poem.

In a poem such as this, short, precise words are essential. It's important to make every syllable count—not just to fill the form. Also, a good cinquain delays its sense of closure until the very last line. Those final two syllables should feel like a climax to the poem.

Hammers

Hammers
are perfect for
driving nails or breaking
things: full piggy banks, geodes—and
silence.

—Avery Strattman

Mystery Machine

What does
this machine do?
I see levers and dials;
I hear gears whirring, smell something
burning!

— Marissa Troff

 12.14B

Writing Poetry

Writing Guidelines Cinquain

Prewriting

- **Choose a topic.** The subject of most cinquains is a noun of some type. This could include an inanimate object, a person, or an activity such as a party, car race, or concert. Select a subject that inspires vivid images for you.
- **Gather details.** Brainstorm a list of descriptive thoughts and feelings associated with the subject.
- **Organize details.** Arrange the ideas in your list by grouping related details together and selecting which ones you might use.

Drafting

- **Follow the poetic conventions for cinquains.** Remember the syllable requirements for each line and repeat your words out loud to judge the rhythm. Iambic rhythm is preferred although not required.
- **Write a draft.** Arrange the descriptive words and thoughts from your list to meet the requirements of a cinquain and to build toward a powerful final line.

Revising

- **Work with a partner.** Read the poem aloud to a trusted partner and ask for an honest response.
- **Fine tune your language.** Review each line and word to be sure they work exactly as you would like. Avoid general statements and vague words in favor of specific ones.

Editing

- **Decide on the use of punctuation.** Using a colon or semicolon to separate words can show the reader where to pause. An exclamation point can emphasize a surprising or powerful word or thought.
- **Make a neat final copy.**

Write a cinquain. Follow the steps above to write your own cinquain in the proper form.

Research Writing

Writing Focus

Research Skills	381
MLA Research Paper	391
Writing Responsibly	439
Documenting Research	447
Making Oral Presentations	461

Learning Language

Work with a partner to learn the following words and expressions from this unit.

1. To **evaluate** means "to look at or judge carefully."
   As you write, how do you evaluate your progress?
2. Something that is **systematic** is orderly or methodical.
   Why is it best to be systematic with homework?
3. To **distinguish** means "to notice differences."
   What distinguishes you from your friends?
4. You make a careful study of a topic when you **research**.
   What are three topics you would like to research?
5. To **carry out** means "to accomplish something."
   What activities do you carry out in school?

Research Writing
Research Skills

Doing research will help you in more ways than you know. If you begin with a topic that's too broad, research can help you narrow it. If you don't know which side of an issue to write about, gathering evidence from experts on the topic can help you take a position. Anyone who has ever done research knows that it can provide not only answers but also additional questions to consider.

That's why it's as important to know *how* to research as it is to know *what* to research. This chapter will serve as a guide to various sources of information—such as primary and secondary sources, where to find them, and how to gauge their reliability.

- **Primary vs. Secondary Sources**
- **Evaluating Sources of Information**
- **Using the Internet**
- **Using the Library**
- **Using Reference Books**

"The outcome of any serious research can only be to make two questions grow where only one grew before."

—Thorstein Veblen

Primary vs. Secondary Sources

Primary sources are original sources (diaries, people, events, surveys). They inform you directly, not through a second person's explanation or interpretation. Ideally, when you research a topic, you should find as much primary information as possible. Using primary sources will allow you to gather evidence from experts on your topic and text written for informed audiences in a field.

Primary sources include . . .

- **Diaries, journals, and letters:** You can often find these in museums, in libraries, or at historic sites.
- **Presentations:** A speaker at a museum or a historic site can give you firsthand information of events he or she lived through, but be aware of the presenter's own interpretation of the events.
- **Interviews:** Talk to an expert on your research topic. You can do this by phone, e-mail, or letter.
- **Surveys and questionnaires:** These tools help you gather a great deal of data from many people.
- **Observation and participation:** Your own observations of a person, a place, or an event provide excellent firsthand information. Participating in an event can give you insights that cannot be discovered through the reports of others.

Secondary sources are third-person accounts found in research done by other people. Much of the news (television, radio, Internet, books, magazines) can be considered a secondary source of information. Keep in mind that, by their very nature, secondary sources represent filtered information that may contain biases.

Primary Sources

1. Reading the journal of a travel guide
2. Listening to a travel guide's presentation on-site
3. Interviewing a shop owner in London

Secondary Sources

1. Exploring a Web site about being a travel guide
2. Reading a magazine about the site
3. Watching a TV documentary about London's retail business

Try It!

List two primary and two secondary sources you might use to learn about the era of your parents' adolescence. Be as specific as you can be. Discuss your ideas with a partner.

Evaluating Sources of Information

You may be able to gather a lot of evidence about your research topic. But before you use any of it, decide whether or not the information is dependable. Use the following questions to help you decide about the reliability of your sources.

Is the source a primary source or a secondary source?

You can usually trust any information you've collected yourself, but be careful with secondary sources. Although many of them are reliable, others may contain outdated or incorrect information.

Is the source an expert?

An expert knows more about a topic than other people. Using an expert's thoughts and opinions can make your paper more believable. If you aren't sure about a source's authority, ask a teacher or librarian what he or she thinks.

Is the information accurate?

Sources that people respect are usually very accurate. Big-city newspapers (*New York Times* or *Chicago Tribune*) and well-known Web sites (CNN or ESPN) are reliable sources of information. Little-known sources that do not support their facts or that contain errors are not reliable.

Is the information fair and complete?

A reliable source should provide information fairly, covering all sides of a subject. If a source presents only one side of a subject, its information may not be accurate. To make themselves sound better, politicians and advertisers often present just their side of a subject. Avoid sources that are one sided; look for those that are balanced.

Is the information current?

Usually, you want to have the most up-to-date information about a subject. Sometimes information changes, and sources can become outdated quickly. Check the copyright page in a book, the issue date of a magazine, and the posting date of online information.

Is the information factual or a complex inference?

As you gather your sources, evaluate the sources to distinguish between factual data and complex inferences, conclusions based on evidence or experience. Some sources contain facts and statistics while others make inferences or conclusions about data. Your report should rely on factual data, but you should carefully consider the inferences in the sources you use.

Using the Internet

Because you can access many resources by surfing the Web, the Internet is a valuable research aid. You can find government publications, encyclopedia entries, business reports, and firsthand observations on the Internet.

Points to Remember

- **Use the Internet wisely.** Sites that include *.edu, .org,* and *.gov* in the Web address are often reliable. These sites are from educational, nonprofit, or government agencies. If you have questions about the reliability of a site, talk to your teacher. (See also page 383.) Remember to check the date of the Web site. Abandoned Web sites may contain outdated information.

- **Try several search engines.** When you type a term into a search engine's input box, the search engine scans its database for matching sites. Then the engine returns recommendations for you to explore. Because there is an enormous amount of information on the Web, no one search engine can handle it all. So employ at least two search engines when you surf the Web. Enter keywords to start your research or enter specific questions to zero in on your topic.

- **Take advantage of links.** When you read a page, watch for links to other sites. These may offer different perspectives or points of view on your topic.

- **Experiment with keywords.** Sometimes you must ask a number of different questions or use different keywords to find the information you need.

- **Ignore Web sites that advertise research papers for sale.** Using these sites is dishonest. Teachers and librarians can recognize and verify when a paper is someone else's work.

- **Learn your school's Internet policy.** Using the computer at school is a privilege. To maintain that privilege, follow your school's Internet policy and any guidelines your parents may have set.

Try It!

With a partner, come up with a possible research topic and enter its keywords into a major search engine. Click on the top ten search results and determine whether each site is a reliable or unreliable source.

TEKS 12.21A

Using the Library

The Internet may be a good place to initiate your research, but a library is often a more valuable place to continue your research. A library offers materials that are more in-depth and reliable than what you find on the Internet. Most libraries contain the following resources.

Books

- **Reference** books include encyclopedias, almanacs, dictionaries, atlases, and directories. Reference books provide a quick overview of research topics.
- **Nonfiction** texts are a good source of facts that can serve as a foundation for your research. Check the copyright dates to be sure you are reading reasonably up-to-date information. Most libraries organize nonfiction using the Dewey decimal system. (See page **387**.)
- **Fiction** can sometimes aid or enhance your research. For example, a historical novel can reveal people's feelings about a particular time in history. (Fiction books are grouped together in alphabetical order by the authors' last names.)

Periodicals

Periodicals (newspapers and magazines) are grouped together in a library. Use the *Readers' Guide to Periodical Literature* to find articles in periodicals. (See page **390**.) You will have to ask the librarian for older issues. Your library may subscribe to online databases of periodicals.

The Media Section

The media section of your library includes DVDs, CD-ROMs, CDs, cassettes, and videotapes. These resources can immerse you in an event. Keep in mind, however, that directors and screenwriters may present events in a way that accommodates their personal views.

Computers

Computers in most libraries are connected to the Internet, although there may be restrictions on their use. Ask a librarian about the use policies at your library.

Try It!

Visit your school or local library. Think of a broad topic and gather evidence about that topic. Look for reference books, fiction and nonfiction books, periodicals, and audio or visual media. Which section of the library was easiest to navigate?

Using the Computer Catalog

Learning to use the library efficiently will help you gather evidence on your research topic. While some libraries still use a card catalog in a cabinet with drawers, most libraries keep their catalog on the computer. Each system varies a bit, so ask for help if necessary. A **computer catalog** lists the books held in your library and affiliated systems. It lets you know if a book is available.

Various Search Methods

When you are using a computer catalog, you can find information about a book with any of the following methods:

- If you know it, enter the **title** of the book.
- If you know the **author** of the book, enter the first and last names.
- A general search of your **subject** will also help you find books on your topic. Enter either the subject or a related keyword.

Sample Computer Catalog Screen

In the illustration below, the key to the right identifies the types of information provided for a particular resource, in this case, a book. Once you locate the book you need, make note of the call number. You will use this to find the book on the shelf.

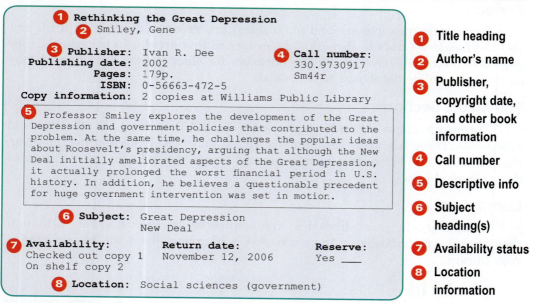

Try It!

Use the computer catalog to see what current newspapers your library subscribes to. Ask the librarian for help if necessary.

Understanding Call Numbers

All nonfiction books in the library have **call numbers**. The books are arranged on the shelves according to these numbers. Call numbers are usually based on the **Dewey decimal classification** system, which divides nonfiction books into 10 subject categories.

000–099	General Works	**500–599**	Sciences
100–199	Philosophy	**600–699**	Technology
200–299	Religion	**700–799**	Arts and Recreation
300–399	Social Sciences	**800–899**	Literature
400–499	Languages	**900–999**	History and Geography

A call number often has a decimal in it, followed by the first letter of an author's name. Note how the following call numbers are ordered on the shelves.

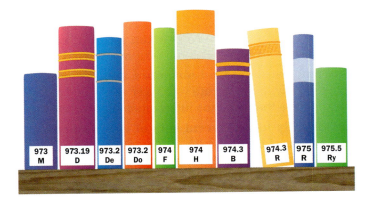

Try It!

Each subject category or class in the Dewey decimal classification system is divided into *divisions*. Identify the division for books listed in the 900s. **Note:** Each division is further divided into *sections* and *subsections*.

Identifying the Parts of a Book

Each part of a book provides valuable information. The **title page** includes the title of the book, the author's name, and the publisher's name and city. The **copyright page** follows with the year the book was published. The **preface, foreword, or introduction** comes before the table of contents and tells why the book was written. The **table of contents** lists the names and page numbers of sections and chapters in the book. At the end of the book, you may find at least one **appendix,** containing various maps, tables, and lists. Finally, the **index** is an alphabetical list of important topics and their page numbers in the book.

Using Reference Books

A reference book is a nonfiction book that contains specific facts or background information. Reference books are reliable sources of information. The reference section includes encyclopedias, dictionaries, almanacs, and so on. Usually, reference books cannot be checked out, so you must use them in the library. As you record source material, be sure to separate factual data that you find in reference books from inferences—conclusions based on evidence or experience—that you find in other sources.

Referring to Encyclopedias

An encyclopedia is a set of books (or a CD-ROM) that contains basic information on topics arranged alphabetically.

Tips for Using Encyclopedias

- **At the end of an article, there is often a list of related articles.**
  You can read these other articles to learn more about your topic.
- **The index can help you find out more about your topic.**
  The index is usually in a separate volume or at the end of the last volume. It lists every article that contains information about a topic. (See below.)
- **Libraries usually have several sets of encyclopedias.**
  Review each set and decide which one best serves your needs. (Always check with your teacher first to see if you can use an encyclopedia as a source for your research.)

Sample Encyclopedia Index

Encyclopedia volume

Page numbers

Related topics

The Great Depression **D:** 331–336 with pictures and illustrations
    Herbert Hoover **H:** 242
    The New Deal **V:** 311–312
    Franklin Delano Roosevelt **V:** 310–312
    See also the related topics in the Great Depression *article.*
    Government Policies **U:** 332
    Public Works Projects **U:** 333
        CCC **C:** 135
        WPA and Parks **P:** 299
        World War II **W:** 276

 12.21A

Consulting Other Reference Books

Most libraries contain several types of reference books in addition to encyclopedias. Avoid over-reliance on one source by consulting several references.

Almanacs

Almanacs are books filled with facts and statistics about many different subjects. *The World Almanac and Book of Facts* contains celebrity profiles; statistics about politics, business, and sports; plus consumer information.

Atlases

Atlases contain detailed maps of the world, continents, countries, and so on. They also contain statistics and related information. Specialized atlases cover topics like outer space and the oceans.

Dictionaries

Dictionaries contain definitions of words and their origins. Biographical dictionaries focus on famous people. Specialized dictionaries deal with science, history, medicine, and other subjects.

Directories

Directories list information about groups of people, businesses, and organizations. The most widely used directories are telephone books.

Periodical Indexes

Periodical indexes list articles in magazines and newspapers. These indexes are arranged alphabetically by subject.

- The *Readers' Guide to Periodical Literature* lists articles from many publications. (See page **390**.)
- The *New York Times Index* lists articles from the *New York Times* newspaper.

Other Reference Books

Some reference books do not fit into any one category but are recognized by their names:

- *Facts on File* includes thousands of short but informative facts about events, discoveries, people, and places.
- *Facts About the Presidents* presents information about all of the presidents of the United States.
- *Bartlett's Familiar Quotations* lists thousands of quotations from famous people.

Using Periodical Guides

Periodical guides are located in the reference or periodical section of the library. These guides alphabetically list topics and articles found in magazines, newspapers, and journals. Some guides are printed volumes, some are CDs, and some are on library Web sites. Ask your librarian for help.

Readers' Guide to Periodical Literature

The *Readers' Guide to Periodical Literature* is a well-known periodical reference source and is found in most libraries. The following tips will help you look up your topic in this resource:

- Articles are always listed alphabetically by author and topic.
- Some topics are subdivided, with each article listed under the appropriate subtopic.
- Cross-references refer to related topic entries where you may find more articles pertinent to your topic.

Sample *Readers' Guide* Format

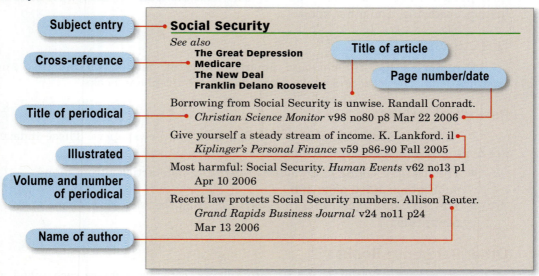

Tip

When you find a listing for your topic, write down the name and issue date of the magazine and the title and page numbers of the article. Your librarian may get the periodical for you, or you may need to find it yourself.

Research Writing
MLA Research Paper

Historians do more than tell what happened during a particular time period. Historians carry out careful research about a person, a place, or an event and then attempt to put their findings into perspective.

Like a historian, when you write a research paper, you need to do more than present the information that you have gathered. You need to analyze the data and present your own interpretation of its impact or importance.

One important aspect of American history is presidential policy. Each presidential administration creates its own policies in a number of areas, from foreign relations to economics. Most of these policies tend to produce both positive and negative effects. In this chapter, you'll learn all the steps necessary to write a research paper that analyzes a particular policy enacted by a president of the United States.

Writing Guidelines

- **Subject:** A presidential policy
- **Purpose:** To research a presidential policy and analyze its effectiveness
- **Form:** Research paper
- **Audience:** Classmates

"Self-confidence is the first requisite to great undertakings."

—Samuel Johnson

Research Paper

While browsing a book of photographs from the Great Depression, Shawna Lopez became interested in this critical period in American history. She decided to write a paper about a presidential policy called the New Deal designed to help Americans get through this troubled time. You will find Shawna's paper on the next eight pages of this chapter. The margin notes point out important features of organization and formatting.

Roosevelt's New Deal:
Success or Failure?

Shawna Lopez
Mr. Collins
Language Arts
March 9, 2011

> **Title Page**
> Center the title about one-third of the way down the page. Center author information two-thirds of the way down.

Roosevelt's New Deal: Success or Failure?

Thesis Statement: Although its success was incomplete, the New Deal saved the United States from collapsing into chaos and gave the nation's citizens the hope they needed to survive.

I. In the 1920s, the U.S. economy roared ahead like a powerful automobile, but beneath the shiny exterior, the economy was corroding.
   A. The value of stocks rose rapidly, and investors grew wealthy.
   B. Workers couldn't afford to buy consumer goods, so businesses cut back on production.
   C. Farm prices lagged, and many farmers lived in poverty.
II. In October 1929, the U.S. economy suddenly collapsed.
   A. The stock market dropped drastically, and investors rushed to sell their shares.
   B. Within weeks, the value of U.S. stocks had dropped by one-third.
   C. Banks had begun to fail, taking their customers' savings with them.
   D. President Herbert Hoover mistakenly believed that the economy would correct itself without government help.

> **Outline**
> Center the title one inch from the top of the page. Double-space throughout. Include the outline after the title page and before the first page of the paper.

Note: Not all teachers require a title page or an outline. If yours does, follow the guidelines above, or use specific instructions provided by your teacher.

1/2"

Lopez 1 1"

1"

The entire paper is double-spaced.

Shawna Lopez
Mr. Collins
Language Arts
9 March 2011

Roosevelt's New Deal: Success or Failure?

Beginning
A dramatic opening grabs the reader's attention.

When he took office on March 4, 1933, President Franklin Delano Roosevelt assumed leadership of a nation mired in poverty and racked by hopelessness. Four years before, a stock market crash had set off the Great Depression, a collapse of the United States economy. Many factories, businesses, and banks closed down, and millions of U.S. citizens lost their jobs. Untold numbers of families had lost their savings and even their homes (Leuchtenburg 1).

1"

As a candidate, Roosevelt had promised a "new deal for the American people" (qtd. in Heale 18). As president, he began to dramatically restructure the U.S. economy with an economic program called the New Deal. The New Deal created jobs, changed banking practices, and prevented many people from losing their savings and their homes (Church). As much as it changed the economy, the New Deal did not end the Great Depression. Although its success was incomplete,the New Deal saved the United States from collapsing into chaos and gave the nation's citizens the hope they needed to survive.

The beginning part leads up to the thesis statement (underlined).

1"

An Economic Meltdown

In the 1920s, the U.S. economy roared ahead like a powerful automobile, but beneath the shiny exterior, the economy was corroding. According to Kennedy in *Freedom from Fear*, "Nearly three decades of barely punctuated economic growth, capped by seven years of unprecedented prosperity, gave to the entire country, an air of masterful confidence in the future" (11). The value of stocks rose rapidly, and investors grew wealthy (Kennedy 10–15). Unfortunately, businesspeople took too much of the profit from their businesses and paid workers too little. Workers couldn't afford to buy consumer goods, so businesses began cutting back on production. Farm prices also lagged, and many farmers lived in poverty (Mintz).

Then, in October 1929, the U.S. economy suddenly collapsed. The stock market dropped drastically, and investors rushed to sell their shares. Within weeks, the value of U.S. stocks had dropped by one-third. The Great Depression had begun (Mintz). Even before this time, banks had begun to fail, taking their customers' savings with them. After 1929, thousands more failed (Badger 31). President Herbert Hoover mistakenly believed that the economy would correct itself without much government help, but the economy only worsened. By 1932, 25 percent of U.S. citizens were unemployed. Many had lost their homes and didn't have the food they needed to survive (Heale 19). As time passed, the nation's Depression became an economic psychological problem. With national spirits at a new low, the country turned to Franklin Roosevelt for help. They put their faith in Roosevelt—and his New Deal.

The New Deal

In the first phase of the New Deal, Roosevelt addressed one of the nation's most pressing problems—the soundness of the banks. Panicked by bank failures, people had made "runs" on banks, pulling out their savings and draining the banks of needed funds. This caused even more failures (Badger 31). To stop this chain reaction, Roosevelt declared a "banking holiday" and closed all the banks. He then presented Congress with legislation to make banks stronger (Freidel 95). When the first banks reopened on March 13, people began to return their money (Mintz). The nation's psychology had begun to shift from despair to hope. Healing had begun.

Roosevelt understood that people needed financial relief, and that a flow of cash would jump-start the economy. In 1933, he introduced the National Industrial Recovery Act (NIRA). Congress approved giving him unprecedented legislative power to make laws to solve the nation's economic woes. With this act he authorized a number of new agencies that put people to work. The Tennessee Valley Authority hired workers to build electrical dams in the rural South. The Civilian Conservation Corps, or CCC, put people to work in forests, planting trees and building roads and shelters. The wages were low—just $30 per month in the CCC (Church), but as with the restructuring of the banks, the psychological effect was critical. People who had lost hope and self-esteem once again became breadwinners, and their confidence began to return.

The New Deal helped citizens in other ways, too. The Home Owners Loan Act and the Agricultural Adjustment Act helped Americans refinance their mortgages and save their homes and farms (Mintz). The Social Security Act established a system by which workers paid money into a government fund that would provide them with a pension when they retired (Leuchtenburg 133). This pension secured the future for senior citizens, among those most vulnerable to economic downturns. The importance of Social Security was more than its economic benefits. Providing a future for the nation's elderly helped promote a feeling of national security that was critical during a very uncertain time.

Bumps in the Road

The newfound hope was real, but NIRA's Title 1 was in trouble. Title 1 attempted to create jobs and increase salaries by regulating labor practices, wages, and prices. It set maximum work hours per week, which forced businesses to hire more workers. It also set minimum wages and guaranteed the right of workers to form unions. Although these were all noble goals, the process to achieve those goals was coercive, cumbersome, and often unequally applied.

Other aspects of the NIRA proved equally problematic. The board that administered the act, the National Recovery Administration (NRA), churned out so many regulations that they became impossible to enforce, and even to understand. Many business owners and labor groups manipulated the regulations to their favor whenever possible, while other businesses simply ignored them (Black 303). The massive regulatory machine also helped turn many businesspeople against the New Deal. In 1935, the Supreme Court ruled against the NIRA. Historian Frank Freidel states, "Chief Justice Hughes was devastating. He held that Roosevelt's code-making [lawmaking] authority was indeed an 'unconstitutional delegation of legislative power' " (161).

The Agricultural Adjustment Act (AAA) met a similar fate. Created to help farmers, the AAA paid farmers to reduce production, which in theory would cause farm prices to rise. Farmers would then make more for the crops they sold. AAA payments came from taxes on companies that processed and sold agricultural products. In fact, the AAA only succeeded in raising farm prices temporarily, and farmers continued to struggle (Black 307–8). In addition, processors hated paying the tax required by the act. They filed suit, and in 1936, the Supreme Court declared the AAA unconstitutional, saying that the agency had no authority to make laws (Black 328–29).

Lopez 6

The End of the New Deal

By 1937, the New Deal had begun to improve the U.S. economy. Unemployment fell to about 12 percent, the lowest in years. Impressed by the improvements, Roosevelt cut back on government spending for New Deal programs (Black 428). This turned out to be a big mistake. By early 1938, the economy was sinking again. The unemployment rate rose to 22.5 percent, and the stock market had taken a major slide. Quickly, Roosevelt reversed position, and the economy began to respond (Black 435–36). Employment rose, and so did industrial production. However, the Depression still gripped the United States, and it would take a bigger force than the New Deal to create an economic boom.

During the 1930s, a depression also gripped Europe. In Germany, the poor economic conditions helped fascist leader Adolph Hitler rise to power (Mintz). In September 1939, Hitler's Germany initiated a world war by invading Poland. In December 1941, after being attacked by Japan, the United States entered the war. Soon U.S. factories converted to production of tanks, planes, bombs, and other war materials. By 1943, employment boomed, and factories were rolling again. The Depression was over, and the United States would enter one of its most productive periods ever (Hartford).

Conclusion

While the New Deal provided jobs for many people and allowed many families to keep their homes and farms,

> Statistics help to paint a clear picture.

> Dates help the reader follow the main points.

it did not succeed in ending the Great Depression. Those who criticize the New Deal often fail to account for its major achievement: It saved the United States from complete collapse. In Europe, the German government lapsed into fascism, largely as a result of a depression there. In the United States, the same might have happened except for Roosevelt and the New Deal. The programs of the New Deal restored the citizens' faith that a democratic, capitalistic system could respond to their needs in the worst of economic times. This restored faith helped democracy and free enterprise to survive. The New Deal also created a new United States, one that would provide a safety net for the old, the infirm, and the suffering, and helped to prevent another economic and social tragedy from happening.

Perhaps just as important, the New Deal helped to convince people of the value of shared sacrifice and innovative vision. Both would prove critical in bringing the nation through another crisis—World War II. Conditioned by years of working together and following the leadership of Franklin Delano Roosevelt, U.S. citizens would meet the challenge of the war as a nation largely unified and willing to make the sacrifices necessary to defeat fascism. Once again, President Roosevelt would ask his nation to follow his creative leadership and make sacrifices for the common good. Once again, Roosevelt would help to kindle the faith and hope so critical to survival in a time of national crisis.

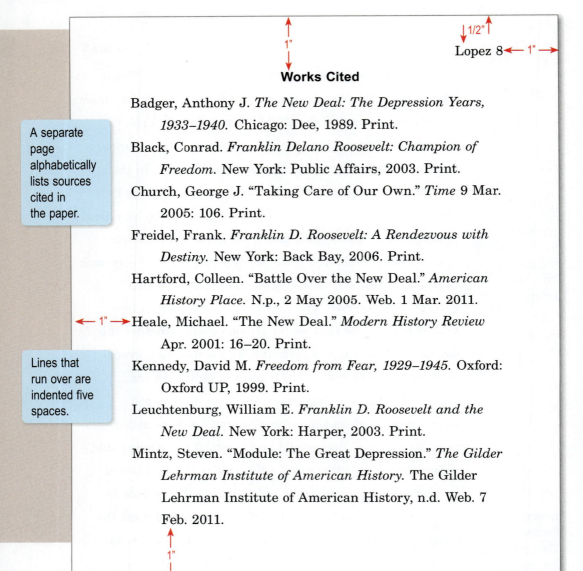

Lopez 8

Works Cited

Badger, Anthony J. *The New Deal: The Depression Years, 1933–1940.* Chicago: Dee, 1989. Print.

Black, Conrad. *Franklin Delano Roosevelt: Champion of Freedom.* New York: Public Affairs, 2003. Print.

Church, George J. "Taking Care of Our Own." *Time* 9 Mar. 2005: 106. Print.

Freidel, Frank. *Franklin D. Roosevelt: A Rendezvous with Destiny.* New York: Back Bay, 2006. Print.

Hartford, Colleen. "Battle Over the New Deal." *American History Place.* N.p., 2 May 2005. Web. 1 Mar. 2011.

Heale, Michael. "The New Deal." *Modern History Review* Apr. 2001: 16–20. Print.

Kennedy, David M. *Freedom from Fear, 1929–1945.* Oxford: Oxford UP, 1999. Print.

Leuchtenburg, William E. *Franklin D. Roosevelt and the New Deal.* New York: Harper, 2003. Print.

Mintz, Steven. "Module: The Great Depression." *The Gilder Lehrman Institute of American History.* The Gilder Lehrman Institute of American History, n.d. Web. 7 Feb. 2011.

A separate page alphabetically lists sources cited in the paper.

Lines that run over are indented five spaces.

Respond to the reading. Now that you have read the sample research paper, answer the following questions.

Organization (1) In a general way, how is the paper organized?
Development of Ideas (2) Name two ways in which the New Deal was successful—and two ways in which it fell short. (3) Why does the writer think the New Deal was important?
Voice (4) Is the voice of the paper convincing? Why or why not?

MLA Research Paper

Prewriting

To develop an effective research paper, you'll need to carry out a great deal of planning and research. During the prewriting stage, you will need to decide on a major research topic, formulate a research question, plan for in-depth research, gather facts and details, establish a thesis, and organize your data.

Keys to Effective Prewriting

1. Brainstorm ideas and consult with others to select a complex topic and formulate a major research question.

2. Formulate a research plan for engaging in in-depth research, including a list of questions you want to answer about the topic.

3. Use a gathering grid to organize your research questions and answers. Use note cards to keep track of longer answers. (See pages 404–405.)

4. Cite the sources of any information you paraphrase or quote.

5. Keep track of the publication details of all your sources. (See page 407.)

6. Gather enough information to offer a clear and complete analysis of your topic.

Prewriting Selecting a Topic

To select a major research topic in the social sciences, Shawna first decided to focus on American presidents because of her interest in American history. She brainstormed a list of presidents she is interested in and consulted with a small group of classmates to come up with some important policies and key points for each.

Topics List

Franklin Roosevelt
New Deal
- response to the Depression
- jump-started the economy
- gave people hope

John F. Kennedy
Alliance for Progress
- help for Latin America
- growth of industry
- land reform

Lyndon Johnson
Great Society
- response to poverty
- focused on civil rights
- expanded Social Security

Make a topics list. Create a list like the one above. Identify two or three topics in the social sciences (such as history, economics, psychology, or education) and key points related to them. If necessary, refer to a textbook, classroom notes, or the Internet for ideas. Then choose the topic you find most interesting for your paper.

Focus on the Texas Traits

Development of Ideas Choose a topic that truly interests you. Also, as you consult with your classmates, discuss whether there will be enough information about your choice. You will need a thorough understanding of the topic to develop an effective analysis.

Assessing Your Topic

You need an appropriate topic to formulate a major research question for your paper. Generally, good topics meet the following criteria.

- **Broad enough to allow in-depth research.** A single rule at your school may not allow in-depth research, but banning books in school libraries would.
- **Important enough to affect people's lives.** A slight change in the price of your school lunch might not have major effects, but changing government aid to school cafeterias might.
- **Invites judgement or assessment.** Studying one voter registration program may not invite a judgement, but assessing voter turnout does.

Formulating a Research Question

A major research question guides all of your research. In most cases, it requires you to interpret and analyze the information you gather. It is probable that you will modify this initial question after you begin research.

Some examples of research questions follow.

- **Who was the most powerful presidential candidate in the 2000 election?**
- **What were the effects of the government's response to Hurricane Katrina?**
- **How did the change in the prescription drug benefit in 2003 affect Medicare recipients?**

To formulate a research question, you need to do some preliminary research on your possible topic. Shawna did some quick research in the following areas.

> What was the New Deal?
> What were some of its successes?
> What were some of its failures?

Her initial research convinced her that her topic was appropriate because it allowed in-depth research, it was important in people's lives, and it invited a judgment or assessment. She formulated the following research question.

> Why was the New Deal so effective?

Prewrite

Assess your topic and formulate a research question. Assess your topic using the criteria above and then do some quick research using the Internet or another reliable resource. Then formulate a major research question that a paper might seek to answer.

Prewriting Using a Gathering Grid

To systematically organize relevant and accurate information, use a graphic organizer such as a gathering grid. Shawna created a gathering grid to organize her research about the New Deal. In the left-hand column, she listed questions she wanted to answer. Across the top, she listed resources that answered those questions. For answers too long to fit in the grid, Shawna used note cards. (See page **405**.) A portion of Shawna's grid is shown below.

Gathering Grid

THE NEW DEAL	Franklin D. Roosevelt and the New Deal (book)	"The New Deal" (magazine article)	The New Deal: The Depression Years, 1933–1940 (book)
Why was the policy created?	See note card 1.		
What were its successes?	TVA built dams for flood control and electricity.	Civilian Conservation Corps	Banking holiday People putting money back in banks
What were its failures?	NIRA was declared unconstitutional.	AAA was struck down by Supreme Court in 1936.	

Create a gathering grid. List questions in the left-hand column of your grid. Across the top, list sources of accurate and relevant information. Fill in the grid with answers you find. Use note cards for longer, more detailed answers.

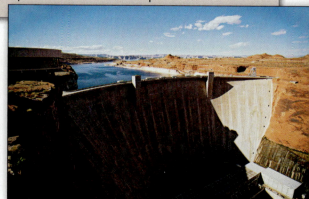

Creating Note Cards

A gathering grid works well for short answers, but when your answers are longer, it's better to use note cards. Number each note card and write a question at the top. Then answer the question with a list, a paraphrase, or a quotation. (See page 406.) To be sure you can accurately cite all researched information, identify the source at the bottom, including the page number if appropriate.

Note Cards

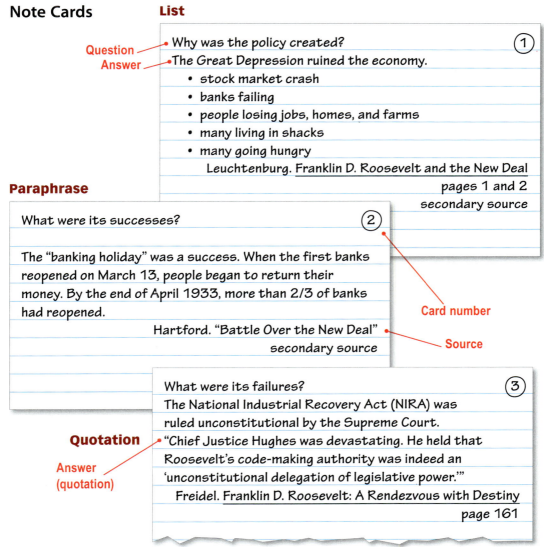

Create note cards. When your answers are too long to fit in a gathering grid, make note cards such as the ones above.

Prewriting Avoiding Plagiarism

Plagiarism means using someone else's words or ideas without giving them credit. Plagiarism is intellectual thievery and must always be avoided. To accurately cite all researched information, take care to note the sources of facts and ideas and indicate whether the note is a paraphrase or summary, or a quotation.

- **Paraphrase or summarize:** When you paraphrase or summarize, you rewrite information in your own words. This is usually the best approach for including information in your paper. Even when you paraphrase or summarize, give credit to the source of the idea.
- **Quote exact words:** To add authority or color to your paper, you may wish to use the exact words from one of your sources. Be sure to include these words in quotation marks and to give credit.

Paraphrasing or Summarizing

> Why was the policy created?
> Panicked by bank failures, people had made "runs" on banks, pulling out their savings and draining the banks of needed funds. This caused even more failures.
>
> Badger. The New Deal
> page 31
> secondary source

Quoting Exact Words

> Why was the policy created?
> "As banks ran into trouble, investors withdrew their assets. [. . .] Their withdrawals put more pressure on the banks. [. . .] As the economy worsened, the banks suffered once more. A total of 2,294 banks failed in 1931, and 1,453 in 1932."
>
> Badger. The New Deal
> page 31

Note: Use ellipses [. . .] in your quotations to show where words from the original source have been left out.

Try It!

Create two note cards for the same key passage from your research. On one card, *quote* a sentence from the passage. On the other card, *paraphrase* or *summarize* the passage. Give credit for the source on each card.

Keeping Track of Your Sources

Keep careful track of the sources you find. To document sources according to MLA style, you'll need to record the following information for each type of source:

- **Book:** Author's name. *Title*. City: Publisher, year of publication. Print.
- **Magazine:** Author's name. "Article title." *Magazine name* date: page numbers. Print.
- **Television:** "Episode Title." *Program title*. Network, Station call letters and Location, date of broadcast. Television.
- **E-mail Interview:** Name of person interviewed. E-mail Interview. date.
- **Internet:** Author's name (if listed). "Article title." *Title of Web site*. Name of sponsoring institution, date of posting or last update. Web. date of access.
- **Newspaper:** Author's name. "Article title." *Newspaper name* date, edition: page numbers. Print.

Source Citations

Book
Black, Conrad. *Franklin Delano Roosevelt: Champion of Freedom*. New York: Public Affairs, 2003. Print.

Magazine
Church, George J. "Taking Care of Our Own: The New Deal Probed the Limits of Government." *Time* 9 Mar. 2005: 106. Print.

Television Program
"F.D.R." *The American Experience*. PBS. WGBH, Boston, 28 Apr. 2006. Television.

E-mail Interview
Lavell, James. E-mail interview. 25 Mar. 2011.

Internet
Powell, Jim. "Fresh Debate about FDR's New Deal." *Individual Liberty, Free Markets, and Peace*. Cato Institute, 2 Dec. 2003. Web. 11 Nov. 2011.

Newspaper
Ringle, Ken. "FDR's Monumental Place in History." *Washington Post* 2 May 2006: A1. Print.

List sources. Keep a list of your sources, using the information above as your guide. Whenever you use a new source, add it to your list.

Prewriting Writing Your Thesis Statement

Once you've organized relevant and accurate information, it's time to write a thesis statement. Your thesis statement expresses the main idea or focus of your research, and it helps guide your writing. All of the other ideas in your paper should support the thesis. You can use the formula below to help you write your thesis statement.

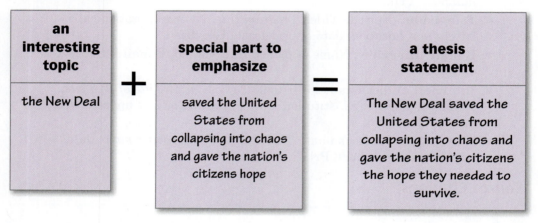

Sample Thesis Statements

Wind power (an interesting topic) **provides a viable energy source in the Plains states** (a special part to emphasize).

A cell that functions abnormally (an interesting topic) **can initiate a process that results in cancer** (a special part to emphasize).

The marketing of high-profile professional athletes (an interesting topic) **has become big business** (a special part to emphasize).

Create your thesis statement. Carefully review your research notes and choose a main point you want to make about your topic. Using the formula above, write a thesis statement for that idea.

Synthesizing Information

Critiquing the Research Process

For most people, it's hard to change an opinion, even if it isn't based on hard evidence. If your research question suggests an analysis or judgment, and you have formed an opinion based on your preliminary research and your previous thoughts, you may be reluctant to change it. However, a good research paper doesn't attempt to prove a preconceived idea. Instead, it follows the research to come to a conclusion.

For example, you might find that a book or Web site you have relied on for information has been questioned by reviewers because of a biased opinion or faulty research, or you may find that your initial research did not address contradictory views. If that is the case, you have three options.

- **Change your research question** to reflect the new and convincing research you have found.
- **Address the concerns in your paper** to acknowledge the questions about the information from a particular source.
- **Find a different source** that is recognized as more reliable and accurate.

Modifying Your Research Question as Necessary

Your major research question was based on some quick research. As you continue to dig deeper into the research on your topic, you may find that your initial assumptions about the topic weren't accurate or complete. If that's the case, it's necessary to modify your research question to fit the information gained from you research.

In the sample research paper, Shawna's initial research question was "Why was the New Deal so effective?" However, as she continued her research, she found that some people questioned the effectiveness of the New Deal. As a result, she modified her research question from "Why was the New Deal so effective?" to "How effective was the New Deal?"

Critique your research process and modify your research question as necessary. Use the guidelines above to critique your research process. If you find that your initial research question did not address the issues the research suggests, modify the question and follow the research to gain a balanced view.

Supporting Your Thesis

Theories and Evidence

A theory is a best guess about something based on your own and others' observations and study. Evidence is factual information based on scientific studies or people's careful observations. A theory needs to be supported by evidence. For example, Newton's theory of gravity has been supported by a great deal of evidence from scientific studies while the theory that the world is flat has been clearly disproved. Some evidence is called anecdotal because it is based on only a single observation or anecdote.

In writing your research paper, your thesis statement is a theory that needs to be supported by evidence. That evidence might involve facts and statistics, scientific experiments, anecdotal evidence, your own observations, or the observations of others. To be convincing, your thesis (theory) must be supported by evidence beyond your own observations, since you are not a recognized expert on the topic.

Creating a Cogent Argument

A cogent argument is one that is compelling or convincing. As you research your topic, you will probably find a range of evidence to support your theory (thesis statement) as well as some that supports contradictory views. It is your job as a researcher to evaluate the evidence (including your own personal observations and views) and create a thesis statement that is supported by evidence from accurate and reliable sources. This will result in a cogent argument, one that is hard to dispute or disprove.

For example, if you are writing on economics, the views of the Treasury Secretary or a Nobel prize winner in economics would probably be more accurate and reliable than those of your classmates or a person running a small business. However, if your classmates or the business owner can add to or illustrate the views of a recognized economics expert, they can help support your thesis and build a cogent argument.

Review your thesis statement and the evidence you have collected to support it. Is the evidence accurate and reliable? Is your argument compelling? If not, look for further research or select other sources to make a stronger argument.

 TEKS 12.23B

Organizing Your Ideas

Selecting Appropriate Formats and Rhetorical Strategies

Your thesis and the evidence to support it can be presented in a variety of ways. Planning a persuasive research paper involves selecting the best formats and rhetorical strategies to make your argument. Your topic and research should guide you in your choices. Some options and examples are shown in the chart below.

Chronological organization	Presents events and ideas according to a timeline "First, on October 15, 2006 . . . Later that year . . ."
Cause and effect	Describes an event or action and the effects of it "When the federal government changed the requirements for . . . ., the effects were far-reaching."
Deductive reasoning	Offers a general idea or rule that is applied to a specific instance "Politicians generally raise money from a variety of special interest groups. . . . In the case of Sen. . . ."
Inductive reasoning	Offers a specific instance that becomes the basis for a general idea or rule "When George Hernandez lost his job, he was forced to use his credit card to pay for basic expenses. . . . Thousands of others like George . . ."
Quotations	Can be provocative or address specific aspects of your evidence or thesis "President Obama said, 'We can no longer . . .'"
Summarizing	Complex topics or ideas benefit from summaries when details are hard to understand "Basically, Medicare works like other forms of medical insurance – people pay in money . . ."
Analyzing	Familiar topics can be analyzed by breaking them into parts and assessing each part "Group insurance plans need to set reasonable rates to be successful. But rates depend on a variety of factors . . ."

Prewrite

Select appropriate formats and rhetorical strategies. Review the formats and strategies listed above. Which ones might work well in your paper? Imagine how each might be used and select the ones that work best.

Anticipating and Answering Critics

Addressing Complexities and Discrepancies

If you have chosen an interesting topic and formulated a thesis, you should find that there are differing opinions on it. It there aren't, you may want to modify your thesis statement because you would be arguing for something that everyone already thinks is true.

Complexities are one reason for differing opinions on topics. Few issues are "black and white" or have a simple correct answer. Complexities are the grey areas that don't allow easy analysis. Discrepancies in facts or logic are also common. For example, one expert might interpret a statistic on student test scores as a positive sign of increased learning while another might suggest the same statistic means that students are lacking in a particular area.

A good research paper acknowledges the complexities and discrepancies associated with a topic and thesis. An author who doesn't address them will be seen as one-sided or lacking in a full understanding of the issue.

Anticipating and Refuting Counter-arguments

While conducting your research, you should have encountered some of the counter-arguments to your thesis. You can also anticipate counter-arguments by playing "the devil's advocate" yourself or having a friend do it. Imagine that you were strongly opposed to your thesis. What would you say or ask in a discussion about the topic? What facts would you point to that would bring your thesis into question?

Once you have identified the counter-arguments, you can plan on how to refute them in your paper. How would you answer the questions posed by others? Preparing to refute counter-arguments forces you to look at your thesis from all sides and to insure that your evidence supports your thesis.

Anticipate and refute counter-arguments. Make a list of differing opinions and counter-arguments to your thesis. Select one or more that are the most important and plan how you will present them and refute them in your paper.

Outlining Your Ideas

An outline is a powerful tool for organizing and planning your research paper. The outline serves as a map or a blueprint to guide your writing. There are two main kinds of outlines: A topic outline lists ideas as words or phrases; a sentence outline lists the ideas as full sentences.

Below is the first part of a sentence outline for the paper on pages **393–400**. The outline begins with a thesis statement. Next, it lists the main point (topic sentence), marked by a Roman numeral, for each middle paragraph. Below each main point is a list of supporting details identified by capital letters.

Sentence Outline

In an outline, if you have a Roman numeral I, you must have at least a Roman numeral II. If you have a capital letter A, you must have at least a capital letter B.

Thesis Statement

Thesis Statement: Although its success was incomplete, the New Deal saved the United States from collapsing into chaos and gave the nation's citizens the hope they needed to survive.

Major Points (I., II., etc.)

I. In the 1920s, the U.S. economy roared ahead like a powerful automobile, but beneath the shiny exterior, the economy was corroding.

Supporting Ideas (A., B., C., etc.)

  A. The value of stocks rose rapidly, and investors grew wealthy.
  B. Workers couldn't afford to buy consumer goods, so businesses cut back on production.
  C. Farm prices lagged, and many farmers lived in poverty.

Continue . . .

II. In October 1929, the U.S. economy suddenly collapsed.
  A. The stock market dropped drastically, and investors rushed to sell their shares.
  B. Within weeks, the value of U.S. stocks had dropped by one-third.
  C. Banks had begun to fail, taking their customers' savings with them.

Prewrite

Create your outline. Write an outline for your paper. Consider formats and rhetorical strategies you might use, as well as counter-arguments and ways to refute them. Be sure that each topic sentence (I., II., III., . . .) supports the thesis statement, and that each detail (A., B., C., . . .) supports its topic. You will use your outline as a guide for writing your first draft.

Drafting

Now that you have organized your research and prepared an outline, it's time to write your first draft. Don't worry about getting everything perfect in the first draft; you'll have a chance to improve your writing later. For now, just get your ideas down on paper in a way that makes sense to you. The following points will help you.

Keys to Effective Writing

1. In your introduction, grab your reader's attention, introduce your topic, and present your thesis statement.

2. Include a topic sentence in each paragraph and stay focused on your thesis.

3. Show the logical progression of thought and develop your ideas with well-chosen details.

4. Engage your reader with your own unique voice.

5. In your conclusion, restate your thesis and leave readers with an insight.

6. Cite the sources of any ideas you paraphrase or quote and list them alphabetically on a works-cited page.

Starting Your Research Paper

The opening part of your paper should grab your reader's attention, introduce your topic, and present your thesis statement. Here are two ways to begin:

- Open with a dramatic situation.
  When he took office on March 4, 1933, President Franklin Delano Roosevelt assumed leadership of a nation mired in poverty and racked by hopelessness.

- Start with an interesting fact.
  By 1932, more than one-quarter of the population of the United States was unemployed.

Introductory Paragraphs

Introduction
The introductory paragraphs grab the reader's attention with a dramatic situation.

Sources are cited correctly.

> When he took office on March 4, 1933, President Franklin Delano Roosevelt assumed leadership of a nation mired in poverty and racked by hopelessness. Four years before, a stock market crash had set off the Great Depression, a collapse of the United States economy. Many factories, businesses, and banks closed down, and millions of U.S. citizens lost their jobs. Untold numbers of families had lost their savings and even their homes (Leuchtenburg 1).
>
> As a candidate, Roosevelt had promised a "new deal for the American people" (Heale). As president, he began to dramatically restructure the U.S. economy with an economic program called the New Deal. The New Deal created jobs, changed banking practices, and prevented many people from losing their savings and their homes (Church 106). As much as it changed the economy, the New Deal did not end the Great Depression. <u>Although its success was incomplete, the New Deal saved the United States from collapsing into chaos and gave the nation's citizens the hope they needed to survive.</u>

The introduction ends with a thesis statement (underlined).

Draft your introductory paragraphs. Using one of the approaches above, grab the reader's interest, introduce your topic, and state your thesis.

Drafting Developing the Middle Part

The middle of your research paper should develop your ideas and provide details that support your thesis statement. Each middle paragraph should cover one main idea. Use your outline to guide your writing.

Middle Paragraphs

Middle
Each paragraph sustains the focus of the thesis statement.

The details in each paragraph support its topic sentence (underlined).

An Economic Meltdown

<u>In the 1920s, the U.S. economy roared ahead like a powerful automobile, but beneath the shiny exterior, the economy was corroding.</u> According to David Kennedy, "Nearly three decades of barely punctuated economic growth, capped by seven years of unprecedented prosperity, gave to the entire country, an air of masterful confidence in the future" (11). The value of stocks rose rapidly, and investors grew wealthy (10–15). Unfortunately, businesspeople took too much of the profit from their businesses and paid workers too little. Workers couldn't afford to buy consumer goods, so businesses began cutting back on production. Farm prices also lagged, and many farmers lived in poverty (Mintz).

<u>Then, in October 1929, the U.S. economy suddenly collapsed.</u> The stock market dropped drastically, and investors rushed to sell their shares. Within weeks, the value of U.S. stocks had dropped by one-third. The Great Depression had begun (Mintz). Even before this time, banks had begun to fail, taking their customers' savings with them. After 1929, thousands more failed (Badger 31). President Herbert Hoover mistakenly believed that the economy would correct itself without much government help, but the economy only worsened. By 1932, 25 percent of U.S. citizens were unemployed. Many had lost their homes and didn't have the food they needed to survive (Heale).

MLA Research Paper

As time passed, the nation's Depression became an economic and psychological problem. With national spirits at a new low, the country turned to Franklin Roosevelt for help. They put their faith in Roosevelt—and his New Deal.

The New Deal

In the first phase of the New Deal, Roosevelt addressed one of the nation's most pressing problems—the soundness of the banks. Panicked by bank failures, people had made "runs" on banks, pulling out their savings and draining the banks of needed funds. This caused even more failures (Badger 31). To stop this chain reaction, Roosevelt declared a "banking holiday" and closed all the banks. He then presented Congress with legislation to make banks stronger (Freidel 95). When the first banks reopened on March 13, people began to return their money (Mintz). The nation's psychology had begun to shift from despair to hope. Healing had begun.

Roosevelt understood that people needed financial relief, and that a flow of cash would jump-start the economy. In 1933, he introduced the National Industrial Recovery Act (NIRA). Congress approved giving him unprecedented legislative power to make laws to solve the nation's . . .

Section heads, which can be numbered, indicate transitions from one main point to the next.

The writer continues to develop ideas with specific details about the policy.

Draft your middle paragraphs. Keep these tips in mind as you write.
1. Use a topic sentence and supporting details in each paragraph.
2. Refer to your outline (page 413) and the keys on page 414 for direction.
3. Add parenthetical references to credit all sources. (See pages 448–450.)

Drafting Concluding Your Research Paper

Your conclusion should sum up your research and bring your paper to a thoughtful close. You should . . .

- remind the reader of the thesis of your paper,
- review your key points, and
- leave the reader with something to think about.

Concluding Paragraphs

Conclusion
The conclusion summarizes the paper's main points and shares the writer's views on the policy's effectiveness.

With a unique insight, the writer gives the reader something to think about.

Conclusion

　　While the New Deal provided jobs for many people and allowed many families to keep their homes and farms, it did not succeed in ending the Great Depression. Those who criticize the New Deal often fail to account for its major achievement: It saved the United States from complete collapse. In Europe, the German government lapsed into fascism, largely as a result of a depression there. In the United States, the same might have happened except for Roosevelt and the New Deal. The programs of the New Deal restored the citizens' faith that a democratic, capitalistic system could respond to their needs in the worst of economic times. This restored faith helped democracy and free enterprise to survive. The New Deal also created a new United States, one that would provide a safety net for the old, the infirm, and the suffering, and helped to prevent another economic and social tragedy from happening.

　　Perhaps just as important, the New Deal helped to convince people of the value of shared sacrifice and innovative vision. Both would prove critical in bringing the nation . . .

Draft your conclusion. Draft your concluding paragraph(s) using the guidelines above.

Creating Your Works-Cited Page

The purpose of a works-cited page is to let your reader find and read the sources you used. The examples on this page—an incomplete list—show the standard MLA format for common types of sources. Also see the guidelines on pages 451–458.

Sample Works-Cited Entries

Book
Black, Conrad. *Franklin Delano Roosevelt: Champion of Freedom.* New York: Public Affairs, 2003. Print.

Magazine
Church, George J. "Taking Care of Our Own: The New Deal Probed the Limits of Government." *Time* 9 Mar. 2005: 106. Print.

Television Program
"F.D.R." *The American Experience.* WGBH, Boston. 28 Apr. 2006. Television.

Interview
Lavelle, James. E-mail interview. 25 Mar. 2011.

Internet
Mintz, Steven. "Module: The Great Depression." *The Gilder Lehrman Institute of American History.* The Gilder Lehrman Institute of American History, n.d. Web. 7 Oct. 2011.

Newspaper
Ringle, Ken. "FDR's Monumental Place in History." *Washington Post* 2 May 2006: A1. Print.

Draft

Create your works-cited page. Check your paper and your source notes to see which sources you actually used. Then follow these directions.

1. Format your sources using the guidelines above and on pages 451–458. (Use a sheet of paper or note cards.)
2. Create your works-cited page, listing sources in alphabetical order. (See page 400.)

How to Tell if Your Paper Is the Right Length

It is hard to say when a paper is long enough, or when it needs to be longer. There is no way to tell for sure until you begin drafting. Your teacher will probably give you an idea of the page range for the paper—say, between 10 and 12 pages—or set a limit on its length. That depends on your teacher and the assignment. A good rule to remember is that your paper should be long enough to cover the subject, but short enough to keep it interesting.

Here are some questions to ask yourself about the length of your paper:

- Have I covered all of the material in my outline? Did I miss anything?
- Does each paragraph contain a topic sentence and supporting details?
- Is each main idea fully developed?
- Is every paragraph focused on the thesis?

Including Graphic Elements in Your Paper

Occasionally you will come across interesting graphs and charts that could support your thesis and help your readers understand complex material. You might also find facts that you could display in a graph or chart or gather in an appendix. For example, in the sample paper, the writer might have chosen to illustrate unemployment statistics during the Great Depression with a line graph showing how the number of unemployed rose or fell from one year to the next. Alternatively, the writer might have included an appendix showing these and other statistics that she could not smoothly incorporate into the structure of the paper.

If you choose to include graphs and charts, they should be placed as close as possible to the text that they refer to. Each chart or graph should be labeled "Fig." (for figure) followed by a number that indicates the sequential order of the graphic elements in your paper. You also need a caption and the source information. These should be placed directly under the graphic element.

Be careful when deciding to add graphic elements to your paper. Remember that graphs, charts, and appendices should enhance the text, not substitute for your written work. They cannot carry the entire weight of the document. If a graph or table does not add new information or clarify important information, do not include it in your paper.

Note: It's a good idea to talk with your teacher about using graphic elements ahead of time. Your teacher might not count the space taken up by illustrations and appendices toward the required page length.

Draft

Determine the correct length. Use the questions above and your teacher's instructions to help you determine whether your draft is long enough or if it needs to be longer.

Revising

In the first draft of your research paper, you connect all of your ideas. As you revise, make sure that your ideas are clear and well supported and that your paper is logically organized and flows smoothly. The following checklist will help you do a thorough revision to improve your paper.

Keys to Effective Revising

1. Make sure that each paragraph is focused on your thesis statement.

2. Make sure that your introduction and conclusion are meaningful, adding depth to your paper.

3. Check for consistency of tone and logical organization.

4. Check that you have developed your ideas with well-chosen details.

5. Make sure that your voice is authentic and original.

6. Use the editing and proofreading marks on pages 638–639.

Revising for Focus and Coherence

When you revise for *focus and coherence*, you check that your writing supports your thesis, and you revise to ensure that your paper has a sense of completeness.

Should I modify my research question?

After researching your topic, you may find that you need to change or modify your research question to improve it. Suppose you are researching the Industrial Revolution, and you develop the following question.

> How did the Industrial Revolution change Great Britain?

Through your research you discover that your topic is too broad. To make your paper more interesting, you decide to narrow your topic.

> How did the Industrial Revolution change the textile industry in England during the 18th and 19th centuries?

This is a more manageable topic because it covers a specific part of the Industrial Revolution.

Don't hesitate to modify your research question if you come across a new or related topic that stirs your curiosity. For example, you might become more interested in how the Industrial Revolution affected the United States than how it changed Great Britain. In that case, you might shift your focus.

> How did the Industrial Revolution influence the development of the textile industry in New England during the 19th century?

While some topics are too broad, other topics may be too narrow. Any question that can be answered briefly or with a "yes" or "no" answer is too narrow. For example, the questions below should be modified.

- Where was the first textile mill in the United States?
- Did the Industrial Revolution affect workers in Massachusetts?

Exercise

Read the following research questions. Identify whether the research questions are too broad or too narrow. Explain why.

1. What were the major inventions of the Industrial Revolution?
2. Which invention is said to have sparked the Industrial Revolution?
3. When did the Industrial Revolution begin?

Evaluate your research question. Ask yourself the following questions: Is my research question too broad? Is it too narrow? Do I feel enthusiastic about it? Decide how you can make it stronger.

Have I determined whether the evidence that supports my theories is weak or strong?

A **theory** is an idea that has not yet been proven. **Evidence** is factual information that proves the theory correct or incorrect. Without adequate evidence to support your theories, you will not be able to create a cogent argument that convinces your readers. The sample essay includes the statement, "By 1937, the New Deal had begun to improve the U.S. economy." This statement is backed up by the following evidence: "Unemployment fell to about 12 percent, the lowest in years."

Keep the following in mind as you gather evidence to support your theories.

1. Your sources should be up-to-date. If you are writing about medical issues, for example, remember that the field of medicine is continually uncovering new facts that might call old theories into question or spark new theories.

2. Your sources should be reliable. A book about the Great Depression written by a professor in American history is probably a more reliable source than a history buff's blog.

3. Avoid using phrases such as "In my opinion. . ." or "It is obvious that . . ." without backing them up with evidence. Your research may have convinced *you* that something is true, but without sharing your evidence, you will disappoint your reader.

Exercise

Examine the following passage and identify the weak evidence. Then explain how the evidence could be made stronger.

1   It is obvious that the Spanish explorer Francisco Vazquez de Coronado did
2   not directly contribute to the settlement of the Southwest in the 1500s. He was
3   disappointed not to find gold and silver. Another factor was the resistance of the
4   native Pueblo peoples.

Check your evidence. Have you provided adequate evidence to support your theories? If not, consider adding factual information from reliable sources.

Focus and Coherence
Reliable evidence is added to support the theory.

President Herbert Hoover mistakenly believed that the economy would correct itself without much government help, but the economy only worsened. By 1932, 25 percent of U.S. citizens were unemployed. Many had lost their homes and didn't have the food they needed to survive. (Heale)

Revising for Organization

When you revise for *organization,* be sure you have used transitional words and phrases to clarify connections within paragraphs, as well as between sections and paragraphs.

How can using transitions improve the clarity of my paper?

In your research paper, you need to explain why and how certain events took place. Generally, cause-and-effect order is a good way to present historical events. To clarify the relationship between causes and effects, and to make your paper read more smoothly, you can use transitional words and phrases such as *then, as a result, hence, because, since, so, therefore, consequently, otherwise,* and *thus.*

In the following examples, see how adding some transitional words and phrases clarifies the relationship between a series of events and their results.

- **As a result of** the stock market crash, investors sold their shares of stock.
- **Therefore,** the value of stocks plummeted.
- **Because** thousands of banks failed, people lost their jobs and their homes, and farmers lost their land.
- **Consequently,** many people struggled to survive during the Great Depression.

Exercise

You can use these transitional words and phrases to improve your own writing. Identify the places in the following paragraph where adding transitions could make the connections clearer.

1.   Drive along any road, cross any bridge, or visit any public park in the United
2. States, and you might see evidence of the Works Progress Administration (WPA).
3. Unemployment soared during the Great Depression. The government stepped in
4. with successful New Deal programs, including the WPA. Millions of people found
5. work while at the same time contributing to their country. Much of what we take for
6. granted would not be here today for us to use and enjoy.

Add transitions. Review your paper, looking for places where you can add transitional words and phrases to clarify connections.

TEKS 12.23B
ELPS 1B, 5F

How do I fix wordiness and repetition in my paper?

During the drafting process, you pay more attention to the content and structure of your paper than to writing tight sentences. Once you have begun the revision process, however, attention to style is essential. Wordiness and repetition may stall the progression of ideas, and your paper will fail to engage your reader. The more direct and concise you can make your writing the better.

Wordy: Once she had finished playing the game, Erika was exhausted.

Better: After the game, Erika was exhausted.

Repetitious: Scientists are working to discover a cure for cancer in order to help cure people with cancer.

Better: Scientists are working to discover a cure for cancer.

Exercise

Practice revising for wordiness and repetition by improving the following sentences.

1. Yesterday morning at 10 a.m., the students in our class went to the museum to see the paintings in the new exhibit that was beginning to show there.
2. There are many reasons why there is so much art in the local museum's collection and so many paintings and sculptures.
3. The museum offers free headsets so visitors can take audio tours of the museum, and the headsets are free of charge.
4. The audio programs are available in a variety of languages, including French, Spanish, Greek, and a number of European languages.

Organization Wordiness is eliminated to improve the flow of the writing.

The importance of Social Security was more than ~~the importance of~~ its economic benefits. Providing a future for the ~~old people in the country~~ **nation's elderly** helped promote a feeling of national security that was critical during a ~~time where people were very unsure about what was going to happen next~~ **very uncertain time**.

Revising for Development of Ideas

When you revise for *development of ideas,* you check that your thesis statement and ideas are developed thoroughly enough to enable the reader to truly understand and appreciate them.

How can I use analysis to support my opinions?

During the course of your research, you have developed a thesis or a positive statement about your topic. If you express an opinion without providing support, however, you have not fulfilled a basic requirement of the research paper assignment. You have to analyze the evidence to make your case.

In the thesis statement, the writer of the sample research report expresses a positive opinion about the success of the New Deal.

> **Although its success was incomplete, the New Deal saved the United States from collapsing into chaos and gave the nation's citizens the hope they needed to survive.**

Without analysis, the statement is simply an unsupported opinion. For example, some readers might argue that the New Deal was not successful to the degree this writer is claiming. It is up to the writer to prove her point with a convincing analysis of the evidence.

Exercise

Read the following examples and determine which of the statements are personal opinion and which provide analysis.

1. By creating programs to help the unemployed, government intervention not only put people back to work but also helped people to feel secure.
2. With the creation of New Deal agencies, the government helped put millions of people back to work.
3. Some of the newly employed became more confident as they were able to buy goods and refinance their mortgages.
4. The New Deal helped Americans in many ways, and it helped to prevent future economic catastrophes.
5. President Roosevelt's New Deal helped to turn the nation around after four years of poverty and hopelessness.
6. The New Deal created jobs, changed the way that banks do business, and prevented many people from losing their life savings and property.

Revise

Identify opinion and analysis. As you revise your paper, look for unsupported personal opinions and provide additional analysis.

How can I avoid summarizing information?

As you revise your research paper, make sure you have developed your ideas by analyzing the material you have gathered and not merely summarized or restated it. A **summary** is a brief restatement of main ideas, in which you express these ideas in your own words. An **analysis** of the same material will look at the material critically by drawing conclusions, comparing and contrasting, making generalizations, and so on.

As you are writing and reviewing your paper, avoid simply listing the facts and ideas that you have gathered. Verify that you have analyzed them and connected your analysis to your thesis.

Read the following passage:

> In the election of 1936, Roosevelt was reelected in a landslide with 60.8 percent of the vote. He won the Electoral College vote with 46 of the 48 states.

Now look at a summary of the passage:

> Roosevelt won the Electoral College and was reelected in 1936 by a wide margin.

Next, look at an analysis of the same information:

> The reelection of Roosevelt in 1936, with a wide margin of votes, can be seen as an affirmation of support for his policies.

Revise

Evaluate your analysis. Check your research paper. Have you analyzed your ideas thoroughly? Are there some places where you have listed, restated, or summarized the facts that you have gathered? If so, revise your work to include an analysis of those ideas.

Development of Ideas
An analysis is added to develop a main idea.

The Civilian Conservation Crops, or CCC, put people to work in forests, planting trees and building roads and shelters. The wages were low—just $30 per month**, but as with the restructuring of the banks, the psychological effect was critical.** People who had lost hope and self-esteem once again became breadwinners **and their confidence began to return.**

Revising for Voice

When you revise for *voice,* check your writing to see that you have used the appropriate word choice and tone for the context and audience.

How formal should the language be in my report?

Although the English language includes many different ways of speaking or writing, standard English is divided into two levels: informal and formal. Informal language includes contractions (such as *can't, won't,* and *wouldn't*), loose sentence structures, and casual diction (word choice). You might use informal language in a journal, a personal essay, or in conversation with friends.

Formal language is often used in informative reports, and you should use it in your research paper. Formal language does not include contractions. You do not need to use long words or write convoluted sentences, but you do want to speak with a tone of authority. Choose words that are exact and write clear, straightforward sentences. Be careful not to shift back and forth between formal and informal language.

Ask yourself these questions when you are revising your research paper:

- Does my paper contain contractions, loose sentence structure, or slang?
- Do I choose precise words to create a formal tone?
- Have I employed schemes and tropes (figures of speech) to clarify meaning?
- Do I create an inconsistent tone by shifting back and forth between formal and informal language?

Exercise

Read the following paragraph. Rewrite the informal sentences to achieve a consistency of tone.

> President Roosevelt pushed through the Social Security Act in 1935 because a bunch of elderly people and others needed support. The act had many critics, who went nuts thinking about the government getting involved with individuals' lives in this way. The act was especially controversial since this was not temporary relief but an ongoing federal program. That's right, ongoing. It's been more than 70 years, and people are still paying into the system. Everybody knows that if you pay into the system, sooner or later you'll receive benefits. If you're lucky, that is!

Evaluate word choice. As you revise your paper, look for places where you might have shifted between formal and informal language. Replace or rearrange words, sentences, and phrases to achieve a consistent tone.

Have I engaged the reader?

If you do not hold the attention of your reader from the beginning to the end of your research paper, you will fail to communicate your ideas. When you are revising your paper, ask yourself the following questions:

- Does the introductory paragraph grab the reader's attention?
- Have I guided my reader through the paper in a logical way?
- Is my paper focused and direct?
- Have I used interesting quotations to emphasize important points?
- Have I avoided stringing together long paragraphs of quotations?
- Have I included interesting details or facts to support my points?
- Have I related interesting stories, or anecdotes?
- Have I avoided bogging the reader down with boring summaries of information he or she may already know a lot about?
- Have I avoided shifting between formal and informal language?
- Have I used an appropriate tone?
- Have I considered using footnotes for necessary but distracting or very technical points?
- Have I used a variety of sentence structures?

Keep in mind that your readers will be most engaged if you use your own, authentic voice. Be formal, but not pretentious. Be enthusiastic, but not informal.

Revise

Evaluate your voice. As you review your paper, imagine that you are having a conversation with your reader. Do you sound enthusiastic about the topic? Does your voice sound authentic and original? Does anything in the paper keep the reader from being engaged?

Voice
A metaphor makes the writing more engaging.

In the 1920s, the U.S. economy ~~seemed to be very strong~~ roared ahead like a powerful automobile but beneath the shiny exterior ~~underneath~~, the economy was ~~weakening~~ corroding.

Revising Using a Checklist

On a piece of paper, write the numbers 1 to 13. If you can answer "yes" to a question below, put a check mark next to that number. If not, continue to work on that part of your research paper.

<u>Revising Checklist</u>

Focus and Coherence

_____ 1. Do I maintain a specific focus and not drift off into other topics?
_____ 2. Have I written a meaningful introduction and conclusion?
_____ 3. Do all of my ideas clearly connect with each other and with the thesis?

Organization

_____ 4. Is my writing logically organized and easy to follow?
_____ 5. Do transitional words and phrases connect ideas?
_____ 6. Have I cited appropriate sources?
_____ 7. Does my conclusion include a summary and my own analysis?

Development of Ideas

_____ 8. Are my ideas thoroughly developed with ample support and specific details?
_____ 9. Is there a clear progression of thought from start to finish?

Voice

_____ 10. Does my voice sound engaging, authentic, and original?
_____ 11. Do I sound knowledgeable and confident?

Conventions

_____ 12. Have I corrected any errors in grammar, mechanics (capitalization and punctuation), and spelling?
_____ 13. Do my sentences flow smoothly?

MLA Research Paper

Editing

When you have finished revising your research paper, check it for conventions in grammar, mechanics (punctuation, capitalization), and spelling.

Keys to Effective Editing

1. Read your paper aloud and listen for words or phrases that may be incorrect.

2. Use a dictionary, a thesaurus, and the "Proofreader's Guide" in the back of this book.

3. Look carefully for errors in grammar, mechanics (punctuation, capitalization), and spelling.

4. Check your paper for proper formatting and for accuracy of citations. (See pages 392–400, 419, and 448–458.)

5. If you use a computer, edit on a printed copy. Then enter your changes on the computer.

6. Use the editing and proofreading marks on pages 638–639.

Grammar

When you edit for *grammar,* you make sure that you have used nouns, verbs, and other parts of speech effectively in your writing.

Have I used noun clauses effectively?

A noun clause takes the place of a noun in a sentence. A noun clause can represent a person, place, or thing. Like all clauses, the noun clause includes a subject and a verb. One way to understand a noun clause is to look at examples of noun clauses in use. In the following sentence, the noun clause is in blue.

What Theodore Roosevelt did changed the United States forever.

In the sentence, *What Theodore Roosevelt did* takes the place of a noun. The noun clause represents the thing that Theodore Roosevelt did. The clause is the subject of the sentence and includes a subject and a verb. Noun clauses can serve as the subject of a sentence, the object of a verb, or the object of a preposition. The following examples show how noun clauses substitute for nouns to perform a variety of tasks. The noun clauses are in blue.

How we can stop climate change is a critical question. **(subject of a verb)**

The settlers did not know **when Texas would join the Union**. **(object of a verb)**

Juan made a call to **whomever he thought could help**. **(object of a preposition)**

The truth is **that many people in the world need more food**. **(subject complement)**

It was unfortunate **that the Great Depression lasted as long as it did**. **(adjective complement)**

Grammar Exercise

Write these sentences on a sheet of paper and underline the noun clauses.

1. Whether the two nations can compromise is not known.
2. So far, voters have not responded to what the candidate said.
3. Scientists are uncertain about what might happen to the beetles.
4. How to meet this goal is what the delegates are discussing.
5. It is unclear how fast the water supply will decrease.

Check your use of noun clauses. Make sure you have used noun clauses effectively in your paper. For more help with noun clauses, see page **768.**

Have I used noun phrases effectively?

Noun phrases are very similar to noun clauses. They take the place of a noun, and in sentences they perform the tasks that nouns accomplish, such as serving as a subject or object.

The main difference between noun phrases and noun clauses lies in their structure. Noun phrases do not include a subject and verb. Here are some examples of noun phrases and how they may be used in sentences. The noun phrases are in blue.

The collapse of the economy was a surprise to almost everyone.

The main source of the river is Harville Lake.

A gallon of gasoline is what we need to drive to the next town.

A cousin of mine took pictures of our family.

Grammar Exercise

Write the following sentences on a sheet of paper and underline the noun phrases.

1. Some people are concerned about the earth's environment.
2. Other people would like to see an end to the health care debate.
3. The economy of the United States is a large and complex structure.
4. Many issues have political and social solutions.

Check your use of noun phrases. Noun phrases can add interest to your writing. Look over your report and examine how you have used noun phrases. Edit to increase the effectiveness of your noun phrases.

Language Learning

Noun clauses include a subject and a verb. Noun phrases do not. Look through your paper to find any noun phrases or clauses. Underline all noun phrases with one color of ink and all noun clauses with another color. Then show the noun phrases and clauses to a partner. Explain the difference between a noun phrase and a noun clause.

Editing for Conventions

Sentence Structure

When you revise for *sentence structure,* you check the way your sentences are structured in order to make them as clear as possible.

Have I used a variety of correctly structured sentences?

Effective writers use a variety of sentence structures to get their ideas across. In addition to simple sentences, you can use compound, complex, and compound-complex sentences to provide variety.

A **compound sentence** consists of two independent clauses. The clauses must be joined by a comma and a coordinating conjunction or a semicolon.

Mr. Flores loved watching baseball, but he did not enjoy football.

I painted the house; I trimmed the lawn.

A **complex sentence** contains an independent clause (shown in black) and one or more dependent clauses (shown in blue).

Since Luis wanted to ride his bike, he filled the tires with air.

Because I wanted to finish my homework on time, I started early, *even though I had other chores to do.*

A **compound-complex sentence** contains two or more independent clauses (shown in black) and a one or more dependent clauses (shown in blue).

Since she needed canned beans, Ai went to the market, but she did not find any there.

Because no one had turned on the lights, the gym was dark *when Albert arrived there,* but he found the switch and turned them on.

Grammar Exercise

Identify each sentence as compound, complex, or compound-complex.

1. Since Ellen could not swim, she wanted to wear a life jacket, because it would keep her safe.
2. I worked all day; I finished the job long after sunset.
3. Although I was the first person there, I did not get my food for almost half an hour.

Check your sentence variety. Edit your paper to include the correct use of a variety of sentence structures.

Mechanics: Spelling

To check your spelling, you can use a number of resources, including software spell-check tools and print and online dictionaries.

What resources can I use to check my spelling?

Software Spellcheck Tools

Chances are, the word processing software you use includes a spell-check tool. The tool will identify words that are spelled incorrectly. What these tools can't do is identify words that are spelled correctly but used improperly.

Print Dictionaries

Print dictionaries are the most reliable resource for checking spelling because they offer a clear definition of each word and the ways in which it is used.

Online Dictionaries

Online dictionaries offer a quick, convenient way to check spelling. However, depending upon the dictionary chosen, they may offer limited definitions.

Exercise

Use a dictionary—you choose which one—to check the spelling in these sentences. On another sheet of paper, write each misspelled word correctly.

1. Historicly, the congress and the senite create laws.
2. The presedent is part of the ezecutive branch of the governmint.
3. In the supreme cort, cases involving the contitution are decieded.
4. All three branches of the government work together to suport the nasion.

Checking your spelling. Read your paper again. Check carefully for misspelled words and for correctly spelled words that have been used incorrectly.

Focus on the Texas Traits

Conventions Checking your spelling helps you get your point across clearly. When your spelling is correct, your readers are able to focus on your message.

Editing for Conventions Using a Checklist

On a piece of paper, write the numbers 1 to 12. If you can answer "yes" to a question, put a check mark next to that number. If not, continue editing for that convention.

Editing for Conventions Checklist

Conventions

MECHANICS: PUNCTUATION AND CAPITALIZATION

_____ 1. Do I correctly punctuate compound and complex sentences?
_____ 2. Have I correctly cited sources in my research paper?
_____ 3. Do I use quotation marks around all quoted words from my sources?
_____ 4. Do I use italics for all words that should be italicized?
_____ 5. Have I correctly formatted a works-cited page?
_____ 6. Have I capitalized proper nouns and adjectives?
_____ 7. Do I begin each sentence with a capital letter?

SPELLING

_____ 8. Have I spelled all words correctly?
_____ 9. Have I double-checked words my spell-checker may have missed?

GRAMMAR

_____ 10. Do I use noun clauses and noun phrases correctly?
_____ 11. Do I use a variety of correctly structured sentences?
_____ 12. Do my subjects and verbs agree?

Italics in MLA Research Papers

Most high school research papers use the Modern Language Association (MLA) format. (See pages **448–458**.) The MLA format requires italics for titles and specialized words. However, be sure to follow your teacher's instructions.

Publishing

Peer Response

When it comes to publishing a high-quality research paper, your classmates can be one of your best sources of support. Letting your peers read your paper and respond with helpful criticism is a great way to discover errors you have overlooked, straighten out any unclear passages, and make sure you present your ideas effectively.

The peer review process requires sensitivity on both sides. You need to consider feedback with an open mind. Your peers need to present all comments about your work respectfully, focusing on helpful suggestions rather than demands for change. Here are some tips to help both writers and responders make the best of peer review.

Writers	Responders
Be willing to accept feedback.	Make respectful suggestions.
Listen and take careful notes.	Focus on the writing, not the writer.
Answer any responder questions.	Point out anything you do not understand.
Identify places where you need help.	Provide specific, not general, advice.

Teacher Feedback

Your teacher is another great source of helpful feedback. A teacher's keen eye can help you to clarify your focus, organize your structure, develop your ideas, strengthen your voice, and avoid errors in conventions. In the chart that follows, you'll see some examples of teacher feedback and how you might respond to it.

Teacher Feedback	Student Response
■ I am having a hard time figuring out the main idea of your paper. ■ I don't see the connection between these two paragraphs. ■ I am not convinced of your argument here. ■ The sentences in the last paragraph are somewhat confusing.	■ Work to state your main idea clearly and directly in the opening paragraph of your paper. Cut out any unrelated ideas. ■ Use transitions to make effective connections between ideas. ■ Provide more details that support and develop your idea. ■ Check conventions to make sure they do not obscure your meaning.

Publishing Sharing Your Paper

When your editing is finished, make a neat final copy of your research paper and proofread it again before sharing it. Make extra copies for family members and friends if you wish. A research paper can also serve as the basis for a speech, a multimedia presentation, or a Web page (See pages **461–473**). You worked hard on your paper, so find the best way to share your writing.

Make a final copy. To format your paper, use the following guidelines. Create a neat final copy to share.

Focusing on Presentation

- Write on a computer and double-space the entire paper.
- Type your name and the page number in the upper right corner of every page.
- Write your name, your teacher's name, the class, and the date in the upper left corner of page 1.
- Skip a line and center your title; skip another line and start your writing.
- Indent every paragraph and leave a one-inch margin on all four sides.
- If your teacher requires a title page and outline, follow his or her instructions. (See page **392**.)

Creating a Title

Give your paper a title that will attract the reader's attention and provide some information about the topic. Try one of these approaches.

- Ask a question:
  Roosevelt's New Deal: Success or Failure?
- Be creative:
  The Big Deal About the New Deal
- Use an idea from your paper:
  The Deal That Saved the Nation
- Use compelling words:
  The New Deal = Relief + Hope

Writing Responsibly

When you write a report based on research you've carried out, it's important to acknowledge your sources. Whether you use direct quotations or simply paraphrase another author's ideas, you commit plagiarism if you do not cite your source. The consequences of stealing copyrighted material vary, but in any case, plagiarism is wrong.

Citing your sources isn't difficult. Additionally, it shows that you've actually done your research, which adds authority to your writing. This chapter will answer your questions about using sources and avoiding plagiarism to produce a responsibly written research paper.

- **Using Sources**
- **Avoiding Plagiarism**
- **Writing Paraphrases**
- **Using Quoted Material**

"Next to the originator of a good sentence is the first quoter of it."
—Ralph Waldo Emerson

12.21A, 12.22A, 12.22C

Using Sources

What does *research* mean? Research means "searching out answers to questions."

Beginning Your Research

- **Consider your topic.** What do you already know about your topic? If you had to write your paper right now, what would you write?
- **Begin with the basics.** An encyclopedia or a Web search will turn up basic information. Use these sources for an overview of the topic.
- **Ask questions.** What do you wonder about your topic? Make a list of questions; then consider what sources you will search to find answers.

Reflecting on Your Research

- **Think about what you have read.** How has your initial research affected your thinking about the topic? What new questions do you have as a result of your reading?
- **Refine your topic, if necessary.** What new questions and ideas have occurred to you? Should you broaden or narrow your topic?

Doing Further Research

- **Focus your efforts.** Look for answers to your new questions.
- **Use the best sources.** Use trustworthy books, periodicals, and Web sites to find answers to your questions. Also consider conducting surveys, arranging personal interviews, and writing letters to experts.

Try It!

Whom could you interview for more information on your topic? Write three or four specific questions for this person, aiming for insight that you wouldn't find in other sources.

Presenting Your Results

- **Make the topic your own.** Your research paper should not just repeat other people's ideas. First and foremost, it should present your own thoughts and understanding of the topic.
- **Paraphrase or quote appropriately.** To support your ideas, paraphrase or quote credible sources as needed. References to other sources should be used only to enhance or support your own thinking.
- **Credit your sources.** Let your reader know the source of each idea you summarize or quote.

Avoiding Plagiarism

You owe it to your sources and your reader to give credit for others' ideas in your research paper. If you don't, you may be guilty of *plagiarism*—the act of presenting someone else's ideas as your own. (See the following pages for examples.) Cite every piece of information you borrow unless you're sure that the information is common knowledge.

Forms of Plagiarism

- **Submitting another writer's paper:** The most blatant form of plagiarism is to put your name on someone else's work (another student's paper, an essay bought from a "paper mill," the text of an article from the Internet, and so on) and turn it in as your own.
- **Using copy-and-paste:** It is unethical to copy phrases, sentences, or larger sections from a source and paste them into your paper without giving credit for the material.
- **Neglecting necessary quotation marks:** Whether it's just a phrase or a larger section of text, if you use the exact words of a source, they must be put in quotation marks and identified with a citation.
- **Paraphrasing without citing a source:** Paraphrasing (rephrasing ideas in your own words) is an important research skill. However, paraphrased ideas must be credited to the source, even if you reword the material entirely.
- **Confusing borrowed material with your own ideas:** While taking research notes, it is important to identify the source of each idea you record. That way, you won't forget whom to credit as you write your paper.

Other Source Abuses

- **Using sources inaccurately:** Be certain that your quotation or paraphrase accurately reflects the meaning of the original. Do not misrepresent the original author's intent.
- **Overusing source material:** Your paper should be primarily your words and thoughts, supported by outside sources. If you simply string together quotations and paraphrases, your voice will be lost.
- **"Plunking" source material:** When you write, smoothly incorporate any information from an outside source. Dropping in or "plunking" a quotation or paraphrased idea without comment creates choppy, disconnected writing.
- **Relying too heavily on one source:** If your writing is dominated by one source, the reader may doubt the depth and integrity of your research.

Original Article

The excerpt below is from an original article about peer-to-peer music sharing. Take note of the examples of plagiarism that follow on the next page.

"Face the Music" by Claire Baughn

. . . **Anyone who uses computer technology like peer-to-peer (P2P) networking to share copyrighted music faces being sued by the music industry.** What the industry is finding out, however, is that prosecuting people who use widely available technology isn't stopping the activity. Recording companies need to understand that **they cannot regulate file-sharing technology the way they regulate the sale of physical objects such as tapes and CD's.**

Members of the Recording Industry Association of America (RIAA) are recording companies trying to protect their financial interests. The RIAA terms P2P networking as "online piracy" even while admitting that the sharing enabled by digital technology has numerous advantages. Unfortunately, RIAA members think that more people sharing music means fewer people buying it, so they are targeting P2P services and their users with copyright infringement lawsuits.

There's no question that copyright is an important part of music; **those who write and perform music deserve to profit from their work.** But are musicians really being hurt by P2P's and other file-sharing devices? A recent study shows that the music industry is affected very little. Researchers from Harvard University have published a study showing that sharing music on P2P networks has no effect on CD sales. In fact, **not only does P2P sharing not *hurt* musicians—it actually *helps* some artists promote their music.** These musicians avoid the industry middleman, delivering their music directly to the consumer. They make music because they love it—not to become rich.

Money is an important factor, but the consumer's right to privacy may be the most emotional part of the issue. Privacy is guaranteed by implication in the Bill of Rights (protected by a number of amendments), and it should apply to Internet users as much as to anyone else. However, the RIAA's approach to discouraging the downloading of copyrighted material requires Internet service providers (ISP's) to identify individuals whose Internet addresses indicate music sharing. (In a number of cases, the ISP's are colleges and universities, drawing them into the fray, as well.) In one instance, Dawnell Leadbetter's ISP gave up her identity to RIAA, and the association threatened her with a lawsuit . . .

Examples of Plagiarism

Below are the three common types of plagiarism, sometimes committed on purpose and sometimes by accident. The plagiarized text is shown in bold type.

🚫 Using copy-and-paste

- In this sample, the writer pastes in two sentences from the original article without using quotation marks or a citation.

  In the land of the free, it's ironic that **anyone who uses computer technology like peer-to-peer (P2P) networking to share copyrighted music faces being sued by the music industry.** These companies seem to forget who made them wealthy in the first place—and, too bad for them, but **they cannot regulate file-sharing technology the way they regulate the sale of physical objects such as tapes and CD's.**

🚫 Neglecting necessary quotation marks

- In the sample below, the writer cites the source of the exact words that she uses from the original article, but she doesn't enclose these words in quotation marks.

  There are good reasons for musicians to copyright what they produce. In a recent article on P2P networking, Claire Baughn acknowledges this fact: **Those who write and perform music deserve to profit from their work** ("Face"). She goes on to say, however, that **not only does P2P sharing not** *hurt* **musicians—it actually** *helps* **some artists promote their music.** Why would the music industry have a problem with it?

🚫 Paraphrasing without citing a source

- Below, the writer accurately paraphrases (restates) a passage from the original article, but she includes no citation.

  Probably the most emotional part of the issue is that of privacy, which is protected by law. Apparently, the RIAA disputes that this protection extends to Internet users, for the group has been demanding that Internet service providers identify music sharers. It's an outrageous abuse of power.

Writing Paraphrases

There are two ways to share information from another source: (1) quote the source directly or (2) paraphrase the source. When you quote directly, you include the exact words of the author and put quotation marks around them. When you paraphrase, you use your own words to restate someone else's ideas. In either case, you must cite your source. To paraphrase, follow the steps below.

1. **Skim the selection first** to get the overall meaning.
2. **Read the selection carefully**, paying attention to key words and phrases.
3. **List the main ideas** on a piece of paper.
4. **Review the selection** again.
5. **Write your paraphrase**; restate the author's ideas using your own words.
   - Stick to the essential information. Drop anecdotes and details.
   - Put quotation marks around key words or phrases taken directly from the source.
   - Arrange the ideas into a smooth, logical order.
6. **Check your paraphrase** for accuracy by asking these questions: *Did I keep the author's ideas and viewpoints clear in my paraphrase? Have I quoted where necessary? Have I cut out enough of the original? Too much? Could another person understand the author's main idea by reading my paraphrase?*

FYI

A *quotation*, a *paraphrase*, and a *summary* are all ways of referencing a source.

- **Quoting:** A quotation states the words of a source exactly. Quoting should be used sparingly in a research paper so that your writing doesn't sound like a patchwork of other people's statements. Use a quotation only when the exact words of the source are essential.
- **Paraphrasing:** In a paraphrase, you recast an idea from a source into your own words. Paraphrasing demonstrates that you understand the idea, and it maintains your voice within your paper. Paraphrasing is more commonly used than quoting or summarizing.
- **Summarizing:** A summary is a condensed version of a source. When you summarize, do so briefly and then provide your own interpretation. A research paper should not be a simple summary of others' work.

Paraphrases

The original passage below is from *Life in a Medieval City,* a book by Edwin Benson. Below it are two sample paraphrases, properly cited.

Original Passage

> The rooms in the houses were quite small, with low ceilings. The small windows, fitted with wooden shutters or glazed with many small panes kept together with strips of lead, lighted the rooms but poorly. The interior walls were of timbering and plaster, often white- or colour-washed. The ventilation and hygienic conditions generally were far from good, as may be imagined from a consideration of the smallness of the houses, the compactness of the city, . . . and especially the primitive system of sanitation, which was content to use the front street as a main sewer. . . .
>
> Rooms were furnished with chairs, tables, benches, chests, bedsteads, and, in some cases, tub-shaped baths. Carpets were to be found only in the houses of the very wealthy. The floors of ordinary houses were covered with rushes and straw. The spit was a much used cooking utensil. Tablecloths, knives, and spoons were in general use, but not the fork before the fifteenth century. At one time, food was manipulated by the fingers. York was advanced in table manners, for it is known that a fork was used in the house of a citizen family here in 1443. . . .

Basic Paraphrase with Quotation

> According to Benson, houses had small rooms and small windows that offered little natural light. Dried straw covered the floors (only the very wealthy had carpets). Basic furniture occupied each room, and in the kitchen were tablecloths, knives, and spoons—"but not the fork before the fifteenth century," although in York "it is known that a fork was used in the house of a citizen family here in 1433." Sanitation at the time was practically nonexistent; the street also served as a sewer (32–33).

Basic Paraphrase

> According to Benson, houses had small rooms and small windows that offered little natural light. Dried straw covered the floors (only the very wealthy had carpets). Basic furniture occupied each room, and in the kitchen were tablecloths, knives, and spoons (but no forks). Sanitation at the time was practically nonexistent; the street also served as a sewer (32–33).

TEKS 12.21A, 12.21C, 12.22C

Using Quoted Material

A quotation can be a single word or an entire paragraph. Choose quotations carefully, keep them as brief as possible, and use them only when they are necessary. When you do quote material directly, be sure that the capitalization, punctuation, and spelling are the same as that in the original work. Clearly mark changes for your reader: (1) changes within the quotation are enclosed in brackets [like this]; (2) explanations of sources are enclosed in parentheses after the closing quotation marks, but before the closing punctuation (like this).

Short Quotations

If a quotation is four typed lines or fewer, work it into the body of your paper and put quotation marks around it.

Long Quotations

Quotations of more than four typed lines should be set off from the rest of the writing by indenting each line one inch from the left margin and double-spacing the material. When quoting two or more paragraphs, indent the first line of each paragraph an additional half inch from the left margin. Do not use quotation marks. (See **666.3**.)

Note: Place the parenthetical reference after the final punctuation mark of the quotation. Generally, a colon is used to introduce quotations set off from the text. (See **656.4**.)

Quoting Poetry

When quoting up to three lines of poetry (or lyrics), use quotation marks and work the lines into your writing. Use a diagonal (/) to show where each line of the poem ends. For quotations of four lines or more, indent each line one inch from the left margin (and double-space the same as the rest of the text). Do not use quotation marks.

Note: To show that you have left out a line or more of verse in a longer quotation, make a line of spaced periods the approximate length of a complete line of the poem.

Partial Quotations

If you want to leave out part of the quotation, use an ellipsis to signify the omission. An ellipsis (. . .) is three periods with a space before and after each one. (See page **676**.)

Note: Do not take out something that will change the author's original meaning.

Documenting Research

Most academic disciplines have their own manuals of style for research paper documentation. The style manual of the Modern Language Association *(MLA Handbook for Writers of Research Papers),* for example, is widely used in the humanities (literature, philosophy, history, and so on), making it the most popular manual in high school and college writing courses. (For complete information about MLA style, refer to the latest version of the *MLA Handbook.*) For papers in social sciences and social studies, the documentation style of the American Psychological Association (APA) is often used.

This chapter will provide you with guidelines for citing sources in both the MLA and the APA styles. *Remember:* Always follow your teacher's directions, which may include special requirements or exceptions for the use of either documentation style. Because these styles continue to evolve, the *Write Source* Web site maintains the most up-to-date information about documenting electronic sources.

- **Guidelines for In-Text Citations**
- **MLA Works-Cited List**
- **APA Reference List**

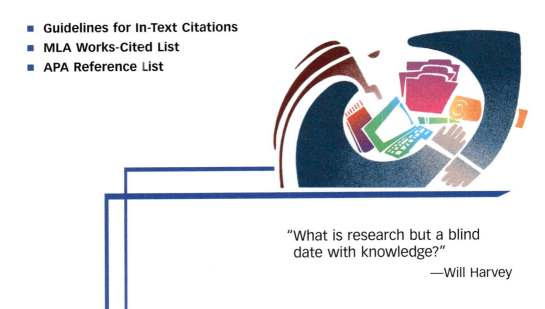

"What is research but a blind date with knowledge?"

—Will Harvey

Guidelines for In-Text Citations

The simplest way to credit a source is to insert the information in parentheses after the words or ideas taken from that source. These in-text citations (often called "parenthetical references") refer to the Works-Cited page at the end of an MLA paper or the References page concluding an APA paper.

Points to Remember

- Make sure each in-text citation clearly points to an entry in your reference list or list of works cited.
  Use the word or words by which the entry is alphabetized.
- Keep citations brief and integrate them into your writing.
- When paraphrasing rather than quoting, make it clear where your borrowing begins and ends. Use stylistic cues to distinguish the source's thoughts ("Kalmbach points out . . . ") from your own ("However, I believe . . . ").
- Place your parenthetical citation at the end of a sentence, before the end punctuation.
- Do not offer page numbers when citing complete works. If you cite a specific part, give the page number, chapter, or section, using the appropriate abbreviations (p. or pp., chap., or sec.). Do not, however, use p. and pp. in MLA parenthetical citations.

MLA	APA
• Place the **author's last name** (or, if unavailable, the first word or two of the title) and/or **page number** (if available) in parentheses following the cited text, except when these items have been included in the text. • For inclusive **page numbers** larger than 99, give only the two digits of the second number (113–14, not 113–114). • Italicize **titles** of books; place quotation marks around titles of articles.	• Place the **author** (or title), **date of the source,** and **page number** (if any), separated by commas, in parentheses, following the cited text, unless these items have been included in the text. • **Titles** of books are italicized; place quotation marks around titles of articles.

Model In-Text Citations

MLA	APA
A Work by One Author	
Genetic engineering was dubbed "eugenics" by a cousin of Darwin's, Sir Francis Galton, in 1885 (Bullough 5).	Bush's 2002 budget was based on revenue estimates that "now appear to have been far too optimistic" (Lemann, 2003, p. 48).
A Work by Two or Three Authors	
Students learned more than a full year's Spanish in ten days using the complete supermemory method (Ostrander and Schroeder 51).	Love changes not just who we are, but who we can become, as well (Lewis, Amini, & Lannon, 2000, p. 25).

Note: For APA, this format also applies to a work by up to five authors. After the first citation, list only the first author followed by *et al.* (meaning "and others").

A Work by Many Authors

This format applies to a work by four or more authors in MLA format or six or more authors in APA format. List only the first author followed by *et al.*

MLA	APA
Communication on the job is more than talking; it is "inseparable from your total behavior" (Culligan et al. 111).	Among children 13 to 14 years old, a direct correlation can be shown between cigarette advertising and smoking (Lopez et al., 2004, p. 75).

A Work by an Unknown Author

When there is no author listed, give the title or a shortened version of the title as it appears on the works-cited or reference page.

MLA	APA
Statistics indicate that drinking water can make up 20 percent of a person's total exposure to lead (*Information* 572).	. . . including a guide to low-impact exercise (*Staying Healthy*, 2004, p. 30).

Personal Communications

For an MLA paper, this parenthetical reference is the same as that for a publication with one author. In an APA paper, cite letters, e-mail messages, phone conversations, and so on as "personal communication" with their full date.

MLA	APA
. . . concern for the wetland frog population (Barzinji).	. . . hiring this spring (R. Fouser, personal communication, December 14, 2004).

A Work Referred to in Another Work

In MLA, use the abbreviation *qtd. in* (quoted in) before the source in your reference. For APA, credit the source by adding *as cited in* within the parentheses.

Quoting Prose

In MLA format, when you are quoting any sort of prose that takes more than four typed lines, do not use quotation marks. Instead, indent each line of the quotation one inch and put the parenthetical citation (the pages and any chapter or other numbers) outside the end punctuation mark of the quotation.

> Allende describes the flying machine that Marcos has assembled:
>> The contraption lay with its stomach on terra firma, heavy and sluggish and looking more like a wounded duck than like one of those newfangled airplanes they were starting to produce in the United States. There was nothing in its appearance to suggest that it could move, much less take flight. (12)

Note: In APA format, quotations of 40 or more words are handled similarly, although the block of lines is indented only 5 spaces, and the abbreviation p. or pp. is included in the parenthetical reference.

Try It!

Paraphrase the passage below and refer to the source in a parenthetical citation in both MLA and APA styles.

"For two years Napoleon held (Europe) at bay, making up for his lack of soldiers by his marvelous military skill and by the enthusiasm which he never failed to arouse in his troops. In 1814, however, surrounded by the troops of Austria, Prussia, Russia, and England, he had to confess himself beaten."

Source: *The World War and What Was Behind It* by L. P. Benezet, published 1918; not paginated

MLA Works-Cited List

The works-cited section of your report lists all of the sources you have referred to in your text. It does not include sources you may have read but did not refer to in your paper. Begin your list on a new page.

List each entry alphabetically by author's last name. If there is no author, use the first word of the title (disregard *A, An, The*). Use a single space after all punctuation in a works-cited entry.

List only the city for the place of publication. If several cities are listed, give only the first.

Additionally, note that publishers' names should be shortened by omitting articles *(a, an, the)*, business abbreviations *(Co., Inc.)*, and descriptive words *(Books, Press)*. Cite the surname alone if the publisher's name includes the name of one person. If it includes the names of more than one person, cite only the first of the surnames. Abbreviate "University Press" as UP. Also use standard abbreviations whenever possible. Lastly, note the medium of publication. The medium for all "hard copy" material is *Print*.

Books
Basic Format

Author's last name, First name. *Book Title*. City: Publisher, year of publication. Medium of publication.

Opie, John. *Ogallala: Water for a Dry Land*. Lincoln: U of Nebraska P, 1993. Print.

Add page numbers if the citation is to only a part of the work. In the rare instance that a book does not state publication information, use the following abbreviations in place of information you cannot supply:

| n.p. | No place of publication given | n.p. | No publisher given |
| n.d. | No date of publication given | n. pag. | No pagination given |

A Work by Two or Three Authors

Haynes, John Earl, and Harvey Klehr. *In Denial: Historians, Communism, & Espionage*. San Francisco: Encounter, 2003. Print.

List the authors in the same order as they appear on the title page. Reverse only the name of the first author.

A Work by Four or More Authors

Schulte-Peevers, Andrea, et al. *Germany*. Victoria: Lonely Planet, 2000. Print.

Two or More Books by the Same Author

List the books alphabetically according to title. After the first entry, substitute three hyphens for the author's name.

Dershowitz, Alan M. *Rights from Wrongs.* New York: Basic, 2005. Print.

---. *Supreme Injustice: How the High Court Hijacked Election 2000.* Oxford: Oxford UP, 2001. Print.

An Anonymous Book

Chase's Calendar of Events 2010. Chicago: Contemporary, 2010. Print.

A Single Work from an Anthology

Mitchell, Joseph. "The Bottom of the Harbor." *American Sea Writing.* Ed. Peter Neill. New York: Library of America, 2000. 584–608. Print.

An Article in a Familiar Reference Book

It is not necessary to give full publication information for familiar reference works (encyclopedias, dictionaries). List the edition and publication year. If an article is initialed, check the index of authors for the author's full name.

Lum, P. Andrea. "Computed Tomography." *World Book.* 2000 ed. Print.

A Government Publication

State the name of the government (country, state, and so on) followed by the name of the agency. Most federal publications are published by the Government Printing Office (GPO).

United States. Dept. of Labor. Bureau of Labor Statistics. *Occupational Outlook Handbook 2000–2001.* Washington: GPO, 2000. Print.

When citing the *Congressional Record,* write *Cong. Rec.,* give the date, page numbers, and medium of publication.

Cong. Rec. 5 Feb. 2002: 5311–15. Print.

A Pamphlet or Brochure

Treat any such publication as you would a book.

Grayson, George W. *The North American Free Trade Agreement.* New York: Foreign Policy Assn., 1993. Print.

If publication information is missing, list the country of publication [in brackets] if known. Beyond that, use n.p. and n.d. as for a book.

Pedestrian Safety. [United States]: n.p., n.d. Print.

One Volume of a Multivolume Work

Cooke, Jacob Ernest, and Milton M. Klein, eds. *North America in Colonial Times.* Vol. 2. New York: Scribner's, 1998. Print.

Note: If you cite two or more volumes in a multivolume work, give the total number of volumes after each title. Offer specific references to volume and page numbers in the parenthetical reference in your text, like this: (2:112–14).

Salzman, Jack, David L. Smith, and Cornel West. *Encyclopedia of African-American Culture and History.* 5 vols. New York: Simon, 1996. Print.

An Introduction, a Preface, a Foreword, or an Afterword

To cite the introduction, preface, foreword, or afterword of a book, list the author of the part first. Then identify the part by type, with no quotation marks or italics, followed by the title of the complete book. Next, identify the author of the work, using the word *By.* (If the book author and the part's author are the same person, give just the last name after *By.*) For a book that gives cover credit to an editor instead of an author, identify the editor as usual. List any page numbers for the part being cited, and, finally, the medium of publication.

Barry, Anne. Afterword. *Making Room for Students.* By Celia Oyler. New York: Teachers College, 1996. Print.

Lefebvre, Mark. Foreword. *The Journey Home.* Ed. Jim Stephens. Madison: North Country, 1989. ix. Print.

Second and Subsequent Edition

An edition refers to the particular publication you are citing, as in the third (3rd) edition.

Joss, Molly W. *Looking Good in Presentations.* 3rd ed. Scottsdale: Coriolis, 1999. Print.

An Edition with Author and Editor

The term *edition* also refers to the work of one person that is prepared by another person, an editor.

Shakespeare, William. *A Midsummer Night's Dream.* Ed. Jane Bachman. Lincolnwood: NTC, 1994. Print.

Periodicals

Basic Format

Author's last name, First name. "Article Title." *Periodical Title* date: page nos. Medium of publication.

Stearns, Denise Heffernan. "Testing by Design." *Middle Ground* Oct. 2000: 21–25. Print.

An Article in a Weekly or Biweekly Magazine

List the author (if identified), article title (in quotation marks), publication title (italicized), full date of publication, page numbers, and medium of publication for the article. Do not include volume and issue numbers.

Goodell, Jeff. "The Uneasy Assimilation." *Rolling Stone* 6 Dec. 2001: 63–66. Print.

An Article in a Monthly or Bimonthly Magazine

As for a weekly or biweekly magazine, list the author (if identified), article title (in quotation marks), and publication title (italicized). Then identify the month(s) and year of the issue, followed by page numbers for the article. However, do not give volume and issue numbers. Finally, list the medium of publication.

"Patent Pamphleteer." *Scientific American* Dec. 2001: 33. Print.

An Article in a Scholarly Journal Paginated by Issue

Scholarly journals are identified by volume number. If each issue is numbered from page 1, your works-cited entry should identify the issue number as well. List the volume number immediately after the journal title, followed by a period and the issue number, the year of publication (in parentheses), the page numbers of the article, and the medium of publication.

Chu, Wujin. "Costs and Benefits of Hard-Sell." *Journal of Marketing Research* 32.2 (1995): 97–102. Print.

An Article in a Scholarly Journal with Continuous Pagination

For scholarly journals that continue pagination from issue to issue, no issue number is needed in the works-cited entry.

Tebble, Nicola J., David W. Thomas, and Patricia Price. "Anxiety and Self-Consciousness in Patients with Minor Facial Lacerations." *Journal of Advanced Nursing* 47 (2004): 417–26. Print.

Note: For articles that are continued on a nonconsecutive page, whatever the publication type, add a plus sign (+) after the first page number.

A Printed Interview

Begin with the name of the person interviewed.

> Cantwell, Maria. "The New Technocrat." By Erika Rasmusson. *Working Woman* Apr. 2001: 20–21. Print.

If the interview is untitled, use *Interview* (no italics) in place of the title.

A Newspaper Article

> Bleakley, Fred R. "Companies' Profits Grew 48% Despite Economy." *Wall Street Journal* 1 May 1995, Midwest ed.: 1. Print.

If a local paper does not name the city, add it in brackets (no italics).

To cite an article in a lettered section of the newspaper, list the section and the page number (A4). If the sections are numbered, however, use a comma after the year (or the edition); then indicate sec. 1, 2, 3, and so on, followed by a colon, the page number (sec. 1: 20), and, lastly, the medium of publication.

> "Bombs—Real and Threatened—Keep Northern Ireland Edgy." *Chicago Tribune* 6 Dec. 2001, sec. 1: 20. Print.

A Newspaper Editorial

If an article is an editorial, put *Editorial* (no italics) after the title.

> "Hospital Power." Editorial. *Bangor Daily News* 14 Sept. 2004: A6. Print.

A Review

Begin with the author (if identified) and title of the review. Use the notation *Rev. of* (no italics) between the title of the review and that of the original work. Identify the author of the original work with the word *by* (no italics). Then follow with publication data for the review.

> Olsen, Jack. "Brains and Industry." Rev. of *Land of Opportunity*, by Sarah Marr. *New York Times* 23 Apr. 1995, sec. 3: 28. Print.

Note: If you cite a review of a work by an editor or a translator, use *ed.* or *trans.* instead of *by*.

An Article with a Title or Quotation Within Its Title

> Morgenstern, Joe. "Sleeper of the Year: *In the Bedroom* Is a Rich Tale of Tragic Love." *Wall Street Journal* 23 Nov. 2001: W1. Print.

Note: Use single quotation marks around the shorter title if it is a title normally punctuated with quotation marks.

 12.21C, 12.23D

Online Sources

When you perform research on the Web, you may find yourself accessing a wide variety of documents. You might need to source scholarly journals, encyclopedias, archives of print publications, and other multimedia resources. The format for most online sources is similar to other media.

It is important to note that MLA style does not require the URLs of Web sources to be included in works-cited lists. URLs often change, and some are so long they cannot be retyped or pasted into a works-cited list without considerable difficulty. You only need to include URL information if the reader will not be able to locate the Web source without it or when your teacher specifically requires it. If a URL is needed, include it immediately following the date of access in angle brackets, ending with a period.

Note: If you must include a line break in a long URL, do so only after a slash, and do not add a hyphen. For a particularly complicated address, give the URL of the site's search page instead.

Basic Format

Author's last name, First name. "Title." *Site Title*. Site sponsor. Date of posting or last update. Medium of publication. Date accessed. <address, if required>.

Tenenbaum, David. "Dust Never Sleeps." *The Why Files*. U of Wisconsin, Board of Regents. 28 July 1999. Web. 26 April 2011. <http://whyfiles.org/shorties/air_dust.html>.

Note: If certain details are not available, go on to the next item in the entry.

An Article in an Online Magazine or Newspaper

Begin with the author's name; the article title in quotation marks; the name of the Web site in italics, the site sponsor, and the date of publication. Include the medium of publication and the date accessed.

Dickerson, John. "Nailing Jello." *Time*. Time, Inc., n.d. 5 Nov. 2001. Web. 9 Dec. 2010.

An Article in an Online Reference Work

Unless the author of the entry is identified, begin with the entry name in quotation marks. Follow with the usual online publication information.

"Eakins, Thomas." *Britannica Concise Encyclopedia*. Encyclopædia Britannica, 2004. Web. 26 Sept. 2010.

An Article in an Online Service

When you use a library to access a subscription service, add the name of the database if known (in italics), the medium of publication, and the date of access.

> Davis, Jerome. "Massacre in Kiev." *Washington Post* 29 Nov. 1999, final ed.: C12. *National Newspapers. ProQuest.* Web. 30 Nov. 2010.

An Online Governmental Publication

As with a governmental publication in print, begin with the name of the government (country, state, and so on) followed by the name of the agency. After the publication title, add the electronic publication information.

> United States. Dept. of Labor. Office of Disability Employment Policy. *Emergency Preparedness for People with Disabilities*. Washington: GPO, 2004. Web.

When citing the *Congressional Record,* the date, page numbers, and the medium of publication are required.

> *Cong. Rec.* 5 Feb. 2002: 5311–15. Web. 22 Jan. 2011.

An Online Multimedia Resource: Painting, Photograph, Musical Composition, Film or Film Clip, Etc.

After the usual information for the type of work being cited, indicate the title of the database or Web site, the medium of publication (Web), and the date of access.

> Goya, Francisco de. *Saturn Devouring His Children*. 1819–1823. Oil on canvas. Museo del Prado, Madrid. *Artchive.* Web. 13 Dec. 2010.

An E-Mail Communication

Identify the author of the e-mail; then list the "Subject" line of the e-mail as a title, in quotation marks. Next, include a description—usually *Message to the author* (no italics), meaning the author of the paper. Finally, give the date of the message and the medium of delivery.

> Barzinji, Atman. "Re: Frog Populations in Wisconsin Wetlands." Message to the author. 1 Jan. 2011. E-mail.

A Discussion Group or Blog Posting

Identify the author of the work, the title of the posting in quotation marks, the Web site name in italics, the publisher, and the posting date. Follow with the medium of publication and the date of access.

> Handel, Sarah. "'12346' Is Not a Good Password." *Blog of the Nation.* Nat'l Public Radio, 7 Oct. 2009. Web. 1 Nov. 2010.

Other Sources: Primary, Personal, and Multimedia

The following examples of works-cited entries illustrate how to cite sources such as television or radio programs, films, live performances, and other miscellaneous nonprint sources.

A Television or Radio Program

"Another Atlantis?" *Deep Sea Detectives*. The History Channel. 13 June 2005. Television.

A Film

The director, distributor, the year of release, and the medium consulted follow the title. Other information may be included if pertinent.

The Aviator. Dir. Martin Scorsese. Perf. Leonardo DiCaprio. Miramax Films, 2004. Film.

A Video Recording

Cite a filmstrip, slide program, videocassette, or DVD just as you would a film. If relevant, include the original release date.

Beyond the Da Vinci Code. A&E Home Video, 2005. DVD.

An Audio Recording

Indicate the medium after the date of publication: *Audiocassette, Audiotape, CD* or *LP* (no italics) before the name of the manufacturer. If you are citing a specific song on a musical recording, place its title in quotation marks before the title of the recording.

Welch, Jack. *Winning*. Harper Audio, 2005. CD.

An Interview by the Author (Yourself)

Brooks, Sarah. Personal interview. 15 Oct. 2010.

A Cartoon or Comic Strip (in Print)

Luckovich, Mike. "The Drawing Board." Cartoon. *Time* 17 Sept. 2001: 18. Print.

A Lecture, a Speech, an Address, or a Reading

If there is a title, use it. Otherwise, use a descriptive label (Lecture, Address, Keynote speech, Reading) at the end of the citation.

Annan, Kofi. Acceptance of Nobel Peace Prize. Oslo City Hall, Oslo, Norway. 10 Dec. 2001. Speech.

APA Reference List

The reference list begins on a separate page and includes all retrievable sources cited in a paper. List the entries alphabetically by author's last name. If no author is given, then list by title (disregarding *A, An,* or *The*).

Leave a single space after all end punctuation marks. Quotation marks are not used for article titles; italicize other titles. Capitalize the first word (and any proper nouns) of book and article titles, as well as the first word after a colon or dash within the title; capitalize the names of periodicals in the usual upper- and lowercase manner.

Books
Basic Format

Author's last name, Initials. (year). *Book title.* Location: Publisher.

Guttman, J. (1999). *The gift wrapped in sorrow: A mother's quest for healing.* Palm Springs, CA: JMJ.

Note: Give the city of publication alone if it is well known. Otherwise, include the state. Include the state or province and the country if outside the United States.

A Book by Two or More Authors

Lynn, J., & Harrold, J. (1999). *Handbook for mortals: Guidance for people facing serious illness.* New York: Oxford UP.

List up to six authors; abbreviate subsequent authors as "et al." List all authors' names in reverse order. Separate authors' names with commas, and include an ampersand (&) before the last.

An Anonymous Book

If an author is listed as "Anonymous," treat it as the author's name. Otherwise, follow this format:

American Medical Association essential guide to asthma. (2003). New York: American Medical Association.

A Single Work from an Anthology

Nichols, J. (2005). Diversity and stability in language. In B. D. Joseph & R. D. Janda (Eds.), *The handbook of historical linguistics* (pp. 283–310). Malden, MA: Blackwell.

An Article in a Reference Book

Lewer, N. (1999). Non-lethal weapons. In *World encyclopedia of peace* (pp. 279–280). Oxford: Pergamon.

Periodicals

Basic Format

Author's last name, Initials. (year, Month day). Article title. Periodical, vol. (issue), pages.

Silberman, S. (2001, December). The geek syndrome. *Wired,* **9(12), 174–183.**

A Journal Article, Two Authors

Newman, P. A., & Nash, E. R. (2005). The unusual southern hemisphere stratosphere winter of 2002. *Journal of the Atmospheric Sciences,* **62(3), 614–628.**

A Journal Article, More Than Six Authors

Watanabe, T., Bihoreau, M-T., McCarthy, L., Kiguwa, S., Hishigaki, H., Tsaji, A., et al. (1999, May 1). A radiation hybrid map of the rat genome containing 5,255 markers. *Nature Genetics,* **22, 27–36.**

A Journal Article, Paginated by Issue

When the page numbering of the issue starts with page 1, the issue number (not italicized) is placed in parentheses after the volume number.

Lewer, N. (1999, summer). Nonlethal weapons. *Forum,* **14(2), 39–45.**

A Newspaper Article

For newspapers, use "p." or "pp." before the page numbers; if the article is not on continuous pages, give all the page numbers, separated by commas.

Stolberg, S. C. (2002, January 4). Breakthrough in pig cloning could aid organ transplants. *The New York Times,* **pp. 1A, 15A.**

Online Sources

Basic Format

Author's last name, Initials. (year, Month day). Article title. Periodical, vol. (issue), pages if available. Retrieved from URL.

Volz, J. (2000, January). Successful aging: The second 50. *Monitor on Psychology,* **31(1). Retrieved from http://www.apa.org/monitor/jan00/cs.html**

Note: If you have read an exact duplicate of a print article online, simply use the basic journal reference, but add [Electronic version] after the title of the article.

Making Oral Presentations

The last time you heard a speech was probably . . . today! Teachers give oral presentations every day. Usually the purpose of their talks is to inform or to demonstrate, but other presentations may attempt to persuade. Whatever the purpose of an oral presentation, it succeeds because of three key factors: familiarity with the material, preparation, and practice.

This chapter offers guidelines and tips for oral presentations. You'll learn how to organize your material, how to bring it to life with visual aids, and how to practice your way to a smooth, effective delivery.

- **Planning Your Presentation**
- **Creating Note Cards**
- **Considering Visual Aids**
- **Practicing Your Speech**
- **Delivering Your Presentation**
- **Evaluating a Presentation**
- **Preparing a Multimedia Report**

"A speech is poetry: cadence, rhythm, imagery, sweep! A speech reminds us that words, like children, have the power to make dance the dullest beanbag of a heart."

—Peggy Noonan

Planning Your Presentation

To transform a research paper into an oral presentation, you need to consider your purpose, your audience, and the content of your paper.

Determining Your Purpose

Your purpose is your reason for giving a presentation.

- **Informative** speeches educate by providing valuable information.
- **Persuasive** speeches argue for or against something.
- **Demonstration** speeches show how to do or make something.

Considering Your Audience

As you think about your audience, keep the following points in mind.

- **Be clear.** Listeners should understand your main points immediately.
- **Anticipate questions** the audience might have and answer them. This helps keep the audience connected.
- **Engage your listeners** through thought-provoking questions, revealing anecdotes, interesting details, and effective visuals.

Reviewing Your Research Paper

During an oral report, obviously your audience cannot go back and listen again to earlier statements, so you must be sure to share your ideas clearly from beginning to end. Review your paper to see how the different parts will work in an oral presentation. Use the following questions as a review guide.

- Will my opening grab the listeners' attention?
- What are the main points that listeners need to know?
- Have I included information from experts on the topic?
- How many supporting details should I include for each main point?
- What visual aids can I use to create interest in my topic? (See page **466**.)
- Will the ending have the proper impact on the listeners?

Try It!

Choose a research paper you've completed. Review it as if you were a member of an audience, hearing the ideas in a presentation. What questions might this audience have about the topic? List them on a sheet of paper and then provide an answer for each one.

Making Oral Presentations

Adapting Your Paper

To create a more effective oral presentation, you may need to rewrite certain parts of your paper. The new beginning below grabs the listeners' attention by using short, punchy phrases. The new ending makes a more immediate connection with the beginning.

Written Introduction (page 393)

> When he took office on March 4, 1933, President Franklin Delano Roosevelt assumed leadership of a nation mired in poverty and racked by hopelessness. Four years before, a stock market crash had set off the Great Depression, a collapse of the United States economy. Many factories, businesses, and banks closed down, and millions of U.S. citizens lost their jobs. . . .

Oral Introduction

> Imagine the changed lives of so many people following the stock market crash of 1929. The Great Depression left families without jobs, savings, even homes. Now imagine the incredible responsibility of the new president four years later. When he took office on March 4, 1933, Franklin Delano Roosevelt . . .

Written Conclusion (pages 398–399)

> While the New Deal provided jobs for many people and allowed many families to keep their homes and farms, it did not succeed in ending the Great Depression. Those who criticize the New Deal often fail to account for its major achievement: It saved the U.S. from complete collapse. . . .

Oral Conclusion

> The New Deal did not halt the Depression, but it improved the nation's morale for years to come. When the U.S. was drawn into World War II, the country met the challenge, largely because of the mind-set established by the New Deal. People knew the value of shared sacrifice and innovative vision and heeded Roosevelt's requests to benefit the common good. Ultimately, the New Deal fostered the recovery of a nation's hope—not once, but twice.

> "Eloquence is in the assembly, not merely in the speaker."
> —William Pitt

Creating Note Cards

If you are giving a prepared speech rather than an oral reading of your paper, you should use note cards to remind you of your main ideas. The guidelines below will help you make effective cards.

Note-Card Guidelines

Write out your entire introduction and conclusion on separate note cards. For the body of your speech, write one point per card, along with specific details.

- Place each main point at the top of a separate note card.
- Write supporting ideas on the lines below the main idea, using key words and phrases to help you remember specific details.
- Number each card.
- Highlight any ideas you want to emphasize.
- Mark the places that call for visual aids.

Three Main Parts to Consider

As you prepare your note cards, keep the following points in mind about the three parts of your oral presentation: the introduction, body, and conclusion.

- **The introduction** should grab the listeners' attention, identify the topic and the focus of your presentation, and provide any essential background information about the topic. (See pages 462–463.)
- **The body** should contain the main points from your paper and present details that will hold your listeners' attention. Remember to note the visual aids that you plan to use.
- **The conclusion** should restate your focus and leave the listeners with a final thought about your topic. (See pages 462–463.)

Try It!

Using one of your recent research papers, adapt the introduction and conclusion for an oral report. Write your complete beginning and ending on separate note cards.

Making Oral Presentations   465

Note Cards

Below are the note cards Shawna used for her oral presentation about the New Deal.

Introduction 1
photo: Depression-era suffering

Imagine the changed lives of so many people following the stock market c[rash] of 1929. The Great Depression left families without jobs, savings, even homes. Now imagine the incredible responsibility of the new president four y[ears] later. When he took office on March 4, 19[...]

The Great Depression 2
photo: another Depression-era picture
- 1920s: U.S. economy out of control, in need of new political policy
- 25 percent of working population unemployed by 1932
- many without enough food or homes

The New Deal 3
photo: TVA workers
- Roosevelt's economic program to restructure economy
- banks being made stronger
- legislation to help people refinance mortgages, save homes
- Social Security to provide for retirement

Unsuccessful programs 4
- NIRA's attempt to regulate labor practices
- too much red tape with NRA; regulations manipulated
- AAA not helping farmers enough

Later years of New Deal 5
chart: unemployment statistics '37–'43
- economic recovery led to funding cut in 1937
- position reversed in '38 due to sinking economy
- economic boom created when U.S. entered WWII

Conclusion 6

The New Deal did not halt the Depression, but it improved the nation's morale for years to come. When the U.S. was drawn into World War II, the country met the challenge, largely because of the mind-set established by the New Deal. People knew the value of shared sacrifice and innovative vision and heeded Roosevelt's . . .

TEKS 12.23A, 12.23B
ELPS 3B, 3F, 3H, 3I

Considering Visual Aids

Consider using visual aids during your speech. They can make your presentation clearer and more meaningful. Here are some examples.

Posters	can include words, pictures, or both.
Photographs	illustrate what you are talking about.
Charts	explain points, compare facts, or give statistics.
Maps	identify or locate specific places being discussed.
Objects	show important items related to your topic.
Computer slides	project your photographs, charts, and maps onto a screen and turn your speech into a multimedia presentation. (See pages 470–471.)

Indicating When to Present Visuals

Write notes on your note cards to indicate where a visual aid would be helpful. Shawna considered the following visuals for her presentation about the New Deal.

- photo of Depression-era unemployment lines
- photo of TVA workers on a dam project
- chart showing unemployment statistics 1937–1943

Try It!

Identify two or three visual aids you could use in your presentation. Explain when and how you would use each one.

Tip

When creating visual aids, keep these points in mind.

- **Make them big.** Your visuals should be large enough for everyone in the audience to see.
- **Keep them simple.** Use labels and short phrases rather than full sentences.
- **Make them eye-catching.** Use color, bold lines, and simple shapes to make the contents clear and interesting.

TEKS 12.23A, 12.23B, 12.23E
ELPS 3C, 3D, 3F, 3H, 3I

Making Oral Presentations

Practicing Your Speech

Practice is the key to giving an effective oral presentation. Knowing what to say and how to say it will help eliminate those butterflies speakers often feel. Here are some hints for an effective practice session.

- **Arrange your note cards in the proper order.** This will eliminate any confusion as you practice.
- **Practice in front of a mirror.** Check your posture and eye contact and be sure your visual aids are easy to see.
- **Practice in front of others.** Friends and family can help you identify parts that need work.
- **Record or videotape a practice presentation.** Do you sound interested in your topic? Are your voice and message clear?
- **Time yourself.** If your teacher has set a time limit, practice staying within it.
- **Speak clearly.** Do not rush your words, especially later when you are in front of your audience.
- **Speak up.** Your voice will sound louder to you than it will to the audience. If you sound too loud to yourself, you are probably sounding just right to your audience.
- **Work on eye contact.** Look down only to glance at a card.
- **Look interested and confident.** This will help engage your listeners.

Practice Checklist

To review each practice session, ask yourself the following questions.

_____ 1. Did I appear at ease?
_____ 2. Could my voice be heard and my words understood?
_____ 3. Did I sound as though I enjoyed and understood my topic?
_____ 4. Were my visual aids interesting and used effectively?
_____ 5. Did I avoid rushing through my speech?
_____ 6. Did I include everything I wanted to say?

Try It!

Practice your presentation. Give your speech to family or friends. Also consider videotaping your speech.

Delivering Your Presentation

When you deliver a speech, concentrate on your voice quality and body language. They communicate as much as your words do.

Controlling Your Voice

Volume, tone, and *pace* are three aspects of your formal speaking voice. If you can control these, your listeners will be able to follow your ideas.

- **Volume** is the loudness of your voice. Imagine that you are speaking to someone in the back of the room and adjust your volume accordingly.
- **Tone** expresses your feelings. Be enthusiastic about your topic and let your voice show that.
- **Pace** is the speed at which you speak. For the most part, speak at a relaxed pace.

Tip

You can make an important point by slowing down, by pausing, by increasing your volume, or by emphasizing individual words.

Considering Your Body Language

Your body language *(posture, gestures,* and *facial expressions)* plays an important role during a speech. Follow the suggestions given below in order to communicate effectively.

- **Assume a straight but relaxed posture.** This tells the audience that you are confident and prepared. If you are using a podium, let your hands rest lightly on the surface.
- **Pause before you begin.** Take a deep breath and relax.
- **Look at your audience.** Try to look toward every section of the room at least once during your speech.
- **Think about what you are saying** and let your facial expressions reflect your true feelings.
- **Point to your visual aids** or use natural gestures to make a point.

Try It!

Deliver your presentation. As you do, be sure to control your voice and exhibit the proper body language.

Evaluating a Presentation

You can use an evaluation sheet to rate a classmate's speech. Circle the best description for each trait. Then offer at least one positive comment and one helpful suggestion.

Peer Evaluation Sheet

Speaker _____ Evaluator _____

1. **Vocal Presentation**

   Volume:
   Clear and loud   Loud enough   A little soft   Mumbled

   Pace:
   Relaxed   A little rushed or slow   Rushed or slow   Hard to follow

   Comments:
   a. _____
   b. _____

2. **Physical Presentation**

   Posture:
   Relaxed, straight   A bit stiff   Fidgeted a lot   Slumped

   Eye contact:
   Excellent contact   Some contact   Quick glances   None

   Comments:
   a. _____
   b. _____

3. **Information**

   Thought provoking   Interesting   A few points   Not informative

   Comments:
   a. _____
   b. _____

4. **Visual Aids**

   Well used   Easy to follow   Not clear   None

   Comments:
   a. _____
   b. _____

Preparing a Multimedia Report

Today's technology allows people to quickly and easily present information in a format that uses more than just spoken words or text on paper. Multimedia reports often combine text with video, audio graphics, and still images to create reports that can be shared across a variety of media, from Web sites to online journals and television.

Here are just a few of the options you can pursue when preparing a multimedia report.

- **Documentary** A documentary is a film that tells the facts about real people and events. To produce a documentary, you will record interviews on digital video and combine them with historical footage, still images, and on-screen titles. Documentary films also include music that helps set a tone for the presentation.

- **Docudrama** A docudrama is a film, usually made for television, that tells a story about real events that have occurred. This format is similar to a documentary film. The main difference is that in a docudrama, actors portray historical figures. The actors use a written script as their guide.

- **Web site** A Web site is a series of interconnected Web pages located on the World Wide Web (WWW). Internet Web sites present information using a wide variety of content, from text and still images to audio and video.

- **Power Presentation** A power presentation is a presentation of digital slides. This format tells a story using a series of slides, each of which contains a small chunk of information. Power presentations are often used in business meetings as well as for training and educational purposes. Slides can include text, graphics, audio, and even video. The presenter often speaks aloud during a power presentation to provide additional information.

In multimedia reports, the producer creates a final product that synthesizes information from multiple points of view and appeals to a specific audience.

Documentaries and Docudramas

Both documentaries and docudramas include three production phases: scripting, shooting, and editing.

Scripting

In a documentary, the script starts as an outline that is used to direct the shooting. Create a script that shows who you want to interview and what you might want them to say. Use the script to plan which questions to ask each person during an interview. Your script should also include notes about where to insert additional footage, still images, graphics, and music. Audio narration, or **voiceover,** would also be included as part of the script.

A docudrama can range in scope from the entire life of a historical figure to the occurrence of a single event. To script a docudrama, start by deciding the scope of your final product. It is a good idea to focus on a few of the most important ideas, characters, or events. Write a script that shows what each character should say and do. Be sure to include directions for props, scenery, lighting, and music.

Shooting

Your audience needs to see and hear your characters and interview subjects to understand the ideas they present. Use enough lights to make sure that the actors and interview subjects can be seen clearly. Use microphones to capture their words without interference from background noise. Make sure everyone knows when to be "quiet on the set!"

Editing

Editing your video means putting it together in a final version that assembles your ideas in an engaging and informative presentation. It includes several steps.

- **Arrange clips** in the order that you want them. Use your script as a guide, but don't be afraid to rearrange some clips to make your point clearer. Shorten clips to cut out ideas that don't relate to the topic.
- **Add titles** at the beginning and credits at the end. You can also add titles to make transitions between different sections of the film.
- **Import music** or other audio that help support your main ideas. If you decide to include music, make sure it doesn't drown out the speakers in your video.

Try It!

Write a script for a scene from a docudrama. Be sure to include lines for the actors and stage directions for props, scenery, lighting, and sound.

Web Sites

The Internet provides a platform for presenting and sharing information about every topic under the sun. Web sites use text, video, graphics, still images, and audio to give visitors a wide range of options. Creating an effective Web site can be challenging, but these tips will help you get the job done.

Use Templates

You do not need to be a computer programmer to build a Web site. Web building software often provides templates that you can use to create your site. The templates let you choose colors and page layouts. You can upload text, audio, video, images, and graphics to fill in a template.

Create a Wireframe

A **wireframe** is a simple diagram that shows the layout of your Web site. It tells how many pages your site will have, and how the pages will be connected. It shows what content and content type will appear on each page.

For a report, you'll probably want to keep it simple. Include a main page that briefly states your ideas. Link to pages where you've stored supporting evidence. Make simple notes about what you want to include on each page. If your report is relatively brief, you may want to present it on a single Web page.

Build Pages

To build the basic site, use the site-building template. Be sure to use the wireframe you have created as your guide.

Upload Content

Now that your basic site is built, upload the **content,** or information you want to present. You have some choices here. Content can include text, video, audio, and still images including graphics and photographs. As you make decisions about content, remember to consider your audience. Your goal is to create a balanced presentation that includes information from multiple points of view. Make sure that you have the right to reproduce each piece of content on the Web.

Try It!

Visit a Web site or explore software that provides Web templates. Familiarize yourself with the templates. Create a wireframe that diagrams a Web site you might build.

Making Oral Presentations

Power Presentations

To create a power presentation, you use computer software that creates a series of "slides." Each slide contains one idea and a few supporting details. Follow these guidelines to create an effective power presentation.

Write an Outline

Use your research materials to create an outline that shows the main ideas and details you want to present and which information will appear on each slide.

Create Your Slides

Use the software program to enter text and visuals on slides. Be brief; you can present more information with audio or by talking as you give the presentation.

Multimedia Report Traits Checklist

Revising Checklist

Focus and Coherence

_____ 1. Have I chosen an appropriate scope for my topic?

Organization

_____ 2. Do my transitions make my report flow smoothly and logically?

Development of Ideas

_____ 3. Do I include ample support and specific details?

Voice

_____ 4. Do I sound interested and enthusiastic?

Conventions

_____ 5. Is my report free of errors?

Try It!

Create a power presentation with text, graphics, and audio.

ELPS 2C, 4C, 5B

Writing Across the Curriculum

Recording Your Learning	475
Writing in Science	481
Writing in Social Studies	493
Writing in Math	511
Writing in the Applied Sciences	521
Writing in the Arts	529
Writing in the Workplace	543

Learning Language

Work with a partner to learn the following words and expressions from this unit.

1. To **reflect** means to think carefully.
   Why do you think it's important to reflect on your mistakes?

2. An assignment's **criteria** are its standards for judgement.
   What criteria did you follow in last night's homework?

3. When you **keep track of** something, you stay informed about it.
   What current events do you keep track of?

Recording Your Learning

Think of the volume of information your brain takes in each day. If you don't keep track of the important things, you risk not remembering them at all. Making connections between new ideas and your prior knowledge helps you understand what you learn. This is why taking notes and reflecting on your learning is so important. Taking notes and keeping a learning log allows you to sort, organize, and process information.

Active listening and purposeful note taking are critical skills to master. Taking good notes and keeping a learning log can help you learn more efficiently, prepare for exams, and save time. In this chapter, you will learn how to sharpen your note-taking skills while listening to a lecture and reading a text. You will also develop strategies for keeping a learning log to reflect on the new ideas and information you study in class.

- **Taking Classroom Notes**
- **Taking Reading Notes**
- **Keeping a Learning Log**

"The pen is the tongue of the mind."
—Miguel de Cervantes

Taking Classroom Notes

Taking good notes helps you remember key lecture points, understand new material, and prepare for tests and writing assignments. Here are a few tips.

Before you take notes . . .

- **Set up your notes** in a three-ring binder so you can insert handouts. A spiral notebook with a pocket is another option.
- **Date each entry** in your notebook and write down the topic.
- **Organize each page.** A two-column format with lecture information on the left and questions on the right works well.

As you take notes . . .

- **Listen for key words.** Pay attention to information that comes after phrases like *for example*, *as a result*, or *most importantly*.
- **Use your own words** as much as possible.
- **Write down questions** as they occur to you.
- **Draw pictures** or quick sketches to capture complex ideas.

After you've taken notes . . .

- **Reread your notes** after class to add any information needed to make the notes clear.
- **Study your notes** to prepare for tests and exams.

The date and topic are noted.

March 6, 2011 – First law of thermodynamics and conservation of energy

First law of thermodynamics:
– Applies principle of conservation of energy
– Conservation of Energy= Energy can be transferred from one system to another in many forms. However, it cannot be created or destroyed. Total energy of an isolated system remains constant.

Main points are underlined.

Key points:
– Fundamental principle of all science, especially physics and chemistry
– Change in internal energy is equal to heat transferred into the system minus energy used in work by the system.
– Can also be stated positively if W (work) is defined as the work done on the system instead of work done by the system.

Dashes set off subpoints.

Formulas:
– $\Delta U = Q - W$, with ΔU =changes in internal energy, Q = heat added to the system, and W = work done by the system.
– Einstein stated that energy and matter are interchangeable, the quantity of energy and matter in the universe being fixed. $E = MC^2$
– Energy (E) is equal to matter (M) times the square of a constant (C).

Recording Your Learning **477**

ELPS 4D, 4G

Taking Reading Notes

Note taking can increase your understanding of reading assignments. Here are some tips on taking reading notes.

Before you take notes . . .
- **Write the date, book title, chapter, and topic** before each entry.
- **Organize each page.** For a two-column format, put your notes on the left and your thoughts and questions on the right.
- **Quickly skim the assigned text.** Read the title, introduction, headings, and chapter summaries. Look at visuals such as graphics, charts, images, and examples.

As you take notes . . .
- **Write down headings or subtopics** and key details under each.
- **Use your own words** to help you understand the material better.
- **Summarize visuals.** Write down or sketch out main ideas.
- **List vocabulary words** and look up definitions later.

After you've taken notes . . .
- **Review your notes.** When you're done reading, write down any other questions you have. Research the answers and add them to your notes.

Questions and thoughts are listed in the second column.

Nov. 12, 2010: Modern Physics, Chapt. 12, Sec. 3 Radioactive Decay

Many nuclei are radioactive or unstable. They eventually decay—emit a particle, transform one nucleus into another, or change to a lower energy state—until a stable nucleus is reached.

– Nucleon number [r= total number of nucleons (neutrons + protons)] must be the same before and after a decay.

– Alpha decay: Nucleus with too many protons—excessive repulsion. Emit a helium nucleus to reduce the repulsion.

– Beta decay: Neutron/proton ratio too great in the nucleus—instability. Neutron turns into a proton and an electron, and electron is emitted.

– Gamma decay: Nucleus is at too high an energy. The nucleus falls down to a lower energy state, emitting a high-energy photon called a gamma particle.

In Beta decay, what if the neutron/proton ratio is too small?

1. positron emission
   A proton turns into a neutron and a positron—a positively charged electron. The positron is emitted.

2. electron capture
   The nucleus "captures" an electron, which turns a proton into a neutron.

Why is radioactive decay important?

When the unstable nuclei of atoms decay and release particles, the result is radiation. Some high-level radiation can cause tissue damage, cancers, and even death.

Notes

Keeping a Learning Log

A learning log is a specialized journal you use to reflect on things you are learning in class. In a learning log, you write about new concepts by connecting them to previous learning or personal experience. Here are some tips for keeping a learning log.

Before you make an entry . . .

- **Set up your learning log** in a binder or notebook.
- **Write the topic and date of each entry** so that you can find it easily.
- **Leave wide margins** so you have room for your own thoughts and questions.

As you make an entry . . .

- **Summarize key concepts** and develop meaningful comparisons.
- **Apply new ideas** to things you already know.
- **Think about questions** you may have about the subject.
- **Predict how the new ideas may prove helpful** in the future.
- **Make personal connections** by explaining what the ideas mean to you.

After you've made an entry . . .

- **Review your entries** periodically to see how your thoughts have been developing.
- **Research any questions** you have and write down the answers.
- **Continue your reflections** by writing new observations in the margins.

Tip

You can use an approach called "stop and write" in your learning log. Stop in the middle of your reading or at the end of a class discussion and write down your thoughts about what you've just learned. This can show how well you understand the topics you are studying. Your learning-log entries can also help you prioritize when you study for exams by showing you which concepts are the most difficult for you to understand.

Try It!

Follow the guidelines above to set up your own learning log. When you have a few minutes during class, stop and write, reflecting on what you are learning. Make personal connections with the ideas.

Learning-Log Entries

Here are some sample learning-log entries made by a student in science class. The student thinks about the ideas discussed about meteorology in class, analyzes them, and applies the theories to current weather trends.

Sept. 28, 2011—El Niño

El Niño is the name for unusually warm ocean temperatures off the coast of Peru. It usually begins around the end of December and lasts several weeks. It has been known to last almost a year. Fish die in the warm waters and the jet stream shifts. El Niño causes warm winters in normally cold states and lots of rain in southern states. Now I understand why we sometimes have hardly any snow. In fact, we sometimes have more rain than snow. Of course, this means ice on the lakes is probably not safe.

Sept. 29, 2011—El Niño

During an El Niño, normal trade winds weaken. Warmer western Pacific water then flows east to Peru. This is the fifth-largest fishing ground in the world. The cold, deep waters are rich in nutrients. This water does not cycle upward during an El Niño.

I didn't know that the fish caught off Peru are ground up into meal for poultry. When there are fewer fish because of El Niño, feed prices go up and so does the price of chicken. I don't pay much attention to chicken prices.

The date and topic are given, and ideas from the class are reviewed.

Questions are listed, and answers from the teacher and other sources are added.

Q. What impact does El Niño have on U.S. weather?
A. In El Niño winters, temperatures are usually warmer in the north central states and cooler than normal in the Southeast and Southwest.

Q. When was the last strong El Niño?
A. We looked this up online on the National Oceanic and Atmospheric Web site. A strong El Niño was visible as warm water spreading from the western Pacific to the eastern Pacific during 1997.

Learning-Log Entries

The following is a learning-log entry a student made after a discussion about student activism in history class.

> **May 12, 2011**
>
> Today we talked about student activism in the 1960s and '70s. I had heard a bit about student protests against the Vietnam War, but I wasn't aware of their extent. Today I also learned more about student activism in other areas, such as civil rights and the environment.
>
> Our classroom discussion about student activism made me think about the Friends of the North Branch Watershed group at our school. They are a group of students who are working to help clean up the North Branch River. Saturday they are holding their annual river cleanup. I think I will go to the event to get ideas for my historical skit on student activism.

A math student used this learning log to reflect on her understanding of the properties of logarithms.

Learning Log

> **January 16, 2011**
>
> Some Properties of Logarithms
>
> 1. $\log(ab) = \log a + \log b$
>
> Example:
> $\log(12) = \log(3 \cdot 4) = \log 3 + \log 4$
>
> 2. $\log\left(\dfrac{a}{b}\right) = \log a - \log b$
>
> Example:
> $\log 4 = \log\left(\dfrac{20}{5}\right) = \log 20 - \log 5$
>
> Logarithms and exponents are related. Logarithm properties actually come from exponent properties.
>
> How to remember properties:
>
> 1. When multiplying the same variable, add the exponents: $a^m \cdot a^n = a^{m+n}$. Taking the log of a product is the same as adding the log of each factor.
>
> 2. To divide the same variables, subtract the exponents:
> $\dfrac{a^m}{a^n} = a^{m-n}$. Taking the log of a quotient is the same as subtracting the log of each part.
>
> In any base, the following rules apply: $\log(ab) = \log a + \log b$; $\log(a/b) = \log a - \log b$; $\log(1/a) = -\log a$; $\log a^b = b \log a$; $\log 1 = 0$ and $\log 0$ is undefined.

Writing in Science

Writing is central to science. It allows scientists to express their hypotheses, to record their observations, and to communicate their conclusions. Writing gives structure to the scientific method and allows scientists to share what they've learned with others.

In science classes—biology, chemistry, physics, botany, geology, astronomy, and oceanography—you can make discoveries about the natural world and learn ways to explore it further. Writing about the practical applications of science in your everyday life requires research skills, accurate observations, and clear explanations.

This chapter covers the types of writing that will help you in your science classes and in applying scientific principles to everyday tasks. Research papers and responses to prompts allow you to share what you've learned with your teacher and others, while practical writing allows you to apply what you've learned to your life.

- **Writing Guidelines: Cause-Effect Essay**
- **Writing Guidelines: Directions**
- **Creating a Multimedia Presentation**
- **Writing Guidelines: Response to an Expository Prompt**

"Aerodynamically, the bumble bee shouldn't be able to fly, but the bumble bee doesn't know it so it goes on flying anyway."

—Mary Kay Ash

Writing Guidelines Cause-Effect Essay

In your science classes, you may be called on to research the causes and effects of scientific phenomena. Your focus can be on one cause and its effects, one effect and multiple causes, or a chain of causes and effects. Follow these guidelines.

Prewriting

- **Select a topic.** If your teacher doesn't assign a specific topic, review your class notes, learning log, and textbook for ideas. Think about topics you have discussed in class. Choose a topic with a number of causes and/or effects that you're interested in finding out more about.
- **Gather details.** Use valid, reliable and relevant primary and secondary sources to research your topic. Your primary sources may include interviews with people who have firsthand experience. Secondary sources such as magazine or newspaper articles may provide important information.
- **Organize your information.** Use your research to identify the topic's causes and effects. The graphics below show several options for organizing a cause-effect essay. Use a similar organizer to plan your draft. Write your thesis statement and list the cause(s) and effect(s).

An essay focused on causes will explain several causes of a single effect.

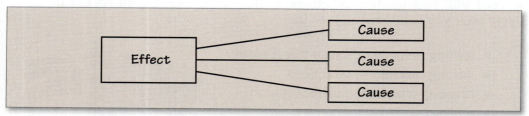

An essay focused on effects will explain several effects of a single cause.

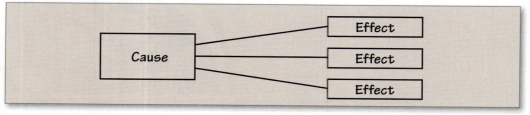

An essay explaining a causal chain will begin with a cause and follow with a series of effects that become the causes of new effects.

Cause-Effect Essay

In this essay, Janet Ledman discusses the causes and effects of flu epidemics in human populations.

The beginning identifies the topic and leads to the thesis statement (underlined).

The first middle paragraph discusses the cause.

The second middle paragraph examines current effects.

Avian Influenza (Bird Flu)

Medical science has solved many riddles in the last 50 years, leading to the defeat of major diseases such as polio and smallpox. On the other hand, as the number of people and the ease of travel between countries increases, the threat of a pandemic (worldwide epidemic) is very real. Currently, health centers around the world are striving to head off such a crisis. <u>Many are concerned that the world is heading for a catastrophic outbreak of avian influenza, often called bird flu.</u>

In several countries, particularly in China, millions of people raise chickens, turkeys, and ducks. Unfortunately, these people often live surrounded by these birds. That means that any serious illness that affects the birds has access to the humans. The proximity of a human population that lacks sufficient hygiene raises the danger level. If mutation occurs, this bird virus could well move from simply infecting birds to infecting people, who then infect other people. This is what happened in the great flu epidemic of 1918 that killed an estimated 50 million people worldwide.

The effects of current strains of avian influenza are severe. For birds, a highly infectious form of the flu usually means death. The loss of these flocks impacts local economies. When humans are infected, fever, sore throat, pneumonia, and acute respiratory distress can easily overwhelm and kill. Young adults, normally able to fight flu, seem to be especially vulnerable. In Hong Kong, eighteen people were infected and six died. Authorities believe they halted the spread of the illness by killing 1.5 million domestic chickens and turkeys. Disease control centers around the world have sent out similar reports of people stricken with the bird flu. If the virus manages to mutate so that human-to-human transmission is possible, death will stalk the world.

Ledman 2

> The **last two middle** paragraphs discuss the possible effects of a pandemic on families, communities, and nations around the world.

At first, an outbreak will mean quarantining individuals and whole families. In the United States, the emphasis on personal freedom and rights will make implementing such action more difficult. But if officials do not act soon enough, the flu will spread. If the local quarantines fail, communities and surrounding areas will be closed off, conceivably restricting travel throughout entire states. Imagine National Guard troops on patrol, preventing anyone from entering or leaving an area the size of a state! Schools and colleges will be closed. Large public gatherings will be banned. People will not go to movies or eat at restaurants. Should the contagion rage in spite of these efforts, nations may close their borders to protect themselves. Those needing help could end up isolated, left to die or recover on their own. Dealing with the millions of patients and deaths would be just the beginning.

Companies, both large and small, would be impacted. The fragile airline industry may cease to exist or be severely scaled back. Trade, particularly of agricultural products, would suffer. Some countries dependent on outside sources for goods and/or food could well collapse into anarchy. Of course, places that cater to tourists would be big losers. During the four months it takes to develop a vaccine to fight the spread of the virus, avian influenza could do untold damage.

> The **ending** summarizes the dilemma for the medical community.

Health officials face a dilemma. Do they act now, spending valuable time and resources to prepare for a pandemic that may not happen, or do they wait? If the flu virus mutates and begins a human-to-human journey, the world will suffer. The risk is too great to ignore, so research concerning avian influenza and its successful treatment will continue.

Drafting Cause-Effect Essay

Once you have gathered and organized your information, you can begin writing the draft of your essay.

Writing Your Beginning

- **Grab your reader's attention.** Use a quotation from an expert, ask a question, or cite an interesting or surprising fact to engage your audience.
- **Identify the topic.** Provide necessary background information about the scientific phenomenon and touch on the main ideas that you will explore in the essay.
- **End with your thesis.** Your introduction should logically lead to a clear thesis statement that expresses the controlling idea of your essay. All the details and evidence that you present in your essay must directly relate to your thesis.

Developing the Middle

- **Connect your ideas.** Follow your graphic organizer or outline as you write the middle of your essay. Include the details you gathered in your research. Be sure to include information on all relevant perspectives in the scientific community as well as an analysis of views that contradict your thesis statement.
- **Support your reasoning.** Use relevant and substantial evidence and well-chosen details to explain the cause(s) and effect(s) of the phenomenon.

Writing Your Ending

- **Summarize your main points.** Conclude by explaining what you learned. Leave the reader with a final thought or question.

Try It!

Write a cause-effect essay. Select a topic that interests you and follow the writing guidelines on this page and on page **482**.

TEKS 12.13C, 12.13D, 12.15A(i–v)
ELPS 1B, 5C, 5D

Revising Improving Your Writing

Use the following checklist as a guide for revising your cause-effect essay.

Revising Checklist

Focus and Coherence

_____ 1. Do all my details and ideas clearly relate to my thesis?

Organization

_____ 2. Do I state my thesis in the introduction, explain cause(s) and effect(s) in the middle, and end with an effective conclusion?

_____ 3. Have I used transitions to connect my ideas?

Development of Ideas

_____ 4. Have I used substantial and relevant evidence and well-chosen details to explain the cause(s) and effect(s)?

_____ 5. Do I use rhetorical devices to explore each idea in depth, so that the reader can appreciate my analysis?

Voice

_____ 6. Have I used an active, engaging voice?

_____ 7. Are my word choice and tone appropriate for my audience?

Editing Checking for Conventions

After you revise your essay, use the following checklist to edit for conventions.

Conventions

_____ 1. Are there any errors in grammar, mechanics (capitalization and punctuation), or spelling?

_____ 2. Do I use a variety of correctly structured sentences that clearly communicate my ideas?

Writing Guidelines Directions

You may be asked to write a set of how-to directions based on scientific knowledge you've learned in class. While this type of writing is more informal than academic writing, it still requires careful attention to detail. Follow these writing guidelines.

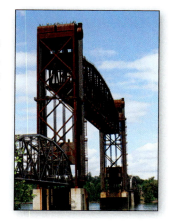

Prewriting

- **Focus on the purpose** of your writing task.
- **Jot down the key points** you want to make. Write out the steps in the process that need to be explained.

Drafting

- **Clearly state your purpose, and keep it in mind** as you write.
- **Express your viewpoint** on the topic, and support it with evidence.
- **Use facts and specific details** to explain each step.
- **Keep your audience in mind.** For example, if you are writing instructions for someone who's doing a project for the first time, you cannot assume anything. Fully explain the names and functions of all ingredients and tools, where supplies are kept, and basic safety precautions. Address potential problems and misunderstandings.
- **Sum up.** Give the reader tips about where to get additional information if needed.

Revising

- **Improve your writing.** Review your first draft for *development of ideas, focus and coherence, and organization*. Ask these questions: *Are my directions clear and complete? Do they follow a logical sequence? Have I included only important details?*
- **Improve your style.** Evaluate your *voice* and *conventions*, asking these questions: *Have I used specific nouns and active verbs? Is technical information accurately explained in accessible language? Have I capitalized words correctly and used punctuation properly?*

Editing

- **Check for conventions.** Proofread your writing for errors in punctuation, capitalization, spelling, and grammar. *Remember:* Even a few errors affect the credibility of your information.
- **Prepare a final copy.** Make a neat final copy for your audience.

Directions

Miguel entered a contest in which he was required to write directions for building a model bridge. He relied on the concepts he had learned in his physics class.

> **Building a Truss Bridge**
>
> **Introduction**
> Trusses are straight structural supports that form triangles against a plane to distribute the weight of a load. A truss bridge is a type of bridge commonly used by railroads. Truss bridges are an efficient bridge design because they are easy to construct, tend to be strong, and are economical due to the amount of materials needed. <u>Building a model truss bridge allows people to appreciate and understand the physics of truss design.</u>
>
> **Materials**
> The following materials are needed to construct a model truss bridge: quarter-inch and half-inch square pine sticks and sixteenth-inch-thick plywood. The necessary tools include a coping saw and woodworkers' glue.
>
> Note: To ensure the integrity of the structure, it is imperative that all materials are accurately measured and precisely cut.
>
> **Building the Base**
> To build the base, place two half-inch pine sticks, each 20 1/2 inches long, four inches apart. Attach them to each other on the ends with four-inch lengths of half-inch pine.
>
> **Forming the Trusses**
> To form the trusses, use the quarter-inch pine to build six equilateral triangles with four-inch sides, and four equilateral triangles with three-inch sides. Set one of the smaller triangles (point up) in front of you. Then place in a row three larger triangles (points up) next to the first one. Finish the row with another small triangle (point up).

*The **beginning** includes a viewpoint supported by facts about why trusses are important and provides a clear statement of purpose (underlined).*

*The **middle** identifies the materials needed and explains how to build the bridge.*

Headings guide the reader and provide an effective formatting structure.

Next, place a 3 1/2-inch piece of the smaller dimension pine from the top of the first small triangle to the top of the first large triangle and from the top of the third large triangle to the top of the second small triangle. Place a four-inch piece of pine from the top of the first large triangle to the top of the second large triangle and then from the top of the second to the top of the third large triangle.

Potential problems will occur if the equilateral triangles are not precisely arranged. This will prevent the trusses from fitting properly and compromise the stablity of the structure. Check that all pieces are properly placed before gluing them together.

Potential problems are addressed.

Carefully glue the triangles together as they are laid out. Then glue small squares of the plywood on top of each of the connecting points. These mimic the plates used in real bridges to both connect and add strength to a joint.

Once you have finished, construct a second truss in the same way.

Putting the Bridge Together

Finally, attach one truss to each side of the base structure built earlier. Connect the joint points on the tops of the two trusses using long enough pine pieces to form triangles. Allow the glue to dry on the model bridge and then test its strength.

Summation

Trusses are an effective way to support the load that a roadbed must carry. Constructed properly, the model bridge can demonstrate how this type of bridge design employs tension and compression to support a significant amount of weight. The triangles, which cannot be pushed out of shape, make the trusses strong.

*The **ending** restates the importance of trusses and the purpose of building a model bridge.*

Try It!

Write a set of how-to directions. Select a topic based on scientific principles that interest you and follow the writing guidelines on page **487**.

Creating a Multimedia Presentation

Creating a multimedia presentation is an effective way to provide how-to instructions. By using video to present the directions, your audience will be able to visualize each step as it is explained. Filming allows you to demonstrate possible problems and misunderstandings, and viewers can pause the video to take notes and complete the steps as they follow the directions.

Planning

- **Outline your presentation.** Use the outline and draft of your directions as a starting point. Decide what information needs to be added, deleted, or rearranged to fit the format of your presentation.
- **Create storyboards.** Sketch the sequence of images. Label screens that will show diagrams, graphics, and/or text and make notes about the audio that will correspond with each screen.

Developing

- **Write your script.** Use index cards or make notes as needed to correlate your audio with each screen shot.
- **Shoot your video.** Check with your teacher or school library or media department if you need technical assistance. Work with a partner if you need help adjusting props or diagrams. Shoot the video in segments, paying attention to multiple points of view. Playback each segment to check for technical errors or mistakes and reshoot as needed before proceeding to the next segment.

Sharing

- **Edit and publish your video.** Most computers have free movie-making software that will allow you to edit your video, add titles and captions, and even create special effects. After you've incorporated feedback from your teacher and peers, you can upload your video to the Web or burn a DVD to share with your class.

Try It!

Follow the guidelines above to adapt your directions for a multimedia presentation. Keep your audience in mind as you plan your presentation.

TEKS 12.13B, 12.13D, 12.15A(i), 12.15A(iii-v)
ELPS 1B, 5C, 5D, 5E, 5G

Writing in Science

Writing Guidelines Response to an Expository Prompt

On a science test, you may be asked to write a response to an expository prompt. This sort of test question is a great way to evaluate your knowledge and understanding of a scientific concept. Use the following tips to make the best of the limited time you will have to respond.

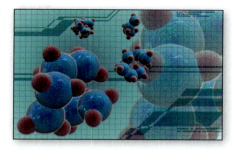

Before you write . . .

- **Understand the prompt.** Review the STRAP questions listed on page 210. Remember that an expository prompt asks you to explain something or to share information.
- **Use your time wisely.** Plan a few minutes for making notes or filling in a graphic organizer before you begin writing, the main portion of time for the actual writing, and another few minutes at the end to check over your response.

As you write . . .

- **Decide on a focus or thesis for your essay.** Keep this main idea or purpose in mind during your writing.
- **Be selective.** Working from your notes, use examples and explanations that directly support your focus.
- **End in a meaningful way.** Close your essay by restating your main idea in a new way.

After you've written your response . . .

- **Check for completeness.** Use the STRAP questions on page 214 as a guide to revision.
- **Check for correctness.** Correct any errors in punctuation, capitalization, spelling, and grammar.

Tip

Many students feel nervous when taking a test, and that is only natural. However, by taking time to plan your response before you begin writing, you can relax and write with confidence.

Response to an Expository Prompt

One student analyzed the following prompt using the STRAP questions (page 210), made a quick list of details about the topic, and then wrote the response below.

Prompt

Two identical pieces of steel are placed in the water. One is shaped like a boat and the other is flat. What happens to each piece of steel? Why did this happen? How can this knowledge be put to practical use? Explain.

The **introduction** proposes an answer to the first part of the prompt.

In the **middle**, the student supports her answer by explaining a scientific principle.

The **conclusion** explains the practical use of the principle.

Displacement

Steel is more dense than water. This means that a flat piece of steel placed in the water will sink. But that same piece of steel formed into a large enough boat will float.

More than 2,200 years ago, Archimedes, a Greek mathematician, noticed that a liquid pushes up on an object placed in it with a force equal to the weight of the liquid displaced by the object. Since the density of a flat piece of steel is greater than the water it displaces, which means it weighs more, the steel will sink.

If a shipbuilder, on the other hand, uses that same amount of steel to build a boat shape of the right size, the boat will be less dense than the water it displaces. This happens because a boat is mostly air with a steel skin. The boat settles into the water, pushes away the amount of water equal to the weight of the boat, and finally floats.

A liquid denser than water, like mercury, would need less volume displaced for the ship to float. A lighter liquid, like alcohol, would need a much greater volume displaced to float the ship.

With this knowledge, shipbuilders can determine the best materials to use in a ship, and how much volume displacement is necessary to float that ship in either freshwater or seawater.

Try It!

Find a science-related prompt and write a response. Use the guidelines on page 491.

Writing in Social Studies

When you write in social studies, you may be asked to do some research and create an essay or other response based on information found in a variety of documents—texts, charts, graphs, maps, photos, and so on. In order to accomplish such a task, you'll need to analyze the documents and summarize important information. You'll also need to organize your information carefully and write a response that satisfies the assignment's criteria.

This chapter models some types of writing you may be asked to do in your social studies classroom, including a historical skit and a report on social studies research using documents.

- **Writing Guidelines: Historical Skit**
- **Planning a Multimedia Presentation**
- **Writing Guidelines: Report on Social Studies Research**

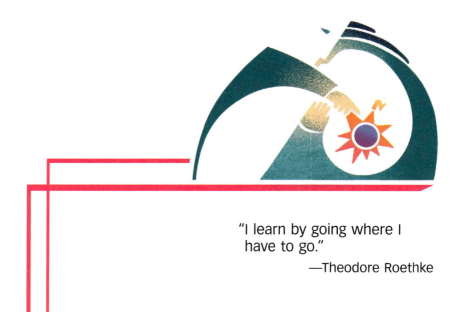

"I learn by going where I have to go."
—Theodore Roethke

Writing Guidelines Historical Skit

A historical skit is a very short play based on an element of history. Skits usually include only a few characters, a brief storyline, a minimal stage set, and a limited number of props. When rendered effectively, a skit brings the audience to a critical moment in time, when people faced a challenge and a moment of decision.

To write your skit, you'll need to do some research and choose a topic and theme. You'll need to select characters to tell your story and choose a setting and a plot. Then you can draft, revise, and edit your skit to produce it for an audience. You can even film it to create a multimedia presentation on the Internet.

Prewriting Doing Some Research

Your social studies teacher may direct you to focus on a particular time or place. The topic, however, may be your choice. To narrow your topic down, focus on a conflict. What challenges did people of that time or place face? Who were the leaders in the struggle? What forces opposed them? What was the result?

Once you've decided on a topic, focus on the theme. To do that, ask: Why were the events important? What lesson can they teach an audience today?

Revolutionary Ideas

In the following example, the teacher asked Luisa and her group to write and produce a skit about the American Revolution. In their research, they discovered an interesting event—a power struggle between two Revolutionary leaders before the capture of Fort Ticonderoga in 1775. They arranged their thoughts in this chart.

Setting	Characters	Plot	Theme
The rebels' camp near Fort Ticonderoga the night before the attack	Captain Johnson, a Connecticut officer Sergeant Hall and Private VanHalbern, two of Ethan Allen's Green Mountain Boys A soldier, loyal to neither leader	Allen and Arnold both claim leadership of the force that will attack the British. If the force cannot decide upon a leader, the men may refuse to fight. The attack may fail.	Is loyalty to one leader more important than loyalty to the cause of liberty?

Try It!

In a group discuss and research an event in history. What story will you tell? Who are the characters? What are the plot and theme?

Drafting Historical Skit

A skit always includes two major components: **stage directions,** including ideas for props, costumes, and lighting, and **dialogue** for the actors. A skit may also include **narration.** A narrator can quickly and easily help set the scene.

- **Begin with some stage directions.** In a skit, stage directions set the scene quickly and with minimal effort. They provide important information about the time period and the way people dressed. Keep the details simple. Your audience's imagination can fill in the gaps.
- **Focus on your main ideas.** Skits are very short, so make every word count by having the characters focus on your main ideas, including your conflict and theme, as soon as possible.
- **Move quickly toward resolution.** Just as you quickly focus on the conflict, you must quickly move toward resolution. The skit ends when the conflict is resolved.
- **Keep theme in mind.** The skit's theme is the life lesson you want your audience to understand. There are two ways to present a theme. An **explicit theme** is stated directly by the characters. An **implicit theme** is not stated directly, but is understood by the audience.

Luisa's group began to draft their skit, keeping the tips above in mind.

(A stage is lit dimly by a lantern. A group of men stand around it, roughly dressed in flannel, wool, and simple tricorn hats. The Green Mountain boys wear a pine spring tucked in their caps.)

NARRATOR: May 10, 1775. A ragged group of Revolutionary soldiers huddle in the cold predawn outside Fort Ticonderoga. The British hold the fort. Soon, the rebels will attack.

CAPTAIN JOHNSON: My men and I have marched here from Connecticut in suport of the rebel cause. We have gathered good rifles and other supplies, which we paid for with our own money. And General George Washington himself has named Benedict Arnold to lead us into battle. My life, and those of my friends and neighbors, is on the line. I'll fight under no other commander but my own.

SERGEANT HALL: I was born and raised not ten miles from this very place. The Green Mountains are my home. I left them for a few short years, to travel at sea to distant ports. I traveled as far as England herself. But my leader here is Ethan Allen of the Green Mountain Boys. I'll follow no one else into battle.

Try It!

Draft your historical skit, using stage direction, dialogue, and narration if you choose. Start in the middle of the conflict, and move quickly toward resolution.

Historical Skit

After revising and editing, Luisa's group had a historical skit that was ready for performance. This is the first part of that skit.

Decision at Ticonderoga

(Stage is lit dimly by a partially-covered lantern. A small group of men stand around it, roughly dressed in flannel and wool. They wear simple tricorn hats. Ethan Allen's Green Mountain boys wear a pine spring tucked in their caps. The Connecticut men wear red ribbons on theirs.)

> Stage directions are kept simple.

NARRATOR: May 10, 1775. A ragged group of Revolutionary soldiers huddle in the cold outside Fort Ticonderoga. The British hold the fort, and before dawn, the rebels must attack, but a conflict among them threatens their cause.

CAPTAIN JOHNSON: My men and I have marched all the way here from Connecticut in support of the rebel cause. General George Washington himself has named Benedict Arnold to lead us into battle. My life, and those of my friends and neighbors, is on the line. I'll fight under no other commander but Arnold.

> The conflict is quickly introduced.

SERGEANT HALL: I was born and raised not ten miles from this very place. The Green Mountains are my home. My leader is Ethan Allen, and no other.

PRIVATE VANHALBERN: Aye! And if your fancy General Arnold will not accept that, all of us will go home. You'll see how your battle fares without us.

CAPTAIN JOHNSON: But Arnold is a trained soldier, not an amateur.

SERGEANT THOMPSON: Hah! While Ethan Allen lacks his schooling, he is a genius nonetheless. Who has kept New York from taking over the Green Mountains all these years? Ethan Allen and none other.

> Multiple viewpoints are presented.

(Another soldier enters, wearing the insignia of neither force.)

THE SOLDIER: They say we will attack within the hour. What are you men jabbering about?

VANHALBERN: Who will lead our force. If it is Arnold, the Green Mountain Boys will go home. If it is Ethan Allen, the Connecticut men will do the same.

TEKS 12.13C
ELPS 1B, 5C, 5D

Writing in Social Studies

Revising Improving Your Writing

Once you have drafted your historical skit, you need to revise and edit it so it is ready for production.

Focus and Coherence

_____ 1. Do I use stage directions to quickly set the scene?
_____ 2. Do my characters focus immediately on the conflict?
_____ 3. Does my dialogue stay on topic without wandering?

Organization

_____ 4. Does the opening of the skit outline the conflict?
_____ 5. Does the middle of the skit include rising action?
_____ 6. Does the end of the skit resolve the conflict?

Development of Ideas

_____ 7. Do I present the conflict clearly?
_____ 8. Do the characters express a variety of viewpoints?
_____ 9. Will the audience understand what is at stake?

Voice

_____ 10. Are my characters' voices unique?
_____ 11. Are they worthy of the audience's attention?
_____ 12. Does the dialogue include appropriate emotion?
_____ 13. Is my dialogue historically appropriate?

Conventions

_____ 14. Have I capitalized proper nouns and adjectives?
_____ 15. Do my subjects and verbs agree in number?
_____ 16. Have I spelled all words correctly?
_____ 17. Have I double-checked the words my spell-checker may have missed?

Try It!

Revise your historical skit for *Focus and Coherence, Development of Ideas, Organization,* and *Voice.* Edit your skit for *Conventions.*

Planning a Multimedia Presentation

Due to its visual nature, a skit suits itself well to a multimedia presentation. It will take some extra planning and work to turn your skit into a new format—a docudrama—but filming it will enable you to share it with a much larger audience. Once your skit has been filmed and edited, you can show it to new audiences using only a monitor and DVD player, or even uploading it to a Web site.

Adjust Your Script

If you have written your script for a live production, you may want to make some adjustments for filming. The script that Luisa's group wrote, for example, calls for a dimly lit set. Such a set, however, might not be conducive to a video shoot. They may want to call for increased lighting, so their main characters can be seen clearly.

In addition, if you are making the effort to broadcast your skit widely, you may want to increase the number of props or costumes to create the proper historical setting. You may also wish to move outside the classroom to shoot "on location" to make the shots more realistic. Luisa's group found a nearby park that could stand in for the forest near Ticonderoga.

Creating a Storyboard

One technique that can help organize your group's ideas before filming begins is to create a storyboard. A storyboard is a series of sketches that outline the sequence of shots or scenes planned for a film. It is an effective way to collaborate with your group to ensure that everyone's ideas about how to film the scenes are considered before filming begins. The traditional way of storyboarding is to actually sketch or draw your ideas for each scene. Today, there are many computer programs that can help you create a storyboard as well.

Prepare the Set

Once you have created a storyboard, you are ready to shoot and should begin preparing the set. Cameras and microphones should be positioned so that they can capture the characters as they speak. Be sure that video equipment such as power cables, lighting stands, and microphones are not visible in camera shots.

Allow Plenty of Time

When you present a live skit, there is nothing that can be done if a mistake is made. However, filming a skit allows you to try again until everything is perfect. Allow time for multiple "takes." In the end, you can choose parts from several takes and edit them together to create a flawless final product.

Filming Your Historical Skit

Shooting a video is a team job. You'll need to work collaboratively with your group, sharing ideas and listening carefully, to create a successful film.

Testing 1, 2, 3!

Before filming, make sure you have all the video equipment you will need. Have all of your costumes and props ready, too. These items should work together to create the proper historical setting and scenery. Your narrator can provide any additional background information that is necessary. Be sure that any images or graphics that you plan to include are also ready to be filmed.

Shooting

Make sure the set is quiet, and there is no unintentional background noise before you begin shooting. Put your actors into position. Encourage them to speak their lines naturally. Shoot several "takes" and choose the best one later.

Editing

Editing your video means putting it together in a final version that assembles your ideas in an engaging and informative presentation. Editing usually includes several steps.

- **Arrange clips** in the order you want them. Use your storyboard as a guide, but don't be afraid to rearrange some clips to make your point clearer. Shorten clips to cut out any ideas that don't relate to the topic.
- **Add a title** at the beginning and credits at the end. You can also add titles to make transitions between different sections of the film.
- **Import music** or sound effects to help create the right atmosphere. Make sure additional audio doesn't drown out your actors' voices.

Uploading to the Web

- Before uploading the video, check the Web site to find out what video formats are acceptable. Save your video in this format, making sure to create and save a backup copy on your own hard drive.
- Upload the video, following the site's instructions. Then send an email, including a description of the video and the site's URL, to your audience of potential viewers.

Try It!

Film your historical skit with your group. Be sure to listen to one another and share ideas to get multiple points of view and to get the most out of the actors, the shoot, and the final product.

TEKS 12.20A, 12.20B, 12.21A, 12.21B, 12.23E

Writing Guidelines Report on Social Studies Research

In social studies class you may be asked to do some research using a variety of documents and to write a report on a social studies topic. To do this, you'll need to brainstorm and choose an appropriate topic, formulate a research question, gather evidence from experts and texts, analyze the documents you find, and synthesize your research into an extended presentation that cites all research in a standard format.

Creating a research report can be a challenge, but its rewards can be great. Exploring a topic in depth can provide you with insight into an unfamiliar subject and help you to better understand the writing process. The ability to gather, organize, and present information is something you'll use over and over again, in college, on the job, and even as you prepare to make decisions such as planning a vacation or buying a home.

Here are a few guidelines that will help you to meet the challenge of writing a report on social studies research using documents.

Prewriting

- **Brainstorm topics.** Your teacher will likely define a broad area of your research, such as a particular time period or event. You'll need to do some more digging and some brainstorming to narrow down a specific topic. Consult with a partner or other classmates about possibilities.
- **Formulate research questions.** These questions will guide your research. Typically, they will be "W" questions.
  - Who influenced the course of historical events?
  - Why did they take the action they did?
  - How did they meet challenges?
  - What is the lasting impact of their actions?
- **Plan research.** Be sure to consider a broad range of media, from primary and secondary print and Web sources to personal interviews. Look for a variety of documents.
- **Gather evidence.** Use note cards to record source information and key points from your research. Be sure to consider multiple perspectives, including opposing views. Gather enough evidence to develop your ideas into a report of sufficient length to adequately address the topic.
- **Analyze evidence in each document.** Consider how your sources relate to your research question—and to each other. Focus on creating your own unique perspective.
- **Organize your facts.** Use a graphic organizer that shows how your ideas connect. The graphic organizer will help you create an outline or time line that will serve as a blueprint for your research.

Working with Sources

Once you've formulated a research question and gathered documents, you need to analyze your evidence. Read or listen carefully to uncover what the evidence can tell you about your topic, and how it can help you create a cogent argument that answers your major research question. Once you've analyzed your evidence, cite your sources properly and summarize key points in your own words.

For her topic, Anna chose to explore the change in voting eligibility that happened in the United States in 1971, when the voting age changed from 21 to 18. Her major research question was "How did 18-year-olds win the right to vote?"

In her research, Anna discovered a pamphlet written by an unidentified young person in 1970. It gave reasons why the voting age should be lowered.

Document One
Old Enough to Fight; Old Enough to Vote!

Every day on the battlefield in Vietnam, young Americans are fighting and dying in service to their country. Some put their lives on the line by choice. Others had no choice, being drafted into the military and forced to serve. Young men aged 18–20 are considered mature enough to carry weapons in a war zone, mature enough to face an enemy in battle, mature enough to sustain wounds and even die for their country. Yet the very country they serve will not allow them the right to vote.

While young Americans can be sent to Vietnam to fight for their country, they have no right to participate in the political process that sends them there. If given a chance, these young Americans can bring in new ideas and new energy to help change our country and the world for the better. For this reason, we call upon the United States to lower the voting age to 18. If we're old enough to fight, we're old enough to vote.

This primary source document states a clear viewpoint: the voting age should be lowered to 18.

Summary: In 1970, many 18–20-year olds were being sent to fight in the Vietnam War. Some young people believed that because they served their country in this way, they deserved the right to vote. They believed that if they could vote, they could make their country—and the world—a better place.

Only the most important information is included in the summary.

Source: U.S. Civic Youth Association. *Old Enough to Fight; Old Enough to Vote.* New York: CYA, 10 Jan. 1970. Print.

TEKS 12.21A, 12.21C, 12.22B, 12.23D

Checking Your Sources

Check a library catalog or search for a topic on the Internet, and you'll instantly have access to hundreds of pages full of ideas, statistics, and opinions. Here are a few tips to help you to identify reliable sources and get the information you need.

Focus on your research questions. It's easy to get sidetracked, especially on the Internet. Consider only those resources that will help answer your questions. Modify your research questions to broaden or narrow your research, as necessary.

Look for the experts. An expert provides accurate information for informed audiences. If you aren't sure about an expert's credentials, ask your teacher. Discard any information that is weak or comes from unreliable sources.

Go with well-known sources. Reliable sources include books, newspapers, magazines, and Web sites produced by major publishers or created by educational institutions, such as universities. Sources that do not support their theories with factual evidence or that contain obvious errors are not considered reliable.

Once you have gathered sources, you can collect information in two ways.

- **Quoting** means using the source's exact words. If you do this, enclose the words in quotation marks and give credit to the source.
- **Paraphrasing** means rewriting ideas in your own words so your paper reflects your own voice. When paraphrasing, you must give credit to the source.

In her research, Anna found the following documents and paraphrased them.

Document Two
Americans Age 18–21 Voting for President, 1972–1996

Year	% Who Registered	% Who Voted	% of Total Voters
1996	45.6	31	3.21
1992	44.9	33.2	3.29
1988	44.9	33.2	3.49
1984	47	36.7	4.05
1980	44.7	35.7	4.71
1976	47.1	38	5.3
1972	36.4	20.8	3.81

Source: "Voter Registration and Turnout in Federal Elections, 1972–1996". United States Election Assistance Commission. 20 March 2007. Web. 1 Nov. 2010.

Paraphrase: From 1972–1996, the participation of young voters generally declined. At the peak in 1976, almost half of those 18–21 registered to vote, and the group that did go to the polls represented 1 out of 20 voters for that election. But after that, participation dropped off. In 1996, fewer than one-third of those 18–21 voted, representing 1 out of 30 votes cast.

Writing in Social Studies

Document Three
Margin of Victory in U.S. Presidential Elections, 1972–1996

Year	% Voting Republican	% Voting Democratic	Winning Party
1996	40.72	49.23	Democratic
1992	37.45	43.01	Democratic
1988	53.77	45.65	Republican
1984	58.77	40.56	Republican
1980	50.75	41.01	Republican
1976	48.02	50.08	Democratic
1972	60.67	37.52	Republican

Source: Leip, Dave. "United States Presidential Election Results." *US Election Atlas.org*. N.p., Web. 1 Nov. 2010.

Statistics are used to make some generalizations.

> The greatest margin of victory was in 1972, with the Republican camp defeating the Democrats by 23.15 percent of the total vote. The smallest margin was in 1976, with the Democrats defeating the Republicans by only 2.08 percent.

Document Four

> "Bad politicians are sent to Washington by good people who don't vote."
> —William E. Simon, former secretary of the United States Treasury

Source: American Bar Association. "Voting: Youth Citizenship." *Abanet.org*. American Bar Assoc. n.d. Web. 31 Oct. 2010.

Inference is used to make the connection.

> There are two ways to connect this to the debate: (1) When very few of the informed young people vote, bad politicians may be voted into office. (2) If more informed young people voted, better politicians may get elected.

Organizing Details

Once you have gathered your information, you need to organize your ideas. Remember, you may wish to revise your plan if the materials you find do not support your argument, ideas, concepts, or themes. The goal is to create a writing plan that will support your thesis logically and effectively.

A **time line** is a great way to organize events chronologically. A **concept map** shows how events and ideas relate to each other. After doing her research, Anna created a concept map to help organize her thoughts.

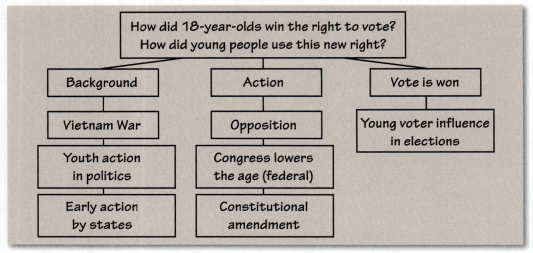

After gathering her ideas in a concept map, Anna used the relationships to create an outline.

I. Reasons people wanted change
    A. Young people's political activism
    B. The Vietnam War
II. Historical support for the youth vote
    A. The first calls for the youth vote
    B. Support by politicians
    C. States taking early action
III. The national campaign
    A. Youth activism
    B. Congress takes action
    C. Confusion in the states
IV. The 26th Amendment
    A. Voting age changed
    B. Applies to both state and federal elections
V. The youth vote
    A. Early enthusiasm
    B. A swift decline
    C. A return to involvement

A Report on Social Studies Research

Using the documents shown on the previous pages, additional documents she discovered during her research, and her own knowledge about the topic, Anna wrote a report on how young citizens aged 18–20 gained the right to vote. She also analyzed how far they have gone toward using the vote to "change the world."

Introduction
The opening provides background about winning the vote and states the thesis.

Middle
Evidence is presented through summaries, paraphrases, and quotations.

Fighting for the Right to Vote

In the 1960s and early 1970s, America's young people faced a dilemma, a dilemma that was huge. Spurred by the Vietnam War, the civil rights movement, and concerns over the environment, many young people became involved in politics. However, because the minimum voting age in federal elections and in many states was 21, the influence they could have over the political direction of the United States was limited. Young people could—and did—publicly state their position on the issues of the day, but they could not vote to elect politicians who shared their views. Working together with like-minded politicians, these young activists used aggressive campaign strategies that produced results. In 1971, the 26th Amndment to the Constitution changed the minimum voting age to 18 (Am. Bar Assoc.). Since then, limited participation by young voters has limited their ability to "change the world" by voting. Yet new trends in more recent elections may indicate that youth voter participation is turning around. The influence of young voters may "change the world" after all.

The idea of a lowered voting age was far from new. In his 1954 State of the Union Address, the president had called for a lowered voting age: "For years our citizens between the ages of 18 and 21 have, in time of peril, been summoned to fight for America. They should participate in the political process that produces this fateful summons." (Eisenhower). The process, however, goes back years earlier. In 1943, Georgia became the first state to grant the right to vote in state elections to those aged 18–20. But young people could still not vote in federal elections. And in the 1960s, as youth began to explore their political power, the demand for the vote reached a tidal wave (Am. Bar Assoc.).

> The campaign tactics are detailed.

Some of the first waves of student activism came during the Civil Rights movement of the 1960s. Young people supported the movement with protests, pamphlets, and "teach-ins." The protests helped to spur the passage the Civil Rights Act of 1964, which outlawed segregation in public accommodations and helped support African Americans' right to vote ("Civil Rights Act"). Young people also pressed for laws that would recognize women as equal to men, and lobbied for protection of the environment.

It was the Vietnam War, however, that provided the most impetus to the drive for youth voting rights. During the war, men aged 18 and older were eligible to be drafted into the military. Thousands of young soldiers served honorably in Vietnam, and many were killed or wounded. Large numbers of young people—both soldiers and civilians—believed the war should be ended, and urged politicians to do so. Without the right to vote, however, they had no true political influence.

> By presenting opposing viewpoints, the writer is able to point out complexities of the time.

Many people were opposed to granting young people the vote, believing that 18-year-olds were too immature. They pointed in particular to protests against the war, some of which had turned violent. The campaign to win the vote featured appeals to other Americans to recognize the sacrifices young people were making for their country and the potential contributions young voters could make to the political system. Young campaigners used pamphlets, posters, and other forms of communication to plead their case. The tone of these materials was aggressive, and even dramatic. One pamphlet announced, "We want the vote and we won't stop asking until we get it." The poster used a stark picture of a soldier to put a human face on the sacrifice made by young American soldiers.

These actions and others by the young people of America helped galvanize the support of sympathetic politicians. Among them was Senator Edward Kennedy. In his call for lowering the voting age, Kennedy said ". . . At the very least, the opportunity to vote should be granted in recognition of the risks an 18-year-old is obliged to assume when he is sent off to fight and perhaps die for his country" (Com. for a Democratic Majority).

In response to this campaign, Congress in 1970 passed a law giving those 18–20 the right to vote in all elections. However, the Supreme Court ruled that the federal government only had the right to set the voting age for federal elections. This created a situation in which an 18-year-old at a voting booth in many states would be able to vote for president and vice-president, but not for candidates in state elections. Following this ruling, Congress proposed an amendment to the Constitution that would give the right to vote to citizens age 18 and over. In 1971, the 26th Amendment was approved by Congress and ratified by the states. The voting age for all elections was now 18 (Am. Bar Assoc.).

Off to a slow start in 1972, the young voters did arrive at the polls in 1976 and made a difference. That year, the Democratic candidate for president won by a slim 2.08 percent margin (Leip). Some believe that the young people's vote made the victory possible. However, others argue that young people's voting record since shows that the potential promised during the youth suffrage campaign will not be realized. Overall, in presidential elections from 1972–1996, fewer than half of eligible 18- to 20-year-olds have voted. More ominously, the number of 18- to 20-year-olds going to the polls steadily declined during those years (Voter Registration and Turnout).

The lack of participation among young voters harms efforts to make America a better place. As former United States Treasury Secretary William E. Simon once remarked, "Bad politicians are sent to Washington by good people who don't vote" (Am. Bar Assoc.). Those who hope that young people can revitalize the American political system have not given up. Campaigns such as Rock the Vote and Youth Vote are working to encourage young people to vote. These efforts may be succeeding. Youth voter participation increased slightly from 2000–2008. In 2004, voting among 18– to 29 year-

> Anticipating counter-arguments, the writer points out discrepancies.

olds increased nine percent over 2000. And the turnout in the 2008 presidential primaries increased 8 percent from 2000 to 2008, perhaps spurred by the "youth appeal" of candidate Barack Obama (Marcelo and Kirby). The increases are not dramatic, and many young people still do not exercise their right to vote. But if the trends continue, youth voters may eventually succeed in their goal to "change the world."

Conclusion
The conclusion restates the thesis and looks at efforts to improve the situation.

Works Cited

American Bar Association. "Voting: Youth Citizenship." *Abanet.org.* n.d. Web. 31 Oct. 2010.

"Civil Rights Act." *Encyclopedia Britannica 2005 Ultimate Reference Suite DVD.* Encyclopedia Britannica, Inc., 2005. DVD.

Committee for a Democratic Majority. "Senator Edward M. Kennedy in His Own Words: Lowering the Voting Age to 18." *TedKennedy.org.* 9 Mar. 1970. Web. 11 Nov. 2010.

Eisenhower, Dwight. "State of the Union, 1954." *AMDOCS Documents for the Study of American History.* n.d. Web. 11 Nov. 2010.

Leip, Dave. "United States Presidential Election Results." *US Election Atlas.org.* n.d. Web. 10 Nov. 2010.

Marcelo, Karlo Barrios, and Emily Hoban Kirby. "Quick Facts About U.S. Young Voters: The Presidential Election Year 2008." *The Center for Information & Research on Civic Learning and Engagement.* Oct. 2008. Web. 10 Nov. 2010.

Voter Registration and Turnout in Federal Elections, 1972–1996. United States Election Assistance Commission. 20 Mar. 2007. Web. 11 Nov. 2010.

U.S. Civic Youth Association. *Old Enough to Fight; Old Enough to Vote.* New York: CYA, 10 Jan. 1970. Print.

Try It!

Do research to find sources you might use for a social studies report on the Great Depression. Create a Works Cited list using MLA style. For more help with citing sources, see pages **451–458**.

Writing in Social Studies

Revising

After Anna created her first draft, she began revising it. She read her draft carefully and looked for places where she could improve support for her ideas by providing examples, improving descriptions, and making effective links between causes and effects. She also worked to eliminate passages that did not support her ideas. Finally, she edited for conventions, by checking for the proper use of grammar, mechanics, spelling, and punctuation.

Writer eliminated redundancy.

Writer made the wording clearer.

Spelling mistakes were fixed.

Specific details were added.

> ### Fighting for the Right to Vote
>
> In the 1960s and early 1970s, America's young people faced a dilemma~~, a dilemma that was huge~~. Spurred by the Vietnam War, the civil rights movement, and concerns over the environment, many young people became involved in politics. However, because the minimum voting age in federal elections and in many states was 21, the influence they could have ~~over the political direction of the United States~~ was limited. Young people could—and did—publicly state their position on the issues of the day, but they could not vote to elect politicians who shared their views. Working together with like-minded politicians, these young activists used aggressive campaign strategies that produced results. In 1971, the 26th Am~~n~~endment to the Constitution changed the minimum voting age to 18 (Am. Bar Assoc.). Since then, limited participation by young voters has limited their ability to "change the world" by voting. Yet new trends in more recent elections may indicate that youth voter participation is turning around. The influence of young voters may "change the world" after all.
>
> The idea of a lowered voting age was far from new. In his 1954 State of the Union Address, ~~the~~ **Dwight D. Eisenhower**, president, had called for a lowered voting age: "For years our citizens between the ages of 18 and 21 have, in time of peril, been summoned to fight for America. They should participate in the political process that produces this fateful summons." (Eisenhower). The process, however, goes back years earlier.

Try It!

Use the checklist on page **510** as you revise your social studies report.

Revising Improving Your Writing

Revising Checklist

Focus and Coherence

____ 1. Is my thesis stated clearly?
____ 2. Is my introduction powerful and engaging?
____ 3. Does my evidence help create a cogent argument?
____ 4. Does my conclusion add some depth to the main idea?

Organization

____ 5. Is my pattern of organization effective?
____ 6. Do my thoughts flow smoothly, leading the reader from one to the other?
____ 7. Do my transitions help to make connections between ideas?
____ 8. Do my ideas build upon each other logically?

Development of Ideas

____ 9. Do I provide ample support for my ideas?
____ 10. Do I include enough specific details?
____ 11. Do I address more than one perspective?
____ 12. Do I provide unique insight into the topic?

Voice

____ 13. Is my voice authentic, personal, and engaging?
____ 14. Do I express my unique ideas about the topic?
____ 15. Do I give credit for other voices I have employed?

Conventions

____ 16. Have I checked that proper nouns are capitalized correctly?
____ 17. Have I double-checked the spelling of names and government organizations?
____ 18. Have I punctuated compound and complex sentences clearly?
____ 19. Do all of my subjects and verbs agree?

Writing in Math

When it comes to math, writing is one of the most valuable learning tools you have at your disposal. As the math becomes more challenging—trigonometry, calculus, advanced algebra—the more essential and helpful writing becomes. Writing, in fact, helps you clarify your thinking and gain mastery over your math course work.

Writing summaries, forming statistical arguments—these forms of writing will sharpen your ability to distill the meaning of mathematical concepts. When you write summaries or arguments, you should be more analytical, carefully displaying your understanding. This chapter will help you with all of your writing in math, from writing summaries to responding to math prompts.

- **Writing Guidelines: Article Summary**
- **Writing Guidelines: Statistical Argument**
- **Writing Guidelines: Response to a Math Prompt**
- **Other Forms of Writing in Math**

"It is impossible to be a mathematician without being a poet in soul."
—Sophia Kovalevskaya

 ELPS 4I, 4G, 5C, 5D, 5G

Writing Guidelines Article Summary

Many magazine articles and news stories include statistics and mathematical concepts. Use the following guidelines when summarizing a math-related article.

Prewriting

- **Select an article.** Find an article that presents figures and statistics to support the story.
- **Read the article.** Try to get an overall feeling for the topic. Then reread it carefully, paying attention to the details.
- **Find the focus.** Write down the main idea of the article.
- **Gather details, including math-related points.** Select only the most important details that support the main idea of the article.

Drafting

- **Write your first draft.** State the main point of the article in your topic sentence. Then provide supporting details. End with a sentence that summarizes your thoughts.

Revising

- **Improve your writing.** Review your first draft for *focus and coherence, organization, development of ideas,* and *voice.* Ask yourself the following questions: *Have I clearly presented the focus of the article? Have I included the most important supporting details? Have I explained any use of mathematical concepts in the article? Is my summary clear? Have I used specific nouns and verbs? Does my summary read smoothly?*

Editing

- **Check for conventions.** Edit your revised draft, correcting any errors in grammar, mechanics, and spelling.
- **Prepare a final copy.** Make all corrections and write a neat final draft.

Try It!

Find an article containing statistics and figures. Using the guidelines above and the sample on the next page, write a summary and create a graph to illustrate the data.

Math-Related Article

A student read the following article and wrote a brief summary, including a graph to illustrate the statistics in the article.

Employment Increase Misleading

A look at the 2009 employment picture of Grange County shows good news and bad news.

According to figures from the State Department of Revenue, employment in Grange County increased 0.86 percent, from 106,972 in December of 2008 to 107,895 in December of 2009. Most of the growth was due to new businesses located in new malls in the towns of Terrell, Point Leon, and Jasper. At first glance, this appears to be a positive trend; however, other factors make the picture less than perfect.

First, it must be noted that most of the new businesses are retail outlets or fast-food chains. Nearly half of workers at these businesses earn no more than minimum wage, many working less than full-time, with no benefits.

Next, while many new jobs have been introduced, many have been lost, due to businesses either moving or closing. The most significant impact was felt by the loss of Yarrow Graphics, accounting for a loss of 297 jobs.

In addition, some local companies closed in the face of new competition. Among them was Point Leon's Main Street Grocery. Owner Jim Hawkins cited an inability to compete with the Mega Bite discount grocery that opened in the town's new mall. Of Main Street's 92 employees, 51 found jobs at the new store, earning significantly less at Mega Bite.

In December of 2008, only 20,774 workers in Grange County were earning minimum wage, while the next year that group rose a startling 47 percent to 30,448. The number of workers earning between $6 and $10 per hour saw a smaller increase of 4 percent, from 32,369 to 33,620. Meanwhile, the number of workers earning higher wages dropped. The largest decrease came in workers earning between $10 and $20 per hour. Their numbers fell from 41,649 in 2005 to 33,804 in 2009—a staggering 19 percent drop. Numbers of those earning more than $20 per hour also fell, a less startling but still significant 18 percent, from 12,180 to 10,023 jobs.

While the county has enjoyed a rise in employment, taxable income has not enjoyed a proportionate rise, tempering any economic celebration.

Article Summary

More Jobs, Not Better Jobs

The article "Employment Increase Misleading" reports on the current employment picture in Grange County. While the number of jobs has increased, salaries have decreased. Both the increase and decrease can be blamed on the types of new businesses in the area. Companies offering high-paying jobs have either relocated or closed down, while new businesses offering low-paying or minimum-wage jobs have proliferated. (See the graph.) Local workers have had to settle for lower pay than they had been earning. So while more people are working, they are earning less.

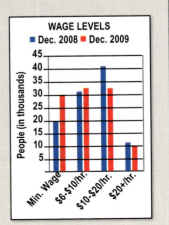

Writing Guidelines Statistical Argument

Use the guidelines below to help you write a persuasive essay containing statistical supporting evidence.

Prewriting

- **Select a topic.** Think about a timely, statistic-driven topic related to your school or community: student dropout rate, state test scores, sports statistics, student volunteer activity, and so on. Choose a topic that interests you and will interest your reader.
- **Gather information.** Research your topic using valid and reliable primary and secondary sources of information. Explore the complete range of relevant perspectives on the topic. Take notes on key facts and figures.
- **Form an opinion.** State an opinion about the topic after reviewing your notes.
- **Plan your essay.** Use an organizing structure appropriate for the audience, purpose, and context. List the logical reasons and various forms of support for your position and against the opposition.

Drafting

- **Write your introduction.** Engage the reader in the topic and clearly state your thesis, or position statement.
- **Develop your middle.** Use your facts and statistics to support your position and to counter objections. When addressing opposing views, be sure to represent information accurately and honestly without taking it out of context. Try to anticipate your audience's response and craft your argument to win support by appealing to logic and emotions.
- **Write your conclusion.** Restate your opinion, summarize the logical reasons for support, and end with a final thought. Put the argument in perspective using firm, decisive language designed to sway a disinterested or opposed audience.

Try It!

Select and research a timely, statistic-driven topic to write about. Gather information and form an opinion about the topic. Then write your argument, using statistics to make your point.

Statistical Argument

The student writing the following persuasive essay uses statistics to emphasize the need for after-school programs.

The introduction includes statistics to introduce the topic.

The opinion statement (underlined) is clearly stated.

In the middle part, statistics help support the opinion.

Happily Ever After

According to the U.S. Department of Labor, of the more than 28 million kids whose parents work outside the home, as many as 15 million have no prearranged supervision after school. Further, Child Trends Research reports that more than 4 million kids—10 percent of children between the ages of 6 and 12—are totally on their own until their parents get home from work. During these unsupervised hours, children are more likely to engage in at-risk behavior or become victims of crime. <u>After-school programs are necessary for the safety of communities and for the future of this country.</u>

After-school programs provide supervision and a safe atmosphere for students. Programs may focus on academic support, enrichment, community service, or even career exploration. These programs have also been shown to improve students' social skills, increase family involvement in children's education, and foster a stronger relationship between children and their community.

Research has shown that after-school programs improve students' academic achievement. In a study by the U.S. Department of Education, high school students involved in extracurricular activities were three times more likely to score in the top 25th percentile of math and reading assessments than those who were not. Following implementation of a city-wide after-school program in Chicago, 75% of schools showed improvement in reading scores and 99% had increases in math.

Students who participate in after-school programs are more likely to stay in school and continue their education after high school. According to the National Federation of High School Associations, students who spent one to four hours a week in extracurricular activities were 60 percent less likely to drop out of school. Of students who participate in ASPIRA, a national organization that runs after-school and summer programs for Hispanic youth, 90 percent enrolled in college or another post-secondary program.

> Additional statistics support other reasons for the position.

After-school programs have also been proven to decrease crime and violence. According to studies by the organization Fight Crime: Invest in Kids, the time period between 3:00 p.m. and 6:00 p.m. is considered a "danger zone," with higher rates of violent crimes involving children. After instituting an after-school program in the San Diego Unified School District, authorities noted a 13.1 percent reduction in after-school arrests, as well as an 11.7 percent reduction in juvenile violent crime. Baltimore police noted a 44 percent reduction in the risk of children being victimized in a high-crime neighborhood following the establishment of an after-school program. In addition, research shows students in who participate in after-school programs are less likely to engage in risky activities such as drug, alcohol, and tobacco use.

> The final middle paragraph identifies counter-arguments and responds to them.

While the benefits of after-school programs are widely recognized, many people do not support using taxpayer dollars to make these programs accessible to all children. Those who do support increases in government funding often prioritize other social and educational services first. However, after-school programs are an investment that is guaranteed to reap rewards. In fact, fully funding after-school programs would save money and reduce the need for the programs that opponents often cite as having a higher priority. Research shows that every dollar invested in an after-school program saves taxpayers $3 in truancy and court costs, as well as the expense of having students repeat a grade or providing them with special education services. A Brandeis University study reported that parents of unsupervised children miss an average of eight days of work per year and make more errors due to situations involving their children. After-school programs help eliminate these situations.

> The **conclusion** restates the opinion and makes a final appeal to the audience.

After-school programs are crucial to protecting not only children, but society in general. When people realize the importance of making such programs accessible to all, they may begin shaping a new world.

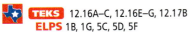

Revising Improving Your Writing

Use the following checklist as a guide for revising your statistical argument.

Revising Checklist

Focus and Coherence

_____ 1. Do all my details and ideas clearly relate to my thesis?

Organization

_____ 2. Do I clearly state my opinion in the introduction, identify reasons for support and address counter-arguments in the middle, and sum up my support in the conclusion?

_____ 3. Is my organizing structure appropriate to the purpose, audience, and context?

Development of Ideas

_____ 4. Have I used logical reasons and trustworthy support?

_____ 5. Have I thoroughly explored each idea, so that the reader can truly appreciate the argument?

Voice

_____ 6. Have I used an active, engaging voice?

_____ 7. Does my formality, style, and tone appeal to the audience and galvanize support for my position?

Editing Checking for Conventions

After revising your essay, use the following checklist to edit for conventions.

Conventions

_____ 1. Are there any errors in grammar, mechanics (capitalization and punctuation), or spelling?

_____ 2. Do I use a variety of correctly structured sentences that clearly communicate my ideas?

Writing Guidelines Response to a Math Prompt

Math prompts propose word problems. You are asked to respond in writing in addition to showing your mathematical calculations and your answers. First you must analyze the prompt and decide what you are supposed to do. Then you respond one step at a time. Follow these guidelines.

Before you write . . .

- **Read the prompt.** Read carefully and watch for key words such as *find, solve, justify, demonstrate,* or *compare*. Then carry out the requested actions only. Be aware that some prompts have more than one part.
- **Gather details and data.** Write down any values, assumptions, or variables provided in the prompt.

As you write . . .

- **Build your solution.** Respond to each part of the prompt. Jot down formulas or equations and sketch brief diagrams if they will help solve the problem. Make the necessary calculations to get an answer and show all your work.

After you've written a first draft . . .

- **Improve your response.** Reread the prompt after you do your calculations. If the problem has more than one part, be sure you have answered every part. Work the problem in another way to check that your solution is correct.
- **Check for conventions.** Check your solution for errors in punctuation, capitalization, spelling, and grammar.
- **Prepare a final copy.** Make a neat copy of your solution.

Writing in Math

Response to a Math Prompt

The following math prompt contains more than one part. The writer provides a solution using words, numbers, and a diagram.

> What is the probability of getting a sum of seven on two dice? First explain what is meant by probability and then solve the problem.

Probability

Probability refers to the number of times the desired result occurs out of the total number of possible outcomes. This problem asks for the number of ways to get a sum of seven on two dice out of all of the possibilities when we roll two dice.

To solve this problem, I need to know the total possible results when throwing two dice (first number indicates result on first die and second number is result on second die):

1,1	1,2	1,3	1,4	1,5	(1,6)
2,1	2,2	2,3	2,4	(2,5)	2,6
3,1	3,2	3,3	(3,4)	3,5	3,6
4,1	4,2	(4,3)	4,4	4,5	4,6
5,1	(5,2)	5,3	5,4	5,5	5,6
(6,1)	6,2	6,3	6,4	6,5	6,6

This gives thirty-six possible results when throwing two dice. Looking at all of the possibilities, there are only six ways to get a sum of seven: 1+6, 2+5, 3+4, 4+3, 5+2, and 6+1. Therefore, the probability of getting a sum of seven would be 1 to 6: $\frac{sum}{total} = \frac{6}{36} = \frac{1}{6}$.

Try It!

Find a math prompt and write a response. Choose a practice prompt from your textbook or one recommended by your teacher. Follow the guidelines on page **518**.

Other Forms of Writing in Math

Definition
Calculus—Write a detailed expository paragraph defining a vector and explaining its function in math.

Narrative
Any Math—Tell about a time you couldn't understand a mathematical principle and how you finally found a way to make it clear.

Compare and Contrast
Algebra—Compare and contrast real numbers and imaginary numbers. Include descriptions, properties, and functions.

Position Paper
Any Math—Defend or oppose the requirement of three years of math to get into college.

Process
Geometry—Explain the process you would use to figure the number of bricks you would need to build a wall around your backyard.

Research
Statistics—Calculate the probability of your favorite baseball team going to the World Series this year. Figure in the statistics of past seasons and each player's performance numbers, along with variables such as injuries, possible trades, and so on.

Writing in the Applied Sciences

Thoughtful logic is at the heart of all scientific thinking and writing. Let's say you need to replace a light switch. You ask questions about what you need to do, and then you search for answers. Whether you go online, read a manual, or ask for advice, in the hands-on world of applied science, it is critical to know every step. Your safety may be at stake. Whenever you are asked to explain something, focus on being clear and complete.

In this chapter, you will learn about essays of explanation and letters of complaint. Apply the solid logic of science and the clarity of good research to all your writing.

- **Writing Guidelines: Explanatory Essay**
- **Writing Guidelines: Career Review**
- **Writing Guidelines: Response to a Prompt**
- **Other Forms of Practical Writing**

"Knowledge is of two kinds. We know a subject ourselves, or we know where we can find information upon it."

—Dr. Samuel Johnson

Writing Guidelines Explanatory Essay

An explanatory essay states a thesis and then provides details that clarify and explain the position given.

Prewriting

- **Select a topic.** If your teacher does not assign a specific topic, review your notes, manual, or textbook for ideas. For example, in a metals fabrication class, you might explain why it is important to prevent electrode contamination.
- **Gather details.** Gather relevant and substantial evidence from a variety of primary and secondary sources and perspectives. Use a graphic organizer to help you arrange your supporting evidence.
- **Plan and organize.** Decide in which order to present your support points. How are they related? Decide on a pattern for moving smoothly from one topic to the next.

Drafting

- **Connect your ideas.** Identify your topic and provide the thesis statement in your introduction. Then present each point, covering one completely and relating it to the controlling idea before moving on to the next. Summarize the main ideas in your conclusion.

Revising

- **Improve your writing.** Examine your work for *focus and coherence, organization, development of ideas,* and *voice.* Rework any ideas that are irrelevant or incomplete. Rearrange words, phrases, and sentences to improve clarity and flow.

Editing

- **Edit for conventions.** Check for a variety of sentence structures. Correct errors in grammar, mechanics, and spelling.
- **Make a neat final copy.**

Try It!

Use the directions above to write an essay of explanation. Select and explain one aspect of a topic.

Explanatory Essay

For her nutrition class, Hanae explained the dangers of a high-protein diet.

The **introduction** identifies the topic and leads to the thesis statement (underlined).

The **middle** addresses the counter-argument and gives reasons that support the thesis.

The **conclusion** wraps up and makes a final statement.

More Than Weight Loss with High-Protein Diets

High-protein diets, which emphasize meat, eggs, seafood, and cheese, have become popular. <u>While this type of diet produces quick weight loss, research shows its dangers far outweigh the benefits.</u>

Many people cite high-protein diets as the most successful method of achieving optimum weight, particularly for those who have a history of struggling with weight loss. However, a 1988 Surgeon General publication called "Nutrition and Health in the United States" discouraged high-protein diets because of the high levels of protein and saturated fat consumed. When carbohydrates needed for complete synthesis of fat are eliminated from the diet, the body faces a challenge: how to burn excess amounts of fat.

Fewer carbohydrates create problems. Fewer high-fiber plant foods combined with an increase in high-fat foods means increased cholesterol levels. Without the high-fiber plant foods, potassium, calcium, and magnesium are reduced and sodium levels rise, increasing the risk of high blood pressure that can lead to heart disease or a stroke. With fewer carbohydrates to help retain body fluids, the body risks dehydration. That strains the kidneys. When excess protein accumulates in the kidneys and is not adequately diluted, a person may develop kidney stones, kidney failure, or gallbladder disease.

The American Heart Association links high-protein diets and osteoporosis, rheumatoid arthritis, and even multiple sclerosis. Most high-protein foods are acidic. The body tries to maintain its alkaline pH balance. To do so, it dissolves bone into phosphorus and calcium to counteract the acid. This bone degeneration is the first step to osteoporosis. The kidneys excrete this bone material, potentially resulting in kidney stones.

Any weight-loss program should improve rather than jeopardize an individual's health. The best diet strategy is to eat a healthy diet, balance protein and carbohydrates, and increase physical activity.

Writing Guidelines Career Review

A career review is a specific type of essay of analysis. It includes the job's requirements, such as education or physical stamina, future advancement possibilities, benefits, and salary.

Prewriting

- **Present your topic.** Explain which job you are analyzing. Remember your purpose. What important factors do you need to consider?
- **Gather details.** Include relevant evidence and details about the requirements, benefits, and future of the job, mentioning anything that makes the career stand out or fall short.
- **Plan and organize.** Cover each area of the career point by point before moving on to the next.

Drafting

- **Include an engaging introduction.** Explain why you are examining this topic and clearly state your thesis.
- **Write the middle.** Analyze the different areas of the topic, point by point.
- **End with an effective conclusion.** Wrap up by sharing one final insight about the topic.

Revising

- **Improve your writing.** Revise for *focus and coherence, organization, development of ideas,* and *voice.* Look for transitions and smooth sentences. Let your interest in the topic show through.

Editing

- **Check for conventions.** Look for and correct any errors in grammar, mechanics, and spelling.
- **Make a clean final copy.**

Writing in the Applied Sciences

Career Review

Jorge's careers class explores the duties and requirements of different careers. Here is his review of a radiology technician career.

> ### Becoming a Radiology Technician
>
> With the aging population in this country, the number of health-related jobs is growing. A top job of the future is that of a radiology technician.
>
> Radiology technicians, or radiographers, have a variety of duties. First of all, they need people skills, as they prepare people for X-rays and explain procedures. If diagnostic dye is used, sometimes technicians must mix the contrast medium as well as administer it to the patient. To administer X-rays, technicians set the level of radiation and the right distance between the machine and the area to be X-rayed. Fine adjustments create the correct angle, density, and contrast for the film to show clear images that allow doctors to make exact diagnoses.
>
> Technical training is required. High school courses in science and computers are a good start. Specialized training is offered in technical schools, colleges, hospitals, and the military. Two-year associate degrees and bachelor's degrees are favored by hospitals. Teaching and administrative positions require four-year degrees.
>
> Most jobs are in hospitals, although positions are also available in doctors' offices, diagnostic imaging centers, and outpatient care centers. Technicians work 40 hours or more per week. In 2007, salaries for radiographers varied between $38,000 to $55,000, but some earn as much as $72,000. Those trained in more complex radiological imaging, such as CT scans and MRI's, find the highest paying jobs.
>
> In summary, the job of radiology technician appears to be interesting, challenging, and important. It's clear that this is a promising career that can make a difference.

The introduction explains the topic.

The middle covers different aspects of the job.

The conclusion offers a summary and a final insight.

Try It!

Select a job or career area and write an analysis of it. Include as much detail as you can to describe the job and give an opinion about it.

Writing Guidelines Response to a Prompt

Before you write . . .

- **Know your time limit.** Set limits for yourself to allow time for prewriting, writing, and revising.
- **Examine the prompt.** Look for key words that will help you determine the following elements:
  - **Subject** What is the topic of your writing?
  - **Purpose** Will you explain, inform, analyze, or persuade?
  - **Focus** What aspect of the subject should you examine?
  - **Form** How will you format your response? As an essay? A letter? A poem? A story?
- **Plan your response.** Write your thesis or opinion statement and use a brief outline or graphic organizer.

As you write . . .

- **Write an effective introduction.** Use a hook to grab your reader's attention. Then introduce your topic and include your thesis statement.
- **Develop the middle.** Develop a clear topic sentence for each paragraph. Support each main point with details, including examples and paraphrases. If you are allowed to look at notes or texts, include quotations and statistics.
- **Write a strong conclusion.** Restate your thesis and offer a final thought. If you are writing a persuasive piece, include a call to action.

After you've written a first draft . . .

- **Read through your work.** Add, cut, or move your details to make your work stronger. Be aware of any time limitation, making the most necessary changes first.
- **Check for conventions.** Correct any errors you find.

Response to a Prompt

Teresa wrote a response to the following prompt in her life-skills class.

> Your landlord has neglected to repair a leaky faucet, a running toilet, and a broken light fixture in your apartment. Write a letter of complaint convincing the landlord to take care of the problems.

The introduction opens with a positive statement and the thesis (underlined).

The middle gives the main points as topic sentences.

The conclusion restates the thesis (underlined) and adds a final statement.

Dear Mr. Miller:

First of all, I want to tell you I enjoy my apartment. It's so spacious, and the neighbors are great. However, I still have the leaking faucet and running toilet in the bathroom and the broken light fixture in the kitchen. Although I mentioned them when I first moved in last month, nothing has been done to fix them. <u>I must complain about the slow response and ask you again to please repair these problems.</u>

The water situation is most serious. The constant dripping is annoying and expensive. I checked my bill with my neighbors, and neither of their bills is as high as mine. They don't have leaks.

The broken kitchen light fixture is also a problem. Without a window in the kitchen, the main fixture is my only light except the stove hood, and it does not light the sink area.

<u>Please take care of these problems.</u> They represent both cost and possible safety issues. Because they were noted as needing fixing on my initial move-in sheet, I ask you to fix them as soon as possible. I do not want to have to contact the Tenants' Union for assistance.

Thank you for your attention to this matter.

Sincerely,

Teresa Hernandez

Try It!

Write a letter of complaint for a real or fictitious situation.

Other Forms of Practical Writing

Process Essay
Architectural Drafting—Explain how to measure a kitchen for new cabinets and countertops.

Essay of Classification
Textile Arts—Explain the different types of needlework and give an example of each.

Essay of Analysis
Auto Mechanics—Analyze the pros and cons of a hydrogen-powered engine and consider its current feasibility for the mass market.

Essay of Explanation
Home Decorating—Explain the various uses of ceramic tile in the home and how to choose the right type of tile for each situation.

Problem-Solution Essay
Advanced Metals Fabrication—Explain the problems encountered by using a contaminated electrode in welding and explain how to repair it.

Persuasive Essay
Health—Write a paper that persuades people they do not need to fear or avoid those who are HIV positive.

Comparison-Contrast Essay
Classic Cooking—Compare the cuisines of Italy and Greece and explain reasons for the differences and similarities.

Writing in the Arts

Archaeologists have found that even before there was language, there was art. Cave paintings told stories and related experiences. But art is more than basic communication. Mahatma Gandhi once said, "True art takes note not merely of form but also of what lies behind." Art is not just visual or aural; it is cerebral, stirring great thoughts as well as deep emotions—thoughts and emotions you can explore and write about.

When you write about art, you can examine your reactions to it and analyze why a piece affects you the way it does. You can examine art's effect on history or its reflection of a particular time period. In this chapter you will learn to respond to art, using your thoughts and emotions to analyze and critique. In writing about art, you will soon gain a better understanding of yourself and others.

- **Writing Guidelines: Research Report**
- **Multimedia Presentation**
- **Writing Guidelines: Performance Review**
- **Writing Guidelines: Response to an Art Prompt**

"I try to apply colors like words that shape poems, like notes that shape music."

—Joan Miro

Writing Guidelines Research Report

You may be asked to write a research report in your art or music class. You may decide to write about a famous painter or analyze a trend in music. The following guidelines will help you create a research report.

Prewriting

- **Choose a subject.** Alone or with other students, brainstorm about your subject. List artists, musical trends, or other ideas that interest you.
- **Look at the list** and narrow down a topic. Ask other students for their ideas about the best approach to your subject.
- **Formulate a research question.** Think about how you will approach your topic. Then phrase that approach as a question to guide your research.
- **Conduct research** about the subject. Check school or public library catalogs for books, look through magazines, and explore Web sites.
- **Explore and synthesize your research materials.** Determine the major theories each source offers regarding your research question. Distinguish these theories from the evidence that supports them (facts, quotations from experts, and so on), summarizing ideas in your notes.
- **Write a thesis statement.** Review your research notes. Then write a thesis statement that clearly identifies the specific topic and focus for your research paper.
- **Plan and organize.** Outline your paper, putting details in the most appropriate order—for example, you may put key points in spatial order, chronological order, or order of importance.
- **Make a revision plan.** To help guide and evaluate your research and writing, write a list of things to look for when you revise your paper.

Drafting

- **Connect your ideas.** Introduce your topic, give background information, and state your thesis.
- **In the middle paragraphs,** support the thesis statement with specific details. Include any counter-arguments or different points of view about your subject. Develop your ideas into a report that is of sufficient length and complexity to address the topic adequately. Use a style guide to ensure that you cite sources and format your paper correctly.
- **Demonstrate good writing skills.** Even in a research report, the way in which you convey information matters. Employing effective rhetorical strategies will strengthen your thesis by emphasizing important supporting points. For a list of some strategies, see pages **634–635**. Consider using strategies like analogy and parallelism, which are appropriate for research writing.
- **In your conclusion,** summarize what you have learned or what you have to say about the subject.

Writing in the Arts

Research Report

You can learn about the arts by studying how different artistic expressions reflect different periods and events throughout history. Tamika Sanders had been studying the migration of African Americans to the northern United States in her history class. She discovered that African American painter Jacob Lawrence had created a series of paintings called *The Great Migration,* and she decided, with permission from both teachers, to make that the topic of a report for her art and history classes.

Tamika Sanders
Mrs. Southwell
History
May 12, 2011

The Great Migration

Painter Jacob Lawrence used art to tell stories—usually through a series of paintings on panels. He became famous for his historical painting series on Harriet Tubman, John Brown, and Frederick Douglass. <u>In the *Migration* series, Lawrence used the panel technique to capture the story of African Americans moving north after the turn of the century.</u>

Lawrence began his career as an artist during the Depression in the Works Progress Administration's federal arts program. His style of telling stories through a series of paintings was influenced by African storytelling traditions, Mexican mural painters, and popular movies. He often planned his series by using a storyboard, in the same way a writer might plan the sequence of events in a film ("Jacob Lawrence").

The *Migration* series was inspired by the people Lawrence grew up with in Harlem, New York. As one writer put it, "Harlem was his universe and his university" (Nesbett and Dubois 67). Many people in his community had moved from the rural South to the urban North during and after World War I. In fact, the Great Migration was the largest movement of black people since Africans had been brought to the Americas and enslaved. Arriving in the North, many blacks found new educational opportunities and more jobs, but often experienced new forms of discrimination and injustice as well ("Great Migration").

The **introduction** presents the thesis statement of the report (underlined).

By likening Lawrence's storyboard to a filmmaker's, the writer uses the rhetorical device analogy to support her thesis.

The **middle** of the report discusses Lawrence's background and the influences that affected his art.

The paintings cover all aspects of the move north. The first panel shows a crowd of stylized figures moving forward toward abstract railroad departure gates labeled "Chicago," "New York," and "St. Louis." Another painting in the series shows a quick, vivid arc of railroad track reflecting the industry where many of the immigrants found employment. Yet another shows well-dressed, haughty, long-time Northern black residents, who often looked down on the poorly dressed, new rural immigrants. Later paintings show the experience of the migrants in the North with images of industry and life in urban settings.

To tell this story in paintings, Lawrence used bold colors, the geometric forms and shapes of his urban home, and intentionally distorted figures to illustrate the universal nature of the migrants' experiences. As in many of his other series paintings, Lawrence repeated motifs, shapes, and words. In the *Migration* series, for example, he repeated the images of a single large spike, chain links, hands, and a hammer to show the continuity in the lives, experiences, and struggles of African American migrants ("Jacob Lawrence").

The *Migration* series made Lawrence commercially successful, but to him, telling the story and the history was most important. In an article written just after Lawrence died, the writer said: "It was also at heart about telling universal stories bigger than any particular man or movement. It illustrated dignity through struggle" (Kimmelman).

Works Cited

The purpose of a works-cited page is to let your reader find and read the sources you used to write your paper. The examples on this page show the standard MLA format for common types of sources. This format is published by the Modern Language Association and is used by many schools, universities, and students, teachers, and publishers. Also see the guidelines on pages **451–458.**

Book
Over the Line: The Art and Life of Jacob Lawrence. Ed. Peter T. Nesbett and Michelle Dubois. Seattle: U of Washington P, 2001. Print.

Encyclopedia
"Great Migration." *Encyclopaedia Britannica Online.* Encyclopaedia Britannica, n.d. Web. 5 Apr. 2011.

Magazine
"Jacob Lawrence: 'Foremost Black Artist.'" *Columns: The University of Washington Alumni Magazine* Sept. 2000. 32. Print.

Internet
Jacob Lawrence: Exploring Stories. Whitney Museum of American Art. 27 Oct. 2009. Web. 9 May 2011.

Newspaper
Kimmelman, Michael. "An Appreciation: Simplicity Can Be Complicated; Jacob Lawrence Found Emotional Authenticity in Art and Life." *New York Times* 14 June 2000: E1. Print.

Interview
Lawrence, Jacob. Interview by Carroll Greene. *Oral History Interviews.* Archives of American Art, Smithsonian Institution. Oct. 1968. Web. 24 Apr. 2011.

Try It!
Work with a partner and write citations for three resources found in your classroom or library. Follow the MLA style that you see in the examples above.

TEKS 12.21B, 12.21C, 12.22A–C, 12.23C, 12.23D
ELPS 1B, 5C, 5D

Revising Improving Your Writing

After you have written a first draft, put it aside for a while to get a fresh perspective. Then revise your work. Use this checklist to help guide your revision.

Focus and Coherence

_____ 1. Have I created a clear thesis?
_____ 2. Have I maintained my focus and not drifted off into other topics?
_____ 3. Do I need to modify the research question?

Organization

_____ 4. Is my writing logically organized to support central ideas, themes, and concepts?
_____ 5. Have I cited appropriate sources using the correct style?

Development of Ideas

_____ 6. Are the ideas thoroughly developed and supported with details?
_____ 7. Have I used strong evidence to create a cogent argument?
_____ 8. Have I incorporated complexities and discrepancies in information?
_____ 9. Have I anticipated and refuted counterarguments?

Voice

_____ 10. Does my voice sound authentic and original?
_____ 11. Do I sound knowledgeable and confident?

Conventions

_____ 12. Have I corrected any errors in grammar, mechanics (capitalization and punctuation), and spelling?

Try It!

Work with a partner as you revise some of your writing about art. Read portions of the work to your partner and use the checklist to make notes about revisions you would like to incorporate into your work.

Multimedia Presentation

We do not learn only by reading. In the same way, we are not limited to sharing what we have learned in just a written report. One way to share information and ideas about your subject is to adapt your report into a multimedia presentation. As a result of this process, you will probably come away with a deeper understanding of your subject, and your audience will be given several different ways to learn about your subject.

Much of what we see and learn comes to us through a variety of media: video, sound, photographs, and graphics. You have probably experienced many multimedia presentations through movies, television, and the Internet. A multimedia presentation integrates media elements. You have a lot of flexibility with a multimedia presentation. Using different media to communicate your ideas can enrich your presentation.

Planning Your Multimedia Presentation

As you begin to plan your presentation, consider the following guidelines.

- **Who is your audience?** Who do you think will be most interested in your subject? Do you want to show your presentation only to your classmates and teacher, or is there a broader audience that might enjoy and learn from it? What is the best way to adapt your report?
- **What is your purpose?** Do you want to entertain, persuade, or inform your audience?
- **What forms of media will you use?** What can you communicate with a multimedia presentation that cannot be explained with text alone? For example, if you decide you want to focus on the historical background of Jacob Lawrence's *Migration* series, you might want to find historical photographs and develop graphics such as maps and charts. If you decide to focus primarily on the paintings, you might create a slide show of the *Migration* series. A number of choices are available.
- **What form will your presentation take?** Will it be a straightforward, expository presentation of facts? Perhaps you will create a narrative or even fictional account of the events and their effect on individuals. Perhaps you will create a montage showing different points of view.

Pre-Production

Take your time to plan your multimedia presentation. You have many options and more flexibility than with your written report. The choice of media should be connected to the content you are trying to adapt. For example, in the sample paper, the descriptions of Jacob Lawrence's paintings are vivid. In a multimedia presentation about the artist's work, the writer might want to find copies of these paintings to project on slides with a narrative voice-over. Additional research will help the writer find historical photographs of Jacob Lawrence in Harlem during the 1920s and 1930s, and so on. For background music, the writer might find recordings of popular songs from the era. Recorded interviews with the subjects might also be available. (Such recordings do exist for Jacob Lawrence.)

Create an Outline for Your Presentation

Think about the best way to organize the information into a logical pattern for your presentation. Reread your finished report. What key ideas and details do you want to share with your audience? Do you want to present the information chronologically, spatially, or in another way? Using a storyboard will help you correctly sequence the information in your report and develop a script. Remember that a strong introduction and conclusion will add depth to your presentation.

Choose the Media

Your multimedia adaptation should combine at least three forms of media. These include (but are not limited to) the following:

- **Graphics** — maps, graphs, charts, diagrams
- **Audio** — narration, music, sound effects
- **Video** — historical footage, filmed narration
- **Photographs** — digital (or developed photos on CDs)
- **Slides** — combination of images for projection

Gathering Your Resources and Tools

You will need to use a range of equipment and software to create and display your presentation. To find the right equipment, speak with your teacher or librarian. Your school may have a media center, which would give you access to recording equipment, video cameras and video editing software, presentation software, projectors, and other equipment.

Try It!

Visit your school library or media center to find out what kinds of resources are available for a multimedia presentation.

Writing in the Arts

Production

When you have created your outline, developed a script, and gathered the materials and tools you need, it is time to put together the audio and visual portions of your presentation. To build a soundtrack and create a visual production, you can begin by doing some of the following.

Audio

- **Create voice-over narration.** You might read aloud some or all of your paper.
- **Assemble recorded voices.** Speaking from different points of view and offering different perspectives on the historical past helps the audience understand the presentation.
- **Find and/or record music.** This can be music from the historical period or music you have written and/or recorded yourself.
- **Include various sound effects.** Experiment with ways to make unusual sounds with ordinary objects.

Visuals

- **Videorecord.** You will need to consider the number and types of shots (such as wide angles and close-ups).
- **Use video-editing software.** Edit footage to make it interesting.
- **Use graphics or presentation software.** Graphics help to visually communicate ideas or concepts.
- **Incorporate photographs and artworks.** Place them in the video or display them separately.
- **Write captions.** Keep them brief, but informative.

Try It!

Discuss the elements of your presentation with a partner. Help each other with the organization and elements of your presentations. Try to eliminate ideas that are distracting or that might be difficult to present. Assist each other in integrating the media smoothly.

Multimedia Report Traits Checklist

Revising Checklist

Focus and Coherence

_____ 1. Have I effectively adapted the report for my audience?
_____ 2. Have I maintained a clear thesis?
_____ 3. Do a strong introduction and conclusion add depth to the presentation?
_____ 4. Do all the elements of my presentation work together?

Organization

_____ 5. Have I followed my outline?
_____ 6. Is my presentation logically organized and easy to follow?

Development of Ideas

_____ 7. Are the ideas thoroughly developed with specific details?
_____ 8. Have I effectively used audio and visual elements to communicate my ideas?

Voice

_____ 9. Is my presentation engaging from start to finish?
_____ 10. Have I expressed my individuality or a unique perspective?

Conventions

_____ 11. Have I corrected any errors in grammar that might disrupt the fluency of my presentation?

Try It!

Rehearse your presentation several times to make sure that all the elements work together. Delete anything that might be distracting.

ELPS 5G

Writing Guidelines Performance Review

You may be asked to write about the arts by reviewing a specific performance. On the other hand, you may enjoy a performance so much that you want to share your thoughts with others through a blog, on your own Web site, or in a letter.

While this type of writing is more informal, or personal, than most academic writing, you should follow basic writing guidelines. A reader will respect your evaluation if your writing shows clarity and insight, so be sure to maintain your focus throughout the review.

Prewriting

- **Focus on what you want to say.**
- **Make notes** on your impressions of an art show or a concert.
- **Write a thesis statement.** Review your notes and state your focus.
- **Plan and organize.** Outline key points you want to make in your review.

Drafting

- **Write freely,** always keeping your main idea in mind. Use your outline as a basic drafting guide.
- **Use examples to support your points.** Whether the reader agrees with you or not, supporting your point of view with solid evidence is important and will gain the reader's respect.
- **Keep your audience in mind** in terms of what you need to explain.
- **Write a strong conclusion.** Sum up why the topic is important enough for you to write about.

Revising

- **Improve your writing.** Check your *development of ideas, organization,* and *voice*. Ask these questions: *Have I created a clear thesis? Have I supported it with a variety of details? Are my details in the best order? Do I sound knowledgeable?*
- **Improve your style.** Check that you have used a variety of sentence structures. Ask these questions: *Does my voice sound authentic and original? Have I explained any technical terms?*

Editing

- **Check for conventions.** Look for errors in grammar, mechanics (punctuation and capitalization), and spelling.
- **Prepare your final copy.** Proofread your review before sharing it.

Performance Review

Greg's school newspaper asked him to write a review about an African dance and drum troupe for the print edition of the paper and for the Web site. Greg took notes at the concert and then wrote about what he learned and about his reaction to the performance itself.

The **introduction** explains who the group is and gives the writer's reaction to the performance.

The **middle** describes the performers, the drums, and the sounds of the event.

The **conclusion** invites readers to discover the group and learn about the special drums.

Feel the Rhythm

Now I know exactly what people mean when they say "you have to feel the rhythm." The pounding rhythm of beating drums and stomping feet went right down to my bones at the performance by African Steps. This dance and drum troupe from King High School shook the rafters in our auditorium during their Black History Month appearance on February 15.

African Steps weaves music and dance together seamlessly. The dancers wear ankle bells and shell bracelets so their movements become part of the pounding rhythm. The drummers' hands dance across the skins, flowing into the choreography.

If you think of drums as simple instruments, you would change your mind after hearing the complex interplay of the many different styles of drums African Steps uses—from pounding bass rhythms to more subtle, almost melodic tones. In introducing themselves, the drummers explained each drum's role. The djembe, for example, has a wide range of sound. It's a hollow drum made from a tree trunk and covered with goatskin. The drum hangs on straps from the musician's shoulders. It's played with the hands only. The kpanlogo gives a smooth but earthy tone.

The powerful, joyful rhythms had even the teachers in the back of the auditorium tapping their feet and swaying. This performance, and the explanations the dancers and drummers gave about the different pieces they performed, helped me appreciate African culture through music and dance. Don't miss the chance to share the experience.

Writing in the Arts

Writing Guidelines Response to an Art Prompt

You may be asked to write a short essay in response to a prompt about art or music as a class assignment or as part of a test. Responding to a prompt allows you to express what you have learned about a specific work of art or style of music. Here are guidelines for responding to an art prompt.

Before you write . . .

- **Understand the prompt.** Read the prompt and focus on what you are asked to do. Should you explain, compare, describe, or persuade?
- **Gather your details.** If permitted, review your notes and research materials. Highlight or jot down important details. Note sources for quotations or facts. If you aren't permitted to use notes or research materials, jot down key facts that you remember about the topic.
- **Organize your details.** Check the prompt for clues that will help you organize your response. For example, if the prompt asks you to describe the jazz classic *Take Five* and discuss how improvisation reshapes the music, you might begin with a general description of the piece and then discuss specific musical themes that serve as springboards for improvisation. You could mention how specific instruments and performers develop the basic themes in creative variations.

As you write . . .

- **Write freely.** Use your notes as a guide and try to include all your main ideas. Many short responses are just one paragraph long. If your prompt calls for an essay, use a new paragraph for each main point.

After you've written a first draft . . .

- **Improve your writing.** Read your draft and cut any details that don't fit the prompt. Add information that will clarify your ideas or help answer the prompt. Make your response as complete as possible.
- **Improve your style.** Make sure that you use a variety of sentence structures and that your response reads smoothly.
- **Check for conventions.** Look for errors in grammar, mechanics, and spelling.

Response to an Art Prompt

In a two-part response, Jasmine discusses the style of artist Paul Cezanne.

Answer the following questions in one or more paragraphs: (1) Why did some consider Cezanne's work primitive? (2) Is the term appropriate in referring to Cezanne's work?

Response #1

Paul Cezanne, a nineteenth-century French painter, is sometimes called the father of modern art. At the time, both his critics and his supporters often used the term "primitive" to refer to his work.

Cezanne's use of pure color with simple brushstrokes and heavy, fluid pigments led many to underestimate his technical skills as an artist and compare his works to those of untutored, "primitive" artists. In addition, his figures were often distorted as he experimented with ways to put down on canvas what his eye was seeing. This approach was often misinterpreted as that of an artist lacking in basic drawing skills. He was obsessed with form and technique rather than with subject. As a result, the public often didn't understand his paintings.

Response #2

Cezanne's early experimental paintings may be called primitive in technique, but as he came closer and closer to putting down on canvas what he saw in nature, he began to use space, mass, and color in a very sophisticated way. Some of his early works, full of emotional intensity, laid the groundwork for the expressionist movement. By the late 1900s, his paintings became more abstract, with buildings and figures evolving into geometric forms. These works set the stage for cubism.

First, the writer explains who Cezanne was and what factors led some to define his work as primitive.

Then the writer gives specific examples.

Next, the writer argues that the term "primitive" isn't appropriate for most of the artist's work.

Try It!

Respond to a short-essay prompt your teacher will supply about a topic you are studying. Write a one- or two-paragraph answer.

Writing in the Workplace

In the workplace, every bit of correspondence reflects the business and the professionalism of the people working there. Despite the changing landscape of business communication, good writing skills remain the bedrock for career success. Whatever the task—writing an e-mail message, a memo, a report, a presentation, or a proposal—it is important to communicate clearly and quickly in this environment.

Even if you remain a student for several more years, you will find yourself using forms of workplace communication. You will write letters and e-mail messages; you will develop multimedia presentations; you will create your résumé. In this chapter, some of the many forms of business writing are covered, along with tips and techniques to strengthen your skills.

- **Writing Guidelines: Business Letters**
- **Writing Guidelines: Résumé**
- **Writing Guidelines: Memo**
- **Writing Guidelines: Job Application**
- **Writing Guidelines: Meeting Agenda**

"In business you get what you want by giving other people what they want."
—Alice Foote MacDougall

Writing Guidelines Business Letters

Writers use business letters to request information, apply for a job, or file a complaint. The basic format of an effective letter is similar whether it is sent through the regular mail or delivered via e-mail.

- The **heading** includes the writer's complete address, either on company stationery, in a computer template, or typed out manually. The heading also includes the day, month, and year. If the address is part of the letterhead, place only the date in the upper left corner.

- The **inside address** includes the recipient's name and complete address. If you are not sure whom should receive the letter or how to correctly spell someone's name, you can call the company to ask. If a person's title is a single word or is very short, include it on the same line as the name, preceded by a comma. If the title is longer, put it on a separate line under the name.

- The **salutation** is the greeting. For business letters, use a colon following the recipient's name, not a comma. Use *Mr.* or *Ms.* followed by the person's last name, unless you happen to be well acquainted with the person. Do not guess at whether a woman prefers *Miss* or *Mrs.* If the person's gender is not obvious from the name, one acceptable solution is to use the full name in the salutation. For example, *Dear Pat Johnson.* If you don't know the name of the person who will read your letter, use a salutation such as one of these:

  - Dear Manager:
  - Dear Sir or Madam:
  - Attention: Human Resources Department
  - Attention: Personnel Director

- The **body** is the main part of the letter. It is organized into three parts. The beginning states why you are writing, the middle provides the needed facts and details, and the ending focuses on what should happen next. In a business letter, double-space between the paragraphs; do not indent. If the letter is longer than one page, on subsequent pages put the reader's name at the top left, the page number in the center, and the date at the right margin.

- The **complimentary closing** ends the message. Use *Sincerely* or *Yours truly*—followed by a comma. Capitalize only the first word.

- The **signature** makes the letter official. Leave four blank lines between the complimentary closing and your typed name. Write your signature in that space.

- The **notes** tell who authored the letter (uppercase initials and a colon), who typed the letter (lowercase initials), who received a copy (after *cc:*), and what enclosures are included (after *Enclosure* or *Encl:*).

Writing in the Workplace

Letter of Inquiry or Request

Plains Union High School offers advertising space in the programs they produce for the school's concerts and plays. Mandisa Kwafume, student liaison for the parents' Band Boosters Club, wrote this letter to solicit more advertising revenue from the business community. (The inside address would change depending on the business owner being contacted.)

Heading

Plains Union High School Band Boosters Club
676 Highway R
Dry Plains, TX 78112
October 6, 2011

Four to Seven Spaces

Inside address

Mr. Rex Neinheus
Area Aquatics
1322 Main Street
Dry Plains, TX 78113

Double Space

Salutation

Dear Mr. Neinheus:

Double Space

Body
The writer explains why she is writing, provides needed details, and suggests a next step.

I am writing on behalf of the Plains Union High School Band Boosters Club. Perhaps you are aware that the high school presents several concerts and plays throughout the year. Did you also know that many local businesses advertise in the programs for these events? Here is your opportunity to join them.

Purchasing an ad in one or more of the programs is a smart business move. The performers' family and friends—most of whom live in the area—read the programs and notice the businesses advertising in them. They'll make an effort to patronize a business that supports the school through advertising.

Enclosed you will find an insertion order for any size advertisement you care to place. You may provide camera-ready copy, or we will be happy to design something for you. Please be sure to indicate which program(s) you prefer for your ad; a checklist is provided.

Thank you for supporting the arts at Plains Union High School.

Double Space

Complimentary closing

Sincerely,

Signature

Mandisa Kwafume   *Four Spaces*

Mandisa Kwafume, Student Liaison

Double Space

**Initials
Copies
Enclosure**

MK: jb
cc: Ms. Felicia Goodman, President
Encl: insertion order

Letter of Application

Lou Roberts wrote the following letter to apply for a summer science research internship position.

24 Hampshire Street
Skones, MT 59781
February 2, 2011

Brian Allman, Director
Office of Biomedical Studies
Medical College of Butte
540 Kings Row
Butte, MT 59702

Dear Mr. Allman:

Please find enclosed my official application for your High School Summer Research Internship Program, as well as the names and contact information for two references. I believe I am qualified for this internship and would love the opportunity to work with the mentors at the Medical College of Butte. Allow me to outline my research interests and career goals.

My interest in biochemistry and cell biology began in my high school science classes this past year. In these classes, we planned and executed several research experiments related to allergic reactions. Investigating the physiology behind these "overreactions" of the immune system proved fascinating.

This internship would be the first step in my ultimate goal of becoming an immunologist. I want to help people who suffer from allergies (myself included) to manage and treat their conditions. Although this career demands intensive training, I can't think of a better introduction to it than this internship.

If you have any specific questions for me, please e-mail me at lrbts@email.net or call me at (406) 555-0515. Thank you for your consideration, and I hope to hear from you soon.

Sincerely,

Lou Roberts

Lou Roberts

Encl: application, references

The opening introduces the writer as well as the purpose of the letter.

The middle paragraphs discuss background, qualifications, and long-range goals.

The closing adds information and thanks the reader.

Writing in the Workplace

Preparing a Letter for Mailing

Letters sent through the mail will get to their destinations faster if they are properly addressed and stamped. Always include a ZIP code.

Addressing the Envelope

Place the return address in the upper left corner, the destination address in the center, and the correct postage in the upper right corner. Some word processing programs will automatically format the return and destination addresses.

LOU ROBERTS
24 HAMPSHIRE STREET
SKONES MT 59781

MR BRIAN ALLMAN
OFFICE OF BIOMEDICAL STUDIES
MEDICAL COLLEGE OF BUTTE
540 KINGS ROW
BUTTE MT 59702

There are two acceptable forms for addressing the envelope: the traditional form and the form preferred by the postal service.

Traditional Form	**Postal Service Form**
Liam O'Donnell	LIAM O'DONNELL
Macalester College	MACALESTER COLLEGE
Admissions Office	ADMISSIONS OFFICE
1600 N. Grand Ave.	1600 N GRAND AVE
St. Paul, MN 55105-1801	ST PAUL MN 55105-1801

Following U.S. Postal Service Guidelines

The official United States Postal Service guidelines are available at any post office or online at www.usps.org.

- Capitalize everything in the address and leave out commas and periods.
- Use the list of common state and street abbreviations found in the *National ZIP Code Directory* or on page **692** of this book.
- Use numbers rather than words for numbered streets (for example, 42ND AVE or 9TH AVE NW).
- If you know the ZIP + 4 code, use it.

Writing Guidelines Résumé

The purpose of a résumé is to interest an employer so he or she will call you for an interview. Instead of simply telling about yourself in a letter, use a special résumé format to highlight your skills, knowledge, work experience, and education, especially as they relate to the position for which you are applying. Prepare a basic version of your résumé. Then, depending upon the requirements of each position, customize your objective and your abilities to match the employer's expectations.

Prewriting

- **Think about your abilities,** experiences, and accomplishments.
- **Gather details** that will create a complete picture of you. Include classes or training taken outside of school, achievements, and other experience such as volunteer work, club duties, and so on.

Drafting

- **Use a traditional résumé format** and organize the information into these parts:
  - Personal contact information
  - Objective
  - Qualifications
  - Specific work experience
  - Education
  - References (Be sure to get permission from each person you wish to use as a reference. It is a good idea to let them know each time you apply for a job so they will be prepared for a phone call.)

Revising

- **Improve your writing** by asking yourself these questions: *Have I included specific, accurate, and complete information? Have I given the most important information first? Have I used a business-like writing style? Have I used words appropriate to the reader? Have I defined any unfamiliar technical terms?*

Editing

- **Check for errors** in grammar, mechanics (punctuation and capitalization), and spelling.
- **Ask someone else** to look over your résumé as well.

Publishing

- **Use text features** such as boldface, columns, bullets, and white space to make your résumé attractive and readable.

TEKS 12.15B(i), 12.15B(ii), 12.15B(v)

Writing in the Workplace

Résumé

A strong résumé is not generic. Here is how one student presented himself in his search for summer employment on a landscaping crew.

> **Victor Rios**
> 250 Lowe Avenue • Sherwood Heights, MI 49065
> Phone 517-555-1662   E-mail vrios@themailstop.com
>
> **Objective:** Seeking full-time summer employment on a landscaping crew.
>
> **Qualifications:**
> - Experienced with landscaping materials and plants
> - Team worker
> - Fast learner
> - Good physical condition
>
> **Experience:** *May–October and winter holiday season 2010*
> Garcia's Gardens & Gifts
> Part-time yard worker and cashier. Became familiar with different kinds of plants, trees, and shrubs and their care.
>
> *October 2009 – March 2010*
> Shop A Lot supermarket
> Part-time stocker and cashier. Often worked with heavy loads.
>
> **Education:** Will graduate from Cayman High School in June; plan to attend Tuyo Community College this fall to work on a degree in horticulture.
>
> Member of my school's chapter of the National FFA Organization; assisted in yearly sale of native-species plants to raise funds for our chapter.
>
> **References:** Available upon request.

The beginning provides contact information and the objective.

The middle lists key details.

The ending notes that references are available.

Writing Guidelines Memo

Memos are short messages in which you ask and answer questions, describe procedures, give short reports, and remind others about deadlines and meetings. Memos are important to the flow of information within any organization. Many routine memos in schools and workplaces are distributed electronically, with hard copies posted on bulletin boards or sent by interoffice mail.

Prewriting

- **Consider your audience** by thinking about who will receive your memo and why.
- **Determine your purpose** and jot down your reason for writing the memo.
- **Gather necessary details** based on what your reader needs to know.

Drafting

- **Prepare the heading** by typing "Memo" and centering it. Include a heading that contains the following information:

    Date: The month, day, and year
    To: The reader's name
    From: Your first and last name (You may initial it before sending.)
    Subject: The memo's topic in a clear, simple statement

- **Organize the body** into three parts:

    Beginning: State why you are writing the memo.
    Middle: Provide all the necessary facts and details. Consider listing the most important points rather than writing them out.
    Ending: Focus on what happens next—the action or response you would like from the reader or readers.

Revising

- **Improve your writing** by asking yourself these questions related to *focus and coherence, organization, development of ideas,* and *voice*: Is my topic clear? Is my purpose obvious? Do I have an effective beginning, middle, and ending? Have I used a positive, friendly tone? Have I explained any unfamiliar terms? Does my memo read smoothly?

Editing

- **Check for conventions.** Correct any errors in grammar, mechanics (punctuation and capitalization), and spelling.
- **Prepare a final copy** of your memo and proofread it before distributing it.

Writing in the Workplace

Memo

Rey Gómez, an assistant to the personnel director, typed up this memo about his company's monthly staff improvement meetings.

The heading identifies the date, recipients, sender, and subject.

The beginning states why you are writing.

The middle shares the necessary details.

The ending makes a call for action.

Memo

Date: October 22, 2011
To: Inter-Tech Staff
From: Rey Gómez, Assistant to the Personnel Director
Subject: New Technology

Our next staff meeting will be held on Thursday, November 18, at 9:00 a.m. in the new training center.

The guest at that meeting will be Dr. G. F. Hollis, a professor at City Technical College. She will speak on the latest technology and how we can expect it to affect us and our work.

Dr. Hollis is planning a winter-term training program that will cover all facets of office technology and communication. Those attending the meeting will receive additional information on the program.

Please sign up with me before the end of the day on Tuesday, November 6, if you plan to attend the meeting.

Try It!

Draft a memo to a group of which you are a member. Follow the guidelines on the previous page and the model above.

Writing Guidelines Job Application

How to Fill Out a Job Application

To give yourself an edge in a competitive job market, it helps to make an excellent first impression by submitting a job application that is neat and complete. Applications that are incomplete or messy give a bad first impression. If you practice filling out job applications ahead of time, it will be easier when you apply for a job.

You can apply for jobs in a number of ways. Some companies require that you complete an online application; others prefer that you apply in person. Depending on the employer, you might be able to take an application home, or you might be asked to fill it in on the spot.

Before you start to fill out the form, read through it carefully. Make sure that you have all the relevant information with you. When you are filling out the form, type or print very clearly with ink, and check your details carefully in order to avoid crossing them out. Fill out all the information that is requested. If a question doesn't apply to you, write N/A (not applicable) in the space. Before you turn in the application, proofread it and make corrections as needed. Make sure that you are submitting the application to the correct person and to the correct address.

You will need to provide all or some of the following information, so make sure you have it with you if you apply in person.

- Name, birth date, address, contact information
- Social Security number
- Education attained
- Extracurricular activities
- Skills related to the position you are applying for
- Previous employer names and contact information
- References

Try It!

Pick up a job application from a prospective employer or download a blank copy of a job application form from the Internet. Then, practice filling out the application.

Writing in the Workplace

Job Application

You might be asked to fill out an application like the one below.

Print neatly. Make sure all numbers are legible.

Personal Information

Last name	First	Middle
Ruiz	Magda	A.

Date: 6-10-2011

Street address: 501 St. Francis Drive

Home phone: 555-123-4567

City, State, Zip: Rivera, Texas 76710

E-mail address: mruiz@server.net

Are you over 18 years of age? yes

Are you employed now? no

Are you legally eligible for employment in the U.S.? yes

Social Security number: 765-43-2110

Include information about your education. Some applications will ask for information about more than one school.

Education

Name and location of shool	No. of years completed	Did you graduate?	Degree or diploma
Dylan High School Rivera, Texas	4	Yes	High school diploma

Give complete information about your employment history. Start with the present or most recent employer.

Employment History

Company Name: Blossoms

Telephone: (555) 555-4321

Address: 92 S. Armijo St., Rivera, Texas

Employed (Month and Year)
From: 10/09   To: 12/10

Name of Supervisor: Marla Thomas

Hourly Rate
Start: $7.00   Last: $8.00

Job title and responsibilites: Customer assistant and cashier

Reason for leaving: Store relocated

Provide the names of people who will give you a positive recommendation.

References

Name	Phone	Business	Years Acquainted
1. Marla Thomas	555-4321	Florist	2
2. Dr. L. Imani	555-9876	Dentist	3
3. Robert Martinez	555-6589	Teacher	1
4.			
5.			

Give information about interests and skills that relate to the job.

Additional Information

Hobbies and Extracurricular Activities: soccer, mountain biking, volunteering at animal shelter

Skills: bilingual (Spanish-English), computer savvy, good with people

Specialized Training: N/A

Sign and date your application.

6-10-2011
Date

Signature: *Magda A. Ruiz*

Writing Guidelines Meeting Agenda

Conducting a Business Meeting

Running a successful business requires clear communication. Many companies have daily or weekly meetings to touch base and set priorities. You might have regular meetings to keep track of an ongoing project, or an occasional meeting about a specific situation that needs to be discussed.

Creating an Agenda

A meeting agenda provides structure and helps make a meeting more productive. An agenda has several purposes:

- It requires the leader or group to set specific goals.
- It sets clear expectations.
- It gives participants the opportunity to prepare.
- It provides a sequence for covering topics.
- It reminds participants what there is left to cover if they are running out of time.

Before the meeting, create an agenda with details about time, length, location, and those required to attend. Circulate the agenda to the attendees, inviting comments and suggestions for new topics by no later than 24 hours before the meeting.

When you receive the agenda with comments, decide how long the meeting will be, and assign time estimates to each agenda item. Then revise and redistribute the agenda.

During the meeting, use the agenda to keep the meeting on track. Adhere to the agenda, but be willing to make adjustments if necessary. Be careful not to let latecomers and others who want to monopolize the meeting interfere with the timing and focus of the agenda.

Assign someone to take minutes of the meeting. These notes can be distributed to the attendees afterwards.

Sample Agenda

As the manager of an online magazine, you decide to call a meeting to discuss a plan about attracting new subscribers.

A good meeting agenda is short and simple. The basic elements are opening and closing the meeting, reports, open discussion, and announcements. Each element is timed.

> Create a time frame for the meeting. Either assign someone to be the timekeeper, or keep track of the time yourself.

Meeting Agenda

May 9, 2011
Main Conference Room
10:00 A.M. – 11:30 A.M.
Attendees: Marketing and Customer Service employees

10:00	Welcome, Introductions (10 minutes)
10:10	Report from Jana Michaelowski (Marketing) about the new subscription campaign (20 minutes)
10:30	Report from Mark Zia (Customer Service) about current status of billing procedure (20 minutes)
10:50	Questions, comments, suggestions (25 minutes)
11:15	Announcements (10 minutes)
11:25	Decide on time and agenda for next meeting. (5 minutes)
11:30	Meeting adjourns.

> Anouncements can be about personnel, company policies, holiday closings, and so on.

Try It!

Draft an agenda for a meeting that you need to run (either a real meeting or one that you make up). Follow the guidelines on the previous page and the model above.

ELPS 2C, 4C, 5B

The Tools of Language

Listening and Speaking	**557**
Using Reference Materials	**561**
Learning the Language of Writing	**565**

Learning Language

Work with a partner to learn the following words and expressions from this unit.

1. When something is *essential*, it is necessary and important.
   What is *essential* to bring with you to class?
2. If you *convey* your ideas, you express them.
   What expressions might *convey* sadness or surprise?
3. When you *synthesize* ideas, you combine and interpret them in a way that makes sense.
   Describe how you might *synthesize* information from two articles on the same subject.
4. When you *figure something out*, you gain a better understanding of it.
   Tell how you *figured out* a new way of doing something.

Listening and Speaking

Strong listening and speaking skills are essential to effective communication. As you mature, you probably find these skills gaining importance in your everyday life. Good speaking skills allow you to communicate clearly with teachers, classmates, bosses, and coworkers. Solid listening skills help you understand lectures and take good notes.

Listening requires you to synthesize a speaker's main ideas and to evaluate and organize information. Speaking allows you to convey ideas and feelings, explain, argue, persuade, inform, and even entertain. In this chapter, you will learn to improve your listening and speaking skills. As they improve, so will your ability to communicate effectively.

- **Listening in Class**
- **Speaking in Class**
- **A Closer Look at Listening and Speaking**

"I like to listen. I have learned a great deal from listening carefully. Most people never listen."

—Ernest Hemingway

Listening in Class

To listen well, you need to go beyond just "hearing" a speaker. Listening takes practice and effort. These tips will help you become a better listener.

- **Know why you're listening.** What is the speaker's message? Will there be an exam? Are you being asked to complete an assignment?
- **Listen for facts.** The 5W and H questions—*who? what? when? where? why?* and *how?*—will help you identify the most important information.
- **Take notes.** As you hear important information, write it in your notebook. Also write down questions and comments in the margins. Review and complete your notes as soon after class as possible.
- **Paraphrase key points.** Restate the speaker's ideas in your own words. Be sure you understand the meaning of new expressions and vocabulary. Seek clarification as needed.

Try It!

Practice your listening skills by taking notes in class or while viewing a documentary on television. Put the speaker's ideas into your own words. Use the margins in your notebook to add your questions and comments.

Multiple Intelligences

- Theory created by Harvard Prof. Howard Gardner
- A person's intelligence is made up of multiple faculties that can work alone or together.
- Faculties = inherent powers & abilities.
- Gardner's 8 Faculties (a.k.a. "Intelligences"): Musical, Bodily-Kinesthetic, Logical-Mathematical, Linguistic, Spatial, Interpersonal, Intrapersonal, Naturalist.
- They provide 8 different ways to teach and learn.

Margin notes:
- Are there more faculties than just these 8?
- Does everyone have all 8 faculties?
- See handout for definitions and examples of faculties.

Speaking in Class

Sharing information in a group discussion is an important skill. A meaningful discussion depends on cooperation. These basic strategies will help you become a better speaker.

Before you speak . . .

- **Listen** carefully and take notes.
- **Think** about what others are saying.
- **Wait** until it's your turn to speak.
- **Plan** how you can add something positive to the discussion.

As you speak . . .

- **Use a loud, clear voice.**
- **Avoid repeating** what's already been said.
- **Support your ideas** with examples, facts, or anecdotes.
- **Maintain eye contact** with others in the group or class.

Tips

- Focus your comments on the topic of the discussion.
- Ask meaningful questions.
- Summarize ideas brought up in the discussion and expand on them.

Try It!

Practice your group discussion skills by taking part in the following discussion activity.

1. As a class, brainstorm discussion topics from current events or as directed by your teacher. Make a list of the topics.
2. Divide into small groups. Each group chooses one topic from the list and takes a turn discussing the topic for 5 to 10 minutes, with the class acting as an audience. There is no preparation time; participants should speak spontaneously about the issue.
3. Following each discussion, the audience analyzes the discussion based on the strategies on this page.

A Closer Look at Listening and Speaking

Improving your listening and speaking skills will help you increase your confidence and effectiveness as a communicator. Follow these basic guidelines in your conversations and discussions.

Good listeners . . .	Good speakers . . .
<ul><li>think about what the speaker is saying.</li><li>stay focused so that they are prepared to respond thoughtfully.</li><li>pay attention to the speaker's tone of voice, gestures, and facial expressions.</li><li>interrupt only when necessary to ask questions.</li></ul>	<ul><li>speak loudly and clearly.</li><li>maintain eye contact with their listeners.</li><li>emphasize their main ideas by changing the tone and volume of their voice.</li><li>explain and clarify information that may be confusing.</li><li>use gestures and body language to enhance their message.</li></ul>

Try It!

Role-playing is an excellent way to practice listening and speaking skills. Try role-playing using this "read-question-answer" activity.

1. Imagine that you are a well-known author speaking to a group of students. Choose an excerpt from a book or a poem you have written. Read it to the group.
2. Have listeners take notes, jotting down questions and comments about "your" writing and the content of the excerpt.
3. Following the reading, role-play a question-answer session in which listeners ask questions and you answer.

Using Reference Materials

In this age of electronic media, you'll find that information is everywhere. From traditional sources such as books and newspapers to Web sites and blogs, there is a wealth of information on just about any subject. The key is learning where to look.

When you begin gathering information on a subject, common references such as encyclopedias and atlases can be very useful. Encyclopedias provide an overview of a topic, and atlases provide maps that help you see connections and understand the locations where events occur.

This chapter focuses on language resources. You will learn about the range of information you can gather from a dictionary. You will also discover how other language resources can help you improve both your speaking and your writing skills.

- **Using a Dictionary**
- **Using Other Reference Materials**

"A new word is like a fresh seed sewn on the ground of discussion."

—Ludwig Wittgenstein

Using a Dictionary

A dictionary gives many types of information:

- **Guide words:** These are the first and last words on the page. Guide words show whether the word you are looking for will be found alphabetically on that page.
- **Entry words:** Each word defined in a dictionary is called an entry word. Entry words are listed alphabetically.
- **Etymology:** Many dictionaries give etymologies (word histories). An etymology tells what language an English word came from, how the word entered our language, and when it was first used.
- **Syllable divisions:** A dictionary tells you where you may divide a word.
- **Pronunciation and accent marks:** A dictionary tells you how to pronounce a word and also provides a key to pronunciation symbols, usually at the bottom of each page.
- **Illustrations:** For some entries, an illustration, a photograph, or a drawing is provided.
- **Parts of speech:** A dictionary tells you what part(s) of speech a word is, using these abbreviations:

n.	**noun**	*tr. v.*	**transitive verb**
pron.	**pronoun**	*interj.*	**interjection**
intr. v.	**intransitive verb**	*conj.*	**conjunction**
adj.	**adjective**	*adv.*	**adverb**
prep.	**preposition**		

- **Spelling and capitalization:** The dictionary shows the correct spelling, as well as capitalization, for words. (For some words, more than one spelling is given.)
- **Definitions:** Some dictionaries are large enough to list all of the meanings for a word. Most standard-size dictionaries, however, will only list the most commonly accepted meanings. Take time to read all of the meanings to be sure that you are using the word correctly.

Try It!

Find a word in a dictionary that is unfamiliar to you. Look at its pronunciation and say it out loud. Then use it correctly in a sentence.

Sample Dictionary Page

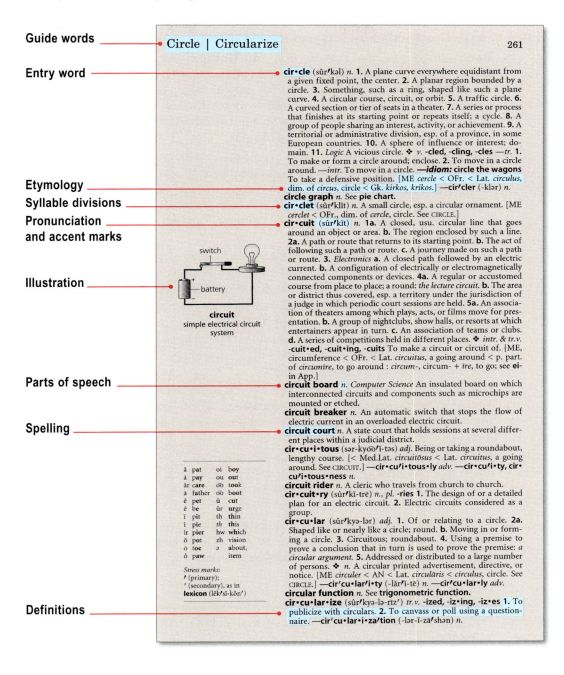

 ELPS 2C, 3B, 3F, 4C

Using Other Reference Materials

Dictionaries are not the only source of information about language. The list below describes some other useful language resources.

- **Books of Synonyms, Antonyms, and Homonyms** A thesaurus is a book of synonyms. It provides lists of words with the same or almost the same meaning and can be helpful for understanding a word or adding variety to your writing. Some thesauruses also contain antonyms (words with opposite meanings) and homonyms (words with the same spelling but different meanings).
- **Dictionaries of Idioms** Idioms are phrases that must be understood as a whole because they cannot be taken literally. For example, if your teacher suggests an activity to "break the ice" on the first day of school, he is offering a way to start a conversation. Dictionaries of idioms can help you understand the common English idioms you read and hear.
- **Dictionaries of Etymology** Dictionaries of etymology, or word history, provide information about where an English word came from, how it came to be used in English, and how long it has been used.
- **Online Dictionaries** These Internet-based dictionaries often provide more information than can be found in a print dictionary. You can search a word and find its meaning, etymology, synonyms, and antonyms. Many online dictionaries also have audio files that allow you to hear the word's pronunciation.
- **Usage Guides** Usage guides can help you determine appropriate language for formal and informal occasions. These guides provide information on grammar, spelling, and punctuation as well as word usage.
- **Pronunciation Dictionaries** A pronunciation dictionary is an electronic resource that allows you to type in or look up a word and hear it pronounced. Most pronunciation dictionaries will provide variations in pronunciation if they exist.
- **Translation Dictionaries** A translation dictionary provides translations of words into other languages. These dictionaries can help you transfer your word knowledge from one language to another.

Try It!

Think of a word or idiom you know and look it up in three of the reference materials listed above. Discuss what you find with a classmate.

ELPS 2C, 4C

Learning the Language of Writing

When it comes to writing, there are many new words and ideas to learn. The *writing process*, the *traits of writing, prewriting, drafting,* and *revising* are just a few of them.

If you play football, you know that there is jargon, or vocabulary, associated with the sport. Without words such as *interception, offense, quarterback, tackle,* and *touchdown,* you would have a hard time playing the game.

The vocabulary related to writing works in the same way. Without knowing the meaning of *thesis, evidence,* and *rhetoric,* you would have a hard time writing an essay or report. This chapter will help you learn the language necessary to write effectively.

- **Language Strategies**
- **Language of the Writing Process**
- **Language of the Writing Traits**
- **Language of the Writing Forms**

"To me, the greatest pleasure of writing is not what it's about, but the inner music the words make."
—Truman Capote

 ELPS 1E, 2C, 2D, 3A, 4C, 5B

Language Strategies

You constantly encounter new words through conversation, reading, and writing. Here are some strategies to help you understand, remember, and use the new language you encounter.

Use Language Patterns

Listen for patterns others use in English conversation.

You hear: This morning, my history teacher assigned a research report. This afternoon, I found out I have a chemistry test.
You can say: Tonight I will study for my test. Tomorrow, I will go to the library.

Try It!

Describe a sequence of events to a partner. Use words to indicate time order, as in the example sentences above.

Pronounce the Word

Listen carefully to new words. Pay close attention to vowel sounds, consonant clusters, and silent letters. Repeat the words.

You hear: Mnemonic devices are learning aids used to help you remember.
You repeat and write down: *mnemonic* **is pronounced "ni MON ik."**

Try It!

When you hear a new word, practice pronouncing it. Also, check in a dictionary to see how the word is spelled.

Use Academic Language

If a teacher uses an unfamiliar word in class, write it down. When you get a chance, look up the word in a dictionary.

You hear: All organisms are made up of one or more cells.
You repeat and write down: organism

Try It!

Listen in class and record unfamiliar words. After you look up the words in a dictionary, try using them in different sentences.

Say It Again

Retell or summarize a spoken message in your own words.

You hear: Explain the significance of the siege at Normandy to the outcome of the war.
You say: Explain the importance of the Normandy invasion to ending the war.

Try It!

Listen carefully to your teacher's instructions and take notes. Then summarize the directions in your own words.

Look for Word Parts You Know

Words often share prefixes, suffixes, or roots, even among language families. For example, the prefix *bio-* means "life" in English, French, Spanish, and German.

Try It!

If you hear an unfamiliar word, try writing it down. See if you recognize any word parts. If so, use the word part to help you determine the meaning of the whole word.

Learn Words in Different Ways

You may hear a word that you know used in an unfamiliar way. Finding the connection to what you know can help you figure out the other meaning.

You think: Nilda said that problems with the community center renovation have been compounded by a loss of funding. In chemistry, a compound is a substance formed by two or more elements. Nilda must mean that the loss of funding poses an additional problem.

Try It!

Listen for familiar words used in unfamiliar ways. Try to determine the logical connection between the two meanings.

Language of the Writing Process

Read the following writing process terms and study their meanings.

Prewrite

The first step of the writing process is to plan your writing. During prewriting, you select a correct genre, or form, to convey your intended meaning to your audience. Sometimes the genre will be given to you. Once you know your genre, you brainstorm or use a graphic organizer to determine an appropriate topic and develop a thesis, or controlling idea.

Draft

When you write a first draft, you structure your ideas based on an outline or notes from your prewriting. You make sure all ideas clearly relate to your thesis, and you use transitions to connect ideas to each other. Various rhetorical devices, or writing techniques, help enhance and add depth to your message.

Revise

Now it is time to read your draft and revise it, or make changes. When you revise, consider these traits: focus and coherence, organization, development of ideas, and voice. Rearrange words, sentences, and paragraphs, and add transitional words and phrases to clarify your meaning.

Edit

When you edit, you look for mistakes in conventions. Conventions include grammar, sentence structure, capitalization, punctuation, and spelling. Correct any errors that you find, and prepare a neat copy for review.

Publish

Have your teacher and peers review your writing. Prepare a final draft in response to their feedback. Then publish your work for the appropriate audience.

Vocabulary: Writing Process

brainstorm	feedback	publish
revise	rhetorical device	thesis
trait	transition	structure

1. **Say the word.** Listen as your teacher reads each word aloud, then repeat the word, paying close attention to consonant clusters such as the *st* in *brainstorm* or the *th* in *thesis*.

2. **Discover the meaning.** With a partner, create word wheels for the vocabulary words. Write each vocabulary word in the center of a word wheel. At the top of the wheel, write your definition of the word. List synonyms on the left, and use the word in an example sentence on the right. At the bottom of the wheel, draw a picture or diagram to show the meaning of the word. Start with the words you already know, and discuss how you can complete each word wheel as you learn about the other words.

3. **Learn more.** Listen intently as your teacher explains the meaning of each vocabulary word. Record key words or phrases that help you figure out each word's meaning, and add the information to your word wheel.

4. **Think about it.** Work with a partner to share ideas about the vocabulary words and answer the questions below.
    - Why might it be helpful to brainstorm ideas for a writing topic?
    - How do transitions guide a reader?
    - In what ways might rhetorical devices help convey meaning?

5. **Show your understanding.** Explain to a partner how each vocabulary word relates to the writing process. Work together to add specific details to create an accurate explanation for each word.

6. **Write about it.** Write a short paragraph describing the writing process. Use at least three of the vocabulary words above in your paragraph.

The Writing Process in Action

Now that you've learned the language of the writing process, it's time to see and experience the process in action. First your teacher will demonstrate each step of the writing process. Then you will complete the steps of the writing process, using the questions below as a guide.

Prewrite

1. What is the correct genre for conveying your message?
2. Who is your audience for this piece of writing?
3. What are some possible topics for your writing?
4. Of the possible topics you brainstormed, which one interests you the most?
5. What is the purpose of your writing?
6. What is the thesis, or controlling idea, of your writing?
7. What details and information support your thesis?
8. What information do you need to gather on your topic?
9. How will you organize your ideas?
10. How do you think your audience will respond to your ideas?
11. What information will you include in your introduction, middle, and conclusion?
12. Do you need to cite your sources?

Draft

1. How can you grab your reader's attention in the introduction?
2. How can you introduce your topic?
3. How can you develop your thesis, or controlling idea?
4. How can you guide readers from one idea to the next?
5. How can you categorize your ideas?
6. How can you organize those ideas into paragraphs that clearly relate to and support your thesis?
7. How can you use rhetorical devices such as simile, metaphor, and parallelism to convey your meaning?
8. What details will help convey your intended meaning to your audience?
9. How can you conclude your writing?

Revise

1. Do all details and ideas relate clearly to your thesis statement?
2. Are there any words, sentences, or paragraphs you should rearrange, add, or delete?
3. Do you develop your ideas logically? Does each sentence and paragraph build on the ones before?
4. Are your word choice and tone appropriate for your audience?
5. Does your writing engage the reader?
6. Do you use transitions to help guide the reader from one idea to the next?
7. Does your writing achieve your purpose and convey your intended meaning?
8. Have you presented the topic in a thoughtful and original way?

Edit

1. Did you follow all the rules of grammar?
2. Does each sentence make sense?
3. Did you follow the rules of capitalization?
4. Did you use correct punctuation to indicate possession and introduce quotations?
5. Are any commas misplaced or missing?
6. Are all the words spelled correctly?

Publish

1. Have you revised your writing in response to feedback from your teacher and peers?
2. Is your writing formatted correctly?
3. Have you selected an appropriate method of publishing to reach your audience?
4. Will additional elements such as images or charts enhance your publication?

Turn and Talk

Talk to a classmate about your writing and the writing process. What were the easiest and most difficult steps? What do you like about your writing? What do you want to improve?

Example: My favorite part of my writing is _____. The step that I found most difficult was _____.

Language of the Writing Traits

Read the following writing trait terms and study their meanings.

Focus and Coherence

Focus and coherence means that all ideas in your writing relate clearly to the thesis, and sentences connect and fit together logically. Everything in the writing should contribute to the composition as a whole and allow the reader to appreciate how ideas are related.

Organization

Your writing should be organized in a way that makes it easy to follow from beginning to end. The organizational pattern should be appropriate for the audience and purpose. Your introduction should capture the reader's attention and identify your topic. The middle paragraphs should build on each other to lead toward an effective conclusion.

Development of Ideas

Details should be used in a way that adds depth to your meaning. Depth means that you layer ideas so that each sentence adds meaning to the one before it. The way you present your ideas should give the reader an appreciation for your point of view.

Voice

Your writing should reflect your own voice, or genuinely express your personality or viewpoint to engage the reader and sound authentic. Voice gives your writing a unique perspective and establishes a relationship between you and the reader.

Conventions

The rules for writing are called conventions. This means that you need to think about grammar, sentence structure, mechanics (capitalization and punctuation), and spelling. Writing that is free of errors allows the reader to focus on and understand your message.

ELPS 2D, 3A, 3D, 3E, 3F, 4C, 5B, 5G

Learning the Language of Writing

Vocabulary: Writing Traits

coherence
depth
organization
composition
development
voice
conventions
mechanics

1. **Say the word.** Listen as your teacher reads the words aloud, then repeat each word, paying close attention to silent letter sounds such as the final *e* in *coherence* and *voice* and the *h* in *mechanics*. Do you have any prior experience with or knowledge of these words?

2. **Discover the meaning.** List the words you know and their meanings in your vocabulary journal. Discuss the words with a partner, taking notes to add to or clarify any meanings. For words you are both unsure of, discuss possible meanings and meanings you may know in other contexts.

3. **Learn more.** Listen as your teacher explains the meaning of each word. Work with your partner to restate the meanings in your own words and add the new information to your journal.

4. **Show your understanding.** Work with a partner to answer the questions below.
   - How can you check for depth in your writing?
   - What are some common errors in mechanics?
   - How can you tell if your writing reflects your voice?

5. **Show it.** Use examples to explain the meaning of each word to a partner. Share your ideas about how each word relates to effective writing. Add examples to your vocabulary journal and include any information that shows connections between the words.

6. **Write about it.** In a short paragraph, explain the five writing traits. Use at least three of the vocabulary words above in your paragraph.

Language of Narrative Writing

A narrative essay tells about a true experience in the writer's life. The experience might be one that took place over a period of time and/or one that changed the writer in some way. Narrative essays often have the same basic organization: a beginning paragraph that gets the reader's attention and identifies the topic, middle paragraphs that tell about the experience in sequential order, and an ending paragraph that tells why the experience was important.

Narrative Essay Organization

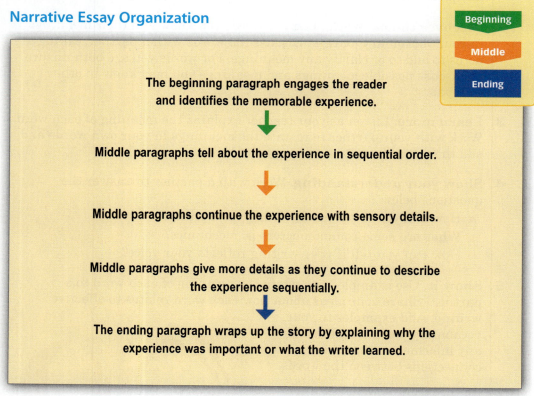

Turn and Talk

Discuss the purpose of each part of the graphic organizer with a partner.

ELPS 2C, 3A, 3D, 3E, 3G, 4C, 4G, 5B, 5G

Vocabulary: Narrative Writing

conclusion	conflict	experience
narrative	narrator	sequential
sensory details	suspense	resolution

1. **Say the word.** Listen as your teacher reads the words aloud. Then repeat each word, paying close attention to short vowel sounds such as the *e* in *sensory* or the *u* in *suspense*.

2. **Discover the meaning.** Some of these vocabulary words appear on page **574** and next to the writing model on pages **136–137**. Work with a partner and make notes about the words you know. Use the writing model to help you figure out what the other words mean.

3. **Learn more.** Listen as your teacher explains the meaning of each word. Take notes on the meanings of the words. Work with your partner to check and correct your earlier notes.

4. **Show your understanding.** Use your notebook to answer the questions below.
   - Where in the narrative does the writer usually reflect upon the situation? Tell why.
   - Why would a narrative be less interesting without suspense?
   - Why is using dialogue important in a narrative essay?

5. **Write it, show it.** In your journal, add notes to help you remember what each word means. You may wish to add synonyms or antonyms of the word. Knowing words with the same or opposite meanings can help you use words correctly in your writing. For example, near the word *conclusion* you could write *ending*.

6. **Write about it.** Write a short paragraph explaining how to write a narrative essay. Use at least three of the vocabulary words above.

Reading the Narrative Model

What Do You Know?

Next you will reread "A Greater Wealth," a sample narrative essay about a boy's relationship with his grandmother on pages **136–137**. What do you know about the lives of your grandparents or other older people? What do you think is most interesting about these people? Have you ever heard stories about their earlier lives? Describe what you know.

Build Background

As you probably know, families can be very complicated. There are many stories that can be told about the history of a family. Sometimes it is difficult to understand all of these stories, usually because they are told in different ways by different people. This often has to do with the person's point of view and sometimes their age. Each generation of a family remembers things a little differently. This can lead to confusion about the sequence of events or the exact details of a story.

Listening

Listen as your teacher or a classmate reads aloud "A Greater Wealth." As you listen, make notes about the order of events. Be prepared to answer the questions below.

1. In what two ways does the writer create detailed and effective images for the reader?
2. How do the writer's thoughts and feelings change over time?
3. Why does the writer say, "Still, I vowed to be attentive, to make myself indispensable to her during her stay"?

Key Words

self-centered	selfish	palatial estate
luxury	regal	wealthy
fascinated	commence	remain
disappointed	riches	

Look at the words in the box. You will see these words when you read the sample essay. With a partner, discuss the meaning of the words. Look them up in a dictionary if you need to. In your discussion, make a prediction about the experience described in the sample essay.

Read Along

Now it's your turn to read. Turn to pages **136–137**. Read the sample narrative essay silently as your teacher or a classmate reads it aloud.

After Reading

Draw a chart such as the one below on a sheet of paper and fill it in with the most important information about the narrative. Add rows and columns to your chart if you would like to include more information. Use your chart to summarize the writing model with a partner.

Actions or Events	Sensory Details	Your Thoughts and Questions
First:		
Next:		
Next:		
Next:		
Last:		

Oral Language: Narrative Writing

When you describe a personal experience, you adjust your narrative for the appropriate audience. For example, you may provide more or less background information depending on your audience's knowledge. You may also adapt the language you use for more formal or informal purposes.

Try It!

Read about the situation below. With a partner, discuss how a narrative about the situation might be adapted for each audience in the list.

Situation

After graduation, a classmate has decided to spend a year before college volunteering to help people in disaster-stricken areas. Her desire to volunteer was inspired by the help aid workers provided to her family and community after a hurricane when she was a child.

Audiences

- another classmate
- the school principal
- a parent

Effective Talk

When you answer a question, you might use a few words, a sentence, or a few sentences. When you use more details, you provide a clearer understanding of your answer.

Read the question and the answers below. In the first box, the question is answered in only a few words. In the second box, a single sentence answers the question. The third answer is the most specific and detailed.

Why do you want to volunteer after graduation?

> to help people

▽

> I want to help other people the way people helped my family and community.

▽

> When I was eight, a hurricane hit my town. The aid workers helped give my family and neighbors a sense of hope. Their kindness impressed me so much that now I've decided it's my turn to give back to others.

Try It!

Select an experience to share with a partner. List your ideas for describing the experience. Then add details that will help your partner understand how you felt about the experience. Use your notes to share your experience orally with your partner. After your description, answer any questions your partner has about the experience.
When you have finished, switch roles.

Language of Expository Writing

Expository writing is writing that analyzes and explains information. A writer's purpose in expository writing is to inform or describe. Types of expository essays may include analyses of opposing ideas or problem analyses. Expository essays commonly follow a similar organizational pattern: an introduction with background information and a thesis statement, body paragraphs with supporting details, and a conclusion that summarizes the information presented in the essay.

Expository Essay Organization

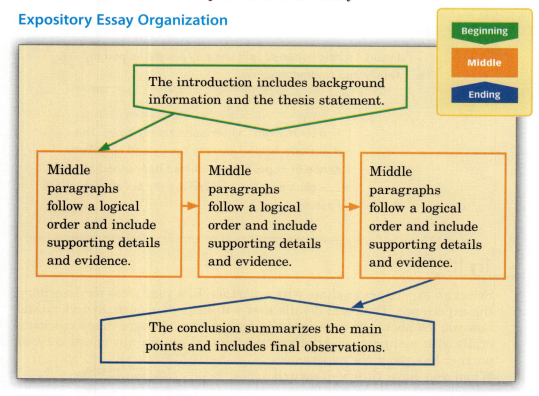

Turn and Talk

Talk with a partner about why you think most expository essays follow an organizational pattern like the one shown.

This organizational pattern makes sense because _____.

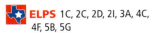

ELPS 1C, 2C, 2D, 2I, 3A, 4C, 4F, 5B, 5G

Learning the Language of Writing 581

Vocabulary: Expository Writing

background	citation	opposing
evidence	expository	reliable
perspective	substantial	valid
source	contradict	

1. **Say the word.** Listen carefully as your teacher reads each vocabulary word aloud. Then repeat each word, paying close attention to consonant clusters such as the *sp* in *perspective*, the *st* in *substantial*, and the *tr* in *contradict*.

2. **Discover the meaning.** Work with a partner to locate some of the vocabulary words on page **580** and in the blue boxes next to the writing model on pages **161–162**. Take notes on what you think the words mean.

3. **Learn more.** Listen as your teacher explains the meaning of each word. Compare the meaning with what you thought the words meant and correct your notes.

4. **Show your understanding.** Use your notebook to answer the questions below.
   - Where should you include citations for your sources?
   - How do you decide if your evidence is valid and reliable?
   - Why should an analysis include information on all relevant perspectives?

5. **Write it, show it.** In your journal, draw pictures or list synonyms to help you remember what each word means. For example, next to *opposing* you could draw two arrows facing each other and write *against*.

6. **Write about it.** Write a short paragraph describing how to write an expository essay. Use the graphic organizer on page **580** as a guide. As you write, use at least three of the vocabulary words above.

Language

TEKS 12.15A
ELPS 1A, 2I, 3A, 3E, 3G,
3H, 3J, 4D, 4F

Reading the Expository Model

What Do You Know?

Next you will reread the writing model of an analysis of opposing ideas "Are Third Parties Viable in U.S. Politics?" on pages 161–162. What do you know about the role of political parties in the United States? Talk to a partner about any prior knowledge you have that relates to U.S. politics.

Build Background

Political parties are organizations that form to gain power in government. They often outline a specific agenda and set of ideas to attract the support of followers. The United States has what is known as a two-party system. This means that the major party candidates (Democrats and Republicans) earn the vast majority of votes in elections. Parties other than the two major parties are known as third parties.

Listening

Listen as your teacher or a classmate reads "Are Third Parties Viable in U.S. Politics?" aloud. As you listen, take note of the thesis statement. Be prepared to answer the questions below.
1. How does the introduction lead to the thesis statement?
2. What opposing views does the writer present?
3. How does the writer conclude the analysis?

Key Words and Phrases

since	however	for example
yet	as long as	in addition
perhaps	those who support	although
according to	those who oppose	people on both sides

Look at the words and phrases in the box. You will see these words and phrases when you read the writing model. With a partner, use the words and phrases to talk about two opposing sides of an issue in your school or community. Then identify areas of agreement between the two sides and discuss your point of view on the issue. As you say the words, pay attention to the way you pronounce consonant clusters such as the *th* in *those* and *although*.

Learning the Language of Writing   583

ELPS 4G, 4J, 4K

Read Along

Now it's your turn to read. Turn to pages 161–162. Read the writing model as your teacher or a classmate reads it aloud.

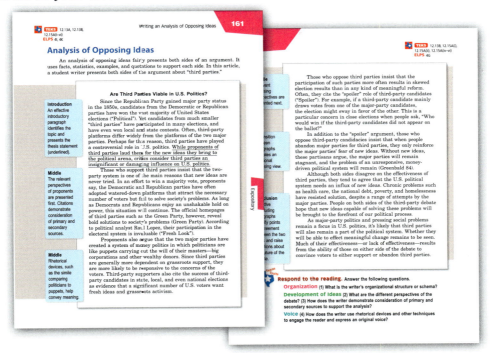

After Reading

Copy the following chart on a sheet of paper and list the arguments for and against third parties. Use your chart to summarize the writing model with a partner.

For	Against

Oral Language: Expository Writing

When you explain information in writing or in speaking, you use an informed voice. Facts, details, and examples help support your ideas. When you speak, techniques such as varying the tone and volume of your voice and using facial expressions and gestures help convey your meaning.

Try It!

Read about the situation below. With a partner, take turns asking each other to explain reasons why people might support or oppose the policy. Use the dialogue as a model. Then discuss whether or not you agree with the policy. Practice effective speaking techniques to express your opinions, ideas, and feelings.

Situation

The high school is adopting a new wellness policy. Effective immediately, candy and soda will not be allowed in the school. In addition, other foods and beverages with high sugar, fat, and sodium content will be strictly limited.

Dialogue

- Speaker 1: Explain why people might support the new wellness policy.
- Speaker 2: Schools should promote healthy habits.
- Speaker 1: Give an example of a situation in which the policy might benefit students with poor nutrition habits.
- Speaker 2: Some students eat soda and candy for lunch. Banning these items would encourage them to make healthier choices.

ELPS 3E, 3G, 3H

Effective Talk

You might explain something in a few words, a sentence, or a few sentences. When you explain with more specificity and detail, your listener gains a better understanding.

Read the question and the answers below. In the first box, the question is answered in a few words. In the second box, the question is answered in a sentence. In the third box, the question is answered in three sentences.

Why does the school want to restrict foods that are high in sugar, fat, and sodium?

> to promote health

> The school wants to promote students' health.

> School officials say that they want to restrict foods that are high in sugar, fat, and sodium to promote students' health. Nutrition is part of the school curriculum, and the school wants to encourage healthy nutrition in addition to teaching about it. School officials also say that poor nutrition habits negatively impact student performance.

Try It!

With a partner, discuss a debate that exists in your school or community. Talk about background information surrounding the debate, and explain the reasons behind the opposing points of view. Use specific details in your discussion.

Language of Persuasive Writing

Persuasive essays attempt to convince the reader to agree with the writer's position. Persuasive essays can take many forms. One of the most common is the problem-solution essay. No matter what the form, most persuasive essays have the same structure: a beginning that includes a position statement, body paragraphs that support the position statement, and an ending that sums up the support and adds perspective.

Persuasive Essay Organization

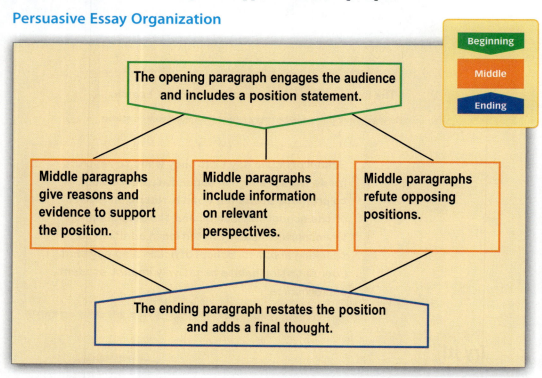

Turn and Talk
Talk with a partner about ways to convince someone to agree with an opinion you have. What is the best way to support an argument?

Learning the Language of Writing

Vocabulary: Persusasive Writing

call to action	counter-argument	issue
objection	persuade	position
problem	reason	solution
support		

1. **Say the word.** Listen as your teacher reads the words. Repeat each word, paying careful attention to your pronunciation. Focus on short vowel sounds such as the *a* in *action,* the initial *o* in *objection,* and the *u* in *support.*

2. **Discover the meaning.** Work with a partner. Read each word and discuss the possible meaning of each. Write down your ideas about what each word means.

3. **Clarify.** Listen as your teacher explains the meaning of each word. In your own words, write down what each vocabulary word means. Ask questions about any definition you do not fully understand.

4. **Show your understanding.** Answer the questions below.
   - Which words relate to people who have an opinion different from the author's?
   - Which word means "a particular point of view"?
   - Which word means "to convince"?

5. **Use a graphic organizer.** Use your vocabulary journal. Choose four words from the vocabulary list. For each vocabulary word, make a word web. In the spaces on the web, write words similar in meaning to the vocabulary word.

6. **Write about it.** Write a short paragraph about a controversial issue. Use at least three of the vocabulary words above as you write.

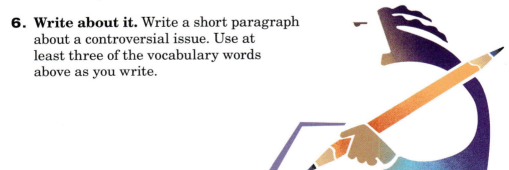

Reading the Persuasive Model

What Do You Know?

You are about to reread "Ban Gifts and Fundraising by Lobbyists," a persuasive writing model on pages 221–222. The essay is about how gifts and fundraising can sometimes influence members of Congress to vote in a certain way. Discuss the issue with a partner. What do you know about what political representatives do? Should lobbyists be allowed to give members of Congress gifts? Why or why not?

Build Background

Members of Congress have a large influence on life in America. They vote on laws that range between controlling pollution to providing medical care for retired citizens. Sometimes, lobbyists give gifts to members of Congress or help them raise election funds. Many people think this is a bad idea. They say that gifts and fundraising can cause members of Congress to vote in a certain way and that gifts and fundraising should be banned.

Listening

Listen as your teacher or a classmate reads "Ban Gifts and Fundraising by Lobbyists" aloud. As you listen, make notes about the problem, the facts that explain the problem, and the proposed solution. Be ready to answer the questions below.

1. What is the writer's position?
2. What are four reasons the writer gives for the proposed solution?
3. With which counter-argument does the writer disagree? Why?

Key Words

banning	constituents	corporate
epidemic	influence	preferential
undue		

Look at the words in the box. You will see these words when you read the sample essay. With a partner, use the words to discuss how gifts and money might influence politicians to do things they ordinarily would not do. Listen carefully to your partner's and your own pronunciation of these words. Pay close attention to short vowel sounds such as the *a* in *banning* and the *i* in *influence*.

Read Along

Now it's your turn to read. Turn to pages 221–222 in this book. Read the writing model as your teacher or a classmate reads it aloud.

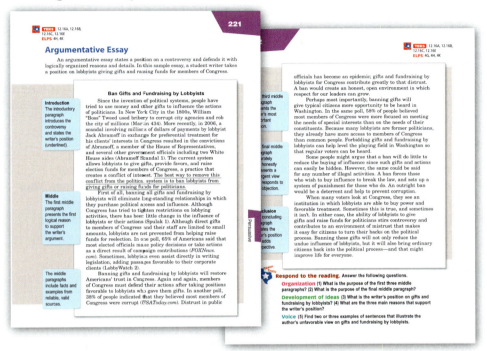

After Reading

The writer of the persuasive essay uses statistics from polls to support the argument that gifts and fundraising by lobbyists should be banned. Use the statistics in the article to answer the following questions.

1. What percentage of Americans believe that most elected officials make decisions or take actions as a direct result of campaign contributions?
2. What percentage of people believe that most members of Congress are corrupt?
3. What percentage of people believe that most members of Congress are more interested in meeting the needs of special interest groups than of their own constituents?

Oral Language: Persuasive Writing

The people who will listen to you or read your writing are called the audience. When you write a persuasive essay, it is important that you consider your audience. What is their relationship to the topic? Which points of your argument will be most convincing to them?

Try It!

Read about the situation below. Then choose two audiences from the list. With a partner, discuss how you might shape a persuasive argument to suit each audience.

Situation

In your city, you and your friends have no place to play outdoor sports. You and your partner have decided to help solve this problem. Your idea is to have the city build an outdoor sports complex. The complex would provide a safe and spacious environment for teens to play sports. Convince your audience that this issue is important and that they should support your efforts.

Audiences

- Taxpayers who would have to pay for the sports complex
- Teens who could use the sports complex
- People who would not use the sports complex

Effective Talk

When you answer a question, you often have a number of options. You might answer with one word, or a few words, or even several sentences. Adding details can provide the information a listener needs to fully understand what you mean.

To see how this works, read the question and the answers below. In the first box, you'll see a very brief answer. In the second box, a few more details are added. In the third box, the answer is even more detailed.

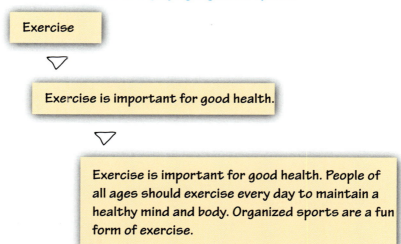

Try It!

Choose a persuasive topic that interests you and your partner. Start by asking the question, "What problem do we want to explore?" Make a list of words and details you would use to describe the problem. Finally, discuss possible solutions to the problem.

Here are some ideas to get you started.

1. What is an issue in your school that needs to be changed?
2. What is something that you would like to improve about your community?

Language of Interpretive Response

An interpretive response to literature is writing in which you discuss something you have read, such as a book or a play. In an interpretive response, you should demonstrate your understanding of a piece of writing and look closely at some aspect of the work or the author's craft. An interpretive response has a beginning, a middle, and an ending that work together to create a cohesive essay.

Interpretive Response Organization

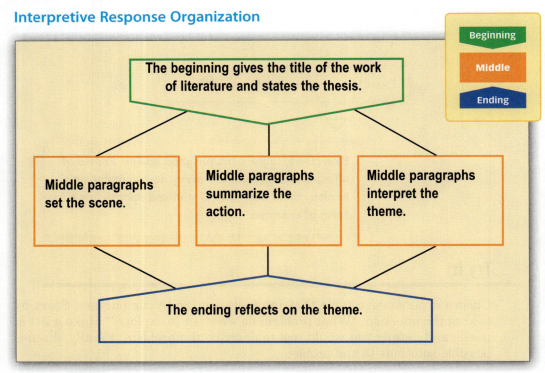

 Turn and Talk

Talk with a partner about how the organizational patterns in an interpretive response differ from those in a narrative essay.

Vocabulary: Interpretive Response

character	action	scene
element	theme	thesis statement
interpretation	quotation	

1. **Say the word.** Listen as your teacher reads the words aloud. Pay close attention to the way each word is pronounced. Repeat each word, focusing on your pronunciation of the silent *h* in *character* and the sound of *ph* in *paragraph*.

2. **Discover the meaning.** Work with a partner to find some of the vocabulary words on page **592** and in the boxes next to the writing model on pages **281–282**. Write notes about what you think the words mean.

3. **Learn more.** Listen as your teacher explains the meaning of each word. Work with your partner to check your notes and revise your definitions.

4. **Show your understanding.** Use your notebook to answer the questions below.
   - Why is it important to have a good thesis statement?
   - Why is it helpful to summarize the action?
   - When does a writer analyze the theme?

5. **Write it, show it.** In your journal, write notes for an interpretive response using as many vocabulary words as possible. You may wish to add synonyms, or words that mean the same thing, to help you remember how to use certain words. For example, near *character* you could write *person*.

6. **Write about it.** Write a short paragraph summarizing the Interpretive Response Organization chart on page **592**. Use at least three of the vocabulary words above in your summary.

Reading the Interpretive Response Model

What Do You Know?

Next you will reread a writing model about a play that focuses on two women who are in an office building on New Year's Eve during a storm. They can't leave because of the weather. One is a business woman, and the other is a cleaning woman. What can bring different people together?

Build Background

The play *Sisters* was first performed in Atlanta in 1987. At that time, many women were beginning to hit a "glass ceiling." People said that women could rise to the top of a company, but it seemed as if there was an invisible barrier. They could only get to a certain point in their careers, and then they went no farther. One of the characters in *Sisters* has hit the "glass ceiling." The other character is still far below.

Marsha A. Jackson began studying theater when she was a teenager. In her plays, she writes about women's lives. She shows how they are sometimes treated differently from men in society. She is an actor and a director as well as a playwright.

Listening

Listen as your teacher or a classmate reads aloud "Stuck with Each Other." As you listen, make notes about the ways that Olivia and Cassie are different. Be prepared to answer the questions below.

1. What is the thesis statement of the writing model?
2. How does the writer show the differences between the characters?
3. Why does the writer use quotations from the play?

Key Words

along with	among	apart
because	begins	powerful
resolve	storm	stuck
together	while	

Look at the words in the box. You will see these words when you read the writing sample. With a partner, use the words to talk about what happens in the play. Then use them to talk about the writer's ideas about the play.

 ELPS 2C, 2G, 2I, 3E, 4C, 4G, 4I, 4J, 4K

Learning the Language of Writing

Read Along

Now it's your turn to read. Turn to pages 281–282. Read the writing model silently as your teacher or a classmate reads it aloud.

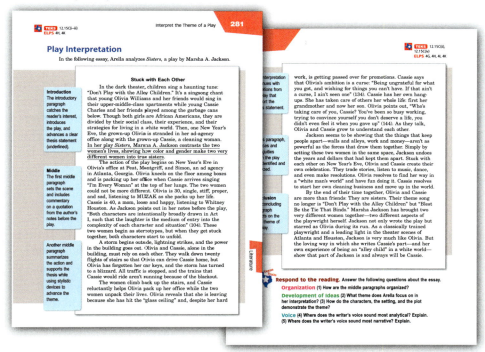

After Reading

Copy the following chart on a sheet of paper. List the main events of the play. Use some of the key words to describe the characters' actions. Share your list with a partner, and use the key words to discuss what you think will happen next.

Main Events
1.
2.
3.

ELPS 1G, 2I, 3E, 3I

Oral Language: Interpretive Response

The person or people who will listen to you or read your writing are called the audience. When you speak or write for your audience, you will choose to use a formal or an informal tone. For example, you might choose a formal tone for an essay that you need to hand in to your teacher. On the other hand, you might choose an informal tone when telling a group of friends about a great book that you just read. You need to decide which tone is appropriate for your audience.

Try It!

Read about the situation below. Then choose two audiences from the list. With a partner, discuss how you might change the way that you talk or write for each audience.

Situation

You read a play where the main character, Arlen, has to change schools. His mother suddenly loses her job, and they have to move. At first Arlen is very upset, because it is the middle of his senior year. He worries about catching up with his studies and fitting in. Every day as he walks between classes at his new school, he sees the same group of students walking together and laughing. He worries that they are laughing at him. Think about what might happen next. Then tell about the play's theme.

Audiences

- Teacher
- Parent
- Classmate
- School principal

Effective Talk

When you answer a question, you might use only a few words to keep your answer short. However, to help your audience better understand your answer, you may need to give more details. In addition, you need to listen carefully to your audience when they are asking questions. Sometimes, you may not understand the question because the person is using complex language. In that case, ask the person to rephrase the question, or use different words to ask the question.

Read the question and the answers below. The answers in the first and second boxes are too short to answer the question. The third box shows the most information and answers the question.

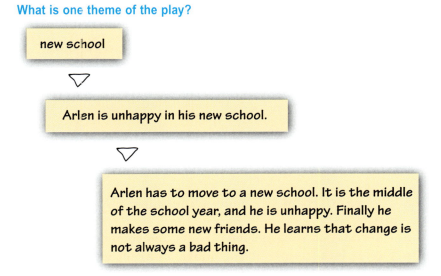

Try It!

Work with a partner. Choose a story or play that you have both recently read. Choose a new question that you would like to discuss. Make notes about details that would give your partner more information about your ideas. Then use your notes to describe your ideas to your partner.

Here are some ideas to get you started.

1. How can you describe the main character?
2. What is the main theme of the literature?
3. What lessons does the main character learn?

Language of Creative Writing

Creative writing tells a fictional story. This type of writing can take the form of a short story, a novel, a play, or poetry. It can inspire many emotions—excitement, joy, sadness, anger, self-reflection, and more. Most creative writing shares the same basic organization and features: an exposition introduces the characters, conflict, and setting; rising action builds to a crisis and climax; and falling action leads to a resolution. The graphic organizer below illustrates the features of most creative writing.

Plot Line

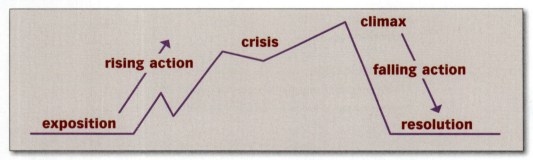

- The **exposition** introduces the main character, conflict, and setting.
- The **rising action** includes events and complications.
- The **crisis** requires the main character to make important decisions.
- In the **climax** the main character risks success or failure and changes as a result.
- The **falling action** shows how the main character reacts to the change.
- The **resolution** brings the story to a satisfying end.

Turn and Talk

Talk with a partner about movies you've seen that contain the elements of fictional writing. Tell the story using the graphic organizer.

ELPS 1C, 2B, 2C, 2I, 3A, 3B, 4C, 4G, 5B, 5G

Learning the Language of Writing

Vocabulary: Creative Writing

crisis	dialogue	exposition
falling action	flashback	metaphor
rising action	resolution	sensory detail

1. **Say the word.** Listen as your teacher reads the words aloud. Pay close attention to short vowel sounds such as the initial *a* in *action* and the *e* in *exposition*. Then repeat each word.

2. **Discover the meaning.** Work with a partner to find some of the vocabulary words on page **598** and in the boxes next to the writing model on pages **345–347**. Think about what you know about creative writing and short stories. Write notes about what you think the words or phrases mean.

3. **Learn more.** Listen as your teacher explains the meaning of each word or phrase. Take notes as necessary, and then work with your partner to write a short definition, in your own words, of each vocabulary word.

4. **Show your understanding.** Use your notebook to answer the following questions.
   - Which happens first in creative writing—a crisis or the falling action? Explain why.
   - What purpose does dialogue serve in a short story?
   - What happens in a flashback?

5. **Write it, show it.** In your journal, add pictures or drawings to help you remember what each word means. You may wish to add synonyms, or words that mean the same thing. For example, near *dialogue* you could write *conversation*.

6. **Write about it.** Write a summary of a story you have recently read or seen on TV or in a movie. Use at least three of the vocabulary words in your summary.

ELPS 1A, 2C, 2G, 2I, 3A, 3E, 3G, 3H, 4C, 4D, 4G

Reading the Creative Model

What Do You Know?

Next you will reread "Soaking," a sample short story on pages **345–347.** It describes a young man's relationship with his parents after he moves back in with them following college and how his life is changed in a single moment. Do you think the relationships between parents and children change when the children move back in as young adults? What kinds of events can force relationships to change?

Build Background

Many young adults move back in with their parents after college and before they begin a career because they need financial help. This situation may be hard for both parents and children because they both tend to treat each other the way they did in the years before college. Even though the teenagers have grown up, parents and children often think and act in some of the same ways they did during the children's teenage years.

Listening

Listen as your teacher or a classmate reads "Soaking" aloud. As you listen, make notes about the main character's thoughts and actions and how he changes. Be prepared to answer the questions below.

1. What is Alejandro's mood before the phone call?
2. Describe the relationship between Alejandro and his sister Sonia.
3. How did Alejandro's feelings for his mother change by the end of the story?

Key Words and Phrases

banged up	every fiber of his being	network
get his act together	get my life in order	nagging
golden opportunity	made it a point	snagged
pick up where they left off		

Look at the words and phrases in the box. You will see these words when you read the sample story. With a partner, use the words to talk about personal relationships and making changes. Pay close attention to your pronunciation of short vowel sounds as you say each word.

ELPS 2C, 2G, 2I, 3E, 3G, 3H, 4C, 4G

Learning the Language of Writing

Read Along

Now it's your turn to read. Turn to pages **345–347**. Read the sample story as your teacher or a classmate reads it aloud.

After Reading

Some of the keywords and phrases in the box on page **600** are expressions that may not seem to make sense. Talk with your partner about the meanings of the words and phrases. Make up funny sentences with them. Follow with more serious sentences to help you understand the true meaning. Ask your teacher for assistance if you need it to understand the true meaning of each expression.

> **Example:**
> When I sharpened the end of the pencil, I made it a point.
> I made it a point to never miss practice.

Summarize the short story, explaining how Alejandro changed.

Oral Language: Creative Writing

The person or people who will listen to you or read your writing are called the audience. When you speak or write, you need to select the right words so your audience will understand your message and the feelings expressed. You will write or speak differently depending on your audience.

Try It!

Read about the story plot below. Then choose two audiences from the list. With a partner, discuss how the words you choose to retell the story might be different for each audience.

Story Plot

Sofia and Michelle have been best friends since first grade. They were both very good students, but in high school Michelle didn't concentrate on her schoolwork. Whenever a big test was coming up, Michelle would ask Sofia for her notes so she could study at the last minute. Finally, Sofia refuses to give Michelle her notes before a test. Sofia tells Michelle she is still her best friend, but she won't do her schoolwork for her. Michelle decides that Sofia is right, and they study together.

Audiences

- A child in second grade
- A teacher
- A classmate

Effective Talk

When you answer a question, you might use a few words, one sentence, or a few sentences. When you use more details to tell about something, the other person will have a better understanding.

Read the question and the answers below. In the first box, there are only a few words. In the second box, a short sentence answers the question. The third answer contains more detail and does a better job answering the question.

What problem does Sofia have with Michelle?

> doesn't do schoolwork

> Michelle wants to use Sofia's schoolwork when Michelle has not done it.

> Sofia and Michelle are best friends but recently Michelle wants to use Sofia's schoolwork when Michelle has not done it. Sofia finally decides she doesn't want to give Michelle her schoolwork.

Try It!

Choose a new question that you would like to talk about with a partner. First make notes about details that would give your partner more information about your ideas. Then use your notes to describe your ideas to your partner.

Here are some ideas to get you started.

1. What problem might you encounter as a member of an after-school team or club?
2. What problem might you face in dealing with a friend?

Language of Research Writing

Research papers involve investigating a topic using a variety of sources. The purpose is to present information about the topic to an audience.

Research writers commonly use MLA style. Research papers written in MLA style have an engaging beginning that identifies the topic and provides a thesis statement. Middle sections include accurate details to support the thesis. Headings can be used to help guide the reader. The ending summarizes the main points and leaves the reader with an insightful thought. Source information is listed on a separate page.

Research Paper Organization

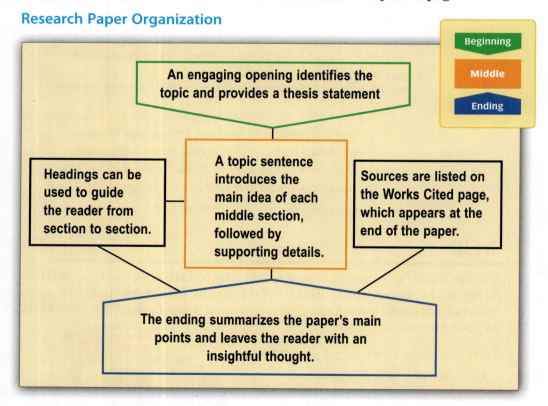

Turn and Talk

Discuss the importance of using accurate details to support your thesis.

ELPS 2B, 2C, 3A, 3B, 4C, 5B, 5G

Vocabulary: Research Writing

headings	outline	paraphrase
quotation	source cited	supporting details
topic sentence	transitions	

1. **Say the word or phrase.** Listen as your teacher reads the words and phrases aloud. Repeat each word carefully, paying close attention to long vowel sounds such as the first *o* in *quotation*, the *i* in *cited*, and the final *a* in *paraphrase*.

2. **Discover the meaning.** Work with a partner to find some of the vocabulary words on page **604** and in the blue margin notes next to the writing model on pages **392–400**. Write notes about what you think the words mean in this context.

3. **Learn more.** Listen as your teacher explains the meaning of each word or phrase. Work with your partner to check and correct the notes that you made earlier.

4. **Show your understanding.** Use the information in your notebook to help you answer the questions below.
   - What is the purpose of including headings in a research paper?
   - What role do transitions play in a research paper?
   - How do you determine when to paraphrase a source instead of using an exact quotation?

5. **Write it, show it.** In your vocabulary journal, you may want to add related words to help you remember what each word means. For example, you may want to write *main ideas* and *major and minor details* next to *outline* to remember what to include in it.

6. **Write about it.** Write a short paragraph describing your past experience writing research papers. Use at least three of the vocabulary words above in your paragraph.

ELPS 1A, 2C, 2G, 2I, 3A, 3E, 3G, 4C, 4D

Reading the Research Writing Model

What Do You Know?

Next you will reread "Roosevelt's New Deal: Success or Failure?," a research writing model on pages 393–400. What do you know about the Great Depression? What do you know about President Franklin Delano Roosevelt? Have you ever heard of his plan called the New Deal?

Build Background

The stock market crash in 1929 began a period in U.S. history known as the Great Depression. During this time, Americans lost their savings when banks closed, workers lost their jobs, homeowners lost their houses, and farmers lost their land. The New Deal was the name given to President Franklin D. Roosevelt's economic plan to help Americans get through this difficult time. It provided aid and created jobs through a variety of government programs and organizations from 1933 to 1939.

Listening

Listen as your teacher or a classmate reads "Roosevelt's New Deal: Success or Failure?" aloud. As you listen, take notes about the New Deal. Be prepared to answer the questions below.

1. Who created the New Deal? When was it created?
2. What was the purpose of the New Deal?
3. How did the government help Americans in need?

Key Words

agencies	bank failures	collapse
economy	Great Depression	legislation
poverty	production	regulations
stock market	unemployment	wages

Look at the words in the box. You will see these words when you read the writing model. With a partner, use the words to talk about the causes and effects of the New Deal. Think about what might have happened to the United States if the New Deal had not been created.

As you say each word, pay attention to your pronunciation. Focus on long vowel sounds such as the *a* in *agencies* and the *e* in *economy*.

Learning the Language of Writing

ELPS 2G, 2I, 4C, 4G, 4I

Read Along

Now it's your turn to read. Turn to pages 393–400 in this book. Read the writing model as your teacher or a classmate reads it aloud. Two pages of the writing model are shown below.

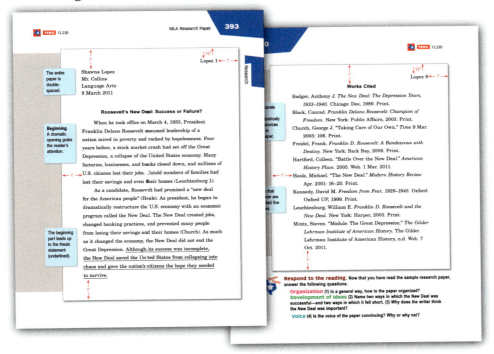

After Reading

On a separate sheet of paper, write the answers to these questions about the writing model.

1. What condition was the U.S. economy in when President Roosevelt took office?
2. What government programs and legislation did the New Deal create?
3. Was the New Deal a success or a failure? Explain your answer.

Oral Language: Research Writing

The person or people who listen to you while you speak or who read your writing are called the audience. When you speak or write, it is important to think about the right words to use so that your audience will understand your thesis. The tone, or the way you write, will be different for each audience.

Try It!

Read about the research topic below. Then choose two audiences from the list. Think about what each audience would be interested in knowing about your topic if you had to retell it. With a partner, discuss how the words and examples you choose might differ for each audience.

Topic

The U.S. Constitution was written in 1787. It is the highest law in the United States. All other laws come from this document. The Constitution explains in detail how the U.S. government works. It creates the office of the president, Congress, and the Supreme Court. The Constitution also limits the powers of the federal government, explains how to pass and change laws, and gives certain freedoms to all American citizens.

Audiences

- A middle-school student
- A person who is visiting from another country
- A parent

Effective Talk

There are a number of ways to answer a question. You might answer with a few words, a sentence, or several sentences. Adding details provides the listener with the information he or she needs to fully understand what you mean.

Read the question and the answers below. In the first box, there is a very brief answer. In the second box, there is a short sentence. The third answer contains more detail and answers the question more effectively.

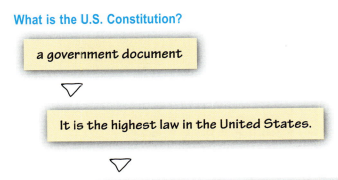

What is the U.S. Constitution?

- a government document
- It is the highest law in the United States.
- The U.S. Constitution creates and explains the system of laws in the United States. All laws come out of the Constitution. It creates the different parts of the U.S. government and gives many rights and freedoms to American citizens.

Try It!

Choose a section of the U.S. Constitution that you would like to research, such as how it limits the powers of the federal government. First make notes about what you want to know about the topic. Then use your notes to describe your ideas to your partner.

Here are some ideas to get you started.

1. How are laws passed in the United States?
2. What rights and freedoms does the U.S. Constitution give to American citizens?

ELPS 2C, 4C, 5B

www.hmheducation.com/tx/writesource

Basic Elements of Writing

Basic Paragraph Skills   611
Basic Essay Skills   623

Learning Language

Work with a partner to learn the following words and expressions from this unit.

1. To **classify** means "to organize by category."
   How are books classified in a library?
2. **Particular** means "specific."
   Describe a particular experience that made you question your beliefs about something.
3. A **method** is a way of doing something.
   What method do you use to manage your homework?
4. A **time-honored** practice is respected because it has been established over a long period of time.
   Identify two time-honored traditions at your school.
5. When you follow someone's **line of thinking**, you understand his or her pattern of thought.
   Explain the line of thinking you used to describe your reasons for doing something.

Basic Paragraph Skills

When it comes to writing well, you must remember these two words: *support* and *organization*. You need to select details that support your main point, and you need to organize those details effectively. That's where the simple, time-honored tradition of paragraphing comes into play. Paragraphs help you organize your thoughts and make it easier for the reader to follow your line of thinking.

In this chapter, you will examine four basic types of paragraphs. Each has a specific purpose, and each requires a particular type of thinking. Then you will look at examples of different ways you can organize your paragraphs to make them most effective. Learning how to write effective paragraphs will give you control of all your academic writing—from essays to research papers.

- **The Parts of a Paragraph**
- **Types of Paragraphs: Narrative, Descriptive, Expository, and Persuasive**
- **Patterns of Organization: Classification, Comparison-Contrast, Cause-Effect, Process, and Climax**

"I often have to write a hundred pages or more before there's a paragraph that's alive."

—Philip Roth

The Parts of a Paragraph

A basic paragraph contains three parts: a topic sentence, body sentences, and a closing sentence. Each detail in the body supports the topic sentence. The following expository paragraph provides information about hot-air ballooning.

Topic Sentence

Body

Closing Sentence

Hot-Air Ballooning

Based on the simple scientific principle that hot air rises, hot-air ballooning has been a popular pastime for more than two centuries. While the idea of a lighter-than-air vehicle had been around since Archimedes, the first functional balloon was created in France in 1783 by brothers Joseph and Etienne Montgolfier, who sent a duck, a chicken, and a sheep into the air for a brief but historical ride. Later that year, the first manned trip was taken by physicist Pilatre de Rozier and the Marquis Francois d'Arlandes, who glided over Paris for 28 minutes. Today's balloons have changed little from those early models, with the balloon envelope designed to trap hot air and lift the structure into the air. The envelope is formed from many strips, called *gores*, pieced together to create a rounded shape. The Montgolfiers' envelope was made of paper, but later balloons were created of silk, and today's models are usually made of ripstop nylon. The tapered bottom edge is open, with a fireproof skirt attached. Early balloons were kept aloft by burning a mixture of straw and manure, but today, propane tanks are used, suspended just below the skirt. Beneath the tanks hangs a basket, usually made of wicker, and large enough for passengers and extra propane tanks. Hot-air ballooning fell out of favor in the nineteenth century with the advent of gas balloons, which could travel farther. Then, in the mid-twentieth century, traditional ballooning had a renaissance. Today people enjoy peaceful scenic rides as well as the sport of balloon racing. Whatever the purpose, balloon enthusiasts throughout the world enjoy gliding on air.

 Respond to the reading. What is the main idea of this paragraph? What specific details in the body support this idea? Name two or three of them.

A Closer Look at the Parts

Every paragraph, whether written to stand alone or to be part of a longer piece of writing, has three parts.

The Topic Sentence

Every topic sentence should do two things: (1) give the specific topic of the paragraph and (2) present a specific feature or feeling about the topic. When writing your topic sentence, you could use the following formula as a guide.

    a specific topic *(hot-air ballooning)*
+ **a particular feature or feeling about the topic** *(has been a popular pastime for more than two centuries)*
= **an effective topic sentence** *(Hot-air ballooning has been a popular pastime for more than two centuries.)*

Tip

You can add phrases or clauses to your topic sentence as long as the basic sentence contains the main point your paragraph will explore.

> *Based on the simple scientific principle that hot air rises,* **hot-air ballooning has been a popular pastime for more than two centuries.**

The Body

Each sentence in the **body** of the paragraph should support the topic sentence while adding new details about the topic.

- Use specific details to make your paragraph interesting.
  Early balloons were kept aloft by burning a mixture of straw and manure.
- Use the method of organization that best suits your topic: classification, order of importance, chronological order, and so on.

The Closing Sentence

The **closing sentence** ends the paragraph. It may restate the topic, summarize the paragraph, or provide a link to the next paragraph.

Whatever the purpose, balloon enthusiasts throughout the world enjoy gliding on air.

Types of Paragraphs

There are four basic types of paragraphs: *narrative, descriptive, expository,* and *persuasive.*

Narrative Paragraph

A **narrative paragraph** tells a story. It may draw from the writer's personal experience or from other sources of information. A narrative paragraph is almost always organized chronologically, or according to time.

Topic Sentence

Body

Closing Sentence

A Good Start

Working in a day care center wasn't my idea of an ideal job, but it was the only one I had been offered, so I steeled myself for a summer surrounded by crazy kids. I was surprised to find the basement was relatively quiet. About eighteen kids of varying ages filled various areas of the main room. Some were building small projects, some were reading, and others were softly practicing musical instruments. I was taken to a back room with high, sunny windows. There, nine little kids were busy around a long table, engrossed in planting a minigarden in long wooden trays. I was an assistant supervisor, and soon we were giggling away, "hoeing" rows with our fingers and carefully planting tiny tomato and pepper seeds. One little girl shyly pulled on my shirt. Her neatly cornrowed hair sparkled in the sunlight as she softly asked me to help her plant some beans. I held a little jar over some newspaper as she carefully poured in some dirt. Then we selected some beans from a small pile. As she gently wriggled them down between the glass and the dirt, she explained that this way we could watch them grow. When we were finished, she gave me a smile and a hug. As we admired our work, I said to myself that this summer might be fun.

Respond to the reading. What is the tone of the story (sad, humorous, angry, and so on)? What details help make the story interesting? Amusing?

Write a narrative paragraph. Share your first job interview or your first tryout for an activity.

Descriptive Paragraph

A **descriptive paragraph** gives the reader a detailed picture of a person, a place, an object, or an event. This type of paragraph should contain a variety of sensory details—specific sights, sounds, smells, tastes, and textures.

Topic Sentence

Body

Closing Sentence

The Garden on the Balcony

In the middle of the city, high above the traffic and pollution, my mother has created a little bit of country on our apartment's balcony. When I step out through the sliding door, I feel as though I have been transported to a secret garden. The sounds of traffic are muffled, creating a soft background that mingles with the lively Tejano music my mom plays. On the left, a wall divides our balcony from our neighbor's. There, my mother has leaned a trellis and planted pots of climbing vines. In the summer, purple and pink trumpet-shaped flowers create a gorgeous cascade of color. In the fall, the leaves glow red. My dad built a slender table that hugs part of the safety wall along the front of the balcony, and there my mother has her herb garden, unusual pots containing lacy-leafed plants that fill the air with savory smells of basil and chive. Along the floor are large and small planters my sister created in her pottery class at the Y. Some overflow with bushy greenery; others contain bright geraniums. On the right, along our other wall, huddles our small gas barbecue. My father hung a board on that wall to hold garden tools and barbecue utensils. Nearby, two small lawn chairs flank a tiny, round wooden table. Two more chairs are folded against the wall, ready for a family dinner. On a stifling summer day, our balcony is our garden in the sky.

Respond to the reading. Does this description create a clear picture of the place being described? Which two or three details are particularly effective?

Write a descriptive paragraph. Describe someone you see in public. Use sensory details to let the reader know exactly how this person "appears" to you.

Expository Paragraph

An **expository paragraph** shares information about a specific topic. It presents facts, gives directions, defines terms, explains a process, and so on. An expository paragraph may use classification, comparison-contrast, cause-effect, problem-solution, or chronological organization.

Topic Sentence

Body

Closing Sentence

Hadrian's Wall

Hadrian's Wall was a monumental undertaking, a stone border that stretched across the northern part of England. Roman emperor Hadrian initiated the building of the wall in 122 C.E. The brick-and-turf wall ran 75 miles from east to west and took 10 years to complete. The wall varied from 8 to 10 feet in depth and from 13 to 16 feet in height. A turret used for signaling was placed each mile along the wall. Fourteen full-sized forts were eventually added along the wall, each housing up to 1,000 troops and employing gates to allow passage to the other side. The importance of the wall changed after Hadrian's death in 138 C.E. when the new emperor, Antoninus Pius, built his own wall—the Antonine Wall—about 100 miles north. In 164 C.E., emperor Marcus Aurelius once again utilized Hadrian's Wall, and it remained in use until the Roman withdrawal from Britain around the fourth century. Although some might argue the wall was built to separate Scotland from England, in fact, the wall is south of the Scottish border. Actually, the wall marked the northern border of the Roman Empire at the time and had several other practical purposes as well. For one, it was an effective warning to northern barbarians not to challenge Rome. It also kept soldiers occupied and provided trade opportunities for the locals. Through the years, stones were taken to build other structures, and today the wall is in disrepair. However, Hadrian's Wall is still a tourist destination, an impressive reminder of an ancient, changing Britain.

Respond to the reading. What is the main point of the above paragraph? Give three examples of details used to support that idea.

Write an expository paragraph. Include plenty of details to support your topic sentence.

Basic Paragraph Skills

Persuasive Paragraph

A **persuasive paragraph** expresses an opinion and tries to convince the reader that the opinion is valid. To be persuasive, a writer must include effective supporting reasons and facts.

Topic Sentence

Body

Closing Sentence

Control the Pet Population

Spaying or neutering is a humane way to treat the growing problem of unwanted animals in the United States. These simple operations can eliminate aggressive behavior and roaming, reducing the risk that a pet may be hit by a car or injured in a fight with another animal. While "fixing" a pet may make it gentler, it will not eliminate the protective behavior desired of watchdogs. Some say that fixing a cat or dog will make it fat and lazy, but it doesn't—overfeeding and lack of exercise do that. Spaying or neutering a pet may actually protect the animal's health, reducing or eliminating the risk of various cancers. Altered pets, in fact, live long, healthy lives. Perhaps the most compelling reason for altering a pet is to reduce the number of unwanted animals that fill pounds and humane societies. According to the American Humane Society, one dog or cat can be responsible for thousands of puppies or kittens born within a seven-year period. Controlling the pet population can reduce the numbers of homeless dogs and cats that roam city streets and the countryside, just trying to survive. These abandoned animals often revert to the wild, posing a threat or nuisance similar to the one posed by coyotes. It's cruel and even dangerous to allow animals to continue having unwanted litters. If people spay or neuter their pets, we can create a healthier, safer world for domestic animals.

Basic Elements

Respond to the reading. What are three main reasons offered for the writer's opinion? Which of these reasons is the most important?

Write a persuasive paragraph. Write a paragraph presenting your opinion. Include at least three strong reasons to support your argument.

Patterns of Organization

On the next five pages, sample paragraphs show basic patterns of organization. Reviewing these samples can help you organize your own writing.

Classification Order

Classification is used when you need to divide or break down a topic into categories. The line diagram below helps to organize the topic of plastics.

Line Diagram

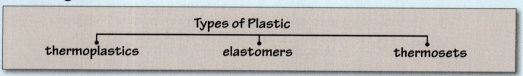

Types of Plastic

Topic Sentence

Since the first plastic, cellulose nitrate, was developed more than 100 years ago, this durable material has become an integral part of daily life. Three structurally different plastics are created by chemically changing natural materials or by synthesizing raw materials. The three types are characterized by their molecular structure, which determines how each type reacts to heat.

Body

Thermoplastics have a branched molecular structure that forms the weakest bond. Pliable at normal temperatures, they melt into a sticky mess with high heat (packaging). Durable *elastomers* have a crosslink structure that allows for flexibility. Once shaped through heating, however, they cannot be reshaped but retain flexibility (tires). *Thermosets*, the most tightly structured plastics, are very hard, with a tightly woven molecular structure that resists reshaping once they are cured. This type of plastic is used to make everything from outlet covers to computer shelves.

Closing Sentence

Different types of plastics, each designed to meet different needs, all play key roles in today's world.

 Respond to the reading. How is the topic classified in this paragraph? What are two things that you learned about the topic?

Comparison-Contrast Order

Organizing by **comparison** allows you to show the similarities or differences between two subjects. A Venn diagram effectively organizes this type of paragraph.

Venn Diagram

Marsupials
- Suckle young
- Permanent pouch
- Have live babies
- More mammal-like
- More than 200 species

Both
- Have a marsupium bone
- One baby per year
- Give babies milk

Monotremes
- Secrete milk on fur
- Temporary pouch
- Lay eggs
- Some reptilian characteristics
- Only three species

Marsupials and Monotremes

Topic Sentence

Australia's marsupials and monotremes are very different from each other. Both types of mammals give birth to one baby per year and possess a marsupium bone that supports a pouch. However, the similarities end there. The monotreme does not possess a permanent pouch, nor does it suckle its young the way marsupials do. It secretes the milk onto its fur, and the baby laps it up. Marsupials give birth to live, undeveloped babies that grow within the mother's pouch; monotremes lay eggs. Physically, monotremes are reptilian-like with horizontal limb orientation, outward-turned rear feet, and the ability to regulate their body temperature. Marsupials have a more vertical bone structure and are warm blooded. There are only three species of monotremes—the platypus and the long- and short-nosed echidna—and they are found only in Australia and New Guinea. There are more than 200 species of marsupials, some of which are found in South America. One species, the opossum, is native to North America. Marsupials and monotremes are amazing and unusual mammals that are very different from each other.

Body

Closing Sentence

Respond to the reading. How many differences between the two topics are identified? Name them.

Cause-Effect Order

The **cause-effect** organizational pattern allows you to discuss the effects of a particular event or happening (the cause). The paragraph below discusses one cause (laughter) and its effects.

Cause-Effect Organizer

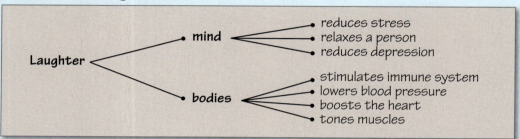

Topic Sentence

Body

Closing Sentence

The Health Benefits of Laughter

A sense of humor can be one of the most powerful forces in our lives, affecting both the mind and the body. Laughter perks up brain function by stimulating the release of chemicals called *endorphins*. These chemicals relax a person, alleviate stress, reduce depression, and provide an overall sense of well-being. Endorphins do more than just make people feel good. Research shows that these chemicals, stimulated by laughter, have an even more important effect on the body. They can help the body deal with pain and even stimulate the immune system. Patients with a positive attitude and a well-developed sense of humor actually get well faster than those who flounder in pain and self-pity. Laughter can positively affect a person in other ways as well, lowering blood pressure and improving heart health. Laughing can even tone muscles. People who laugh hard may experience a side ache. That's because laughing actually stimulates the muscles. Although not a substitute for a real workout, belly laughs provide healthy exercise. So that old saying, "Laughter is the best medicine," may be true.

 Respond to the reading. What are two ways laughter can affect us? Give two supporting details for each.

Process Organization

Process organization uses a step-by-step approach to explain a process. You start by introducing the topic and then follow with an appropriate series of steps.

Process Diagram

The Process of Cheese Making
Step 1: bacteria culture added to milk to produce lactic acid
Step 2: milk separates and rennet stirred in
Step 3: curds cut and drained, solids heated
Step 4: curds salted and put in press
Step 5: cheese coated with wax

Cheese Making

Topic Sentence

Cheese making was a chore for pioneers, but today many people enjoy making cheese. Although the process has been modernized, cheese is still made by souring and curdling milk and then separating liquids from the solids.

Body

To begin, warm milk is "ripened" by the addition of a bacterial culture. This starter culture produces lactic acid in the milk, which facilitates the separation of the milk into curds (solids) and whey (liquid). Then rennet, a chemical derived from either an animal or vegetable source, is stirred into the mixture to further coagulate the milk solids. Once the curds are set, they are cut into smaller pieces and drained, and the solids are heated gradually until firm. The curds are drained again and then salted and put into a cheese press to squeeze out the remaining whey. During the pressing process, the cheese is turned regularly to facilitate drying. Once the cheese has dried, it may be coated with a special wax to preserve it. Some cheeses can be eaten right away while others are best left to age for better flavor.

Closing Sentence

With a little effort and know-how, anyone can make delicious homemade cheese.

Respond to the reading. What transitional words or phrases are used to connect ideas? Name three.

Climax Organization

Climax (specific to general) is a method of organization in which the specific details lead up to an important summary statement. (If a topic sentence is used, it is placed at the end.) The paragraph below shows the excitement building as the writer waits for a concert to begin.

Details List

Leading up to a concert
- house lights dimmed
- multicolored spotlights begin
- sound builds
- feet stamping, hand clapping, whistling
- guitar blasts
- flash of light, shower of sparks

Opening Sentence

Body

Summary/ Topic Sentence

Anxiously Waiting

As the lights dimmed in the amphitheater, multicolored spotlights began to circle overhead, bouncing off the ceiling and swirling over the heads of the crowd. The sound began to build. At first, it sounded like thunder rumbling in the distance, but soon it grew to a deafening roar. People all around were stamping their feet, clapping their hands, and whistling through their fingers to show that they were ready for the show to begin. The crowd noise was soon drowned out by a blast of bass guitar and drums that seemed to come out of nowhere. Behind a blinding flash of light and a shower of glittering sparks, the band appeared on stage and began to play. At last, the concert had begun.

Respond to the reading. What types of details does the writer use to build to the climax? Give two examples of effective details.

Basic Essay Skills

As you take more advanced classes, you will find that most of your writing assignments are in the form of essays—from essay tests to responses to literature. In these essays, you will explain, argue, or describe your thinking on a particular topic. The approach you take in each essay will depend on the guidelines established by your instructor and on your own judgment about how the topic should be presented. You may decide a traditional, straightforward approach works best, or you may find a more creative approach effective.

No matter which approach you take, developing an essay can be a challenge. You must have a good understanding of your topic and confidence in your position on that topic. Then you must develop your ideas so that your reader can clearly understand your thinking. The information in this chapter serves as a basic guide to essay writing.

- **Understanding the Basic Parts**
- **Outlining Your ideas**
- **Writing Thesis Statements**
- **Creating Great Beginnings**
- **Developing the Middle Part**
- **Using Transitions**
- **Shaping Great Endings**
- **Key Terms, Techniques, and Forms**

"Writing is the best way to talk without being interrupted."
—Jules Renard

Understanding the Basic Parts

Each part of an essay—the introduction, middle, and conclusion—plays an important role. To develop your writing, refer to the suggestions below and to the writing models earlier in this book.

Beginning Your opening paragraph should capture your reader's attention and state your thesis. Here are several ways to capture your reader's attention:

- Tell a dramatic or exciting story (anecdote) about the topic.
- Ask an intriguing question or two.
- Provide a few surprising facts or statistics.
- Provide an interesting quotation.
- Explain your personal experience or involvement with the topic.

Middle The middle paragraphs should support your thesis statement. They provide information that fully explains the thesis statement. For example, in an essay about the changes in the cartoon animation industry, each middle paragraph could focus on one main trend in that industry. Follow your own outline while writing this section.

Ending Your closing paragraph should summarize your thesis and leave the reader with something to think about. Here are some strategies for creating a strong closing:

- Review your main points.
- Emphasize the special importance of one main point.
- Answer any questions the reader may still have.
- Draw a conclusion and put the information in perspective.
- Provide a significant final thought for the reader.

Outlining Your Ideas

Once you've established a general pattern of development, you're ready to organize the main points and supporting details that you will cover in your essay. To help you organize this information, it may be wise to use a list, a topic outline, or a sentence outline.

Topic Outline

An outline is an orderly listing of related ideas. In a **topic outline**, each new idea is stated as a word or phrase rather than as a complete sentence. Before you start, write your working thesis statement at the top of your paper to keep you focused on the subject of your essay. Do not attempt to outline your opening and closing paragraphs unless specifically asked to do so.

> Introduction
> I. Effects of malnutrition on the body
>   A. Extreme weight loss and stunted growth
>   B. Frequent infections
>   C. Less resistance to diseases
> II. Extreme forms of malnutrition
>   A. Marasmus
>   B. Kwashiorkor
> III. Effects of malnutrition on development
>   A. Limited ability to walk and to talk
>   B. Stunted intellectual development
>   C. Effects continuing into adulthood
> Conclusion

Sentence Outline

A **sentence outline** contains more detail than a topic outline, and each new idea is expressed as a complete sentence. A sentence outline is often required for longer essays or research papers.

> Introduction
> I. Genetic engineering is a form of biotechnology.
>   A. Scientists can manipulate genes.
>   B. Genes can be copied and moved to cells in other species.
>   C. Scientists can recombine genes and clone entire organisms.
> II. Genetic engineering affects animal and plant breeding.
>   A. Past species—improvement efforts proved unpredictable.
>   B. Now development time is cut dramatically with better results.
>   C. Animals are potential chemical factories, and new animals can be created and patented.
> III. Genetic engineering is feared by some.
>   A. Dangerous organisms could be released.
>   B. Public confidence in scientists has been undermined.
> Conclusion

Writing Thesis Statements

In most cases, a thesis statement takes a stand or expresses a specific feature or feeling about your topic. An effective thesis statement gives you the necessary direction to develop your essay.

Using a Formula

    a specific topic (*multicultural education*)
+ **a particular feature or feeling about the topic** (*is vital to a society made up of many different peoples*)
= **an effective thesis statement** (*Multicultural education is vital to a society made up of many different peoples.*)

Sample Thesis Statements

Writing Assignment: Examine a psychological theme in a novel.
Specific Topic: *Animal Dreams*
Thesis Statement: In *Animal Dreams* by Barbara Kingsolver (**topic**), a woman's search for personal identity is juxtaposed with her father's identity loss to Alzheimer's (**particular feature**).

Writing Assignment: Defend a strongly held principle.
Specific Topic: The use of chemicals in food production
Thesis Statement: The use of chemicals in food production (**topic**) needs to be more stringently regulated (**particular stand**).

Writing Assignment: Review a music concert.
Specific Topic: The hip hop group Word
Thesis Statement: The hip hop group Word (**topic**) combines a powerful message with an infectious rhythm (**particular feeling**).

Thesis Checklist

Be sure that your thesis statement . . .
_____ identifies a limited, specific topic,
_____ focuses on a particular feature or feeling about the topic,
_____ can be supported with convincing facts and details, and
_____ meets the requirements of the assignment.

Creating Great Beginnings

The opening paragraph of an essay should grab the reader's attention, identify your topic, and present your thesis. Try one of these approaches to start an opening paragraph:

- **Start with an interesting fact.**
  Recently, the question has come up about whether astronauts ever really did walk on the moon.

- **Ask an interesting question.**
  What if the government had set up an elaborate hoax to make people think astronauts had landed on the moon?

- **Start with a quotation.**
  "The body of physical evidence that humans did walk on the moon is simply overwhelming." So says Dr. Robert Park, Director of the Washington office of the American Physical Society and a known critic of NASA's manned space program.

Trying a Beginning Strategy

If you have trouble coming up with a good opening paragraph, follow the step-by-step example below.

First sentence: Grab the reader's attention with an opening sentence (see approaches above).

> Recently, the question has come up about whether astronauts ever really did walk on the moon.

Second sentence: Give some background information about the topic.

> The creators of a television exposé show suggest that the whole moon landing was really staged in a movie studio.

Third sentence: Introduce the specific topic of the essay in a way that builds up to the thesis statement.

> However, this criticism has not gone unchallenged by NASA scientists.

Fourth sentence: Give the thesis statement of the paper (see page **626**).

> The fact is, there is overwhelming evidence to support the country's claims that astronauts have in fact walked on the moon.

Developing the Middle Part

The middle part of an essay is where you do most of the work. In this part, you develop the main points that support your thesis statement.

Use your outline or other planning notes as a guide when you write this section. However, new ideas may pop into your head as you go along. You may incorporate these ideas into your draft or make a note to research the ideas later.

Advancing Your Thesis

Keep these points in mind as you explain and develop your thesis statement.

- **Cover your main points.** Develop each main point in a paragraph or series of paragraphs.
- **Give background information.** If necessary, provide some history to put the topic in context.
- **Define terms.** Clarify any terms that your reader is not likely to know.
- **Order the main points.** Present the main ideas in a logical order (according to your outline).

Testing Your Ideas

When you write the middle part of an essay, you're testing your first thoughts about your topic. Here are some ways to test your ideas as you write.

- **Raise questions.** Anticipate any questions the reader may have about your topic.
- **Consider alternative ideas.** Take inventory of your thesis as you go along: Do you need to strengthen or rethink it? Also look at your main points from different angles.
- **Answer objections.** Address different points of view about your topic.

Building a Coherent Structure

Each middle paragraph should include main points and details that logically develop your thesis.

- **Develop one paragraph at a time.** Start a new paragraph whenever you shift to another main idea about the topic.
- **Connect your main points.** Use transitional phrases to link each new paragraph with the preceding one. (See page **629**.)

Basic Essay Skills

Using Transitions

Transitions can be used to connect one sentence to another sentence within a paragraph, or to connect one paragraph to another within a longer essay or report. The lists that follow show a number of transitions and how they are used. Each **colored list** is a group of transitions that could work well together in a piece of writing.

Words used to show location

above	around	between	inside	outside
across	behind	by	into	over
against	below	down	near	throughout
along	beneath	in back of	next to	to the right
among	beside	in front of	on top of	under

Above	In front of	On top of		
Below	Beside	Next to		
To the left	In back of	Beneath		
To the right				

Words used to show time

about	before	in the end	second	today
after	during	later	soon	tomorrow
as soon as	finally	meanwhile	then	until
at	first	next	to begin	yesterday

First	To begin	Now	First	Before
Second	To continue	Soon	Then	During
Third	To conclude	Eventually	Next	After
Finally			In the end	

Words used to compare things

also	both	like	one way	
as	in the same way	likewise	similarly	

In the same way	One way		
Also	Another way		
Similarly	Both		

Basic Elements

Words used to contrast (show differences)

although	even though	on the other hand	still
but	however	otherwise	yet

On the other hand   Although
Even though   Yet
Still   Nevertheless

Words used to emphasize a point

again	for this reason	to emphasize	truly
especially	in fact	to repeat	

For this reason   Truly   In fact
Especially   To emphasize   To repeat

Words used to conclude or summarize

all in all	because	in conclusion	therefore
as a result	finally	lastly	to sum it up

Because   As a result   To sum it up   Therefore
In conclusion   All in all   Because   Finally

Words used to add information

additionally	and	finally	moreover
again	another	for example	next
along with	as well	for instance	other
also	besides	in addition	

For example   For instance   Next   Another
Additionally   Besides   Moreover   Along with
Finally   Next   Also   As well

Words used to clarify

for example	for instance	in other words	that is

For instance   For example
In other words   Equally important

Shaping Great Endings

The closing paragraph of a paper should summarize your thesis and leave the reader with something to think about. When writing your closing paragraph, use two or more of the following approaches:

- **Review** your main points.
- **Emphasize** the special importance of one main point.
- **Answer any questions** the reader may still have.
- **Draw a conclusion** and put the information in perspective.
- **Provide a significant final thought** for the reader.

Trying an Ending Strategy

If you have trouble coming up with an effective closing paragraph, follow the step-by-step example below.

First sentence: Reflect on the topic. Start by reflecting on the material presented previously about the topic.

> The moon landing was real and was an important milestone in the history of the United States space program.

Second sentence: Add another point. Include a final point of interest that you didn't mention before.

> If the landing had been merely a hoax, other countries such as Russia and China could have easily staged their own "moon landing," but they didn't.

Third sentence: Emphasize the most important point. Stress the importance of one or more key points that support the thesis.

> The information gathered by the moon astronauts, along with the rocks they brought home, proved invaluable to modern technology.

Fourth sentence: Wrap up the topic or draw a conclusion. Add one final thought about the topic or draw a conclusion from the points you've presented in the writing.

> The moon walk was real—as real as the new industries and materials developed during its planning, and as real as the pride people still feel when they remember those remarkable astronauts who took that first "giant leap for mankind."

ELPS 2C, 4C

Learning Key Writing Terms

The next two pages include important terms related to writing. Refer to these pages whenever you have a question about the vocabulary associated with any part of the writing process.

Balance	Arranging words or phrases in a way that gives them equal importance
Body	The main part of a piece of writing, containing details that support or develop the thesis statement
Brainstorming	Collecting ideas by thinking freely about all the possibilities; used most often in groups
Central idea	The main point of a piece of writing, often stated in a thesis statement or a topic sentence
Closing sentence	The summary or final sentence in a piece of writing
Coherence	The logical arrangement of ideas that makes them clear and easy to follow
Dialogue	Written conversation between two or more people
Emphasis	Giving great importance to a specific idea in a piece of writing
Exposition	Writing that explains and informs
Figurative language	Language that goes beyond the normal meaning of the words used, often called "figures of speech"
Focus (thesis)	The specific part of a topic that is written about in an essay
Generalization	A general statement that gives an overall view rather than focusing on specific details
Grammar	The rules that govern the standard structure and features of a language
Idiom	A phrase or an expression that means something different from what the words actually say
	The answer was really out in left field. (This means the answer was not even close to being correct.)
	Next year you'll sing a different tune. (This means you'll think differently.)
Jargon	The special language of a certain group or occupation
	The weaver pointed out the fabric's unique warp and woof.
	Computer jargon: **byte icon server virus**

Limiting the subject	Narrowing a general subject to a more specific one
Literal	The actual dictionary meaning of a word; language that means exactly what it appears to mean
Loaded words	Words slanted for or against the subject **The new tax bill helps the rich and hurts the poor.**
Logic	Correctly using facts, examples, and reasons to support a point
Modifiers	Words, phrases, or clauses that limit or describe another word or group of words
Objective	Writing that gives factual information without adding feelings or opinions (See *subjective*.)
Poetic license	A writer's freedom to bend the rules of writing to achieve a certain effect
Point of view	The position or angle from which a story is told (See page **354**.)
Prose	Writing in standard sentence form
Purpose	The specific goal of the writing
Style	The author's unique choice of words and sentences
Subjective	Writing that includes the writer's feelings, attitudes, and opinions (See *objective*.)
Supporting details	Facts or ideas used to sustain the main point
Syntax	The order and relationship of words in a sentence
Theme	The main point or unifying idea of a piece of writing
Thesis statement	A statement of the purpose, or main idea, of an essay
Tone	The writer's attitude toward the subject
Topic	The specific subject of a piece of writing
Topic sentence	The sentence that carries the main idea of a paragraph
Transitions	Words or phrases that connect or tie ideas together
Unity	A sense of solidarity in writing in which each sentence helps to develop the main idea
Usage	The way in which people use language (*Standard* language follows the rules; *nonstandard* language does not.)
Voice	A writer's personal tone or feeling that comes across in a piece of writing

Using Writing Techniques

Experiment with some of these techniques in your own essays and stories.

Allusion	A reference to a familiar person, place, thing, or event **Mario threw me my mitt. "Hey, Babe Ruth, you forgot this!"**
Analogy	A comparison of similar ideas or objects to help clarify one of them **The mind of a bigot is like the pupil of the eye: The more light you shine on it, the more it will contract.** —Oliver Wendell Holmes, Jr.
Anecdote	A brief story used to illustrate or make a point **It is said that the last words John Adams uttered were "Thomas Jefferson survives." Ironically, Jefferson had died just a few hours earlier. Both deaths occurred on July 4, 1826—the 50th anniversary of the Declaration of Independence shepherded by the two great men.** (This ironic anecdote intensifies the importance of both men in our nation's history.)
Colloquialism	A common word or phrase suitable for everyday conversation but not for formal speech or writing **"Cool" and "rad" are colloquialisms suggesting approval.**
Exaggeration	An overstatement or a stretching of the truth to emphasize a point (See *hyperbole* and *overstatement*.) **We opened up the boat's engine and sped along at a million miles an hour.**
Flashback	A technique in which a writer interrupts a story to go back and relive an earlier time or event **I stopped at the gate, panting. Suddenly I was seven years old again, and my brother was there, calling me "chicken" from the edge of the stone well. Then I opened my eyes and heard only the crickets chirping. The years, the well, and my brother were gone. I turned back to the road, determined to get home before nightfall.**
Foreshadowing	Hints about what will happen next in a story **As Mai explained why she had to break their date, she noticed Luke looking past her. Turning, she saw Meg smiling—at Luke.**
Hyperbole	(hi-púr-bə-lē) Exaggeration used to emphasize a point **The music was loud enough to make your ears bleed.**
Irony	An expression in which the author says one thing but means just the opposite **As we all know, there's nothing students love more than homework.**

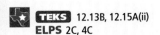

Basic Essay Skills

Juxtaposition	Putting two words or ideas close together to create a contrasting of ideas or an ironic meaning **Ah, the** sweet smell **of** fuel emissions**!**
Local color	The use of details that are common in a certain place
Metaphor	A figure of speech that compares two things without using the words *like* or *as* **The sheep were** dense, dancing clouds **scuttling across the road.**
Overstatement	An exaggeration or a stretching of the truth (See *exaggeration* and *hyperbole*.) **If I eat one more piece of turkey,** I will burst**!**
Oxymoron	Connecting two words with opposite meanings **small fortune cruel kindness original copy**
Paradox	A true statement that says two opposite things **As I crossed the finish line dead last, I felt a surge of triumph.**
Parallelism	Repeating similar grammatical structures (words, phrases, or sentences) to give writing rhythm We cannot undo, we will not forget, **and** we should not ignore **the pain of the past.**
Personification	A figure of speech in which a nonhuman thing is given human characteristics **The computer spit out my disk.**
Pun	A phrase that uses words that sound the same in a way that gives them a funny effect **I call my dog Trousers because he** pants **so much.**
Simile	A figure of speech that compares two things using *like* or *as* **Her silent anger was** like a rock wall**, hard and impenetrable.**
Slang	Informal words or phrases used by a particular group of people **cool it hang out shoot the curl**
Symbol	A concrete object used to represent an idea
Understatement	The opposite of exaggeration; using very calm language to call attention to an object or an idea **The accident was fairly minor; I only broke both legs and arms.**

Basic Elements

Knowing the Different Forms

Finding the right form for your writing is just as important as finding the right topic. When you are selecting a form, be sure to ask yourself whom you're writing for (your *audience*) and why you're writing (your *purpose*).

Anecdote	A brief story that helps to make a point
Autobiography	A writer's story of his or her own life
Biography	A writer's story of someone else's life
Book review	An essay offering an opinion about a book (not to be confused with *literary analysis*)
Cause and effect	An examination of an event, the forces leading up to that event, and the effects following the event
Character sketch	A brief description of a specific character showing some aspect of that character's personality
Descriptive writing	Writing with sensory details that allow the reader to clearly visualize a person, a place, a thing, or an idea
Editorial	A letter or an article offering an opinion, an idea, or a solution
Essay	A thoughtful piece of writing in which ideas are explained, analyzed, or evaluated
Expository writing	Writing that explains something by presenting its steps, causes, or kinds
Eyewitness account	A report giving specific details of an event
Fable	A short story that teaches a lesson or moral, often using talking animals as the main characters
Fantasy	A story set in an imaginary world in which the characters usually have supernatural powers or abilities
Freewriting	Spontaneous, rapid writing to explore your thoughts about a topic of interest
Historical fiction	An invented story based on an actual historical event
Interview	Writing based on facts and details obtained through speaking with another person
Journal writing	Writing regularly to record personal observations, thoughts, and ideas

Literary analysis	A careful examination or interpretation of some aspect of a piece of literature
Myth	A traditional story intended to explain a mystery of nature, religion, or culture
Novel	A book-length story with several characters and a well-developed plot, usually with one or more subplots
Personal narrative	Writing that shares an event or experience from the writer's personal life
Persuasive writing	Writing intended to persuade the reader to follow the writer's way of thinking about something
Play	A form that uses dialogue to tell a story, usually meant to be performed in front of an audience
Poem	A creative expression that may use rhyme, rhythm, and imagery
Problem-solution	Writing that presents a problem followed by a proposed solution
Process paper	Writing that explains how a process works, or how to do or make something
Profile	An essay that describes an individual or re-creates a time period
Proposal	Writing that includes specific information about an idea or a project that is being considered for approval
Research report	An essay that shares information about a topic that has been thoroughly researched
Response to literature	Writing that is a reaction to something the writer has read
Science fiction	Writing based on real or imaginary science and often set in the future
Short story	A short fictional piece with only a few characters and one conflict or problem
Summary	Writing that presents the most important ideas from a longer piece of writing
Tall tale	A humorous, exaggerated story about a character or an animal that does impossible things
Tragedy	Literature in which the hero fails or is destroyed because of a serious character flaw

TEKS 12.13D, 12.17B, 12.18A, 12.19A
ELPS IB, 5C, 5D, 5E, 5F

Editing and Proofreading

The editing and proofreading marks on page **639** allow you to make changes to your drafts quickly and easily while keeping a record for your reference. Follow the guidelines below to use the editing and proofreading marks.

When you write . . .

- **Double-space your drafts.** This will allow room for you, your teacher, and your peers to mark changes.
- **Try to get all of your ideas on paper.** Editing and proofreading is easier when most of the information you need is already in your draft. This will help your reviewers understand your meaning, too.

As you edit . . .

- **Mark changes clearly.** Study the symbols, meaning, and examples of the editing and proofreading marks and use them correctly. Use a colored pen or pencil so you can easily see the changes.

To produce your final copy . . .

- **Carefully implement the changes.** If you are writing by hand, rewrite one sentence at a time, checking to make sure you have copied it correctly. If your are using a computer, input the changes one at a time, checking them off as you go.
- **Proof your changes.** After you have implemented your changes, carefully check that you have made them correctly. Be sure you haven't introduced any new errors.

Editing Checklist

Use the following checklist to edit your work. Be sure to check that your writing also meets the requirements specific to your genre, audience, and purpose.

_____ Have I followed the rules of capitalization?
_____ Are my sentences punctuated correctly?
_____ Have I used a variety of sentence structures?
_____ Are all the details necessary and clear?
_____ Do my subjects and verbs agree?
_____ Are all words spelled correctly?
_____ Do all the words, phrases, sentences, and paragraphs make my meaning clear?

Editing and Proofreading   **639**

Editing and Proofreading Marks

Use the symbols and letters below to show where and how your writing needs to be changed. Your teachers and peers may also use these symbols to point out errors in your writing or to suggest areas for improvement.

Symbols	Meaning	Example	Corrected Example
≡	Capitalize a letter.	George orwell wrote *1984*.	George **O**rwell wrote *1984*.
/	Make a capital letter lowercase.	His novel explores life without personal Freedom.	His novel explores life without personal **f**reedom.
⊙	Insert (add) a period.	*1984* focuses on a parallel world in the future.It is . . .	*1984* focuses on a parallel world in the future**.** It is . . .
◯ or sp.	Correct spelling.	Winston Smith tries to escape the (tyrany).	Winston Smith tries to escape the **tyranny**.
⌿	Delete (take out) or replace.	His every movement is scrutinized.	His every **move** is scrutinized.
∧	Insert here.	Winston and Julia create a plan. (complicated)	Winston and Julia create a **complicated** plan.
∧ ∧ ∧	Insert a comma, a colon, or a semicolon.	Together they profess their allegiance against the Party.	Together**,** they profess their allegiance against the Party.
∨ ∨ ∨	Insert an apostrophe or quotation marks.	OBrien is not a member of the Brotherhood.	O**'**Brien is not a member of the Brotherhood.
? ! ∧ ∧	Insert a question mark or an exclamation point.	Broken, Winston screams, "Not me"	Broken, Winston screams, "Not me**!**"
¶	Start a new paragraph.	¶Winston is a changed man after he . . .	Winston is a changed man after he . . .
∼	Switch words or letters.	Julia (admits ultimately) her betrayal.	Julia **ultimately admits** her betrayal.

Basic Elements

ELPS 2C, 4C, 5B

Proofreader's Guide

Checking Mechanics	641
Understanding Idioms	702
Using the Right Word	708
Parts of Speech	728
Understanding Sentences	762

Learning Language

Work with a partner to learn the following words from this unit.

1. When you **address** someone, you talk to that person directly.
   Would you look an enemy in the eyes or look down when you **address** him?

2. To **unearth** something is to discover it.
   Tell about a secret you have **unearthed**.

3. When you **speculate**, you guess.
   What can you **speculate** about your future?

4. If you **omit** something, you leave it out.
   If you needed to shorten a research paper, what part would you **omit**?

Checking Mechanics

Period

641.1 At the End of a Sentence

Use a **period** at the end of a sentence that makes a statement, requests something, or gives a mild command.

> (Statement) **The man who does not read good books has no advantage over the man who can't read them.**
> —Mark Twain
>
> (Request) **Please bring your folders and notebooks to class.**
>
> (Mild command) **Listen carefully so that you understand these instructions.**

Note: It is not necessary to place a period after a statement that has parentheses around it and is part of another sentence.

My dog Bobot (I don't quite remember how he acquired this name) is a Chesapeake Bay retriever—a hunting dog—who is afraid of loud noises.

641.2 After an Initial or an Abbreviation

Place a period after an initial or an abbreviation (in American English).

Ms. Sen. D.D.S. M.F.A. M.D. Jr. U.S. p.m. a.m.
Edna St. Vincent Millay   Booker T. Washington   D. H. Lawrence

Note: When an abbreviation is the last word in a sentence, use only one period at the end of the sentence.

Jaleesa eyed each door until she found the name Fletcher B. Gale, M.D.

641.3 As a Decimal Point

A period is used as a decimal point.

New York City has a budget of $46.9 billion to serve its 8.1 million people.

Exclamation Point

641.4 To Express Strong Feeling

Use the **exclamation point** (sparingly) to express strong feeling. You may place it after a word, a phrase, or a sentence.

> **"When I was a child," Marci told her son, "we didn't have cell phones, answering machines, or cable TV. Imagine that!"**

Question Mark

642.1 Direct Question

Place a **question mark** at the end of a direct question.

> How should I do this? I wondered. Am I supposed to give my dog his medication with a treat? Or should I try to hide it in his food?
>
> Where did my body end and the crystal and white world begin?
>
> —Ralph Ellison, *Invisible Man*

When a question ends with a quotation that is also a question, use only one question mark, and place it within the quotation marks.

> On road trips, do you remember driving your parents crazy by asking, "Are we there yet?"

Note: Do not use a question mark after an indirect question.

> When I went backstage on opening night, I asked Mr. Mayans where my costume was.
>
> Marta asked me if I finished my calculus homework yet.

642.2 To Show Uncertainty

Use a question mark within parentheses to show uncertainty.

> This summer marks the 20th season (?) of the American Players Theatre.

642.3 Short Question Within a Sentence

Use a question mark for a short question within parentheses.

> We crept so quietly (had they heard us?) past the kitchen door and back to our room.

Use a question mark for a short question within dashes.

> He woke up at 4 a.m. with his heart beating fast—who hasn't had a nightmare, at one time or another?—but he soon forgot the dream and went back to sleep.

Practice

Periods, Exclamation Points, and Question Marks

 For each line in the paragraphs below, write where periods, exclamation points, or question marks are needed. Write the word preceding each mark. (Write "none" if no marks are needed.)

1   Herme was persistent about going after the job that he wanted

2   "A wildland firefighter" his mother exclaimed "Why did you choose a
3   job like that"

4   "Actually, Ma," Herme answered, "someday I want to be a smoke
5   jumper, like T J Brookes"

6   His mother got that "I'm going to win this argument" look on her face
7   "A smoke jumper" she cried out "I don't think so Mrs Wagero, down at the
8   church, she told me all about Terrance, Jr, the smoke jumper He still almost
9   gives his mama a heart attack every time he fights one of those wildfires No
10 You will *not* be a smoke jumper"

11 Herme picked up his backpack, kissed his mother good-bye, and headed
12 for the door The state employment office opened at eight The starting pay
13 for a tech trainee was just $700 an hour, but to Herme the low wage was
14 worth it—just to train as a wildland
15 firefighter, that was enough

Model

Model the following sentences to practice punctuating a sentence with a tag question (a short question at the end of a statement) correctly.

That's the Russian faith all over, isn't it? . . . Surely that's Russian, isn't it?
—Fyodor M. Dostoevsky, *The Brothers Karamazov*

Comma

644.1 Between Two Independent Clauses

Use a **comma** between two independent clauses that are joined by a coordinating conjunction *(and, but, or, nor, for, yet, so)*.

> I want to teach English in Latin America, but I need to study Spanish for at least another year before I can apply.

Note: Do not confuse a sentence containing a compound verb for a compound sentence.

> I had to erase my drawing and start all over.

644.2 To Separate Adjectives

Use commas to separate two or more adjectives that *equally* modify the same noun. (Note: Do not use a comma between the last adjective and the noun.)

> Bao's eyes met the hard, bright lights hanging directly above her.
> —Julie Ament, student writer

A Closer Look

To determine whether adjectives modify equally—and should, therefore, be separated by commas—use these two tests:

1. Shift the order of the adjectives; if the sentence is clear, the adjectives modify equally. (In the example below, *hot* and *smelly* can be shifted and the sentence is still clear; *usual* and *morning* cannot.)

2. Insert *and* between the adjectives; if the sentence reads well, use a comma when the *and* is omitted. (The word *and* can be inserted between *hot* and *smelly*, but *and* does not make sense between *usual* and *morning*.)

> Matty was tired of working in the hot, smelly kitchen and decided to take her usual morning walk.

644.3 To Separate Contrasted Elements

Use commas to separate contrasted elements within a sentence. Often the word or phrase that is set off is preceded by *not*.

> Since the stereotypes were about Asians, and not African Americans, no such reaction occurred.
> —Emmeline Chen, "Eliminating the Lighter Shades of Stereotyping"

Mechanics

Practice

Commas 1
- Between Two Independent Clauses
- To Separate Adjectives
- To Separate Contrasted Elements

Indicate where commas are needed in the following sentences by writing the commas along with the words that surround them.

1. The newspaper printed a correction that Dr. Ellen Ochoa is Hispanic not Hawaiian.

2. Ellen was the first Hispanic female astronaut and she was also the inventor of optical analysis systems.

3. Her mother was a determined hardworking single parent who earned a college degree while raising five children.

4. Ellen possesses a powerful never-ending commitment to learn.

5. She is most often recognized as an astronaut not as an inventor.

6. Ellen completed a brief vigorous training program before her first shuttle ride.

7. "Usually it takes quite a bit longer but I got lucky," she said.

8. Ellen was accepted into the space program in 1991 and in 1993 she completed her first shuttle mission.

9. Few people know that she is also a talented experienced flutist.

10. Ochoa says, "Many doors opened for me when I completed college and I encourage all Latinas to seek out interesting challenging careers."

Model

Model the following sentence to practice using commas to separate adjectives.

> She had a quiet, unthreatening way about her that made older, uglier, fatter people take to her despite her beauty.
> —Maeve Binchy, *Scarlet Feather*

Comma (continued)

646.1 To Set Off Appositives

A specific kind of explanatory word or phrase called an **appositive** identifies or renames a preceding noun or pronoun.

> **Benson,** our uninhibited and enthusiastic Yorkshire terrier, **joined our family on my sister's fifteenth birthday.**
> —Chad Hockerman, student writer

Note: Do not use commas with *restrictive appositives*. A restrictive appositive is essential to the basic meaning of the sentence.

> **Sixteen-year-old student** Ray Perez **was awarded an athletic scholarship.**

646.2 Between Items in a Series

Use commas to separate individual words, phrases, or clauses in a series. (A series contains at least three items.)

> **The chef bought organic** broccoli, spinach, and corn **at the farmers market.** (words)
> I found a space, paid the rent, and set up my office **for my new business.** (phrases)

Note: Do not use commas when all the words in a series are connected with *or, nor,* or *and*.

> **He had his car cleaned** and **waxed** and **vacuumed out.**

646.3 After Introductory Phrases and Clauses

Use a comma after an introductory participial phrase.

> Determined to finish the sweater by Friday, **my grandmother knit night and day.**

Use a comma after a long introductory prepositional phrase or after two or more short ones.

> In the oddest places and at the strangest times, **my grandmother can be found knitting madly away.**

Note: You may omit the comma if the introductory phrase is short.

> Before breakfast **my grandmother knits.**

Use a comma after an introductory adverb (subordinate) clause.

> After the practice was over, **Tina walked home.**

Note: A comma is not used if an adverb clause *follows* the main clause and is needed to complete the meaning of the sentence.

> **Tina practiced hard** because she feared losing.

However, a comma is used if the adverb clause following the main clause begins with *although, even though, while,* or another conjunction expressing a contrast.

> **Tina walked home,** even though it was raining very hard.

Mechanics 647

Practice

Commas 2
- To Set Off Appositives
- Between Items in a Series
- After Introductory Phrases and Clauses

Indicate where commas are needed in the following sentences by writing the commas along with the words that surround them. If no commas are needed, write "none needed."

1. The idea of contact lenses the common substitute for glasses has been around for hundreds of years.

2. Leonardo da Vinci the Italian artist inventor and scientist sketched ideas for contacts in 1508.

3. More than a hundred years later Rene Descartes the French mathematician suggested placing a lens directly on the eye.

4. Though the idea had been around for centuries it was 1887 before the first contact lenses were produced.

5. The first glass lenses were made by F. A. Muller a German glassblower.

6. After centuries of ideas and experimentation today's contact wearers have their choice of hard soft or gas-permeable lenses.

7. Today about 90 percent of contacts sold in the United States are soft lenses.

8. Remi has a pair each of hazel blue and green lenses to suit her varying moods.

Model

Model the following sentences to practice using commas between items in a series, after introductory phrases, and to set off appositives.

Bill Post ran forward, gathered his little family in his arms for a moment, and then quickly ushered them toward the safety of the house.
—Thomas Steinbeck, "The Night Guide"

A few days before the shooting, Director Yu, a lecturer at a cinema school in Shanghai, gave Huping a small book to read.
—Ha Jin, "A Tiger-Fighter Is Hard to Find"

Comma (continued)

648.1 To Enclose Parenthetical Elements

Use commas to separate parenthetical elements, such as an explanatory word or phrase, within a sentence.

They stood together, away from the pile of stones in the corner, **and their jokes were quiet, and they smiled rather than laughed.**
—Shirley Jackson, "The Lottery"

Allison meandered into class, late as usual, **and sat down.**

648.2 To Set Off Nonrestrictive Phrases and Clauses

Use commas to set off **nonrestrictive** (unnecessary) clauses and participial phrases. A nonrestrictive clause or participial phrase adds information that is not necessary to the basic meaning of the sentence. For example, if the clause or phrase (in red) were left out in the two examples below, the meaning of the sentences would remain clear. Therefore, commas are used to set them off.

The Altena Fitness Center and Visker Gymnasium, which were built last year, **are busy every day.** (nonrestrictive clause)

Students and faculty, improving their health through exercise, **use both facilities throughout the week.** (nonrestrictive phrase)

Do not use commas to set off a **restrictive** (necessary) clause or participial phrase, which helps to define a noun or pronoun. It adds information that the reader needs to know in order to understand the sentence. For example, if the clause and phrase (in red) were dropped from the examples below, the meaning wouldn't be the same. Therefore, commas are *not* used.

The handball court that has a sign-up sheet by the door **must be reserved.**
The clause identifies which handball court must be reserved.
(restrictive clause)

Individuals wanting to use this court **must sign up a day in advance.**
(restrictive phrase)

A Closer Look

Use *that* to introduce restrictive (necessary) clauses; use *which* to introduce nonrestrictive (unnecessary) clauses. When the two words are used in this way, the reader can quickly distinguish necessary and unnecessary information.

The treadmill that monitors heart rate **is the one you must use.**
(The reader needs the information to find the right treadmill.)

This treadmill, which we got last year, **is required for your program.** (The main clause tells the reader which treadmill to use; the other clause gives additional, unnecessary information.)

Mechanics

Practice

Commas 3
- To Enclose Parenthetical Elements
- To Set Off Nonrestrictive Phrases and Clauses

Indicate where commas are needed in the following sentences by writing the commas along with the words that surround them. If no commas are needed, write "none needed."

1. The classic *Star Trek* series the one with Kirk and Spock was on television for only three seasons.

2. The show which was created by Gene Roddenbery was canceled because of low ratings.

3. Fans called "Trekkies" wanting the show to return waged a letter-writing campaign.

4. The show returned in syndicated reruns and became very popular.

5. *Star Trek* movies some great and others not so great led to a new television series: *Star Trek: The Next Generation*.

6. The new show known for its Shakespearean references starred Patrick Stewart as Captain Jean-Luc Picard.

7. The series that stars William Shatner and Leonard Nimoy remains popular with *Star Trek* fans.

8. Vendors sell merchandise everything you can think of with a *Star Trek* logo at conventions.

Model

Model the following sentence to practice using commas to set off nonrestrictive clauses.

> I . . . developed a very practiced smile, which I call my "Noh smile" because it resembles a Noh mask whose features are frozen.
> —Arthur Golden, *Memoirs of a Geisha*

Comma (continued)

650.1 To Set Off Dates

Use commas to set off items in a date.

> On September 30, 1997, my little sister entered our lives.
> He began working out on December 1, 2005, but quit by May 1, 2006.

However, when only the month and year are given, no commas are needed.

> He began working out in December 2005 but quit by May 2006.

When a full date appears in the middle of a sentence, a comma follows the year.

> On June 7, 1924, my great-grandfather met his future wife.

650.2 To Set Off Items in Addresses

Use commas to set off items in an address. (No comma is placed between the state and ZIP code.)

> Mail the box to Friends of Wildlife, Box 402, Spokane, Washington 20077.

When a city and state (or country) appear in the middle of a sentence, a comma follows the last item in the address.

> Several charitable organizations in Juneau, Alaska, pool their funds.

650.3 In Numbers

Use commas to separate numerals in large numbers in order to distinguish hundreds, thousands, millions, and so forth.

> 1,101   25,000   7,642,020

650.4 To Enclose Titles or Initials

Use commas to enclose a title or initials and names that follow a surname (a last name).

> Letitia O'Reilly, M.D., is our family physician.
> Hickok, J. B., and Cody, William F., are two popular Western heroes.

650.5 Before Tags

Use a comma before a tag, which is a short statement or question at the end of a sentence.

> He's the candidate who lost the election, isn't he?
> You're not going to like this casserole, I know.

650.6 Following Conjunctive Adverbs and Transitional Phrases

Use a comma following conjunctive adverbs such as *however, instead,* and *nevertheless,* and transitional phrases such as *for example, in fact,* and *as a result.* (Also see 654.2.)

> Jaleel is bright and studies hard; however, he suffers from test anxiety.
> Pablo was born in the Andes; as a result, he loves mountains.

Practice

Commas 4
- To Set Off Dates
- To Enclose Titles
- Before Tags
- Following Conjunctive Adverbs and Transitional Phrases

Indicate where commas are needed in the following sentences by writing the commas along with the words that surround them. If no commas are needed, write "none needed."

1. Cori Ramos is planning to attend USC this fall right?

2. I'm looking forward to graduation; however I'll miss high school and my friends.

3. The article written by Sanjay Singh M.D. is about fibromyalgia treatments.

4. On August 24 2006 many astronomers announced that Pluto is not a planet.

5. Many people were upset by the decision; in fact there is a strong movement to restore Pluto's status.

6. Special-effects technology is improving all the time; furthermore there is a need for specialists in this field.

7. Maya Angelou Ph.D. will speak at my sister's graduation ceremony.

8. My cousin started biking competitively in April 2000.

9. He didn't expect to lose did he?

10. He looked forward to winning at least second place; after all he had trained so long and hard.

Model

Model the following sentence to practice using a comma before a tag.

> **Though both sentences have a certain on-the-money ring to them, the first one sounds better, doesn't it?**
> —June Casagrande, *Grammar Snobs Are Great Big Meanies*

Comma (continued)

652.1 To Set Off Dialogue

Use commas to set off the speaker's exact words from the rest of the sentence. (It may be helpful to remember that the comma is always to the left of the quotation mark.)

"It's like they knew we were coming," **said Mary, pointing at the dozens of people standing on the dock.**

652.2 To Set Off Interjections

Use a comma to separate an interjection or a weak exclamation from the rest of the sentence.

Hey, **how do you expect me to remember all these rules?**
Wow, **I had no idea that she wears contacts.**

652.3 To Set Off Interruptions

Use commas to set off a word, a phrase, or a clause that interrupts the movement of a sentence. Such expressions usually can be identified through the following tests: (1) They may be omitted without changing the meaning of a sentence. (2) They may be placed nearly anywhere in the sentence without changing its meaning.

George, well, **he's happy with what he can get.**
The safest way to cross this street, as a general rule, **is with the light.**

652.4 In Direct Address

Use commas to separate a noun of direct address from the rest of the sentence. A *noun of direct address* is the noun that names the person(s) spoken to.

"You wouldn't understand yet, son, **but your daddy's gonna make a transaction. . . . "**
—Lorraine Hansberry, *A Raisin in the Sun*

Quineisha, **why aren't you answering your phone?**

652.5 For Clarity or Emphasis

You may use a comma for clarity or for emphasis. There will be times when none of the traditional rules call for a comma, but one will be needed to prevent confusion or to emphasize an important idea.

It may be that those who do most, dream most. **(emphasis)**
—Stephen Leacock

What the crew does, does **affect our voyage. (clarity)**

Mechanics

Practice

Commas 5
- To Set Off Dialogue
- To Set Off Interjections
- To Set Off Interruptions
- In Direct Address
- For Clarity or Emphasis

 Indicate where commas are needed in the following sentences by writing the commas along with the words that surround them.

1. What now dear reader shall we make of our telescope?
   —Johannes Kepler

2. The world as a rule does not live on beaches and in country clubs.
   —F. Scott Fitzgerald

3. Whatever you do do with all your might.
   —Marcus Tullius Cicero

4. As the poet said "Only God can make a tree."
   —Woody Allen

5. Don't criticize what you don't understand son.
   —Elvis Presley

6. "Now I have asked you a question my friend" said Mr. Jaggers.
   —Charles Dickens, *Great Expectations*

7. Well all I know is what I read in the papers.
   —Will Rogers

Model

Model the following sentences to practice using a comma to set off an interruption, to set off dialogue, and in direct address.

On the Web, right now, Clark was hunting for someplace to buy roofing.
   —Alice Munro, "The Runaway"

"General, sir," Mortenson shouted, "I think we're heading the wrong way."
   —Greg Mortenson and David O. Relin, *Three Cups of Tea*

Semicolon

654.1 To Join Two Independent Clauses

Use a **semicolon** to join two or more closely related independent clauses that are not connected with a coordinating conjunction. (Independent clauses can stand alone as separate sentences.)

> He never brags about being a gifted writer; his books speak for themselves.
>
> The forest was quiet; not a creature made a sound as the red-tailed hawk circled above.

Note: When independent clauses are especially long or contain commas, a semicolon may punctuate the sentence, even though a coordinating conjunction connects the clauses.

> We waited all day in that wide line, tired travelers pressing in from all sides; and when we needed drinks or sandwiches, I would squeeze my way to the cafeteria and back.

654.2 With Conjunctive Adverbs and Transitional Phrases

A semicolon is used *before* a conjunctive adverb or transitional phrase (with a comma after it) when the word connects two independent clauses in a compound sentence.

> Many actors move to New York City hoping to make it big; however, they often discover that the fierce competition for acting jobs makes it extremely unlikely for them to succeed.

Common Conjunctive Adverbs

also, besides, finally, however, indeed, instead, meanwhile, moreover, nevertheless, next, still, then, therefore, thus

Common Transitional Phrases

after all, as a matter of fact, as a result, at any rate, at the same time, even so, for example, for instance, in addition, in conclusion, in fact, in other words, in the first place, on the contrary, on the other hand

654.3 To Separate Groups That Contain Commas

A semicolon is used to separate groups of words that already contain commas.

> Every Saturday night my little brother gathers up his things—goggles, shower cap, and snorkel; bubble bath, soap, and shampoo; tapes, stereo, and rubber duck—and heads for the tub.

Mechanics

Practice

Semicolons
- To Join Two Independent Clauses
- With Conjunctive Adverbs
- To Separate Groups That Contain Commas

Indicate where a semicolon is needed in the following sentences by writing the semicolon along with the words that surround it.

1. Everyone is talking about the weather they wonder why significant weather events are happening more frequently.

2. Weather is news these days—hurricanes, cyclones, and tornadoes flash floods, droughts, and tsunamis even snow in the deep South.

3. Unusual weather events have always been a part of the earth's climate consider January 1997, when snow fell near the bridge between Florida's mainland and the Keys.

4. In 2006, El Niño raised water temperatures in the Pacific Ocean moveover, it affected many countries.

5. Wetter conditions than normal affect Chile, Peru, and Ecuador southern Brazil and northern Argentina and Mexico's northwest states.

6. Earth is warming this may be the reason for the unusual weather events.

7. As the climate grows warmer, evaporation will increase therefore, there will be heavier rainfalls.

8. Higher ocean temperatures might change the path of hurricanes look for them to track more often through the Caribbean or to make landfall along the east coast of the United States.

Model

Model the following sentence to practice using a semicolon to join two independent clauses.

> The trees echoed with birdsong; a warm southeasterly breeze carried the sweetness of lime blossom. —Michelle Paver, *Spirit Walker*

Colon

656.1 After a Salutation

Use a **colon** after the salutation of a business letter.
    Dear Judge Parker**:**   Dear Governor Whitman**:**

656.2 Between Numerals Indicating Time

Use a colon between the hours, minutes, and seconds of a number indicating time.
    8**:**30 p.m.   9**:**45 a.m.   10**:**24**:**55

656.3 For Emphasis

Use a colon to emphasize a word, a phrase, a clause, or a sentence that explains or adds impact to the main clause.
    One goal of space exploration is to find the element essential to the support of human life**:** water.

656.4 To Introduce a Quotation

Use a colon to formally introduce a quotation, a sentence, or a question.
    Directly a voice in the corner rang out wild and clear**:** "I've got him! I've got him!"
                                                           —Mark Twain, *Roughing It*

656.5 To Introduce a List

A colon is used to introduce a list.
    He is a successful politician**:** attractive, articulate, and well-funded.

A Closer Look

Do not use a colon between a verb and its object or complement, or between a preposition and its object.

        Incorrect: Min has: a snowmobile, an ATV, and a canoe.
           Correct: Min has plenty of toys: a snowmobile, an ATV, and a canoe.
        Incorrect: I watch a TV show about: cooking wild game.
           Correct: I watch a TV show about a new subject: cooking wild game.

656.6 Between a Title and a Subtitle

Use a colon to distinguish between a title and a subtitle, volume and page, and chapter and verse in literature.
    Encyclopedia Americana IV**:** 211   Psalm 23**:**1–6   Bass**:** *A Handbook of Strategies*

Mechanics

Practice

Colons

- After a Salutation
- Between Numerals Indicating Time
- For Emphasis
- To Introduce a Quotation
- To Introduce a List
- Between a Title and a Subtitle

 Indicate where a colon is needed in the following sentences by writing the colon along with the words or numbers that surround it.

1. Darnell found the following items in his backpack two notebooks, some dirty socks, his cell phone charger, a comb, and a twenty-dollar bill.

2. Last weekend, Salli bought the DVD of *The Chronicles of Narnia The Lion, the Witch, and the Wardrobe*.

3. Dad reminded me of the inevitable "Real life begins after graduation."

4. The letter began, "Dear Mr. Parker Welcome to Lingston University!"

5. Tanisha plans to take the 813 a.m. train to Chicago; she'll arrive home tonight at 745.

6. Malcolm Gladwell's book *The Tipping Point How Little Things Can Make A Big Difference* is about sudden, unexpected changes in our society.

7. I have a lot to do on Saturday attend my brother's softball game, help Mom clean the basement, and install some new software on my computer.

8. Kennedy couldn't stop herself from thinking about Juan Was he just using "work" as an excuse to not see her?

Model

Model the following sentence to practice using colons to introduce a list.

> It's more than just the way I look: refugee-skinny with absolutely no chest to speak of, hair the color of dirt, connect-the-dot freckles on my cheeks that, let me tell you, do not fade with lemon juice or sunscreen or even, sadly, sandpaper.
>
> —Jodi Picoult, *My Sister's Keeper*

Hyphen

658.1 In Compound Words

Use the **hyphen** to make some compound words.

    great-great-grandfather   **maid-in-waiting**   **three-year-old**

658.2 To Create New Words

Use a hyphen to form new words beginning with the prefixes *self-, ex-, all-,* and *half-*. Also use a hyphen to join any prefix to a proper noun, a proper adjective, or the official name of an office. Use a hyphen before the suffix *-elect*.

    self-contained   **ex-governor**   **all-inclusive**   **half-painted**
    pre-Cambrian   **mid-December**   **president-elect**

Use a hyphen to join the prefix *great-* only to the names of relatives.

    great-aunt, great-grandfather (correct)   **great-hall** (incorrect)

658.3 To Form an Adjective

Use a hyphen to join two or more words that serve as a single adjective (a single-thought adjective) before a noun.

    Sonia, who volunteers at the soup kitchen on her days off, is a big-hearted woman.

Use common sense to determine whether a compound adjective might be misread if it is not hyphenated. Generally, hyphenate a compound adjective that is composed of . . .

- a phrase   **heat-and-serve meal**   **off-and-on relationship**
- a noun + adjective   **oven-safe handles**   **book-smart student**
- a noun + participle (*ing* or *ed* form of a verb)   **bone-chilling story**

658.4 To Join Letters and Words

Use a hyphen to join a capital letter or lowercase letter to a noun or participle. (Check your dictionary if you're not sure of the hyphenation.)

    T-shirt   **S-curve**   **G-rated**   **x-axis**

A Closer Look

When words forming the adjective come after the noun, do not hyphenate them.

    In real life I am large and big boned.

When the first of these words is an adverb ending in *-ly,* do not use a hyphen.

    delicately prepared pastry

Also, do not use a hyphen when a number or a letter is the final element in a single-thought adjective.

    class B movie

Practice

Hyphens 1
- **In Compound Words**
- **To Create New Words**
- **To Form an Adjective**
- **To Join Letters and Words**

For each sentence below, correctly write the words that should be hyphenated. Some sentences contain more than one hyphenated word.

1. The three year old Detroit based store is going out of business.

2. My great great uncle was an all or nothing sort, a self made man who earned his fortune in land speculation during the 1840s.

3. Some thought provoking arguments were raised in this award winning film.

4. My brother in law got a small business loan to open his restaurant.

5. Senator elect Ricchio spoke last night at the Italian American club.

6. The race car driver approached the S curve at an unsafe speed.

7. Dana's great grandpa is a self sufficient, fun loving person.

8. He decided to take Web based lessons to learn how to play the banjo.

9. Saied has a ten dollar credit on his prepaid phone card.

10. Tovah bought a yellow V neck T shirt at the mall.

Model

Model the following sentences to practice using hyphens to form adjectives and to create new words.

> The stones which Deucalion threw sprang up as full-grown men, strong, and handsome, and brave.   —James Baldwin, "The Flood"

> He did look cautiously behind it first, as if he half-expected to be terrified with the sight of Marley's pigtail sticking out into the hall.
> —Charles Dickens, *A Christmas Carol*

Hyphen (continued)

660.1 Between Numbers and Fractions

Use a hyphen to join the words in compound numbers from *twenty-one* to *ninety-nine* when it is necessary to write them out (see **690**).

Use a hyphen between the numerator and denominator of a fraction, but not when one or both of those elements are already hyphenated.

    four-tenths   **five-sixteenths**   **(7/32) seven thirty-seconds**

660.2 In a Special Series

Use hyphens when two or more words have a common element that is omitted in all but the last term.

    The ship has lovely two-, four-, or six-person cabins.

660.3 To Join Numbers

Use a hyphen, or an endash, to join numbers indicating the life span of a person or the score in a contest or a vote.

    We can thank Louis Pasteur (1822-1895) for pasteurized milk.
    In the 2007 Rose Bowl, USC defeated Michigan 32-18.

660.4 To Prevent Confusion

Use a hyphen with prefixes or suffixes to avoid confusion or awkward spelling.

    re-create (not *recreate*) the image   **re-cover** (not *recover*) the sofa

660.5 To Divide a Word

Use a hyphen to divide a word, only between its syllables, at the end of a line of print. Always place the hyphen after the syllable at the end of the line—never before a syllable at the beginning of the following line.

Guidelines for Dividing with Hyphens

1. Always divide a compound word between its basic units: **sister-in-law**, not **sis-ter-in-law**.
2. Avoid dividing a word of five or fewer letters: **paper, study, July.**
3. Avoid dividing the last word in a paragraph.
4. Never divide a one-syllable word: **rained, skills, through.**
5. Never divide a one-letter syllable from the rest of the word: **omit-ted**, not **o-mitted.**
6. When a vowel is a syllable by itself, divide the word after the vowel: **epi-sode**, not **ep-isode.**
7. Never divide abbreviations or contractions: **shouldn't**, not **should-n't.**
8. Never divide the last word in more than two lines in a row.

Practice

Hyphens 2

- Between Numbers and Fractions
- In a Special Series
- To Join Numbers
- To Prevent Confusion
- To Divide a Word

For each sentence below, correctly write the word(s) that should be hyphenated or are incorrectly hyphenated.

1. The unusual foliage has a shelllike coating.

2. Your assignment is to write an 800 to 1,000 word persuasive essay.

3. Say what you will, but I believe these arguments about money have stra-ined our relationship.

4. Even one thirty second of an inch error in measurement will result in an inaccurate reading.

5. Cut the board into two, four, and six inch lengths.

6. Dr. Mahan's degree is in chemistry, but he is always ready with one histo-rical fact or another to explain his lessons.

7. Two thirds of the crowd left when the score was 33 10 in the fourth quarter.

8. My boss asked me to resign the form after rereading sections 5 7.

9. Prior to the exam, the proctor gave this instruction: "You will need to o-mit question number six from your answers due to a printing error."

10. Sergei wrote of yesterday's Moscowwide electrical outage in his e-mail.

11. By 2015, more than one half of the world's population will live in urban areas.

12. Ramona created six and eight sided paper snowflakes.

Model

Model the following sentence to practice using hyphens in a special series.

Two-, three-, and four-column notebooks are available at the bookstore.

Apostrophe

662.1 In Contractions

Use an **apostrophe** to show that one or more letters have been left out of a word group to form a contraction.

hadn't – *o* is left out   **they'd** – *woul* is left out   **it's** – *i* is left out

Note: Use an apostrophe to show that one or more numerals or letters have been left out of numbers or words in order to show special pronunciation.

class of '09 – *20* is left out   **g'day** – *ood* is left out

662.2 To Form Singular Possessives

Add an apostrophe and *s* to form the possessive of most singular nouns.

Spock's ears   Captain **Kirk's** singing   the **ship's** escape plan

Note: When a singular noun ends with an *s* or a *z* sound, you may form the possessive by adding just an apostrophe. When the singular noun is a one-syllable word, however, you usually add both an apostrophe and an *s* to form the possessive.

San **Carlos'** government (or) San **Carlos's** government (two-syllable word)
Ross's essay (one-syllable word)   the **class's** field trip (one-syllable word)

662.3 To Form Plural Possessives

The possessive form of plural nouns ending in *s* is usually made by adding just an apostrophe.

students' homework   **bosses'** orders

For plural nouns not ending in *s*, an apostrophe and *s* must be added.

children's book   **men's** department

A Closer Look

It will help you to punctuate correctly if you remember that the word immediately before the apostrophe is the owner.

girl's guitar (*girl* is the owner)   **boss's** order (*boss* is the owner)
girls' guitars (*girls* are the owners)   **bosses'** order (*bosses* are the owners)

662.4 To Show Shared Possession

When possession is shared by more than one noun, use the possessive form for the last noun in the series.

Hoshi, Linda, and Nakiva's water skis (All three own the same skis.)
Hoshi's, Linda's, and Nakiva's water skis (Each owns her own skis.)

Mechanics

Practice

Apostrophes 1
- In Contractions
- To Form Singular Possessives
- To Form Plural Possessives
- To Show Shared Possession

For each sentence, write the contraction for or the possessive form of the word or words in parentheses.

1. *(Ravi, Simone, and Lucas)* biology classes went on a field trip together.

2. They had to take two buses because everyone *(would not)* fit on one.

3. *(Mount Ranier)* Sunrise Area was the destination for the *(students)* trip.

4. Simone said, "*(I have)* never been here before. I hope *(it will)* be fun!"

5. The *(classes)* assignment was to observe and investigate an *(alpine ecosystem)* fragility.

6. The *(teachers)* lesson plans provided excellent insight into the *(mountain)* ecological systems.

7. *(Ravi and Simone)* shoes *(were not)* appropriate for a three-mile hike.

8. Ravi wished *(he had)* worn hiking boots.

9. *(Mr. Sullivan and Mrs. Ling)* first-aid kit was put to good use.

10. *(It is)* a good thing that *(they are)* always prepared; the kids *(would have)* suffered without bandages for their blisters.

Model

Model the following sentences to practice using apostrophes to form singular and plural possessives.

Take each man's censure, but reserve thy judgment.
—William Shakespeare, *Hamlet*

The notion that nutmeg could ward off the plague survived longer than many another old wives' tales.
—Simon Winchester, *Krakatoa*

Apostrophe (continued)

664.1 To Show Possession with Indefinite Pronouns

Form the possessive of an indefinite pronoun by placing an apostrophe and an *s* on the last word (see **732.1** and **734.3**).

> everyone's   anyone's   somebody's
>
> It is everybody's responsibility to keep his or her locker orderly.

In expressions using *else,* add the apostrophe and *s* after the last word.

> This is somebody else's mess, not mine.

664.2 To Show Possession in Compound Nouns

Form the possessive of a compound noun by placing the possessive ending after the last word.

> the secretary of the interior's (singular) agenda
> her lady-in-waiting's (singular) day off

If forming a possessive of a plural compound noun creates an awkward construction, you may replace the possessive with an *of* phrase. (All four forms below are correct.)

> their fathers-in-law's (plural) birthdays
> or the birthdays of their fathers-in-law (plural)
> the ambassadors-at-large's (plural) plans
> or the plans of the ambassadors-at-large (plural)

664.3 To Express Time or Amount

Use an apostrophe and an *s* with an adjective that is part of an expression indicating time or amount.

> a penny's worth   two cents' worth   this morning's meeting
> yesterday's news   a day's wage   six months' pay

664.4 To Form Certain Plurals

Use an apostrophe and *s* to form the plural of a letter, a number, a sign, or a word discussed as a word.

> B – B's   C – C's   8 – 8's   + – +'s   and – and's
>
> Ms. D'Aquisto says our conversations contain too many like's and no way's.

Note: If two apostrophes are called for in the same word, omit the second one.

> Follow closely the do's and don'ts (not don't's) on the checklist.

Practice

Apostrophes 2
- To Show Possession with Indefinite Pronouns
- To Show Possession in Compound Nouns
- To Express Time or Amount
- To Form Certain Plurals

Write each underlined word in the following paragraphs with the apostrophe placed correctly.

Each day, I drink about five **(1)** dollars worth of coffee. You might share **(2)** everyone elses opinion that I drink too much coffee, but that's not true—no **(3)** ifs, ands or buts about it! I buy only one cup of coffee a day, and it's always one of the **(4)** Super 20s at Sergio's Coffee Shop. (Each specialty cup of coffee holds 20 ounces.)

The shop is staffed by Sergio's family members, and these **(5)** Italian Americans cooking is superb. Sergio uses his **(6)** sister-in-laws recipes for the special coffee drinks, and she works in the shop as a barista. Her Almond Joy Super 20 (I love it!) is a flavored latte that's **(7)** everybodys favorite. Some of the other Super 20 flavors are **(8)** Cs in 3s (cappuccino with chocolate and caramel syrups) and **(9)** Anyones Guess, which is **(10)** todays flavor of the day.

Model

Model the following sentences to practice using apostrophes to express time or amount and to show possession with indefinite pronouns.

> I never did a day's work in my life. It was all fun.
> —Thomas Edison

> Everybody's business is nobody's business, and nobody's business is my business.
> —Clara Barton

Quotation Marks

666.1 To Set Off Direct Quotations

Place **quotation marks** before and after the words in direct quotations.

"Please give the liver and onions a try," she said. "I think you'll like it."

In a quoted passage, put brackets around any word or punctuation mark that is not part of the original quotation. (See **678.1**.)

If you quote only part of the original passage, be sure to construct a sentence that is both accurate and grammatically correct.

Much of the restructuring of the Postal Service has involved "turning over large parts of its work to the private sector."

666.2 Placement of Punctuation

Always place periods and commas inside quotation marks.

"Well, that's a relief," said Isabel. "I thought we wouldn't make it to the theater in time for the previews."

Place an exclamation point or a question mark *inside* quotation marks when it punctuates the quotation and *outside* when it punctuates the main sentence.

"Am I dreaming?"   Had she heard him say, "Here's the key to your new car"?

Always place semicolons or colons outside quotation marks.

I wrote about James Joyce's "The Dead"; I found it thought provoking.

666.3 For Long Quotations

If you quote more than one paragraph, place quotation marks before each paragraph and at the end of the last paragraph (Example A). If a quotation has more than four lines on a page, you may set it off from the text by indenting 10 spaces from the left margin (block form). Do not use quotation marks either before or after the quoted material, unless they appear in the original (Example B).

Example A

"_____
_____
_____.
    "_____
_____
_____.
    "_____."

Example B

_____.
_____
_____
_____.
_____

Mechanics

Practice

Quotation Marks 1
- To Set Off Direct Quotations
- Placement of Punctuation
- For Long Quotations

Indicate where quotation marks are needed in the following paragraphs by writing the quotation marks along with the words and other punctuation after or before them. (Use ellipses to show omitted words in your answers.)

1   I couldn't believe what I held in my hands. It was a yellowed letter
2 that I'd discovered tucked among the pages of an old scrapbook in our attic.
3 Mom, look at this. I said. It's a love letter. I handed her the fragile page
4 filled with the following almost illegible scrawl.

5   This letter brings the same old theme, which instead of growing
6   old by telling only grows brighter. This proves that my love for
7   you is stronger with each passing day. My happiness can not be
8   any greater than since I met you, my darling Ella. Being apart
9   from you, far across the sea, seems like an eternity to me. I long
10   to see your smile again, to hold your hands, and to look into your
11   beautiful eyes.

12   Mom sighed. This letter is from your great-grandfather to his wife,
13 Ella, she said. Grandma told me once that Grandpa Doty had written her
14 some wonderful letters. She also told me how they fell in love.

15   It really was a love-at-first-sight story. Ella and William, a soldier,
16 met a few weeks before he was scheduled to leave for England. It was
17 during World War I, and many soldiers were dying in the war overseas.
18 The day before he shipped out, they ran off and got married against their
19 parents' wishes.

20   William wrote to Ella almost every day, and I wouldn't be surprised
21 if we find more letters up here. Now I can't wait to go through all this old
22 stuff! Mom said.

23   I can't either, I answered. All of a sudden, cleaning the attic was a
24 treasure hunt instead of a chore.

Model

Model the following sentence to practice correct placement of punctuation with quotation marks.

It is not a lucky word, this name "impossible"; no good comes of those who have it so often in their mouths.
—Thomas Carlyle

Quotation Marks (continued)

668.1 Quotation Marks Within Quotations

Use single quotation marks to punctuate a quotation within a quotation. Use double quotation marks if you need to distinguish a quotation within a quotation within a quotation.

"For tomorrow," said Mr. Botts, "read 'Unlighted Lamps.'"
Sue asked, "Did you hear Mr. Botts say, 'Read "Unlighted Lamps"'?"

668.2 For Special Words

You may use quotation marks (1) to distinguish a word that is being discussed, (2) to indicate that a word is unfamiliar slang, or (3) to point out that a word is being used in a special way.

(1) As any English teacher will tell you, the word "whom" is rarely used correctly.
(2) I . . . asked the bartender where I could hear "chanky-chank," as Cajuns called their music.
—William Least Heat-Moon, *Blue Highways*
(3) Tom pushed the wheelchair across the street, showed the lady his "honest" smile . . . and stole her purse.

Note: You may use italics (underlining) in place of quotation marks in each of these three situations. (See 670.3.)

668.3 To Punctuate Titles

Use **quotation marks** to punctuate titles of songs, poems, short stories, one-act plays, lectures, episodes of radio or television programs, chapters of books, unpublished works, electronic files, and articles found in magazines, newspapers, encyclopedias, or online sources. (For punctuation of other titles, see 670.2.)

"Santa Lucia" (song)
"The Chameleon" (short story)
"Twentieth-Century Memories" (lecture)
"Affordable Adventures" (magazine article)
"Dire Prophecy of the Howling Dog" (chapter in a book)
"Dancing with Debra" (television episode)
"Miss Julie" (one-act play)

Note: Punctuate one title within another title as follows:
"Clarkson's 'Breakaway' Hits the Waves"
(title of a song in title of an article)

Mechanics

Practice

Quotation Marks 2
- **Quotation Marks Within Quotations**
- **For Special Words**
- **To Punctuate Titles**

Write the word or words that should be enclosed in quotation marks in the following sentences.

1. Parker's poem entitled North to Midnight was accepted for publication in the national magazine *Know It!*

2. Tremain said, Did you see that ridiculous *Enquirer* article, Pterodactyls Found Alive in Tanzanian Cave?

3. The real estate agent used words like spacious, open, and airy to describe the home's sunroom.

4. Dad says that I should check out the drum solo in the song Away by an old rock group called Rain Sign.

5. Melissa's essay was titled The Natural State and told of the clear lakes, streams, and abundance of natural wildlife in Arkansas.

6. Rob asked, Have you read *Walden Pond* for English class?

7. His favorite episode of *Deadliest Catch* is Race Against the Ice.

8. Employees at the soda bottling company are subject to pop quizzes.

Model

Model the following sentences to practice using quotation marks within quotations.

In my new pen pal's latest e-mail, he wrote about his musical tastes: "The Beatles are my all-time favorite band, and my favorite Beatles songs are probably 'Paperback Writer' and 'Hey Jude.' I like lots of newer bands, too, though."

"I was lucky," said Jane. "The proctor announced, 'Put your pencils down,' just as I was filling in the last answer."

Italics (Underlining)

670.1 Handwritten and Printed Material

Italics is a printer's term for a style of type that is slightly slanted. In this sentence, the word *happiness* is printed in italics. In material that is handwritten or typed on a machine that cannot print in italics, underline each word or letter that should be in italics.

> *My Ántonia* is the story of a strong and determined pioneer woman.
> (printed)
> Willa Cather's <u>My Ántonia</u> describes pioneer life in America.
> (typed or handwritten)

670.2 In Titles

Use italics to indicate the titles of magazines, newspapers, pamphlets, books, full-length plays, films, videos, radio and television programs, book-length poems, ballets, operas, paintings, lengthy musical compositions, sculptures, cassettes, CD's, legal cases, and the names of ships and aircraft. (For punctuation of other titles, see **668.3**.)

> *Newsweek* (magazine)   *Cold Sassy Tree* (book)
> *Shakespeare in Love* (film)   *Law & Order* (television program)
> *Caring for Your Kitten* (pamphlet)   *Hedda Gabler* (full-length play)
> *Chicago Tribune* (newspaper)   *The Thinker* (sculpture)

670.3 For Special Uses

Use italics for a number, letter, or word that is being discussed or used in a special way. (Sometimes quotation marks are used for this reason. See **668.2**.)

> I hope that this letter *I* on my report card stands for *incredible* and not *incomplete*.

670.4 For Foreign Words

Use italics for foreign words that have not been adopted into the English language; also use italics for scientific names.

> The voyageurs—tough men with natural *bonhomie*—discovered the shy *Castor canadensis*, or North American beaver.

670.5 For Emphasis

Use italics for words that require particular emphasis.

> I guess it really *was* worth it to put in extra study time.

Practice

Italics (Underlining)
- **In Titles**
- **For Special Uses**
- **For Foreign Words**
- **For Emphasis**

 Write and underline the word or words that should be italicized in the following sentences.

1. In algebra, we use the letters Z, Q, R, and C respectively to represent integers, rational, real, and complex numbers.

2. Giana hugged the queen—quite a faux pas, she later learned.

3. I enjoy planning trips to places I read about in National Geographic magazine.

4. Vinny did say that he would be late, remember?

5. Robin wrote a humorous opera called Diary of a Soccer Mom's Daughter.

6. Did you mix up the words bring and take?

7. "Not now!" Amber cried when her computer froze in the middle of a message.

8. She would have to call her cousin in New York about some tickets for the show Rent.

Model

Model the following sentence to practice using italics (underlining) for emphasis.

"As yet," cried the stranger—his cheek glowing and his eye flashing with enthusiasm—"as yet, I have done *nothing*."
—Nathaniel Hawthorne, "The Ambitious Guest"

Parentheses

672.1 To Set Off Explanatory Material

You may use **parentheses** to set off explanatory or added material that interrupts the normal sentence structure.

> Benson (our dog) sits in on our piano lessons (on the piano bench), much to the teacher's surprise and amusement.
> —Chad Hockerman, student writer

Note: Place question marks and exclamation points within the parentheses when they mark the added material.

> Ivan at once concluded (the rascal!) that I had a passion for dances, and . . . wanted to drag me off to a dancing class.
> —Fyodor Dostoevsky, "A Novel in Nine Letters"

672.2 With Full Sentences

When using a full sentence within another sentence, do not capitalize it or use a period inside the parentheses.

> Because the weather in the mountains can be unpredictable (it sometimes hails in the summer), make sure you take a poncho and warm clothes with you when you go hiking.

When the parenthetical sentence comes after the period of the main sentence, capitalize and punctuate it the same way you would any other complete sentence.

> They kiss and hug when they say "hello," and I love this. (In Korea, people are much more formal; they just shake hands and bow to each other.)
> —Sue Chong, "He Said I Was Too American"

Note: For unavoidable parentheses within parentheses (. . . [. . .] . . .), use brackets. Avoid overuse of parentheses by using commas instead.

Diagonal

672.3 To Show a Choice

Use a **diagonal** (also called a *slash* or *forward slash*) between two words, as in *and/or*, to indicate that either is acceptable.

> Press the load/eject button.
> Don't worry; this is indoor/outdoor carpet.

672.4 When Quoting Poetry

When quoting more than one line of poetry, use a diagonal to show where each line of poetry ends. (Insert a space on each side of the diagonal.)

> "Let not the wind / Example find, / To do more harm than it purposeth."
> —John Donne, from "A Valediction: Of Weeping"

Mechanics

Practice

Parentheses and Diagonals
- To Set Off Explanatory Material
- With Full Sentences
- To Show a Choice
- When Quoting Poetry

For the following sentences, write the word or words that should be enclosed in parentheses or divided by a diagonal. (Include parentheses or diagonals.)

1. Thai food have you tried it? is gaining popularity.

2. Old-style Thai cooking features the foods of a "waterborne lifestyle." This means ingredients like aquatic animals, plants, and herbs.

3. Americanized Thai food a unique blend of flavors is influenced by centuries-old Eastern and Western cultures.

4. Choose a curry dish and or a spiced salad to begin your meal.

5. Thai food everything is served in bite-sized pieces never needs a knife.

6. The server provides his her patrons with just a fork and a spoon.

7. You might want to try Khao Phat and Phat Thai one of the popular rice and noodle dishes when you visit a Thai restaurant.

Rewrite the haiku poem below as if you were quoting it in the text of an essay.

8. Moored to the heavens
   The wistful moon and bound stars
   Dream about dancing.

Model

Model the following sentence to practice parentheses to set off explanatory material.

> We asked people in the street (outside the Palladium Theatre, as it happens, at about 5 p.m.) if they used proper punctuation when sending text messages.
> —Lynne Truss, *Eats, Shoots and Leaves*

Dash

674.1 To Indicate a Sudden Break

Use a **dash** to indicate a sudden break or change in the sentence.

> Near the semester's end—and this is not always due to poor planning—some students may find themselves in a real crunch.

Note: Dashes are often used in place of commas. Use dashes when you want to give special emphasis; use commas when there is no need for emphasis.

674.2 To Set Off an Introductory Series

Use a dash to set off an introductory series from the clause that explains the series.

> A good book, a cup of tea, a comfortable chair—these things always saved my mother's sanity.

674.3 To Set Off Parenthetical Material

You may use a dash to set off parenthetical material—material that explains or clarifies a word or a phrase.

> A single incident—a tornado that came without warning—changed the face of the small town forever.

674.4 To Indicate Interrupted Speech

Use a dash to show interrupted or faltering speech in dialogue.

> Sojourner: Mama, why are you—
> Mama: Isabelle, do as I say!
> —Sandy Asher, *A Woman Called Truth*

674.5 For Emphasis

Use a dash to emphasize a word, a series, a phrase, or a clause.

> After several hours of hearing the high-pitched yipping, Petra finally realized what it was—coyote pups.

> After years of trial and error, Belther made history with his invention—the unicycle.

Practice

Dashes

- To Indicate a Sudden Break
- To Set Off an Introductory Series
- To Set Off Parenthetical Material
- To Indicate Interrupted Speech
- For Emphasis

 A word, a phrase, or a clause follows each sentence below. Rewrite the sentences to include those words, set off by one or two dashes.

1. The strange sound came from Old Ike's cornfield; I couldn't tell if it was human, or not. (*a low, guttural groaning*)

2. One would never guess that this colorful bird is considered a pest in Australia. (*the rainbow lorikeet*)

3. The members of Lemuel's band, Elixer K8, finally reached their long-sought-after goal. (*hearing their song played on the radio*)

4. That's all I need for a relaxing day on the beach. (*a cold drink, sunscreen, my MP3 player, and a good book*)

5. At 8:00 p.m. Saul arrived to take Trina to the prom. (*almost two hours late*)

6. Tony Akgulian spoke out in favor of a citywide graduation party sponsored by the Downtown Association. (*fifth-district alderman*)

7. Jarvis borrowed his brother's leather jacket to wear at the audition. (*the "lucky" jacket*)

8. Edward had applied to these prestigious schools. (*Princeton, Harvard, and Yale*)

Model

Model the following sentence to practice using dashes to set off parenthetical material.

> When I first beheld this apparition—for I could scarcely regard it as less—my wonder and my terror were extreme.
>
> —Edgar Allan Poe, "The Black Cat"

Ellipsis

676.1 To Show Omitted Words

Use an **ellipsis** (three periods with one space before and after each period) to show that one or more words have been omitted in a quotation.

(Original)
We the people of the United States, in order to form a more perfect Union, establish justice, insure domestic tranquility, provide for the common defense, promote the general welfare, and secure the blessings of liberty to ourselves and our posterity, do ordain and establish this Constitution for the United States of America.
—Preamble, U.S. Constitution

(Quotation)
"We the people . . . in order to form a more perfect Union . . . establish this Constitution for the United States of America."

676.2 At the End of a Sentence

If words from a quotation are omitted at the end of a sentence, place the ellipsis after the period that marks the conclusion of the sentence.

"Studies serve for delight, for ornament, for ability. . . . So every defect of the mind may have a special receipt."
—Sir Francis Bacon, from "Of Studies"

Note: If the quoted material is a complete sentence (even if it was not complete in the original), use a period, then an ellipsis.

(Original)
I am tired; my heart is sick and sad. From where the sun now stands I will fight no more forever.
—Chief Joseph of the Nez Percé

(Quotation)
"I am tired. . . . From where the sun now stands I will fight no more forever."
or
"I am tired. . . . I will fight no more. . . . "

676.3 To Show a Pause

Use an ellipsis to indicate a pause.

I brought my trembling hand to my focusing eyes. It was oozing, it was red, it was . . . it was . . . a tomato!
—Laura Baginski, student writer

Mechanics 677

TEKS 12.18A

Practice

Ellipses

- **To Show Omitted Words**
- **At the End of a Sentence**
- **To Show a Pause**

 For the following paragraph, select the least important information to replace with ellipses. Write the shortened paragraph on your paper.

1 Have you ever tried making a tasty, cheesy, wonderful, homemade
2 pizza from scratch? Making a pizza is easy to achieve, especially if you use
3 a bread machine. Combine the following easy-to-find ingredients in the pan
4 of the bread machine: 3 1/2 cups flour, 1 cup warm water, 2 tablespoons
5 dry yeast, 2 tablespoons honey (you can leave this ingredient out if you
6 want to; it's entirely up to you), 1/4 cup olive oil, and about 1/2 teaspoon of
7 salt (more or less, to your preferred taste). Set the machine to the "dough
8 only" setting and push the start button. When it is ready, place the dough
9 on a wood cutting board or another flat surface. Throw some flour on the
10 surface and flatten the dough with your hands or a sturdy rolling pin. Work
11 it until it's the size of the pan you plan to cook it on (a round pizza pan or
12 a cookie sheet works well). Rub a little olive oil onto the pan and then press
13 the dough evenly into the pan. Prick some small holes in the crust with a
14 fork. This will help to keep it from bubbling up while cooking, and it also
15 helps to hold the sauce, as well. Top the crust with pizza sauce, a lot of
16 tasty mozzarella cheese, and whatever other kinds of toppings that you like
17 on your pizza. Bake the pizza in a 400-degree oven until the crust is light
18 brown. Enjoy eating your pizza!

Exercise

For each of the following situations, write a sentence or two in which you use an ellipsis to show a pause.

Your best friend has asked a special person to the prom dance. You want to know if the answer was "yes."

You are surprised by the contents of a letter that you've just read.

Mechanics

Brackets

678.1 To Set Off Clarifying Information

Use **brackets** before and after words that are added to clarify what another person has said or written.

> It [my hand] began to itch after I touched the poison ivy by mistake.

Note: The brackets indicate that the words *my hand* are not part of the quotation but were added for clarification.

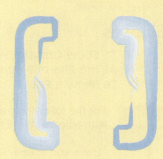

678.2 Around an Editorial Correction

Place brackets around an editorial correction inserted within quoted material.

> "Brooklyn alone has 8 percent of lead poisoning [victims] nationwide," said Marjorie Moore.
> —Donna Actie, student writer

Note: The brackets indicate that the word *victims* replaced the author's original word.

Place brackets around the letters *sic* (Latin for "as such"); the letters indicate that an error appearing in the material being quoted was made by the original speaker or writer.

> "When I'm queen," mused Lucy, "I'll show these blockheads whose [sic] got beauty and brains."

678.3 To Set Off Added Words

Place brackets around comments that have been added to a quotation.

> "Congratulations to the astronomy club's softball team, which put in, shall we say, a 'stellar' performance." [groans]

Punctuation Marks

´	Accent, acute	,	Comma	( )	Parentheses
`	Accent, grave	†	Dagger	.	Period
'	Apostrophe	—	Dash	?	Question mark
*	Asterisk	/	Diagonal/Slash	" "	Quotation marks
{ }	Brace	¨ (ü)	Dieresis	§	Section
[ ]	Brackets	...	Ellipsis	;	Semicolon
^	Caret	!	Exclamation point	~	Tilde
ç	Cedilla	-	Hyphen	__	Underscore
^	Circumflex	...	Leaders		
:	Colon	¶	Paragraph		

Practice

Brackets

- **To Set Off Clarifying Information**
- **Around an Editorial Correction**
- **To Set Off Added Words**

 Follow the directions for each activity below.

1. In the following quotation, the speaker is talking about solar flares. Rewrite the quotation, using the words *solar flares* in brackets to clarify the quotation.

    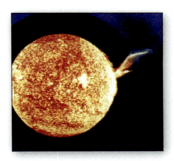

    "Early records indicate that the sun went through a period of inactivity in the late seventeenth century," Dr. Johnson explained. "Very few were seen from about 1645 to 1715."

2. Quote the following statement and show that the error was made by the original author, Jean le Fleur.

    Many belief that the "Kennedy curse" began with the death of Joseph Kennedy during World War II.

3. In the following quotation, replace the speaker's use of the word *motorsport* with the words *auto racing*. Place brackets around your editorial correction.

    According to David Carls, a local race-car enthusiast, "Motorsport is probably the world's most popular spectator sport because everybody dreams of being able to drive a car that fast—legally."

4. Use brackets to add the writer's comment, a yawn, to these sentences.

    All of this endless talk about a referendum is getting old. Put it on a ballot and take it to the people!

Model

Model the following sentence to practice using brackets to set off clarifying information.

He [a physicist] is an atom's way of knowing about atoms.
—George Wald

Capitalization

680.1 Proper Nouns and Adjectives

Capitalize proper nouns and proper adjectives (those derived from proper nouns). The chart below provides a quick overview of capitalization rules. The pages following explain some specific rules of capitalization.

Capitalization at a Glance

Names of people	Alice Walker, Matilda, Jim, Mr. Roker
Days of the week, months	Sunday, Tuesday, June, August
Holidays, holy days	Thanksgiving, Easter, Hanukkah
Periods, events in history	Middle Ages, the Battle of Bunker Hill
Official documents	Declaration of Independence
Special events	Elgin Community Spring Gala
Languages, nationalities, religions	French, Canadian, Islam
Political parties	Republican Party, Socialist Party
Trade names	Oscar Mayer hot dogs, Pontiac Sunbird
Official titles used with names	Mayor John Spitzer, Senator Feinstein
Formal epithets	Alexander the Great

Geographical names

Planets, heavenly bodies	Earth, Jupiter, the Milky Way
Continents	Africa, South America
Countries	Ireland, Grenada, Sri Lanka
States, provinces	Ohio, Utah, Nova Scotia
Cities, towns, villages	El Paso, Burlington, Wonewoc
Streets, roads, highways	Park Avenue, Route 66, Interstate 90
Landforms	the Rocky Mountains, the Sahara Desert
Bodies of water	Yellowstone Lake, Pumpkin Creek
Buildings, monuments	Elkhorn High School, Gateway Arch
Public areas	Times Square, Sequoia National Park

Mechanics

Practice

Capitalization 1

■ **Proper Nouns and Adjectives**

For each sentence below, write the word or words that should be capitalized.

1. Charles the bald was the youngest son of louis the pious, emperor and king of the franks.

2. The fugitive slave law of 1793 provided the return of runaway slaves to their owners.

3. Swahili, also known as "kiswahili," is a complex language spoken in east africa.

4. To avoid using the word "crock-pot," a registered trademark, use "slow cooker" instead.

5. The swallows day parade is an annual event in orange county, california.

6. The dixie highway stretched as far north as ontario, canada, and reached as far south as florida city, florida.

7. Lake powell, lake mead, and lake nassar are all man-made lakes.

8. In which u.s. city can you find the united nations secretariat building?

9. It is located in the turtle bay neighborhood (in the borough of manhattan) in new york city.

10. The building was featured in the movies *the pink panther strikes again* and *the interpreter.*

Model

Model the following sentence to practice capitalizing proper nouns and adjectives.

It was early February, in the middle of the peaceful lull that settles over Venice every year between New Year's Day and Carnival.
—John Berendt, *The City of Fallen Angels*

 12.18A

Capitalization (continued)

682.1 First Words

Capitalize the first word of every sentence, including the first word of a full-sentence direct quotation.

> Jane was nervous and excited. In a trembling voice, she whispered to her brother, "Did you see that cougar? It was on the trail just behind us." At that moment, they heard a noise on the path behind them.

682.2 Sentences in Parentheses

Capitalize the first word in a sentence enclosed in parentheses, but do not capitalize the first word if the parenthetical appears within another sentence.

> Shamelessly she winked at me and grinned again. (That grin! She could have taken it off her face and put it on the table.)
> —Jean Stafford, "Bad Characters"

> Damien's aunt (she's a wild woman) plays bingo every Saturday night.

682.3 Sentences Following Colons

Capitalize the first word in a complete sentence that follows a colon when (1) you want to emphasize the sentence or (2) the sentence is a quotation.

> When we quarreled and made horrible faces at one another, Mother knew what to say: "Your faces will stay that way, and no one will marry you."

682.4 Sections of the Country

Capitalize words that indicate particular sections of the country; do not capitalize words that simply indicate direction.

> Mr. Johnson is from the **Southwest**. (section of the country)
> After moving **north** to Montana, he had to buy winter clothes. (direction)

682.5 Certain Religious Words

Capitalize nouns that refer to the Supreme Being, the word *Bible,* the books of the Bible, and the names for other holy books.

> God   Jehovah   Buddha   the Savior   Allah   Bible   Dharma

682.6 Titles

Capitalize the first word of a title, the last word, and every word in between except articles (*a, an, the*), short prepositions, and coordinating conjunctions. Follow this rule for titles of books, newspapers, magazines, poems, plays, songs, articles, films, works of art, photographs, and stories.

> *Washington Post*   "The Diary of a Madman"   *Nights of Rain and Stars*

Practice

Capitalization 2

- **First Words**
- **Sentences in Parentheses**
- **Sentences Following Colons**
- **Sections of the Country**
- **Certain Religious Words**
- **Titles**

 Find the words or word groups that are not correctly capitalized in the following paragraphs. Write the line number in which each error appears, followed by the corrected word(s).

1 There was a cavernous rumble. Reed said, "over there!" He was
2 pointing at a giant supercell. (these rotating thunderstorms can spawn
3 tornadoes.) I felt a huge adrenaline rush as we watched the storm ramble
4 toward us from the Southwest.

5 Soon enough, the expected happened: a black rope slithered down
6 from the wall cloud. I shouted, "we have a tornado!" Reed, a seasoned storm
7 chaser from the midwest, grabbed my arm, and we bolted for his truck.

8 I thanked god that I was assigned to chase with Reed. as a
9 filmmaker, I was excited to see his photogrammetric analysis of the
10 storm. (Tornado photogrammetry is the use of film or video to
11 determine wind speed.) Some of his weather photography was featured
12 in a recent edition of *national geographic* magazine.

13 The tornado was gone as abruptly as it had appeared. the wind had
14 died down, and an eerie green atmosphere blanketed the Area. Reed started
15 his truck, ready to pursue the next storm to hit this area of the deep south.

Model

Model the following sentence to practice capitalizing sections of the country.

The Avalon Peninsula is the easternmost prow of North America—a vaguely H-shaped chunk of land that is very nearly an island itself.
—Scott Weidensaul, *Return to Wild America*

Capitalization (continued)

684.1 Words Used as Names

Capitalize words like *father, mother, uncle,* and *senator* when they are used as titles with a personal name or when they are substituted for proper nouns (especially in direct address).

We've missed you, Aunt Lucinda! (*Aunt* is part of the name.)
I hope Mayor Bates arrives soon. (*Mayor* is part of the name.)

A Closer Look

To test whether a word is being substituted for a proper noun, simply read the sentence with a proper noun in place of the word. If the proper noun fits in the sentence, the word being tested should be capitalized; otherwise, the word should not be capitalized.

Did Mom (Sue) say we could go? (*Sue* works in this sentence.)
Did your mom (Sue) say you could go? (*Sue* does not work here.)

Note: Usually the word is not capitalized if it follows a possessive —*my, his, your*—as it does in the second sentence above.

684.2 Letters

Capitalize the letters used to indicate form or shape.
U-turn   I-beam   S-curve   T-shirt   V-shaped

684.3 Organizations

Capitalize the name of an organization, an association, or a team.
Lake Ontario Sailors   American Indian Movement   Democratic Party

684.4 Abbreviations

Capitalize abbreviations of titles and organizations. (Some other abbreviations are also capitalized. See pages **692–694**.)
AAA   CEO   NAACP   M.D.   Ph.D.

684.5 Titles of Courses

Capitalize words like *sociology* and *history* when they are used as titles of specific courses; do not capitalize these words when they name a field of study.

Who teaches History 202? (title of a specific course)
It's the same professor who teaches my sociology course. (a field of study)

Note: The words *freshman, sophomore, junior,* and *senior* are not capitalized unless they are part of an official title.
Rosa is a senior this year and is in charge of the Senior Class Banquet.

Mechanics

Practice

Capitalization 3
- Words Used as Names
- Letters
- Organizations
- Abbreviations
- Titles of Courses

Find the words that are incorrectly lowercased in the following memo. Write the line number along with the words that should be capitalized.

1 **Date:**   December 8, 2011
2 **To:**   senator Robert Flanagan
3 **From:**   Mayor Dana Stepanski of Rockdale
4 **Subject:**   Update on Rerouting r.r. 27

5   Representatives from madd (mothers against drunk driving) have
6 gathered 2,500 signatures in support of rerouting the s-curve on Rural
7 Route 27. Monica Curtis, ph.d, president of the Rockdale chapter of MADD
8 and chairperson of the environmental and safety department at McKay
9 College, presented our city council with the petition.

10   Professor Curtis teaches the highway traffic safety course at the
11 college. She pointed out that r.r. 27 has had more accidents than any other
12 state highway in River Rock County. The petition addresses the issue of
13 accidents on the S-curve in 2008-2009. As you know, there have been six
14 fatalities on the curve, and the highway investigation committee reports
15 seventeen accidents there in 2008-2009.

16   This issue needs to be addressed. Please let me know when you are
17 available to meet with me to develop a proposal to present to governor
18 Billingsly.

Model

Model the following sentence to practice capitalizing titles of courses.
I love math, so I can't wait to take Calculus II in college next year.

Plurals

686.1 Most Nouns

Form the **plurals** of most nouns by adding *s* to the singular.
    cheerleader – cheerleaders
    sign – signs
    crate – crates

686.2 Nouns Ending in *sh, ch, x, s,* and *z*

Form the plurals of nouns ending in *sh, ch, x, s,* and *z* by adding *es* to the singular.
    lunch – lunches   dish – dishes   mess – messes   fox – foxes

Exception: When the final *ch* sounds like *k*, add an *s* (*monarchs*).

686.3 Nouns Ending in *y*

The plurals of common nouns that end in *y*—preceded by a consonant—are formed by changing the *y* to *i* and adding *es*.
    fly – flies   jalopy – jalopies

Form the plurals of nouns that end in *y*—preceded by a vowel—by adding only an *s*.
    donkey – donkeys   monkey – monkeys

Note: Form the plurals of all proper nouns ending in *y* by adding *s* (*Kathys*).

686.4 Nouns Ending in *o*

The plurals of nouns ending in *o*—preceded by a vowel—are formed by adding an *s*.
    radio – radios   rodeo – rodeos   studio – studios   duo – duos

The plurals of most nouns ending in *o*—preceded by a consonant—are formed by adding *es*.
    echo – echoes   hero – heroes   tomato – tomatoes

Exception: Musical terms always form plurals by adding *s*.
    alto – altos   banjo – banjos   solo – solos   piano – pianos

686.5 Nouns Ending in *ful*

Form the plurals of nouns that end in *ful* by adding an *s* at the end of the word.
    two tankfuls   three pailfuls   four mouthfuls

Note: Do not confuse these examples with *three pails full* (when you are referring to three separate pails full of something) or *two tanks full*.

686.6 Compound Nouns

Form the plurals of most compound nouns by adding *s* or *es* to the important word in the compound.
    brothers-in-law   maids of honor   secretaries of state

Practice

Plurals 1

- **Most Nouns**
- **Nouns Ending in *sh, ch, x, s,* and *z***
- **Nouns Ending in *y***
- **Nouns Ending in *o***
- **Nouns Ending in *ful***
- **Compound Nouns**

 Write the correct plurals of the underlined word or words in each sentence.

1. Ten local artist will present their renderings of church at Gallery One.

2. The Knight of Columbus are sponsoring the exhibit.

3. Two husband-wife duo will show their joint work of art.

4. The Buchinsky will exhibit their sculptures called "The Three Faithful."

5. These works feature mystery associated with historical mosque.

6. Carol and Franco Diaz will show religious folk art created from Mexican box.

7. Echo in Time and other paintings by Margaret Cliffton can be found in the hallway of the gallery.

8. Visitors can view a demonstration of fabric art using chintz.

9. They will also be able to sign up for art class at the gallery.

10. A highlight of the exhibit will be Fr. Anthony Spinozza's pen-and-ink drawing of Roman church from early century.

11. Several art studio will be open for tours Sunday afternoon.

12. Jacob Barr will entertain at the event with his original piano solo.

Model

Model the following sentences to practice using the plurals of nouns ending in *sh* and *ch*.

> We would often be sorry if our wishes were gratified. —Aesop

> It is just the little touches after the average man would quit that make the master's fame. —Orison Swett Marden

Plurals (continued)

688.1 Nouns Ending in *f* or *fe*

Form the plurals of nouns that end in *f* or *fe* in one of two ways: If the final *f* sound is still heard in the plural form of the word, simply add *s*; but if the final *f* sound becomes a *v* sound, change the *f* to *ve* and add *s*.

> **Plural ends with *f* sound:** roof – roofs; chief – chiefs
> **Plural ends with *v* sound:** wife – wives; loaf – loaves

Note: Several words are correct with either ending.

> **Plural ends with either sound:** hoof – hooves/hoofs

688.2 Irregular Spelling

A number of words form a plural by taking on an irregular spelling.

> crisis – crises   child – children   radius – radii
> criterion – criteria   goose – geese   die – dice

Note: Some of these words are acceptable with the commonly used *s* or *es* ending.

> index   indices/indexes   cactus – cacti/cactuses

Some nouns remain unchanged when used as plurals.

> deer   sheep   salmon   aircraft   series

688.3 Words Discussed as Words

The plurals of symbols, letters, numbers, and words being discussed as words are formed by adding an apostrophe and an *s*.

> Dad yelled a lot of *wow*'s and *yippee*'s when he saw my A's and B's.

Note: You may omit the apostrophe if it does not cause any confusion.

> the three R's or Rs   YMCA's or YMCAs

688.4 Collective Nouns

A collective noun may be singular or plural depending upon how it's used. A collective noun is singular when it refers to a group considered as one unit; it is plural when it refers to the individuals in the group.

> **The class was on its best behavior.** (group as a unit)
> **The class are preparing for their final exams.** (individuals in the group)

If it seems awkward to use a plural verb with a collective noun, add a clearly plural noun such as *members* to the sentence (changing the noun to an adjective), or make the collective noun the object of a preposition that follows the plural noun.

> **The class members are preparing for their final exams.**
> **The students in the class are preparing for their final exams.**

Practice

Plurals 2
- **Nouns Ending in *f* or *fe***
- **Irregular Spelling**
- **Words Discussed as Words**
- **Collective Nouns**

 Write the correct plurals of the underlined word or words in each sentence.

1. Football is a game of four quarters and two <u>half</u>.
2. Early colonists shouted *<u>huzzah</u>* instead of *<u>hurray</u>*.
3. <u>Chef</u> sometimes use bay <u>leaf</u> to season soups and stews.
4. Scientists found <u>fungus</u> and <u>bacterium</u> in the samples.
5. How many English words contain two <u>*u*</u> in a row?
6. <u>Man</u>, <u>woman</u>, and <u>child</u> waited in line for the latest Harry Potter book.
7. I determine if I want to read certain books by first reading <u>synopsis</u>.
8. On our drive through the country, we saw <u>deer</u>, <u>sheep</u>, and <u>sheaf</u> of wheat.
9. "All the <u>*and*</u> and <u>*but*</u> in this sentence should give you a clue, Dave," said the teacher, "that it's a run-on."
10. Have you ever wondered why <u>goose</u> have no <u>tooth</u>?

 For each sentence below, choose the correct pronoun (in parentheses).

11. The committee gathered *(their, its)* luggage at the airport.
12. The committee presented *(their, its)* findings at the convention.

Exercise

Write one or two sentences using the plurals of all the following words.

index, phenomenon, thief, life, offspring

Numbers

690.1 Numerals or Words

Numbers from one to nine are usually written as words; numbers 10 and over are usually written as numerals. However, numbers being compared or contrasted should be kept in the same style.

    8 to 11 years old   eight to eleven years old

You may use a combination of numerals and words for very large numbers.

    1.5 million   3 billion to 3.2 billion   6 trillion

If numbers are used infrequently in a piece of writing, you may spell out those that can be written in no more than two words.

    ten   twenty-five   two hundred   ten thousand

690.2 Numerals Only

Use numerals for the following forms: decimals, percentages, chapters, pages, addresses, phone numbers, identification numbers, and statistics.

    26.2   8 percent   Highway 36   chapter 7
    pages 287–89   July 6, 1945   44 B.C.E.   a vote of 23 to 4

Always use numerals with abbreviations and symbols.

    8%   10 mm   3 cc   8 oz   90° C   24 mph   6' 3"

690.3 Words Only

Use words to express numbers that begin a sentence.

    Fourteen students "forgot" their assignments.

Note: Change the sentence structure if this rule creates a clumsy construction.

    Clumsy: *Six hundred thirty-nine* teachers were laid off this year.
    Better: This year, 639 teachers were laid off.

Use words for numbers that come before a compound modifier if that modifier includes a numeral.

    They made twelve 10-foot sub sandwiches for the picnic.

690.4 Time and Money

If time is expressed with an abbreviation, use numerals; if it is expressed in words, spell out the number.

    4:00 A.M. (or) four o'clock

If an amount of money is spelled out, so is the currency; use a numeral if a symbol is used.

    twenty dollars (or) $20

Practice

Numbers

- **Numerals or Words**
- **Numerals Only**
- **Words Only**
- **Time and Money**

 For each sentence below, write the underlined numbers the correct way. If a number is already correctly presented, write "correct."

1. The <u>two-thousand-and-four</u> tsunami was the deadliest in history.
2. It struck at <u>seven-fifty-three</u> A.M. local time on December 26.
3. Initial estimates of the death toll neared <u>300,000</u> people.
4. The earthquake that caused it registered <u>nine-point-one</u> on the Richter scale.
5. The quake lasted between <u>500</u> and <u>six hundred</u> seconds.
6. The tsunami created waves up to <u>thirty</u> meters (<u>100</u> feet).
7. <u>Sixty-six</u> percent of the fishing fleet was destroyed in coastal areas.
8. Energy released by the quake equaled about as much as the United States typically uses in <u>11</u> days.
9. The quake caused the earth to wobble on its axis about <u>1</u> inch in the direction of <u>one-hundred forty-five</u> degrees east longitude.
10. <u>16</u> coral-reef atolls crushed by sea waves could be uninhabitable for decades.
11. <u>Three billion dollars</u> in aid was provided by world countries.
12. Many children aged <u>six to 18</u> contributed aid to victims.

Model

Model the following sentences to practice using numbers and numerals correctly.

    In the future, everyone will be famous for 15 minutes.
                                                     —Andy Warhol

    Fifteen years ago, Congress took a significant step in implementing national health insurance for the aged with the establishment of Medicare.
        —Select Committee on Aging, "Medicare: A Fifteen-Year Perspective"

Abbreviations

692.1 Formal and Informal Abbreviations

An **abbreviation** is the shortened form of a word or phrase. Some abbreviations are always acceptable in both formal and informal writing:

  Mr.   Mrs.   Jr.   Ms.   Dr.   a.m. (A.M.)   p.m. (P.M.)

Note: In most of your writing, you do not abbreviate the names of states, countries, months, days, or units of measure. However, you may use the abbreviation *U.S.* after it has been spelled out once. Do not abbreviate the words *Street, Company,* and similar words, especially when they are part of a proper name. Also, do not use signs or symbols (%, &, #, @) in place of words. The dollar sign, however, is appropriate with numerals ($325).

692.2 Correspondence Abbreviations

United States

	Standard	Postal
Alabama	Ala.	AL
Alaska	Alaska	AK
Arizona	Ariz.	AZ
Arkansas	Ark.	AR
California	Calif.	CA
Colorado	Colo.	CO
Connecticut	Conn.	CT
Delaware	Del.	DE
District of Columbia	D.C.	DC
Florida	Fla.	FL
Georgia	Ga.	GA
Guam	Guam	GU
Hawaii	Hawaii	HI
Idaho	Idaho	ID
Illinois	Ill.	IL
Indiana	Ind.	IN
Iowa	Iowa	IA
Kansas	Kan.	KS
Kentucky	Ky.	KY
Louisiana	La.	LA
Maine	Maine	ME
Maryland	Md.	MD
Massachusetts	Mass.	MA
Michigan	Mich.	MI
Minnesota	Minn.	MN
Mississippi	Miss.	MS
Missouri	Mo.	MO
Montana	Mont.	MT
Nebraska	Neb.	NE
Nevada	Nev.	NV
New Hampshire	N.H.	NH
New Jersey	N.J.	NJ
New Mexico	N.M.	NM
New York	N.Y.	NY
North Carolina	N.C.	NC
North Dakota	N.D.	ND
Ohio	Ohio	OH
Oklahoma	Okla.	OK
Oregon	Ore.	OR
Pennsylvania	Pa.	PA
Puerto Rico	P.R.	PR
Rhode Island	R.I.	RI
South Carolina	S.C.	SC
South Dakota	S.D.	SD
Tennessee	Tenn.	TN
Texas	Texas	TX
Utah	Utah	UT
Vermont	Vt.	VT
Virginia	Va.	VA
Virgin Islands	V.I.	VI
Washington	Wash.	WA
West Virginia	W.Va.	WV
Wisconsin	Wis.	WI
Wyoming	Wyo.	WY

Canadian Provinces

	Standard	Postal
Alberta	Alta.	AB
British Columbia	B.C.	BC
Labrador	Lab.	NL
Manitoba	Man.	MB
New Brunswick	N.B.	NB
Newfoundland	N.F.	NL
Northwest Territories	N.W.T.	NT
Nova Scotia	N.S.	NS
Nunavut	—	NU
Ontario	Ont.	ON
Prince Edward Island	P.E.I.	PE
Quebec	Que.	QC
Saskatchewan	Sask.	SK
Yukon Territory	Y.T.	YT

Addresses

	Standard	Postal
Apartment	Apt.	APT
Avenue	Ave.	AVE
Boulevard	Blvd.	BLVD
Circle	Cir.	CIR
Court	Ct.	CT
Drive	Dr.	DR
East	E.	E
Expressway	Expy.	EXPY
Freeway	Fwy.	FWY
Heights	Hts.	HTS
Highway	Hwy.	HWY
Hospital	Hosp.	HOSP
Junction	Junc.	JCT
Lake	L.	LK
Lakes	Ls.	LKS
Lane	Ln.	LN
Meadows	Mdws.	MDWS
North	N.	N
Palms	Palms	PLMS
Park	Pk.	PK
Parkway	Pky.	PKY
Place	Pl.	PL
Plaza	Plaza	PLZ
Post Office Box	P.O. Box	PO BOX
Ridge	Rdg.	RDG
River	R.	RV
Road	Rd.	RD
Room	Rm.	RM
Rural	R.	R
Rural Route	R.R.	RR
Shore	Sh.	SH
South	S.	S
Square	Sq.	SQ
Station	Sta.	STA
Street	St.	ST
Suite	Ste.	STE
Terrace	Ter.	TER
Turnpike	Tpke.	TPKE
Union	Un.	UN
View	View	VW
Village	Vil.	VLG
West	W.	W

693.1 Other Common Abbreviations

abr. abridged; abridgment
AC, ac alternating current
ack. acknowledge; acknowledgment
acv actual cash value
A.D. in the year of the Lord (Latin *anno Domini*)
AM amplitude modulation
A.M., a.m. before noon (Latin *ante meridiem*)
ASAP as soon as possible
avg., av. average
BBB Better Business Bureau
B.C. before Christ
B.C.E. before the Common Era
bibliog. bibliographer; bibliography
biog. biographer; biographical; biography
C 1. Celsius 2. centigrade 3. coulomb
c. 1. circa (about) 2. cup
cc 1. cubic centimeter 2. carbon copy
CDT, C.D.T. central daylight time
C.E. of the Common Era
chap. chapter
cm centimeter
c.o., c/o care of
COD, C.O.D 1. cash on delivery 2. collect on delivery
co-op. cooperative
CST, C.S.T. central standard time
cu., c cubic
D.A. district attorney
d.b.a. doing business as
DC, dc direct current
dec. deceased
dept. department
DST, D.S.T. daylight saving time
dup. duplicate
DVD digital video disc
ea. each
ed. edition; editor
EDT, E.D.T. eastern daylight time
e.g. for example (Latin *exempli gratia*)
EST, E.S.T. eastern standard time
etc. and so forth (Latin *et cetera*)
ex. example
F Fahrenheit
FM frequency modulation
F.O.B., f.o.b. free on board
ft foot
g 1. gram 2. gravity
gal. gallon
gloss. glossary
GNP gross national product
hdqrs, HQ headquarters
HIV human immunodeficiency virus

Hon. Honorable (title)
hp horsepower
HTML hypertext markup language
Hz hertz
ibid. in the same place (Latin *ibidem*)
id. the same (Latin *idem*)
i.e. that is (Latin *id est*)
illus. illustration
inc. incorporated
IQ, I.Q. intelligence quotient
IRS Internal Revenue Service
ISBN International Standard Book Number
Jr. junior
K 1. kelvin (temperature unit) 2. Kelvin (temperature scale)
kc kilocycle
kg kilogram
km kilometer
kn knot
kW kilowatt
l liter
lat. latitude
lb, lb. pound (Latin *libra*)
l.c. lowercase
lit. literary; literature
log logarithm
long. longitude
Ltd., ltd. limited
m meter
M.A. master of arts (Latin *Magister Artium*)
Mc, mc megacycle
M.C., m.c. master of ceremonies
M.D. doctor of medicine (Latin *medicinae doctor*)
mdse. merchandise
mfg. manufacturing
mg milligram
mi. 1. mile 2. mill (monetary unit)
misc. miscellaneous
ml milliliter
mm millimeter
mpg, m.p.g. miles per gallon
mph, m.p.h. miles per hour
MS 1. manuscript 2. Mississippi 3. multiple sclerosis
Ms., Ms title of courtesy for a woman
MST, M.S.T. mountain standard time
neg. negative
N.S.F., n.s.f. not sufficient funds
oz, oz. ounce
PA 1. public-address system 2. Pennsylvania
pct. percent
pd. paid

PDT, P.D.T. Pacific daylight time
PFC, Pfc. private first class
pg., p. page
P.M., p.m. after noon (Latin *post meridiem*)
P.O. 1. personnel officer 2. purchase order 3. postal order; post office 4. (also **p.o.**) petty officer
pop. population
POW, P.O.W. prisoner of war
pp. pages
ppd. 1. postpaid 2. prepaid
PR, P.R. 1. public relations 2. Puerto Rico
P.S. post script
psi, p.s.i. pounds per square inch
PST, P.S.T. Pacific standard time
PTA, P.T.A. Parent Teacher Association
qt. quart
RF radio frequency
RN registered nurse
R.P.M., rpm revolutions per minute
R.S.V.P., r.s.v.p. please reply (French *répondez s'il vous plaît*)
SASE self-addressed stamped envelope
SCSI small computer system interface
SOS 1. international distress signal 2. any call for help
Sr. 1. senior (after surname) 2. sister (religious)
ST standard time
St. 1. saint 2. strait 3. street
std. standard
syn. synonymous; synonym
TBA to be announced
tbs, tbsp tablespoon
TM trademark
tsp teaspoon
UHF, uhf ultra high frequency
UPC universal product code
UV ultraviolet
V 1. *Physics:* velocity 2. *Electricity:* volt 3. volume
V.A., VA Veterans Administration
VHF, vhf very high frequency
VIP *Informal:* very important person
vol. 1. volume 2. volunteer
vs. versus
W 1. *Electricity:* watt 2. *Physics:* (also **w**) work 3. west
whse., whs. warehouse
wkly. weekly
w/o without
wt. weight
yd yard (measurement)

Acronyms and Initialisms

694.1 Acronyms

An **acronym** is a word formed from the first (or first few) letters of words in a phrase. Even though acronyms are abbreviations, they require no periods.

radar	radio detecting and ranging
CARE	Cooperative for American Relief Everywhere
NASA	National Aeronautics and Space Administration
VISTA	Volunteers in Service to America
LAN	local area network

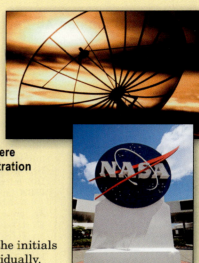

694.2 Initialisms

An **initialism** is similar to an acronym except that the initials used to form this abbreviation are pronounced individually.

CIA	Central Intelligence Agency
FBI	Federal Bureau of Investigation
FHA	Federal Housing Administration

694.3 Common Acronyms and Initialisms

ADD	attention deficit disorder	**LLC**	limited liability company
AIDS	acquired immunodeficiency syndrome	**MADD**	Mothers Against Drunk Driving
AKA	also known as	**MRI**	magnetic resonance imaging
ATM	automatic teller machine	**NASA**	National Aeronautics and Space Administration
BMI	body mass index	**NATO**	North Atlantic Treaty Organization
CD	compact disc; certificate of deposit	**OPEC**	Organization of Petroleum-Exporting Countries
DMV	Department of Motor Vehicles	**OSHA**	Occupational Safety and Health Administration
ETA	estimated time of arrival	**PAC**	political action committee
FAA	Federal Aviation Administration	**PDF**	portable document format
FCC	Federal Communications Commission	**PETA**	People for the Ethical Treatment of Animals
FDA	Food and Drug Administration	**PIN**	personal identification number
FDIC	Federal Deposit Insurance Corporation	**PSA**	public service announcement
FEMA	Federal Emergency Management Agency	**ROTC**	Reserve Officers' Training Corps
FTC	Federal Trade Commission	**SADD**	Students Against Destructive Decisions
FYI	for your information	**SUV**	sport utility vehicle
GPS	global positioning system	**SWAT**	special weapons and tactics
HDTV	high-definition television	**TDD**	telecommunications device for the deaf
IRS	Internal Revenue Service		
IT	information technology		
JPEG	Joint Photographic Experts Group		
LCD	liquid crystal display		

Practice

Abbreviations, Acronyms, and Initialisms

Write the correct abbreviation for the underlined word or words.

1. Find the <u>universal product code</u> on this <u>digital video disc</u>.
2. Luis lives at 1279 <u>North</u> Bethesda <u>Circle</u>, Watch Hill, <u>Rhode Island</u>.
3. During the awards ceremony, the <u>master of ceremonies</u> introduced the <u>very important persons</u>.
4. The program begins at 8:00 <u>ante meridiem, eastern daylight time</u>.
5. The National 4-H <u>headquarters</u> is in Washington, <u>District of Columbia</u>.
6. All books have an <u>International Standard Book Number</u>.
7. <u>Mister</u> Jenkins took a class to learn <u>hypertext markup language</u>.
8. My grandfather is in a <u>Veterans Administration</u> hospital in <u>Iowa</u>.
9. Anwar Singh, <u>doctor of medicine</u>, spoke about the <u>human immunodeficiency virus</u>.
10. Under "time" for next week's meeting, someone had written "<u>to be announced</u>."
11. Look for a maximum <u>pounds per square inch</u> stamp on your tires before adding air.
12. The <u>longitude</u> of Tuscaloosa, <u>Alabama</u>, is 87.62 degrees; the <u>latitude</u> is 33.23 degrees.

Model

Model the following acronyms and initialisms to come up with your own abbreviations. (Write at least one acronym and one initialism.)

    BOYS — Bradford Orchid and Yam Society
    JUSTICE — Jesuit University Students Together in Concerned Empowerment
    ZFF — Zephyr Flower Flats
    DHS — Department of Homeland Security

Spelling Rules

696.1 Write *i* before *e*

Write *i* before *e* except after *c,* or when sounded like *a* as in *neighbor* and *weigh.*

   relief   receive   perceive   reign   freight   beige

Exceptions: There are a number of exceptions to this rule, including these: *neither, leisure, seize, weird, species, science.*

696.2 Words with Consonant Endings

When a one-syllable word *(bat)* ends in a consonant *(t)* preceded by one vowel *(a),* double the final consonant before adding a suffix that begins with a vowel *(batting).*

   sum—summary   god—goddess

Note: When a multisyllabic word *(control)* ends in a consonant *(l)* preceded by one vowel *(o),* the accent is on the last syllable *(con trol´),* and the suffix begins with a vowel *(ing)*—the same rule holds true: Double the final consonant *(controlling).*

   prefer—preferred   begin—beginning
   forget—forgettable   admit—admittance

696.3 Words with a Silent *e*

If a word ends with a silent *e,* drop the *e* before adding a suffix that begins with a vowel. Do not drop the *e* when the suffix begins with a consonant.

   state—stating—statement   like—liking—likeness
   use—using—useful   nine—ninety—nineteen

Exceptions: *judgment, truly, argument, ninth*

696.4 Words Ending in *y*

When *y* is the last letter in a word and the *y* is preceded by a consonant, change the *y* to *i* before adding any suffix except those beginning with *i.*

   fry—fries—frying   hurry—hurried—hurrying   lady—ladies
   ply—pliable   happy—happiness   beauty—beautiful

When *y* is the last letter in a word and the *y* is preceded by a vowel, do not change the *y* to *i* before adding a suffix.

   play—plays—playful   stay—stays—staying
   employ—employed

Important reminder: Never trust your spelling even to the best spell-checker. Use a dictionary for words your spell-checker does not cover.

Practice

Spelling 1

Find the 12 words that are misspelled in the following paragraph and write them correctly. (Each misspelled word is in the "Commonly Misspelled Words" list on pages 698–699.)

1   A playright is a person who writes dramatic literture. Sophocles and
2   Euripides, ancent Greeks, created some of the earliest plays around the
3   fifth century B.C.E. The dramatic forms of comedy and traggedy are usualy
4   studied in asociation with the life of William Shakespeare. He was a brilliant
5   writer during England's Elizabethan period. Shakespeare's works have
6   withstood the test of time. Performances of his plays are still presented by
7   modern-day proffesional theater groups in America and abroad. Undoutably,
8   the works of these early authors were instramental in influencing the
9   creation of modern drama.

Model

Model the following sentences to practice using the spelling rules that deal with adding a suffix.

A playwright lives in an occupied country. And if you can't live that way, you don't stay.
—Arthur Miller

It's discouraging to think how many people are shocked by honesty and how few by deceit.
—Noel Coward

Commonly Misspelled Words

A
abbreviate
abrupt
absence
absolute (ly)
absurd
abundance
academic
accelerate
accept (ance)
accessible
accessory
accidentally
accommodate
accompany
accomplish
accumulate
accurate
accustom (ed)
ache
achieve (ment)
acknowledge
acquaintance
acquired
across
address
adequate
adjustment
admissible
admittance
adolescent
advantageous
advertisement
advisable
aggravate
aggression
alcohol
alleviate
almost
alternative
although
aluminum
amateur
analysis
analyze
anarchy
ancient
anecdote
anesthetic
annihilate
announce
annual
anonymous
answer
anxious
apologize
apparatus
apparent (ly)
appearance
appetite
applies
appreciate
appropriate
approximately
architect
arctic
argument
arithmetic
arrangement
artificial
ascend
assistance
association
athlete
attendance
attire
attitude
audience
authority
available

B
balance
balloon
bargain
basically
beautiful
beginning
believe
benefit (ed)
biscuit
bought
boycott
brevity
brilliant
Britain
bureau
business

C
cafeteria
caffeine
calculator
calendar
campaign
canceled
candidate
catastrophe
category
caught
cavalry
celebration
cemetery
certificate
changeable
chief
chocolate
circuit
circumstance
civilization
colonel
colossal
column
commercial
commitment
committed
committee
comparative
comparison
competitively
conceivable
condemn
condescend
conference
conferred
confidential
congratulate
conscience
conscientious
conscious
consequence
consumer
contaminate
convenience
cooperate
correspondence
cough
coupon
courageous
courteous
creditor
criticism
criticize
curiosity
curious
cylinder

D
dealt
deceitful
deceive
decision
defense
deferred
definite (ly)
definition
delicious
descend
describe
description
despair
desperate
destruction
development
diameter
diaphragm
diarrhea
dictionary
dining
disagreeable
disappear
disappoint
disastrous
discipline
discrimination
discuss
dismissal
dissatisfied
dissect
distinctly
dormitory
doubt
drought
duplicate
dyeing
dying

E
earliest
efficiency
eighth
elaborate
eligible
eliminate
ellipse
embarrass
emphasize
employee
enclosure
encourage
endeavor
English
enormous
enough
enrichment
enthusiastic
entirely
entrance
environment
equipment
equipped
equivalent
especially
essential
eventually
exaggerate
examination
exceed
excellent
excessive
excite
executive
exercise
exhaust (ed)
exhibition
exhilaration
existence
expensive
experience
explanation
exquisite
extinguish
extraordinary
extremely

F-G
facilities
familiar
fascinate
fashion
fatigue (d)
feature
February
fiery
financially
flourish
forcible
foreign
forfeit
fortunate
forty
fourth
freight
friend
fulfill
gauge
generally
generous
genuine
glimpse
gnarled
gnaw
government
gradual
grammar
gratitude
grievous
grocery
guard
guidance

H
happiness
harass
harmonize
height
hemorrhage
hereditary
hindrance
hoping
hopping
hospitable
humorous

Mechanics

hygiene
hymn
hypocrisy

I-J

ignorance
illiterate
illustrate
imaginary
immediately
immense
incidentally
inconvenience
incredible
indefinitely
independence
indispensable
industrial
industrious
inevitable
infinite
inflation
innocence
inoculation
inquiry
installation
instrumental
intelligence
interesting
interfere
interrupt
investigate
irregular
irresistible
issuing
itinerary
jealous (y)
jewelry
journal
judgment

K-L

knowledge
laboratory
laugh
lawyer
league
legacy
legalize
legitimate
leisure

liaison
license
lightning
likable
liquid
literature
loneliness

M-N

maintenance
maneuver
manufacture
marriage
mathematics
medieval
memento
menagerie
merchandise
merely
mileage
miniature
miscellaneous
mischievous
misspell
moat
mobile
mortgage
multiplied
muscle
musician
mustache
mutual
mysterious
naive
nauseous
necessary
neither
neurotic
nevertheless
nighttime
ninety
noticeable
nuclear
nuisance

O-P

obstacle
obvious
occasion
occupant
occupation

occurred
occurrence
official
often
omitted
opinion
opponent
opportunity
opposite
optimism
ordinarily
organization
original
outrageous
pamphlet
parallel
paralyze
partial
particularly
pastime
patience
peculiar
pedestal
performance
permanent
permissible
perseverance
personal (ly)
personality
perspiration
persuade
petition
phenomenon
physical
physician
picnicking
planned
playwright
plead
pneumonia
politician
ponder
positively
possession
practically
precede
precious
preference
prejudice
preparation
presence
prevalent
primitive

privilege
probably
proceed
professional
professor
prominent
pronounce
pronunciation
protein
psychology
puny
purchase
pursuing

Q-R

qualified
quality
quantity
questionnaire
quiet
quite
quizzes
recede
receipt
receive
recipe
recognize
recommend
reference
referred
regard
regimen
religious
repel
repetition
residue
responsibility
restaurant
rheumatism
rhythm
ridiculous
robot
roommate

S

sacrifice
salary
sandwich
satisfactory
scarcely
scenic

schedule
scholar
science
secretary
seize
separate
sergeant
several
severely
sheriff
shrubbery
siege
signature
signify
silhouette
similar
simultaneous
sincerely
skiing
skunk
society
solar
sophomore
souvenir
spaghetti
specific
specimen
statue
stomach
stopped
strength
strictly
submission
substitute
subtle
succeed
success
sufficient
supersede
suppose
surprise
suspicious
symbolism
sympathy
synthetic

T-U

tariff
technique
temperature
temporary
tendency

thermostat
thorough (ly)
though
throughout
tongue
tornado
tortoise
tragedy
transferred
tremendous
tried
trite
truly
unanimous
undoubtedly
unfortunately
unique
unnecessary
until
urgent
usable
usher
usually

V

vacuum
vague
valuable
variety
vengeance
versatile
vicinity
villain
visibility
visual

W

waif
Wednesday
weird
wholly
width
women
wrath
wreckage

Y

yesterday
yield
yolk

Steps to Becoming a Better Speller

1. **Be patient.**
   Becoming a good speller takes time.

2. **Check the correct pronunciation of each word you are attempting to spell.**
   Knowing the correct pronunciation of a word can help you remember its spelling.

3. **Note the meaning and history of each word as you are checking the dictionary for pronunciation.**
   Knowing the meaning and history of a word provides you with a better notion of how the word is properly used, and this can help you remember its spelling.

4. **Before you close the dictionary, practice spelling the word.**
   Look away from the page and try to "see" the word in your mind. Then write it on a piece of paper. Check your spelling in the dictionary; repeat the process until you are able to spell the word correctly.

5. **Learn some spelling rules.**
   For four of the most useful rules, see page **696**.

6. **Make a list of the words that you often misspell.**
   Select the first 10 and practice spelling them.

   STEP A: Read each word carefully; then write it on a piece of paper. Check to see that you've spelled it correctly. Repeat this step for the words that you misspelled.

   STEP B: When you have finished your first 10 words, ask someone to read them to you as you write them again. Then check for misspellings. If you find none, congratulations! (Repeat both steps with your next 10 words, and so on.)

7. **Write often.**

Mechanics

Practice

Spelling 2

For each quotation below, fill in the letters to spell the correct word from the list of "Commonly Misspelled Words" (pages **698–699**).

1. Television is instantaneous and s____u__t_____s: Everyone gets the message at the same time.
   —William J. Donnelly

2. It takes time to p_____e men to do even what is for their own good.
   —Thomas Jefferson

3. The g____r l____ stump has as tender a bud as the sapling.
   —Henry David Thoreau

4. Only strong personalities can endure history; the weak ones are e__t____g_____d by it.
   —Friedrich Nietzsche

5. The day is but a Scandinavian night; the winter is an a _ c ____ c summer.
   —Henry David Thoreau

6. I have noted that persons with bad j____g_____t are most insistent that we do what they think best.
   —Lionel Abel

7. R____e_____n is tedious.
   —Mason Cooley

8. No l__g__c__ is so rich as honesty.
   —William Shakespeare

9. S_____ is counted sweetest by those who ne'er succeed.
   —Emily Dickinson

10. No guest is so welcome in a friend's house that he will not become a n_____a_____ after three days.
    —Titus Maccius Plautus

Model

Model the following sentence to practice using the spelling rule for writing *i* before *e*.

Time folded in on itself then. What is left lies in clear yet disjointed pieces in my head.
—Sue Monk Kidd, *The Secret Life of Bees*

Understanding Idioms

Idioms are phrases that are used in a special way. You can't understand an idiom just by knowing the meaning of each word in the phrase. You must learn it as a whole. For example, the idiom *bury the hatchet* means "to settle an argument," even though the individual words in the phrase mean something much different. This section will help you learn some of the common idioms in American English.

apple of his eye	Eagle Lake is the apple of his eye. (something he likes very much)
as plain as day	The mistake in the ad was as plain as day. (very clear)
as the crow flies	New London is 200 miles from here as the crow flies. (in a straight line)
at a snail's pace	My last hour at work passes at a snail's pace. (very, very slowly)
axe to grind	The manager has an axe to grind with that umpire. (disagreement to settle)
bad apple	There are no bad apples in this class. (bad influences)
beat around the bush	Don't beat around the bush; answer the question. (avoid getting to the point)
benefit of the doubt	Mom gave me the benefit of the doubt when I said I'd tried to be on time. (belief when the truth is unclear)
beyond the shadow of a doubt	Beyond the shadow of a doubt, this is my best science project. (for certain)
blew my top	When I saw the broken statue, I blew my top. (showed great anger)
bone to pick	Alison had a bone to pick with the student who copied her paper. (problem to settle)
brain drain	When the magnet school opened nearby, we feared our school would experience brain drain. (the best moving away)
break the ice	The nervous ninth graders were afraid to break the ice. (start a conversation)
burn the midnight oil	Devon had to burn the midnight oil to finish his report. (work late into the night)

Understanding Idioms

bury the hatchet	My sisters were told to bury the hatchet immediately. (settle an argument)
by the skin of her teeth	Sumey avoided an accident by the skin of her teeth. (just barely)
champing at the bit	The skiers were champing at the bit to get on the slopes. (eager, excited)
chicken feed	The prize was chicken feed to some people. (not worth much money)
chip off the old block	Frank's just like his father. He's a chip off the old block. (just like someone else)
clean as a whistle	My boss told me to make sure the place was as clean as a whistle before I left. (very clean)
cold shoulder	I wanted to fit in with that group, but they gave me the cold shoulder. (ignored me)
crack of dawn	Ali delivers his papers at the crack of dawn. (first light of day, early morning)
cry wolf	If you cry wolf too often, no one will believe you. (say you are in trouble when you aren't)
dead of night	Hearing a loud noise in the dead of night frightened Bill. (middle of the night)
dirt cheap	A lot of clothes at that store are dirt cheap. (inexpensive, costing very little money)
doesn't hold a candle to	That award doesn't hold a candle to a gold medal. (is not as good as)
drop in the bucket	The contributions were a drop in the bucket. (a small amount compared to what's needed)
everything from A to Z	That catalog lists everything from A to Z. (a lot of different things)
face the music	Todd had to face the music when he broke the window. (deal with the punishment)
fish out of water	He felt like a fish out of water in the new math class. (someone in an unfamiliar place)
fit for a king	The food at the athletic banquet was fit for a king. (very special)

flew off the handle	Bill flew off the handle when he saw a reckless driver near the school. (became very angry)
floating on air	Celine was floating on air at the prom. (feeling very happy)
food for thought	The boys' foolish and dangerous prank gave us food for thought. (something to think about)
get down to business	After sharing several jokes, Mr. Sell said we should get down to business. (start working)
get the upper hand	The wrestler moved quickly on his opponent in order to get the upper hand. (gain the advantage)
give their all	Student volunteers give their all to help others. (work as hard as they can)
go fly a kite	Charlene stared at her nosy brother and said, "Go fly a kite." (go away)
has a green thumb	Talk to Mrs. Smith about your sick plant. She has a green thumb. (is good at growing plants)
has a heart of gold	Joe has a heart of gold and will always help a friend or stranger in need. (is very kind and generous)
hit a home run	Rhonda hit a home run with her speech. (succeeded, or did well)
hit the ceiling	When my parents saw my grades, they hit the ceiling. (were very angry)
hit the hay	Exhausted from the hike, Jamal hit the hay without eating supper. (went to bed)
in a nutshell	Can you, in a nutshell, tell us your goals for this year? (in summary)
in one ear and out the other	Sharl, concerned about her pet, let the lecture go in one ear and out the other. (without really listening)
in the black	My aunt's gift shop is finally in the black. (making money)
in the nick of time	Janelle caught the falling vase in the nick of time. (just in time)
in the red	Many businesses start out in the red. (in debt)
in the same boat	The new tax bill meant everyone would be in the same boat. (in a similar situation)

iron out	Joe will meet with the work crew to iron out their complaints. (solve, work out)
it goes without saying	It goes without saying that saving money is a good idea. (it is clear)
it stands to reason	It stands to reason that your stamina will increase if you run every day. (it makes sense)
keep a stiff upper lip	Keep a stiff upper lip when you visit the doctor. (be brave)
keep it under your hat	Keep it under your hat about the pop quiz. (don't tell anyone)
knock on wood	My uncle knocked on wood after he said he had never had the flu. (did something for good luck)
knuckle down	After wasting half the day, we were told to knuckle down. (work hard)
learn the ropes	It takes every new employee a few months to learn the ropes. (get to know how things are done)
leave no stone unturned	The police plan to leave no stone unturned at the crime scene. (check everything)
lend someone a hand	You will feel good if you lend someone a hand. (help someone)
let the cat out of the bag	Tom let the cat out of the bag when he mentioned the surprise party. (told a secret)
let's face it	Let's face it. You don't like rap. (let's admit it)
look high and low	We looked high and low for Jan's dog. (looked everywhere)
lose face	In some cultures, one student's bad grades can cause the whole family to lose face. (be embarrassed)
needle in a haystack	Trying to find a person in New York is like trying to find a needle in a haystack. (something impossible to find)
nose to the grindstone	With all of these assignments, I have to keep my nose to the grindstone. (work hard)
on cloud nine	After talking to my girlfriend, I was on cloud nine. (feeling very happy)
on pins and needles	Emiko was on pins and needles during the championship game. (feeling nervous)

out the window	Once the rain started, our plans were out the window. (ruined)
over and above	Over and above the required work, Will cleaned up the lab. (in addition to)
pain in the neck	Franklin knew the report would be a pain in the neck. (very annoying)
pull your leg	Cary was only pulling your leg. (telling you a little lie as a joke)
put his foot in his mouth	Lane put his foot in his mouth when he answered the question. (said something embarrassing)
put the cart before the horse	Tonya put the cart before the horse when she sealed the envelope before inserting the letter. (did something in the wrong order)
put your best foot forward	When applying for a job, you should put your best foot forward. (do the best that you can do)
red-letter day	Sovann had a red-letter day because she did so well on her math test. (very good day)
rock the boat	I was told not to rock the boat. (cause trouble)
rude awakening	Jake will have a rude awakening when he sees the bill for his computer. (sudden, unpleasant surprise)
save face	His gift was clearly an attempt to save face. (fix an embarrassing situation)
see eye to eye	We see eye to eye about the need for a new school. (are in agreement)
shake a leg	I told Mako to shake a leg so that we wouldn't be late. (hurry)
shift into high gear	Greg had to shift into high gear to finish the test in time. (speed up, hurry)
sight for sore eyes	My grandmother's smiling face was a sight for sore eyes. (good to see)
sight unseen	Liz bought the coat sight unseen. (without seeing it first)
sink or swim	Whether you sink or swim in school depends on your study habits. (fail or succeed)

Understanding Idioms

spilled the beans	Suddenly, Kesia realized that she had spilled the beans about Sharon's birthday gift. (revealed a secret)
spring chicken	Although Mr. Gordon isn't a spring chicken, he sure knows how to talk to kids. (young person)
stick to your guns	Know what you believe, and stick to your guns. (don't change your mind)
sweet tooth	Chocolate is often the candy of choice for those with a sweet tooth. (a love for sweets, like candy and cake)
take a dim view	My sister will take a dim view of that movie. (disapprove)
take it with a grain of salt	When you read that advertisement, take it with a grain of salt. (don't believe everything)
take the bull by the horns	It's time to take the bull by the horns so the project gets done on time. (take control)
through thick and thin	Those two girls have remained friends through thick and thin. (in good times and in bad times)
time flies	Time flies as you grow older. (time passes quickly)
time to kill	Grace had time to kill, so she read a book. (extra time)
to go overboard	The class was told not to go overboard. A $50.00 donation was fine. (to do too much)
toe the line	The new teacher made everyone toe the line. (follow the rules)
tongue-tied	He can talk easily with friends, but in class he is usually tongue-tied. (not knowing what to say)
turn over a new leaf	After another bad grade, Mike decided to turn over a new leaf in school. (make a new start)
two peas in a pod	Ever since kindergarten, Lil and Eve have been like two peas in a pod. (very much alike)
under the weather	Guy was feeling under the weather this morning. (sick)
wallflower	Cho used to be a wallflower, but now she talks to everyone. (a shy person)
word of mouth	Joseph learns a lot about his favorite team by word of mouth. (talking with other people)

Using the Right Word

a lot ■ *A lot* (always two words) is a vague descriptive phrase that should be used sparingly.

> You can learn a lot just by reading.

accept, except ■ The verb *accept* means "to receive" or "to believe"; the preposition *except* means "other than."

> The principal accepted the boy's story about the broken window, but she asked why no one except him saw the ball accidentally slip from his hand.

adapt, adopt ■ *Adapt* means "to adjust or change to fit"; *adopt* means "to choose and treat as your own" (a child, an idea).

> After a lengthy period of study, Malcolm X adopted the Islamic faith and adapted to its lifestyle.

affect, effect ■ The verb *affect* means "to influence"; the verb *effect* means "to produce, accomplish, complete."

> Ming's hard work effected an A on the test, which positively affected her semester grade.

The noun *effect* means the "result."

> Good grades have a calming effect on parents.

aisle, isle ■ An *aisle* is a passage between things; an *isle* is a small island.

> Many airline passengers on their way to the Isle of Capri prefer an aisle seat.

all right ■ *All right* is always two words (not *alright*).

allusion, illusion ■ *Allusion* is an indirect reference to someone or something; *illusion* is a false picture or idea.

> My little sister, under the illusion that she's movie-star material, makes frequent allusions to her future fans.

already, all ready ■ *Already* is an adverb meaning "before this time" or "by this time." *All ready* is an adjective meaning "fully prepared."

Note: Use *all ready* if you can substitute *ready* alone in the sentence.

> Although I've already had some dessert, I am all ready for some ice cream from the street vendor.

Practice

Using the Right Word 1

accept, except; affect, effect; aisle, isle; already, all ready

 Find the words that are used incorrectly. Write the line number followed by the right word.

1   Parnel, feeling a bit depressed, is watching TV: an ancient movie
2 from the 1950s in which the wealthy escape to the Isle of Capri. Here's the
3 dashing Cary Grant, breakfasting on a veranda overlooking a lush valley.
4 There's his lovely lady Audrey Hepburn, all ready growing restless with the
5 relaxation. Cary knows, of course, it is up to him to effect a change in her
6 attitude, and sets about doing so. Getting Audrey to except this life of leisure
7 won't be easy, but, darn it, he's determined!
8   Obviously, the movie has a big affect on Parnel. He dreams he is Cary,
9 except with better-looking hair. He is making his way down the isle of a
10 small jet, which is all first class. He finds himself at the open door, all ready
11 to jump out. Cary/Parnel checks to make sure his parachute is secure; even
12 dreaming, he does not want to think about
13 how skydiving without a parachute will affect
14 his looks. He jumps . . . he falls gently . . . he
15 screams as he . . . hears his alarm clock.

Learning Language

Many words in English have silent letters. The letter *s* in *aisle* and *isle* are examples of silent letters. You will have to remember the *s* when spelling, but leave it out when pronouncing the words.

Work with a partner to practice pronouncing these words. Then, make a list of other words with silent letters. You will find at least one more in the list on page **708**. Practice pronouncing all the words correctly.

altogether, all together ■ *Altogether* means "entirely." The phrase *all together* means "in a group" or "all at once."

"There is altogether too much gridlock," complained the Democrats. All together, the Republicans yelled, "No way!"

among, between ■ *Among* is typically used when speaking of more than two persons or things. *Between* is used when speaking of only two.

The three of us talked among ourselves to decide between going out or eating in.

amount, number ■ *Amount* is used for bulk measurement. *Number* is used to count separate units. (See also *fewer, less*.)

A substantial amount of honey spilled all over a number of my CD's.

annual, biannual, semiannual, biennial, perennial ■ An *annual* event happens once every year. A *biannual* or *semiannual* event happens twice a year. A *biennial* event happens every two years. A *perennial* event is one that is persistent or constant.

Dad's annual family reunion gets bigger every year.
We're going shopping at the department store's semiannual white sale.
Due to dwindling attendance, the county fair is now a biennial celebration.
A perennial plant persists for several years.

anyway ■ Do not add an *s* to *anyway*.

ascent, assent ■ *Ascent* is the act of rising or climbing; *assent* is "to agree to something after some consideration" (or such an agreement).

We completed our ascent of the butte with the assent of the landowner.

bad, badly ■ *Bad* is an adjective. *Badly* is an adverb.

This apple is bad, but one bad apple doesn't always ruin the whole bushel.
In today's game, Sumey passed badly.

base, bass ■ *Base* is the foundation or the lower part of something. *Bass* (pronounced like *base*) is a deep sound or a musical instrument. *Bass* (rhyming with *class*) is a fish.

A car's wheel base is the distance between the centers of the front and rear wheels.
Luther is the bass player in his bluegrass band.

beside, besides ■ *Beside* means "by the side of." *Besides* means "in addition to."

Mother always grew roses beside the trash bin. Besides looking nice, they also gave off a sweet smell that masked odors.

ELPS 2C, 3A, 4C

Using the Right Word

711

Practice

Using the Right Word 2

among, between; amount, number; annual, biannual, semiannual, biennial, perennial; ascent, assent; beside, besides

In each paragraph below, find the word or words that are used incorrectly. Then write the right word(s) correctly. If there are no incorrect words, write "none."

1. Among serious gardeners here in Watertown, the biennial sale at Garden Emporium—every March and October—is anticipated most. It offers the widest assortment of spring and fall perennials in the area, including a good amount of jonquils and hostas. Besides that, they also offer volume discounts.

2. When it comes to choosing among one automaker's model and another manufacturer's car, buyers have their work cut out for them. Some makes are so similar that it's hard to tell them apart, even when they're right beside each other. In such a case, though, it's the dollar amount on the window sticker that will help the car shopper decide.

3. It was getting difficult to organize the pinecone collectors' convention each year, so we decided to make it a biennial event instead. We were sure the members of the Cone Collectors of America would assent to this change; they had been "pining" for it for years!

4. Jorge's assent in the amateur golf rankings is the result of consistent practice. He is now positioned between Dave Vasquez, the regional leader, and Marty White, winner of last year's Daily Cup tournament. Jorge's goal is to make it to the Jetar-Bettim Annual Tourney, to be held in Carson, Nevada, this year.

Learning Language

Vowels in English make both long and short sounds. For example, the *a* in *base* makes a long sound, while the *a* in *bass* (the fish) makes a short sound. Listen to the differences as your teacher pronounces the words on page 710. Then repeat the words, being careful to use the correct long or short vowel sounds.

board, bored ▪ *Board* is a piece of wood. *Board* is also an administrative group or council.

    The school board approved the purchase of fifty 1- by 6-inch pine boards.

Bored is the past tense of the verb "bore," which may mean "to make a hole by drilling" or "to become weary out of dullness."

    Watching television bored Joe, so he took his drill and bored a hole in the wall where he could hang his new clock.

brake, break ▪ *Brake* is a device used to stop a vehicle. *Break* means "to separate or to destroy."

    I hope the brakes on my car never break.

bring, take ▪ *Bring* suggests the action is directed toward the speaker; *take* suggests the action is directed away from the speaker.

    Bring home some garbage bags so I can take the trash outside.

can, may ▪ *Can* suggests ability while *may* suggests permission.

    "Can I go to the mall?" means "Am I physically able to go to the mall?"
    "May I go to the mall?" asks permission to go.

capital, capitol ▪ The noun *capital* refers to a city or to money. The adjective *capital* means "major or important." *Capitol* refers to a building.

    The state capital is home to the capitol building for a capital reason. The state government contributed capital for its construction.

cent, sent, scent ▪ *Cent* is a coin; *sent* is the past tense of the verb "send"; *scent* is an odor or a smell.

    For forty-one cents, I sent my girlfriend a mushy love poem in a perfumed envelope. She adored the scent but hated the poem.

cereal, serial ▪ *Cereal* is a grain, often made into breakfast food. *Serial* relates to something in a series.

    Mohammed enjoys reading serial novels while he eats a bowl of cereal.

chord, cord ▪ *Chord* may mean "an emotion" or "a combination of musical tones sounded at the same time." A *cord* is a string or a rope.

    The guitar player strummed the opening chord to the group's hit song, which struck a responsive chord with the audience.

chose, choose ▪ *Chose* (choz) is the past tense of the verb *choose* (chooz).

    Last quarter I chose to read Chitra Divakaruni's *The Unknown Errors of Our Lives*—a fascinating book about Indian immigrants.

 ELPS 2C, 3A, 4C, 5B

Using the Right Word   713

Practice

Using the Right Word 3

brake, break; cereal, serial; chord, cord; chose, choose

Write the correct choice from those given in parentheses.

1. Ms. Alford drove to the dealership to have her *(brake, break)* system inspected.

2. During a service call, most computer manufacturers require that you state the *(cereal, serial)* number of your product before they will answer any questions.

3. It is now possible for new parents to save the blood from the umbilical *(chord, cord)* that once connected their baby to his or her mother.

4. Aunt Margaret gave me two options for dinner; then she told me to *(choose, chose)* the one I'd like to make!

5. Nasim is going to *(brake, break)* a leg if he continues to snowboard without the proper equipment.

6. *(Cereal, Serial)* is an important ingredient in dog food, but it should not be the first in the list of ingredients.

7. The power *(chord, cord)* is commonly used in rock music.

8. Mae *(choose, chose)* from among dozens of fresh fruits and vegetables at the farmers' market.

9. *(Cereal, Serial)* dramas became known as "soaps" because detergent manufacturers often sponsored them.

10. You can *(brake, break)* the record for consecutive pogo-stick jumps by bouncing 177,738 times.

Model

Model the following sentences to practice using the words *chord* and *cord* correctly. Notice the silent *h* in *chord*, and be sure to pronounce it correctly.

[A] chord in music is analogous to a word in language.   —Sigmund Spaeth

No cord or cable can draw so forcibly, or bind so fast, as love can do with a single thread.   —Robert Burton

 ELPS 2C, 4C, 5B

coarse, course ■ *Coarse* means "rough or crude"; *course* means "a path or direction taken." *Course* also means "a class or a series of studies."

> Fletcher, known for using coarse language, was barred from the golf course until he took an etiquette course.

complement, compliment ■ *Complement* refers to that which completes or fulfills. *Compliment* is an expression of admiration or praise.

> Kimberly smiled, thinking she had received a compliment when Carlos said that her new Chihuahua complemented her personality.

continual, continuous ■ *Continual* refers to something that happens again and again with some breaks or pauses; *continuous* refers to something that keeps happening, uninterrupted.

> Sunlight hits Iowa on a continual basis; sunlight hits Earth continuously.

counsel, council ■ When used as a noun, *counsel* means "advice"; when used as a verb, it means "to advise." *Council* refers to a group that advises.

> The student council counseled all freshmen to join a school club. That's good counsel.

desert, dessert ■ The noun *desert* (děz´ərt) refers to barren wilderness. *Dessert* (dĭ zûrt´) is food served at the end of a meal.

> The scorpion tiptoed through the moonlit desert, searching for dessert.

The noun *desert* (dĭ zûrt´) can also mean "deserved reward or punishment." The verb *desert* (dĭ zûrt´) means "to abandon."

> The burglar's hiding place deserted him when the spotlight swung his way; his subsequent arrest was his just desert.

die, dye ■ *Die* (dying) means "to stop living." *Dye* (dyeing) is used to change the color of something.

different from, different than ■ Use *different from* in a comparison of two things. *Different than* should be used only when followed by a clause.

> Carlos is quite different from his brother.
> Both are different than they were as children.

farther, further ■ *Farther* refers to a physical distance; *further* refers to additional time, quantity, or degree.

> Alaska extends farther north than Iceland does.
> Further information can be obtained in an atlas.

fewer, less ■ *Fewer* refers to the number of separate units; *less* refers to bulk quantity.

> Because we have fewer orders for cakes, we'll buy less sugar and flour.

Using the Right Word

Practice

Using the Right Word 4

complement, compliment; continual, continuous; desert, dessert; different from, different than; fewer, less

Write the correct choice from those given in parentheses.

1. *(Continually, Continuously)* rising at 5:30 a.m. to get to school by 7:00 is not my ideal way of life.

2. The stray dog would *(desert, dessert)* us after we fed him a few times.

3. How are tostadas *(different from, different than)* sopes?

4. Not all women consider being whistled at a *(complement, compliment)*.

5. Aunt Lulu would always let me eat *(desert, dessert)* first.

6. Generally speaking, a hybrid vehicle burns *(fewer, less)* gallons of gas over the same distance than a gas-only vehicle does.

7. Min braids cornrows *(differently from, differently than)* Rae Lin does.

8. We've had *(fewer, less)* sunshine this month than in any other this year.

9. Mr. Allen's neighbors began to worry about the *(continual, continuous)* music—the same CD—blaring from his apartment.

10. The hoodia plant grows wild only in the Kalahari *(Desert, Dessert)* of Africa.

11. My red jacket would be the perfect *(complement, compliment)* to your outfit!

12. Is a medal a fair *(desert, dessert)* for breaking a record in the Olympics?

Model

Model the following sentences to practice using the words *complement* and *compliment* correctly.

> There may be as much nobility in being last as in being first, because the two positions are equally necessary in the world, the one to complement the other.
> —José Ortega Y Gasset

> We were told our campaign wasn't sufficiently slick. We regard that as a compliment.
> —Margaret Thatcher

flair, flare ■ *Flair* refers to style or natural talent; *flare* means "to light up quickly" or "burst out" (or an object that does so).

> Ronni was thrilled with Jorge's flair for decorating—until one of his strategically placed candles flared, marring the wall.

good, well ■ *Good* is an adjective; *well* is nearly always an adverb. (When *well* is used to describe a state of health, it is an adjective: He was happy to be *well* again.)

> The CD player works well.
>
> Our team looks good this season.

heal, heel ■ *Heal* means "to mend or restore to health." A *heel* is the back part of a foot.

> Achilles died because a poison arrow pierced his heel and caused a wound that would not heal.

healthful, healthy ■ *Healthful* means "causing or improving health"; *healthy* means "possessing health."

> Healthful foods build healthy bodies.

hear, here ■ You *hear* with your ears. *Here* means "the area close by."

heard, herd ■ *Heard* is the past tense of the verb "hear"; *herd* is a large group of animals.

hole, whole ■ A *hole* is a cavity or hollow place. *Whole* means "complete."

idle, idol ■ *Idle* means "not working." An *idol* is someone or something that is worshipped.

> The once-popular actress, who had been idle lately, wistfully recalled her days as an idol.

immigrate, emigrate ■ *Immigrate* means "to come into a new country or environment." *Emigrate* means "to go out of one country to live in another."

> Martin Ulferts immigrated to this country in 1882. He was only three years old when he emigrated from Germany.

imply, infer ■ *Imply* means "to suggest or express indirectly"; *infer* means "to draw a conclusion from facts." (A writer or speaker implies; a reader or listener infers.)

> Dad implied by his comment that I should drive more carefully, and I inferred that he was concerned for both me and his new car.

Practice

Using the Right Word 5

flair, flare; good, well; idle, idol; imply, infer

 Write the correct choice from those given in parentheses.

1. The groupings of pampas grass definitely add *(flair, flare)* to Jacinda's flower garden.

2. Tempers *(flaired, flared)* as it became evident that the "contest" was a hoax and there would be no winners.

3. After five months of winterlike conditions, it felt *(good, well)* to soak up some sun in the park.

4. I didn't sleep so *(good, well)* last night; nightmares plagued me.

5. Uncle Isaac's old jalopy has sat *(idle, idol)* in the barn for 15 years.

6. A dozen candles surrounded the *(idle, idol)* on the small altar.

7. Does wearing torn jeans *(imply, infer)* a lack of funds to purchase nicer clothing?

8. Satish *(implied, inferred)* from his boss's cold stare that he was in trouble.

9. Because Mia wasn't feeling *(good, well)*, she opted out of going to the mall with her friends.

10. The group stranded on a pleasure boat shot a *(flair, flare)* into the sky in hopes that rescuers would come.

Learning Language

Listen as your teacher reads the above sentences aloud. Notice that in many cases the two options in parentheses sound exactly the same. Other pairs of words that sound the same are: *plain/plane, fair/fare, sea/see,* and *tail/tale.* With a partner, read these pairs of words aloud. Discuss what the words mean. Then use the words in sentences. Share reading the sentences with your partner and try to identify the correct word, based on context.

 ELPS 2C, 4C, 5B

insure, ensure ■ *Insure* means "to secure from financial harm or loss." *Ensure* means "to make certain of something."

> To ensure that you can legally drive that new car, you'll have to insure it.

it's, its ■ *It's* is the contraction of "it is." *Its* is the possessive form of "it."

> It's hard to believe, but the movie *Shrek* still holds its appeal for many kids.

later, latter ■ *Later* means "after a period of time." *Latter* refers to the second of two things mentioned.

> Later that year we had our second baby and adopted a stray kitten. The latter was far more welcomed by our toddler.

lay, lie ■ *Lay* means "to place." *Lay* is a transitive verb. (See **742.1**.)

> Lay your books on the big table.

Lie means "to recline," and *lay* is the past tense of *lie*. *Lie* is an intransitive verb. (See **742.1**.)

> In this heat, the children must lie down for a nap. Yesterday they lay down without one complaint. Sometimes they have lain in the hammocks to rest.

lead, led ■ *Lead* (lēd) is the present tense of the verb meaning "to guide." The past tense of the verb is *led* (lĕd). The noun *lead* (lĕd) is a metal.

> We were led along the path that leads to an abandoned lead mine.

learn, teach ■ *Learn* means "to acquire information." *Teach* means "to give information."

> I learn better when people teach with real-world examples.

leave, let ■ *Leave* means "to allow something to remain behind." *Let* means "to permit."

> Would you let me leave my bike at your house?

lend, borrow ■ *Lend* means "to give for temporary use." *Borrow* means "to receive for temporary use."

> I told Mom I needed to borrow $18 for a CD, but she said she could only lend money for school supplies.

like, as ■ When *like* is used as a preposition meaning "similar to," it can be followed only by a noun, pronoun, or noun phrase; when *as* is used as a subordinating conjunction, it introduces a subordinate clause.

> You could become a gymnast like her, as you work and practice hard.

medal, meddle ■ *Medal* is an award. *Meddle* means "to interfere."

> Some parents meddle in the awards process to be sure that their kids get medals.

ELPS 2C, 4C, 5B

Using the Right Word

Practice

Using the Right Word 6

insure, ensure; it's, its; lay, lie; lend, borrow; medal, meddle

Find the words that are used incorrectly. Write the line number followed by the right word.

1   Mr. and Mrs. Hartleson entered the bank together. They desperately
2 needed to borrow $10,000 to cover some overdue payments. They could no
3 longer lay low—they had to take action now to insure their stake in the new
4 condo development in which they had invested.
5   "Please let me handle this," said Mrs. Hartleson to her spouse. "You
6 can insure my success in this endeavor if you promise not to meddle."
7   If Mr. Hartleson was offended, he did not show it. "That's fair," he said.
8 "I know you are laying your professional reputation on the line here." Then
9 he added, "Its obvious that you'll deserve a medal if you pull this off." He
10 patted her on the back.
11   They were uneasy; if the bank would not borrow them the money, they
12 would be in serious financial trouble. Mr. Hartleson had recently been forced
13 to take a cut in pay, and although Mrs. Hartleson herself was a banker, this
14 time she was on the other side of the fence. *This* bank—and it's loan officers,
15 who looked decidedly unfriendly today—was going to sit in judgment.
16 Anxious sweat formed on the back of her neck.

Model

Model the following sentences to practice using the words *lend* and *borrow* correctly.

> **We don't inherit the earth from our ancestors; we borrow it from our children.**
> —David Brower

> **Parents lend children their experience and a vicarious memory; children endow their parents with a vicarious immortality.**
> —George Santayana

metal, mettle ■ *Metal* is a chemical element like iron or gold. *Mettle* is "strength of spirit."

> Grandad's mettle during battle left him with some metal in his shoulder.

miner, minor ■ A *miner* digs for valuable ore. A *minor* is a person who is not legally an adult. A *minor* problem is one of no great importance.

moral, morale ■ A *moral* is a lesson drawn from a story; as an adjective, it relates to the principles of right and wrong. *Morale* refers to someone's attitude.

> Ms. Ladue considers it her moral obligation to go to church every day.
> The students' morale sank after their defeat in the forensics competition.

passed, past ■ *Passed* is a verb. *Past* can be used as a noun, an adjective, or a preposition.

> That old pickup truck passed my sports car! (verb)
> Many senior citizens hold dearly to the past. (noun)
> Tilly's past life as a circus worker must have been . . . interesting. (adjective)
> Who can walk past a bakery without looking in the window? (preposition)

peace, piece ■ *Peace* means "tranquility or freedom from war." *Piece* is a part or fragment.

> Grandma sits in the peace and quiet of the parlor, enjoying a piece of pie.

peak, peek, pique ■ A *peak* is a high point. *Peek* means "brief look" (or "look briefly"). *Pique*, as a verb, means "to excite by challenging"; as a noun, it is a feeling of resentment.

> The peak of Dr. Fedder's professional life was his ability to pique children's interest in his work. "Peek at this slide," he said to the eager students.

pedal, peddle, petal ■ A *pedal* is a foot lever; as a verb, it means "to ride a bike." *Peddle* means "to go from place to place selling something." A *petal* is part of a flower.

> Don Miller paints beautiful petals on his homemade birdhouses. Then he pedals through the flea market every weekend to peddle them.

personal, personnel ■ *Personal* means "private." *Personnel* are people working at a particular job.

plain, plane ■ *Plain* means "an area of land that is flat or level"; it also means "clearly seen or clearly understood."

> It's plain to see why settlers of the Great Plains had trouble moving west.

Plane means "flat, level"; the noun *plane* is a tool used to smooth the surface of wood.

> I used a plane to make the board plane and smooth.

Plane also means "a level of existence or consciousness."

Using the Right Word

Practice

Using the Right Word 7

metal, mettle; peak, peek, pique; personal, personnel; plain, plane

Write the correct choice from those given in parentheses.

1. "A *(plain, plane)* 'yes' or 'no' will suffice," admonished the defense attorney.

2. My illness is of a rather *(personal, personnel)* nature, and I'd rather not discuss it.

3. There is nothing that can *(peak, peek, pique)* my curiosity like an unfamiliar word.

4. It takes unusual *(metal, mettle)* to persevere despite harsh conditions.

5. As a child, Dale would *(peak, peek, pique)* down through the stairway railings, watching the people at his parents' parties.

6. Adding sand to paint transforms the wall from a *(plain, plane)* surface to a more interesting, texturized one.

7. Whereas many kitchen appliances used to be made of *(metal, mettle)*, today they are more likely to be plastic.

8. Just as Terry reached what he thought was the *(peak, peek, pique)* of his endurance, he got a second wind.

9. You must go to the *(personal, personnel)* office down the hall to report an on-the-job injury.

10. Abi left the meeting in a *(peak, peek, pique)* following Nathan's presentation of her idea as his own.

Model

Model the following sentences to practice using the words *plain* and *plane* correctly.

Man cannot live on the human plane; he must be either above or below it.
—Eric Gill

Any woman who has brains and willing hands finds twenty remunerative occupations open to her where formerly she would have found merely the inevitable two—plain sewing, or the dull little boys.
—Clara Lanza

poor, pour, pore ■ *Poor* means "needy or pitiable." *Pour* means "to cause to flow in a stream." A *pore* is an opening in the skin.

> Tough exams on late spring days make my poor pores pour sweat.

principal, principle ■ As an adjective, *principal* means "primary." As a noun, it can mean "a school administrator" or "a sum of money." *Principle* means "idea or doctrine."

> His principal concern is fitness. (adjective) The principal retired. (noun)
> During the first year of a loan, you pay more interest than principal. (noun)
> The principle of *caveat emptor* is "Let the buyer beware."

quiet, quit, quite ■ *Quiet* is the opposite of "noisy." *Quit* means "to stop." *Quite* means "completely or entirely."

quote, quotation ■ *Quote* is a verb; *quotation* is a noun.

> The quotation I used was from Woody Allen. You may quote me on that.

real, really, very ■ Do not use *real* in place of the adverbs *very* or *really*.

> Mother's cake is usually very (not *real*) tasty, but this one is really stale!

right, write, wright, rite ■ *Right* means "correct or proper"; it also refers to that which a person has a legal claim to, as in *copyright*. *Write* means "to inscribe or record." A *wright* is a person who makes or builds something. *Rite* refers to a ritual or ceremonial act.

> Write this down: It is the right of the shipwright to perform the rite of christening—breaking a bottle of champagne on the stern of the ship.

ring, wring ■ *Ring* means "encircle" or "to sound by striking." *Wring* means "to squeeze or twist."

> At the beach, Grandma would ring her head with a large scarf. Once, it blew into the sea, so she had me wring it out.

scene, seen ■ *Scene* refers to the setting or location where something happens; it also may mean "sight or spectacle." *Seen* is a form of the verb "see."

> Serena had seen her boyfriend making a scene; she cringed.

seam, seem ■ *Seam* (noun) is a line formed by connecting two pieces. *Seem* (verb) means "to appear to exist."

> The ragged seams in his old coat seem to match the creases in his face.

set, sit ■ *Set* means "to place." *Sit* means "to put the body in a seated position." *Set* is transitive; *sit* is intransitive. (See **742.1**.)

> How can you just sit there and watch as I set all these chairs in place?

Using the Right Word

Practice

Using the Right Word 8

principal, principle; quote, quotation; real, really, very; right, write, wright, rite

In each paragraph below, find the word or words that are used incorrectly. Then write the right word(s) correctly. If there are no incorrect words, write "none."

1. Given the circumstances, uttering the quote from last night's *Daily Show* may not have been appropriate—but it *was* really funny. Unfortunately, it tends to lose its humor when you have to write it 50 times as a punishment from the principal.

2. Mario has had several real good stories published. Eventually he would like to be a well-known playwrite, but for now his principle concern is finishing a novel begun last year. He hopes to have it published by his twenty-first birthday.

3. Once a month, Jim performs a right of cleansing in which he drinks only water, rests, does yoga, and meditates for a full day. He says this ritual is based on the principle that regular "bathing" should apply not only to the outside of the body, but to its insides and to the mind, as well. He hasn't talked me into trying it myself, but it certainly hasn't seemed to do *him* any harm.

4. In any writing in which you quote another person's words, it is only right to acknowledge the source. To not do so is to steal—a real transgression in the world of publishing. Avoid plagiarism: Be sure to cite your quotations.

Learning Language

In many English words, *wr* represents the same sound as *r*. This is why there is so much confusion among the words *right*, *write*, *wright*, and *rite*. Pay close attention as your teacher pronounces these words and repeat the words to be sure you pronounce them correctly. With a partner, discuss these words and other words with a silent *w*. Write sentences with the words.

 ELPS 2C, 4C, 5B

sight, cite, site ■ *Sight* means "the act of seeing"; a *sight* is what is seen. *Cite* means "to quote" or "to summon," as before a court. *Site* means "location."

In her report, the general contractor cited several problems at the downtown job site. For one, the loading area was a chaotic sight.

sole, soul ■ *Sole* means "single, only one"; *sole* also refers to the bottom surface of the foot. *Soul* refers to the spiritual part of a person.

As the sole inhabitant of the island, he put his heart and soul into his farming.

stationary, stationery ■ *Stationary* means "not movable"; *stationery* refers to the paper and envelopes used to write letters.

steal, steel ■ *Steal* means "to take something without permission"; *steel* is a type of metal.

It takes nerves of steel to brazenly steal another's possessions in broad daylight.

than, then ■ *Than* is used in a comparison; *then* tells when.

Abigail shouted that her big brother was bigger than my big brother. Then she ran away.

their, there, they're ■ *Their* is a possessive personal pronoun. *There* is an adverb used to point out location. *They're* is the contraction for "they are."

They're a well-dressed couple. Do you see them there, with their matching jackets?

threw, through ■ *Threw* is the past tense of "throw." *Through* means "from beginning to end."

Through seven innings, Danielle threw just seven strikes.

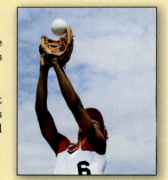

to, too, two ■ *To* is a preposition that can mean "in the direction of." *To* is also used to form an infinitive. *Too* means "also" or "very." *Two* is a number.

vain, vane, vein ■ *Vain* means "valueless or fruitless"; it may also mean "holding a high regard for oneself." *Vane* is a flat piece of material set up to show which way the wind blows. *Vein* refers to a blood vessel or a mineral deposit.

The vain prospector, boasting about the vein of silver he'd uncovered, paused to look up at the turning weather vane.

vary, very ■ *Vary* means "to change." *Very* means "to a high degree."

Though the weather may vary from day to day, generally, it is very pleasant.

Using the Right Word

Practice

Using the Right Word 9

sight, cite, site; stationary, stationery; than, then; vain, vane, vein

  Select the correct word from the list above to complete each sentence.

1. With so many other means to send messages these days, is _____ obsolete?

2. A _____ from the leg is often used in heart bypass surgery.

3. A journalist may be out of a job if he or she does not _____ sources precisely.

4. The road curves around a large, _____ boulder.

5. According to the _____ atop the roof, the wind is coming from the north today.

6. Masafumi started to jack up the car, but _____ he remembered that he had to loosen the lug nuts first.

7. A person who accurately predicts future events is said to have "second _____."

8. Some might mistake someone with a high level of self-confidence for a _____ person.

9. An affordable _____ for a home is becoming increasingly hard to find.

10. Rather _____ taking the bus to school every day, Jasmine rides her bike when she can.

Learning Language

The *th* sounds in words such as *than*, *there*, and *through* can be confusing because the consonant cluster *th* makes two different sounds. Listen as your teacher pronounces the words, and repeat them carefully. Then, discuss the different words with a partner.

vial, vile ■ A *vial* is a small container for liquid. *Vile* is an adjective meaning "foul, despicable."

It's a vile job, but someone has to clean these lab vials.

waist, waste ■ *Waist* is the part of the body just above the hips. The verb *waste* means "to spend or use carelessly" or "to wear away or decay"; the noun *waste* refers to material that is unused or useless.

Her waist is small because she wastes no opportunity to exercise.

wait, weight ■ *Wait* means "to stay somewhere expecting something." *Weight* refers to a degree or unit of heaviness.

ware, wear, where ■ *Ware* refers to a product that is sold; *wear* means "to have on or to carry on one's body"; *where* asks "in what place?" or "in what situation?"

The designer boasted, "Where can anybody wear my ware? Anywhere."

way, weigh ■ *Way* means "path or route." *Weigh* means "to measure weight" or "to have a certain heaviness."

My dogs weigh too much. The best way to reduce their weight is a daily run in the park.

weather, whether ■ *Weather* refers to the condition of the atmosphere. *Whether* refers to a possibility.

Due to the weather, the coach wondered whether he should cancel the meet.

which, that ■ Use *which* to refer to objects or animals in a nonrestrictive clause (set off with commas). Use *that* to refer to objects or animals in a restrictive clause. (For more information about these types of clauses, see **648.2**.)

The birds, which stay in the area all winter, know where the feeders are located.
The food that attracts the most birds is sunflower seed.

who, whom ■ Use *who* to refer to people. *Who* is used as the subject of a verb in an independent clause or in a relative clause. *Whom* is used as the object of a preposition or as a direct object.

To whom do we owe our thanks for these pizzas? And who ordered anchovies?

who's, whose ■ *Who's* is the contraction for "who is." *Whose* is a pronoun that can show possession or ownership.

Cody, whose car is new, will drive. Who's going to read the map?

your, you're ■ *Your* is a possessive pronoun. *You're* is the contraction for "you are."

Take your boots if you're going out in that snow.

ELPS 2C, 3A, 4C

Using the Right Word

Practice

Using the Right Word 10

waist, waste; which, that; who, whom; who's, whose; your, you're

For each numbered sentence, write the correct choice from the words given in parentheses.

(1) If *(your, you're)* like the average American, you generate about four pounds of garbage each day. **(2)** While some of it gets recycled or incinerated, most of the country's *(waist, waste)* ends up in landfills. **(3)** These burial sites for anything *(which, that)* can't be recycled are filling up fast as people produce more trash, and environmental problems sometimes follow.

(4) *(Who's, Whose)* the culprit? **(5)** It's not just one group of people *(who, whom)* share responsibility for America's growing trash predicament. Of course, individuals and organizations should try to reuse and recycle as much as they can. **(6)** A growing problem, however, is companies promoting disposable goods, *(which, that)* ultimately end up in a landfill. **(7)** It's *(your, you're)* choice whether to buy such items, so avoid them when possible.

(8) *(Who's, Whose)* job is it to make sure a landfill is safe? Although the federal Environmental Protection Agency's regulations must be met, each state has its own laws. Elected municipal officials also legislate actions related to landfills, so be sure to vote for those **(9)** *(who, whom)* you trust with the environment.

Learning Language

When two vowels are together in a word, the first vowel often makes a long sound and the second is silent, such as in the word *waist*. Long vowel sounds are also common in words ending in silent *e* such as *vile* and *site*. Listen as your teacher pronounces these and other words with long vowel sounds. Then, practice pronouncing the words on your own.

Parts of Speech

Words in the English language are used in eight different ways. For this reason, there are eight parts of speech.

728.1 Noun

A word that names a person, a place, a thing, or an idea
> Governor Smith-Jones   Oregon   hospital   religion

728.2 Pronoun

A word used in place of a noun
> I   you   she   him   who   everyone   these   neither   theirs   themselves   which

728.3 Verb

A word that expresses an action or a state of being
> float   sniff   discover   seem   were   was

728.4 Adjective

A word that describes a noun or a pronoun
> young   big   grim   Canadian   longer

728.5 Adverb

A word that describes a verb, an adjective, or another adverb
> briefly   forward   regally   slowly   better

728.6 Preposition

The first word or words in a prepositional phrase (which functions as an adjective or an adverb)
> away   from   under   before   with   for   out of

728.7 Conjunction

A word that connects other words or groups of words
> and   but   although   because   either, or   so

728.8 Interjection

A word that shows strong emotion or surprise
> Oh no!   Yipes!   Good grief!   Well, . . .

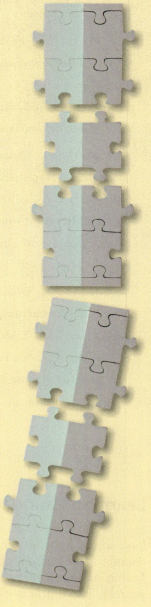

Noun

A **noun** is a word that names something: a person, a place, a thing, or an idea.

    governor   Oregon   hospital   Buddhism   love

Classes of Nouns

The five classes of nouns are *proper, common, concrete, abstract,* and *collective.*

729.1 Proper Noun

A **proper noun** names a particular person, place, thing, or idea. Proper nouns are always capitalized.

    Jackie Robinson   Brooklyn   World Series
    Christianity   Ebbets Field   Hinduism

729.2 Common Noun

A **common noun** does not name a particular person, place, thing, or idea. Common nouns are not capitalized.

    person   woman   president   park   baseball   government

729.3 Concrete Noun

A **concrete noun** names a thing that is tangible (can be seen, touched, heard, smelled, or tasted). Concrete nouns are either proper or common.

    child   Grand Canyon   music
    aroma   fireworks   Becky

729.4 Abstract Noun

An **abstract noun** names an idea, a condition, or a feeling—in other words, something that cannot be touched, smelled, tasted, seen, or heard.

    New Deal   greed   poverty   progress   freedom   awe

729.5 Collective Noun

A **collective noun** names a group or a unit.

    United States   Portland Cementers   team   crowd   community

Forms of Nouns

Nouns are grouped according to their *number, gender,* and *case.*

730.1 Number of a Noun

Number indicates whether the noun is singular or plural.

A **singular noun** refers to one person, place, thing, or idea.
actor   stadium   Canadian   bully   truth   child   person

A **plural noun** refers to more than one person, place, thing, or idea.
actors   stadiums   Canadians   bullies   truths   children   people

730.2 Gender of a Noun

Gender indicates whether a noun is masculine, feminine, neuter, or indefinite.

Masculine:
uncle   brother   men   bull   rooster   stallion

Feminine:
aunt   sister   women   cow   hen   filly

Neuter **(without gender):**
tree   cobweb   amoeba   closet

Indefinite (masculine or feminine):
president   plumber   doctor   parent

730.3 Case of a Noun

Case tells how nouns are related to other words used with them. There are three cases: *nominative, possessive,* and *objective.*

- A **nominative case** noun can be the subject of a clause.
    > Humberto's car broke down again. That incompetent mechanic created additional problems when he tried to fix it.

    A nominative noun can also be a predicate noun (or predicate nominative), which follows a "be" verb *(am, is, are, was, were, be, being, been)* and renames the subject. In the sentence below, *type* renames *Mr. Cattanzara.*
    > Mr. Cattanzara was a different type than those in the neighborhood.
    > —Bernard Malamud, "A Summer's Reading"

- A **possessive case** noun shows possession or ownership.
    > The inspector's approval meant that the restaurant could finally reopen.

- An **objective case** noun can be a direct object, an indirect object, or an object of the preposition.
    > Marna always gives Mylo science fiction books for his birthday.

    (*Mylo* is the indirect object and *books* is the direct object of the verb *gives. Birthday* is the object of the preposition *for.*)

Grammar Practice

Nouns

- **Classes of Nouns**
- **Number of a Noun**
- **Case of a Noun**

For each underlined noun, classify it as *proper* or *common* and *singular* or *plural*. Also indicate whether it is a *collective* noun and identify its case as *nominative*, *possessive*, or *objective*.

1. <u>Maddy</u>, my cat, is extremely overweight, but she is on a special <u>diet</u> now.

2. The life sciences <u>faculty</u> at Lee's school have judged our science <u>fair</u> for years.

3. Did your <u>father</u> ever see <u>Herb's</u> guitar?

4. We've had great <u>luck</u> to have six gorgeous <u>days</u> in a row!

5. This type of <u>iguana</u> is wild in <u>Mexico</u>.

6. My <u>niece</u> loves to see marching <u>bands</u> in city parades.

7. Juanita cooks <u>dinner</u> for her family on every <u>Thursday</u>.

8. <u>Ladybugs</u> must be squeezing in through cracks in the window <u>frame</u>.

9. His <u>computer's</u> hard drive is corrupt and needs replacing, according to the guy in the <u>Information Technology Department</u>.

10. Perhaps the <u>games</u> that his <u>son</u> installed caused the problem.

Model

Model the following sentences to practice using abstract nouns in the objective case.

Politics is made up largely of irrelevancies.
—Dalton Camp

She tells enough white lies to ice a wedding cake.
—Margot Asquith

Pronoun

A **pronoun** is a word used in place of a noun.

I, you, she, it, which, that, themselves, whoever, me, he, they, mine, ours

The three types of pronouns are *simple, compound,* and *phrasal.*

- Simple: I, you, he, she, it, we, they, who, what
- Compound: myself, someone, anybody, everything, itself, whoever
- Phrasal: one another, each other

All pronouns have **antecedents**. An antecedent is the noun that the pronoun refers to or replaces.

Mr. O'Connor is a popular teacher. Hundreds of students have taken his class on American literature. He always makes the class interesting, and students work extra hard for him.

(*Mr. O'Connor* is the antecedent of *his, he,* and *him.*)

Note: Each pronoun must agree with its antecedent. (See page 780.)

732.1 Classes of Pronouns

The six classes of pronouns are *personal, reflexive and intensive, relative, indefinite, interrogative,* and *demonstrative.*

Personal
I, me, my, mine / we, us, our, ours
you, your, yours / they, them, their, theirs
he, him, his, she, her, hers, it, its

Reflexive and Intensive
myself, yourself, himself, herself, itself, ourselves, yourselves, themselves

Relative
what, who, whose, whom, which, that

Indefinite

all	both	everything	nobody	several
another	each	few	none	some
any	each one	many	no one	somebody
anybody	either	most	nothing	someone
anyone	everybody	much	one	something
anything	everyone	neither	other	such

Interrogative
who, whose, whom, which, what

Demonstrative
this, that, these, those

Parts of Speech **733**

Grammar Practice

Pronouns 1

■ **Antecedents**

Find the pronoun in each sentence below. Write the pronoun—labeled as *simple*, *compound*, or *phrasal*—and its antecedent.

1. Dominique carefully chose the ingredients for her salad.

2. Bonita and Lora took down each other's phone number.

3. Gesturing at the pot of rice and beans, Claude said, "Is that for lunch?"

4. The toddlers—twins, by the look of things—grabbed the toy from the child-care provider and proclaimed, "Do ourselves!"

5. Uh-oh, the cell phone is displaying gibberish on its screen.

6. The honor-roll students lined up, and each one approached the stage to receive an award.

7. Dr. Lopez encouraged the crowd: "Everyone here has the potential to make a difference!"

8. Petra decided to change the tire herself.

9. Some of the lug nuts were rusty, and Petra had difficulty loosening them.

10. Petra positioned the jack and raised it up to the car's frame.

Model

Model the following sentences to practice using compound and phrasal pronouns.

The most important thing is to be whatever you are without shame.
—Rod Steiger

Hearing voices no one else can hear isn't a good sign, even in the wizarding world.
—J. K. Rowling, *Harry Potter and the Chamber of Secrets*

Pronoun (continued)

734.1 Personal Pronouns

A **personal pronoun** can take the place of any noun.

>Our coach made her point loud and clear when she raised her voice.

- A **reflexive pronoun** is formed by adding *-self* or *-selves* to a personal pronoun. A reflexive pronoun can be a direct object, an indirect object, an object of the preposition, or a predicate nominative.

  >Miss Sally Sunshine loves herself. (direct object of *loves*)
  >Tomisha does not seem herself today. (predicate nominative)

- An **intensive pronoun** is a reflexive pronoun that intensifies or emphasizes the noun or pronoun it refers to.

  >Leo himself taught his children to invest their lives in others.

734.2 Relative Pronouns

A **relative pronoun** relates or connects an adjective clause to the noun or pronoun it modifies.

>Students who study regularly get the best grades. Surprise!
>The dance, which we had looked forward to for weeks, was canceled.

(The relative pronoun *who* relates the adjective clause to *students*; *which* relates the adjective clause to *dance*.)

734.3 Indefinite Pronouns

An **indefinite pronoun** refers to unnamed or unknown people or things.

>I wonder why anybody would want to travel around the world alone; if you know anybody who has done this, I would love to meet him or her. (The antecedent of *anybody* is unknown.)

734.4 Interrogative Pronouns

An **interrogative pronoun** asks a question.

>"Who gave you my name? Who told you to call me? What do you think I can do to help you?"

734.5 Demonstrative Pronouns

A **demonstrative pronoun** points out people, places, or things without naming them.

>This shouldn't be too hard.   That looks about right.
>These are the best ones.   Those ought to be thrown out.

Note: When one of these words precedes a noun, it functions as an adjective, not a pronoun. (See 754.1.)

>That movie bothers me. (*That* is an adjective.)

Grammar Practice

Pronouns 2
- **Personal Pronouns**
- **Reflexive and Intensive Pronouns**
- **Relative Pronouns**
- **Indefinite Pronouns**
- **Interrogative Pronouns**
- **Demonstrative Pronouns**

 Write down the pronouns in the paragraphs below and label their class.

1   In March 1989, a geomagnetic storm caused a malfunction in Quebec's
2   power grid. In only a minute and a half, a complete blackout that left 6
3   million people without power disrupted critical services (transportation, fire
4   and police protection)—and everything else—for nine hours.

5   What is a geomagnetic storm? You may have heard of it as a solar
6   storm. These storms are responsible for the incredible light displays
7   known as the auroras, but they also cause temporary disruptions of radio
8   transmissions, navigation systems, and, as evidenced above, power grids.
9   This is how it happens: A solar eruption causes an incredible solar wind
10 shock wave that strikes Earth's magnetic field a day or so later. The shock
11 waves change the electric currents in the atmosphere, which, in turn, are
12 attracted to electric transmission lines. The added current in the lines
13 overheats transformers, causing them to fail.

14   The utility companies themselves are not to blame since the storms
15 can't be prevented. Instead, they have plans to ride out the storms. That
16 may not be the best strategy, but the companies' only existing alternative is
17 installing complex, costly devices to block the extra current. With any luck,
18 nobody will have to cope with a solar storm causing a large-scale blackout.

Model

Model the following sentences to practice using demonstrative pronouns.

> I was thought to be "stuck up." I wasn't. I was just sure of myself. This is and always has been an unforgivable quality to the unsure.
> —Bette Davis

Forms of Personal Pronouns

The form of a personal pronoun indicates its *number* (singular or plural), its *person* (first, second, third), its *case* (nominative, possessive, or objective), and its *gender* (masculine, feminine, or neuter).

736.1 Number of a Pronoun

Personal pronouns are singular or plural. The singular personal pronouns include *my, him, he, she, it*. The plural personal pronouns include *we, you, them, our*. (*You* can be singular or plural.) Notice in the caption below that the first *you* is singular and the second *you* is plural.

"Larry, you need to keep all four tires on the road when turning. Are you still with us back there?"

736.2 Person of a Pronoun

The **person** of a pronoun indicates whether the person, place, thing, or idea represented by the pronoun is speaking, is spoken to, or is spoken about.

- **First person** is used in place of the name of the speaker or speakers.

    "We can't pick up the phone every time it rings," said my mother; "I don't like being interrupted if I'm in the middle of something. They can wait until I call them back."

- **Second person** pronouns name the person or persons spoken to.

    "If you let me borrow your binoculars, will you show me again how to use them?" I said.

- **Third person** pronouns name the person or thing spoken about.

    She had hardly realized the news, further than to understand that she had been brought . . . face to face with something unexpected and final. It did not even occur to her to ask for any explanation.
    —Joseph Conrad, "The Idiots"

Grammar Practice

Pronouns 3

- **Number of a Pronoun**
- **Person of a Pronoun**

Identify the person and number of each underlined pronoun.

1. "<u>You</u> should rent the first season of *Friends* on DVD," Pasha said when <u>she</u> heard that <u>I</u> had never seen it.

2. <u>We</u> read *Things Fall Apart*, by Chinua Achebe, in <u>our</u> Contemporary Literature class.

3. <u>She</u> got to the gym just in time to see <u>her</u> boyfriend sink the winning basket.

4. "Will <u>you</u> call <u>us</u> if you're running late?" the parents asked the teens.

5. <u>I</u> am eager to try scuba diving in the ocean this summer.

6. Luisa, when are <u>you</u> picking <u>them</u> up at the airport?

7. Whether or not <u>they</u> called <u>him</u> to go to the movie, he was going to see <u>it</u>.

8. <u>I</u> can't believe that Li Ming didn't invite <u>them</u> to opening night.

9. "<u>You</u> have until Friday to complete <u>your</u> term papers," Mr. Weatherby told his students.

Model

Model the following sentence to practice using first- and third-person pronouns correctly.

> **I had been encouraged early on by my mother and my grandmother to be a high achiever, and I got hooked on the accolades they showered on me.**
> —Dana Buchman, *A Special Education*

738.1 Case of a Pronoun

The **case** of each pronoun tells how it is related to the other words used with it. There are three cases: *nominative, possessive,* and *objective.*

- A **nominative case** pronoun can be the subject of a clause. The following are nominative forms: *I, you, he, she, it, we, they.*

    I like life when things go well. You must live life in order to love life.

A nominative pronoun is a *predicate nominative* if it follows a "be" verb (*am, is, are, was, were, be, being, been*) or another linking verb (*appear, become, feel,* etc.) and renames the subject.

    "Oh, it's only she who scared me just now," said Mama to Papa, glancing over her shoulder.
    "Yes, it is I," said Mai in a superior tone.

- **Possessive case** pronouns show possession or ownership. Apostrophes, however, are not used with personal pronouns. (Pronouns in the possessive case can also be classified as adjectives.)

    But as I placed my hand upon his shoulder, there came a strong shudder over his whole person.
    —Edgar Allan Poe, "The Fall of the House of Usher"

- An **objective case** pronoun can be a direct object, an indirect object, or an object of the preposition.

    The kids loved it! We lit a campfire for them and told them old ghost stories.
    (*It* is the direct object of the verb *loved. Them* is the object of the preposition *for* and the indirect object of the verb *told.*)

Number, Person, and Case of Personal Pronouns

	Nominative	Possessive	Objective
First Person Singular	I	my, mine	me
Second Person Singular	you	your, yours	you
Third Person Singular	he	his	him
	she	her, hers	her
	it	its	it
	Nominative	Possessive	Objective
First Person Plural	we	our, ours	us
Second Person Plural	you	your, yours	you
Third Person Plural	they	their, theirs	them

738.2 Gender of a Pronoun

Gender indicates whether a pronoun is masculine, feminine, or neuter.

Masculine: **he him his**   Feminine: **she her hers**

Neuter (without gender): **it its**

Grammar Practice

Pronouns 4
- **Case of a Pronoun**
- **Gender of a Pronoun**

Identify each underlined pronoun as *nominative, possessive,* or *objective.* If the pronoun is gender specific, write its gender, too.

(1) <u>My</u> sister-in-law Sookie and **(2)** <u>I</u> went shopping for my brother's birthday present. He's into snowboarding, and Sookie wanted to get **(3)** <u>him</u> a new board before **(4)** <u>they</u> went on **(5)** <u>their</u> vacation to the mountains. Snowboarding is a sport that Sookie knows **(6)** <u>nothing</u> about, so **(7)** <u>she</u> called **(8)** <u>her</u> amazing brother-in-law (that would be **(9)** <u>I</u>) to help her shop.

When **(10)** <u>we</u> got to the sporting goods store, I asked Sookie, "How much do **(11)** <u>you</u> want to spend?"

She said, "I want to get **(12)** <u>your</u> brother a good quality board, but **(13)** <u>it</u> should be one that really stands out."

Just then, I saw **(14)** <u>it</u>, and I pointed it out to Sookie. **(15)** <u>Its</u> jazzy, yellow design screamed at **(16)** <u>us</u> from across the aisle. (I wished that it were **(17)** <u>mine</u>.) Sookie looked at it closely and said, "**(18)** <u>It</u> is perfect! Let's get it for him."

Model

Model the following sentences to practice using nominative- and objective-case pronouns.

Computers are useless. They can only give you answers.
—Pablo Picasso

There was a definite process by which one made people into friends, and it involved talking to them and listening to them for hours at a time.
—Rebecca West

Verb

A **verb** is a word that expresses action (*run, carried, declared*) or state of being (*is, are, seemed*).

Classes of Verbs

740.1 Linking Verbs

A **linking verb** links the subject to a noun or an adjective in the predicate.
> In the outfield, the boy **felt** confident.
> He **was** the best fielder around.

Common Linking Verbs

is	are	was	were	be	been	am

Additional Linking Verbs

smell	seem	grow	become	appear	sound
taste	feel	get	remain	stay	look	turn

Note: The verbs listed as "additional linking verbs" function as linking verbs when they do not show actual action. An adjective usually follows these linking verbs. (When they do show action, an adverb or a direct object may follow them. In this case, they are action verbs.)

> Linking: This fruit **smells** rotten.
> Action: Maya always **smells** fruit carefully before eating it.

740.2 Auxiliary Verbs

Auxiliary verbs, or helping verbs, are used to form some of the **tenses** (**744.3**), the **mood** (**750.1**), and the **voice** (**748.2**) of the main verb. (In the example below, the auxiliary verbs are in **red**; the main verbs are in **blue**.)

> The road to the hospital **was** obscured by sheets of rain that **were** whipping along the ground. The streetlights **had** gone out, and it **was** impossible to see the curb where the water **was** gushing like a river.

Common Auxiliary Verbs

is	was	being	did	have	would	shall	might
am	were	been	does	had	could	can	must
are	be	do	has	should	will	may	

Grammar Practice

Verbs 1
- **Linking Verbs**
- **Auxiliary Verbs**

Label each underlined verb in the paragraph below as a *linking verb*, an *auxiliary verb*, or *neither*.

Laisha **(1)** <u>is</u> a real estate agent. She **(2)** <u>has</u> decided to have an addition to her house built. Although the addition **(3)** <u>is</u> going to cost a lot of money, Laisha **(4)** <u>feels</u> good about it. She **(5)** <u>has</u> no experience working with contractors, so she **(6)** <u>will</u> read as much as she can about it beforehand. She **(7)** <u>does</u> not want to seem like an easy target for unscrupulous businesses. She will **(8)** <u>sound</u> authoritative and **(9)** <u>appear</u> as though she's done this before. She will not **(10)** <u>be</u> weak in any negotiations. She **(11)** <u>looks</u> forward to the experience as one that **(12)** <u>can</u> improve her job skills.

Model

Model the following sentences to practice using linking and auxiliary verbs correctly.

The hallmark of creative people is their mental flexibility.
—Roger von Oech, *A Kick in the Seat of the Pants*

Our ability to delude ourselves may be an important survival tool.
—Jane Wagner

742.1 Action Verbs: Transitive and Intransitive

An **intransitive verb** communicates an action that is complete in itself. It does not need an object to receive the action.

> The boy *flew* on his skateboard. He *jumped* and *flipped* and *twisted*.

A **transitive verb** (red) is an action verb that needs an object (blue) to complete its meaning.

> The city council *passed* a strict noise ordinance.
> Raul *takes* pictures for the student paper.

While some action verbs are only transitive *or* intransitive, some can be either, depending on how they are used.

> He finally *stopped* to rest. (intransitive)
> He finally *stopped* the show. (transitive)

742.2 Objects with Transitive Verbs

- A **direct object** receives the action of a transitive verb directly from the subject. Without it, the transitive verb's meaning is incomplete.

    > The boy *kicked* his skateboard forward. (*Skateboard* is the direct object.)
    > Then he *put* one foot on it and rode like a pro.

- An **indirect object** also receives the action of a transitive verb, but indirectly. An indirect object names the person *to whom or for whom* something is done. (An indirect object can also name the thing *to what or for what* something is done.)

    > Ms. Oakfield *showed* us pictures of the solar system.
    > (*Us* is the indirect object.)
    > She *gave* Tony an A on his project.

Note: When the word naming the indirect receiver of the action is in a prepositional phrase, it is no longer considered an indirect object.

> Ms. Oakfield *showed* pictures of the solar system to us.
> (*Us* is the object of the preposition *to*.)

Grammar Practice

Verbs 2

- Transitive and Intransitive Verbs
- Direct and Indirect Objects

For each underlined verb, indicate whether it is transitive or intransitive. For transitive verbs, write the direct object, too. If there is an indirect object, write and label it, as well.

For Dad's birthday, Mom and I **(1)** are giving him a gift he won't easily forget: a skydiving lesson. A small local airport **(2)** offers lessons from certified instructors. The plane **(3)** will fly at about 10,000 feet, and Dad will tandem-jump with the instructor. Then will come the scary part: free-falling! (Even though the free fall **(4)** lasts only about 45 seconds, I bet it will seem longer.) Once the instructor **(5)** releases the parachute, they will **(6)** float for about five minutes before reaching the ground.

If Dad **(7)** likes skydiving enough to do more jumps, he **(8)** can jump by himself eventually. For the first dozen or so jumps, however, an instructor **(9)** must supervise his efforts. He or she **(10)** shows students important things—such as the location of the pull cord for the reserve parachute.

Learning Language

Some verbs describe an action that is complete in itself. (He ***stopped*** [verb] to rest.) In some sentences, verbs need an object to complete the meaning. (He ***stopped*** [verb] the ***show*** [object].) Look at the verbs on this page. With a partner, discuss the meaning of each verb. Next, take turns reading the sentences aloud while the other partner listens carefully. Stop at the underlined verb in each sentence. Ask your partner: Is the action of the verb complete? Does it need another word or words to make sense? What does it mean?

Forms of Verbs

A verb has different forms depending on its *number, person, tense, voice,* and *mood*.

744.1 Number of a Verb

Number indicates whether a verb is singular or plural. In a clause, the verb (in blue below) and its subject (in red) must both be singular or both be plural.

- **Singular**
    One large island floats off Italy's "toe."
    Italy's northern countryside includes the truly spectacular Alps.
- **Plural**
    Five small islands float inside Michigan's "thumb."
    The Porcupine Mountains rise above the shores of Lake Superior.

744.2 Person of a Verb

Person indicates whether the subject of the verb is first, second, or third person (is speaking, is spoken to, or is spoken about). The form of the verb usually changes only when a present-tense verb is used with a third-person singular subject.

	Singular	Plural
First Person	I sniff	we sniff
Second Person	you sniff	you sniff
Third Person	he/she/it sniffs	they sniff

744.3 Tense of a Verb

Tenses can affect the sense of time in a piece of writing. Each verb has three principal parts: the *present, past,* and *past participle*. All six tenses are formed from these principal parts. The past and past participle of regular verbs are formed by adding *ed* to the present form. For irregular verbs, the past and past participle are usually different words; however, a few have the same form in all three principal parts.

744.4 Simple Tenses

- **Present tense** expresses action that takes place in the present, or action that happens continually, regularly.
    In September, sophomores smirk and joke about the "little freshies."
- **Past tense** expresses action that took place in the past.
    They forgot that just ninety days separated them from freshman status.
- **Future tense** expresses action that may take place in the future.
    They will recall this in three years when they will be freshmen again.

Grammar Practice

Verbs 3

- Number of a Verb
- Person of a Verb
- Simple Tenses of a Verb

 Find the verbs in the following sentences. Write each, followed by its person and number and its tense.

1. I think of Leonardo da Vinci as an artist, but he was quite an inventor, as well.

2. He created designs for a diving suit, a revolving bridge, and a helicopter.

3. Can you imagine such intelligence?

4. Flocks of starlings race after the lawn mower, seeking a meal of the bugs set loose by the blades.

5. Mahender attends Blakely School for the Blind.

6. The radio station will feature an interview with Alejandro Isassi at 4:20 this afternoon.

7. You look as red as a ripe tomato!

8. Alfonso and Lela will call me when they are ready to go.

9. After I brushed my teeth, Rachelle offered me a warm brownie.

10. The British Virgin Islands attract tourists from around the world.

11. Jaime, please fold your clothes and put them away.

12. The summer solstice will occur at 5:16 p.m. on June 21, 2011.

Learning Language

Verb tenses tell about time: the past (Lela **called** me yesterday), the present (Lela **calls** me every day), and the future (Lela **will call** me tomorrow). With a partner, identify the meaning and the tenses of the verbs in the above sentences. Use the past tense to tell each other a story about something that happened in your past. Then, use the future to tell about your plans for the weekend.

ELPS 5D, 5E

Forms of Verbs (continued)

746.1 Perfect Tenses

- **Present perfect tense** expresses action that began in the past but continues in the present or is completed in the present.
  Our boat has weathered worse storms than this one.
- **Past perfect tense** expresses an action in the past that occurred before another past action.
  They reported, wrongly, that the hurricane had missed the island.
- **Future perfect tense** expresses action that will begin in the future and be completed by a specific time in the future.
  By this time tomorrow, the hurricane will have smashed into the coast.

746.2 Irregular Verbs

Common Irregular Verbs and Their Principal Parts

Present Tense	Past Tense	Past Participle	Present Tense	Past Tense	Past Participle	Present Tense	Past Tense	Past Participle
am, be	was, were	been	go	went	gone	shrink	shrank	shrunk
begin	began	begun	grow	grew	grown	sing	sang, sung	sung
bite	bit	bitten	hang (execute)	hanged	hanged	sink	sank, sunk	sunk
blow	blew	blown				sit	sat	sat
break	broke	broken	hang (suspend)	hung	hung	slay	slew	slain
bring	brought	brought				speak	spoke	spoken
buy	bought	bought	hide	hid	hidden, hid	spring	sprang, sprung	sprung
catch	caught	caught	know	knew	known			
choose	chose	chosen	lay	laid	laid	steal	stole	stolen
come	came	come	lead	led	led	strive	strove	striven
dive	dove	dived	leave	left	left	swear	swore	sworn
do	did	done	lie (recline)	lay	lain	swim	swam	swum
draw	drew	drawn				swing	swung	swung
drink	drank	drunk	lie (deceive)	lied	lied	take	took	taken
drive	drove	driven				teach	taught	taught
eat	ate	eaten	lose	lost	lost	tear	tore	torn
fall	fell	fallen	make	made	made	throw	threw	thrown
fight	fought	fought	ride	rode	ridden	wake	waked, woke	waked, woken
flee	fled	fled	ring	rang	rung			
fly	flew	flown	rise	rose	risen	wear	wore	worn
forsake	forsook	forsaken	run	ran	run	weave	weaved, wove	weaved, woven
freeze	froze	frozen	see	saw	seen			
get	got	gotten	shake	shook	shaken	wring	wrung	wrung
give	gave	given	show	showed	shown	write	wrote	written

These verbs are the same in all principal parts: *burst, cost, cut, hurt, let, put, set,* and *spread.*

ELPS 5D, 5E

Grammar Practice

Verbs 4

- **Perfect-Tense Verbs**
- **Irregular Verbs**

 Write the past participle of the verb in parentheses to complete each sentence. Indicate whether the verb is *present perfect, past perfect,* or *future perfect.*

1. Melford hadn't *(see)* the cat in a while; he assumed that she had *(lie)* in a patch of sunlight for most of the afternoon.

2. I'm sure I have *(eat)* at this restaurant before, since I have never *(sit)* in a booth like this anywhere else!

3. By the time this batter will have *(swing)* at another pitch, the guy on second base will have *(run)* to third.

4. Colleen has *(lead)* her niece's scout troop for three years, and she's *(do)* a great job.

5. The vase, teetering on the edge of the shelf for so long, had finally *(fall)* and *(break)* into little pieces.

6. Odds are that Noney will have *(catch)* some serious tanning-booth rays before she heads to Florida this spring; she has *(grow)* rather fond of her skin's orangey glow.

7. D'Shawn had *(choose)* Melanie's watercolor painting over the others because he liked the way she had *(draw)* bare trees over the colors in dark ink.

8. Dad has *(lay)* his last brick; by tomorrow he will have *(throw)* out the trowel that he used for so many years.

Model

Model the following sentences to practice using irregular perfect tense verbs correctly.

> A person who talks fast often says things she hasn't thought of yet.
> —Caron Warner Lieber

> The only ones among you who will be really happy are those who have sought and found how to serve.
> —Albert Schweitzer

748.1 Continuous Tenses

- A **present-continuous tense** verb expresses action that is not completed at the time of stating it. The present continuous tense is formed by adding *am*, *is*, or *are* to the *-ing* form of the main verb.

    Scientists are learning a great deal from their study of the sky.

- A **past-continuous tense** verb expresses action that was happening at a certain time in the past. This tense is formed by adding *was* or *were* to the *-ing* form of the main verb.

    Astronomers were beginning their quest for knowledge hundreds of years ago.

- A **future-continuous tense** verb expresses action that will take place at a certain time in the future. This tense is formed by adding *will be* to the *-ing* form of the main verb.

    Someday astronauts will be going to Mars.

    This tense can also be formed by adding a phrase noting the future (*are going to*) plus *be* to the *-ing* form of the main verb.

    They are going to be performing many experiments.

748.2 Voice of a Verb

Voice indicates whether the subject is acting or being acted upon.

- **Active voice** indicates that the subject of the verb is, has been, or will be doing something.

    For many years Lou Brock held the base-stealing record.

    Active voice makes your writing more direct and lively.

- **Passive voice** indicates that the subject of the verb is being, has been, or will be acted upon.

    For many years the base-stealing record was held by Lou Brock.

Note: With a passive verb, the person or thing creating the action is not always stated.

The ordinance was overturned. (Who did the overturning?)

Tense	Active Voice		Passive Voice	
	Singular	Plural	Singular	Plural
Present	I see you see he/she/it sees	we see you see they see	I am seen you are seen he/she/it is seen	we are seen you are seen they are seen
Past	I/he saw you saw	we/they saw you saw	I/it was seen you were seen	we/they were seen you were seen
Future	I/you/he will see	we/you/they will see	I/you/it will be seen	we/you/they will be seen

Grammar Practice

Verbs 5

- **Continuous Tenses**
- **Voice of a Verb**

In each sentence below, identify the verb in the underlined group of words as *present continuous, past continuous,* or *future continuous.*

1. The students <u>are going to be creating their own Web page designs</u>.
2. Aliyya and her brother, Haani, <u>are working in their family's restaurant</u>.
3. Construction workers <u>were finally repaving</u> the pothole-filled road.
4. Rufus and I <u>are looking forward</u> to the first game of the season.
5. <u>You will be graduating soon</u>.
6. In my programming course, <u>I am learning</u> how to create lifelike animations.
7. <u>Darius was leaning against the wall</u>, waiting his turn in the long line.
8. Wolf <u>spiders were building an intricate web</u> on our front porch.
9. <u>Will they be laying their eggs</u> there soon?
10. Those <u>spiders aren't going to be catching many bugs</u> in that web.

Model

Model the following sentences, but change the passive voice to the active voice.

> Some people claim that the first modern computer was invented by Konrad Zuse in 1941.

> The wise are instructed by reason; ordinary minds by experience; the stupid, by necessity; and brutes by instinct.
> —Cicero

> The new budget was debated for months by both parties in Congress.

750.1 Mood of a Verb

The **mood** of a verb indicates the tone or attitude with which a statement is made.

- **Indicative mood** is used to state a fact or to ask a question.

    Sometimes I'd **yell** questions at the rocks and trees, and across gorges, or **yodel**, "What is the meaning of the void?" The answer **was** perfect silence, so I **knew**.
    —Jack Kerouac, "Alone on a Mountain Top"

- **Imperative mood** is used to give a command.

"Whatever you do, don't fly your kite during a storm."
—Mrs. Abiah Franklin

- **Subjunctive mood** is used to express a condition that is contrary to fact or highly doubtful, a wish, a posibility, a suggestion, or a necessity.

    Use the subjunctive to express a wish.
       I wish I **were** able to run the marathon tomorrow, but I have a cold.

    Use the subjunctive to state a condition that is contrary to fact.
       If I **had** wings, I would fly around the world.

    Use the subjunctive *were* after *as though* or *as if* to express an unreal condition.
       Mrs. Young acted as if she **were** sixteen again.

    Use the subjunctive *be* in "that" clauses to express a demand, a request, or a suggestion. It is sometimes used in legal decisions or parliamentary motions.
       It is moved and supported that no more than 6 million quad **be used** to explore the planet Earth.

Grammar Practice

Verbs 6

- **Mood of a Verb**

Write whether each statement shows *indicative*, *imperative*, or *subjunctive* mood.

1. If I were eighteen, I could vote in the November election.
2. Stop at my house after school and pick up Jana's homework.
3. Have you heard that Matthias got a job at Gordon's garage?
4. Be certain the air conditioning is operating by tomorrow!
5. Because someone else called in sick today, I'm working until ten tonight.
6. Pedro acts as if he were a shoo-in for the lead role.
7. Notice how Dot sands the table with fine-grain sandpaper.
8. Why do you like the idea of earlier start times for high schools?
9. I've decided to enroll in a technical college this fall.
10. Get off the freeway at the next exit.
11. The vice principal peered at the boys as though they were criminals.
12. Before you leave the house, make sure you empty the dishwasher and put the dishes away.
13. Tino proposed to his parents that he be permitted to be out until 1:00 a.m. on weekends.
14. Please take the garbage out.

Learning Language

In a small group, describe street signs that you have seen. Decide which signs contain imperatives—verbs that give commands. Explain what the signs are telling drivers to do. Discuss the importance of street signs for driving and ask: What would happen if drivers did not obey the signs?

Verbals

A **verbal** is a word that is derived from a verb but does not function as a verb in a sentence. Instead, a verbal acts as another part of speech—noun, adjective, or adverb. There are three types of verbals: *gerunds, infinitives,* and *participles*. Each is often part of a verbal phrase.

752.1 Gerunds

A **gerund** is a verb form that ends in *ing* and is used as a noun.

Swimming is my favorite pastime. (subject)
I began **swimming** at the age of six months.
(direct object)
The hardest part of **swimming** is the resulting sore muscles.
(object of the preposition *of*)
Swimming in chlorinated pools makes my eyes red.
(gerund phrase used as a subject)

752.2 Infinitives

An **infinitive** is a verb form that is usually introduced by *to*; the infinitive may be used as a noun, an adjective, or an adverb.

Most people find it easy **to swim**. (adverb modifying an adjective)
To swim the English Channel must be a thrill. (infinitive phrase as noun)
The urge **to swim in tropical waters** is more common. (infinitive phrase as adjective)

752.3 Participles

A **participle** is a verb form ending in *ing* or *ed* that acts as an adjective.

The workers **raking leaves** are tired and hungry.
(participial phrase modifying *workers*)
The bags full of **raked** leaves are evidence of their hard work.
(participle modifying *leaves*)
Smiling faces greeted my father when he returned from a business trip.
(participle modifying *faces*)

Note: The past participle of an irregular verb can also act as an adjective.
That rake is obviously **broken**.
It's a **known** fact that leaves make good compost.

Grammar Practice

Verbals

- **Gerunds**
- **Infinitives**
- **Participles**

 Label each underlined phrase in the following paragraphs as a *gerund phrase*, a *participial phrase*, or an *infinitive phrase*. Also state the function of each infinitive phrase (*noun, adjective,* or *adverb*).

You may have heard the term "hijab" in the news lately. **(1)** <u>Derived from the Arabic word "hajaba,"</u> the word means "to hide from view." In the religion of Islam, passages in the holy book refer to the requirement for women **(2)** <u>to cover their heads and bodies</u>. Today, some people—**(3)** <u>Muslims included</u>—find hijab a controversial matter.

On one side of the issue are tradition and pride. Many women who observe hijab are comfortable with **(4)** <u>making the statement about their religious identity</u>. **(5)** <u>To maintain their religious beliefs</u> is more important than **(6)** <u>fitting in</u> to any other society. They are of the opinion that their way of dress forces others **(7)** <u>to judge them</u> for their intelligence and ability rather than for their looks and sexuality.

Some Muslim communities interpret hijab more loosely. Although **(8)** <u>covering the entire body</u> is not strictly enforced, families and the culture itself still expect women to dress modestly. Usually **(9)** <u>consisting of long-sleeved shirts or dresses</u>, long skirts or pants, and a scarf over the hair, this attire is acceptable to many **(10)** <u>working Muslim women</u>.

Model

Model the following sentences to practice using an infinitive as a noun.

To fulfill a dream, to be allowed to sweat over lonely labor, to be given the chance to create is the meat and potatoes of life. The money is the gravy.
—Bette Davis, *The Lonely Life*

What would you attempt to do if you knew you could not fail?
—Robert Schuller

Adjective

An **adjective** describes or modifies a noun or a pronoun. The articles *a*, *an*, and *the* are also adjectives.

    The young driver peeked through **the big** steering wheel.
    (*The* and *young* modify *driver*; *the* and *big* modify *steering wheel*.)

754.1 Types of Adjectives

A **proper adjective** is created from a proper noun and is capitalized.
    In **Canada** (proper noun), **you will find many cultures and climates.**
    Canadian (proper adjective) **winters can be harsh.**

A **predicate adjective** follows a form of the "be" verb (or other linking verb) and describes the subject.
    Late autumn seems grim to those who love summer. (*Grim* modifies *autumn*.)

Note: Some words can be either adjectives or pronouns (*that, these, all, each, both, many, some,* and so on). These words are adjectives when they come before the nouns they modify; they are pronouns when they stand alone.
    Jiao made both goals. (*Both* modifies *goals*; it is an adjective.)
    Both were scored in the final period. (*Both* stands alone; it is a pronoun.)

754.2 Forms of Adjectives

Adjectives have three forms: *positive, comparative,* and *superlative.*

- The **positive form** describes a noun or a pronoun without comparing it to anyone or anything else.
    The first game was long and tiresome.

- The **comparative form** (*-er, more,* or *less*) compares two persons, places, things, or ideas.
    The second game was longer and more tiresome than the first.

- The **superlative form** (*-est, most,* or *least*) compares three or more persons, places, things, or ideas.
    The third game was the longest and most tiresome of all.

Note: Use *more* and *most* (or *less* and *least*)—instead of adding a suffix—with many adjectives of two or more syllables.

Positive	Comparative	Superlative
big	bigger	biggest
helpful	more helpful	most helpful
painful	less painful	least painful

Grammar Practice

Adjectives

- Types of Adjectives
- Forms of Adjectives

Write the adjectives (not including articles) in each of the following sentences. Label *proper*, *predicate*, *comparative*, and *superlative* adjectives. (Some adjectives will have two labels.)

1. The new warehouse seems much larger than the old one.
2. I hope to scale Mt. Everest—the highest mountain in the world.
3. African sunsets on the Serengeti Plain are gorgeous.
4. Of all the bands, One Step Back was the most enjoyable.
5. Hunter looks handsome in his royal blue tuxedo.
6. Shineece's Chihuahua is smaller than any dog I have ever seen.
7. Olga crocheted long, multicolored scarves for both grandmothers.
8. Didn't second-hour geometry class seem longer than usual?
9. The Chinese culture was brought to life through Shaiming's amazing presentation.
10. The highway worker's bright orange vest really made her stand out against the gray-brown background of the bare trees lining the country road.

Learning Language

An adjective describes a noun or a pronoun. The words *long*, *smart*, *American*, and *sunny* are examples of adjectives. Think of a person you admire and write ten adjectives that describe the person. Then use the adjectives as you describe the person to a partner.

Adverb

An **adverb** describes or modifies a verb, an adjective, or another adverb.

> **She sneezed loudly.** (*Loudly* modifies the verb *sneezed*.)
> **Her sneezes are really dramatic.** (*Really* modifies the adjective *dramatic*.)
> **The sneeze exploded very noisily.** (*Very* modifies the adverb *noisily*.)

An adverb usually tells *when, where, how,* or *how much.*

756.1 Types of Adverbs

Adverbs can be cataloged in four basic ways: *time, place, manner,* and *degree.*

> **Time** (These adverbs tell *when, how often,* and *how long.*)
> today, yesterday   daily, weekly   briefly, eternally

> **Place** (These adverbs tell *where, to where,* and *from where.*)
> here, there   nearby, beyond   backward, forward

> **Manner** (These adverbs often end in *ly* and tell *how* something is done.)
> precisely   effectively   regally   smoothly   well

> **Degree** (These adverbs tell *how much* or *how little.*)
> substantially   greatly   entirely   partly   too

Note: Some adverbs can be written with or without the *ly* ending. When in doubt, use the *ly* form.

> slow, slowly   loud, loudly   fair, fairly   tight, tightly   quick, quickly

756.2 Forms of Adverbs

Adverbs of manner have three forms: *positive, comparative,* and *superlative.*

- The **positive form** describes a verb, an adjective, or another adverb without comparing it to anyone or anything else.
  > **Model X vacuum cleans well and runs quietly.**

- The **comparative form** (*-er, more,* or *less*) compares how two things are done.
  > **Model Y vacuum cleans better and runs more quietly than model X does.**

- The **superlative form** (*-est, most,* or *least*) compares how three or more things are done.
  > **Model Z vacuum cleans best and runs most quietly of all.**

Irregular Forms

Positive	Comparative	Superlative
well	better	best
fast	faster	fastest
remorsefully	more remorsefully	most remorsefully

Grammar Practice

Adverbs

- **Types of Adverbs**
- **Forms of Adverbs**

 Write the adverbs in each of the following sentences (some sentences have more than one). Identify each as an adverb of *time, place, manner,* or *degree*. For an adverb of manner, also identify it as *positive, comparative,* or *superlative*.

1. Of all the board members, the mayor reacted most enthusiastically to our proposal.

2. P. J. sat there lazily while I foolishly hauled his boxes to the car alone.

3. Jason rode his motorbike clear across the course in minutes.

4. An immense cargo carrier roared deafeningly overhead.

5. Yesterday, my brother discovered that I'd accidentally dented his pickup truck.

6. I observed an affectionate side of Arnell when he spoke very gently to his nephew.

7. The speaker shared a very interesting anecdote.

8. His was one of the most finely planned science projects at the fair.

9. I performed well on last year's SAT's, but I slipped behind on my final exams.

10. Mr. and Mrs. O'Leary indulgently had their colorful tropical drinks delivered poolside.

Model

Model the following sentences to practice using comparative and superlative adverbs.

People always call it luck when you've acted more sensibly than they have.
—Anne Tyler, *Celestial Navigation*

Practice shows that those who speak the most knowingly and confidently often end up with the assignment to get the job done.
—Bill Swanson, *Swanson's Unwritten Rules of Management*

Preposition

A **preposition** is the first word (or group of words) in a prepositional phrase. It shows the relationship between its object (a noun or a pronoun that follows the preposition) and another word in the sentence. The first noun or pronoun following a preposition is its object.

>To make a mustache, Natasha placed the hairy caterpillar under her nose.
>(*Under* shows the relationship between the verb, *placed*, and the object of the preposition, *nose*.)
>The drowsy insect clung obediently to the girl's upper lip.
>(The first noun following the preposition *to* is *lip; lip* is the object of the preposition.)

758.1 Prepositional Phrases

A **prepositional phrase** includes the preposition, the object of the preposition, and the modifiers of the object. A prepositional phrase functions as an adverb or as an adjective.

>Some people run away from caterpillars.
>(The phrase functions as an adverb and modifies the verb *run*.)
>However, little kids with inquisitive minds enjoy their company.
>(The phrase functions as an adjective and modifies the noun *kids*.)

Note: A preposition is always followed by an object; if there is no object, the word is an adverb, not a preposition.

>Natasha never played with caterpillars before. (The word *before* is not followed by an object; therefore, it functions as an adverb that modifies *played*, a verb.)

Common Prepositions

aboard	before	from	of	save
about	behind	from among	off	since
above	below	from between	on	subsequent to
according to	beneath	from under	on account of	through
across	beside	in	on behalf of	throughout
across from	besides	in addition to	onto	till
after	between	in back of	on top of	to
against	beyond	in behalf of	opposite	together with
along	by	in front of	out	toward
alongside	by means of	in place of	out of	under
along with	concerning	in regard to	outside of	underneath
amid	considering	inside	over	until
among	despite	inside of	over to	unto
apart from	down	in spite of	owing to	up
around	down from	instead of	past	upon
aside from	during	into	prior to	up to
at	except	like	regarding	with
away from	except for	near	round	within
because of	for	near to	round about	without

Grammar Practice

Prepositions

- **Prepositional Phrases**

 For each underlined prepositional phrase, indicate whether it functions as an adjective or an adverb.

Nearly all my life, **(1)** <u>except the last three years</u>, was spent **(2)** <u>at home</u>. I never traveled much, and in fact, never expected to become a traveler, and above all an unwilling heroine **(3)** <u>in the North-West troubles</u>. I had several sisters and brothers. I was the eldest **(4)** <u>of the family</u>, and as such, **(5)** <u>for many years</u> had to devote my time **(6)** <u>to household cares</u>. My school days seem now the pleasantest period **(7)** <u>of my early life</u>.

From Two Months in the Camp of Big Bear by
Theresa Gowanlock and Theresa Delaney

If this journey had taken place **(8)** <u>during my days</u> **(9)** <u>of study and happiness</u>, it would have afforded me inexpressible pleasure. But a blight had come **(10)** <u>over my existence</u>, and I only visited these people **(11)** <u>for the sake</u> of the information they might give me **(12)** <u>on the subject</u> in which my interest was so terribly profound. Company was irksome to me; when alone, I could fill my mind **(13)** <u>with the sights</u> of heaven and earth; the voice of Henry soothed me, and I could thus cheat myself **(14)** <u>into a transitory peace</u>.

From Frankenstein by Mary Wollstonecraft Shelley

Learning Language

When you do shared reading in class, you read along while a classmate or your teacher reads aloud. With a partner, do shared reading of the passages above. One of you will read aloud as the other follows along. When you get to an underlined phrase, speak it aloud together. Write down the first word of every underlined phrase and look for other examples of them on this page or in the rest of your textbook.

Conjunction

A **conjunction** connects individual words or groups of words. There are three kinds of conjunctions: *coordinating, correlative,* and *subordinating*.

760.1 Coordinating Conjunctions

Coordinating conjunctions usually connect a word to a word, a phrase to a phrase, or a clause to a clause. The words, phrases, or clauses joined by a coordinating conjunction are equal in importance or are of the same type.

> She knew it would be *difficult to go to college* **and** *scary to live in a new town,* **but** *she had a lot of support from her family.*

(*And* connects the two parts of a compound predicate; *but* connects two independent clauses that could stand on their own.)

760.2 Correlative Conjunctions

Correlative conjunctions are conjunctions used in pairs.

> They were **not only** exhausted by the day's journey **but also** sunburned.

760.3 Subordinating Conjunctions

Subordinating conjunctions connect two clauses that are *not* equally important, thereby showing the relationship between them. A subordinating conjunction connects a dependent clause to an independent clause in order to complete the meaning of the dependent clause.

> A brown trout will study the bait **before** he eats it. (The clause *before he eats it* is dependent. It depends on the rest of the sentence to complete its meaning.)

Kinds of Conjunctions

Coordinating: **and, but, or, nor, for, yet, so**

Correlative: **either, or; neither, nor; not only, but also; both, and; whether, or**

Subordinating: **after, although, as, as if, as long as, as though, because, before, if, in order that, provided that, since, so that, that, though, till, unless, until, when, where, whereas, while**

Note: Relative pronouns (**734.2**) and conjunctive adverbs (**654.2**) can also connect clauses.

Interjection

An **interjection** communicates strong emotion or surprise. Punctuation—a comma or an exclamation point—sets off an interjection from the rest of the sentence.

> **Oh no!** The TV broke. **Good grief!** I have nothing to do! **Yikes,** I'll go mad!

Grammar Practice

Conjunctions

 Write the 14 conjunctions you find in the following paragraph and label them *coordinating*, *subordinating*, or *correlative*. (Write both correlative conjunctions as one answer.)

1 A very special baby was born on July 17, 1990. His given name was
2 Matthew Joseph Thaddeus Stepanek, but everyone knew him as "Mattie."
3 Mattie was special; not only was he born with a rare neuromuscular disease,
4 but he also was destined to become a well-known peacemaker and poet.
5 Mattie used a wheelchair to get around because he was unable to walk. He
6 also needed a ventilator so he could breathe. The pain and discomfort of his
7 illness never stopped him from writing and speaking about world peace.
8 Although he was often very ill in his short life (he died on June 22, 2004), he
9 neither complained nor wanted people to feel sorry for him. Before his death,
10 he published eight books of poetry, and five made it to the *New York Times*
11 best-seller list. Mattie also appeared on numerous talk shows to discuss his
12 philosophies about peace efforts and global tolerance. After he died, former
13 President Jimmy Carter delivered the eulogy at his funeral (the two had
14 been friends since 2002, bonding over their passion for peacemaking). Carter
15 said that he had known many kings and queens, but Mattie was the most
16 extraordinary person he had ever met. Matthew Joseph Thaddeus Stepanek
17 was indeed a remarkable young man, and he left us with these final
18 thought-provoking words: "Remember to play after every storm."

Model

Model the follow sentences to practice using interjections effectively.

Oh no! Look out! That car is going too fast.

"This is fantastic!" Mr. Rumsfeld blurted. **"I've got a laser pointer! Holy mackerel!"**

—Eric Schmitt, *The New York Times*

Understanding Sentences

Constructing Sentences

A **sentence** is made up of one or more words that express a complete thought. Sentences begin with a capital letter; they end with a period, a question mark, or an exclamation point.

> What should we do this afternoon? We could have a picnic. No, I hate the ants!

Using Subjects and Predicates

A sentence usually has a **subject** and a **predicate**. The subject is the part of the sentence about which something is said. The predicate, which contains the verb, is the part of the sentence that says something about the subject.

> **We** write from aspiration and antagonism, as well as from experience.
> —Ralph Waldo Emerson

762.1 The Subject

The **subject** is the part of the sentence about which something is said. The subject is always a noun; a pronoun; or a word, clause, or phrase that functions as a noun (such as a gerund or a gerund phrase or an infinitive).

> **Wolves** howl. (noun)
> **They** howl for a variety of reasons. (pronoun)
> **To establish their turf** may be one reason. (infinitive phrase)
> **Searching for "lost" pack members** may be another. (gerund phrase)
> **That wolves and dogs are similar animals** seems obvious. (noun clause)

- A **simple subject** is the subject without its modifiers.
   > Most wildlife **biologists** disapprove of crossbreeding wolves and dogs.

- A **complete subject** is the subject with all of its modifiers.
   > **Most wildlife biologists** disapprove of crossbreeding wolves and dogs.

- A **compound subject** is composed of two or more simple subjects.
   > Wise **breeders** and **owners** know that wolf-dog puppies can display unexpected, destructive behaviors.

762.2 Delayed Subject

In sentences that begin with *There* or *It* followed by a form of the "be" verb, the subject comes after the verb. The subject is also delayed in questions.

> There was **nothing** in the refrigerator. (The subject is *nothing*; the verb is *was*.)
> Where is my **sandwich**? (The subject is *sandwich*; the verb is *is*.)

Grammar Practice

Constructing Sentences 1

- **Simple, Complete, and Compound Subjects**
- **Delayed Subjects**

 Write the complete subject of each independent clause (and each dependent clause in a complex or compound-complex sentence). Circle the simple subject or subjects.

(1) In 1953, General Motors introduced an automobile destined to become one of the most popular cars in American history. **(2)** It was the Chevrolet Corvette. **(3)** It wasn't the Corvette's performance that was striking; the design sold the car. **(4)** You could only buy the '53 "Vettes" in white, and all were convertibles. **(5)** The red vinyl interior, soft black top, and red rims around the whitewall tires defined the design. **(6)** There was nothing else like it on the road. **(7)** The suggested retail price for the base model amounted to about $3,500.

(8) GM created only 300 of the '53 Corvettes, but the limited number was unintentional. **(9)** The powerful corporate giant got a late start building the cars. **(10)** A temporary manufacturing plant in Flint, Michigan, was the production site. **(11)** The plant and assembly line required time to set up, so workers were able to make just 300 cars before the start of the 1954 model year.

(12) About 225 of the '53 Corvettes still exist today, representing the rarest of all model-year Corvettes. **(13)** Whoever owns one of these automobiles holds a valuable collector's piece worth more than $105,000. **(14)** There is a nice little sum!

Model

Model the following sentence to practice using a compound subject.

> Junipero Serra, the Majorca-born missionary who headed the effort, and his small band of Franciscan followers built a chain of missions from San Diego in the south to San Rafael in the north.
> — H. W. Brands, *The Age of Gold*

764.1 Predicates

The **predicate** is the part of the sentence that shows action or says something about the subject.

> Giant squid **do exist**.

- A **simple predicate** is the verb without its modifiers.
  > One giant squid **measured** nearly 60 feet long.

- A **complete predicate** is the simple predicate with all its modifiers.
  > One giant squid **measured nearly 60 feet long**.
  > (*Measured* is the simple predicate; *nearly 60 feet long* modifies *measured*.)

- Compound and complex sentences have more than one predicate.
  > The sperm whale **has an enormous head** that **is approximately a third of its entire length**.
  > A whale **is a mammal**, but a squid **is a mollusk**.

- A **compound predicate** is composed of two or more simple predicates.
  > A squid **grasps** its prey with tentacles and **bites** it with its beak.

Note: A sentence can have a **compound subject** and a **compound predicate**.
> Both **sperm whales** and **giant squid** **live** and occasionally **clash** in the deep waters off New Zealand's South Island.

- A **direct object** is part of the predicate and receives the action of the verb. (See **742.2**.)
  > Sperm whales sometimes eat **giant squid**.
  > (The direct object *giant squid* receives the action of the verb *eat* by answering the question *whales eat what*?)

Note: The **direct object** may be compound.
> In the past, whalers harvested **oil**, **spermaceti**, and **ambergris** from slain sperm whales.

764.2 Understood Subjects and Predicates

Either the subject or the predicate may be "missing" from a sentence, but both must be clearly **understood**.

> **Who** is in the hot-air balloon?
> (*Who* is the subject; *is in the hot-air balloon* is the predicate.)
>
> **No one**.
> (*No one* is the subject; the predicate *is in the hot-air balloon* is understood.)
>
> **Get out of the way**!
> (The subject *you* is understood; *get out of the way* is the predicate.)

Understanding Sentences

Grammar Practice

Constructing Sentences 2

- **Simple, Complete, and Compound Predicates**

 Write the complete predicate of each sentence. Circle the simple predicate or predicates. In sentences with a direct object, underline it.

1. Danica Patrick finished fourth in the 2005 Indianapolis 500.

2. She led for 19 laps and became the first woman driver ever to lead the race.

3. Her car stalled in the pits about halfway through the 500-mile race.

4. She restarted the car but dropped to the middle of the field.

5. Her fourth-place finish was the highest ever for a female driver.

6. Danica won the 2005 title of Rookie of the Year.

7. At 10 years old, Danica began racing go-carts.

8. Today Danica drives Indy cars for the Rahal-Letterman racing team.

9. In the 2006 Indy race, Danica finished in eighth place.

10. Think about how exciting that would have been!

Model

Model the following sentence to practice using a compound predicate.

When I get bored, I drive downtown and get a great parking spot, then sit in my car and count how many people ask me if I'm leaving. —Steven Wright

Using Phrases

A **phrase** is a group of related words that function as a single part of speech.

766.1 Types of Phrases

- An **appositive phrase,** which follows a noun or a pronoun and renames it, consists of a noun and its modifiers. An appositive adds new information about the noun or pronoun it follows.

    The Trans-Siberian Railroad, the world's longest railway, **stretches from Moscow to Vladivostok.**
    (The appositive phrase renames *Trans-Siberian Railroad* and provides new information.)

- An **adjective phrase** modifies a noun or pronoun. It often begins with a preposition. One form of adjective phrase is a **participial phrase**, a verbal that consists of a past or present participle and its modifiers.

    Actors with extensive training **are more likely than others to be cast in plays.**
    (The adjective phrase modifies the noun *actors*.)

    She is extremely well-traveled.
    (The adjective phrase modifies the pronoun *She*; it tells "how much.")

    Following his nose, **the beagle took off like a jackrabbit.**
    (The adjective phrase modifies the noun *beagle*.)

    The raccoons, warned by the rustling, **took cover.**
    (The adjective phrase modifies the noun *raccoons*.)

- An **adverb phrase** modifies a verb. It is composed of the adverbs that modify verbs, adjectives, or clauses.

    He beat his opponent in the chess game very easily.
    (The adverb phrase modifies the verb *beat*.)

- A **noun phrase** consists of a pronoun or noun with any associated modifiers. Noun phrases can be a *gerund* or an *infinitive*. (See **752.1 and 752.2**.) They may serve as subjects, direct objects, indirect objects, or objects of prepositions.

    - A **gerund phrase** consists of a gerund and its modifiers. The whole phrase functions as a noun.

        Spotting the tiny mouse **was easy for the hawk.**
        (The gerund phrase is used as the subject of the sentence.)

        The mouse escaped by ducking under a rock.
        (The gerund phrase is the object of the preposition *by*.)

    - An **infinitive phrase** consists of an infinitive and its modifiers. The whole phrase functions either as a noun, an adjective, or an adverb.

        To shake every voter's hand **was the candidate's goal.**
        (The infinitive phrase functions as a noun used as the subject.)

        Your efforts to clean the chalkboard **are appreciated.**
        (The infinitive phrase is used as an adjective modifying *efforts*.)

        Please watch carefully to see the difference.
        (The infinitive phrase is used as an adverb modifying *watch*.)

Understanding Sentences   767

Grammar Practice

Constructing Sentences 3
- **Appositive Phrases**
- **Adjective Phrases**
- **Adverb Phrases**
- **Noun Phrases**

Identify each underlined phrase as an *appositive, adjective, adverb,* or *noun* phrase. (One phrase below will have two correct answers.)

1. The citizens approved a referendum for <u>increasing library funds</u>.
2. Kai, <u>my best friend for ten years</u>, will be my college roommate.
3. You can find fashionable boots <u>in the department store</u>.
4. James dreams about <u>becoming an ER doctor</u>.
5. <u>To avoid <u>burning the burgers</u></u>, Ryan watched them closely.
6. Paul Anka, <u>the dog on the television show *Gilmore Girls*</u>, is named after a famous teen idol.
7. The student <u>chosen as valedictorian</u> will speak at the graduation ceremony.
8. <u>Camping in the woods</u> at this time of year is dangerous.
9. The camper <u>clearing the snow from the site</u> is building up a good appetite.
10. The best exercise, <u>walking every day</u>, costs only the price of a good pair of shoes.

Model

Model the following sentence to practice using a gerund phrase.

    For me, singing sad songs often has a way of healing a situation.
                                                  —Reba McEntire

Using Phrases (continued)

- A **verb phrase** consists of a main verb preceded by one or more helping verbs.

    Snow **has been falling** for days. (*Has been falling* is a verb phrase.)

- A **prepositional phrase** is a group of words beginning with a preposition and ending with a noun or a pronoun. Prepositional phrases function mainly as adjectives and adverbs.

    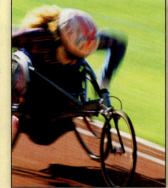

    Reach for that catnip ball **behind the couch**.
    (The prepositional phrase *behind the couch* is used as an adjective modifying *catnip ball*.)

    Zach won the wheelchair race **in record time**.
    (*In record time* is used as an adverb modifying the verb *won*.)

- An **absolute phrase** consists of a noun and a participle (plus the participle's object, if there is one, and any modifiers). An absolute phrase functions as a modifier that adds information to the entire sentence. Absolute phrases are always set off with commas.

    Its wheels clattering rhythmically over the rails, the train rolled into town. (The noun *wheels* is modified by the present participle *clattering*. The entire phrase modifies the rest of the sentence.)

Using Clauses

A **clause** is a group of related words that has both a subject and a predicate.

768.1 Independent and Dependent Clauses

An **independent clause** presents a complete thought and can stand alone as a sentence; a **dependent clause** (also called a *subordinate clause*) does not present a complete thought and cannot stand alone as a sentence.

  Sparrows make nests in cattle barns (independent clause) **so that they can stay warm during the winter** (dependent clause).

768.2 Types of Dependent Clauses

There are three basic types of dependent clauses: *adverb*, *noun*, and *adjective*.

- An **adverb clause** is used like an adverb to modify a verb, an adjective, or an adverb. Adverb clauses begin with a subordinating conjunction. (See **760.3**.)

    If I study hard, I will pass this test. (The adverb clause modifies the verb *will pass*.)

- A **noun clause** is used in place of a noun.

    However, the teacher said **that the essay questions are based only on the last two chapters**. (The noun clause functions as a direct object.)

- An **adjective clause** modifies a noun or a pronoun.

    Tomorrow's test, **which covers the entire book**, is half essay and half short answers. (The adjective clause modifies the noun *test*.)

Understanding Sentences

Grammar Practice

Constructing Sentences 4

- **Verb Phrases**
- **Prepositional Phrases**
- **Absolute Phrases**
- **Independent Clauses**
- **Dependent Clauses**

For each underlined group of words, write whether it is a *verb phrase*, a *prepositional phrase*, or an *absolute phrase*.

1. Mara <u>did not find</u> the resources needed <u>for the assignment</u>.

2. <u>The school year nearly finished</u>, Hannah and Sally made plans <u>for the summer</u>.

3. My sister <u>will meet</u> us at the coffee shop at three o'clock.

4. <u>After the race</u>, Huan beelined for the water fountain, <u>his chest heaving</u>.

5. He <u>was having</u> difficulty breathing.

For each underlined group of words, write whether it is an *independent clause* or a *dependent clause*. If it is a dependent clause, also identify its type.

6. Nobody except Jaleesa knows <u>where the party will be</u>.

7. She took the job <u>so that she could pay her college tuition</u>.

8. <u>Ms. Klema has been giving me extra help</u>, and my grades are improving.

9. The house <u>that we used to live in</u> was sold.

10. <u>My back hurts so much</u> because I fell yesterday.

Model

Model the following sentence to practice using prepositional phrases effectively.

> At the house, a small white gate opened from the lane into a country garden, which in summer would shine with bunched roses and morning glories and tresses of sweet pea.
>
> —Frank Delaney, *Ireland*

Using Sentence Variety

A **sentence** may be classified according to the type of statement it makes, the way it is constructed, and its arrangement of words.

770.1 Kinds of Sentences

The five basic kinds of sentences are *declarative, interrogative, imperative, exclamatory,* and *conditional.*

- **Declarative sentences** make statements. They tell us something about a person, a place, a thing, or an idea. Although declarative sentences make up the bulk of most academic writing, there are overwhelmingly diverse ways in which to express them.

    The Statue of Liberty stands in New York Harbor.
    For over a century, it has greeted immigrants and visitors to America.

- **Interrogative sentences** ask questions.

    Did you know that the Statue of Liberty is made of copper and stands more than 150 feet tall?
    Are we allowed to climb all the way to the top?

- **Imperative sentences** make commands.

    Stanley, please purchase a ticket.

    They often contain an understood subject *(you)* as in the examples below.

    Go see the Statue of Liberty.
    After a few weeks of physical conditioning, climb its 168 stairs.

- **Exclamatory sentences** communicate strong emotion or surprise.

    Climbing 168 stairs is not a dumb idea!
    Just muster some of that old pioneering spirit, that desire to try something new, that never-say-die attitude that made America great!

- **Conditional sentences** express wishes ("if . . . then" statements) or conditions contrary to fact.

    If I could design a country's flag, I would use six colors behind a sun, a star, and a moon.
    I would feel as if I were representing many cultures in my design.

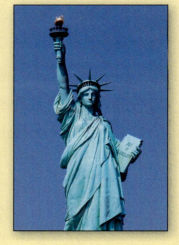

Grammar Practice

Kinds of Sentences

Write the kind of statement each sentence makes: *declarative, interrogative, imperative, exclamatory,* or *conditional.*

1. A superstition is an illogical belief that comes from fear or ignorance.

2. You should hear some of these unusual, old superstitions!

3. If you carry a hoe into the house, you should carry it out walking backward to avoid bad luck.

4. Always close a front door with your face toward it.

5. Do you believe that an apple a day keeps the doctor away?

6. Seeing a single crow is unlucky, but seeing two means good luck.

7. Have you heard that a dead beetle tied around the neck is a cure for whooping cough?

8. When eating a fish, start at the tail and work toward the head.

9. We are what we believe ourselves to be.

10. If you believe in superstition, it will always follow you.

Learning Language

An imperative sentence tells you to do something. Normally imperatives begin with a verb: ***Do** your homework.* Working with a partner, use imperatives to give each other commands. Have your partner follow your directions. Then trade places and follow your partner's directions.

772.1 Types of Sentence Constructions

A sentence may be *simple, compound, complex,* or *compound-complex.* It all depends on the relationship between independent and dependent clauses.

- A **simple sentence** can have a single subject or a compound subject. It can have a single predicate or a compound predicate. However, a simple sentence has only one independent clause, and it has no dependent clauses.

    My back aches.
    (single subject; single predicate)
    My teeth and my eyes hurt.
    (compound subject; single predicate)
    My throat and nose feel sore and look red.
    (compound subject; compound predicate)
    I must have caught the flu from the sick kids in class.
    (independent clause with two phrases: *from the sick kids* and *in class*)

- A **compound sentence** consists of two independent clauses. The clauses must be joined by a comma and a coordinating conjunction or by a semicolon.

    I usually don't mind missing school, but this is not fun.
    I feel too sick to watch TV; I feel too sick to eat.

Note: The comma can be omitted when the clauses are very short.

    I wept and I wept.

- A **complex sentence** contains one independent clause (in black) and one or more dependent clauses (in red).

    When I get back to school, I'm actually going to appreciate it.
    (dependent clause; independent clause)
    I won't even complain about math class, although I might be talking out of my head because I'm feverish.
    (independent clause; two dependent clauses)

- A **compound-complex sentence** contains two or more independent clauses (in black) and one or more dependent clauses (in red).

    Yes, I have a bad flu, and because I need to get well soon, I won't think about school just yet.
    (two independent clauses; one dependent clause)
    The best remedy for those who suffer with flu symptoms is plenty of rest and fluids, but the chicken soup that Grandma makes for me always helps, too.
    (two independent clauses; two dependent clauses)

Understanding Sentences

Grammar Practice

Types of Sentence Constructions

 Identify each of the following sentences as a *simple, compound, complex,* or *compound-complex* sentence.

1. The Tomb of the Unknowns is guarded 24 hours a day, 365 days a year, in all kinds of weather.

2. The Third United States Infantry is labeled "The Old Guard."

3. "The Old Guard" guards the tomb, and it follows strict rules.

4. Its procedure is precise.

5. A sentinel, man or woman, marches 21 paces past the tomb.

6. He makes a crisp 90-degree turn; he faces east for 21 seconds.

7. The sentinel makes another 90-degree turn, and then he faces north and stands for 21 seconds.

8. He quickly moves his rifle.

9. He places its barrel on his shoulder, facing away from the tomb, to show that he stands between the tomb and any threat.

10. After this procedure is completed, it is repeated, and this goes on 24 hours each day.

11. The Tomb of the Unknowns, located in Arlington National Cemetery, contains the remains of several unknown American soldiers.

12. The unknown soldiers were killed in both World Wars, the Korean War, and the Vietnam War.

Model

Model the following sentence to practice forming a compound sentence.

Windows rattled and floors shook; the sound was a giant hand shaking Lydia Kilkenny's sleeping shoulders.
—Myla Goldberg, *Wickett's Remedy*

774.1 Arrangements of Sentences

Depending on the arrangement of the words and the placement of emphasis, a sentence may also be classified as *loose, balanced, periodic,* or *cumulative.*

- A **loose sentence** expresses the main thought near the beginning and adds explanatory material as needed.

    We hauled out the boxes of food and set up the camp stove, all the time battling the hot wind that would not stop, even when we screamed into the sky.

    The earliest television shows were like radio with pictures—much more talking and fewer visual effects.

- A **balanced sentence** is constructed so that it emphasizes a similarity or a contrast between two or more of its parts (words, phrases, or clauses).

    The wind in our ears drove us crazy and pushed us on.
    (The similar wording emphasizes the main idea in this sentence.)

    Some people dislike contemporary art because they do not understand it; perhaps that is because they do not understand the point of contemporary art.

- A **periodic sentence** is one that postpones the crucial or most surprising idea until the end.

    Following my mother's repeated threats to ground me for life, I decided it was time to propose a compromise.

    A writer can do what most people cannot—tell absolute truths and absolute lies.

- A **cumulative sentence** places the general idea in the middle of the sentence with modifying clauses and phrases coming before and after.

    With careful thought and extra attention to detail, I wrote out my plan for being a model teenager, a teen who cared about neatness and reliability.

    After several months, Mark became more comfortable teaching English to Chinese students, especially when he began to learn Chinese.

Note: Writers often experiment with arrangement in order to have a variety of sentences in a particular piece of writing. Remember, however, that the arrangement of a sentence indicates the importance of the ideas within it. Don't rearrange sentences so much that your original emphasis is lost.

Grammar Practice

Arrangements of Sentences

Classify each of the following sentences as *loose, balanced, periodic,* or *cumulative*.

(1) Although she knew little about her ancestors, Soo Jin found genealogy intriguing. **(2)** Last summer, at a family reunion, she got a surprise. **(3)** A distant cousin presented her with her great-grandmother's diary, which was written in Korean. **(4)** Soo Jin was ecstatic, anticipating the family stories this book held.

(5) With great care, Soo Jin opened this heirloom from her ancestry, something she thought she would never do. **(6)** Until now, Soo Jin had not worried about learning Korean. **(7)** She hoped that someone at the reunion could read it, but she was disappointed. **(8)** She needed to find a translator, someone to unlock the diary's secrets.

(9) As it turned out, Mrs. Kim, a volunteer at the youth center, read Korean, and she helped Soo Jin. **(10)** Together, they enjoyed translating the diary.

Learning Language

Sentences can be formed in different ways. Read the following sentences with a partner. Look at the different parts. Where is the basic meaning found in each sentence?

- At home, Kiama learned how to cook, and it was easy.
- Most pets have simple needs—to be fed and to be loved.
- Do not keep secrets or tell secrets.

With a partner, take turns reading a sentence from the above passage. Take notes about the main part in each sentence.

Getting Sentence Parts to Agree

Agreement of Subject and Verb

A verb must agree in number (singular or plural) with its subject.

>The student was proud of her quarter grades.

Note: Do not be confused by words that come between the subject and verb.

>The manager, as well as the players, is required to display good sportsmanship. (*Manager*, not *players*, is the subject.)

776.1 Compound Subjects

Compound subjects joined by *or* or *nor* take a singular verb (when they are singular subjects).

>Neither Bev nor Kendra goes to the street dances.

Note: When one of the subjects joined by *or* or *nor* is singular and one is plural, the verb must agree with the subject nearer the verb.

>Neither Yoshi nor his friends sing in the band anymore. (The plural subject *friends* is nearer the verb, so the plural verb *sing* is correct.)

Compound subjects connected with *and* require a plural verb.

>Strength and balance are necessary for gymnastics.

776.2 Delayed Subjects

Delayed subjects occur when the verb comes before the subject in a sentence. In these inverted sentences, the delayed subject must agree with the verb.

>There are many hardworking students in our schools.
>There is present among many young people today a will to succeed.
>(*Students* and *will* are the true subjects of these sentences, not *there*.)

776.3 "Be" Verbs

When a sentence contains a form of the "be" verb—and a noun comes before and after that verb—the verb must agree with the subject, not the *complement* (the noun coming after the verb).

>The cause of his problem was the bad brakes.
>The bad brakes were the cause of his problem.

776.4 Special Cases

Some nouns that are **plural in form but singular in meaning** take a singular verb: *mumps, measles, news, mathematics, economics, gallows, shambles*.

>Measles is still considered a serious disease in many parts of the world.

Some nouns that are plural in form but singular in meaning take a plural verb: *scissors, trousers, tidings*.

>The scissors disappear whenever I need them.

ELPS 5D

Understanding Sentences

Grammar Practice

Agreement of Subject and Verb 1

 For each sentence, write the correct verb from the choice given in parentheses.

1. Neither the school board nor the superintendent *(have, has)* made a decision.
2. On our flight to Italy *(was, were)* several athletes from Team USA.
3. There *(is, are)* too many abandoned animals at the shelter.
4. Someone who adopts one of these animals *(saves, save)* it from an uncertain fate.
5. *(Is, Are)* you interested in adopting a shelter dog?
6. Dwayne or his sisters *(is, are)* going to college in Montana.
7. Great—there *(go, goes)* our train to Chicago!
8. *(Were, Was)* Nina's parents asking about the trip?
9. The Downtown Committee *(is, are)* planning a fall harvest fair.
10. Kandi, Robyn, or Lyndsay *(have, has)* a laptop you might borrow.
11. I can't understand why the soda machines *(are, is)* gone.
12. My dad, as well as his golf partner, *(was, were)* asked to play in the tournament.

Model

Model the following sentences to practice correct subject-verb agreement.

Her cheekbones were still high and strong, but the skin was parched and ruddy.
— Jeannette Walls, *The Glass Castle: A Memoir*

Blue jeans are the most beautiful things since the gondola.
—Diana Vreeland

Agreement of Subject and Verb (continued)

778.1 Collective Nouns

Collective nouns *(faculty, committee, team, congress, species, crowd, army, pair, squad)* take a singular verb when they refer to a group as a unit; collective nouns take a plural verb when they refer to the individuals within the group.

> The favored team is losing, and the crowd is getting ugly. (Both *team* and *crowd* are considered units in this sentence, requiring the singular verb *is*.)
>
> The pair reunite after 20 years apart.
> (Here, *pair* refers to two individuals, so the plural verb *reunite* is required.)

778.2 Indefinite Pronouns

Some **indefinite pronouns** are singular: *each, either, neither, one, everybody, another, anybody, everyone, nobody, everything, somebody,* and *someone*. They require a singular verb.

> Everybody is invited to the cafeteria for refreshments.

Some **indefinite pronouns** are plural: *both, few, many,* and *several*.

> Several like trail-mix bars. Many ask for frozen yogurt, too.

Some **indefinite pronouns** are singular or plural. (See page 246.)

Note: Do not be confused by words or phrases that come between the indefinite pronoun and the verb.

> One of the participants is (not *are*) going to have to stay late to clean up.

A Closer Look

Some **indefinite pronouns** can be either singular or plural: *all, any, most, none,* and *some*. These pronouns are singular if the number of the noun in the prepositional phrase is singular; they are plural if the noun is plural.

> Most of the food complaints are coming from the seniors.
> (*Complaints* is plural, so *most* is plural.)
>
> Most of the tabletop is sticky.
> (*Tabletop* is singular, so *most* is singular.)

778.3 Relative Pronouns

When a **relative pronoun** *(who, which, that)* is used as the subject of a clause, the number of the verb is determined by the antecedent of the pronoun. (The antecedent is the word to which the pronoun refers.)

> This is one of the books that are required for geography class.
> (The relative pronoun *that* requires the plural verb *are* because its antecedent, *books*, is plural.)

Note: To test this type of sentence for agreement, read the "of" phrase first.

> Of the books that are required for geography class, this is one.

Grammar Practice

Agreement of Subject and Verb 2

For each numbered sentence, write the correct verb from the choice given in parentheses.

(1) Imagine that you are a young person who *(live, lives)* in Florida during the first half of the twentieth century. **(2)** You are excited that one of your state's most famous athletes *(is, are)* Babe Didrikson. **(3)** Many girls your age *(credit, credits)* her as a role model. **(4)** Most of the local papers *(carry, carries)* stories about her versatile athletic abilities. **(5)** Because of Babe's basketball skills, her high school team *(play, plays)* in a women's national basketball championship. **(6)** Everyone *(is, are)* thrilled when she sets world records at the Olympics in the 80-yard dash and javelin throw.

(7) Babe's career *(don't, doesn't)* stop there. She pitches on a women's baseball team, and then she tries tennis. **(8)** This is one of the sports that *(is, are)* a problem for Babe. **(9)** The U.S. Lawn Tennis Association *(bar, bars)* her from the game because she plays too well. **(10)** By spring of 1934, Babe *(become, becomes)* famous as one of the top competitors on the professional golf circuit. **(11)** The Associated Press *(take, takes)* notice. **(12)** Its members *(vote, votes)* Babe Didrikson Zaharias the Top Woman Athlete of the Half Century (1900–1949).

Model

Model the following sentences to practice subject-verb agreement.

Everybody likes a compliment.
—Abraham Lincoln

Most of the luxuries and many of the so-called comforts of life are not only not indispensable, but positive hindrances to the elevation of mankind.
—Henry David Thoreau

ELPS 5D, 5E

Agreement of Pronoun and Antecedent

A pronoun must agree in number, person, and gender with its *antecedent*. (The *antecedent* is the word to which the pronoun refers.)

Cal brought **his** gerbil to school. (The antecedent of *his* is *Cal*. Both the pronoun and its antecedent are singular, third person, and masculine; therefore, the pronoun is said to "agree" with its antecedent.)

780.1 Agreement in Number

Use a **singular pronoun** to refer to such antecedents as *each, either, neither, one, anyone, anybody, everyone, everybody, somebody, another, nobody,* and *a person*.

Neither of the brothers likes **his** (not **their**) room.

Two or more singular antecedents joined by *or* or *nor* are also referred to by a **singular pronoun**.

Either **Connie** or **Sue** left **her** headset in the library.

If one of the antecedents joined by *or* or *nor* is singular and one is plural, the pronoun should agree with the nearer antecedent.

Neither the **manager** nor the **players** were crazy about **their** new uniforms.

Use a **plural pronoun** to refer to plural antecedents as well as compound subjects joined by *and*.

Jared and **Carlos** are finishing **their** assignments.

780.2 Agreement in Gender

Use a **masculine** or **feminine pronoun** depending upon the gender of the antecedent.

Tristan would like to bring **his** dog along on the trip.
Claire is always complaining that **her** feet are cold.

Use a **neuter** pronoun when the antecedent has no gender.

The ancient **weeping willow** is losing many of **its** branches.

When *a person* or *everyone* is used to refer to both sexes or either sex, you will have to choose whether to offer optional pronouns or rewrite the sentence.

A person should be allowed to choose **her** or **his** own footwear. (optional pronouns)

People should be allowed to choose **their** own footwear. (rewritten in plural form)

Understanding Sentences

Grammar Practice

Agreement of Pronoun and Antecedent

For each sentence, write the correct pronoun from the choice given in parentheses.

1. Leah and Abdul made plans to go to *(their, her)* senior prom.
2. Sidnie helped her brother fill out *(his, their)* income tax form.
3. Most of the wall had crayon marks all over *(it, them)*.
4. Each college-bound student should have received *(his or her, their)* application materials by now.
5. Francisco or Rory will babysit for *(their, his)* sister this Saturday night.
6. Chuck's new pants were too long, and he didn't know how to hem *(it, them)*.
7. Most of the team's shirts had commemorative patches on *(it, them)*.
8. Either Mr. Ramos or his son lost *(his, their)* drill at the work site.
9. My Princess Diana rosebush has black spots on *(its, her)* leaves.
10. I asked everyone to bring *(his or her, their)* ideas to the meeting.
11. Neither my motorcycle nor any bicycles had dents on *(it, them)* as a result of the hail.
12. Did anyone leave *(their, his or her)* cell phone at my house last night?

Model

Model the following sentences to practice pronoun-antecedent agreement.

> A good person will resist an evil system with his or her whole soul.
> —Mohandas Karamchand Gandhi

> Far away, there in the sunshine, are my highest aspirations. I may not reach them, but I can look up and see their beauty, believe in them, and try to follow where they lead.
> —Louisa May Alcott

Diagramming Sentences

A **graphic diagram** of a sentence is a picture of how the words in that sentence are related and how they fit together to form a complete thought.

782.1 Simple Sentence with One Subject and One Verb

Chris fishes.

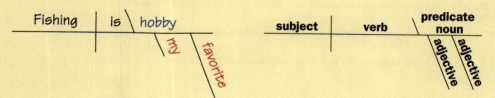

782.2 Simple Sentence with a Predicate Adjective

Fish are delicious.

782.3 Simple Sentence with a Predicate Noun and Adjectives

Fishing is my favorite hobby.

Note: When possessive pronouns *(my, his, their,* etc.) are used as adjectives, they are placed on a diagonal line under the word they modify.

782.4 Simple Sentence with an Indirect and Direct Object

My grandpa gave us a trout.

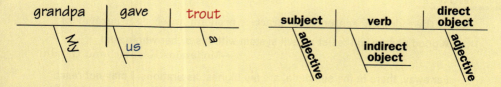

Note: Articles *(a, an, the)* are adjectives and are placed on a diagonal line under the word they modify.

Understanding Sentences 783

Grammar Practice

Sentence Diagramming 1

Diagram the following sentences.

1. Jerry MacDonald studies ancient fossils.
2. The New Mexico desert is his workplace.
3. His discoveries are incredible!
4. The Paleozoic Trackways Project was his best find.
5. Jerry dug.
6. He unearthed interesting tracks.
7. He showed some colleagues his discovery.
8. The tracks were prehistoric.
9. They gave us a new understanding.
10. Paleontology is exciting!

Half a truth is often a great lie. —Benjamin Franklin

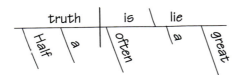

Model

Model the following proverbs to practice writing simple sentences with direct objects.

The early bird catches the worm.
The big thieves hang the little ones.

Diagramming Sentences (continued)

784.1 Simple Sentence with a Prepositional Phrase

I like fishing by myself.

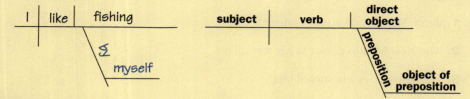

784.2 Simple Sentence with a Compound Subject and Verb

The team and fans clapped and cheered.

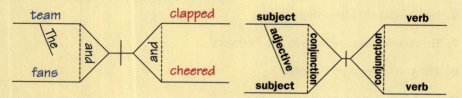

784.3 Compound Sentence

The team scored, and the crowd cheered wildly.

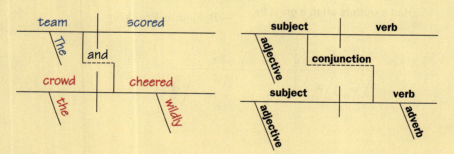

784.4 Complex Sentence with a Subordinate Clause

Before Erin scored, the crowd sat quietly.

Grammar Practice

Sentence Diagramming 2

 Diagram the following sentences.

1. Jamar completed the first leg of the triathlon.
2. Landon and his dad explored caves with a guide.
3. In our high school, the principal has the toughest job.
4. The guard on duty at the mall always wears a uniform.
5. I will be tired when I get home from the game.
6. Geeta and Melissa went to the sale and bought some shoes.
7. You can grow awesome flowers, but it takes a "green thumb."
8. Some students are unprepared and so do not have control over their futures.
9. Hector went for a swim in the lake.
10. Lauren laughed, but her dad frowned.

Art knows no limit, and the artists will never achieve perfection.
—Bente Borsum

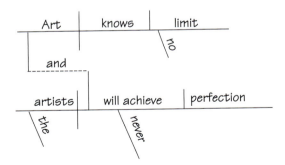

Model

Model the following sentences to practice writing compound and complex sentences.

If at first you don't succeed, you're running about average. —M. H. Alderson

I think, therefore I am. —Rene Descartes

Texas Essential Knowledge and Skills for English Language Arts

The English Language Arts and Reading TEKS specify the skills you need to master by the end of English IV. To help you understand what is required of you, we have provided a list of the skills you will practice and learn during this school year. The second column shows where these TEKS are addressed in this program.

TEKS 12.13 Writing/Writing Process

Students use elements of the writing process (planning, drafting, revising, editing, and publishing) to compose text. Students are expected to:

A	plan a first draft by selecting the correct genre for conveying the intended meaning to multiple audiences, determining appropriate topics through a range of strategies (e.g., discussion, background reading, personal interests, interviews), and developing a thesis or controlling idea	pages 2, 3, 9, 10, 14, 15, 17, 48–50, 61, 92–94, 138, 152, 153, 155, 158–161, 163, 164, 167, 202, 211, 218, 219, 223, 224, 226, 262, 271, 284, 288, 334–337, 339, 348, 349, 408, 482, 485, 526, 624, 626, 636, 637
B	structure ideas in a sustained and persuasive way (e.g., using outlines, note taking, graphic organizers, lists) and develop drafts in timed and open-ended situations that include transitions and the rhetorical devices to convey meaning	pages 9, 10, 17–19, 48–50, 60, 62, 64–66, 98, 100–103, 106, 139, 140, 153, 155, 161–163, 168, 170, 172, 173, 211–213, 218, 223, 230–233, 270–273, 280, 285, 288, 290, 291, 293, 294, 299, 302, 335, 337, 338, 341, 344–349, 352, 413, 424, 482, 491, 509, 526, 618–622, 625, 628–630, 634, 635
C	revise drafts to clarify meaning and achieve specific rhetorical purposes, consistency of tone, and logical organization by rearranging the words, sentences, and paragraphs to employ tropes (e.g., metaphors, similes, analogies, hyperbole, understatement, rhetorical questions, irony), schemes (e.g., parallelism, antithesis, inverted word order, repetition, reversed structures), and by adding transitional words and phrases	pages 9, 11, 20, 21, 23–25, 48–50, 108–114, 142, 143, 154, 175–184, 207, 214, 235–237, 244, 267, 274, 275, 302, 304, 340, 341, 353, 424, 428, 429, 486, 497, 509, 510
D	edit drafts for grammar, mechanics, and spelling	pages 9, 11, 26–27, 48–50, 122–126, 144, 145, 154, 185–190, 208, 214, 245–247, 249, 268, 280, 326, 340, 341, 353, 486, 491, 509, 510, 526, 638, 639 pages 3–14, 16, 18–27, 29–36, 39–41, 43, 44, 47, 48, 51–56, 65, 66
E	revise final draft in response to feedback from peers and teacher and publish written work for appropriate audiences	pages 9, 22, 23, 28, 48–50, 116–120, 128–133, 191, 251, 268, 311, 326, 437, 438

*Page References in *Student Edition*
*Page References in *SkillsBook*

TEKS 12.14 Writing/Literary Texts

Students write literary texts to express their ideas and feelings about real or imagined people, events, and ideas. Students are responsible for at least two forms of literary writing. Students are expected to:

A	write an engaging story with a well-developed conflict and resolution, a clear theme, complex and non-stereotypical characters, a range of literary strategies (e.g., dialogue, suspense), devices to enhance the plot, and sensory details that define the mood or tone	pages 136–143, 146, 147, 150–154, 343–354, 598, 622
B	write a poem that reflects an awareness of poetic conventions and traditions within different forms (e.g., sonnets, ballads, free verse)	pages 368–379
C	write a script with an explicit or implicit theme, using a variety of literary techniques	pages 356–366, 494–496

TEKS 12.15 Writing/Expository and Procedural Texts

Students write expository and procedural or work-related texts to communicate ideas and information to specific audiences for specific purposes. Students are expected to:

A	write an analytical essay of sufficient length that includes: (i) effective introductory and concluding paragraphs and a variety of sentence structures (ii) rhetorical devices, and transitions between paragraphs (iii) a clear thesis statement or controlling idea (iv) a clear organizational schema for conveying ideas (v) relevant and substantial evidence and well-chosen details (vi) information on all relevant perspectives and consideration of the validity, reliability, and relevance of primary and secondary sources (vii) an analysis of views and information that contradict the thesis statement and the evidence presented for it	pages 54–56, 61, 63, 66, 158–181, 184, 185, 188, 200–201, 203–207, 232, 299, 300, 482–486, 491, 492, 522–525, 580, 582, 618–620, 627–631, 634, 635
B	write procedural and work-related documents (e.g., résumés, proposals, college applications, operation manuals) that include: (i) a clearly stated purpose combined with a well-supported viewpoint on the topic (ii) appropriate formatting structures (e.g., headings, graphics, white space) (iii) relevant questions that engage readers and address their potential problems and misunderstandings (iv) accurate technical information in accessible language (v) appropriate organizational structures supported by facts and details (documented if appropriate)	pages 487–489, 544–555, 621

*Page References in *Student Edition*
*Page References in *SkillsBook*

C	write an interpretation of an expository or a literary text that: (i) advances a clear thesis statement (ii) addresses the writing skills for an analytical essay including references to and commentary on quotations from the text (iii) analyzes the aesthetic effects of an author's use of stylistic or rhetorical devices (iv) identifies and analyzes ambiguities, nuances, and complexities within the text (v) anticipates and responds to readers' questions and contradictory information	pages 279–282, 286, 287, 291–294, 296–301, 303, 318, 320–325, 328–332, 592
D	produce a multimedia presentation (e.g., documentary, class newspaper, docudrama, infomercial, visual or textual parodies, theatrical production) with graphics, images, and sound that appeals to a specific audience and synthesizes information from multiple points of view	pages 470–473, 490, 498, 499, 535–538

⭐ TEKS 12.16 Writing/Persuasive Texts

Students write persuasive texts to influence the attitudes or actions of a specific audience on specific issues. Students are expected to write an argumentative essay (e.g., evaluative essays, proposals) to the appropriate audience that includes:

A	a clear thesis or position based on logical reasons with various forms of support (e.g., hard evidence, reason, common sense, cultural assumptions)	pages 14, 17–19, 220–223, 226, 229, 236, 237, 244, 260, 264, 272, 273, 514, 517, 586, 588
B	accurate and honest representation of divergent views (i.e., in the author's own words and not out of context)	pages 19, 221–223, 227, 229, 230, 233, 244, 261, 264, 272, 273, 514, 517, 586, 588
C	an organizing structure appropriate to the purpose, audience, and context	pages 14, 17–19, 221–223, 228–234, 238, 239, 244, 248, 265, 272, 273, 514, 517, 586, 590
D	information on the complete range of relevant perspectives	pages 14, 15, 220, 227, 229, 244, 263, 514, 586
E	demonstrated consideration of the validity and reliability of all primary and secondary sources used	pages 16, 221–225, 260, 261, 263, 514, 517
F	language attentively crafted to move a disinterested or opposed audience, using specific rhetorical devices to back up assertions (e.g., appeals to logic, emotions, ethical beliefs)	pages 14, 25, 240–243, 261, 266, 267, 272, 273, 517
G	an awareness and anticipation of audience response that is reflected in different levels of formality, style, and tone	pages 24, 25, 227, 242–244, 261, 266, 267, 517

*Page References in *Student Edition*
*Page References in *SkillsBook*

Texas Essential Knowledge and Skills

TEKS 12.17 Oral and Written Conventions/Conventions

Students understand the function of and use the conventions of academic language when speaking and writing. Students will continue to apply earlier standards with greater complexity. Students are expected to:

A	use and understand the function of different types of clauses and phrases (e.g., adjectival, noun, adverbial clauses and phrases)	pages 144, 186, 247, 306, 307, 310, 432, 433, 436, 766–769 pages 121–132, 212–213
B	use a variety of correctly structured sentences (e.g., compound, complex, compound-complex)	pages 86, 187, 248, 250, 308, 310, 434, 436, 517, 638, 770–775 pages 118, 119, 133–139, 149–156, 181–184, 211, 214, 217, 220, 221, 223

TEKS 12.18 Oral and Written Conventions/Handwriting, Capitalization, and Punctuation

Students write legibly and use appropriate capitalization and punctuation conventions in their compositions. Students are expected to:

A	correctly and consistently use conventions of punctuation and capitalization	pages 85, 249, 250, 305, 309, 310, 431, 638, 639, 641–685 pages 3–44, 65, 66, 187–194, 198

TEKS 12.19 Oral and Written Conventions/Spelling

Students spell correctly. Students are expected to:

A	spell correctly, including using various resources to determine and check correct spellings	pages 84, 250, 305, 310, 431, 435, 436, 638, 639, 696–701 pages 47, 48, 51–56, 65, 66, 195, 200, 201

TEKS 12.20 Research/Research Plan

Students ask open-ended research questions and develop a plan for answering them. Students are expected to:

A	brainstorm, consult with others, decide upon a topic, and formulate a major research question to address the major research topic	pages 92–94, 195, 200, 201, 401, 402, 500, 530
B	formulate a plan for engaging in in-depth research on a complex, multi-faceted topic	pages 95, 401, 500

*Page References in *Student Edition*
*Page References in *SkillsBook*

TEKS 12.21 Research/Gathering Sources

Students determine, locate, and explore the full range of relevant sources addressing a research question and systematically record the information they gather. Students are expected to:

A	follow the research plan to gather evidence from experts on the topic and texts written for informed audiences in the field, distinguishing between reliable and unreliable sources and avoiding over-reliance on one source	pages 95, 382–390, 440, 441, 443, 446, 500, 502, 503
B	systematically organize relevant and accurate information to support central ideas, concepts, and themes, outline ideas into conceptual maps/timelines, and separate factual data from complex inferences	pages 100–104, 106, 404, 408, 413, 500, 503, 504, 510, 534
C	paraphrase, summarize, quote, and accurately cite all researched information according to a standard format (e.g., author, title, page number), differentiating among primary, secondary, and other sources	pages 105, 382, 401, 405–407, 419, 444–446, 448–460, 501–503, 505, 530, 531, 534

TEKS 12.22 Research/Synthesizing Information

Students clarify research questions and evaluate and synthesize collected information. Students are expected to:

A	modify the major research question as necessary to refocus the research plan	pages 403, 409, 422, 440, 530, 534
B	differentiate between theories and the evidence that supports them and determine whether the evidence found is weak or strong and how that evidence helps create a cogent argument	pages 410, 423, 501, 502, 510, 530, 534
C	critique the research process at each step to implement changes as the need occurs and is identified	pages 409, 440, 441, 443, 446, 530, 534

*Page References in *Student Edition*
*Page References in *SkillsBook*

TEKS 12.23 Research/Organizing and Presenting Ideas

Students organize and present their ideas and information according to the purpose of the research and their audience. Students are expected to synthesize the research into an extended written or oral presentation that:

A	provides an analysis that supports and develops personal opinions, as opposed to simply restating existing information	pages 415–418, 426, 427, 463–469, 604
B	uses a variety of formats and rhetorical strategies to argue for the thesis	pages 411, 415–418, 424, 425, 463–469, 509, 531
C	develops an argument that incorporates the complexities of and discrepancies in information from multiple sources and perspectives while anticipating and refuting counter-arguments	pages 412, 507, 530, 534
D	uses a style manual (e.g., *Modern Language Association*, *Chicago Manual of Style*) to document sources and format written materials	pages 392, 393, 400, 407, 415, 417, 419, 431, 436, 448–460, 501–503, 506, 508, 510, 531, 533, 534
E	is of sufficient length and complexity to address the topic	pages 420, 467–469, 500, 508, 530

*Page References in *Student Edition*
*Page References in *SkillsBook*

English Language Proficiency Standards

The English Language Proficiency Standards (ELPS) outline expectations for students who are learning English. The chart below, which contains a selected list of the ELPS, includes descriptions of activities and interactions that will help you develop your knowledge of English. The second column shows where these skills are specifically addressed in this program.

ELPS 2 Cross-curricular second language acquisition/listening

The student is expected to:

D	monitor understanding of spoken language during classroom instruction and interactions and seek clarification as needed	pages 54, 78, 116, 119, 176, 476, 478–480, 558, 560, 566, 567, 573, 581, 587, 597

ELPS 3 Cross-curricular second language acquisition/speaking

The student is expected to:

A	practice producing sounds of newly acquired vocabulary such as long and short vowels, silent letters, and consonant clusters to pronounce English words in a manner that is increasingly comprehensible	pages 566, 569, 573, 575, 581, 582, 587, 593, 599, 600, 605, 606, 709, 711, 713, 723, 725, 727
G	express opinions, ideas, and feelings ranging from communicating single words and short phrases to participating in extended discussions on a variety of social and grade-appropriate academic topics	pages 6, 8, 11, 12, 22, 53, 56, 61, 101, 103, 110, 114, 166, 176, 278, 559, 560, 569, 571, 575, 578–580, 582, 584–586, 588, 591, 592, 597, 600–604, 606, 608, 609
H	narrate, describe, and explain with increasing specificity and detail as more English is acquired	pages 22, 54, 68, 176, 467, 468, 559, 569, 574, 578, 579, 582, 584, 585, 588, 591, 592, 594, 597, 598, 600–603, 609, 745, 755

ELPS 4 Cross-curricular second language acquisition/reading

The student is expected to:

C	develop basic sight vocabulary, derive meaning of environmental print, and comprehend English vocabulary and language structures used routinely in written classroom materials	pages 6, 46, 48, 50, 134, 156, 176, 180, 182–184, 186, 187, 216, 247, 276, 308, 342, 344, 349, 354, 359, 360, 374, 375, 380, 474, 520, 528, 556, 562, 564–566, 568, 569, 572, 573, 575, 576, 579, 581, 587, 588, 593, 595, 598–601, 605–607, 610, 632–637, 640, 708–727, 751

*Page References in *Student Edition*
*Page References in *SkillsBook*

English Language Proficiency Standards

ELPS 5 Cross-curricular second language acquisition/writing

The student is expected to:

B write using newly acquired basic vocabulary and content-based grade-level vocabulary

pages 66, 156, 172, 182–184, 216, 232, 276, 299, 306, 342, 380, 471, 474, 556, 566, 569, 573, 575, 581, 587, 593, 599, 605, 610, 629, 630, 640, 708, 710, 712–724, 726

G narrate, describe, and explain with increasing specificity and detail to fulfill content area writing needs as more English is acquired.

pages 35, 49, 62, 66, 93, 140, 169–174, 205, 207, 215, 229–231, 233, 234, 273, 275, 279, 286, 290–294, 302, 304, 324, 330, 331, 341, 351–352, 415–418, 424, 471, 485, 487, 489, 491, 492, 512, 522, 525, 539, 550–551, 569, 573–575, 581, 599, 605, 614–617

*Page References in *Student Edition*
*Page References in *SkillsBook*

Credits

Text:

P. 563: Copyright © 2010 by Houghton Mifflin Harcourt Publishing Company. Adapted and reproduced by permission from *The American Heritage College Dictionary,* Fourth Edition.

Photos:

P. 2 Element; **3, 584** ©Image Source Pink/Alamy; **4, 35, 133, 360, 376, 404, 462, 470, 482, 487, 518, 528** (bottom), **541, 551, 560** (left), **608, 631, 663, 679, 694** (top), **716** (bottom), **733, 737, 739, 764, 780** (right) ©Photodisc/Getty Images; **20, 24, 26, 32, 526, 723, 727, 731, 780** (left) ©Photos.com/Jupiter Images; **96** HRW Photo; **104, 141, 169, 229, 289, 375** (top), **414, 448, 479, 484, 492, 613** (top), **655, 665, 669, 681, 711, 716** (top), **729, 743, 752, 771** (bottom), **773** ©Corbis; **108** ©Todd Davison/Getty Images; **112** ©Jose Luis Pelaez, Inc./Getty Images; **114** ©image 100/Corbis; **endsheet, 118, 651,** ©Ablestock.com/Jupiter Images; **125** ©Vladimir Wrange/Alamy; **137** ©Blend Images/Getty Images; **151** (left) ©Artville/Getty Images; **151** (right) ©James Woodson/Digital Vision/Getty Images; **159** ©Jacobs Stock Photography/Getty Images; **163, 223, 283, 401** ©Rubberball/SuperStock; **175, 235, 295, 421, 596** ©Stockbyte/Getty Images; **185, 245, 305, 431** Digital Studios; **191** ©Thomas Northcut/Getty Images; **234, 374** (top), **671, 724** ©SuperStock RF/SuperStock; **262, 373** ©BananaStock/AGE Fotostock; **272, 528** (top) ©Digital Vision/Getty Images; **284** ©Wire Design/Getty Images; **308** ©Steve Gorton/Getty Images; **311** ©Blue Jean Images/Getty Images; **347** ©Caspar Benson/Getty Images; **374** (bottom) ©2007 Ron Chapple Stock/Cutcaster.com; **375** (bottom) ©Paul Katz/Getty Images; **378** (top) Tim Fuller/Harcourt; **378** (bottom) ©2010 JupiterImages Corporation; **402** ©Cutcaster.com/Ritu Jethani; **438** ©Steven Nudson/Alamy; **451** Harcourt; **742** (right) ©Brand X Pictures/Getty Images; **491** ©ArtBox Images/Getty Images; **524, 647, 709** ©Alamy; **532** ©Jupiter; **540** ©VStock/Alamy; **559** John Langford/HRW Photo; **560** (right) ©Inspirestock/Getty Images; **578** ©Somos/Veer/Getty Images; **590** ©Nancy Ney/Photodisc/Getty Images; **602** ©Jupiterimages/Brand X Pictures/Getty Images; **613** (bottom) ©Alexey Stiop/Alamy; **622** ©1bestofphoto/Alamy; **627** Courtesy of NASA; **643** ©Robert McGouey/Alamy; **649** ©Mark S/Cutcaster.com; **671** ©Superstock; **673** ©Yevgen Timashov/Alamy; **674** ©Deddeda/Design Pics/Corbis; **690, 712** HMH Collection; **694** (bottom) ©Leabrooks Photography/Alamy; **696** ©Southern Stock/Getty Images; **697, 742** (left, middle) ©Comstock/Getty Images; **714** ©ColorBlind Images/Getty Images; **719** ©Tanya Constantine/Getty Images; **728** ©imagebroker/Alamy; **741** ©David Sacks/Getty Images; **749** ©Hu Zhao/Alamy; **767** ©Getty Images; **768** ©Paul Radenfeld/Getty Images; **769** ©Dex Image/Alamy; **770** ©Image DJ/Alamy; **771** (top) ©LeighSmithImages/Alamy; **775** ©WizData,inc./Alamy; **777** ©JUPITERIMAGES/Thinkstock/Alamy.

Index

The index will help you find specific information in this book. Entries in italics are from the "Using the Right Word" section. The colored boxes will contain information you will use often.

A

abbreviations, 692–693
  acronyms, 694.1, 694.3
  capitalization, 684.4
  correspondence, 692.2
  formal and informal, 692.1
  initialisms, 694.2–694.3
  punctuation, 641.2
  works cited section, 451
absolute phrase, 768
abstract nouns, 729.4
academic language, 48–49, 57–58, 81, 354, 374–375, 566, 632–637
accept/except, 708
acronyms, 694.1, 694.3
action, 140
action verbs, 742.1
active voice, 188, 748.2
adapt/adopt, 708
address
  correspondence, 547, 650.2, 692.2
  direct, 652.4
adjectives
  clauses, 247, 768.2
  comparative, 754.2
  compound, 658.3
  defined, 728.4, 754–755
  effective use of, 82
  equal, 644.2
  forms of, 754.2
  participles as, 752.3
  phrases, 144, 758.1
  positive, 754.2
  predicate, 754.1, 782.2–782.3
  prepositional phrase as, 758.1
  problems, 82
  proper, 680.1, 754.1
  punctuation, 644.2
  superlative, 754.2
  types of, 754.1

adverbs, 756–759
  clauses, 306, 768.2
  comparative, 756.2
  conjunctive, 650.6, 654.2
  defined, 728.5, 756–757
  forms of, 756.2
  infinitive phrase as, 766.1
  irregular forms, 756.2
  -ly endings, 756.1
  phrases, 307, 758.1, 766.1, 768.2
  positive, 756.2
  prepositional phrase as, 307, 758.1, 768.2
  superlative, 756.2
  types of, 756.1
affect/effect, 708
afterword, citing, 453
agenda, business, 554–555
agreement, 776–781
  "be" verbs, 776.3
  collective nouns, 778.1
  compound subjects, 776.1
  delayed subjects, 776.2
  indefinite pronouns, 778.2
  pronoun-antecedent, 125, 732, 780–781
  relative pronouns, 778.3
  special cases, 776.4
  subject-verb, 124, 246, 744, 776–779
aisle/isle, 708
alliteration, 372, 374
all right, 708
allusion, 634
allusion/illusion, 708
almanac, 389
a lot, 708
already/all ready, 708
altogether/all together, 710
American Psychological Association, *see* APA.
among/between, 710

amount, expressing, 664.3
amount/number, 710
analogy, 634
analysis, 6, 103, 410–411, 426–427, 528, *see also specific topics.*
analytical voice, 303
anapestic rhythm, 375
anecdotes, 57, 153, 225, 243, 634, 636
annual/biannual, 710
anonymous works, citing, 449, 452–453, 459
antagonist, 354
antecedent-pronoun agreement, 125, 732, 780–781
anthologies, citing, 452, 459
anticipator modifiers, 88
antonyms, books of, 564
anyway, 710
APA citations, 447–450, 459–460
apostrophes, 662–665
  in contractions, 662.1
  errors in, 125
  to express time or amount, 664.3
  to form certain plurals, 664.4
  to form plural possessives, 662.3
  to form singular possessives, 662.2
  plurals for words as words, 688.3
  to show possession, 126, 662.4, 664.1–664.2
application letter, 546
applied sciences, writing in the, 521–528
appositive phrases, 766.1
appositives, 646.1

argumentative essay, 217–258
  cogent arguments, 410
  drafting, 103, 229–234
  editing, 245–250
  evaluating, 252–257
  goals, 220
  prewriting, 223–228
  publishing, 251
  reflecting on writing, 258
  revising, 235–244, 251
  statistical argument, math, 514–517
argument/counter-argument chart, 263
articles
  citing, 455–457, 459–460
  math summary, 512–513
arts, writing in the, 529–542
  performance review, 539–540
  prompts, response to, 541–542
  research reports, 530–538
ascent/assent, 710
as/like, 718
assessment, 31, 34–45, 403, 409, *see also* evaluating; peer response; prompts, response to.
assonance, 372, 374
atlas, 389
audio/audio recordings, 385, 458, 536–537
audio play, 364–366
authors of works, 386, 390, 448–453, 458–460
autobiography, 636
auxiliary verbs, 740.2

B

background, 141, 287, 576, 582, 588, 594, 600, 606
bad/badly, 710
balance, 632
balanced sentence, 774.1
base/bass, 710
Basics of Life list, 93

beginnings, writing, *see also* drafting; introductions; *specific steps in writing process.*
  applied science, 523, 525, 527
  arts, 531, 540
  big picture, 60, 100
  creating great, 627
  creative writing, 345, 351, 356, 361, 366
  defined, 624
  expository, 161, 170–171, 200, 205, 212, 328, 331, 580
  math, 515
  narrative, 136, 140, 150, 153, 574
  one writer's process, 13–32
  persuasive, 219, 221, 230–231, 260, 265, 272, 586
  research reports, 393, 415, 440, 604
  response to literature, 281, 290–292, 320, 324, 328, 331, 338, 592
  science, 483, 485, 488, 492
  social studies, 496, 505
  workplace writing, 549, 551
beside/besides, 710
between/among, 710
"be" verbs, 740.1–740.2, 776.3
biannual/annual/biennial, 710
big picture, 60, 90, 100, 140, 170, 230, 290
biography, 636
board/bored, 712
bodies of water, capitalization, 680
body, writing, *see also* middles, writing.
  business letter, 544–546
  defined, 612
  descriptive, 615
  expository, 616
  narrative, 614
  oral presentations, 463
  organizational patterns, 618–622
  persuasive, 617
  research reports, 463
  as writing term, 632

body language, 468
body sentences, 159, 219, 279, 612–613
books
  book review, 636
  citing, 407, 419, 448–453, 459, 533
  indexes, 388
  in libraries, 385
  parts of, 387
  reference books, 385, 388–390
  titles, 668.3, 682.6
borrow/lend, 718
brackets, 678.1–678.3
brainstorming, 632
brake/break, 712
break, sudden, 674.1
bring/take, 712
brochures, citing, 452
buildings, capitalization, 680
business agenda, 554–555
business letters, 544–547

call numbers, 386–387
call to action, 106
can/may, 712
capital/capitol, 712
capitalization, 189, 680–685
  abbreviations, 684.4
  certain religious words, 682.5
  first words, 682.1
  geographic directions, 189
  historical periods and events, 189
  letters, 684.2
  organizations, 684.3
  proper adjectives, 680.1
  proper nouns, 680.1, 684.1
  sections of the country, 682.4
  sentences following colons, 682.3
  sentences in parentheses, 682.2
  titles, 189, 682.6, 684.5
  words used as names, 684.1
card catalog, 386

career review essay, 524–525
cartoons, citing, 458
case
  of nouns, 730.3
  of pronouns, 186, 738.1
cause-effect organization, 63, 66, 411, 482, 620, 636
cause-effect writing, 482–486, 636
central idea, 632, *see also* themes.
cent/sent/scent, 712
cereal/serial, 712
characters, 348, 351, 354, 359–360
character sketch, 636
charts. *See* **graphic organizers**
checklist, constructive criticism, 120
checklist, editing
  creative writing, 353, 363, 366
  expository, 190, 208, 214
  narrative, 145
  persuasive, 250, 268, 274
  research reports, 436
  response to literature, 310, 326, 332, 340
  in writing process, 26–27
checklist, practice presenting, 467
checklist, punctuation, 85
checklist, revising
  arts, 534, 538
  creative writing, 353, 363, 366
  expository, 178, 184, 207
  math, 517
  narrative, 143, 154
  persuasive, 244, 267
  research reports, 430
  response to literature, 304, 325
  science, 486
  in writing process, 111
checklist, thesis, 626
checklist, traits 50
choice, showing, 672.3

chord/cord, 712
chose/choose, 712
chronological order, 63, 66, 411
cinquains (quintet), 378–379
cite/site/sight, 724
cities, capitalization of, 680
citing sources, 407, 419, 447–460
  APA guidelines, 447–450, 459–460
  arts, 533
  authors of works, 386, 390
  books, 407, 419, 448–453, 459
  Internet, 407, 419, 456–457, 533
  in-text, 448–450
  MLA guidelines, 400, 419, 451–458
  plagiarism, 105, 406, 441–443
  works-cited section, 400, 419, 451–458, 508, 533
clarity, 424, 630, 652.5, 678.1
classes
  of nouns, 729
  of pronouns, 732.1
  of verbs, 740–743
classification, 604, 618
classification essay, 528
clauses, 768–769
  adjective, 247, 768.2
  adverb, 306, 768.2
  dependent, 768.1–768.2
  independent, 308–309, 644.1, 654.1, 760.1, 768.1
  introductory, 646.3
  nonrestrictive, 124, 648.2
  noun, 432, 768.2
  punctuation, 644.1, 648.2
  restrictive, 648.2
  subordinate, 247, 308, 768.1, 784.4
  "who" clauses, 126
climax, 139, 342, 344–345, 352, 354
climax organizational pattern, 622

closing, business letter, 544–546
closing sentences, *see also* endings, writing.
  big picture, 60
  defined, 612–613
  descriptive writing, 615
  expository, 159, 170, 616
  narrative, 614
  organizational patterns, 618–622
  persuasive, 219, 230, 617
  response to literature, 279, 290
  as writing term, 632
cluster diagrams, 92, 211, 271
coarse/course, 714
coherence, 237, 572, 628, 632, *see also* focus and coherence (trait).
collective nouns, 688.6, 729.5, 778.1
college entrance essay, 149–155
colloquialisms, 79, 634
colons, 656–657
  after a salutation, 656.1
  for emphasis, 656.3
  to introduce a list, 656.5
  to introduce a quotation, 656.4
  between numerals indicating time, 656.2
  between titles and subtitles, 656.6
comic strips, citing, 458
commas, 644–653
  after introductory clauses/phrases, 646.3
  for clarity or emphasis, 652.5
  in direct address, 652.4
  to enclose parenthetical elements, 648.1
  to enclose titles or initials, 650.4
  following conjunctive adverbs, 650.6
  following transitional phrases, 650.6
  introductory words, phrases, clauses, 249

nonrestrictive phrases/ clauses, 648.2
in numbers, 650.3
problems, 89, 124–125
to separate adjectives, 644.2
to separate contrasted elements, 644.3
to separate independent clauses, 644.1
to separate items in a series, 646.2
to set off appositives, 646.1
to set off dates, 650.1
to set off dialogue, 652.1
to set off interjections, 652.2
to set off interruptions, 652.3
to set off items in addresses, 650.2
before tags, 650.5
"who" clauses, 126
comma splices, 89, 124
common ground, 167, 172
community publishing, 129
comparative adjectives, 754.2
comparative adverbs, 756.2
comparative suffixes, 754.2, 756.2
comparison, 58, 619, 629
comparison-contrast, 61, 63, 66, 75, 520, 528, 619
complement/compliment, 714
completeness, 54
complete predicates, 764.1
complete subjects, 762.1
complexity, 412, 506–507, 530, 534
complex sentences, 308, 772.1
complications, plot, 139, 592
complimentary closing, 544–546
compound adjectives, 658.3
compound-complex sentences, 308, 434, 772.1
compound nouns, 664.2, 686.6
compound predicates, 764
compound pronouns, 732
compound sentences, 124, 308, 434, 772.1

compound subjects, 246, 762.1, 776.1
compound words, 658.1
computer catalog, library, 386
computers, in libraries, 385
concept map, 504
concessions, opposing viewpoint chart, 264
conclusions, *see also* endings, writing.
creative writing, 361, 366
expository, 170, 174, 331
focused, 56
forming, 106
parts of an essay, 624
persuasive, 234, 238, 265
in plot line, 139, 592
research reports, 418, 463
response to literature, 290, 294, 324, 331
science, 485
transition words, 630
concrete nouns, 729.3
conditional sentences, 770.1
conflict, 139, 351–352, 354, 359, 592
confusion, and hyphens, 660.4
conjunctions, 760–761
coordinating, 760.1
correlative, 760.2
defined, 728.7
subordinating, 306, 760.3
conjunctive adverbs, 650.6, 654.2
connotation, 182
consonance, 374
constructive criticism, 116–117, 119–120, *see also* holistic scoring guide; peer response.
continents, capitalization, 680
continual/continuous, 714
continuous tense, 748.1
contractions, 428, 662.1
contradictory evidence and ideas, 169, 200–201, 206–207, 298, 485
contrast, 630

contrasted elements, 644.3
controlling ideas, 152. *See also* thesis statements
controversy, 156, 165, *see also* argumentative essay.
controversy chart/map, 158, 164
conventions (trait), 83–89, *see also* editing.
arts, 534, 538
checking, 11, 26–27, 49–50
creative writing, 353, 363, 366
described, 48–50
expository, 160, 190, 208, 214
holistic scoring, 37
learning language, 572
math, 517
narrative, 144–145, 154
peer response, 119
persuasive, 14, 220, 246–250, 268, 274
research reports, 430, 432–436, 473
response to literature, 280, 306–310, 326, 332, 340
science, 486
social studies, 497, 510
conventions, poetic, 371–372, 374–375
convey, as term, 556
correction marks, 639
correlative conjunctions, 760.2
correspondence
address, 547, 650.2, 692.2
business letters, 544–547
e-mail, 457
counsel/council, 714
counter-arguments, 216, 412, 506–507, 530, 534
countering objections, 227
counterpoints, 73
country, capitalization, 680, 682.4
couplets, 368
courses, capitalization, 684.5
cover sheet, portfolio, 132

creative writing, 342–379
  audio play, 364–366
  defined, 598
  drafting, 351–352, 361–362, 366, 371–372, 377, 379
  editing, 353, 363, 366, 373, 377, 379
  graphic organizers, 344, 349, 359–360, 362
  language of, 598–603
  oral language, 602–603
  organizational patterns, 598
  playwriting, 355–366
  plot, 344–347
  poetry, 367–379
  prewriting, 348–350, 359–360, 364, 370, 377, 379
  publishing, 363, 366, 373
  reading the model, 600–601
  revising, 353, 363, 366, 373, 377, 379
  stories, 343–354
  and traits, 353, 363, 366, 373
  vocabulary (key words), 599
crisis, 344, 352
criteria, 474
criticism, *see* holistic scoring.
criticism, constructive, 116–117, 119, *see also* holistic scoring guide; peer response.
critics, 412
critique of research process, 409
cross-curricular writing, 474
cumulative sentences, 87, 774.1
curriculum, writing across, *see* cross-curricular writing.
cycle (process) diagram, 65

D

dactylic rhythm, 375
dash, 674–676
  for emphasis, 674.5
  to indicate a sudden break, 674.1
  to indicate interrupted speech, 674.4
  to set off an introductory series, 674.2
  to set off parenthetical material, 674.3
dates, 2, 650.1
debate, 216
decimal points, period as, 641.3
declarative sentences, 770.1
deductive organizational patterns, 411
deductive writing, 62
definition diagram, 65
definition essay, 520
definitions
  as detail, 58
  dictionary, 562–563
degree, adverbs to show, 756.1
delayed subjects, 762.2, 776.2
demonstrative pronouns, 732.1, 734.6
denotation, 183
dependent clause, 768.1–768.2
depth, 114
descriptive writing, 69, 71–72, 102–103, 615, 636
desert/dessert, 714
design, effective, 28, 133
details
  action, 140
  anecdotes, 57, 153, 225, 243, 634, 636
  comparison, 58, 619, 629
  definitions, 58
  dialogue, 72, 78, 140, 349, 604, 632, 652.1
  examples, 57, 73, 180
  facts, 57, 73, 153, 180, 225
  levels of, 104
  point-counterpoint, 73
  to present ideas, 72–73, 181
  quotes, *see* quotations.
  reasons, 58, 73, 226
  sensory, 140
  statistics, 57, 153, 180, 225
  unnecessary, 177

details, gathering
  creative writing, 370
  expository, 166, 206
  narrative, 152
  prewriting, 10, 16
  supporting, 57–58, 287, 410, 426, 633
  thoughts, 68, 94, 96, 349, 471
developing ideas, *see* ideas, development of (trait).
Dewey decimal system, 387
diagonals, 672, 672.3–672.4
diagramming sentences, 782–785
diagrams, *see* graphic organizers.
dialogue, 72, 78, 140, 349, 495, 604, 632, 652.1
diction, 79
dictionaries, 389, 435, 562–564
die/dye, 714
different from/different than, 714
digital slides (power presentations), 470, 473
direct address, 652.4
directions, writing, 487–490
direct objects, 730.3, 738.1, 742.2, 764.1, 782.4
directories, 389
direct questions, 642.1
direct quotations, 666.1, 682.1
discussion group, citing, 457
distinguish, as term, 380
divergent views, 300
docudramas, 470–471
documentaries, 470–471
documenting research, 447–460

drafting, 99–106
  in action, 10, 570
  applied sciences, 522, 524
  arts, 530, 539
  beginnings, 101
  big picture, 100
  creative writing, 351–352, 361–362, 366, 371–372, 377, 379
  defined, 568

endings, 106
expository, 169–174, 205–206, 212–213
first draft, 18–19, 99–106
keys to effective, 169, 229, 289, 414
math, 512, 514
middles, 102–105
narrative, 140, 153
persuasive, 229–234, 265–266, 272–273
research reports, 414–420
response to literature, 289–294, 324, 331, 336–339
science, 485, 487
social studies, 495
and traits, 49
workplace writing, 548, 550
in writing process, 9–10, 18–19, 99–106, 570

drama, *see* playwriting.
dramatic irony, 360
DVDs, citing, 407
dye/die, 714

E

editing, 121–126, *see also* conventions (trait).
in action, 11, 123, 571
applied sciences, 522, 524
arts, 539
as basic writing element, 638–639
common errors, 124–125
conventions, checking for, 26, *see also* checklist, editing.
creative writing, 353, 363, 366, 373, 377, 379
defined, 568
expository, 185–190, 214
keys to effective, 185, 245, 305, 425, 431
math, 512, 517
multimedia presentation, 471
narrative, 144–145, 154
persuasive, 245–250, 268, 274
problems, 126
research reports, 431–436
response to literature, 305–310, 326, 332, 340
science, 486–487
social studies, 497
and traits, 49
workplace writing, 548, 550
in writing process, 9, 26–27, 121–126, 571

editing marks, 639
editorial corrections, 678.2
editorials, citing, 455
editorial writing, 259–268, 636
editors within edition, citing, 453
effect/affect, 708
effective, as term, 6
elements
defined, 276
of expository text, 330
of fiction, 354
of novel, 322
ellipsis, 676.1–676.3
emigrate/immigrate, 716
emphasis, 630, 632, 652.5, 656.3, 656.5, 670.5
encyclopedias, 388, 533
endings, writing, *see also* closing sentences; conclusions; *specific steps in writing process.*
applied science, 523, 525, 527
arts, 532, 540
big picture, 60, 100
creating great, 631

creative writing, 358, 361, 366
defined, 624
expository, 162, 170, 174, 201, 205, 213, 329, 331, 580
interpretive response, 282, 290, 294, 321, 324, 329, 331, 347, 592
math, 516
narrative, 137, 140, 142, 151, 153, 574
one writer's process, 13–32

persuasive, 219, 222, 230, 234, 261, 265, 273, 586
prompts, response to literature, 339
research reports, 400, 418, 604
science, 484–485, 489, 492
social studies, 496, 508
workplace writing, 549, 551
end rhyme, 375
English Language Proficiency Standards (ELPS), *see* language learning.
English sonnets, 368
enjambment, 371, 375
ensure/insure, 718
entry words, dictionary, 562–563
envelope for business letter, 547
epithets, capitalization, 680
essay organizing patterns, 61
essay skills, 623–639
creating great beginnings, 627
creating great endings, 631
creating great middles, 628
editing and proofreading, 638–639
key writing terms, 632–633
list of writing forms, 636–637
outlining, 625
parts of an essay, 624
thesis statements, 626
transitions, 629–630
as writing form, 636
writing techniques, 634–635
essential, as term, 556
etymology, dictionary, 562–564
evaluating
defined, 380
expository, 192–198
holistic scoring guide, 33–45
information sources, 383
narrative, 146–147
peer response, 115–120, 437, 469
persuasive, 252–257
research reports, 469

Index

response to literature, 312–317
strength of evidence, 423
evaluation collection grid, 64
events, 680
events, play map, 285
evidence, 206, 410, 423
exaggeration, 634
examples, 57, 73, 180
except/accept, 708
exclamation points, 641.4
exclamatory sentences, 770.1
experience, 5, 134, 640
explain, 102
explain a process organizing pattern, 61
explanatory essay, 522–523, 528
explanatory materials, 672.1
exposition, 344, 598, 604, 632

expository writing, 156–215
applied sciences, 521–528
arts, 529–542
career review, 524–525
conventions (trait), 160, 190, 208, 214
defined, 580
drafting, 169–174, 205–206, 212–213
editing, 185–190, 214
elements of, 330
evaluating, 192–198
explanatory essay, 522–523
expository essay organization, 580
focus and coherence (trait), 160, 176–177, 184, 206–207
goals, 160
grammar, 186–187
graphic organizers, 158, 164, 202, 204, 211, 583
ideas, development of (trait), 69, 71, 160, 164, 180–181, 184, 202, 207
keys to effective, 163, 169, 175, 185
language of, 580–585
math, 511–520
mechanics, 189

opposing ideas, analyzing, 157–198
oral language, 584–585
organization (trait), 160, 178–179, 184, 207
organizational patterns, 580
paragraphs, 159, 588, 616
prewriting, 163–168, 202–204, 210–211
problems, analyzing, 199–208
prompts, response to, 209–215, 491–492, 526–527
publishing, 191
reading the model, 582–583
recording learning, 475–480
reflecting on writing, 198
response to, 327–332
revising, 175–184, 207, 214
science, 481–492
sentence structure, editing for, 188
social studies, 493–510
test-taking tips, 215
and traits, 160
vocabulary (key words), 581
voice (trait), 160, 182–184, 207
workplace, 543–555
as writing form, 636

external conflict, 359
eyewitness account, 636

fable, 636
facts, 57, 73, 153, 180, 225
fairness in presentation, 240–241
falling action, 344
fantasy, 636
farther/further, 714
feminine pronouns, 780.2
fewer/less, 714
fiction
elements of, 354
in library, 385
figurative language, 632
figures of speech, 81, 374
films, citing, 457–458

first drafts, 18–19, 99–106
first-person pronouns, 736.2
first words, capitalization, 682.1
five W's chart, 65
flair/flare, 716
flashback, 634
focus, 46, 52–53, 55, 96, 297, 348, 632

focus and coherence (trait), 51–58
arts, 534, 538
big picture, 100
completeness, 54
conclusions, 56
creative writing, 353, 363, 366, 373
described, 48
details to support, 57–58
expository, 160, 176–177, 184, 206–207
focused conclusions, 56
focused introductions, 55
holistic scoring, 35–36
learning language, 572
math, 517
multimedia presentations, 473
narrative, 138, 143, 154
peer response, 118
persuasive, 14, 220, 236–237, 244, 267
prewriting, 49
research reports, 422–423, 430, 473
response to literature, 280, 296–297, 304, 325, 340
revising for, *see* revising for focus and coherence (trait).
science, 486
social studies, 497, 510
in writing process, 20, 49

foreign words, 670.4
foreshadowing, 634
forewords, 453
formal abbreviations, 692.1
formal epithets, capitalization, 680
formal language, 79, 266, 428
formal voice, 242

formatting, 28, 419, 470
forms of writing, *see* writing forms.
formula, 276
fractions, 660.1
free-verse poetry, 376–377
freewriting, 93–94
future continuous tense, 748.1
future perfect tense, 746.1
future tense, 744.4

G

gaps, avoiding, 74
gathering details, *see* details, gathering.
gathering grid, 404
gender, 730.2, 738.2, 780.2
generalization, 632
general subject prompt, college essay, 155
genre, 90, 92, 96, *see also* writing forms.
geographic directions, capitalization, 189
geographic names, capitalization, 680
gerund phrases, 752.1, 766.1
gerunds, 752.1, 766.1
goals, 14, 160, 220, 280
good-or-bad conclusions, 106
good/well, 716
government publications, citing, 452, 457

grammar, 728–761, *see also* sentences.
  adjectives, 728.4, 754–755
  adverbs, 728.5, 756–757
  checking, 26, *see also* checklist, editing; conventions (trait).
  conjunctions, 728.7, 760–761
  dictionary, 562–563
  expository, 186–187
  interjections, 728.8, 754
  narrative, 144–145
  nouns, 728.1, 729–731
  persuasive, 246–247
  prepositions, 728.6, 758–759
  pronouns, 728.2, 732–739
  research reports, 432–433
  response to literature, 306–307
  using the right word, 708–727
  verbals, 752–753
  verbs, 728.3, 740–751
  as writing term, 632

graphic organizers, *see also* lists; outlines.
  argument/counter-argument chart, 263
  brief list, 98
  cause-effect organizer, 64, 411, 482, 620
  cluster diagram, 92, 211, 271
  concept map, 504
  controversy chart/map, 158, 164
  creative writing, 344, 349, 359–360, 362
  definition diagram, 65
  evaluation collection grid, 64
  expository, 158, 164, 202, 204, 211
  five W's chart, 65
  gathering grid, 404
  line diagram, 65, 337, 618
  math, 519
  narrative, 138
  opposing viewpoint-concession chart, 264
  organization (trait), 64–65
  persuasive, 218, 224, 226, 262–264, 271
  play map, 278, 285
  plot line, 139, 598
  problem-solution web, 64
  process (cycle) diagram, 65
  pro-con chart, 15, 218
  Q-and-A charts, 138
  quick list, 211, 271
  reading writing chart, 577, 583
  research reports, 402, 404, 420
  response to literature, 278, 284–285, 335, 337
  science, 482
  sensory charts, 65
  social studies, 504
  table, 519
  T-bar, 271
  T-chart, 211, 271
  thought map, 349
  time line, 64, 211, 504
  two-column chart, 204
  Venn diagram, 65, 211, 619
  "why" chart, 226
  "why not" chart, 227
  writing process, 15, 17
graphics, 536–537
graphs, 420
guide words, dictionary, 562–563

H

handwritten material, 28, 670.1
headings, 544–546
heal/heel, 716
healthful/healthy, 716
heard/herd, 716
hear/here, 716
helping verbs, 740.2
highways, capitalization, 680
historical fiction, 636
historical skit, 494–499
history, capitalization, 189, 680
hole/whole, 716
holidays, capitalization, 680
holistic scoring guide, 33–45
  effectiveness of writing, 34
  expository, 192–198
  narrative, 146–147
  persuasive, 252–257
  research reports, 469
  response to literature, 312–317
  sample essay with errors, 38–45
  scale and points, 34–36
  scoring guide, 34, 36–37
  and traits, 31, 34–37

Index

homonyms, books of, 564
homophones (word pairs), 708–727
hyperbole, 81, 374, 634
hyphens, 658–661
   in compound words, 658.1
   to create new words, 658.2
   to divide a word, 660.5
   to form an adjective, 658.3
   general guidelines, 660
   to join letters and words, 658.4
   to join numbers, 660.3
   between numbers and fractions, 660.1
   to prevent confusion, 660.4
   in a special series, 660.2

I

iambic pentameter, 368–369, 371
iambic rhythm, 375
i before *e,* 688.2, 696.1
ideas, *see also* opposing ideas, analysis and response to.
   central idea, 632
   contradictory, 298
   creative, 68
   developing, *see* drafting; ideas, development of (trait).
   linking, *see* transitions.
   seed idea, 4
   testing, in middles, 628

ideas, development of (trait), 67–74
   arts, 534, 538
   big picture, 100
   creative thinking, 68
   creative writing, 353, 363, 366, 373
   described, 24–25, 48–49
   developing ideas, 70
   drafting, 49
   expository, 71, 160, 164, 170, 180–184, 202, 207
   gaps, avoiding, 74
   holistic scoring, 37
   interpretive response, 280, 284, 300–301, 304, 325, 340
   learning language, 572
   math, 517
   multimedia presentations, 473
   narrative, 71, 143, 154
   peer response, 118
   persuasive, 14, 71, 220, 227, 240–241, 244, 262, 267
   presenting ideas, 72–73, 181
   research reports, 402, 426–427, 430, 473
   revising, *see* revising for ideas, development of (trait).
   science, 486
   social studies, 497, 510
   starting points, 69
   writing forms, 69

idioms, 564, 632, 702–707
idle/idol, 716
illusion/allusion, 708
illustrations, dictionary, 562–563
immigrate/emigrate, 716
imperative mood, 750.1
imperative sentences, 770.1
imply/infer, 716
importance, order of, 63, 66
indefinite pronouns, 246, 664.1, 732.1, 734.4, 778.2
independent clauses, 308–309, 644.1, 654.1, 760.1, 768.1
indexes, 388–389
indicate, as term, 342
indicative mood, 750.1
indirect objects, 730.3, 738.1, 742.2, 782.4
inductive reasoning, 411
infer/imply, 716
infinitive phrases, 752.2, 766.1
influences in your life prompt, college essay, 155
informal abbreviations, 692.1
informal language, 79, 266, 428, 578, 596, 608, 632–635
informal voice, 242
information, adding, 95, 112, 409, 630
information sources
   citing, *see* citing sources
   Internet, 384
   libraries, 385–387
   on note cards, 16, 166
   paraphrasing, 16, 502
   persuasive, 224–225
   primary, 95, 165–166, 203, 263, 382–383, 458
   quoting, 16, 502
   reference materials, 385, 388–390, 452, 456, 459, 561–564
   secondary, 95, 166, 203, 263, 382–383
   source notes, 16, 407
   summarizing, 501
   tracking, 407
initialisms, 694.2–694.3
initials, punctuation, 650.4
inquiry, letter of, 545
inside address, letter, 544–546
insure/ensure, 718
intensive pronouns, 732.1, 734.1
interjections, 652.2, 728.8, 754, 760
internal conflict, 359
internal dialogue, 349
internal rhyme, 375
Internet
   blog, citing, 457
   blog, publishing to, 191
   e-mail, citing, 457
   government publication, citing, 457
   media sources, 165
   multimedia resource, citing, 457
   periodicals, citing, 456
   research, 384
   Web sites, building, 133, 472
   Web sites, citing, 456–457
   Web sites, publishing to, 133, 199, 470

interpretive response, 276–341
  conventions (trait), 280, 306–310, 326, 332, 340
  defined, 592
  drafting, 289–294, 324, 331, 336–339
  editing, 305–310, 326, 332, 340
  evaluating, 312–317
  expository text, analyzing, 327–332
  focus and coherence (trait), 280, 296–297, 304, 325, 340
  goals, 280
  grammar, 306–307
  graphic organizers, 278, 284–285, 335, 337
  ideas, development of (trait), 280, 284, 300–301, 304, 325, 340
  keys to effective, 283, 289, 295, 305
  language of, 592–597
  mechanics, 309
  novel, analyzing, 319–326
  oral language, 596–597
  organization (trait), 280, 298–299, 304, 325, 340
  organizational patterns, 592
  paragraphs, 279
  play, analyzing themes of, 277–318
  prewriting, 283–288, 322–323, 330, 334–335
  prompts, 333–341, *see also* prompts, response to.
  publishing, 311, 326, 332
  reflecting on writing, 318
  response to literature essay organization, 592
  revising, 295–304, 325, 340
  sentence structure, editing for, 308
  test-taking tips, 341 themes of a play, analyzing, 277–318
  vocabulary (key words), 593
  voice (trait), 280, 302–304, 325, 340

interrogative pronouns, 732.1, 734.5
interrogative sentences, 770.1
interrupter modifiers, 88
interruptions, 652.3, 674.4
interviews, 455, 458, 533, 636
in-text citations, 448–450
intransitive verbs, 742.1
introductions, *see also* beginnings, writing.
  citing, 453
  expository, 159, 170–171, 176, 331
  focused, 55
  parts of an essay, 624
  persuasive, 231, 238, 265
  playwriting, 361, 366
  research reports, 415, 463
  response to literature, 290–291, 324, 331
  science, 485
introductory series, 674.2
introductory words, clauses, phrases, 249, 646.3
irony, 360, 634
irregular adverbs, 756.2
irregular plurals, 84
irregular verbs, 187, 746.2
isle/aisle, 708
Italian sonnets, 369
italics (underlining), 670–671
  for emphasis, 670.5
  for foreign words, 670.4
  in handwritten and printed material, 670.1
  MLA research reports, 436
  for special uses, 670.3
  in titles, 670.2
it's/its, 125, 718

jargon, 79, 632
job application, 552–553
journals
  citing, 454
  writer's notebook, 2–5, 92
juxtaposition, 635

keys to effective writing
  expository, 163, 169, 175, 185
  persuasive, 223, 229, 235, 245
  research reports, 401, 414, 421, 431
  response to literature, 283, 289, 295, 305
key words, *see* vocabulary (key words).
key writing terms, 632–633
knew/new, 718
know/no, 718

L

land forms, capitalization, 680
language, *see* learning language.
language levels, 242
languages, capitalization, 680
later/latter, 718
lay/lie, 718
lead/led, 718
learning language, 556–609
learning language, creative writing, 598–603
learning language, expository, 580–585
learning language, language strategies, 566–567
learning language, learning strategies
  distinguish between formal/informal English, 79, 207, 242, 244, 261, 266–267, 272, 428, 517, 578, 584, 590, 596, 602, 608
  monitor language production and employ self-corrective techniques, 119, 175–190, 207–208, 214, 235–251, 267–268, 274, 297–309, 486–487, 491, 497, 510, 517, 534, 638
  use basic or academic language, 6, 46, 90, 134, 156, 182–184, 215–216, 276, 342, 380, 474, 556, 566, 569, 573, 575–576,

Index

581–582, 587–588, 593–594, 598–600, 605–606, 610, 629–630, 632–638
use prior knowledge, 478, 576, 582, 588, 594, 600, 606
use strategic techniques, 211, 264, 271, 275, 567, 569, 581, 587, 599

learning language, listening
collaborate with peers, 8, 11, 22, 53, 68, 73, 82, 110, 116–117, 176, 187, 247, 251, 278, 311, 469, 494, 499, 530, 571, 574, 576, 578–582, 584, 586–590, 592–601, 604, 606–609, 743, 771
follow directions, 771
learn basic/academic vocabulary, 6, 46, 90, 134, 156, 187, 216, 276, 342, 380, 474, 556, 558, 564–567, 569, 575, 581, 587–588, 593–595, 599–600, 605–606, 610, 632–637, 640, 708–727
learn language structures/expressions, 6, 80, 90, 134, 156, 216, 276, 342, 380, 474, 556, 558, 564, 566, 579, 584, 589, 594, 599–600, 609, 640, 701–702
monitor understanding, 54, 78, 116, 119, 176, 476, 478–480, 558, 560, 566–567, 569, 573, 581, 587, 597
recognize elements of English sound system, 587–588, 593, 599, 605
respond to questions/requests, 110, 570–571, 576, 581–582, 587–589, 593–594, 597, 599–600, 606–607
summarize/retell spoken messages, 479–480, 558, 567, 578, 599, 604
take notes, 53, 68, 166, 469, 476, 479–480, 558, 567, 576, 579, 581, 588, 594, 597, 599–600, 606–609
understand general meaning, important details, or main points, 176, 469, 558, 588–589, 594–595, 600–601, 606–607, 609

understand implicit ideas and information, 469, 558, 591, 597, 603, 609
use visual, contextual, or linguistic support, 166, 176, 476, 478–480, 560

learning language, narrative, 574–579

learning language, persuasive, 586–591

learning language, reading
comprehend English language structures or vocabulary, 6, 46, 48–49, 90, 134, 156, 180, 182–184, 186, 216, 247, 276, 308, 342, 344, 347, 354, 359–360, 374–375, 380, 474, 520, 528, 556, 562, 564–566, 568–569, 572–573, 575–576, 579, 581–582, 587–588, 593, 595, 598–601, 605–606, 610, 632–637, 640, 708–727
develop background knowledge, vocabulary or grasp of language structures, 55, 215, 275, 311, 326, 341, 565–566, 576, 581–582, 587–588, 594
develop basic sight vocabulary, 6, 46, 48–49, 90, 134, 156, 172, 182–184, 187, 216, 276, 342, 380, 474, 556, 562, 564–566, 576, 579, 587, 595, 600, 606–607, 610, 640, 708–727
distinguish main ideas/details, 161, 200–201, 260–261, 272–273, 282, 320–321, 328–329, 338–339, 512–513, 577, 583, 589, 595, 607
employ analytical skills/perform critical analyses, 35, 45, 148, 160–161, 176, 200–202, 215, 221–222, 260–261, 272–273, 280–282, 320–321, 328–329, 334–335, 338–339, 345–347, 356–358, 415–418, 423–424, 426–430, 483, 488–489, 492, 523, 525, 542, 577, 583, 589, 595

employ inferential skills, 200–201, 336–337, 576–577, 583, 589, 595
enhance and confirm understanding, 55, 215, 275, 311, 326, 341, 576, 581–582, 589
find supporting text evidence, 200–201, 336–337, 576–577, 589, 595
read silently, 221–222, 281–282, 345–347, 356–358, 483, 488–489, 492, 523, 525, 540, 542, 577
respond to questions, retell material, or participate in shared reading, 55, 137, 151, 162, 176, 203, 222, 261, 282, 298, 321, 329, 339, 344, 347, 358, 400, 567, 576, 577, 583, 588–589, 593–595, 599–600, 61, 607, 775
summarize text, 201, 477–478, 513, 567, 577, 583, 759
take notes, 166, 336–337, 341, 404–406, 477–480, 567, 576, 579, 594, 599–600, 775
understand supporting ideas/details, 161, 200–201, 260–261, 272–273, 282, 320–321, 328–329, 338–339, 513, 577, 583, 589, 595, 607
use prereading supports, 46, 285, 477–478, 576, 582, 588, 594, 600, 606
use visual/contextual and peer/teacher support, 55, 215, 275, 311, 326, 341, 576, 581–582, 587–588

learning language, research reports, 604–609

learning language, response to literature, 592–597

learning language, speaking
adapt spoken language, 463, 466–468, 578, 582, 584, 590, 596, 598, 602, 608
ask for and give information, 466–469, 573

build academic language proficiency, 467, 564, 569, 573, 575

describe, explain, or narrate with specificity/detail, 22, 54, 68, 176, 467–468, 559, 569, 574, 578–579, 582, 584–585, 588, 591–592, 594, 597–598, 600–603, 609, 745, 755

express feelings, ideas, or opinions, 6, 8, 11–12, 22, 53, 56, 61, 101, 103, 110, 114, 117, 166, 176, 278, 348, 559–560, 569, 571, 575, 578–580, 582, 584–586, 588, 591–592, 597, 600–604, 606, 608–609

identify/describe with high-frequency English words, 48, 466, 559, 564, 587, 593–594, 599, 605, 717

learn routine language, retell stories/basic information, 48, 466, 559, 564, 594, 599, 605, 717

produce sounds of new vocabulary, 566, 569, 573, 575, 581–582, 587, 593, 599–600, 605–606, 709, 711, 713, 723, 725, 727

respond orally to wide variety of media, 580, 586, 592, 598

share information, 6, 8, 12, 22, 48, 53, 61, 63, 110, 187, 247, 268, 278, 284, 294, 311, 326, 332, 339, 382–383, 494, 499, 530, 559, 569, 571, 573–576, 578–580, 582, 584–588, 590–592, 594–596, 598, 600–604, 606, 608–609

use variety of connecting words, grammatical structures and sentences, 467, 603

learning language, writing

describe, explain, or narrate with specificity/detail, 35, 49, 62, 66, 93, 140, 169–174, 205, 207, 215, 229–231, 233–234, 273, 275, 279, 286, 290–294, 302, 304, 324, 330–331, 341, 351–352, 415–418,

424, 471, 485, 487, 489, 491–492, 512, 522, 525, 531, 539, 451–542, 569, 573–575, 581, 599, 605, 614–617

edit writing for grammar and usage, 26–27, 111, 122–126, 128, 145, 185–188, 190, 208, 214, 245–246, 250, 268, 274, 280, 305–307, 310, 326, 332, 340–341, 430–431, 436, 486, 497, 510, 512, 517, 534, 638, 732–733, 744–747, 776–781

employ complex grammatical structures, 26–27, 122–123, 145, 185–188, 190, 208, 214, 245, 250, 274, 305–307, 310, 491, 526, 638, 662–665, 732–733, 744, 746–747, 780–781

spell with increasing accuracy, 26–27, 84, 122–123, 145, 185, 190, 208, 214, 245, 250, 268, 274, 305, 310, 326, 332, 340, 353, 363, 430–431, 435–436, 486–487, 497, 510, 512, 517, 534, 638–639, 696–701

use newly acquired basic/content-based vocabulary, 66, 156, 172, 182–184, 216, 232, 276, 299, 306, 342, 380, 471, 474, 556, 566, 569, 573, 575, 581, 587, 593, 599, 605, 610, 629–630, 708, 710, 712–724, 726

use variety of connecting words, sentence lengths, or patterns, 66, 86–88, 119, 144–145, 185, 208, 244, 247–248, 250, 268, 302, 306–310, 332, 353, 425, 430, 432–434, 436, 487, 517, 526, 638, 766–770, 772–774

learning log, 453, 478–480

learn/teach, 718

leave/let, 718

lectures, citing, 458

lend/borrow, 718

length
of quotations, 446, 666.3
of research reports, 420
of sentences, 86, 248

less/fewer, 714

letters, of the alphabet, 658.4, 684.2, 688.3

letters, writing, *see* correspondence.

levels of detail, 104

levels of language, 242

libraries, 385–387

like/as, 718

limiting the subject, 633

line breaks, poetry, 375

line diagrams, 65, 618

lingering questions, 106

linking verbs, 740.2

listening, *see also* learning language, listening.
in class, 558, 560
creative writing, 600
expository, 582
narrative, 576
persuasive, 588
research reports, 606
response to literature, 594

lists
Basics-of-Life, 93
brief, 98
current-issues, 202
details, 622
information sources, 165
organized, 17
punctuation, 656.5, 678, 694
quick, 211, 271
selecting topics, 92
topics, 138, 202, 262, 284, 402
writing forms, 636–637

literal, as writing term, 633

literary analysis, 637, *see also* response to literature.

literary terms, *see specific terms, such as* plot; *specific writings, such as* creative writing.

literature, response to, *see* response to literature.

literature connection, 160, 220, 280

Index 807

loaded words, 633
local color, 635
location, 629
logic, 633
logical progression of ideas, 62
loose sentences, 774.1

M

magazines, 160, 385, 407, 419, 454–455, 533, *see also* periodicals.
main characters, 360
manner, adverbs to show, 756.1
masculine pronouns, 780.2
math, writing in, 511–520
may/can, 712
meaning of words, 567
mechanics, 641–701
  abbreviations, 692–693
  acronyms, 694–695
  capitalization, 189, 680–685
  checklist, 26, 122, *see also* checklist, editing.
  initialisms, 694–695
  numbers, 690–691
  plurals, 686–689
  writing form, 189, 249, 309, 435
medal/meddle, 718
media, 165, 385, 536–537
memo, workplace, 550–551
metal/mettle, 720
metaphors, 80, 374, 635
method, as term, 610
middles, writing, *see also* specific steps in writing process.
  applied science, 523, 525, 527
  arts, 531–532, 540
  big picture, 60, 100
  creating great, 628
  creative writing, 345–347, 356–358, 361, 366
  defined, 624
  expository, 161–162, 170, 172–173, 200–201, 205, 212–213, 328–329, 331, 580
  levels of detail, 104
  math, 515–516
  narrative, 136–137, 140, 150–151, 153, 574
  one writer's process, 13–32
  persuasive, 219, 221–222, 230, 232–233, 239, 260–261, 265, 272–273, 586
  prompts, response to literature, 338–339
  research reports, 394–399, 416–417, 604
  response to literature, 281–282, 286, 290, 292–293, 320–321, 324, 328–329, 331, 592
  science, 483–485, 488–489, 492
  social studies, 496, 505–507
  workplace writing, 549, 551
miner/minor, 720
misspelled words, common, 698–699
MLA guidelines, 391–438
  drafting, 414–420
  editing, 431–436
  in-text citations, 448–450
  outline, 413
  peer response, 437
  prewriting, 401–413
  publishing, 437–438
  research report sample, 392–400
  revising, 421–430
  works-cited section, 400, 419, 451–458, 508, 533
model for reading, *see* reading strategies.
Modern Language Association, *see* MLA guidelines.
modifiers, 88, 633
moment of truth, 139
money, expressing, 690.4
monthly/bimonthly magazines, citing, 454–455
months, capitalization, 680
monuments, capitalization, 680
mood, 142, 350, 354
mood, of verbs, 750.1
moral/morale, 720
motivation, character, 359
multimedia presentations, 458, 470–473, 490, 498–499, 535–537
multivolume works, citing, 453
musicals, citing, 457
myth, 637

N

names, capitalization, 680, 684.1
narrative, as term, 640
narrative voice, 302
narrative writing, 134–155
  college entrance essay, 149–155
  conventions (trait), 144–145, 154
  defined, 574
  drafting, 140, 153
  editing, 144–145, 154
  evaluating, 146–147
  focus and coherence (trait), 138, 143, 154
  grammar, 144–145
  graphic organizers, 138, 577
  ideas, development of (trait), 69, 71, 143, 154
  language of, 574–579
  math, 520
  oral language, 578–579
  organization (trait), 139, 143, 154
  organizational patterns, 574
  organizational patterns, 574
  paragraphs, 614
  personal narrative, 135–148
  prewriting, 138–139, 152
  prompts, 155
  publishing, 145, 155
  reading the model, 576–577
  reflecting on writing, 148
  revising, 141–143, 154
  vocabulary (key words), 575
  voice (trait), 143, 154

narrator, 354
nationalities, capitalization, 680
neuter pronouns, 780.2
newspapers, 220, 385, 407, 419, 455, 460, 533
New York Times Index, 389
nominative case, 186, 730.3, 738.1
nonfiction texts, in library, 385
nonrestrictive phrases/ clauses, 124, 648.2
note, business letter, 544–546
notebook, writer's, 2–5, 92
note cards, 16, 166, 405–406, 464–465, 471
note taking, 476–480, 558
nouns
　abstract, 729.4
　capitalization of proper, 684.1
　cases, 730.3
　classes of, 729
　clause, 432, 768.2
　collective, 688.6, 729.5, 778.1
　common, 729.2
　compound, 664.2, 686.6
　concrete, 729.3
　defined, 728.1, 729–731
　direct objects, 730.3
　forms of, 730
　gender, 730.2
　indirect objects, 730.3
　metaphors with, 80
　nominative case, 730.3
　number of, 730.1
　objective case, 730.3
　object of a preposition, 758.1
　phrase, 433, 766.1
　plural, 730.1
　plurals, 686–691
　possessive case, 730.3
　predicate, 730.3, 782.3
　proper, 680.1, 684.1, 729.1
　singular, 730.1
novel, 322, 637
novel, analysis and response to, 319–326
nuance, 296

O

objections, 227, 232
objective, 359, 633
objective case, 186, 730.3, 738.1
object pronouns, 126
objects
　direct and indirect, 730.3, 738.1, 742.2, 764.1, 782.4
　of a preposition, 730.3, 738.1, 758.1
　with transitive verbs, 742.2
octave, 369
official documents, capitalization, 680
official titles, capitalization, 680
omitted words, 676.1
online, *see* Internet.
onomatopoeia, 375
open-ended prompts, college essay, 155
opening letter, portfolio, 131
opening sentences, *see* topic sentences.
opinions, 426
opposing ideas, analysis and response to, 157–198
　drafting, 169–174
　editing, 185–190
　evaluating, 192–198
　goals, 160
　introduction, 159
　persuasive writing, 264
　prewriting, 163–168
　publishing, 191
　reflecting on writing, 198
　revising, 175–184

number, 690–691
　of nouns, 730.1
　numerals or words, 656.2, 690.1–690.3
　of pronouns, 736.1, 738, 780.1
　punctuating, 650.3, 660.1, 660.3
　time and money, 690.4
　verbs, 744.1
number/amount, 710

opposing viewpoint-concession chart, 264
oral language
　creative writing, 602–603
　expository, 584–585
　narrative, 578–579
　persuasive, 590–591
　research reports, 608–609
　response to literature, 596–597
　speaking in class, 559–560
oral presentations, 461–473
　audio and visual aids, 466
　delivering, 468
　evaluating, 469
　multimedia, 458, 470–473, 490, 498–499, 535–537
　note cards, 464–465
　planning, 462–463
　practicing, 467
　research reports, 470–473
order of importance organizational pattern, 63, 66

organization (trait), 59–66
　arts, 534, 538
　big picture, 60, 100
　checklist for effective writing, 50
　creative writing, 353, 363, 373
　described, 48
　expository, 160, 178–179, 184, 207
　graphic organizers, 64–65
　holistic scoring, 35–36
　interpretive response, 280, 298–299, 304, 325, 340
　learning language, 572
　logical progression of ideas, 62
　math, 517
　multimedia presentations, 473
　narrative, 139, 143, 154
　organizational patterns, 63
　outlines, 17
　peer response, 118
　persuasive, 14, 220, 238–239, 244, 267

Index

research reports, 424–425, 430, 473
revising for, *see* revising for organization (trait).
science, 486
social studies, 497, 510
thesis statements, 61
transitions, 66
in writing process, 20, 49

organizational patterns
analyzing, 411
cause-effect, 63, 66, 411, 432, 620
chronological order, 63, 66, 411
classification, 618
climax, 622
comparison-contrast, 63, 66, 619
creative writing, 598
deductive, 62, 411
expository, 580
inductive, 411
in language, 566
logical progression of ideas, 62
narrative, 574
order of importance, 63, 66
paragraphs, 618–622
persuasive, 586
problem-solution, 63, 66
process organization, 621
quotations, 411
research reports, 411, 604
response to literature, 592
summarizing, 411
transitional words/phrases, 66
organization of details, *see* details, organizing.
organizations, capitalization, 684.3
organized lists, 17
organizers, graphic, *see* graphic organizers.
outlines
creating, 625
multimedia presentations, 473, 536
persuasive, 228

prewriting, 17
research reports, 392, 413, 504
response to literature, 288
sentence, 168, 228, 288, 413, 513, 625
topic, 17, 98, 168, 625
overstatement, 635
oxymoron, 635

P

paintings, citing, 457
pairs of words (homophones), 708–727
pamphlets, citing, 452
paradox, 635
paragraphs, 611–622
body sentences, 159, 219, 279, 612–613, *see also* middles, writing.
classification order, 618
closing, *see* closing sentences.
descriptive, 615
expository, 171, 174, 205, 616, *see also* expository writing.
first draft, 18–19, 99–106
narrative, 614, *see also* narrative writing.
opening, *see* topic sentences.
organizational patterns, 618–622
parts of, 612–613
persuasive, 219, 617, *see also* persuasive writing.
response to literature, 279
skills writing, 611–622
topic sentence, 612–613, *see also* topic sentences.
types of, 614–617
parallel series, 187
paraphrasing, 16, 405–406, 442–445, 502
parentheses, 672.1–672.2
parenthetical material, 648.1, 674.3
partial quotations, 446
participial phrases, 752.3, 766.1
participles, 752.3
parts of speech, 728–761

adjectives, 728.4, 754–755
adverbs, 728.5, 756–757
conjunctions, 728.7, 760–761
dictionary, 562–563
interjections, 728.8, 754
nouns, 728.1, 729–731
prepositions, 728.6, 758–759
pronouns, 728.2, 732–739
verbals, 752–753
verbs, 728.3, 740–751
passed/past, 720
passive voice, 188, 748.2
past continuous tense, 748.1
past participles, 744.3, 746.2
past perfect tense, 746.1–746.2
past tense, 187, 744.4
patterns of organization, *see* organizational patterns.
pauses, 676.3
peace/piece, 720
peak/peek/pique, 720
pedal/peddle/petal, 720
peer response, 22–23, 115–120, 437, 469
perennial/semiannual, 710
perfect tense, 746.1
performance review, 539–540
periodical guides, 390
periodical indexes, 389
periodicals, 385, 389, 407, 454–456, 460
periodic sentences, 774.1
periods, 641
after an abbreviation/initial, 641.2
as a decimal point, 641.3
to end a sentence, 641.1
in parentheses, 641.1
periods of history, capitalization, 189, 680
person
of pronoun, 736.2, 738
of verb, 744.2
personal narrative, 135–148, 574
personal/personnel, 720
personal pronouns, 732.1, 734.1, 736–738

personal sources, citing, 450, 458
personification, 81, 372, 374, 635
persuasive paragraphs, 617
persuasive writing, 216–275
  applied sciences, 528
  argumentative essay, 217–258
  conventions (trait), 14, 220, 246–250, 268, 274
  defined, 586
  drafting, 229–234, 265–266, 272–273
  editing, 245–250, 268, 274
  editorial writing, 259–268
  evaluating, 252–257
  focus and coherence (trait), 14, 220, 236–237, 244, 267
  goals, 220
  graphic organizers, 218, 224, 226, 262–264, 271
  ideas, development of (trait), 14, 71, 220, 227, 240–241, 244, 262, 267
  keys to effective, 223, 229, 235, 245
  language of, 586–592
  oral language, 590–591
  organization (trait), 14, 220, 238–239, 244, 267
  organizational patterns, 586
  paragraphs, 219, 617
  prewriting, 223–228, 262–264, 270–271
  prompts, response to, 269–275
  publishing, 251, 268
  reading the model, 515–516, 588–589
  reflecting on writing, 32, 258
  revising, 235–244, 251, 267, 274, 517
  sentence structure, editing for, 248
  statistical argument, 514–517
  test-taking tips, 275
  vocabulary (key words), 587
  voice (trait), 14, 220, 242–244, 266–267
  as writing form, 637

photographs, citing, 457
phrasal pronouns, 732.1
phrases, 766–768
  absolute, 768
  adjective, 144, 758.1
  adverb, 307, 758.1, 766.1, 768.2
  appositive, 766.1
  defined, 766
  gerund, 752.1, 766.1
  infinitive, 752.2, 766.1
  introductory, 646.3
  nonrestrictive, 124, 648.2
  noun, 433, 766
  participial, 752.3, 766.1
  prepositional, 144, 758.1, 768, 784.1
  restrictive, 648.2
  transitions, 66, 629–630
  types of, 766.1
  verb, 768
  verbal, 766.1
place, adverbs to show, 756.1
plagiarism, 105, 406, 441–443
plain/plane, 720
planning writing, *see* prewriting.
play, 637
play map, 278, 285
plays, themes in, analysis and response to, 277–318
  drafting, 289–294
  editing, 305–310
  evaluating, 312–317
  goals, 280
  prewriting, 283–288
  publishing, 311
  reflecting on writing, 318
  revising, 295–304
playwriting, 355–366, *see also* scripts.
plot, 344–347, 354
plot line, 139, 354, 598
plurals, 686–689
  collective nouns, 688.4, 778.1
  compound nouns, 686.6
  irregular, 84
  irregular spelling, 688.2
  nouns, 686–689, 730.1
  nouns ending in *f* or *fe*, 688.1

nouns ending in *ful*, 686.5
nouns ending in *o*, 686.4
nouns ending in *sh, ch, x, s,* and *z*, 686.2
nouns ending in *y*, 686.3
possessives, 662.3
pronouns, 736.1, 780.1
punctuation of, 662, 664.4
regular, 84
subjects, 776
verbs, 744.1, 748.2, 776
words discussed as words, 688.3
podcasts, citing, 457
poem, 637
poetic conventions, 371–372, 374–375
poetic license, 633
poetry, quoting, 446, 672.4
poetry, writing, 367–379
  cinquains (quintet), 378–379
  drafting, 371–372, 377, 379
  editing, 373, 377, 379
  English sonnets, 368
  free-verse, 376–377
  prewriting, 370, 377, 379
  publishing, 373
  revising, 373, 377, 379
  sonnets, 368–369
  techniques and conventions, 371–372, 374–375
point-counterpoint, 73
point of view, 354, 633
policy as detail, 94
political parties, capitalization, 680
poor/pour/pore, 722
portfolios, 130–132
position papers, math, 520
position statements, 226, 230–231, 236, *see also* thesis statements.
positive adjectives, 754.2
positive adverbs, 756.2
possessive case, 186, 738.1
possessive nouns, 730.3
possessive pronouns, 664.1
possessives, punctuation, 662, 664

Index

postal guidelines, 547, 692.2
power (digital slides) presentations, 470, 473
practical writing
applied sciences, 521–528
expository writing, 156–215
workplace writing, 543–555
practicing presentations, 467
predicate adjectives, 754.1, 782.2–782.3
predicate nouns, 730.3
predicates, 762, 764.1–764.2, 782.2–782.3
preface, 453
prefixes, 567, 658.2
prepositional phrases, 144, 758.1, 768, 784.1
prepositions, 758–759
common, 758
defined, 728.6
object of, 730.3, 738.1, 758.1
pre-production, multimedia, 536
presentations, *see also* publishing.
expository, 191
multimedia, 458, 470–473, 490, 498–499, 535–537
oral, 461–473
research reports, 438, 461–473
present continuous tense, 748.1
present perfect tense, 746.1
present tense, 187, 744.4
previewing, 14
prewriting, 91–98
in action, 10, 570
applied sciences, 522, 524
arts, 530, 539
creative writing, 348–350, 359–360, 364, 370, 377, 379
defined, 568
expository, 163–168, 202–204, 210–211
keys to effective, 163, 169, 223, 283, 393, 401
math, 512, 514

interpretive response, 283–288, 322–323, 330, 334–335
narrative, 138–139, 152
persuasive, 223–228, 262–264, 270–271
research reports, 401–413
science, 482, 487
social studies, 500
thesis statement, forming, 97
and traits, 49
workplace writing, 548, 550
in writing process, 9–10, 15–17, 91–98, 568, 570

primary sources, 95, 165–166, 203, 263, 382–383, 458
principal/principle, 722
printed material, italics in, 670.1
print media, 165
problems, analyzing, 199–208
problem-solution organizational pattern, 61, 63, 66
problem-solution web, 64
problem-solution writing, 528, 637
process (cycle) diagram, 65, 621
process of writing, *see* writing process.
process organizational patterns, 621
process writing, 487–490, 520, 528, 637
pro-con chart, 15, 218
production, multimedia, 466, 536–537
profile, 637
prompts, response to
applied sciences, 526–527
arts, 541–542
college essay, 155
expository, 209–215, 491–492
literature, 333–341
math, 518–519
persuasive, 269–275
science, 491–492

pronouns
-antecedent agreement, 125, 732, 780–781
case, 186, 738.1
classes of, 732.1
compound or simple, 732
defined, 728.2, 732–739
demonstrative, 732.1, 734.6
first-person, 736.2
gender, 738.2, 780.2
indefinite, 246, 664.1, 732.1, 734.4, 778.2
intensive, 732.1, 734.1
interrogative, 732.1, 734.5
neuter, 780.2
nominative case, 186, 738.1
number, 736.1, 738, 780.1
objective case, 186, 738.1
object, 126
person, 736.2, 738
personal, 732.1, 734.1, 736–738
phrasal, 732
plural, 736.1, 780.1
possessive, 664.1
possessive case, 186, 738.1
reciprocal, 734.3
reflexive, 732.1, 734.1
relative, 732.1, 734.2, 760.3, 778.3
second-person, 736.2
singular, 736.1, 780.1
subject, 738.1
third-person, 736.2
types of, 732.1, 734–737
pronunciation, 562–564, 566
proofreader's guide, *see also* checklist, editing.
idioms, 702–707
mechanics, 641–701
parts of speech, 728–761
punctuation, 641–679
right words, using, 708–727
sentences, 762–785
proofreading, 49, 638–639
proofreading marks, 639
proper adjectives, 680.1, 754.1
proper nouns, 680.1, 684.1, 729.1
proposals, 637

pros and cons, 167, 172–173, 271
prose, 450, 633
protagonist, 354
provinces, capitalization, 680
public areas, capitalization, 680

publishing, 127–133, *see also* presentations.
  in action, 11, 571
  creative writing, 363, 366, 373
  defined, 568
  design, 28
  expository, 191
  Internet, 133
  narrative, 145, 155
  peer response, 437
  persuasive, 251, 268
  places for, 129
  portfolios, 130–132
  preparing for, 128
  research reports, 437–438
  response to literature, 311, 326, 332
  and traits, 49
  workplace writing, 548
  in writing process, 9, 11, 28–31, 127–133, 571

pun, 635
punctuation, 641–679
  apostrophes, 662–665
  brackets, 678–679
  colons, 656–657
  commas, 644–653
  common, 85
  conventions (trait), 85
  dash, 674–676
  diagonals, 672
  ellipsis, 676–677
  exclamation points, 641.4
  hyphens, 658–661
  introductory words, phrases, clauses, 249
  italics (underlining), 670–671
  list of marks, 678
  parentheses, 672
  parenthetical elements, 225
  periods, 641
  question marks, 642

  quotation marks, 295, 666–669
  semicolons, 654–655
purpose, 77, 96, 462, 633

Q

Q-and-A chart, 138
quatrains, 368
question marks, 642.1–642.3
questions
  answering, with oral language, 579, 585, 603, 609
  details, gathering, 94
  direct, 642.1
  ideas, developing, 71
  lingering, 106
  Q-and-A chart, 138
  research questions, 403, 405, 409, 422
  response to literature, 298
  STRAP, 210–211, 214, 270
quick lists, 211, 271
quiet/quit/quite, 722
quintet (cinquains), 378–379
quotation marks, 666–669
  for long quotations, 666.3
  placement of punctuation when using, 666.2
  to punctuate titles, 668.3
  within quotations, 668.1
  to set off direct quotations, 666.1, 682.1
  for special words, 668.2
quotations
  as detail, 58
  direct, 666.1, 682.1
  expository, 166, 180
  introducing, 656.4
  length of, 446
  narrative, 153
  on note cards, 16, 405–406
  novels, 322
  as organizational pattern, 411
  paraphrasing with, 445
  partial, 446
  persuasive, 225
  poetry, 446
  to present ideas, 72

  problems, 105
  from prose, 450
  punctuation, *see* quotation marks.
  research reports, 405–406
  response to literature, 287, 301, 322
  within titles of works, citing, 455
  using, 105, 444
  without citation, 442–443
quote/quotation, 722
quoting sources, 502

R

radio programs, citing, 458
random, as term, 216
Readers' Guide to Periodical Literature, 390
readings, citing, 458
reading strategies, *see also* learning language, reading.
  creative writing model, 600–601
  expository model, 582–583
  narrative model, 576–577
  persuasive model, 588–589
  research model, 606–607
  response to literature model, 594–596
real/really/very, 722
reasons, 58, 73, 226
reasons for writing, 1–5
reciprocal pronouns, 734.3
recording learning, 475–480
redundant, as term, 90
reference materials, 385, 388–390, 452, 456, 459, 561–564
reflect, as term, 474
reflecting on writing
  critique of research process, 409
  expository writing, 32, 198
  narrative writing, 148
  persuasive writing, 258
  research reports, 440
  response to literature, 318

Index

revising, 109
   thesis statements, 103
   writing process, 15
reflective writing, 103
reflexive pronouns, 732.1, 734.1
regular plurals, 84
relative pronouns, 732.1, 734.2, 760.3, 778.3
relevant, as term, 156
religion, capitalization, 680, 682.5
repetition, 375, 425, 567
request, letter of, 545
research, as term, 380
research question, 403, 409, 422, 500

research reports, writing, 380–473, 530–538
   arts, 530–538
   citations, 400, 533
   conventions (trait), 430, 432–436, 473, 534
   documenting research, 447–460, 500–503
   drafting, 414–420
   editing, 431–436
   focus and coherence (trait), 422–423, 430, 473
   grammar, 432–433
   graphic organizers, 402, 404, 504
   ideas, development of (trait), 402, 426–427, 430, 473
   keys to effective, 401, 414, 421, 431
   language of, 604–609
   mechanics, 435
   MLA research report, 391–438
   multimedia presentations, 470–473
   note cards, 405–406, 464–465
   oral language, 608–609
   oral presentations, 461–473
   organization (trait), 424–425, 430, 473, 504
   organizational patterns, 604
   outline, 392, 413, 504

   peer response, 437
   practice checklist, 467
   presentations, 438, 461–473
   prewriting, 401–413, 500–504
   publishing, 437–438
   reading the model, 505–508, 606–607
   researching, 440, 500–503
   responsible writing, 439–446
   revising, 421–430, 509–510
   sentence structure, editing for, 434
   skills and sources, 381–390, 500–503
   social studies, 500–510
   title page, 392
   vocabulary (key words), 605
   voice (trait), 428–430, 473
   works-cited section, 400, 419, 451–458, 508, 533

research skills, 381–390, 500–503
resolution, 344–345, 354
response, peer, 115–120, 437, 469
response to literature, *see* interpretive response.
responsible writing, 439–446
restrictive clauses, 648.2
resume, 548–549
retelling, as language strategy, 567
return address, 547
reviews, 455, 462

revising, 20–25, 107–114
   in action, 11, 112–113, 571
   applied sciences, 522, 524
   arts, 534, 538–539
   basic guidelines, 108
   checklist for, 111
   creative writing, 353, 363, 366, 373, 377, 379
   defined, 568
   depth, 114
   expository, 175–184, 207, 214
   first revision, 20–21

   keys to effective, 175, 235, 295, 421
   math, 512, 517
   methods for, 109–110
   multimedia presentations, 473
   narrative, 141–143, 154
   peer response, 22–23
   persuasive, 235–244, 251, 267, 274
   research reports, 421–430
   response to literature, 295–304, 325, 340
   science, 486–487
   social studies, 497, 509–510
   and traits, 49
   workplace writing, 548, 550
   in writing process, 9, 11, 20–25, 107–114, 568, 571

revising for focus and coherence (trait), 20, 49
   arts, 534, 538
   creative writing, 353, 363, 366, 373
   expository, 176–177, 184, 207
   math, 517
   narrative, 138, 143, 154
   persuasive, 236–237, 244, 267
   research reports, 422–423, 430
   response to literature, 296–297, 304, 325, 340
   science, 486
   social studies, 497, 510
revising for ideas,
   development of (trait), 24–25
   arts, 534, 538
   creative writing, 353, 363, 366, 373
   expository, 180–181, 184, 207
   math, 517
   narrative, 143, 154
   persuasive, 240–241, 244, 267
   research reports, 426–427, 430
   response to literature, 300–301, 304, 325, 340
   science, 486
   social studies, 497, 510

revising for organization (trait), 20, 49
  arts, 534, 538
  creative writing, 353, 363, 373
  expository, 178–179, 184, 207
  math, 517
  narrative, 143, 154
  persuasive, 238–239, 244, 267
  research reports, 424–425, 430
  response to literature, 298–299, 304, 325, 340
  science, 486
  social studies, 497, 510
revising for voice (trait), 24–25, 49
  arts, 534, 538
  creative writing, 353, 363, 366, 373
  expository, 182–184, 207
  math, 517
  narrative, 143, 154
  persuasive, 242–244, 267
  research reports, 428–430
  response to literature, 302–304, 325, 340
  science, 486
  social studies, 497, 510
rhetorical devices, 20, 299, 323, 411
rhyme, 371, 375
rhyme scheme, 368–369
rhythm, 371, 375
right words, using, 708–727
right/write/wright/rite, 722
ring/wring, 722
rising action, 344–345
roads, capitalization, 680
roots of words, 567
rubrics, *see* holistic scoring guide.
run-on sentences, 89

S

salutation, 544–546, 656.1
scenes, play, 361
scene/seen, 722
scheme, rhyme, 368–369
scholarly journals, citing, 454
school publications, 129
science, writing in, 481–492
science fiction, 637
scoring guide, 33–35, *see also* holistic scoring guide.
scripts, 471, 494–499, *see also* playwriting.
seam/seem, 722
search methods, 384, 386
secondary characters, 360
secondary sources, 95, 166, 203, 263, 382–383
second editions, citing, 453
second-person pronouns, 736.2
seed idea, 4
semiannual/perennial, 710
semicolons, 654–655
  conjunctive adverbs, 654.2
  correct usage, 309
  to join independent clauses, 654.1
  to separate groups that contain commas, 654.3
  transitional phrases, 654.2
semiformal voice, 242
sensory charts, 65
sensory details, 140
sentence fragments, 89
sentence outlines, 168, 228, 288, 413, 625
sentences
  agreement of parts, 776–781
  arrangement of, 774.1
  awkward, 89
  balanced, 774.1
  beginnings of, 86
  body, 159, 219, 279, 612–613
  clauses, 768–769
  closing, *see* closing sentences.

comma splices, 89
complete, 762
complex, 308, 772.1
compound, 308, 434, 772.1
compound-complex, 308, 434, 772.1
conditional, 770.1
constructing, 772.1
conventions (trait), 86–89
creating great beginnings, 627
creating great endings, 631
creating great middles, 628
cumulative, 87, 774.1
declarative, 770.1
defined, 774
exclamatory, 770.1
expanding, 87,
fragments, 89
imperative, 770.1
interrogative, 770.1
kinds of, 770.1
length of, 86, 248
levels of details, 104
loose, 774.1
opening, *see* topic sentences.
periodic, 774.1
phrases, 766–768
predicates, 762, 764.1–764.2, 782.2–782.3
problems, 89
run-ons, 89
simple, 434, 772.1
subjects, 762, 764.2
subject-verb agreement, 124, 246, 744, 776–779
variety, 86, 770–775
sentences, diagramming, 782–785
  complex sentences with a subordinate clause, 784.4
  compound sentences, 784.3
  simple sentences with a compound subject and verb, 784.2
  simple sentences with an indirect and direct object, 782.4
  simple sentences with a prepositional phrase, 784.1

Index

simple sentences with one subject and one verb, 782.1
simple sentences with predicate adjectives, 782.2
simple sentences with predicate noun and adjectives, 782.3
sentence structure, editing for, 26, 188, 248, 308, 434, *see also* checklist, editing.
sent/scent/cent, 712
serial/cereal, 712
series, 125, 187, 646.2, 660.2, 674.2
series comma, 125, 646.2
sestet, 369
set/sit, 722
setting, 351, 354
shared possession, 662.4
short stories, 343–354, 598, 637
showcase portfolios, 130–132
sight/cite/site, 724
signal words, 179
signature, business letter, 544–546
silent *e,* 696.3
similes, 374
simple predicate, 764.1
simple pronouns, 732
simple sentence, 434, 772.1
simple subject, 762.1
singular nouns, 730.1
singular possessives, 662.2
singular pronouns, 736.1, 780.1
singular verbs, 748.2
site/sight/cite, 724
sit/set, 722
situational irony, 360
slang, 79, 635
skit, *see* historical skit.
social studies, writing in, 493–510
  historical skit, 494–499
  learning log, 480
  research reports, 500–510
sole/soul, 724

sonnets, 368–369
sounds of poetry, 374–375
source notes, 407
sources, information, *see* information sources.
speaking in class, 559–560, *see also* learning language, speaking; oral language.
special cases of agreement, 776.4
special events, capitalization, 680
special words, punctuation, 668.2
speech
  figures of, 81, 374
  interrupted, 674.4
  parts of, 728–761
spell-check software, 84, 435
spelling, 696–701, *see also* checklist, editing.
  commonly misspelled words, 698–699
  dictionary, 562–563
  i before *e,* 688.2, 696.1
  irregular plurals, 688.2
  plurals, 84
  proofreading marks, 639
  research reports, 435
  spell-check software, 84, 435
  tips for improved, 700
  words ending in *y,* 696.4
  words with consonant endings, 696.2
  words with silent *e,* 696.3
stage directions, 362, 495
states
  capitalization, 680
  postal abbreviations, 547, 692.2
stationary/stationery, 724
statistical argument, math, 514–517
statistics, 57, 153, 180, 225, 503
steal/steel, 724
stereotypes, 342
stories, 343–354, 598, 637

storyboard, 498
STRAP questions, 210–211, 214, 270
strategies, language, 566–567, *see also* learning language, learning strategies; reading strategies.
student (peer) response, 115–120, 437, 469
style, 266, 323, 633
subject for writing, 386, 390, *see also* topics, selecting.
subjective, as term, 633
subject noun, 730.3
subject pronoun, 738.1
subjects (grammar)
  complete, 762.1
  compound, 246, 762.1, 776.1
  delayed, 762.2, 776.2
  diagramming sentences, 782.1–782.2
  in sentences, 762, 764.2
  simple, 762.1
subject-verb agreement, 124, 246, 744, 776–779
subjunctive mood, 750.1
subordinate clause, 247, 308, 768.1, 784.4
subordinating conjunctions, 306, 760.3
subsequent editions, citing, 453
subtitles, 656.6
suffixes, 567, 658.2, 754.2
summary, 56, 406, 411, 427, 444, 501, 513, 630, 637
superlative adjectives, 754.2
superlative adverbs, 756.2
supporting details, 57–58, 287, 410, 426, 633
suspense, 134, 140, 352
syllable division, dictionary, 562–563
symbols, 349, 635
synonyms, books of, 564
syntax, 633
synthesizing information, 409, 556

table of contents, 131
tables, 519
tags, 650.5
take/bring, 712
taking notes, 476–480, 558
tall tale, 637
T-charts, 211, 271
teach/learn, 718
television programs, citing, 407, 419, 458
templates, multimedia, 472
terms, key writing, 632–633
test-taking tips, 215, 275, 341, *see also* holistic scoring guide.
Texas Writing Traits, *see* traits of writing.
than/then, 724
that/which, 648, 726
their/there/they're, 724
themes, 354, *see also* plays, themes in, analysis and response to.
theories, 410, 423
thesaurus, 564
thesis, 52, 69, 296, 410, 628
thesis checklist, 626
thesis statements, *see also* drafting; prewriting; topic sentences.
    conclusions, 56
    expository, 167, 170–171, 204
    forming, 17, 97
    introductions, 55
    organization (trait), 61
    persuasive, 264
    research reports, 408, 413
    response to literature, 279, 286, 290, 323, 337
    supporting, 18–19
    as writing term, 633
third-person pronouns, 736.2
thought map, 349
thoughts, 68, 94, 96, 471
threw/through, 724
time, 629, 656.2, 664.3, 690.4, 756.1

time lines, 64, 211, 504
title page, 392
titles of courses, 684.5
titles of people, 189, 641.2, 650.4
titles of works
    capitalization, 682.6
    citing, 455
    expository, 190, 207
    in-text citations, 448
    italics in, 670.2
    library computer catalog, 386
    persuasive, 250, 267
    punctuation, 656.6, 668.3
    Readers' Guide, 390
    research reports, 438
    response to literature, 310
tone, 142, 266, 350, 354, 633
tools of language, 556–609
    learning language, 565–609
    listening in class, 558, 560
    reference materials, 561–564
    speaking in class, 559–560
topic outlines, 17, 98, 168, 625
topics, 8, 15, 70–71, 96, 633
topics, selecting
    cluster for, 92
    freewriting for, 93
    list for, 92–93
    narrative, 138
    persuasive, 224, 262
    poetry, 370
    prewriting, 92–93
    research reports, 402–403
    response to literature, 284
    writer's notebook, 3
topic sentences, *see also* beginnings, writing; thesis statements.
    defined, 612–613
    descriptive writing, 615
    expository, 159, 167, 170, 177, 616
    narrative, 614
    persuasive, 219, 230, 617
    prompts, response to, 335
    response to literature, 290
    as writing term, 633
topics lists, 138, 202, 262, 284, 402
to/too/two, 724

trade names, capitalization, 680
tragedy, 637
trailing modifiers, 88
traits of writing, 46–89, *see also specific traits.*
    big picture, 60, 100
    checklist, 50
    conventions, 14, 48, 83–89
    expository, 14, 160
    focus and coherence, 14, 48, 51–58
    holistic scoring, 34–37
    ideas, development of, 14, 48, 67–74
    language of, 572
    organization, 14, 48, 59–66
    peer response, 118–119
    persuasive, 220
    previewing, 14
    respond to the reading, 137, 151, 162, 222, 261, 282, 321, 329, 339, 347, 358, 368–369, 400
    response to literature, 280
    revising, 9, 11, 20–25
    understanding, 47–50
    vocabulary (key words), 573
    voice, 14, 48, 75–82
    writing process, 20, 24–26, 46–89
transitional phrases, 650.6, 654.2
transitions
    expository, 172
    organization (trait), 66
    in organizational patterns, 66, 572
    persuasive, 232
    research reports, 424
    response to literature, 299
    words/phrases for, 66, 629–630
    as writing term, 633
    in writing process, 19
transitive verbs, 742.1–742.2
translation dictionaries, 564
trochaic rhythm, 375
two-column chart, 204
two/to/too, 724

uncertainty, punctuation, 642.2
understatement, 81, 635
understood subject/ predicate, 764.2
unity, 633
usage, 633
usage guides, 564
U.S. Postal Service, 547, 692.2

vain/vein/vane, 724
variety of sentences, 86, 770–775
vary/very, 724
Venn diagrams, 65, 211, 619
verbal irony, 360
verbals, 752–753
  gerunds, 752.1, 766.1
  infinitives, 752.2, 766.1
  participles, 752.3, 766.1
verbs, 740–751
  action, 742.1
  active voice, 188, 748.2
  auxiliary, 740.2
  be, 740.1–740.2, 776.3
  classes of, 740–743
  defined, 728.3, 740
  forms of, 744
  helping, 740.2
  intransitive, 742.1
  irregular, 746.2
  linking, 740.1
  metaphors with, 80
  mood, 750.1
  number of, 744.1
  passive voice, 188, 748.2
  person, 744.2
  phrase, 768
  plural, 744.1, 748.2
  regular, 744.3
  singular, 748.2
  subject-verb agreement, 124, 246, 744, 776–779
  transitive, 742.1–742.2

verb tense
  continuous, 748.1
  defined, 744.3
  future, 744.4
  future continuous, 748.1
  future perfect, 746.1
  past, 744.4
  past continuous, 748.1
  past participles, 744.3, 746.2
  past perfect, 746.1–746.2
  past tense, 187
  perfect, 746.1
  present, 187, 744.4
  present continuous, 748.1
  present perfect, 746.1
  simple, 744.4
very/real/really, 722
vial/vile, 726
videos, 385, 407, 458, 470–471, 498–499, 536–537
visuals/visual aids, 466, 536
vocabulary (key words)
  creative writing, 599
  expository, 581
  narrative, 575
  persuasive, 587
  prompts, 334
  research reports, 605
  response to literature, 593
  writing process, 569
  writing traits, 573
voice
  active, 188, 748.2
  adjectives, effective use of 82
  adjusting, 77
  analytical, 303
  developing, 76
  dialogue, 78
  diction, 79
  engaging, 429
  figures of speech, 81
  formality, 242
  metaphors, 80
  narrative, 302
  oral presentations, 468
  passive, 188, 748.2
  persuasive, 242–243
  research reports, 468
  tone, 142, 266, 350, 354, 633
  as writing term, 633

voice (trait), 75–82
  arts, 534, 538
  big picture, 100
  checklist for effective writing, 50
  creative writing, 353, 363, 366, 373
  described, 48
  expository, 160, 182–184, 207
  figures of speech, 81
  holistic scoring, 37
  learning language, 572
  math, 517
  narrative, 143, 154
  peer response, 119
  persuasive, 14, 220, 242–244, 266–267
  research reports, 428–430, 473
  response to literature, 280, 302–304, 325, 340
  revising for, *see* revising for voice (trait).
  science, 486
  social studies, 497, 510
  and writing process, 24–25, 49

waist/waste, 726
wait/weight, 726
ware/wear/where, 726
warm-up, 158, 218, 278
way/weigh, 726
weather/whether, 726
Web sites, 133, 457, 470, 472, 499
weekly/biweekly magazines, citing, 454
weigh/way, 726
well/good, 716
which/that, 726
"who" clauses, 126
whole/hole, 716
who's/whose, 726
who/whom, 726
"why" chart, 226

"why not" chart, 227
wireframes, 472
wordiness, 425
words
  added, 678.3
  compound, 658.1, 686.6
  connotation, 182
  creating new, 658.2, 660.2
  denotation, 183
  division of, 660.5
  pairs (homophones), 708–727
  parts, as language strategy, 567
  transitions, 66, 629–630
  using the right word, 708–727
workplace, writing in the, 543–555
  business letter, 544–547
  job application, 552–553
  meeting agenda, 554–555
  memo, 550–551
  resume, 548–549
works-cited section, 400, 419, 451–458, 508, 533
wring/ring, 722
Writer's Market, 129
writer's notebook, 2–5, 92
Write Source Holistic Scoring Guide, 34, 36–37, *see also* holistic scoring guide.
Write Source Web address, 133
write/wright/rite/right, 722
writing across the curriculum, *see* cross-curricular writing.
writing elements, 610–639
  editing/proofreading marks, 639
  essay-writing skills, 623–639
  paragraph skills, 611–622
writing forms, 636–637
  creative writing, 342–379
  expository writing, 156–215
  narrative writing, 134–155
  persuasive writing, 216–275
  research reports, 380–473
  response to literature, 276–341
writing portfolios, 130–132

writing process, 6–133, *see also* keys to effective writing.
  defined, 9, 568
  drafting, 9–10, 18–19, 99–106, 568
  editing, 9, 11, 26–27, 121–126, 568
  goal previewing, 14
  graphic organizers, 15, 17
  one writer's, 13–32
  peer response, 115–120, 437, 469
  prewriting, 9–10, 15–17, 91–98, 568, 570
  publishing, 9, 11, 28–31, 127–133, 568
  revising, 9, 11, 20–25, 107–114, 568, 571
  and traits, 20, 24–26, 46–89
  vocabulary (key words), 569

writing techniques
  essay skills, 634–635
  poetry, 374–375
writing traits, *see* traits of writing.

your/you're, 726